RealWorld Evaluation

Working Under Budget, Time, Data, and Political Constraints

2

EDITION

Michael Bamberger

Independent Consultant, Former World Bank Senior Sociologist

Jim Rugh

Independent Consultant

Linda Mabry

Washington State University Vancouver

SAGE

Los Angeles | London | New Delhi
Singapore | Washington DC

Los Angeles | London | New Delhi
Singapore | Washington DC

FOR INFORMATION:

SAGE Publications, Inc.
2455 Teller Road
Thousand Oaks, California 91320
E-mail: order@sagepub.com

SAGE Publications Ltd.
1 Oliver's Yard
55 City Road
London EC1Y 1SP
United Kingdom

SAGE Publications India Pvt. Ltd.
B 1/I 1 Mohan Cooperative Industrial Area
Mathura Road, New Delhi 110 044
India

SAGE Publications Asia-Pacific Pte. Ltd.
33 Pekin Street #02-01
Far East Square
Singapore 048763

Acquisitions Editor: Vicki Knight
Associate Editor: Lauren Habib
Editorial Assistant: Kalie Koscielak
Production Editor: Astrid Virding
Copy Editor: Kim Husband, Talia Greenberg, and Gillian Dickens
Typesetter: C&M Digitals (P) Ltd.
Proofreader: Dennis W. Webb
Indexer: Will Ragsdale
Cover Designers: Anupama Krishnan and Candice Harman
Marketing Manager: Helen Salmon
Permissions Editor: Adele Hutchinson

Printed in the United States of America

Library of Congress Cataloging-in-Publication Data

Bamberger, Michael.

RealWorld evaluation : working under budget, time, data, and political constraints / Michael Bamberger, Jim Rugh, Linda Mabry. — 2nd ed.

p. cm.
Includes bibliographical references and index.

ISBN 978-1-4129-7962-7 (pbk. : acid-free paper)

1. Evaluation research (Social action programs)—Developing countries. 2. Economic development projects—Developing countries—Evaluation. I. Rugh, Jim. II. Mabry, Linda. III. Title.

H62.5.D44B36 2012
001.4—dc23   2011033238

This book is printed on acid-free paper.

11 12 13 14 15 10 9 8 7 6 5 4 3 2 1

RealWorld Evaluation

2
EDITION

For Elizabeth, in appreciation for all your support and encouragement over the years. It is always good to have quilter in your corner.

—Michael

I want to express my deep appreciation to my many esteemed colleagues from whom I have learned much. These include those who joined my table when I was awarded the AEA 2010 Alva and Gunnar Myrdal Practice Award: co-author Michael Bamberger, Thomaz Chianca, Ana Coghlan, Ross Conner, Anne Cullen, Michael Hendricks, Michael Quinn Patton, Patricia Rogers, and Megan Steinke.

—Jim

To evaluators everywhere working to improve programs and society through practice that is not only competent but also marked by sensitivity and integrity.

—Linda

Brief Contents

Detailed Contents

List of Figures

List of Tables

List of Boxes

Preface

This book addresses the challenges of conducting program evaluations in real-world contexts where evaluators and the agencies commissioning evaluations face budget and time constraints and where critical data are not available or are of poor quality. Evaluators must also adapt the evaluation to a range of political pressures and influences and must work within organizational systems that often involve many different agencies and actors and where administrative procedures may not be well suited to the conduct of a rigorous evaluation. Evaluators are also often subject to pressures from many sides concerning the "right" evaluation methods to use, what should be studied (and not studied), who should be involved, and how and to whom the findings should be disseminated. While trying to juggle and reconcile all of the constraints (factors), it is also essential for the evaluator to follow standards of professional practice and to adhere to evaluation codes of conduct.

We were inspired to write a book about *RealWorld Evaluation* (**RWE**) because it became clear from our evaluation workshops and consultancies that most of the above topics were not systematically addressed in most evaluation textbooks. So while it was very easy to find textbooks and workshops explaining how to conduct a rigorous impact evaluation when budget and time are not major constraints, as well as when critical data are either available or can be collected, it was very difficult for evaluators and for agencies commissioning or using evaluations to provide practical guidance on how to conduct evaluations of an acceptable level of rigor and validity when working under budget, time, and data constraints, as well as when seeking to reconcile different political perspectives while working within organizational structures not well suited to conducting a rigorous evaluation.

Since the publication of the first edition of *RealWorld Evaluation* in 2006, there have been a number of important developments in the field of program evaluation, and the second edition has been considerably expanded to address these new issues as well as the feedback we continue to receive from the RWE workshops (see following box). These include continuing debates on appropriate evaluation designs, the challenges of evaluating complex development programs, how to manage evaluations and promote the institutionalization of evaluation systems, the emergence of mixed methods as a distinct approach to evaluation design, new developments in program theory, and the need to find ways to reduce sample size while ensuring statistically acceptable standards. Encompassing all of these is the recognition of the importance of following professional evaluation standards and codes of conduct and an understanding of the complex ethical issues affecting evaluation practice.

What's New in the Second Edition?

- A greater focus on responsible professional practice, codes of conduct, and the importance of ethical standards for all evaluations.
- Some new perspectives on the debate over the "best" evaluation designs. While experimental designs can address the important issues of selection bias, such statistical designs are potentially vulnerable to a number of important threats to validity. These include process and contextual analysis, collecting information on sensitive topics and from difficult-to-reach groups, difficulties in adapting to changes in the evaluation design, and implementation strategies. Experience also suggests that strong statistical designs can be applied only in a very small proportion of evaluations.
- There are many instances in which well-designed nonexperimental designs will be the best option for assessing outcomes of many programs, particularly for evaluating complex programs and even "simple" programs that involve complex processes of behavioral change.
- The importance of understanding the setting within which the evaluation is designed, implemented, and used.
- Program theory as a central building block of most evaluation designs. The expanded discussion incorporates theory of change, contextual and process analysis, multilevel logic models, using competing theories, and trajectory analysis.
- The range of evaluation design options has been considerably expanded, and case studies are included (Appendix F) to illustrate how each of the 19 designs has been applied in the field.
- Greater emphasis is given to the benefits of mixed-method evaluation designs.
- A new chapter has been added on the evaluation of complicated and complex development interventions. Conventional pretest–posttest comparison group designs can rarely be applied to the increasing proportion of development assistance channeled through complex interventions, and a range of promising new approaches—still very much "work in progress"—is presented.
- Two new chapters on organizing and managing evaluations and strengthening evaluation capacity. This includes a discussion of strategies for promoting the institutionalization of evaluation systems at the sector and national levels.
- The discussion of quality assurance and threats to validity has been expanded, and checklists and worksheets are included (Appendixes A–E) on how to assess the validity of quantitative, qualitative, and mixed-method designs.

The RWE approach, originally called "shoestring evaluation," initially focused on problems of conducting evaluations in developing countries under budget, time, and data constraints. However, it soon became clear that despite the widespread use of evaluation in industrialized countries such as the United States, Canada, Europe, Australia, New Zealand, and Japan, many evaluators in these countries faced similar constraints. It also became clear that for many evaluators, political and organizational constraints were seen as bigger challenges than budget and time. Consequently, RWE now addresses a broader range of challenges and constraints faced by evaluators in both developing and developed countries.

Intended Audiences

The book is intended for four main audiences. First are the **evaluation practitioners** who design, conduct, and advise on evaluation methodology and use. Second are the *users of evaluation*, including agencies who commission evaluations, the staff of agencies or programs being evaluated, policymakers, academics, groups affected by the programs being evaluated, advocacy groups, public opinion, and the media. The third audience consists of the *managers of individual evaluations and of evaluation systems*. These include evaluation offices in donor agencies and national implementing agencies, evaluation managers in consulting firms and research agencies, and national and sector agencies that plan and coordinate national or sector evaluation strategies. The fourth is the *university and research community* where evaluation methodology is taught and is one of the main sources of evaluation expertise. Each audience includes both people who are relatively new to the field of evaluation and the "old hands" who have been involved in evaluation for a long time. Of course, there is considerable overlap between these four audiences. For example, many university faculty members also conduct evaluations and advise on their use, and many evaluation practitioners also teach.

For people relatively new to the field of evaluation, the book can also be used as an introductory text on the general principles of evaluation, while for experienced evaluators, the book addresses the special issues involved in conducting evaluations under RealWorld constraints. Our experience from having organized workshops in more than 20 countries (see Acknowledgments below) is that there is widespread interest in learning how to conduct adequately rigorous evaluations when it is not possible to follow standard research/evaluation methodologies. These obviously are questions that most evaluation practitioners and evaluation users frequently face. Although many evaluators are familiar with the *fast-and-dirty* evaluation studies that largely ignore concerns about rigor and validity of conclusions, very few have systematically addressed the challenge of how to ensure maximum methodological rigor under a particular set of RealWorld constraints. As indicated earlier, to the best of our knowledge, no previous evaluation textbook systematically addresses all these questions.

The following table provides a brief summary of the organization of this book. We hope this "road map" will help you know where you are and where you want to go as you explore this book.

A Reader's Guide to RealWorld Evaluation (Second Edition)

	Preface	Introduction to the second edition of this RWE book
Part I: The Seven Steps of the RealWorld Evaluation Approach		
Chapter 1	An overview of the full RWE approach	This chapter provides a preview of the seven steps and the basics of how the RWE tools and techniques can help evaluators and their clients cope with a variety of constraints typically faced when conducting evaluations in the RealWorld.
Chapters 2–8	Presentation of the seven steps of the RWE approach	Relatively nontechnical discussion that provides an introduction to the different stages of an evaluation. Cross-referenced to more detailed discussion of these topics in Part II.
Part II: A Review of Evaluation Methods and Approaches and Their Application in RealWorld Evaluation: *For those who would like to dig deeper*		
Chapter 9	Ensuring competent and ethical practice in the conduct of the evaluation	The basic "good practice" principles and standards that guide the evaluation profession.

(Continued)

(Continued)

Chapter 10	Theory-based evaluation	Theory-based evaluation is an essential building block in the RWE approach.
Chapter 11	Evaluation designs	Reviews the stages in the selection of an evaluation design and presents a wide range of experimental, quasi-experimental, and nonexperimental designs. Statistical rigor is only one of several dimensions of a methodologically sound design, and strong statistical designs are often weak on other important dimensions, while there are many situations in which nonexperimental designs are the best option. Appendix F presents case studies illustrating how each of the 19 designs has been used in the field.
Chapter 12	Quantitative approaches and methods	Reviews and contrasts the key elements of QUANT and QUAL approaches to evaluation. Shows how mixed-method design can combine the strengths of both approaches. Mixed methods is an integrated strategy involving unique approaches at each stage of the evaluation.
Chapter 13	Qualitative approaches and methods	
Chapter 14	Mixed-methods approaches	
Chapter 15	Sampling for RealWorld evaluations	Reviews approaches to sample design for QUANT, QUAL, and mixed-method evaluations. Explains the role of statistical power and effect size in estimating sample size. Introduces Lot Quality Acceptance Sampling (LQAS) as a practical operational tool for working with small samples.
Chapter 16	Evaluating complex, multicomponent development interventions	Discusses the move toward more complex, multicomponent, national-level development support and the demand that this creates for new evaluation designs as conventional evaluation designs can rarely be applied at these levels. A range of promising new approaches is discussed.
Part III: Organizing and Managing Evaluations and Strengthening Evaluation Capacity: *For readers involved with the funding and management of evaluations*		
Chapter 17	Organizing and managing evaluations	Defines and discusses the main stages in the preparation, recruitment of evaluators, implementation, dissemination, and use of an evaluation.
Chapter 18	Strengthening evaluation capacity at the agency and national levels	This covers quality assurance and threats-to-validity checklists, working with program management to design "evaluation-ready" projects, evaluation capacity development, and institutionalizing evaluation systems.
Chapter 19	Conclusions and challenges for the road ahead	Our final comments on some of the main approaches and issues discussed in the book.

We wish you success in your evaluation work and hope the book will help you conduct, use, and teach about evaluation in RealWorld contexts!

Acknowledgments

This book benefited greatly from the advice and encouragement of Lucia Fort, Raymond Gervais, Michael Hendricks, Patrick Leung, Michael Patton, Mike Ponder, Michael Scriven, and Brett S. Sharp. Special thanks to Professor Gary Miron and his graduate students at the Western Michigan Evaluation Center for their detailed critiques of the first edition. We also thank Susan Kistler and her colleagues in the American Evaluation Association; Karen Ginsberg, Barbara Levine, Linda Morra, and Ray Rist at the International Program for Development Evaluation Training (IPDET); Dr. Sivagnanasothy, Mallika Samaranayake, and Soma de Silva of the Sri Lankan Evaluation Association; Patrick Grasso, Keith MacKay, Markus Goldberg, Manuel Castro, and Maurya West Meiers at the World Bank; Nobuko Fujita at the Foundation for Advanced Studies in International Development in Tokyo; Mary Cole at the Development Bank for Southern Africa; Zenda Ofir of the African Evaluation Association; Alexey Kuzmin of the International Program Evaluation Network; Esteban Tapella and Pablo Rodríguez Bilella of ReLAC; Marcia Paterno Joppert of Rede Brasileira de Monitoramento e Avaliação (Brazilian M&E Network); Anzel Schonfeldt and Benita Van-Wyk of the South African Monitoring and Evaluation Association; Ram Chandra Khanal and Ramesh Tuladhar of the South Asian Community of Evaluators; Beate Bull and her colleagues at NORAD; Verena Knippel and her colleagues at Sida; Sophie Punte and her colleagues at ESCAP; Cate Rogers and her colleagues at AusAID; and the Atlanta-area Evaluation Association, among others, for offering the opportunity to organize workshops and seminars on Shoestring Evaluation and RealWorld Evaluation as the approach developed over the past 10 years. These include the constructive feedback we received from colleagues during our RWE workshops in many countries, including Canada, Japan, Russia, the Ukraine, Portugal, the Czech Republic, Norway, Sweden, South Africa, Sierra Leone, Egypt, the Philippines, Sri Lanka, Bangladesh, Nepal, India, Indonesia, Costa Rica, and Brazil, in addition to multiple AEA conferences in the United States.

We would also like to express our appreciation to the following reviewers whose thoughtful comments helped strengthen many of the chapters: John R. Mathiason, Syracuse University; Gary Miron, Western Michigan University; Robin Anderson, James Madison University; Paige L. Tompkins, Mercer University; John E. Paul, University of North Carolina at Chapel Hill; Sheryl P. Kubiak, Michigan State University; Tom Ricketts, University of North Carolina Gillings School of Global Public Health; W. E. Bickel, University of Pittsburgh; Michael D. Niles, Missouri Western State University; Dia Sekayi, Mercer University; Pamela A. Larde, Mercer University; Deborah D. Wright, The DCW Group, LLC; Terry Dalton, University of Denver; and Mara L. Schoeny, George Mason University. Thanks also to reviewers who preferred to remain anonymous.

Finally, we would like to thank the many people at Sage Publications who helped guide us through the publication process: Vicki Knight, Acquisitions Editor; Helen Salmon, Executive Marketing Manager; Lauren Habib, Senior Associate Editor; Kale Koscielak, Editorial Assistant; Astrid Virding, Senior Project Editor; the three copy editors: Kim Husband, Talia Greenberg and Gillian Dickens; and Candice Harman, cover designer.

About the Authors

Michael Bamberger has almost 40 years of experience in development evaluation, including a decade working with nongovernmental organizations in Latin America, almost 25 years working on evaluation with the World Bank in most of the social and economic sectors and in most regions of the world, and 10 years as an independent evaluation consultant, including programs with 10 United Nations agencies and multilateral and bilateral development agencies. He has published three books and several monographs and handbooks on development evaluation, as well as numerous articles in professional journals. He has been active for 20 years with the American Evaluation Association, serving on the Board and as Chair of the International Committee. He has served on the Editorial Advisory Board of *New Directions for Evaluation*, the *Journal of Development Effectiveness*, the *Journal of Mixed Methods Research*, and the *American Journal of Evaluation* and is a regular reviewer for several professional evaluation journals. He has taught program evaluation in more than 30 countries in Africa, Latin America, Asia, and the Middle East and, since 2002, has been on the Faculty of the International Program for Development Evaluation Training (IPDET) in Ottawa, Ontario, Canada; since 2001, has also lectured at the Foundation for Advanced Studies on International Development (FASID) in Tokyo.

Jim Rugh has been professionally involved for 47 years in rural community development in Africa, Asia, Appalachia and other parts of the world. For the past 31 years he has specialized in international program evaluation. He served as head of Design, Monitoring and Evaluation for Accountability and Learning for CARE International for 12 years. He has also evaluated and provided advice for strengthening the M&E systems of a number of other International NGOs. He is recognized as a leader in the international evaluation profession. He has served as the American Evaluation Association (AEA) Representative to and Vice President of the International Organization for Cooperation in Evaluation (IOCE), the global umbrella of national and regional professional evaluation associations. Jim has led numerous workshops on the topic of RealWorld Evaluation for many organizations and networks in many countries. In recognition of his contributions to the evaluation profession he was awarded the 2010 Alva and Gunnar Myrdal Practice Award by AEA.

Linda Mabry is a faculty member at Washington State University specializing in program evaluation, student assessment, and research and evaluation methodology. She currently serves as president of the Oregon Program Evaluation Network and on the editorial board for *Studies in Educational Evaluation*. She has served in a variety of leadership positions for the American Evaluation Association, including the Board of Directors, chair of the Task Force on Educational Accountability, and chair of the Theories of Evaluation topical interest group. She has also served on the Board of Trustees for the National Center for the Improvement of Educational Assessments and on the Performance Assessment Review Board of New York. She has conducted evaluations for the U.S. Department of Education, National Science Foundation, National Endowment for the Arts, the Jacob Javits Foundation, Hewlett-Packard Corporation, Ameritech Corporation, ATT-Comcast Corporation, the New York City Fund for Public Education, the Chicago Arts Partnerships in Education, the Chicago Teachers Academy of Mathematics and Science, and a variety of university, state, and school agencies. She has published in a number of scholarly journals and written several books, including *Evaluation and the Postmodern Dilemma* (1997) and *Portfolios Plus: A Critical Guide to Performance Assessment* (1999).

PART I

The Seven Steps of the RealWorld Evaluation Approach

CHAPTER 1

Overview: RealWorld Evaluation and the Contexts in Which It Is Used

The chapter begins with an overview of the RealWorld Evaluation (RWE) approach, the contexts in which RealWorld evaluations are conducted, and the many different constraints, pressures, and influences under which evaluations are formulated, conducted, disseminated, and used. The RWE approach was originally developed to address four of the most common constraints evaluators face: budget, time, and data constraints, and political influences. Subsequently, issues concerning organizational structures and management and administrative arrangements were added as additional challenges. The two most common RWE scenarios are reviewed. The first is when the evaluator is brought in at the start of the project but with constraints on the types of information that can be collected or the designs that can be used. The second and probably the more common scenario is when the evaluator is not called in until the project has been operating for some time and may even be almost completed. In most of these cases, no baseline data have been collected and usually no comparison (control) group has been identified.

1. Welcome to RealWorld Evaluation

Most evaluators are familiar with situations in which programs have been underway for some time or perhaps are almost completed before implementing or funding agencies begin to think seriously about evaluating the extent to which the programs are achieving their objectives and producing the intended **impacts**. Usually, the belated interest in evaluation is motivated by the need for solid **evidence**[1] on which to base decisions about whether the program should be continued or perhaps expanded. When the evaluations do finally get underway, many have to be

---

[1]Bold technical terms are defined in the glossary at the end of this book.

conducted under budget and time constraints, often with limited access to baseline data and comparison groups. Consequently, it is difficult, if not impossible, to apply many of the methodologically most robust evaluation designs.

Although more resources are allocated to evaluation in developed countries, many evaluators in the United States, Canada, Europe, Japan, and Australasia report that they operate under similar constraints to those faced by their colleagues in developing countries.[2] As if these problems were not enough, many evaluations in both developed and developing countries are often conducted in *political* environments in which funding agencies, clients, and key stakeholders have strongly held views on what the "right" evaluation methods should be, what types and amounts of information should be collected, and which groups should and should not be asked to comment on (or even see) the **findings**. New evaluators soon discover that "technical" issues such as whether to use randomized selection of project and control groups; the choice of qualitative, quantitative, or mixed-method designs; and whom to interview and what questions to ask can provoke strong reactions from clients and stakeholders.

Despite the difficult circumstances under which many evaluations have to be conducted, there is a growing demand from funding agencies, governments, civil society, and intended beneficiaries for systematic impact evaluations, including whether the program could and/or should be continued or expanded to other communities or locations. Consequently, there is a strong demand from many sides for evaluators to answer basic questions such as these:

- Did the project meet its objectives?
- Did it have an impact?
- Who benefited and who did not?
- Should the program continue or be replicated elsewhere?

There is also an increasing awareness that evaluation conclusions need to be supported by sound evidence and not just opinions—although there are often major disagreements as to what constitutes credible evidence.[3]

The pressures of conducting evaluations under budget and time constraints, missing baseline data, and political pressures have often resulted in inattention to sound research design or to identifying and addressing factors affecting the validity of the findings. The RWE approach presented in this book was developed in response to the demand for guidance on how to conduct evaluations when faced by these kinds of constraints, accommodating organizational structures and administrative procedures, while at the same time ensuring maximum possible methodological rigor within the particular evaluation context.

---

[2]One of our colleagues who has worked with major U.S. foundations that support community-level initiatives stated that there is a huge unmet need in the United States for material on how to conduct evaluations when working with very limited financial and professional resources. He stated that his "and other foundations make lots of small grants. There is often not enough money in the grants to hire an external consultant. And the recipients of these small grants don't have the capacity to do internal evaluation. The evaluation work done by these nonprofits is usually pretty bad. I don't really know of any materials targeted to this group."

[3]For two recent publications on the question of credible evidence see: Donaldson, S., C. Christie and M. Mark. 2009. *What Counts as Credible Evidence in Applied Research and Evaluation Practice?* Thousand Oaks: Sage; and Rieper, O., F. Leeuw, and T. Ling. 2010. *The Evidence Book: Concepts, Generation and Use of Evidence.* New Brunswick, NJ, and London: Transaction Publishers.

RWE is based on the following seven-step approach, summarized more specifically in Figure 1.1 and described in detail in Chapters 2 through 8:

- Step 1: *Planning and scoping the evaluation.* Before thinking about the evaluation design, it is important to fully understand the purpose of the evaluation, the information needs and expectations of the clients and stakeholders, and the constraints and pressures under which they are working. What is the client's bottom line? What do different stakeholders really want from the evaluation, and how will the results be used? Clarifying these questions is particularly critical for RWE because difficult choices will often have to be made to accommodate budget and time constraints or to recognize the limitations of the available data. This step also includes getting agreement on the articulation of the **program theory or logic model** (discussed in more detail in Chapter 10, which in addition to clarifying the underlying model on which the program is based, can also help identify the critical hypothesis or the linkages in the program implementation model on which the limited evaluation resources should focus). The scoping phase also involves identifying some different basic evaluation design strategies available for addressing the cost, time, and data constraints that a particular evaluation will face and then assessing the strengths and weaknesses (threats to validity and adequacy) of each option. The different design options are then discussed with clients, emphasizing the trade-offs involved in each option, and an agreement is then reached on which design would be most feasible and acceptable to the client. (We get into more detailed coverage of evaluation designs in Chapter 11.)
- Step 2: *Strategies for addressing budget constraints.* How many evaluators have been told by the client, "We really need a rigorous and professional evaluation as it is important to assess impacts, but . . . unfortunately our budget has been cut" Step 2 describes options for reducing costs. These include: simplifying the evaluation design; reducing the amount of data to be collected; making greater use of secondary data; revising the sample design and size, and streamlining data collection and analysis.
- Step 3: *Strategies for addressing time constraints.* In addition to many of the approaches used in Step 2, strategies include: planning ahead to avoid delays and bottlenecks, particularly during the short periods when outside consultants are involved; building impact-related indicators into routine project monitoring data collection and using videoconferencing to reduce travel and to permit more frequent interactions between the evaluation team and agency staff
- Step 4: *Strategies for addressing data constraints:* These include ways to address common problems concerning the lack of important data or data quality and reliability when the evaluation is not commissioned until late in the project cycle. Thus one needs to consider a number of approaches for *reconstructing* baseline data. These include using secondary data sources, recall, key informants, focus groups, construct mapping and participatory group techniques such as PRA. The chapter covers techniques for collecting information on sensitive topics and on difficult-to-reach groups. Many of these groups are the poorest and most vulnerable sectors of the community, and reaching them is often more costly and time-consuming; consequently, there will often be pressures to ignore these difficult questions and inaccessible groups.
- Step 5: *Understanding and coping with political factors influencing how the evaluation is designed, implemented, disseminated or used:* Identify the key actors and their political perspectives and understanding how these affect their orientation to the evaluation and developing strategies to address the political realities without compromising the evaluation. We identify common political issues arising at the outset of an evaluation, during

Figure 1.1   The RealWorld Evaluation Approach

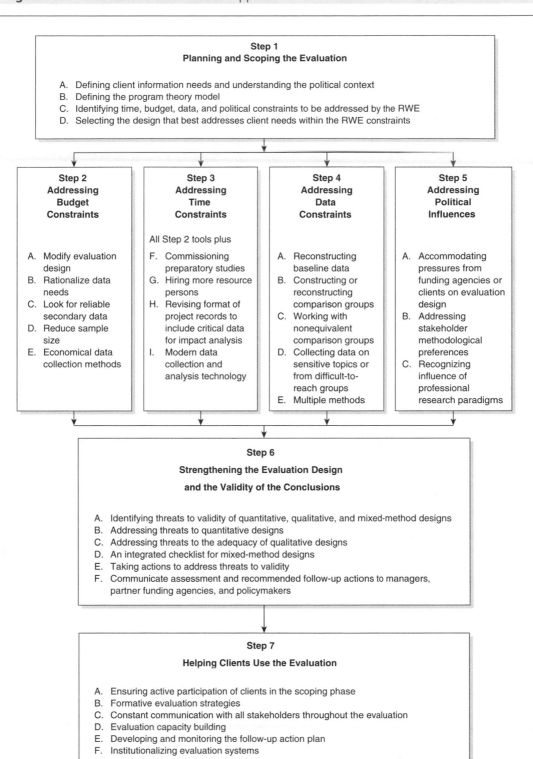

Step 1
Planning and Scoping the Evaluation

A. Defining client information needs and understanding the political context
B. Defining the program theory model
C. Identifying time, budget, data, and political constraints to be addressed by the RWE
D. Selecting the design that best addresses client needs within the RWE constraints

Step 2 **Addressing** **Budget** **Constraints**	**Step 3** **Addressing** **Time** **Constraints**	**Step 4** **Addressing** **Data** **Constraints**	**Step 5** **Addressing** **Political** **Influences**
	All Step 2 tools plus		
A. Modify evaluation design B. Rationalize data needs C. Look for reliable secondary data D. Reduce sample size E. Economical data collection methods	F. Commissioning preparatory studies G. Hiring more resource persons H. Revising format of project records to include critical data for impact analysis I. Modern data collection and analysis technology	A. Reconstructing baseline data B. Constructing or reconstructing comparison groups C. Working with nonequivalent comparison groups D. Collecting data on sensitive topics or from difficult-to-reach groups E. Multiple methods	A. Accommodating pressures from funding agencies or clients on evaluation design B. Addressing stakeholder methodological preferences C. Recognizing influence of professional research paradigms

Step 6

Strengthening the Evaluation Design

and the Validity of the Conclusions

A. Identifying threats to validity of quantitative, qualitative, and mixed-method designs
B. Addressing threats to quantitative designs
C. Addressing threats to the adequacy of qualitative designs
D. An integrated checklist for mixed-method designs
E. Taking actions to address threats to validity
F. Communicate assessment and recommended follow-up actions to managers, partner funding agencies, and policymakers

Step 7

Helping Clients Use the Evaluation

A. Ensuring active participation of clients in the scoping phase
B. Formative evaluation strategies
C. Constant communication with all stakeholders throughout the evaluation
D. Evaluation capacity building
E. Developing and monitoring the follow-up action plan
F. Institutionalizing evaluation systems

implementation, and during reporting and use of the evaluation, and we propose strategies for addressing all these issues. We also discuss some important professional and ethical issues concerning who should be given information on the evaluation and when. Often, the client would like to limit who sees and is invited to comment on the evaluation draft, whereas the evaluator may feel that the report should be given to the mass media and to the different stakeholder groups potentially affected by the project. We will return to these ethical issues throughout the book.

- Step 6: *Strengthening the Evaluation Design and the Validity of the Conclusions* discusses the analysis of threats to validity affecting the findings and recommendations of the evaluation and how these can be addressed once they have been identified. We present worksheets that have been developed for assessing the validity of QUANT, QUAL and mixed method designs respectively, and for communicating the assessment and the recommended follow-up to managers and policy-makers.

- Step 7: *Helping clients use the evaluation.* Ensure that clients and other key stakeholders are actively involved from the start and that they "buy into" the evaluation; maintaining contact with clients throughout the evaluation and ensuring that by the time the major reports are published, they do not contain any surprises for the client; and adapting the presentation of findings to the preferred communication style of different stakeholders. On a broader level this also involves helping institutionalize evaluation systems at the sector and national level (see Chapters 17 and 18).

2. The RealWorld Evaluation Context

The RWE approach was developed to assist the many evaluators in both developing and developed countries who must conduct evaluations with budget, time, data, and political constraints. In one common scenario, the client delays contracting an evaluator until late in the project when the funding agency (government, international development agency, foundation, etc.) is about to decide whether to continue to support a project or possibly launch a larger second phase. Such tardiness occurs even when evaluation was built into the original project agreement (see Box 1.1). With the decision point approaching, the funding agency may suddenly realize that it

---

BOX 1.1
A FAMILIAR EVALUATION STORY

When a social development fund was launched in an African country a few years ago, it was suggested that a baseline study be conducted as the first phase of a longitudinal impact evaluation study. The project manager asked, "What is the point of spending money and time on a baseline study when we do not know if the project model will work in our country?" He also indicated that staff members were under pressure to launch the project and could not spend time on something that would not be useful until the project was completed. Three years later, when the possibility of a second project was being discussed, consultants were called in to conduct an impact evaluation study. It was agreed that it was unfortunate that no baseline data were available to permit a rigorous measurement of the changes produced by the project. The consultants had to try to reconstruct baseline data using methods described in Chapter 5.

does not have solid information on which to base a decision about future funding of the project, or the project-implementing agency may realize it does not have the evidence needed to support its claim that the project is achieving its objectives. An evaluator called in at this point may be told it is essential to conduct the evaluation by a certain date and to produce "rigorous" findings regarding project impact although, unfortunately, no comparable baseline data are available.

In other scenarios, the evaluator may be called in early to help develop the monitoring and evaluation (M&E) plan but may find that for budget, political, or methodological reasons, it will not be possible to collect data on a comparison group for purposes of determining program impact by comparing participants with nonparticipants (a **counterfactual**). In some cases, it may not even be possible to collect baseline data on the project population for purposes of analyzing progress or impact over time. Data constraints may also result from difficulties of collecting information on sensitive topics such as HIV/AIDS, domestic violence, postconflict reconstruction, or illegal economic activities (e.g., commercial sex workers, narcotics, or political corruption).

Determining the most appropriate evaluation design under these kinds of circumstances can be a complicated juggling act involving trade-offs between available resources and acceptable standards of evaluation practice. Often, the client's concerns are more about budgets and deadlines, and basic principles of evaluation may receive a lower priority. Box 1.2 illustrates this difficult trade-off between budgets and deadlines on the one hand and desired standards of methodological rigor on the other. Failure to reach satisfactory resolution of these trade-offs may also contribute to a much-lamented problem: low use of evaluation results (see Chelimsky 1994; Operations Evaluation Department 2005; Patton 1997). RWE is a response to the all-too-real difficulties in the practical world of evaluation.

BOX 1.2
REALWORLD EVALUATION CONSTRAINTS IN THE EVALUATION OF AN EDUCATION PROJECT IN EGYPT

This excerpt from a meta-evaluation (review of evaluation methodologies and practices) by CARE International illustrates the many RealWorld constraints facing evaluation in the field.

The evaluators mentioned that the methodology they employed had to be more subjective and anecdotal than they would have desired. The decision not to use their preferred (more rigorous) quantitative design was made due to the limited time available (2 weeks for all data gathering) and the geographic spread, size, and diversity of the target population. Although they felt that a random or weighted sampling would lead to statistically significant or statistically representative findings, it was not realistic given time and other limitations. Instead, the team employed other techniques to try to ensure that the information gathered was as comprehensive and thorough and followed, as closely as possible, accepted approaches to classroom and teacher observation within the very severe time constraints.

The meta-evaluation, recognizing that it is not possible to achieve acceptable standards of evaluation rigor within these time and budget constraints, suggested that CARE may need to re-examine some of its evaluation policies to determine if the desire (or limitations imposed by the donors) to economize on evaluation costs and duration is working at cross-purposes with the level of rigor it hopes to achieve.

SOURCE: Russon (2005:12–13).

3. The Four Types of Constraints Addressed by the RealWorld Approach

Table 1.1 illustrates the different ways in which RWE constraints are combined in the typical contexts in which evaluations are conducted. In some cases, the evaluator faces a single constraint. For example, the budget may be limited, but there is plenty of time. Or the evaluation may begin at the start of the project with no time constraint, but the evaluator is told that for political or ethical reasons, it will not be possible to collect data on a comparison group. Many unlucky evaluators find themselves simultaneously contending with several or all of these constraints!

Table 1.1   RealWorld Evaluation Scenarios: Conducting Impact Evaluations with Time, Budget, Data, and Political Constraints

The constraints under which the evaluation must be conducted				
Time	Budget	Data	Political	Typical Evaluation Scenarios
X				The evaluator is called in late in the project and told that the evaluation must be completed by a certain date so that it can be used in a decision-making process or contribute to a report. The budget may be adequate, but it may be difficult to collect or analyze survey data within the time frame.
	X			The evaluation is allocated only a small budget, but there is not necessarily excessive time pressure. However, it will be difficult to collect sample survey data because of the limited budget.
		X		The evaluator is not called in until the project is well advanced. Consequently, no baseline survey has been conducted either on the project population or on a comparison group. The evaluation does have an adequate scope, either to analyze existing household survey data or to collect additional data. In some cases, the intended project impacts may also concern changes in sensitive areas, such as domestic violence, community conflict, women's empowerment, community leadership styles, or corruption, on which it is difficult to collect reliable data even when time and budget are not constraints.
			X	The funding agency or a government regulatory body has requirements concerning acceptable evaluation methods. For example: In the United States, the No Child Left Behind Act of 2001 includes funding preference for certain types of research designs. In other cases, a client or funding agency may specifically request qualitative data, tests of statistical significance regarding measured program effects, or both.
			X	There is overwhelming indication that the evaluation is being commissioned for political purposes. For example, an evaluation of the effects of conservation policy might be commissioned to stall its expansion.
			X	There is reason to suspect that the evaluation will be used for political purposes other than or contrary to those articulated in preliminary discussions. For example, an evaluator might suspect that an evaluation of charter schools might be used (and even misused) by a client with known advocacy for privatization of education.

The constraints under which the evaluation must be conducted				
Time	Budget	Data	Political	**Typical Evaluation Scenarios**
X	X			The evaluator has to operate under time pressure and with a limited budget. Secondary survey data may be available, but there is little time or few resources to analyze it.
X		X		The evaluator has little time and no access to baseline data or a comparison group. Funds are available to collect additional data, but the survey design is constrained by the tight deadlines.
	X	X		The evaluator is called in late and has no access to baseline data or comparison groups. The budget is limited, but time is not a constraint.
X	X	X		The evaluator is called in late, is given a limited budget, and has no access to baseline survey data; and no comparison group has been identified.

NOTE: To simplify the table, the possible combinations of political constraints with the other three factors have not been included in the table.

3.1 Budget Constraints

Sometimes funds for the evaluation were not included in the original project budget, and the evaluation must be conducted with a much smaller budget than would normally be allocated. As a result, it may not be possible to collect the desirable data or to reconstruct baseline or comparison group data. Lack of funds may create or exacerbate time constraints because evaluators may not be able to spend as much time in the field as they consider necessary. Box 1.3 makes the point that it is important to understand whether the main constraint is budget or time (or both), because the best strategy will often be different in each case.

BOX 1.3
BUDGET AND TIME CONSTRAINTS HAVE DIFFERENT IMPLICATIONS FOR THE EVALUATION DESIGN

While budget and time constraints often have similar consequences for the evaluation design, in other cases they can require very different approaches. For example, if an evaluation must be completed by a certain date, the process of data collection can often be speeded up by bringing in consultants, hiring more experienced researchers, or increasing the number of **interviewers**. All these measures may require significant budget increases. If, on the other hand, budget is the main constraint, the decision might be made to contract with a local university that would use cheaper though less experienced graduate students who might require more time for data collection because they cannot work fulltime.

3.2 Time Constraints

The most common time constraint is when the evaluator is not called in until the project is already well advanced and the evaluation has to be conducted within a much shorter period of time than the evaluator considers necessary—in terms of a longitudinal perspective over the life of the project, the time allotted for conducting the end-of-project evaluation, or both. Time constraints often make it impossible to conduct a pretest–posttest evaluation design with a baseline study that can be repeated after the project has been implemented. The time available for planning stakeholder consultations, site visits and fieldwork, and data analysis may also have to be drastically reduced to meet the report deadline. These time pressures are particularly problematic for an evaluator who is not familiar with the area or even the country and who does not have time for familiarization and for building confidence with the communities and the agencies involved with the study. The combination of time and budget constraints frequently means that foreign evaluators (and out-of-town U.S. evaluators) can be in the country or the state for only a short period of time—often requiring them to use shortcuts that they recognize as methodologically questionable.

3.3 Data Constraints

When the evaluation does not start until late in the project cycle, there is usually little or no comparable baseline information available on the conditions of the target group before the start of the project. Even if project records are available, they are often not organized in the form needed for comparative before-and-after analysis, or they measure activities and outputs but not outcomes. Project records and other documentary data often suffer from reporting biases or poor record-keeping standards. Even when secondary data are available for a period close to the project starting date, they usually do not fully match the project populations. For example, employment data may cover only larger companies, whereas many project families work in smaller firms in the informal sector, or school records may cover public schools but not religious and other private schools.

Most clients are interested in collecting data only on the groups or communities with which they are working. They may also be concerned that collection of information on nonbeneficiaries might create expectations of financial compensation or other benefits (for which the project has no budget), which further discourages the collection of data on a comparison group. Even if funds are available, it is also often difficult to identify a comparison group, because many project areas have unique characteristics. Where intended project impacts concern sensitive topics such as women's empowerment, contraceptive usage, or domestic violence, especially in paternalistic societies, information may be difficult to collect even when funds are available (see Box 1.4). Similar data problems can arise

---

BOX 1.4
PROBLEMS IN CAPTURING INFORMATION
FROM OR ABOUT WOMEN

- Many household surveys only interview the "household head," who is often considered to be the male. He often does not have all the information on female household members or gives low priority to their concerns. Many men, for example, say their wives are happy to spend several hours per day walking to collect water or fuel because they "sing and chat with their friends as they walk."

- Women are often interviewed in the presence of other household members where they may not feel free to express their views.
- Donor agencies often insist that women be invited to attend community meetings to discuss proposed projects. However, the women often do not feel free to speak in public, or they always say they agree with their husbands.
- In many parts of the world, sexual harassment is one of the main reasons women do not use public transport. However, it is culturally impossible for women to mention this to an outside interviewer, so this major problem is often not captured in surveys.

when working with difficult-to-reach groups such as drug addicts, criminals, ethnic minorities, migrants, or illegal residents.

3.4 Political Influences

We use the term *political influences and constraints* in a broad sense to refer not only to pressures from government agencies and politicians but also to include the requirements of funding or regulatory agencies, pressures from stakeholders, and differences of opinion within an evaluation team regarding evaluation approaches or methods.

Evaluations are frequently conducted in contexts in which political and ethical issues affect design and use. All programs affect some portion of the public, and most programs consume public funds, always limited and often scarce. Decisions based on evaluation results may intensify competition for funding, expand or terminate programs needed by some and paid for by others, or advance the agenda of a politically oriented group. Box 1.5 gives an example of how political pressures often affect the evaluation design—in this case, forbidding the use of a comparison group.

BOX 1.5
POLITICAL INFLUENCE ON THE EVALUATION OF A POWER PROJECT IN ASIA

Consultants were asked to design an evaluation to assess the impacts of a hydroelectric power project in an Asian country that would involve the forced resettlement of a number of villages in the area where the dam was to be constructed. Families who had title to their land would receive compensation. The consultants proposed that the evaluation should include a comparison group of families who did not have land title. They were informed by the power authority that it would not be possible to do this because this would create expectations that these families would also receive compensation for being relocated, and funds for this were not included in the project budget.

While evaluators are always quick to spot the political or ideological biases of their clients and stakeholders, they are often less aware (or open) about their own ideological orientations. Many of the ongoing debates between quantitative and qualitative evaluators are fueled by the search for the "correct" or "best" research **paradigm**.

4. Additional Organizational and Administrative Challenges

In addition to budget, time, data, and political constraints, all evaluations must conform to the organizational arrangements under which they are commissioned and the administrative procedures of the different agencies involved in commissioning, financing, managing, and using the evaluations. Often there will be a number of different agencies involved in the evaluation, and it is not uncommon for them to have different goals for the evaluation. These may involve the kinds of information to be obtained; the preferred methodology; preferences with respect to the stakeholders that should be involved and who is asked to comment on or approve the evaluation reports; the extent and form in which target populations are or are not involved; and how and to which audiences the evaluation will be disseminated and used. When different international agencies are involved, the basic logistics of arranging joint missions to the country where the evaluation is being conducted can be a major challenge, sometimes delaying implementation for significant periods of time.

Balancing the preferences and operating styles of different agencies can be a major challenge for the evaluation team, particularly in cases where there may be differences of opinion among stakeholders or lack of definition of their respective roles.

Even when only a single agency is involved, their administrative and operating procedures may provide further constraints and challenges for the evaluator. For example, when local counterparts have to be contracted, the procurement procedures of the funding agency or the host government may produce long delays or require the use of contractual procedures that do not work well for a particular evaluation. In other cases, the requirement to prepare an inception report and to delay the start of fieldwork until different departments have commented on the report can cause significant delays in the start of the evaluation. In some cases, the date for the completion of the evaluation report is not changed, despite time lost waiting for feedback, so that the effective time for consultants to work on the evaluation may be significantly reduced. Another common problem is that a fixed amount of time is allowed for fieldwork in every country, despite the fact that in some cases it is well known that considerable numbers of days are likely to be lost while arranging travel to difficult-to-reach parts of the country or while waiting for government clearance for travel. Often, when the evaluation consultants bring up these logistical problems, the evaluation manager will respond, "I entirely agree with you, but unfortunately, this is our administrative policy, so you will just have to do the best you can."

5. The RealWorld Approach to Evaluation Challenges

Although RWE does not develop many new data collection or analysis methods, the approach makes several contributions to the conduct of evaluations under RealWorld budget, time, data, and political constraints. First, it presents ways to draw from a wide range of evaluation approaches and methods to address the four types of constraints described earlier. The systematic use of mixed methods is emphasized throughout. Using mixed-method approaches is considered critical for several reasons: (a) It permits the evaluator to draw on the widest possible range of evaluation methods and tools, (b) it increases the validity of conclusions by providing two or more independent estimates of key indicators (triangulation), (c) it permits a deeper and richer analysis and interpretation of the context in which a program operates, and (d) it offers ways to reduce the costs or time of data collection (see Chapters 3, 4, and 14).

Second, RWE's seven-step approach offers corrective measures that can be introduced in different phases of the evaluation process, some even after a draft evaluation report has been produced, helping to enhance the quality of the evaluation. Quality promotes credibility and utility of findings, which, in turn, help ensure that evaluation contributes to the public good.

Third, many quantitative evaluations rely on a pretest–posttest with statistical counterfactual design to estimate the changes and impacts produced by a project or program. This approach, when used in isolation, has two serious limitations: (a) It does not take into account the different socioeconomic and political contexts affecting each project, and (b) it implicitly assumes that each project is implemented as planned and in exactly the same way in each location. One of the contributions of RWE is to look inside the "**black box**" of the project implementation process to examine what actually happens during implementation and how much variation there is between different project sites (see Box 1.6). It also focuses on quality of implementation. This is a critical contribution because in many RealWorld contexts, some project components are not implemented at all or the quality is so low that it is hardly surprising that the intended impacts were not achieved. In other cases, the intended impacts were achieved, but what went on within the project was quite different from what had been planned!

BOX 1.6
GETTING INSIDE THE "BLACK BOX"

Many impact evaluations assume that projects are implemented exactly as planned and in exactly the same way in each location. In fact, there are often major differences in how each project is implemented depending on local cultural, economic, administrative, and political factors. In some cases, the pretest–posttest evaluation is faithfully conducted without realizing that some of the project components were never implemented at all. Women did not apply for loans because it was too far to travel to the bank in town, teachers did not come to school during the planting season, textbooks never reached many of the schools, and parents in some areas did not send their daughters to school.

Unless the evaluation looks inside the "black box" of the project's implementation process, many of the findings of an impact evaluation can be very misleading and of little practical utility.

---

6. Who Uses RealWorld Evaluation, for What Purposes, and When?

There are two main users of RWE: First, evaluation practitioners will find it useful to use RWE for a number of reasons. For example:

- To identify ways to conduct adequately rigorous evaluations given limitations of time and financial resources

- To overcome data constraints, particularly the lack of baseline and comparison data
- To identify and address factors affecting the validity and adequacy of the findings of the evaluation

Second, *government agencies, international development agencies, and foundations* who commission evaluations and/or use evaluation findings will find the RWE approach useful for these reasons:

- To identify ways to reduce the costs and time of evaluations—or at least be aware of what an adequate budget and time frame would be required to conduct the kind of evaluation they may have in mind
- To be more fully aware of the various constraints under which an evaluation is to be conducted, and what can be done to address those constraints
- To understand the implications of different RWE strategies on the ability of the evaluation to respond to the purposes for which it was commissioned

Table 1.2 Who Uses RWE, for What Purposes, and When?

When does the evaluation start?	Evaluation practitioners who design or implement the evaluation	Managers and funding agencies
At the beginning of a project (baseline)	<ul><li>Identify a life-of-project evaluation design that will meet the needs of key stakeholders, given anticipated budget, time, and data constraints</li><li>Advise management how to reduce costs and time while achieving evaluation objectives</li><li>Negotiate with managers to relax some of the constraints (e.g., provide adequate budget and time) to reduce some of the threats to validity and adequacy</li><li>Advise management on plans for a baseline study consistent with evaluation objectives</li></ul>	<ul><li>Be realistic in estimating the budget and time required for the proposed evaluation design, including the baseline study</li><li>Assess the relevance, required level of rigor, and quality of the proposed life-of-project evaluation design</li></ul>
During project implementation	<ul><li>Identify ways to produce the best evaluation under budget, time, and data constraints</li><li>Identify ways for relevant monitoring data to be collected and documented that inform implementers and are relevant for evaluation purposes</li><li>If there was no baseline, reconstruct baseline data</li><li>Ensure maximum quality under existing constraints</li></ul>	<ul><li>Identify ways to strengthen the ongoing monitoring and evaluation (these measures may be directly implemented by project management or funding agencies or recommended to the agency conducting the evaluation)</li><li>Keep data collection minimized and prioritized on information that informs decision making and learning</li></ul>

When does the evaluation start?	Evaluation practitioners who design or implement the evaluation	Managers and funding agencies
At the end of the project	• Identify ways to meet evaluation objectives within limitations of budget, time, political considerations, and data availability • Use the RWE checklist to identify and deal with threats to validity and reliability • Reconstruct baseline data • Ensure maximum quality under existing constraints	• Be clear on the purpose of evaluation and the relevant degree of rigor required • Identify ways to correct weaknesses in the evaluation within the budget and time constraints and/or be willing to allocate more funds and time to achieve required credibility

Table 1.2 shows that RWE can be conducted at three different points in a project or program: at the start during the planning stage, when the project is already being implemented, or at the end. When the evaluation begins at the start of the project, RWE is used (a) to understand client information needs and the political context within which the evaluation will be conducted, (b) to help identify different options for minimizing costs or time required for evaluation while still providing adequately valid information to meet stakeholders' needs, (c) for deciding what evaluation design would be appropriate, (d) for deciding what data need to be collected by the monitoring system during the implementation of the project, and (e) for deciding how to make the best use of available data.

When the evaluation does not begin until project implementation is already underway, RWE is used to identify and assess the different evaluation design options that can be used within the budget and time constraints and to consider ways to reconstruct baseline data. Attention will be given to assessing the strengths and weaknesses of monitoring and administrative data available from the project and the availability and quality of secondary data from other sources. The feasibility of constructing a comparison group may also be considered. When the evaluation does not begin until toward the end of the project (or when the project has already ended), RWE is used in a similar way to the previous situation except that the design options are more limited because it is no longer possible to directly observe the project implementation process. One of the innovative RWE approaches is to suggest measures that can be taken to strengthen the validity of the findings even up to the point when the draft final evaluation report is being reviewed.

SUMMARY

- Many evaluations are affected by budget, time, and data constraints or by political influences that limit the design options and data collection methodologies available to the evaluator. We call these the *RWE constraints*.
- RealWorld evaluators most frequently face one of two main scenarios. The first is when the evaluator is called in at the start of the project but the choice of evaluation design is constrained by budget or time pressures, by technical and administrative difficulties in collecting certain kinds of data, or by pressures from clients and stakeholders.

- The second and probably the most common scenario is when the evaluator is not called in until the project has been underway some time or may even be nearing completion. Often the evaluator is again subject to budget and time constraints and political pressures, but even when budget and time are adequate, it is usually the case that no systematic baseline data have been collected and usually no comparison group has been identified.
- We have found that the RealWorld Evaluation approach is applicable to varying degrees in all countries.

FURTHER READING

American Evaluation Association. 2004. *Guiding Principles for Evaluators.*Fairhaven, MA: Author. Retrieved from www.eval.org/Publications/GuidingPrinciples.asp

The evaluation guidelines approved by the American Evaluation Association.

Morra-Imas, L. and R. Rist. 2009. *The Road to Results: Designing and Conducting Effective Development Evaluations.* Washington, DC: World Bank.

Covers many of the topics addressed by RWE.

Operations Evaluation Department. 2004. *Influential Evaluations: Evaluations That Improved Performance and Impacts of Development Programs.* Washington, DC: World Bank.

Case studies of evaluations that had a demonstrable influence on clients and stakeholders and a discussion of the factors determining whether evaluations will be used.

Patton, M. Q. 2008. *Utilization-Focused Evaluation.* 4th ed. Thousand Oaks, CA: Sage.

One of the most cited texts on how to design evaluations that will be utilized.

Patton, M.Q. 2011. Developmental *Evaluation: Applying Complexity Concepts to Enhance Innovation and Use.* New York: Guilford.

Discussion of the limitations of conventional impact evaluation designs, particularly for the evaluation of complex and evolving programs.

Rossi, P., M. Lipsey, and H. Freeman. 2004. *Evaluation: A Systematic Approach.* 7th ed. Thousand Oaks, CA: Sage.

Chapter 2 introduces the evaluator–stakeholder relationship, and Chapter 12 discusses the social context of evaluation and the ethical issues discussed in this chapter.

Russon, C. and G. Russon, eds. 2005. *International Perspectives on Evaluation Standards.* New Directions for Evaluation, No. 104. San Francisco: Jossey-Bass.

Discussion of the experiences and issues when other countries in different regions consider adopting and/or adapting U.S. evaluation standards.

CHAPTER 2

First Clarify the Purpose: Scoping the Evaluation

n this chapter, we introduce Step 1 of the RealWorld Evaluation (**RWE**) approach—"scoping the evaluation." We begin by considering the widely different expectations that **clients** can have about the purpose and nature of evaluation and what they understand by and expect from an impact evaluation. It is important to understand client information needs, their assumptions on how the evaluation should be conducted, and how clients expect to use the information produced by the evaluation. We also point to the need to identify other **stakeholders** and the nature and degree to which they should be involved in an evaluation. We then discuss the use of **program theory models** to articulate the assumptions on which the project **design** was based and to ensure that the evaluation focuses on the key issues and hypotheses of concern to stakeholders. Program theory also helps us understand how project implementation, **outcomes**, and **impacts** are affected by the political, economic, institutional, environmental, and cultural context within which each individual project is implemented. RWEs use both qualitative (**QUAL**) and quantitative (**QUANT**) evaluation methodologies, and there should be no a priori preference for either. There are many advantages in using mixed-method designs that draw on the strengths of both QUAL and QUANT methodologies. The chapter concludes by showing how the information collected during the scoping phase is used to preliminarily identify the cost, time, data, and political constraints that a particular evaluation will face and how this analysis is used to identify and assess the possible RWE designs that could be used for this particular evaluation.

1. Stakeholder Expectations of Impact Evaluations

There is a wide variety of understandings of what is involved in conducting an impact evaluation and what can be expected from the results. These include those who believe that every impact evaluation must be a sophisticated, "scientific," randomized, or quasi-experimental design.[1] On the other end of

---

[1]See, for example, the MIT's Poverty Action Lab (www.povertyactionlab.com), and the International Initiative for Impact Evaluation (3ie; www.3ieimpact.org).

the continuum are those who believe that QUAL methods are needed to understand programs and their impacts in the ways in which they are experienced by stakeholders. And there are those who prefer multisite or multiprogram studies of issues or themes to examine broader impact. Although decisions on the choice of evaluation methods are partly based on the methodological preferences of the evaluators and the agencies commissioning the evaluation, they are also influenced by the size and complexity of the program (we use the term *program* to cover projects, broader programs, and multicomponent interventions) being evaluated, the context within which the intervention is implemented, and the specific purpose of the evaluation. As we will explore in more depth in subsequent chapters, RWE budget, time, data, and political constraints can also affect the choice of methods.

Figure 2.1   Step 1: Scoping the Evaluation

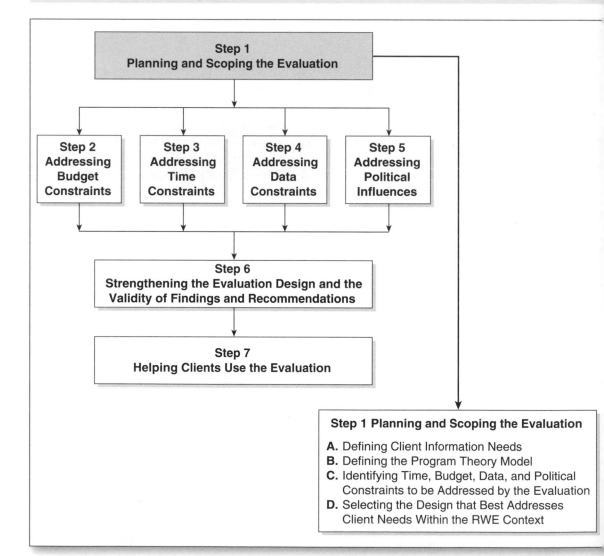

2. Understanding Information Needs

Whether plans for evaluating an intervention (project or program)[2] begin at the time it is designed or are not thought about until near the end of its life, those responsible for commissioning and conducting the evaluation will need to consider its purpose and therefore what design and methodologies would be appropriate and feasible. Table 1.1 (Chapter 1) shows that RWE can be used at the beginning of a program, during implementation, or at the end; it also describes the purposes for which evaluations are used by evaluation practitioners and clients/users at each of these points in the program cycle. The process of defining the evaluation purpose begins with a stakeholder analysis conducted by the evaluation team to understand the expectations of key stakeholders and often to negotiate with them what should and can be done, given constraints of money, time, data availability, and political considerations.

A clear understanding of the priorities and information needs of clients and other key stakeholders is an essential first step in the design of a good evaluation and an effective way for the RealWorld evaluator to eliminate unnecessary data collection and analysis, hence reducing cost and time. The timing, focus, and level of detail of the evaluation should be determined by information needs and the types of decisions to which the evaluation must contribute.

While it is usually a simple matter to define the clients (those commissioning the evaluation), a more difficult issue is to define the range of **stakeholders** whose concerns should be taken into account in the evaluation design, implementation, and dissemination. Time and budget constraints often create pressures that limit the range of stakeholders that can be consulted and involved. The evaluator should try to assess whether these constraints exclude some important groups—particularly, vulnerable groups who may be difficult to reach and less likely to be included in the planning, implementation, and use of the evaluation. It is sometimes useful to distinguish between primary stakeholders, who are consulted regularly throughout the intervention and the evaluation and whose opinions are normally taken into consideration, and secondary stakeholders, whose role in the evaluation is less clearly defined and who may or may not be consulted on a regular basis. Evaluators and clients may sometimes disagree on who is a stakeholder and who should see draft reports and be consulted. This can become a sensitive issue if the evaluator believes that certain groups who are affected by the project should be consulted and the client wishes to limit consultations to the primary stakeholders.

Typically, an evaluator (or evaluation team) is commissioned to conduct an evaluation according to the terms set forth by the client (manager representing the implementing agency or donor). Some agencies call these the **Terms of Reference (ToR)**, while other agencies refer to the Scope or Statement of Work (SoW). But should a conscientious evaluator challenge an implicit paradigm that "the client knows best" by proposing that other stakeholders' perspectives be included and that the evaluation be made relevant to them? As Robert Chambers (1997) asks, "Whose reality counts?"

Related to the previous point, *Realist Evaluation* (Pawson and Tilley 1997; Pawson 2006) suggests asking the following questions:

1. Who benefits from the program?

2. How do they benefit?

---

[2]We use the term "intervention" to cover all types of development initiatives that are funded by government, donor agencies or non-government organizations.

3. When do they benefit?

4. Why?

5. Who does not benefit and why?

An understanding of the perspectives gained by such questions can greatly strengthen the design of an evaluation and the definition of the stakeholder groups that should be consulted.

An important part of the scoping phase is to clarify the **evaluand**, that is, what is being evaluated. As White and Bamberger (2008) have pointed out, evaluators need to pay more attention to the "factual" (the evaluand), as many evaluation designs are based on wrong or at least untested assumptions about how the program actually works. So among issues that need to be addressed during the evaluability assessment are:

1. How well developed and tested is the program theory?

2. If the program is still in a pilot development phase, the evaluation will need to assess how well the program's organization and delivery systems work. It is not possible (or it is risky) to conduct a rigorous assessment of impacts if the basic systems are not yet tested or working.

3. If the program has been operating for some time and is well tested, it is possible to consider a more rigorous assessment of outcomes and impacts.

Table 2.1 presents a checklist identifying 14 dimensions of the evaluation scenario that must be taken into consideration when designing the evaluation. The first 11 dimensions describe the characteristics of the evaluand (program being evaluated), while the final three refer to methodological dimensions referring both to client and stakeholder preferences and what is feasible within budget, time, and data constraints. It is recommended that evaluators should refer to this checklist when considering the most appropriate evaluation design. For example, the appropriate evaluation design would be quite different when evaluating a complex, national-level intervention with a large evaluation budget and for which the evaluation is being planned before the intervention begins than it would be for the evaluation of a small project with a small evaluation budget and for which the evaluation does not begin until the project is nearing completion. The purpose of the evaluation will also influence the appropriate evaluation design, as will the type of client who commissions (pays for) the evaluation and the skills and preferences of the consultant(s) hired to conduct the evaluation. A review of this checklist shows that it makes no sense to discuss the "best" evaluation design until all of these dimensions are fully understood.

Even when the evaluation design options have been narrowed down on the basis of these factors, there will still often be several different ways that that the evaluation could be designed. The methodological dimensions are also important as the evaluation design must reflect the methodological preferences of the client and key stakeholders as well as the constraints imposed by the evaluation scenario.

An evaluability assessment may reveal that the scope of the original ToR may need to be modified if some of the proposed questions cannot be addressed at this time and within the constraints of the evaluation. For example:

1. It may be too early in the life of the program to reasonably expect to measure impacts.

2. The lack of comparative data may limit the use of more rigorous statistical designs.

Table 2.1 Evaluation Purpose and Context

This table identifies some of the characteristics and dimensions of the evaluand (thing to be evaluated) that need to be taken into consideration as decisions about the design of the evaluation are made.	
I. Characteristics of the evaluand and the purpose and nature of the evaluation	
1. Basic purpose of evaluation[a]	a. Developmental, i.e., support innovative exploration of evolving approaches for addressing problems b. Formative, i.e., learning and improvement of planned intervention during the implementation process in order to improve the process itself c. Summative, i.e., accountability and judgment of the overall merit, worth, value, and significance of completed program. (Though this can feel like a postmortem, summative evaluation can inform major decisions about future programming.)
2. Other purposes of evaluation	a. Compliance with stated program plan b. Impact: existing or potential achievement of higher level outcomes, e.g., improved quality of life of intended beneficiaries c. Adapting an intervention to a new context d. Adapting an existing program to a major change e. To help make resource allocation decisions on competing or best alternatives f. To help identify emerging problems and build consensus on the causes of a problem and how to respond g. To support public sector reform and innovation
3. Complexity of the evaluand[b]	a. *Simple project*: few intervention components, defined timeline b. *Complicated program*: sector program with various components, often combining several individual projects c. *Complex situations*: e.g., general budget support or multiprogram interventions often involving several funding agencies and operating at the national or cross-country level or evolving situations such as natural disasters, violent conflict, or other dramatic changes
4. The local and national context within which the evaluation will be implemented	a. Economic context b. Political context c. Policy, legal, and administrative context d. Organizations and agencies involved in the project e. Natural environment f. Characteristics and culture of the target population, politics, history, socio-economic context, values, relative peace or conflict, needs and interests of stakeholders
5. Geographic level	a. Program or sector level (which could involve multiple countries) b. Multinational/regional (several countries) c. National (one country) d. Subnational region (e.g., district or province) e. One or a few local communities
6. Scale of intervention[c]	a. Small (e.g., less than 5,000 individuals or households) b. Medium (e.g., up to 50,000 units) c. Large (e.g., more than 50,000 units)

(Continued)

(Continued)

7. Size of the evaluation budget[d]	a. Small (e.g., less than 5% of program budget) b. Moderate (e.g., up to 15% of program budget) c. Generous (e.g., more than 15%—for example, a major purpose is research to test a new intervention)
8. When evaluation commissioned	a. Start of intervention (baseline/pretest) b. Midterm c. End of intervention (posttest) d. After intervention completed (ex-post)
9. Duration of the evaluation	a. Continues throughout intervention cycle b. Evaluation commissioned late in the intervention cycle but sufficient time is budgeted to conduct required data collection and analysis c. Great time pressure (the evaluation must be completed in weeks or a few months)
10. Client	a. Donor agency b. Planning ministry c. Implementing agency d. Civil society or other
11. Who conducts the evaluation	a. Internal evaluator (or evaluation team) b. External consultant(s) (individual or team) c. Mixed team combining external and internal members
II. Methodological dimensions	
12. Statistical rigor (client preference and what is feasible)	a. Statistically strong evaluation design b. Statistically weaker design c. Nonexperimental design
13. QUANT–QUAL preference	a. All or mostly quantitative methods and data b. All or mostly qualitative methods and evidence c. Appropriate mix of QUANT and QUAL
14. Data source(s)	a. Direct collection from units of study b. Secondary sources c. Appropriate mix of primary and secondary sources

[a]Adapted from Patton (2010a, as summarized in Exhibit 2.2, pp. 44–46, and Exhibit 10.1, pp. 308–313) and Morra-Imas and Rist 2009 (Box 1.1, p. 15), with additional categories added by the present authors to reflect other purposes of funding agencies and clients

[b] The concept of complexity is discussed in Chapter 15.

[c]The concepts of "large" and "small" with respect to cost and scale are relative. What might be considered "small-scale" or "low-cost" by a major donor might be considered very large by a nongovernmental organization (NGO).

[d]Though we give relative budget percentages for illustrative purposes, obviously the actual amount available for evaluation makes a significant difference on the kind of evaluation that can be undertaken.

3. The absence of relevant secondary data or its poor quality and reliability may limit the possibility of reconstructing reliable baseline data.

4. Political or ethical constraints may limit the evaluation design (e.g., selecting control individuals or groups for randomized control trials), the people who can be interviewed, or the questions that can be asked.

In addition to the above considerations, there is, of course, need for an adequate understanding of the context within which the evaluation is to be conducted. Many evaluation designs are based on a limited or incorrect understanding of the evaluation context—often assuming that the project was able to be implemented as planned, without understanding the many political, cultural, organizational, economic, and perhaps environmental factors that could constrain how the project is actually implemented and who benefits. Some of the factors that could be considered include:

1. The ethnic composition of the target population and any conflicts and divisions that could make it difficult for the project to reach and benefit the whole population.

2. The need to understand gender relations.

3. Population movements and demographic trends.

4. How the local and national political context may affect the project.

Meeting as early as possible with clients and key stakeholders helps ensure that the reasons for commissioning the evaluation are understood, as well as some of the perspectives gained by asking the kinds of questions suggested above. It is particularly important to understand policy and operational decisions to which the evaluation will contribute and to agree on the level of precision required in making these decisions. Typical questions that decision makers must address include the following:

1. Is there evidence that the project achieved (or will achieve) its objectives? Which objectives were (or will be) achieved and which were not (or will not be) achieved? Why?

2. Did the project aim for the right objectives? Were the underlying causes of the problem(s) the project is designed to ameliorate accurately diagnosed and adequately addressed?

3. Are outcomes sustainable and benefits likely to continue?

4. What internal and/or external contextual factors determine the degree of success or failure?

5. Did the program satisfy the OECD/DAC criteria of relevance, effectiveness, efficiency, impact, and sustainability?

Many of these questions do not require a high level of statistical precision, but they do require reliable answers to additional questions, such as:

1. Are there measurable changes in the characteristics of the **target population** with respect to the impacts the project was intended to produce?

2. What impact has the project had on different subsets of the target population, including the poorest and most vulnerable groups? Are there different impacts on men and women? Are there ethnic, religious, or similar groups who do not benefit or who are affected negatively?

3. Is it likely the same impacts could be achieved if the project were implemented in a different setting or on a larger scale?

4. It may also be useful to address the realist evaluation questions referred to earlier: Who benefits from the program? How do they benefit? When do they benefit? Why? Who does not benefit and why?

The RealWorld evaluator needs to distinguish between critical issues that must be explored in depth and those that are less critical and can be studied less intensively or eliminated completely. It is also essential to understand when the client needs rigorous statistical or QUANT analysis to legitimize the evaluation **findings** to members of Congress, funding agencies, or those critical of the program and when more general analysis and findings would be acceptable. Answers to such questions can have a major impact on the evaluation design, budget, and time required.

3. Developing the Program Theory Model

A program theory is "an explicit theory or model of how the program causes the intended or observed outcomes" (Rogers, Petrosino, Huebner, and Hacsi 2000:5). All programs are based on an explicit or implicit hypothesis or theory about how intended program outputs are to lead to desired outcomes and impacts and the factors constraining or facilitating their achievement. While program theory models can be used in all evaluations, they are particularly useful for RWE as a framework upon which to design the evaluation and to identify critical areas and issues on which limited evaluation resources or time should focus. A program theory model may help explain whether failure to achieve objectives is due to faulty expectations or ineffective project implementation (Lipsey 1993; Weiss 1997).

Though program theory may be spelled out in project documents (e.g., a results-based management or logical framework or flow chart, often to meet donor requirements), more often, the **logic model** must be elicited or at least verified by the evaluator through consultations with program staff members, program participants, and partner agencies. Developing a program theory model is often an iterative process in which an initial model is constructed by the evaluator on the basis of preliminary consultations and then discussed and modified through further consultations.

Program theory models are relatively easy to describe for projects, as these normally have a relatively simple structure with a limited number of inputs intended to achieve relatively well-defined and measurable outputs and outcomes. They also have a relatively linear structure (see discussion in Chapters 9 and 15) and often a defined start and end date. All of these are particularly true when projects are funded by donor agencies, which usually will base the loan or grant on a clearly defined project document, or when they are funded by a government agency under a specific budget line item. However, many projects that are supported by local or international NGOs will often, but not always, have less clearly defined objectives and often no defined end date. As we will see, program theory can be applied in these latter cases, but a more creative and participatory approach will often be required to identify objectives and the underlying assumptions on which the project is based.

As interventions become larger and more complex, it becomes harder to apply program theory models. When applied to programs with a number of different components, it will often become necessary to use a multilevel program theory model (Rogers 2008; Funnell and Rogers 2011). The application of program theory models at the program and complex intervention levels is discussed in Chapters 10 and 16.

Figure 2.2 illustrates how a program theory model can be applied to a typical project. The model describes the seven stages of the project cycle:[3]

1. *Design.* How the project was designed (e.g., was it top-down, were there participatory consultations, was a standard blueprint used, or was it adapted to the local context)?

2. *Inputs.* The financial, human, material, technological, and information resources used in the project

3. *Implementation process.* The actions taken or work performed through which inputs, such as funds, technical assistance, and other types of resources, are mobilized to produce specific outputs; to what extent and how intended beneficiaries were involved

4. *Outputs.* Products and services resulting directly from program activities

5. *Outcomes.* The intended or achieved short- and medium-term effects of an intervention's outputs. Outcomes represent changes in development conditions that occur between the

Figure 2.2 A Simple Program Theory Model

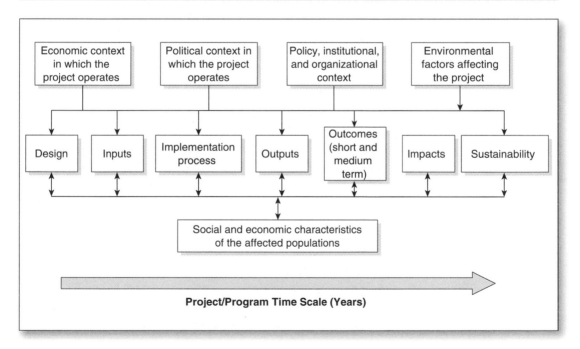

---

[3]Several of the definitions given here are adapted from Organization for Economic Cooperation and Development—Development Assistance Committee (OECD-DAC) (2002). This source is widely used by the evaluation departments of international development agencies.

completion of outputs and the achievement of impact. Higher-level outcomes, often referred to as impacts, usually require acknowledging the collective efforts (plausible contributions) of partners and other actors.

6. *Impacts*. Long-term economic, sociocultural, institutional, environmental, technological, or other effects on identifiable populations or groups produced by a project, directly or indirectly, intended or unintended

7. *Sustainability*. Continuation of benefits after a project has been completed

Although the first four components of this model—design, inputs, implementation processes, and outputs—may be directly controllable by those managing the project, by contrast, the outcomes, impacts, and sustainability depend to a considerable degree on external factors over which the project agency usually has little or no control. Some forms of logic models (e.g., log frames) refer to these as *assumptions*. Since the success of a project achieving higher-level results depend on those external assumptions to be fulfilled, it is important that they be verified. If essential external conditions change, it will be necessary for the project design to be changed accordingly to adapt to those changes.

BOX 2.1
DEFINING OUTCOMES AND IMPACTS

Outcomes are defined by OEC/DAC (2002) as "the likely or achieved short and medium term effects of an intervention's outputs." In this book, we focus on impact evaluations. However, it needs to be recognized that there is a wide variety of definitions of and assumptions related to the meaning of *impact* and to the related term *outcomes.* In simple terms, impact evaluation goes beyond an examination of outputs or even intermediary outcomes produced by a project's interventions to determine higher-level and longer-term effects.

The definition of impact adopted by the OECD-DAC (2002) is "Positive and negative, primary and secondary long-term effects produced by a development intervention on identifiable population groups, directly or indirectly, intended or unintended. These effects can be economic, socio-cultural, institutional, environmental, technological or of other types." This definition emphasizes that an impact evaluation is conducted late in the project cycle to assess the long-term effects, but the definition does not require that a particular methodology be used. On the other hand, many quantitative researchers define impact evaluation in terms of the methodology, stating that impacts can only be assessed through the definition of a statistical counterfactual (generated through experimental or quasi-experimental designs), but most of these definitions do not state the point in the project cycle at which an impact evaluation can be conducted. They also typically measure intermediary outcomes directly attributable to specific interventions.

There are other definitions or nuances, including the following:

- Some writers consider that outcomes are the observed changes in the variables the project seeks to affect, whereas impacts are the proportion of the changes that can be attributed to the project. Outcomes (changes in conditions) can be observed,

> whereas impacts (the influence a project had on those changes) can only be inferred through the use of an analytical process such as a quasi-experimental design.
>
> - Some define impact as "higher-level" outcomes (CARE International's definition is "equitable and durable improvements in human wellbeing and social justice"; CARE International 2003) whether or not changes at these levels can be directly attributable to a project. A project can be held accountable for direct attribution to outputs and more immediate outcomes/short-term effects, and thus to their plausible contributions to higher-level sustainable impact, along with other influences that must be identified and acknowledged.
>
> - The dictionary definition of impact refers to influence, the effect or impression of one thing on another—for example, what difference did the project make?
>
> - But influence on what? A project could have an "impact" on staff paychecks, on direct (but superficial) benefits of services provided to participants, on the capacities of local organizations, on the conditions of the target population, on the empowerment of individuals and community groups, on national policy, on the achievement of the Millennium Development Goals[4] . . . the list could go on. There needs to be agreement among stakeholders (including intended beneficiaries, donors, and partners) on what "success" (and therefore impact) would look like. It depends on their values and expectations—and on what is reasonable to expect from a time- and resource-bound project.
>
> - There are those who refer to impact in terms of scope or scale—for example, how many people's lives were influenced (impacted) in some way?
>
> - Others refer to it in terms of degree or depth—that is, whether a project had a minor influence or made a significant difference in the quality of life of beneficiaries in important ways.
>
> - There are also the intended/unintended dimensions of impact, desired/negative impact, and direct/indirect impact (e.g., multiplier effect of people adopting a practice beyond those who participated directly in a project).

And, of course, there is the assumption (that needs to be verified by measurement or projection) that whatever impact there was will be *sustainable*—that is, will continue after the external influence of a project has ended.

Some of the different ways in which the concept of impact is used in evaluation are described in Box 2.1. There are also a number of agencies that do not use the concept of impact, believing that it is methodologically or philosophically too difficult to define, measure, or interpret. However, because the purpose of most development interventions is to contribute to long-term effects (improvements in the well-being of the target populations) rather than just to produce short-term observable outcomes, we go along with the majority of development practitioners and try to evaluate impacts—while fully recognizing all the methodological and philosophical limitations on how well impacts can be measured/assessed/inferred, particularly in many RWE contexts.

An **evaluability assessment** may also be conducted during the scoping phase. This is an assessment of the feasibility of assessing project outputs, outcomes, and impacts with the available

---

[4]See www.un.org/millenniumgoals.

resources and data. While design, inputs, implementation processes, and outputs can be directly observed, measured, and documented by the project's monitoring system, indicators of outcomes and impacts usually require additional data collection (e.g., sample surveys or in-depth QUAL data collection), often using one of the designs discussed in Chapter 11. Whether the project makes plausible contributions to such outcomes and impacts must be tested or inferred. And unless there is an ex-post evaluation conducted some time after the project finished operating, sustainable impact can only be inferred and not directly observed. Consequently, one of the purposes of the evaluability assessment (if it is conducted) is to determine whether resources will permit collecting the types of additional data required to assess outcomes and impacts.

Outcomes are the short- and medium-term effects and impacts are the long-term effects of a project. In other words, these are the changes that can be wholly or partly attributed to the interventions of the project, perhaps by a **counterfactual** that estimates what would have been the economic, sociocultural, institutional, or other conditions of the intended beneficiaries in the absence of the project's interventions. The difference between the observed conditions of the beneficiaries and the counterfactual is the estimated impact of the project. The methodology for assessing project impacts through a variety of evaluation designs is discussed in Chapter 11.

The logic model depicted in Figure 2.2 also identifies five sets of **contextual variables** that may affect implementation and outcomes. These include the economic, political, organizational, operational, and environmental settings of the project and the socioeconomic and cultural characteristics of the affected populations (Hentschel 1999; Patton 2008). The following are examples of how each of these contextual variables can affect the project and how their analysis can strengthen interpretation of evaluation findings:

- *Economic factors:* In a dynamic economy in which jobs are being created and demand for products and services is growing, people are often more willing to invest time or resources in developing marketable skills or in launching small businesses. It is often hypothesized, for example, that parents are more willing to pay for their daughters to stay in school (and to forego the daughters' assistance with domestic and farming activities) if labor market conditions create the expectation that extra education will help them get better jobs.

- *Political factors:* Support from local government agencies (who happen to be from the same political party as the national or state government sponsoring a project) can significantly improve project performance by mobilizing community support or providing free resources such as transport, workers, or buildings. Inversely, politically induced opposition to a project can seriously affect its success or even its ability to operate. Sometimes projects can become affected by political campaigns. In Zambia in the late 1970s, a donor agency was trying to convince the Ministry of Housing to charge full economic rent for low-cost housing. One of the candidates in the municipal election campaign promised families that if he was elected, all rents would be subsidized, which contributed to the reluctance of families to pay their rent to the project.

- *Organizational and institutional factors:* Many projects require support from government agencies and other organizations such as **NGOs** (nongovernmental organizations) or religious organizations. The effectiveness of this cooperation can vary considerably from one community, district, or city to another. In some cases, this is due to personalities, in other cases to local politics, but in many cases, it is mainly due to differences in staff, financial, or other resources. Sometimes something as basic as the Ministry of Health in one town having a jeep, whereas in the next location it does not, can have a major impact on the level and effectiveness of support.

- *Environmental factors:* Agricultural and rural development projects are directly affected by variations in the local environment. The new grain varieties being introduced may prosper well on flat land but not on hillsides, or they may be very sensitive to variations in seasonal rainfall. Urban development projects may be affected by erosion or flooding. All these factors may produce dramatic differences in crop yield or in the success of water and sanitation projects.

- *Socioeconomic and cultural characteristics of the target communities.* Many countries in Africa and other developing regions have literally hundreds of different tribal groups, each with its own farming practices, rules concerning use of natural resources, marriage practices, and attitudes concerning the mobility and economic participation of women. In one village in Uganda, bicycles proved an effective way to transport water and reduce women's time burden (because water was carried in square metal jerry cans that could easily be transported on the bicycle's luggage rack), but in a neighboring village, bicycles failed to produce this benefit because water was transported in round clay pots that could not easily be transported on a luggage rack.

An analysis of these contextual factors can often help explain why two identical projects may have very different outcomes in different communities. In one community, the economy may be thriving, whereas in another it is in decline—so parents are more willing to pay for their daughters' continued education in the first than in the second; in one community, most of the farm land is flat and well drained, whereas in the next community, most of the land is hilly and the new variety of grain does not prosper. For these reasons, evaluators are strongly encouraged to incorporate contextual analysis into the evaluation design.

A key element of program theory models is the identification and monitoring of critical assumptions about inputs, implementation processes, and the expected linkages with outcomes. There are two types of assumptions: internal and external. Internal assumptions, or hypotheses, describe the logical cause-and-effect links between interventions and outcomes. External assumptions refer to factors beyond the direct control of a project—for example, whether the project should address policy issues rather than take it for granted that it can have no influence over them. Even those external factors that truly cannot be changed by the project need to be monitored if the success of the project depends on the correctness of those assumptions or on needed adjustments in response to changing external conditions.

3.1. Program Theory as a Management Tool

Program theory is widely used as a management tool to define and monitor progress toward the achievement of program objectives (results, goals, outcomes, and impacts), to test the validity of the assumptions on which program design is based, and to draw lessons for the design and implementation of future projects. In order to do this, the program theory is represented graphically by a logic model that is then translated into a set of tables that operationalize inputs, outputs, outcomes, and impacts with related indicators that can be measured and against which progress can be tracked. Today, the most common framework for doing this is results-based management (RBM), which is a refinement of logical framework analysis. RBM is discussed in Chapter 10.

An important management tool is the incorporation of a results chain (see Chapter 10) that spells out in more detail the steps through which the outputs, outcomes, and impacts are to be achieved. When these are not fully achieved, the results chain enables management to identify the link in the chain at which the problems arose. The results chain is also a valuable tool for designing the evaluation, as it helps identify the critical hypotheses and assumptions that need to be tested by the evaluation.

4. Identifying the Constraints to Be Addressed by RWE and Determining the Appropriate Evaluation Design

The final part of Step 1 of the RWE approach includes preliminary identification of those budget, time, data, and political constraints that can be anticipated. This can lead to a determination of which of the options for Steps 2, 3, 4, and 5 will need to be used. Once the evaluators have identified what they consider to be the best options for addressing these constraints, the proposed strategy will then be discussed with the client and, ideally, key stakeholders. Often this may involve a period, sometimes quite long, of negotiation and revision of the proposed strategy. In some cases, the evaluation team may try to convince the client that the requested reductions in budget or time are not possible without prejudicing the purposes for which the evaluation is being conducted. If the client is not able or willing to increase the budget or allow for more time, the evaluators may in some cases decide to withdraw from the project, but typically some compromise can be reached. However, in these cases, it is extremely important for the client to understand the types of information, findings, and recommendations that can and cannot be provided within these constraints and the levels of precision, validity, and adequacy that the evaluation can be expected to achieve. Importantly, the client should also understand how these compromises are likely to affect the credibility of the findings with different stakeholders.

Chapters 3 through 6 review the options for addressing budget, time, data, and political constraints, respectively.

5. Developing Designs Suitable for RealWorld Evaluation Conditions

We now address a very important decision that needs to be made by those commissioning and those responsible for conducting an evaluation: What evaluation design would be most appropriate for responding to the priority questions determined during the assessment of client needs, and which design options are even possible, given the constraints and the stage the project has reached? As we saw in Table 1.1, the earlier in the life of the project this decision is made, the more options there are. Though the subject of evaluation designs will be covered in more detail in Chapter 11, we provide a brief introduction here.

Table 2.2 presents a framework for classifying the evaluation design structures. They are classified in terms of when the evaluation began, whether baseline (or only posttest) data were collected, whether a **comparison group** design was used, and if so, how the comparison group was selected. These structures or **scenarios** should only be considered as the skeleton of the evaluation design, and a wide range of different methodologies (quantitative, qualitative, and mixed-method) can be used within each structure. Given the ongoing debates concerning whether there is a "best" evaluation design, it is important to stress that we do not believe there is a single best design and that the choice

Table 2.2 Seven Basic Impact Evaluation Design Frameworks

Key: P = Project participants C = Control/comparison group (Note 1) P_1, P_2, C_1, C_2 = First and second and any subsequent observations X = Project intervention	Start of project (baseline/ pretest) (Note 2)	Project intervention (Note 3)	Midterm evaluation	End of project evaluation (endline)	Postproject evaluation (some time after intervention ended) (ex-post)
Time period for evaluation event:	T_1		T_2	T_3	T_4
1. *Longitudinal design* with pretest (baseline), midterm, posttest (endline), and ex-post observations of both project and comparison groups.	P_1 C_1	X	P_2 C_2	P_3 C_3	P_4 C_4
2. *Pretest + posttest project and comparison group design* i.e., before-and-after plus with-and-without comparisons.	P_1 C_1	X		P_2 C_2	
3. Truncated *pretest + posttest of project and comparison groups where the initial study is not conducted until the project has been underway for some time* (most commonly at the midterm evaluation)		X	P_1 C_1	P_2 C_2	
4. *Pretest + posttest comparison of project group combined with posttest (only) of comparison group*	P_1	X		P_2 C_1	
5. *Posttest(only) comparison of project and comparison groups*		X		P_1 C_1	
6. *Pretest + posttest of project group (no counterfactual comparison group)*	P_1	X		P_2	
7. *Posttest(only) analysis of project group (no baseline or statistical comparison group)*		X		P_1	

NOTES:

(1) Technically, a *control group* is only used in an experimental design, as randomization supposedly ensures there is no systematic difference in the distribution of subject characteristics between the two groups (i.e., selection *controls* for differences) and a comparison group is used in quasi-experimental designs in which different selection procedures are used for the nontreatment group (sometimes called a "nonequivalent control group"). However, we will follow the common practice of using *comparison group* as shorthand for all kinds of matched groups, except when we wish to specifically indicate that randomization was used, in which case we will use the term *control group*.

(2) In this simplified table, the point at which data are first collected on the project group (P_1) is also the time at which the evaluation begins. In Table 11.3 (Chapter 11), we distinguish between evaluations that start at the beginning of the project (and in which baseline data are collected through primary data collection) and evaluations that start late in the project but in which baseline data are obtained from secondary sources or through the baseline reconstruction techniques discussed in Chapter 5.

(3) The project intervention is usually a process that occurs over time, that is, past the midterm to the end of the life of the project.

of the appropriate design must be made on the basis of the purpose of the evaluation and a review of types of evaluation presented earlier.

It is useful at this point to distinguish between designs that are statistically strong (experimental and quasi-experimental designs 1, 2, and perhaps 3 in Table 2.2) and methodologically sound designs. Box 2.2 argues that many of the "strong designs" referred to in the research literature are, in fact, only strong in their ability to address statistical threats to selection bias, but they are potentially

---

BOX 2.2
POTENTIAL METHODOLOGICAL WEAKNESSES IN MANY STATISTICALLY STRONG EVALUATION DESIGNS

Many evaluation designs that are commonly referred to in the evaluation literature are, in fact, only strong with respect to their ability to control for sources of statistical selection bias. The reasons that they are statistically strong (e.g., randomization or statistical matching of samples, strict and inflexible rules concerning how data are collected, and administration of the same survey instrument to the same or equivalent samples before and after the project implementation) make these quantitative designs potentially weak in other respects, including:

- *Weak construct validity*: Many statistical designs are not based on a program theory model (although it is perfectly possible to incorporate a program theory model).
- *No or insufficient analysis of the project implementation process*
- *No consideration of contextual variables* that can explain differences in outcomes in different project locations
- *Mono-method bias*: Many quantitative designs collect all of their data from a single instrument, most commonly a structured questionnaire. This increases the risk of bias or incomplete information, as it is not possible to compare estimates obtained from different independent sources.
- *Difficulties in collecting information on sensitive topics*: Many quantitative approaches use data collection methods such as structured questionnaires.
- *Inflexibility and difficulty in adapting the design to changes in the project design or the context in which it is implemented*

Two conclusions result from these potential methodological weaknesses in strong statistical designs. First, it is important, when discussing the merits of different evaluation designs, to always distinguish between "strong statistical designs" and "methodologically strong designs." While statistical evaluations can be designed to ensure all-round methodological strength, this is frequently not done, so that many statistically strong designs can be vulnerable in other ways. Similarly, it is possible to have qualitative or mixed-method designs that might be considered weak in terms of conventional quantitative terms but that may use designs that are methodologically sound in other ways. Second, it is almost always possible to strengthen the methodology of all evaluation designs, quantitative, qualitative, and mixed-method, by incorporating the essential evaluation design components discussed in the following text (see Table 2.3).

weak with respect to other important methodological areas. These questions are discussed in more detail in Chapter 11 and in Chapters 12, 13, and 14, in which the relative strengths and weaknesses of quantitative, qualitative, and mixed-method designs are compared.

The evaluation design frameworks presented in Table 2.2 could be classified into three categories depending on whether there is a control/comparison group and, if so, how it is selected:

- *Experimental designs* (randomized control trials) in which subjects are randomly assigned to the project and treatment groups. This is the strongest statistical design in terms of control for selection bias but, as noted in Box 2.2, these designs have a number of potential methodological weaknesses when used in isolation.
- *Quasi-experimental designs* in which a comparison group is used, but it is selected separately from the project group so that there are potential problems of selection bias. When large samples are used or good secondary data are available, it is possible to use statistical matching procedures such as propensity score matching. When this is not possible, judgmental matching procedures, which are statistically weaker, must be used. While these designs can reduce the effects of statistical selection bias, as in the case of experimental designs, when used in isolation, they are subject to a range of methodological challenges.
- *Nonexperimental designs* that do not use a statistical comparison group. While these designs are often used when an evaluation must be conducted under time and budget constraints and where as a consequence the methodology is often weak, many other evaluations use methodologically strong qualitative and mixed-method designs (see Chapters 13 and 14).

So this framework should be considered as a starting point for identifying the most appropriate evaluation design and not as a list of evaluation designs and certainly not as a ranking of "strong" and "weak" designs.

5.1. How the Sources of Data Affect the Choice of Evaluation Design

As indicated earlier, evaluations can be based mainly on primary data collection, they can use a combination of primary and secondary data, or they can be based mainly on secondary data from surveys that have already been conducted. When good-quality secondary data are available, the range of design options is increased: pretest/posttest comparison designs can be used even when the evaluation does not start until late in the program cycle. It becomes more feasible to use a comparison group, and the procedures for selecting a comparison group can be strengthened.

Whichever design is selected, the RWE approach strongly recommends that the basic statistical design be complemented by a number of mixed-method design components to address some of the weaknesses of the statistical designs. Table 2.3 describes six essential components of all RWE evaluation designs.

While these frameworks and designs have often been discussed within the context of QUANT evaluation designs, the scenarios (e.g., whether or not the evaluation begins with a baseline assessment, whether there are to be before-and-after comparisons, whether or not there is some form of counterfactual analysis) apply equally to QUAL and mixed-method evaluations. Most QUANT evaluations are based on either an experimental or a quasi-experimental design in that they seek to directly measure changes in a set of QUANT variables and to assess whether the changes are

Table 2.3 Essential Evaluation Design Components to Complement Any of the Basic Evaluation Designs

Essential evaluation design component	Why required	How to implement
1. Basing the evaluation on a program theory model	The purpose of an evaluation is not just to estimate "how much" change has occurred but also to explain "why" and "how" the changes were produced. Clients also wish to know to what extent the changes were due to the intervention and whether similar changes would be likely to occur if the program is replicated in other contexts. In order to achieve the above objectives, it is necessary to explain the underlying theory and the key assumptions on which the program is based and to identify how these can be tested in the evaluation.	The design and use of program theory are discussed in Chapter 10. That chapter also illustrates how the theory can be articulated graphically through a logic model.
2. Process analysis	Project outcomes are affected by how well a project is implemented and by what happens during implementation. Without process analysis, it is not possible to assess whether failure to achieve outcomes is due to design failure or to implementation failure.	See Chapter 10.
3. Multiple data collection methods	Many evaluations use a single method of data collection. For QUANT designs, typically, data are collected using a structured questionnaire. This is not adequate for collecting information on sensitive topics or on multidimensional indicators.	See Chapters 13 and 14.
4. Contextual analysis	Projects implemented in an identical way in different locations will often have different outcomes due to different local economic, political, or organizational contexts or different socioeconomic characteristics of target communities. This can result in wrong estimations of project impact, often leading to underestimation of impacts (due to increased variance of the estimations).	See Chapter 10.
5. Identification and use of available secondary data	Many evaluations do not identify and use all of the available secondary data. Secondary data can often reduce the costs of data collection and provide independent estimates of key variables.	See Chapter 5.
6. Triangulation	The validity of data and the quality and depth of interpretation of findings are enhanced when two or more independent estimates can be compared.	See Chapters 13 and 14.

associated with the project interventions. Even if using QUAL methods to determine people's perspectives of changes that have taken place, there will be discussion of what things were like before the intervention started, what changes might be attributed to the project, and how these might compare with what has happened in other communities. These considerations make it possible to identify a set of evaluation designs that cover most RWE scenarios and that include QUANT, QUAL, and mixed-method approaches. Table 2.4 provides a decision tree matrix to help decide which design is possible under different scenarios.

Table 2.4 Determining Possible Evaluation Designs[a]

Question[b]	If the Answer Is Yes	If the Answer Is No
1. Was the evaluation pre-planned? That is, was the evaluation design included in the project's monitoring and evaluation plan from the beginning?	Use that pre-existing plan as the guide for the project evaluation. The evaluation should include an assessment of the appropriateness of the monitoring and evaluation plan and should acknowledge and use it as much as possible.	This is going to have to be an ad hoc, one-off evaluation (e.g., Design 5 or 7). This limits the rigor of the evaluation design, but there are things that can be done, even so.
2. Was there a baseline (pretest)?	That will make a "before and after" (Design 1, 2, 4, or 6) possible—if the baseline was done in a way that can be compared with the posttest (end-of-project evaluation).	Too bad. You'll either have to make do with retrospective analysis, a "with and without" (comparison group at endline only, Design 5) or cope with a "one snapshot" limitation.
3. Was there a comparison group for the baseline?	Recommend Design 1 or 2 if there can be the same or a comparable control group for the posttest (see next question).	Too bad. Could still use Design 3 or 4, hoping that the posttest comparison group was similar to the participants at the beginning of the project.
4. Even if there was no comparison group in the baseline, can there be a comparison group for the posttest (end-of-project evaluation)?	Design 3, 4, or 5 could be used. Do all possible to verify that the comparison group was similar to the participants at the beginning in all ways except for the intervention.	Consider looking for secondary data that may give general trends in the population to compare with the group that participated in the project.
5. Was reliable monitoring information collected on outcome and/or impact indicators during project implementation?	Very helpful! Quasi-experimental longitudinal Design 1 may be possible, including examining trends over time.	Well, pretest + posttest with comparison group (Design 2) isn't bad. You might still look for secondary data indicating trends.
6. Will it be possible to conduct an ex-post evaluation sometime (e.g., several years) after the end of the project?	An extended longitudinal Design 1 will provide more certain evidence of sustainability (or lack thereof).	Without an ex-post evaluation, predictions about sustainability will have to be made based on the quality of the project's process and intermediary outcomes.

[a]These are the kinds of questions that should be asked by an evaluation team when called in to evaluate an ongoing project. Obviously, if these questions are considered at the time a project is designed, the evaluation plan can be stronger. Otherwise, the evaluation team will have to cope as well as it can with the given situation. See Table 2.2 for the Designs referenced here.

[b]Readers not familiar with any of the terms used in this table are referred to Chapter 11, where all the evaluation designs are discussed.

To repeat the caveat mentioned previously, it should be noted that whereas the various quasi-experimental evaluation designs given in Table 2.2 are more commonly associated with QUANT methods, whether there can be a before–after and/or a with–without comparison applies to both

QUANT and QUAL methodologies. The major differences between these designs have to do with the stage of the project at which the evaluation team collects data (e.g., baseline, midterm, final, ex-post). A separate distinction has to do with whether the data collection *methods* are QUANT, QUAL, or mixed and whether they also rely on secondary sources or the **recall**[5] perspectives of key informants and participants.

In the situation depicted by Design 7 (posttest analysis without baseline or comparison group), for example, the evaluators would not only want to measure (QUANT approach) or describe (QUAL approach) the present status of the condition the project aimed to change (indicator or other form of evidence), they would also need to find some evidence of how that condition changed over the life of the project and a comparison of how that change may have been different for those participating in the project compared with others under similar conditions who did not. This calls for finding secondary data or collecting the perspectives of knowledgeable people and the use of recall. Whether the evaluator does that by measurement (collecting numbers) or descriptions (words) has to do with methodology. How much of that data is obtained from primary sources (e.g., surveys, observation, key informants) or from secondary sources has to do with evaluation design.

5.2. Determining Appropriate Methods

A key decision is whether the evaluation will use QUANT, QUAL, or a combination of methodologies (mixed methods). We emphasize throughout this book that although we see many advantages to using a purposeful mix of methods, both to address RWE constraints and to gain multiple perspectives, there is no "best" evaluation methodology. The choice of research methods is determined by a number of different factors that, in addition to the types of questions to be addressed, include the professional orientation of the client and also that of the evaluation practitioner. The list of questions in the next section can help determine which methods are most suitable for the purposes for an evaluation and the conditions under which it is to be conducted.

6. Developing the Terms of Reference (Statement of Work) for the Evaluation

Those commissioning evaluations may find the following set of questions helpful when preparing the Terms of Reference (ToR) or Scope of Work (SoW) for the evaluation. (This topic is covered with more detail in Chapter 16.) The evaluators might also find this checklist helpful, particularly for identifying points not covered in the ToR and that must be clarified with the client before the evaluation is designed.

1. Who asked for the evaluation? Who are the key stakeholders? Do they have preconceived ideas regarding the purpose for the evaluation and expected findings (political considerations)?

---

[5]Recall techniques (see Chapter 5) involve asking individuals or groups to give their recollections of their personal situation or the situation of their community at an earlier point in time. For impact evaluations, the earlier time will usually be the time at which the project was starting.

2. Who should be involved in planning the evaluation?

3. Who should be involved in implementing the evaluation?

4. What are the key questions to be answered?

5. Will this be a **developmental** or **formative** or **summative** evaluation? Is its purpose primarily for learning and improving, or accountability, or a combination of both?

6. Will there be a next phase, or will other projects be designed based on the findings of this evaluation?

7. What decisions will be made in response to the findings of this evaluation? By whom?

8. What is the appropriate level of rigor needed to collect and analyze the information needed to inform those decisions?

9. What is the scope/scale of the evaluation/**evaluand** (program or intervention being evaluated)?

10. How much time will be needed/available?

11. What financial resources are needed/available?

12. What evaluation design would be required/is possible under the circumstances?

13. Should the evaluation rely mainly on QUANT methods, QUAL methods, or a combination of the two?

14. Should participatory methods be used? If so, who should be included? What roles should they play?

15. Can/should there be a survey of individuals, households, or other entities?

16. Who should be interviewed?

17. What sample design and size are required/feasible?

18. What form of analysis will best answer the key questions (see the fourth question above)?

19. Who are the audiences for the report(s)?

20. How will the findings be communicated to each audience?

SUMMARY

- Clients and other stakeholders can have widely varying expectations of what an impact evaluation is and what it can produce. These can range from detailed statistical measurements to case studies on how a program has affected the lives of individual communities, families, or schools.
- An evaluation should be based on a sound understanding of why the evaluation is being commissioned, how the findings will be used, and the political context within which it will be conducted. Understanding the client's *bottom line*—what information and analysis are essential and what would simply be "nice to have"—is critical when decisions have to be made on what can and cannot be cut in the light of budget and time constraints.

- All programs are based on an explicit or implicit model of how the program is expected to operate, how the intended program outputs and impacts are to be achieved, and the factors facilitating or constraining achievement. Defining the program theory helps focus the evaluation and identify the key hypotheses and linkages that the evaluation must test.

- The scoping step should end with an agreement between the client and the evaluator on the RWE design that best responds to the purposes for which the evaluation is being commissioned while at the same time adapting to the budget, time, data, and political constraints under which it must be conducted.

FURTHER READING

Altschuld, J. and D. Kumar. 2010. *Needs Assessment: An Overview.* Thousand Oaks, CA. Sage.

This is the introduction to a five-volume needs assessment kit. It explains the importance and applications of needs assessment in different organizational contexts and provides a three-step generic needs assessment model that can be applied in many different organizational contexts.

Carvalho, S. and H. White. 2004. "Theory Based Evaluation: The Case of Social Funds." *American Journal of Evaluation* 25(2):141–60.

An example of the application of program theory to the evaluation of social investment funds (a widely used model for providing health, education, water supply, and other local infrastructure in developing countries). The article illustrates how program theory can be reconstructed during the evaluation when it was not defined in the project documents. The article is also interesting because it presents the concept of an "anti-theory" based on the views of critics as to the potential negative outcomes of the project interventions.

Chambers, R. 1997. *Whose Reality Counts? Putting the First Last.* London, UK: ITDG.

Making the case for ensuring that all stakeholders and affected groups, particularly the poorest and most vulnerable, are involved in program design, implementation, and evaluation

Donaldson, S. 2007. *Program Theory-Driven Evaluation Science: Strategies and Applications.* Thousand Oaks, CA: Sage.

Recent overview of program theory. Includes eight case studies illustrating diverse applications of program theory.

MercyCorps. 2005. *Design, Monitoring and Evaluation Guidebook.* Portland, OR: MercyCorps.

Includes chapters on project design and criteria for useful evaluations.

Morra-Imas, L. and R. Rist. 2009. *The Road to Results: Designing and Conducting Effective Development Evaluations.* Washington, DC: World Bank.

Very practical guidance for the evaluation of international development programs. Includes understanding the context, developing the program theory of change, considering the evaluation approach and design, developing evaluation questions, and much more.

Patton, M. Q. 2008. *Utilization-Focused Evaluation.* 4th ed. Thousand Oaks, CA: Sage.

Probably the most widely cited text on how to ensure that evaluations respond to the needs of stakeholders and that the findings will be used.

Pawson, R. and N. Tilley. 1997. *Realist Evaluation.* London: Sage.

They argue convincingly for the need for a better understanding of the intervention, what happens during implementation, who benefits, and why.

Rogers, P., T. Hacsi, A. Petrosino, and T. Huebner, eds. 2000. *Program Theory in Evaluation: Challenges and Opportunities.* New Directions for Evaluation, No. 87. San Francisco: Jossey-Bass.

A useful overview of program and still relevant even though published in 2000. All the chapters include extensive reference sources.

Rogers, P. 2008. "Using Programme Theory to Evaluate Complicated and Complex Aspects of Interventions." *Evaluation.* 14(1): 29-48.

Introduction to the concept of complexity and the challenges of applying logic models to complex programs. Also includes a review of recent developments in logic modeling that help address the challenges of modeling complex programs.

Thomas, A. and G. Mohan. 2007. *Research Skills for Policy and Development: How to Find Out Fast.* London: Sage/The Open University.

This publication explains how research is designed and used to contribute to policy and action. It focuses on the kinds of information that policymakers need and shows the wide variety of sources and methods that can be used to generate this information. Chapter 1, "Information Needs and Policy Change," illustrates the kinds of information required for different kinds of policy decisions and makes the important point that as the policy context changes, so do the information needs. Researchers and evaluators must be sufficiently attuned to the policy environment to be able to adapt the focus of their evaluation.

Rossi, P., M. Lipsey, and H. Freeman. 2004. *Evaluation: A Systematic Approach.* 7th ed. Thousand Oaks, CA. Sage.

This classic textbook has a number of chapters covering the topics discussed in this chapter including: tailoring evaluations; identifying issues and formulating questions; assessing the needs for a program; and expressing and assessing program theory

Weiss, C. H. 2001. "Theory-Based Evaluation: Theories of Change for Poverty Based Programs." Pp. 103–14 in *Evaluation and Poverty Reduction,* edited by O. Feinstein and R. Picciotto. New Brunswick, NJ: Transaction.

A discussion of how program theory models can be applied to the evaluation of poverty reduction programs.

White, H., and M. Bamberger. 2008. *Impact Evaluation in Official Development Agencies.* Sussex, UK: IDS Bulletin.

Considerations for the determination of evaluation designs, based on extensive experience with international agencies.

CHAPTER 3

Not Enough Money: Addressing Budget Constraints

S tep 2 of the RealWorld Evaluation (**RWE**) approach identifies five strategies for conducting an evaluation on a tight budget (see Figure 3.1). These strategies include simplifying the evaluation **design**, clarifying **client** information needs so as reduce the amount of data to be collected or the types of analysis required, making greater user of secondary data, reducing the sample size, and reducing the costs of data collection. Finally, we identify some of the common threats to validity and adequacy of the evaluation conclusions that occur when measures are taken to reduce costs.

Often, **project** and program budgets include insufficient funds for evaluation, or by the time managers become concerned with **impact** issues, evaluation funds have been re-allocated to other activities. This chapter describes five strategies for addressing the budget constraints that evaluators often face (see Box 3.1 and Table 3.1):

1. Simplify the evaluation design (see also Chapter 11).

2. Clarify client information needs, seeking ways to cut out the collection of nonessential information (see also Chapter 2).

3. Look for reliable secondary data (see also Chapter 5).

4. Reduce the sample size (see also Chapter 15).

5. Use more economical data collection methods.

1. Simplifying the Evaluation Design

One way to significantly reduce the costs and time of the evaluation is to simplify the evaluation design. A review of the evaluation scenarios identified in Chapter 2 (Table 2.1) may suggest some ways in which the evaluation design could be simplified. For example, the purpose of the evaluation (points 1 and 2 in the table) and the methodological preferences of the client (points 12–14) might suggest that a relatively simple design would be acceptable.

Figure 3.1 Step 2: Addressing Budget Constraints

```
┌─────────────────────────────────┐
│           Step 1                │
│  Planning and Scoping the       │
│         Evaluation              │
└─────────────────────────────────┘

┌──────────┐ ┌──────────┐ ┌──────────┐ ┌──────────┐
│  Step 2  │ │  Step 3  │ │  Step 4  │ │  Step 5  │
│Addressing│ │Addressing│ │Addressing│ │Addressing│
│  Budget  │ │   Time   │ │   Data   │ │Political │
│Constraints│ │Constraints│ │Constraints│ │Influences│
└──────────┘ └──────────┘ └──────────┘ └──────────┘

┌─────────────────────────────────┐
│           Step 6                │
│ Strengthening the Evaluation    │
│  Design and the Validity of     │
│  Findings and Recommendations   │
└─────────────────────────────────┘

┌─────────────────────────────────┐
│           Step 7                │
│ Helping Clients Use the         │
│         Evaluation              │
└─────────────────────────────────┘

┌─────────────────────────────────┐
│ Step 2  Addressing Budget       │
│         Constraints             │
│ A. Modify the Evaluation Design │
│ B. Clarify Client Information   │
│    Needs                        │
│ C. Look for Reliable Secondary  │
│    Data                         │
│ D. Reduce Sample Size           │
│ E. Economical Data Collection   │
│    Methods                      │
└─────────────────────────────────┘
```

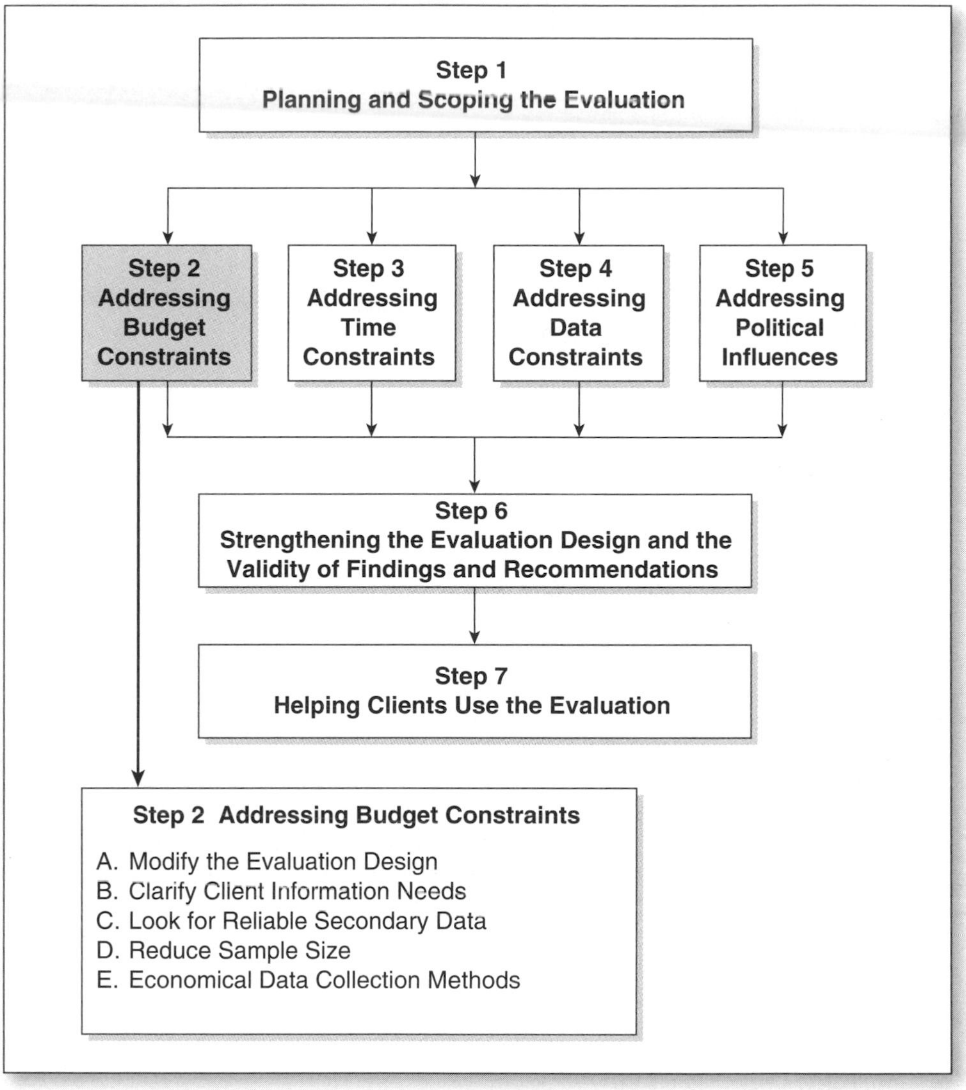

Of course, the analysis of the scenarios might also suggest that a more sophisticated and expensive design is required. When client preferences and the purpose of the evaluation permit simplification, this will often result in reducing the number of interviews or concentrating the interviews in a smaller number of physical locations so that travel time and cost can be reduced. The cost and time reduction strategies are easier to define for quantitative (QUANT) evaluations because interviews all have a similar duration and there is normally a standard cost for each interview. Consequently, it is easy to estimate the cost savings if the number of interviews is reduced. However, the cost reduction strategies are not so clearly defined for most qualitative (QUAL) evaluations because the time required to prepare a case study or conduct participant observation can vary greatly and is difficult to estimate in advance.

BOX 3.1
FIVE QUESTIONS TO HELP MAKE THE BUDGET GO FARTHER

1. Can we use a simpler and cheaper evaluation design?

2. Do we really need to collect all of this information?

3. Has someone already collected some of the information that we need?

4. Can we reduce the number of interviews, observations, cases, and so on without sacrificing the necessary precision?

5. Is there a cheaper way to collect the information?

Table 3.1   Reducing Costs of Data Collection and Analysis for Quantitative and Qualitative Evaluations

Quantitative Evaluations	Qualitative Evaluations
A. Simplifying the Evaluation Design[a]	
All these designs produce potential cost savings (see Table 3.3)[b]. • Truncated longitudinal design (Design 3): study starts at midterm • Pretest–posttest project group with posttest analysis of project and comparison groups (Design 4.1b): eliminates baseline comparison group • Posttest comparison of project and control group (Design 5): eliminates baseline • Pretest–posttest comparison of project group (Design 6): eliminates comparison group • Evaluation based on posttest data from project group (Design 7): eliminates comparison group and baseline project group	• Prioritize and focus on critical issues • Reduce the number of site visits or the time period over which observations are made • Reduce the amount and cost of data collection • Reduce the number of persons or groups studied
B. Clarifying Client Information Needs	
Prioritize data needs with the client to eliminate the collection of nonessential data.	

Quantitative Evaluations	Qualitative Evaluations
C. Using Existing Data	
• Census or surveys covering project areas • Data from project records • Records from schools, health centers, and other public-service agencies	• Newspapers and other mass media • Records from community organizations • Dissertations and other university studies (for both QUAL and QUANT)
D. Reducing Sample Size	
• Lower the level of required precision (lower precision = smaller sample) • Reduce types of disaggregation required (less disaggregation = smaller sample) • Use stratified sample designs (to reduce total interviews) • Use cluster sampling (lower travel costs)	• Consider critical or quota sampling rather than comprehensive or representative sampling • Reduce the number of persons or groups studied
E. Reducing Costs of Data Collection, Input, and Analysis	
• Self-administered questionnaires (with literate populations) • Direct observation—instead of surveys (sometimes saves money but not always) • Automatic counters and other nonobtrusive methods • Direct inputting of survey data through handheld devices • Optical scanning of survey forms and electronic surveys	• Decrease the number or period of observations • Prioritize informants • Employ and train university students, student nurses, and community residents to collect data (for both QUAL and QUANT) • Data input through handheld devices
Mixed-Method Designs	
• Triangulation to compensate for reduced sample size • Focus groups and community forums instead of household surveys • PRA and other participatory methods	

[a]See Table 3.2 for the listing of designs and Chapter 12 for a discussion of the designs.

[b]See the seven evaluation design models in Box 3.3 and Table 2.2.

1.1. Simplifying the Evaluation Design for Quantitative Evaluations

RWE approaches are used when the evaluation must be designed and implemented with budget as well as time, data, and political constraints. This means that many of the standard impact evaluation designs cannot be used. Chapter 11 reviews the principles of experimental and quasi-experimental designs and explains why the technically stronger QUANT designs cannot be used in many RWE contexts. Consequently, the RealWorld evaluator must make compromises on elements of the stronger designs because of the budget and other constraints and therefore must recognize the additional threats to the validity of the evaluation conclusions when weaker designs are used. Box 3.2 also points out that technically "robust" designs must be correctly implemented if they are not to lose their methodological strength.

> ## BOX 3.2
> ## "ROBUST" DESIGNS REQUIRE CORRECT DESIGN AND IMPLEMENTATION!
>
> The fact that a "robust" design is selected does not guarantee methodologically sound conclusions unless a study is properly designed, implemented, and analyzed. If the sample is not properly selected, the survey instrument is not properly designed and administered, there is a high nonresponse rate, or if triangulation and other quality-control procedures are not used, then the conclusions may be of questionable validity. See Chapter 15 for a discussion of these issues.

Chapter 2 describes the seven basic impact evaluation design frameworks depending on when the evaluation begins (start, middle, or end of the project), at how many points in the project cycle data are collected (start, during implementation, at project completion, after project completion), and whether comparison group data are collected at the same time as data on the project population. Chapter 11 elaborates on this framework, showing that there are several design options for each of these frameworks depending on (a) whether the project and comparison groups are matched statistically (the strongest option) or judgmentally (a weaker option when secondary data are not available for statistical matching) and (b) whether baseline data are collected at the start of the project (the strongest option) or reconstructed when the evaluation does not start until late in the project (usually a weaker option). Table 11.3 (pp. 220–222) shows that the combination of the seven design frameworks with these two additional factors produces a total of 19 impact evaluation design options. Although there are a number of other factors that also affect methodological rigor (e.g., how carefully the evaluation is administered, the adequacy of the data collection instrument for collecting key information, the ability to identify and interview all sectors of the target population), it is possible to classify all of these designs into the following categories:

- The strongest statistical designs (Designs 1.1 and 2.1)
- Strong statistical designs (Designs 2.2 and 2.3)
- Acceptable statistical designs (Designs 2.3, 2.4 and 2.5)
- Weaker statistical designs (Designs 3.1, 4.1, and 5.1)
- Nonexperimental designs (Designs 6.1, 6.2, 6.3, 6.4, and 7.1). These designs do not include a matched comparison group and, consequently, it is not possible to define a conventional counterfactual to answer the question "what would have been the condition of the project population if the project had not taken place?" So from the statistical perspective, these designs are very weak. However, there are many situations in which some of these designs can be the strongest methodological design available, as they are better suited than QUANT designs for evaluating complex programs that are implemented through many steps and produce complicated behavioral changes or that are subject to the influence of many contextual factors.

There is a direct relationship between the methodological soundness of the evaluation design and the number of observation points at which surveys are conducted or other forms of data are collected. In the strongest designs (Designs 1.1 and 2.1), information is collected on both the project population and a **comparison group** before the project begins (baseline or pretest) and when the project has ended (posttest). For Design 1.1, data are also collected during project implementation and after the project has been operating for some time. These two designs also use random assignment of subjects to the project and control groups, and when properly implemented, they provide robust estimates of whether there are statistically significant differences between the project and comparison groups with respect to the indicators of project impact.

Design 2.2 cannot use random assignment but is a strong design because it is possible to use statistical matching for the project and comparison groups. Design 2.3 (regression discontinuity) can also provide strong and unbiased statistical estimates. It has the advantage that much of the baseline data can be obtained from administrative records so that data collection costs are lower (see Appendix F, pp. 556–602, for an explanation of this design and an example of its application).

Designs 2.4 and 2.5 are considered acceptable statistical designs. Design 2.4 (pipeline design) has the advantages that it is cheaper because when projects are implemented in phases over time, the Phase 2 beneficiaries can be used as the comparison group for Phase 1 (if certain conditions, discussed in Chapter 11 and Appendix F, are satisfied). This eliminates the cost and time required to identify and interview an external comparison group. Design 2.5 is similar to Design 2.2 except that judgmental matching, rather than statistical matching, of the two samples is used.

The weaker statistical designs (Designs 3.1, 4.1, and 5.1) either involve the elimination of baseline data collection for one or both samples or delay in the collection of baseline data until the project has been operating for some time.

However, with the possible exception of the regression discontinuity design, the strongest statistical designs are also the most expensive because they require that information be collected on two groups (project and comparison group) and at two or more points in time (at least before and after the project's interventions). Each of the cheaper and methodologically weaker statistical designs eliminates collection of data at one or more of these four points.

Table 3.3 estimates the cost savings from using the weaker statistical designs. These are rough estimates based on the assumption that eliminating any one of the four data collection points (pre- and posttest for project and comparison groups) will reduce the costs of data collection by about 25%. However, there are still certain fixed costs such as instrument design, sample selection, and interviewer training that are still required. It can be seen that some designs, such as the posttest-only comparison, may reduce the cost of the evaluation by up to 40%. It is more difficult to estimate the cost savings from the use of nonexperimental designs (Designs 6.1 through 7.1), as there is much greater variation in how each design is used. For example, a longitudinal design might only involve three or four visits to a community over the course of the year, but other designs may require constant contact or even living in the community for some time. The only nonexperimental design (NED) in which it is easier to estimate cost savings is Design 7.1, as this is often the default design that is used when budget and time constraints do not permit the use of other more rigorous designs. Often, this design only allows a short visit to the project locations, so there are considerable cost savings (which can be as much as 80%).

When estimating cost and time requirements, it is important to remember there is an important trade-off between cost and time savings on the one hand and validity of the evaluation findings on the other. All these less robust designs eliminate or weaken one or more of the pretest or posttest observations on the project or **comparison group** and, consequently, increase vulnerability to the

Table 3.2 Overview of Most Common RWE Impact Evaluation Designs Classified by Their Statistical Strength

Design[a]		
Strongest statistical designs (randomized assignment to project and comparison groups)		
1.1	Longitudinal comparison groups randomized design	Data collected at start, during implementation, end, and some time after project completion
2.1	Pretest–posttest comparison group randomized design	Data collected at start and end of project
Strong statistical designs (quasi-experimental designs with different selection procedures for project and comparison groups)		
2.2 A+B[b]	Pretest–posttest comparison group design with statistical matching	Groups matched using techniques such as propensity score matching
2.3	Regression discontinuity	Groups just above (participants) and below (comparison) selection cutoff point are compared to detect change in intercept or slope of regression line
Acceptable statistical designs		
2.4	Pipeline comparison group design	Phase 2 beneficiaries used as comparison group for Phase 1
2.5 A+B	Pretest–posttest comparison group design with judgmental matching	Consultation with experts and key informants combined with rapid diagnostic studies to select best match for project group
Weaker statistical designs		
3.1	Truncated pretest–posttest comparison group design	Baseline not conducted until project implementation has started
4.1 A+B	Pretest–posttest design with no comparison group baseline	
5.1	Posttest-only comparison group design	Data only available for posttest comparison with no baseline reference
Nonexperimental designs (no comparison group)		
6.1	Single-case design	Pretest–posttest comparison of single case with repeated application of intervention
6.2	Longitudinal design	Continuous observation of the project group over the life of the project
6.3	Interrupted time series	When time series data are available before and after project intervention, analysis examines whether there is a change in the line at the project intervention point
6.4 A+B	Pretest-posttest project group design	
7.1	Posttest-only project group design	This is often the default design that is used when the evaluation must be conducted with significant budget and time constraints

NOTES:

[a]This table is a summary of Table 11.3 in Chapter 11. See Appendix F for examples of each design.

[b]Some designs have two options. Option A is when the evaluation is commissioned at the start of the project so that primary baseline data can be collected. Option B is when the evaluation is not commissioned until late in the project and baseline data are "reconstructed" using secondary data, recall, key informants, or the other techniques discussed in Chapter 5. Normally, Option B is methodologically weaker, as baseline estimates may be less reliable due to the passage of time.

Table 3.3 Estimated Cost Savings for Less Robust RWE Designs Compared With Design 2.2[a]

Design		Estimated Cost Saving Compared with Design 2.2[a]
	Quasi-experimental designs (QEDs)	
2.4	Pipeline design[b]	10–20%
2.5	Pretest–posttest with judgmental matching	0%
3.1	Truncated longitudinal design	5–10%
4.1	No comparison group baseline study	10–20%
5.1	No baseline study for either group	30–40%
	Nonexperimental designs (NEDs)[c]	
6.1	Single-case design	Variable
6.2	Longitudinal design	Variable
6.3	Interrupted time series	60–70%
6.4	Pretest–posttest project group design	30–40%
7.1	Posttest-only project group	60–80%

NOTES:

[a]The estimated cost savings are based on the percentage reduction in the total number of interviews, but take into account that there are fixed costs, such as questionnaire design and training.

[b]The potential cost reductions come from the lower cost of selecting and interviewing the comparison group because it is selected from the same community as the project group. It is also likely that respondents would be more willing to cooperate, as they will be receiving benefits in a later phase, so the response rate might be higher.

[c]There is much greater variation in the design of NEDs, ranging from rapid and economical designs to expensive designs lasting over periods of years in some cases. So it is very difficult to estimate average costs and potential savings. The exception is Design 7.1, which is usually conducted on a small budget and with very limited time in the field.

four types of "threats to validity" described in Chapter 7 and Appendixes 1 through 5. It should be noted, however, that even the two most robust designs (Designs 1.1 and 2.1) are subject to a number of threats to validity (see Chapters 7 and 11 and Shadish, Cook, and Campbell 2002 for a more extended discussion).

Whenever weaker evaluation designs are used, it is strongly recommended to try to budget some additional resources and time to strengthen the design through the use of some of the "essential design components" listed in Table 2.3 (Chapter 2). Some of these strategies such as incorporating a program theory model or using triangulation may not greatly increase cost or time but can make a major contribution to strengthening the validity and utility of the evaluation findings and recommendations.

1.2. Simplifying the Design for Qualitative Evaluations

As indicated earlier, while some QUAL methods follow precise implementation guidelines (e.g., for some focus group techniques or some observation methods), in most cases, the researcher is given much more flexibility in terms of how the methods are applied. In fact, many QUAL evaluators would not accept the concept of standard designs.

Table 3.1 gives examples of how some but not all QUAL designs can be simplified to reduce costs. One approach is to identify and prioritize the critical issues that must be addressed and then to integrate all the tools to focus on the critical questions. Another option is to use recall to reduce the number of visits or the time period over which the observations are made. For example, respondents can tell the researcher about the time they spent traveling to collect fuel and water without the researcher having to accompany them on the trips. The possibility can also be considered of reducing the number of members of the household or community to be included in the study. Finally, it may be possible to simplify the research hypotheses so as to reduce the amount of data and the collection costs. For example, if the hypothesis concerns only differences of behavior between women of different age groups in the same ethnic group, the study will be simpler (and perhaps cheaper) than if both age and ethnicity are being studied.

2. Clarifying Client Information Needs

The costs and time required for data collection can sometimes be significantly reduced through a clearer definition of the information required by the client and the kinds of decisions to which the evaluation will contribute. Some of the ways to elicit this information were discussed in Chapter 2. The approaches and issues in the clarification of information needs are often but not always similar for QUANT and QUAL evaluations.

3. Using Existing Data

Often, secondary data can be identified that obviate or reduce the need for the collection of primary data (see Chapter 5). Typical examples include the following (also see Table 3.1):

- Census or survey data covering the project and comparison communities. Many governments conduct periodic national household surveys that usually contain information on the socioeconomic conditions of households and communities and include information of interest to the evaluation. If the results can be disaggregated to the specific population reached by a project with adequate statistical validity, such secondary data can be helpful in a project evaluation.
- Data from project monitoring records (e.g., household income, type of housing, school attendance, microloans approved).
- Records from schools (e.g., enrollment, attendance, test scores), health centers (e.g., number of patients, types of illness), and other public-service agencies (e.g., water supply and sanitation, public transport).
- Newspapers and other mass media often have extensive coverage on economic and social issues that projects address (e.g., quality and availability of schools, access to health and sanitation facilities, public transport, etc.).

- Records from community organizations (minutes of meetings, photographs, posters, etc.).
- Dissertations and other academic studies.

The identification and evaluation of the validity of secondary data are discussed in Chapter 5.

4. Reducing Costs by Reducing Sample Size

4.1. Adjusting the Sample Size to Client Information Needs and the Kinds of Decisions to Which the Evaluation Will Contribute

Often, sample sizes are defined by survey researchers without reference to the kinds of decisions to be made by clients and the level of precision[1] actually required. Many clients assume that sample size is a purely technical question and that the evaluator should tell the client what is the "right" sample strategy and size. When sample size is not appropriately related to the purpose of the evaluation, how the results are to be used, and the required level of precision, larger and more costly samples may be used than are really necessary. However, in other cases, the sample may not be large enough to support the kinds of analysis required by the client. *It is absolutely essential to involve the client in decisions on the size and structure of the sample.*

The role of the evaluator is to understand the client's information needs and how the evaluation **findings** are to be used. It is critical to understand whether very precise statistical estimates are required or whether this is an exploratory study in which only general estimates of potential impacts are required. The evaluator must also present the trade-offs between precision and statistical credibility of the findings on the one hand and cost to the client on the other and agree together on the best option to provide the required information within the available budget (and time). In many cases, it is possible to reduce costs by cutting out some kinds of information or analysis included in the initial **terms of reference**, but the decision to do so should be made jointly between the client and the evaluator.

Dane (2011:Chapter 5) provides a useful explanation for clients who are not research specialists on the differences between different kinds of samples and the benefits of each. This can be helpful when discussing the trade-offs between cost and statistical rigor.

4.2. Factors Affecting Sample Size for Quantitative Evaluations

The required sample size can vary greatly according to the characteristics of the population, the nature of the project intervention, and the purpose of the evaluation. Table 3.4 lists 11 factors that affect the required sample size. All these factors are discussed in more detail in Chapter 15 (Sections 3 and 4).

The most important concepts in determining sample size are the **effect size** and the **power of the test.** The effect size refers to the size of the change (effect) that the **program** produces.

---

[1]*Precision* refers to the level of statistical significance used to accept that an observed project effect does not occur by chance (that an effect as strong as the one observed is not due to *pseudo effects* caused by factors unrelated to the project). The convention is to accept a 95% confidence level that the observed effect is not simply due to *statistical noise* (spurious factors). Where a higher level of precision is required, the confidence level can be increased to 99% (or even higher), but this will involve a substantial increase in the size and cost of the sample. See Chapter 15, Section 4.6, for more details.

Table 3.4   Factors Affecting the Sample Size

Factor	Explanation	Influence on Sample Size
1. The purpose of the evaluation	Is this an exploratory study, or are very precise statistical estimates required?	The more precise the required results, the larger the sample.
2. Will a one- or two-tailed test be used? (Is the direction of the expected change known?)	If the purpose of the evaluation is to test whether positive outcomes have increased or negative ones have declined, then a one-tailed test can be used. If the purpose is to test whether there has been "a significant change" without knowing the direction, a two-tailed test is required (see Chapter 15, Section 4.5).	The sample size will be approximately 40% larger for a two-tailed test.
3. Is only the project group interviewed?	In some evaluation designs, only subjects from the project group are interviewed. This is the case if information on the total population is available from previous studies or secondary data. Normally, a comparison group must also be selected and interviewed.	The sample size will be doubled if the same number of people must be interviewed in both the project and comparison groups.
4. Homogeneity of the group	If there is little variation among the population with respect to the outcome variable, then the standard deviation will be small.	The smaller the standard deviation (i.e., variability), the smaller the required sample.
5. The effect size	Effect size is the amount of increase the project is expected to produce (see Chapter 15, Section 4.2).	The smaller the effect size, the larger the required sample.
6. The efficiency with which the project is implemented	When project administration is poor, different individuals or groups may receive different combinations of services. The quality of the services can also vary. This makes it difficult to determine if lower-than-expected outcomes are due to poor project design or to the fact that many subjects are not receiving all intended services.	The poorer the quality and efficiency of the project, the larger the required sample.
7. The required level of disaggregation	In some cases, the client requires only global estimates of impact for the total project population. In other cases, it is necessary to provide disaggregated results for different project sites, for variations in the package of services provided, or for different socioeconomic groups (sex, age, ethnicity, etc.).	The greater the required disaggregation, the larger the sample.
8. The sample design	Sampling procedures such as stratification can often reduce the variance of the estimates and increase precision.	Well-designed stratification may reduce sample size.
9. The level of statistical precision	"Beyond a reasonable doubt" is usually defined as meaning there is less than a 1 in 20 possibility that an impact as large as this could have occurred by chance (defined as the "0.05 confidence level"). If less precise results are acceptable, it is possible to reduce sample size by accepting a lower confidence level—for example, a 1 in 10 possibility that the result occurred by chance.	The higher the confidence level, the larger the sample.

Factor	Explanation	Influence on Sample Size
10. The power of the test	The statistical power of the test refers to the probability that when a project has "real" effect, this will be rejected by the statistical significance test. The conventional power level is 0.8, meaning that there is only a 20% chance that a real effect would be rejected. Where a higher level of precision is required, the power can be raised to 0.9 or higher (see Chapter 15, Section 4.4).	The higher the required power level, the larger the sample.
11. Finite population correction factor	The finite population correction factor reduces the required sample size by the proportion that the sample represents of the population (see Chapter 15, Section 4.6, p. 380).	The greater the proportion the sample represents of the total population, the smaller the sample.

Where possible, use a **standardized effect size**[2] measure so that comparisons can be made between different projects using the same treatment or between projects using different treatments to produce the same effect. To estimate required sample size, it is necessary to define the minimum acceptable effect size (**MAES**). This is the minimum change (effect) that the client requires the evaluation to be able to test. Table 15.1 (Chapter 15, p. 372) presents eight different criteria that can be used to specify the MAES. In some cases, MAES is simply the expected effect size, whereas in other cases, it is derived from a comparison with other similar programs ("the project must be able to achieve an effect size at least as great as Project X"), or it might be determined by a policy objective ("to reduce the number of families with incomes less than $X"). The MAES is agreed to in consultation between the client and the evaluator. Once MAES and the required power of the test (see below) have been defined, the required sample size can be estimated.

A key determinant of the sample size is that *the smaller the effect size, the larger the required sample.* Because many projects can be expected to produce only a relatively small effect size, the required sample size to test for this effect will often be much larger than clients might have wished. In some cases, it may be concluded that the required sample size cannot be afforded, and a decision may have to be made to revise the objectives of the evaluation or even not to conduct the evaluation. This example emphasizes the importance of conducting an **evaluability assessment** during the scoping phase of the evaluation to ensure that the stated evaluation objectives could be achieved within budget, time, and data constraints (see Chapter 2).

The second key concept is the statistical power of the test (see Chapter 15). Statistical power is defined as "the probability that an estimate will be statistically significant when, in fact it represents a real effect of a given magnitude" (Rossi, Lipsey, and Freeman 2004:309). Figure 15.2 (p. 377) shows that when the effect size is small, there is a high probability that the statistical test may fail to detect the project effect even when it is real. In this figure, the power of the test is only 0.4, meaning that if 100 samples were selected, in 60 of these, the statistical test would fail to detect that the project had

---

[2]The standardized effect size is defined as the mean of the sample minus the population mean divided by the population standard deviation (see Chapter 15, Section 4.2).

an effect—even though the effect was real. There are two important rules with respect to sample size:

1. The smaller the effect size, the lower the power of the test.

2. The power of the test can be raised by increasing the sample size.

Table 3.5 illustrates how the required sample size is affected by the minimum decrease in health expenditures that an evaluation must be able to detect (Gertler et al. 2011, p. 186, Table 11.2). In this example, the statistical power is set at 0.9, which is reasonably high. In order to be able to detect a reduction as small as $1, a total sample size (combining treatment and comparison group) of 2,688 would be required. However, in order to detect a reduction as small as $2, the required sample size would drop to 672, and for a minimum of $3, only 300 interviews would be required. If a lower level of statistical power (0.8) could be accepted, the respective sample sizes would drop to 2,008 (compared to 2,688 with power = 0.9), 502 (compared to 672), and 224 (compared to 300). This example clearly illustrates the need for the client to define clearly the size of the effect that it must be possible to detect, as this has a dramatic effect on the sample size.

Table 3.5   Sample Size Required for Various Minimum Detectable Effects (Decrease in Household Health Expenditures), Power = 0.9. No clustering

Minimum detectable effect	Treatment group	Comparison group	Total sample
$1	1,344	1,344	2,688
$2	336	336	672
$3	150	150	300

SOURCE: Gertler et al. (2011) Table 11.2.

Table 15.4 (pp. 385–386) illustrates how effect size and the power of the test affect sample size. Using standard assumptions discussed in Chapter 15, and setting the statistical power level at 0.8, the table shows that if the project was expected to produce a relatively large change (an adjusted effect size of 0.5), then a sample of only 19 subjects would be required for both the project and comparison groups (a total of 38 subjects). However, if the project was expected to produce only a small change (an adjusted effect size of 0.2), then the sample size for each group would increase to 154 (a total of 308 subjects). In this latter case, if the client indicated that a higher statistical power must be used (setting the power of the test at 0.9 instead of 0.8), the total sample size would increase from 308 to 424.

Effect of the Level of Disaggregation on the Required Sample Size

In many cases, clients require a comparison of project impacts on different sectors of the target population, such as different regions, male- and female-headed households, people of different socioeconomic levels, or people who have received different project options or combinations of services. Each additional level or type of disaggregation normally requires a corresponding increase in sample size. Consequently, in cases where some of the levels of disaggregation can be eliminated (e.g., estimating impact on the total project population rather than for each region), it is often possible to achieve significant reductions in sample size. When the levels of disaggregation are reduced because of money constraints, other methods, such as key informant interviews, if representative and reliable, may be used to obtain information on differential impacts on various sectors within the community with at least some degree of validity.

4.3. Factors Affecting the Size of Qualitative Samples

Because QUAL sampling has different objectives from QUANT, it is usually not possible to estimate the required sample size with the same degree of statistical exactitude. The following are some of the factors affecting sample size for QUAL evaluations:

- QUAL samples can be considered as having four dimensions: (1) the number of subjects or units of observation (schools, families, drug dealers), (2) the number of physical locations in which observation takes place (the home, the place of work, the street, the bar), (3) the period of time over which the observations take place, and (4) the frequency of observations (hourly, daily, weekly, etc.). Consequently, sample costs and time can be saved by reducing the number of subjects, reducing the number of physical locations (observe only in the street or only in the school), and the duration of the study or the number of time periods over which observations are made (every day for a week, every day for a month, once a week for a year).
- The required levels of disaggregation must be determined. The more categories (types of schools, ethnic groups, farming systems) that must be compared, the larger the required sample.

The decision on the number of subjects, locations, or duration of the study or units of analysis (communities, schools, prostitutes) usually depends on the professional judgment of the researcher, and there are usually no precise rules as to whether, for example, four or six families would be the appropriate number to study or whether the observations should continue over one week or one month. Researchers are often tempted to increase the number of subjects or the duration because each additional case or observation period offers added dimensions. If pressed, however, it is often (but not always) possible for the evaluator to reduce the number of cases or observations without compromising the purpose of the evaluation.

4.4. Factors Affecting the Size of Mixed-Method Samples

Mixed-method evaluation designs combine QUANT and QUAL data collection and analysis. Consequently, decisions on sample size will usually combine decisions on both QUANT and QUAL components discussed above. Chapter 15 discusses determinants of mixed-method sample size (Section 6).

Mixed-method approaches can sometimes reduce sample size by creative combining of different techniques of data collection and the use of triangulation to check for consistency. For example, instead of conducting a sample survey to estimate community travel patterns, these might be estimated by combining observation with focus groups and key informants. Triangulation is a key element of the strategy to check for consistency and to explore further if findings from different sources are inconsistent. On the other hand, mixed methods will often try to ensure the representativity of QUAL data, and this may require a larger sample of QUAL cases than might have been the case for a purely QUAL design.

4.5. Practical Tools for Working With Small Samples: The Example of Lot Quality Acceptance Sampling (LQAS)

Lot quality acceptance sampling (LQAS) is an example of an approach designed to work with small, economical, and easily administered samples that has recently been gaining in popularity (Valadez and Devkota 2002). Originally developed to assess the achievement of coverage targets for local health delivery systems, LQAS has now been used to assess immunization coverage, antenatal care, oral rehydration, growth monitoring, family planning, disease incidence, and natural disaster relief.

LQAS is used to assess whether *coverage benchmarks* have been achieved in particular project locations. An example of a benchmark would be ensuring that 80% of families have received oral rehydration kits and orientation or that 70% of farmers have received information on new seed varieties. A major advantage of this approach is that a sample of 19 (households, farmers, etc.) will normally be sufficient to estimate whether any level of benchmark coverage has been achieved with no greater than a 10% error (see Chapter 15, Section 7.1). The findings are very simple to analyze, as the number of required positive responses is defined for any given benchmark coverage level. For example, if the target coverage level is 80%, then the sample of 19 families (farms, etc.) must include at least 13 cases in which the service had been satisfactorily received. If the target coverage was 60%, then the sample must find at least nine satisfactory cases. So in addition to the advantage of very small samples, an LQAS study is very easy for health workers, agricultural extension workers, and other nonresearch specialists to administer and interpret.

5. Reducing Costs of Data Collection and Analysis

Considerable cost savings can often be achieved through reducing the length and complexity of the data-collection instruments. The elimination of nonessential information can significantly reduce the length of the data-collection instrument or the duration of the observation. Examples of areas in which the amount of information can often be reduced include (a) demographic information on each household member, (b) amount of information on agricultural production and food consumption in a community, and (c) information on urban or rural travel patterns. It is again important to define information requirements with the client and not to arbitrarily eliminate information simply to produce a shorter data-collection instrument. For many QUAL studies, the amount and type of information cannot be defined as easily as for QUANT surveys, and consequently, the list of questions or issues cannot be pruned quite so easily. While the original QUAL design—questions, issues, methods, instruments—is available for pruning from the start, the pruning process is more complicated. With emergent designs, issues and questions arise as the research progresses, and often, many of what prove to be the critical issues were not even included on the initial lists of questions. However, the following are examples of ways to reduce the amount of information to be collected:

- The range of topics can be reduced to those of greatest priority.
- The number of interviewees can be reduced.
- The number and types of documents to be analyzed can be reduced.
- The time period studied can be shortened.

A number of alternatives can significantly reduce the costs of data collection for both QUAL and QUANT evaluations (see Table 3.1). Examples include the following:

- Collect information on community attitudes, time use, access to and use of services, and the like through **PRA** (participatory rural appraisal) group interview methods and **focus groups** rather than through household surveys or interviews with individuals. It is important to note, however, that well-designed focus groups are in themselves time consuming and, in some cases, can be more costly than surveys. Focus groups require identifying appropriate interviewees, arranging times that all members of the group can get together, preparing and field-testing the interview protocol, transcribing and validating the interview data, and conducting content analysis. In contrast, a survey requires only preparing, field-testing, administering the survey, and aggregating responses to items. The relative costs of the two approaches will, of course, depend on the proposed sample size for the survey.
- Replace surveys with direct observation—for example, to study time use, travel patterns, and use of community facilities. It is again important to note that although some types of observation can be quite rapid and economical (e.g., observation of pedestrian and vehicular travel patterns in areas with relatively few roads), in other cases, observing enough to ensure the validity of observation data and doing content analysis is not necessarily faster than a survey.
- Use key informants to obtain information on community behavior and use of services.
- Use self-administered instruments such as surveys, self-evaluations, reflection or response forms, diaries, and journals to collect data on income and expenditure, travel patterns, or time use.
- Make maximum use of preexisting data, including project records.
- Photography and videotaping can sometimes provide useful and economical documentary **evidence** on the changing quality of houses and roads, as well as on use of public transport services (Heath 2004; Kumar 1993; Patton 2002b).

Many of these suggestions involve methodological **triangulation** (Denzin 1989) to obtain conformational data in two or more ways or from two or more data sources. Triangulation is particularly important for RealWorld evaluators faced by budget and time constraints. The *triangulation by method and source* can help determine the accuracy of information when only limited amounts of data can be collected. Box 3.3 presents three illustrations of reducing the cost and time of data collection.

BOX 3.3
ECONOMICAL METHODS OF DATA COLLECTION

1. In Bulgaria, a rapid midterm assessment was conducted of a project to reduce the environmental contamination produced by a major metallurgical factory. Key informant interviews, review of project records, and direct observation were combined to provide economical ways to assess compliance with safety and environmental regulations and to assess reductions in the level of environmental contamination. A survey of key stakeholders was conducted to obtain independent assessments of the findings reported in the evaluation. The evaluation cost less than $5,000 and was completed in less than two months.

SOURCE: Dimitrov (2005).

2. An evaluation of the impacts of a slum-upgrading project in Manila, the Philippines, assessed the impact of the housing investments made by poor families on their consumption of basic necessities. A randomly selected sample of 100 households was asked to keep a daily record of every item of income and expenditure over a period of a year. Households recorded this information themselves in diaries, and the evaluation team of the National Housing Authority made weekly visits to a sample of households to ensure quality control. The only direct cost, other than a small proportion of staff salaries, was the purchase of small gifts for the families each month. Because the study covered only project participants, most of whom were very favorable toward the project, the response rate was maintained at almost 100% throughout the year. This proved to be a very economical way to collect high-quality income and expenditure data and permitted the use of an interrupted time series design with 365 (daily) observation points, although with little analysis of external influences.

SOURCE: Valadez and Bamberger (1994:255–573).

An assessment of the impacts of community management on the quality and maintenance of village water supply in Indonesia combined direct observation of the quality and use of water with participatory group assessments of water supply and interviews with key informants. The use of group interviews and direct observation proved a much more economical way to assess project impacts than conventional household sample surveys.

SOURCE: Dayal, van Wijk, and Mukherjee (2000).

6. Common Threats to Validity of Budget Constraints

Box 3.4 identifies some of the most common threats to validity and adequacy of evaluation conclusions that must be addressed when assessing the different approaches to budget constraints discussed in this chapter. Similar tables are included for reference in the following two chapters to identify the respective threats to validity when taking measures to reduce time or when working with limited data. It is recommended that readers who are not familiar with the concepts of threats to validity read Chapter 7 and then to return to this section.

BOX 3.4
THREATS TO ADEQUACY AND VALIDITY RELATING TO BUDGET CONSTRAINTS

NOTE. The numbers refer to the RWE "Integrated Checklist for Assessing the Adequacy and Validity of Quantitative, Qualitative, and Mixed-Method Designs" (see Appendix C). All the concepts are discussed and defined in Chapter 7.

Checklist 2. Internal Design Validity (Reliability and Dependability)

1. *How context rich and meaningful ("thick") are the descriptions?* Budget pressures often reduce the richness of the data collected.

3. *Did triangulation among complementary methods and data sources produce generally converging conclusions?* Budget constraints often reduce the use of triangulation because the application of different data-collection methods usually increases costs.

5. *Are areas of uncertainty identified? Was negative evidence sought, found?* Budget pressures can reduce the search for negative evidence.

8. *Were data collected across the full range of appropriate settings, times, respondents, etc.?* Budget pressures frequently result in the elimination of some groups—often, the most difficult to reach.

16. *History.* Budget pressures often constrain ability to control for historical differences between project and comparison areas.

24. *Use of less rigorous designs due to budget and time constraints.*

Checklist 3. Statistical Conclusion Validity

1. *The sample is too small to detect program effects.* Budget pressures often result in the sample size being reduced below the minimum size required to satisfy power analysis criteria (see Chapter 15, Section 4.6).

5 & 10. *Restriction of range and extrapolation from truncated/incomplete database.* Time pressures sometimes result in samples or secondary data with more limited coverage.

Checklist 4. Construct Validity

3. *Use of a single method to measure a construct (monomethod bias).* Budget pressures may limit the number of data collection methods or the number of independent indicators of key variables.

(Continued)

(Continued)

12. *Using indicators and constructs developed in other countries without pretesting in the local context.* Budget pressures often result in inadequate testing and customization of instruments.

Checklist 5. External Validity, Transferability, and Fittingness

7. These are often not adequately addressed when budget is a factor.

9. *Does the sample design theoretically permit generalization to other populations?* Simplifying sample design to save time can sometimes reduce representativity of the sample.

SUMMARY

- Five strategies can be considered for reducing costs of evaluation planning, data collection, and analysis. (It should be noted that each of these may reduce the validity of results obtained.)
- The first is to simplify the evaluation design, usually by eliminating the collection of data on the project or comparison group before the project begins (pretest) or on the comparison group after the project is implemented (posttest) (see Chapter 11). In the simplest design, when data are collected on only the posttest project group, the data-collection budget can be reduced by as much as 80%.
- The second is to agree with clients on the elimination of nonessential information from the data collection instruments.
- The third is to maximize the use of existing documentation (secondary data). See Chapter 5 for more details.
- The fourth is to reduce the sample size. Although this can produce significant savings, if the sample becomes too small, there is the danger of failing to detect statistically significant project effects even when they do exist. See Chapter 15 Section 4 for more details.
- The fifth is to reduce the costs of data collection through methods such as the use of self-administered questionnaires, direct observation (instead of surveys), automatic counters, inputting data through handheld devices, reducing the number of periods of observation, prioritizing informants, and hiring and training students, nurses, and other more economical data collectors. It should be noted, however, that although these methods may reduce the cost of data collection, they will not necessarily reduce or may even increase the costs of data analysis.
- Most of the above strategies for reducing costs involve trade-offs because they pose threats to the validity of the evaluation findings and recommendations. The chapter concludes with a brief introduction to the assessment of threats to validity discussed in more detail in Chapter 7.

FURTHER READING

Aron, A., E. Coups, and E. Aron. 2010. *Statistics for the Behavioral and Social Sciences: A Brief Course.* 5th ed. Upper Saddle River, NJ: Prentice Hall.

This is a thorough but easily understandable review of all the statistical concepts discussed in this chapter.

Beebe, J. 2001. *Rapid Assessment Process: An Introduction.* Walnut Creek, CA: Altamira.

A clear overview of how to reduce the time required to conduct ethnographic studies of communities, programs, or organizations. Many of the techniques are also useful for reducing costs. Chapter 5 ("Trusting RAP") discusses some of the issues when conducting rapid evaluations but does not include a thorough discussion of threats to validity.

Bickman, L. and D. Rog. 2009. *The SAGE Handbook of Applied Social Research Methods. (2d ed.)* Thousand Oaks, CA: Sage.

A comprehensive review of evaluation research methodology. The following chapters are particularly useful for the present chapter: Chapter 1 (Applied Research Design), Chapter 5 (Randomized Control Trials), Chapter 6 (Quasi-Experimentation), and Chapter 7 (Designing a Qualitative Study).

Dane, F. 2011. *Evaluating Research: Methodology for People Who Need to Read Research.* Thousand Oaks, CA: Sage.

Explanation of the research designs discussed in this chapter from the perspective of people who read and use research. Chapters 7 (Experimental Research), 8 (Quasi-Experimental Research), and 12 (Evaluation Research) are particularly relevant for the present chapter.

Valadez, J. and B. R. Devkota. 2002. "Decentralized Supervision of Community Health Programs: Using LQAS in Two Districts of Southern Nepal" in *Community-Based Health Care: Lessons from Bangladesh and Boston,* edited by Raj Wyon. Management Sciences for Health.

Nontechnical explanation of how to use lot quality acceptance sampling, which is one of the techniques that is becoming popular for working with small samples.

CHAPTER 4

Not Enough Time: Addressing Scheduling and Other Time Constraints

S tep 3 of the RealWorld Evaluation (**RWE**) approach identifies strategies to address time constraints (see Figure 4.1). The first five strategies are similar to those described in Chapter 3 for reducing costs. Additional strategies that can reduce time constraints but that might in some cases increase the cost of the evaluation include reducing time pressures on expensive external (national or international) consultants, hiring more resource people (e.g., interviewers, supervisors, data analysts), and incorporating indicators for future **impact** evaluations into some of the administrative data forms routinely collected by most **programs**. The final option is to use modern technology to speed up data collection, input, and analysis. We conclude by identifying the particular threats to validity and adequacy (see Chapter 7) that arise when time-saving strategies are used.

1. Similarities and Differences Between Time and Budget Constraints

While most cost-saving methods also save time, it is important to clarify in each case whether the main constraint is time or money (or both) because there are some important differences in the approaches to be used. Both budget and time constraints may result from a low priority given to evaluation, but some ways to save time require additional expenditure. Consequently, it is important to clarify with the client whether additional resources can be made available to help save time or whether the evaluation is subject to both time and budget constraints.

There are two different ways to think about time saving. The first is a reduction of the *level of effort* (total staff time) required to complete the data collection and analysis. The second way concerns the total *duration* of data collection or analysis. This distinction is important because the

Figure 4.1 Step 3: Addressing Time Constraints

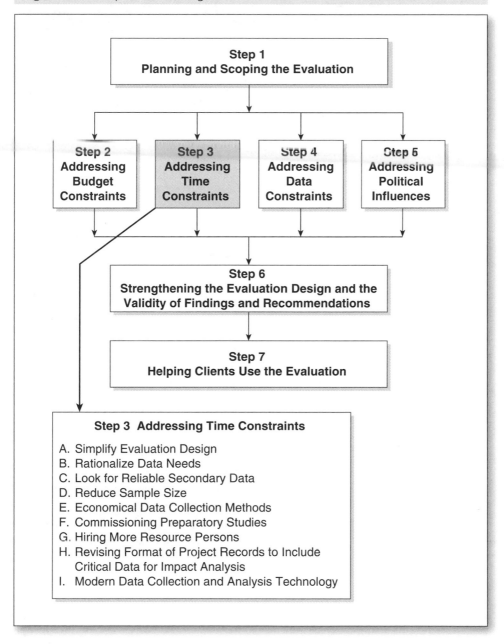

best approach to use will often depend on whether it is more important to reduce the level of effort or the duration of the evaluation. The following paragraph illustrates the differences between these two concepts.

> ## BOX 4.1
> ## TWO KINDS OF TIME SAVING
>
> It is important to distinguish between approaches that reduce the *duration* of an evaluation (it is completed over a period of six months instead of one year) and those that reduce the *level of effort* (fewer staff weeks required to actually conduct the evaluation). Asking households in a low-income community in Manila to keep a diary of their daily expenditures over one year did not reduce the duration of the evaluation, but it significantly reduced the level of effort of National Housing Authority evaluation staff. On the other hand, increasing the size of the field research team can reduce the duration of the data collection and analysis but does not reduce and may even increase the level of effort because larger research teams require more planning and coordination.
>
> SOURCE: Valadez and Bamberger (1994).

An evaluation of the impacts of a slum-upgrading project in Manila, the Philippines, on household expenditures required the collection of household income and expenditure data over a period of one year to observe how expenditures on food and other basic necessities were affected by increased investment in house improvements (see Box 4.1). The original plan was to conduct a panel study in which **interviewers** would visit a sample of households once a week over a 12-month period to record information on all household expenditures and sources of income. However, it was decided instead to ask 100 families to keep daily records of income and expenditure over the year. In return, they would be able to select a small gift at the end of every month. This method of data collection proved successful and saved a considerable amount of *effort* for the evaluation team. However, it did not reduce the *duration* of the study, which still lasted 12 months. In a different situation, the *duration* of a study (not appropriate in this example because it was necessary to collect data over a 12-month period) could be reduced by increasing the number of interviewers. It is always important when talking about saving time to clarify whether the goal is to reduce effort or duration.

Table 4.1 identifies nine general approaches that can be used to reduce time. The first five approaches are similar to those discussed in Chapter 3 for reducing costs: simplifying the evaluation **design**, clarifying client information needs, using secondary data, reducing sample size, and using cheaper and faster methods of data collection. The final four—reducing time pressures on external consultants, increasing the size of the research team, incorporating indicators for future impact studies into project records, and using modern data-collection and -analysis technology—do not necessarily reduce costs and may in fact increase them. Each of these nine approaches is discussed in this chapter. The point is made that it is important to clarify whether the constraint facing the evaluation team is to reduce time, reduce costs, or both, because the strategies can be different in each case. In particular, there are a number of time-saving strategies that may significantly increase costs.

Table 4.1 Options for Reducing the Time Required for Data Collection and Analysis in Quantitative and Qualitative Evaluations

Approaches that reduce both time and costs (see Chapter 3 for description of QUANT and QUAL applications)		
1. Simplifying the evaluation design		
2. Clarifying and prioritizing client information needs		
3. Using existing documentary data		
4. Reducing sample size		
5. Using cheaper and faster methods of data collection (see also Table 4.2)		

Additional approaches that save time but may not save money and often increase costs		
	Quantitative	**Qualitative**
1. Reducing time constraints on external (often foreign) consultants or subcontractors		
a. Commissioning the advance collection and organization of available data by local consultants	a. Compilation of secondary data and initial assessment of quality and relevance for the study (applicable also to QUAL studies)	a. Compilation of research literature and sources such as mass media materials, photographs
b. Commissioning exploratory studies by a local consultant to identify some of the key issues and the characteristics of the population prior to the arrival of the external consultant	b. Rapid surveys to obtain demographic, economic, or other relevant data on the target populations to help develop the sample design and the preparation of the sampling frame (list or map with the location of all families or other subjects in the population studied). Rapid studies can also be used to obtain preliminary estimates of, for example, education or literacy scores.	b. Rapid ethnographic studies, focusing on key concepts and issues to be covered in the study and to lay the groundwork for the external consultants
c. Videoconferences involving external and local consultants prior to the visit of the external consultant to do advance planning and save time	c. Establish rapport with the community and local leaders and officials to facilitate the smooth implementation of the study and to avoid bureaucratic delays (e.g., obtaining documents required to start the study)	c. Photos, videos, and tape recordings that can be sent to external consultants to document the conditions of the communities during different times of year (e.g., the monsoons and the dry season). This can be important if consultants are not able to visit the region in every season.
		d. Establish rapport (as for QUANT).

(Continued)

(Continued)

	Quantitative	Qualitative

2. Hiring more data collectors
 	
  a. Increasing the number of interviewers and supervisors
 	
  b. Hiring more experienced interviewers and supervisors can reduce the time required for training and can increase the efficiency and speed of the regular data collectors.
 	
  c. Subcontracting data collection or analysis
	All these approaches are applicable to QUANT studies.	Some of these approaches can be applied to QUAL studies, but it is often more difficult to recruit more experienced and qualified local researchers.

3. Revising format of project records to include critical data for impact analysis	Include indicators on access and use of services as well as relevant household or individual characteristics—particularly impact indicators.	Encourage/enable project staff to record more than project activities, e.g., to document observations of changes in conditions in beneficiaries' households.
4. Modern data-collection and -analysis technology	a. Handheld computers for data input b. Optical scanning c. Automatic counters d. QUANT computer software for data analysis and presentation	a. E-mail surveys used for both QUAL and QUANT studies b. Video cameras and tape recorders c. Photography d. GPS mapping and aerial photography to observe demographic patterns, agricultural practices, and condition of infrastructure over a large area, saving considerable amounts of time required to reach remote villages and areas. e. QUAL computer software for data analysis and presentation (does not always save time because the main purpose is to permit more comprehensive analysis)

BOX 4.2
TIME CONSTRAINTS AFFECTING THE EVALUATION OF A WATER AND SANITATION PROJECT IN MOZAMBIQUE

The design and implementation of an evaluation of a water and sanitation project in Mozambique was assessed as part of a meta-evaluation of CARE International's approach to the evaluation of its projects. It was assumed that important data would be easily accessible and that all required fieldwork could be completed in 10 days. However, the review of the terms of reference for the evaluation found that the time actually needed for fieldwork was much longer than originally planned.

"The Terms of Reference (TOR) required a final review of a three year project over a three week period, with 10 days in the field with the project staff and one week report writing. The TOR assumed easy access to necessary data, but in the event it has taken more than four weeks to obtain full details of communities benefiting and construction details, and also budget and expenditure details. There was no mention [in the TOR] of the lack of any surveys or regular monitoring of impact, which made it necessary to undertake a full End of Project Survey during the period of the evaluation. This is normally a separate exercise taking several weeks to design, test, train enumerators, collect field data and analyze it, and as a result it took up a large proportion of the evaluation time, but impact could not have been assessed without it."

SOURCE: Russon (2005).

Box 4.2 illustrates a common situation in which it is not possible to complete fieldwork within the very short period of time originally planned (in this case, 10 days) because the data are often more difficult to find or collect than had originally been assumed. This often means that while the team is in the field, a rapid decision has to be made to either limit the scope of the evaluation or extend the time (and resources) allowed for fieldwork.

2. Simplifying the Evaluation Design

In Table 3.2 (Chapter 3), we described the seven evaluation frameworks and the 19 most common evaluation design options (combining the framework with how the project and comparison groups were matched and when the evaluation began). In Chapter 3, we also pointed out that some of the methodologically weaker designs can cut costs by 50% or more. When these designs are applied to saving time rather than to costs, the distinction between reducing effort and reducing duration is important. The duration of the evaluation can be reduced by selecting any of the designs that collect data only at the end of the project (option B for Designs 2.2, 2.5, 4.1, and 6.4). In contrast, the level of effort is reduced by selecting designs that do not include a pretest and/or posttest comparison group (Designs 2.2, 2.5, 4.1, and 6.4) as well as those that do not collect baseline data (Designs 5.1 and 7.1).

As discussed in Chapter 3, although many of these designs can significantly reduce time or cost, they do so by relaxing or eliminating many of the quality-control and validity measures that are part of standard evaluation methodology. It is, therefore, important to assess the trade-offs between staying within the evaluation time frame and not exposing the evaluation to threats to quality that may compromise the validity of the conclusions. The general principles for assessing threats to validity are discussed in Chapter 7.

3. Clarifying Client Information Needs and Deadlines

Because in many cases there is a potential trade-off between reducing the time required for data collection or analysis and the quality and coverage of the evaluation, it is important to understand the client's priorities, options, and critical deadlines. The following are typical options to clarify with the client: ·

- Is it essential that the evaluation be completed and the full report presented by a certain date? *or*

- Would it be acceptable to prepare for this deadline a short summary report outlining key **findings** and recommendations? Would this allow more time to complete the full final report?
- Is it more important to complete the report by a certain date (even if this will affect quality) or to extend the time period to ensure a better-quality report?

It is essential for the evaluator to understand why these deadlines are critical and what kinds of decisions or actions must be taken. Some dates are critical, but the client needs only certain specific information by that date and not the whole report, such as, "Is the project going well?" "Will the evaluation recommend that the project should continue?" "Will additional funds for the evaluation have to be requested in the next budget?" It often takes time to establish exactly what is required, but it may save time later by asking questions such as the following:

- What information is essential and what could be dropped or reduced?
- What level of **precision** and how much detail are required for the essential information? For example, is it necessary to have separate estimates for each subgroup (e.g., male and female beneficiaries, each separate project location), or is a general estimate acceptable? Is it necessary to analyze all project components and services or only the most important?
- Is it possible to obtain additional resources (e.g., money, staff, computer access, vehicles) to speed up data collection and analysis?

Once the deadlines are clearly understood, it is important to establish a collaborative relationship with the client, working together to produce the best report possible by this date. Evaluators can easily find themselves in an adversarial relationship in which the client is pressuring them to produce more information by a certain date and the evaluator is seen as obstinately opposing every request. It is important to discuss and agree ahead of time on what can and cannot be produced by a particular date and why.

Then, in negotiating design and methods, it is important that the client understand the trade-offs and potential threats to quality when time-saving approaches are used.

4. Using Existing Documentary Data

Using existing documentary data can be an important time saver if, for example, available surveys or government reports can lessen the need to collect new data. However, existing data must always be carefully assessed to determine when and how the data were collected and for what purpose; these characteristics can sometimes limit their usefulness for the current evaluation. This is a particular challenge when there is not sufficient time to fully assess the strengths and limitations of particular documents or data sources because there is a temptation to use them despite potential biases or other problems.

5. Reducing Sample Size

We saw in Chapter 3 that reducing sample size can potentially save a significant amount of time and money during the data-collection phase. However, smaller samples usually increase sampling error and limit the ability of the evaluation to determine whether the project has produced its intended effects. Smaller samples often increase the need to introduce quality controls and to use mixed methods (such as combining sample survey with participant observation, key informant interviews, and focus groups) to permit triangulation. The use of mixed methods will often increase the duration of data collection and analysis, thus losing some of the time savings from using smaller samples.

However, because many of these mixed methods can, and often should, be conducted at the same time as the survey, the overall time for the evaluation can be significantly reduced if resources are available to hire additional researchers to conduct these additional collections of data for the study—at the same time that other QUAL or QUANT data collection is underway.

6. Rapid Data-Collection Methods

Emphasis in QUAL studies is often placed on iterative learning and understanding through frequent contact, often over a long period of time. Given the need to adapt many of these methods to the time constraints under which most program evaluations take place, an international development literature (which is apparently not well known in the United States) has developed in which the focus is on rapid methods of data collection (see annotated bibliography at the end of this chapter). Many of these approaches are adapted from traditional ethnographic methods. While many of these approaches can be implemented very rapidly, most of these rapid applications do not systematically address the increased threats to validity to which the findings may be subjected, and there are serious limitations on the validity of findings. There is a need for further work in this area to assess the trade-offs between time, quality, and validity and to define the situations in which the use of these rapid methods can be justified. Box 4.3 gives examples of a number of different methods for rapid data collection. These include participant observation, the use of diaries, group consultations, rapid ethnographic methods, and exit studies as people are leaving a meeting or service facility.

BOX 4.3
EXAMPLES OF RAPID DATA COLLECTION METHODS

1. The cost-saving data-collection methods from Bulgaria, the Philippines, and Indonesia described in Box 3.5 also helped save time. The Bulgarian study was completed in less than two months and required only about two weeks of fieldwork. The use of diaries to record expenditures in the Philippines made it necessary for the monitor to visit a subsample of households only once a week for quality control, and the participatory group discussion techniques in Indonesia obviated the necessity for small surveys to obtain information on the use of water and sanitation services and significantly reduced the time required for data collection.

2. Rapid ethnographic methods make it possible to conduct diagnostic studies of communities, programs, or organizations that would traditionally require several months of field research to be completed in one to six weeks (see Box 4.4).

3. Asking people leaving a meeting or the office of a public service agency to answer a single question (such as "Would you recommend a friend or neighbor to use this service?") makes it possible to conduct a very rapid and economical attitude survey.

BOX 4.4
RAPID ETHNOGRAPHIC METHODS (RAP)

Beebe states that the *rapid assessment process* means a "minimum of 4 days and, in most situations, a maximum of 6 weeks." He further states that "RAP recognizes that there are times when results are needed almost immediately and that the *rapid* production of results involves compromises and requires special attention to methodology if the results are to be meaningful." He emphasizes that "rapid does not mean rushed, and spending too little time or being rushed during the process can reduce RAP to *research tourism.*" According to Beebe, RAP uses most of the standard ethnographic methods, but the defining characteristics of RAP are the following:

- Intensive *team-based* ethnographic enquiry
- Systematic use of triangulation
- Iterative data analysis
- Additional data collection to quickly develop a preliminary understanding of a situation from the insider's perspective

SOURCE: Beebe (2001:xvi).

Table 4.2 identifies a number of rapid QUAL and QUANT methods and gives examples of how time requirements can be reduced. The following are some of the ways to reduce time required for applying QUAL methods:

- Focus groups: The selection and recruitment of participants and the conducting and analysis can be subcontracted to specialists such as market research firms. More researchers can be contracted so that several focus groups can be conducted simultaneously (rather than one at a time as is often done).
- Community interviews, perhaps using **PRA** (participatory rural appraisal) techniques (Kumar 2002) can be used to collect information from groups (e.g., on agricultural practices and crop production, on children's health and nutrition) rather than conducting surveys with households.
- Exit surveys can be used to obtain rapid feedback on meetings and other community activities.
- Community informants or community groups (such as secondary school children or women's organizations) can be trained to collect information or to talk about what they know.

Examples of rapid QUANT methods include these:

- Rapid surveys using very short questionnaires. When only a few questions are asked, the time taken to collect and analyze data is dramatically reduced.
- A number of specialized sampling techniques can significantly reduce the number of interviews required to assess use of, and satisfaction with, public services (see the discussion of lot quality acceptance sampling in Chapter 15, Section 7.1, and Valadez and Devkota 2002).

Table 4.2   Rapid Data-Collection Methods: The Effect on Duration of the Evaluation and the Level of Effort

	Ways to Reduce Time Requirements	Reducing Duration (elapsed time) or Level of Effort (staff time)	
		Duration	Effort
A. Mainly qualitative methods			
Key informant interviews	Key informants can save time either by providing data (regarding agricultural prices, people leaving and joining the community, school attendance and absenteeism), helping researchers focus on key issues, or pointing out faster ways to obtain information. Ways to reduce time of key informant interviews: • Reduce the number of informants. • Limit the number of issues covered. • Hire more researchers to conduct the interviews or to tape interviews for the researcher to review. Do this with caution; it is important for the researcher to maintain personal contact with key people in the community.	√ √ √	√ √
Focus groups and community interviews	• Subcontract to focus group specialists such as market research firms. • Conduct several focus groups simultaneously instead of sequentially. • Collect information from meetings rather than surveys. Information on topics such as access to and use of water and sanitation, agricultural practices, and gender division of labor in farming can be obtained in group interviews, possibly combined with the distribution of self-administered surveys. • *Note: It is important to use techniques that ensure the views of all participants are captured (time pressures mean that more vulnerable and harder-to-access groups may be left out).*	√ √ √	√ √
Structured observation	• Observation can sometimes, but not always, be faster than surveys—for example, observation of the gender division of labor in different kinds of agricultural production, who attends meetings and participates in discussions, types of conflict observed in public places in the community.	√	
Use of existing documents and artifacts	• Many kinds of existing data can be collected and reviewed more rapidly than new data can be collected—for example, school attendance records, newspapers and other mass media, minutes of community meetings, health center records, surveys in target communities conducted by research institutions.	√	√
Using community groups to collect information	• Organization of rapid community studies (QUAL and QUANT) using community interviewers (local schoolteachers often cooperate with this).	√	
Photos and videos	• Giving disposable cameras or camcorders to community informants to take photos (or make videos) illustrating, for example, community problems.	√	√

(Continued)

(Continued)

	Ways to Reduce Time Requirements	Reducing Duration (elapsed time) or Level of Effort (staff time)	
		Duration	Effort
Triangulation	• Having several interviewers simultaneously interview and separately record their observations on the same key respondents rather than having separate interviews. This can save elapsed time if it replaces several separate interviews with the same person.	√	
B. Mainly quantitative methods			
Rapid surveys with short questionnaires and small samples	• Reducing the number of questions and the size of the sample can significantly reduce the time required to conduct a survey. • Increasing the number of interviewers.	√ √	√
Reduce sample sizes	• There are specialized sampling techniques such as lot quality acceptance sampling (Valadez and Bamberger 1994) designed to provide estimates of the use or quality of public services such as health and education with very small samples. Samples of 14 to 19 households may be sufficient to assess use or quality of a single health center.	√	√
Triangulation (used also in QUAL and mixed methods)	• Obtaining independent estimates from different sources (e.g., survey and observation) sometimes makes it possible to obtain estimates from smaller samples, hence saving both elapsed time and effort.	√	√
Rapid exit surveys	• People leaving a meeting or exiting a service facility can be asked to write their views on the meeting or service on an index card. These can then be posted on a wall or notice board to provide rapid feedback to clients. • Often only one key question will be asked. For example, "Would you recommend a neighbor to come to the next meeting or use this center?"	√ √	√ √
Use of existing data	• Previous surveys or other data sources may eliminate the need to collect certain data. • Previous survey findings can reduce the time required for sample design by providing information on the standard deviation (how narrowly or widely subjects are distributed around the mean) of key variables. This may make it possible to reduce sample size or to save time through more efficient stratification or cluster sampling. (These terms are defined in Chapter 15 Section 3.)	√ √	√
Observation checklists	• Observation checklists can often eliminate the need for certain surveys (e.g., pedestrian and vehicular traffic flows, use of community facilities, time required to collect water and fuel).	√	√
Automatic counters	• Recording people entering buildings or using services such as water.	√	√

	Ways to Reduce Time Requirements	Reducing Duration (elapsed time) or Level of Effort (staff time)	
		Duration	Effort
C. Mixed methods			
• Triangulation (used also in QUAL and QUANT methods)	• Triangulating data from several quantitative and qualitative methods may sometimes make it possible to obtain estimates from smaller samples, hence saving effort and elapsed time. This is not always the case because use of several different data-collection methods has obvious time/cost implications.	√	√
• Rapid quantification of participatory assessment methods and focus groups	• Short and rapid sample surveys can be combined with numerical estimates obtained from community interviews and focus groups to provide estimates of, for example, service usage, unemployment rates, time use for a community or other population group.	√	√

NOTE: It is often difficult to differentiate between saving time and reducing effort. It is also important to stress that saving time by increasing the size of the team will usually increase the budget. Hence, the need to clarify with the client whether the major constraint is time, budget, or both.

- Observation checklists can be used to collect numerical information on use of community service, transport patterns, or the types of goods on sale in the community or the market.
- Using triangulation to combine QUANT and QUAL estimates of key variables. The use of QUAL indicators to confirm or question QUANT estimates (e.g., of income, proportion of the population with access to public services) can often reduce the required sample size and reduced the time required for data collection.
- Complementing participatory assessments or focus groups with short and rapid surveys can provide rapid QUANT estimates of service usage, unemployment rates, transport patterns, and so on.

Box 4.5 illustrates the use of mixed methods in a study of poverty and survival strategies of poor families in Colombia. The study, which would normally have required two to three months, was completed in four weeks.

BOX 4.5
REDUCING THE TIME REQUIRED TO
CONDUCT A MIXED-METHOD STUDY OF SURVIVAL
STRATEGIES OF LOW-INCOME HOUSEHOLDS

A study was conducted in low-income areas of Cartagena, Colombia, to estimate the importance of interhousehold transfers of money and goods as a survival strategy for poor urban households. The study, combining a sample survey of 160 households and

(Continued)

(Continued)

the preparation of in-depth case studies on the interhousehold transfer patterns of 5 households, was designed, conducted, and analyzed in only four weeks and used a total of only 40 person days. This was achieved by reducing the number of survey questions to the absolute minimum and planning the timing of the interviews to ensure high response rates. The main time inputs were the following:

	Days
Designing and testing the survey instrument	7.5
Sample design	2
Selecting, training, and debriefing interviewers	7
Conducting 160 QUANT interviews	6
Designing QUAL study	8
Developing and testing methodology	2
Conducting case studies	8
Total staff days	40.5 days
Total duration of the study	4 weeks

A study of this size and complexity would normally require at least two to three months to design, implement, and analyze.

SOURCE: Wansbrough, Jones, and Kappaz (2000).

7. Reducing Time Pressure on Outside Consultants

In this discussion, it is helpful to distinguish between the *outside consultant* coming from a different area of the country or from a different country, the *local consultant* who comes from the city or area where the evaluation is being conducted, and the *in-house staff* working with the agency being evaluated or possibly from a planning agency (e.g., the planning department in the Ministry of Health or the national planning agency). Each of these people can play a different role in the evaluation. The issues discussed here are similar for situations in which the external consultant is working in his or her own country (a developed country such as the United States or Europe) or where that person is brought in from another country (e.g., a consultant from France working on an evaluation in Ethiopia). Some of the issues discussed are more relevant to a large country where the national consultant has to travel a long distance so that the timing of the interventions has to be well planned and coordinated.

Many evaluations contract an outside consultant, usually from a different part of the country or from a different country. Although there are well-funded evaluations in which the outside consultant is contracted for long periods of time and may visit the project or program on a regular basis, for

RWEs, the outside consultant is usually contracted for a relatively short period of time (often defined in terms of the number of person days) and is seen as an expensive and scarce resource.

The outside consultant(s) may either be responsible for conducting the whole evaluation, with support from local agency staff and local consultants, or he or she may have a specific role to play (e.g., helping with the research design and the development and testing of the data-collection instruments). Both because of the high cost and the short time availability of the outside consultant, it is important to ensure that his or her time is used effectively, particularly ensuring that time is not spent on activities that could have been done as well (or better) by local staff and consultants. One way to save time is to collect background data and possibly conduct preliminary exploratory studies prior to the arrival of the outside consultant. A typical exploratory study might involve preparing initial reports on the social and economic characteristics of the target groups or communities and describing key features of the programs or projects to be studied, how they operate, and how they are perceived. In some cases, a preliminary list of potential key informants and possible participants in focus groups might also be prepared.

Some of this material can be collected by project staff; in other cases, it may be necessary to commission local consultants. Very often, the client or funding agency will have a standard procedure for contracting short-term consultants and perhaps a roster of local consultants from which consultants must be selected based on a description of the work. In other cases, a request for proposals may be sent out in response to a description of the task (this procedure will often significantly increase the timeline). Whichever procedure is used, precise **terms of reference** should be prepared. The contract should also include some time for local consultants, if any, to work with the outside consultant during the evaluation and, ideally, time for follow-up activities after the completion of the evaluation report by the external consultant.

Review of existing data and exploratory studies might be commissioned to collect background information on the program, characteristics of the **target population**, and context or setting. This information is then available when the outside consultant officially starts work. There may be more flexibility concerning the use of local personnel and resources. Videoconferencing is often a useful way to establish contact and rapport with external consultants and to speed up preparatory activities (note the caution in Box 4.6) and reduce time pressures during the external consultant's usually short site visit by developing trust and a good working relationship in advance.

BOX 4.6
BE CONSIDERATE OF NATIONAL STAFF WHEN PLANNING
"CONVENIENT" VIDEOCONFERENCING

While videoconferencing may seem very convenient and simple for the international consultants, it is important to recognize potential problems for national staff. An obvious point is the difference in time zones. A comfortable 10 a.m. start in Washington or London may be late at night in Asia. One of the authors also discovered later that staff from an Indian agency had to drive for 12 hours (in each direction) to get to the videoconference center in New Delhi. Many local staff may be reluctant to mention these problems when agreeing to participate in the videoconference. Over the past few years, the advances in the videoconferencing software for use with desktop computers has significantly reduced some of these logistical problems.

8. Hiring More Resource People

The time required for data collection can often be significantly reduced by spreading the workload among a greater number of interviewers or other data collectors. However, increasing the number of interviewers will often require additional time for training and may increase the complexity of coordination, so unless it is well planned, the desired time savings may not be achieved. There may also be a risk of reduced quality of information collected. Subcontracting portions of the data collection to private firms with the requisite experience, personnel, and facilities can also help reduce time overall.

Creating an evaluation team that includes both QUAL evaluators and QUANT evaluators may ensure full and appropriate use of both QUANT and QUAL methods of data collection and analysis, but that often considerably increases the time needed for the study because of the number of data collection and analysis methods being used and the need for discussion of their appropriate bundling and balancing. The time required for team building and creating understanding and confidence among professionals from different disciplines or approaches has often resulted in overemphasis of one type of data and relative neglect of another.

9. Building Outcome Indicators into Project Records

Where evaluation is considered at the time the project implementation is planned and where projects and personnel demonstrate flexibility, it may be possible to modify project-monitoring records and forms so that information regarding specific evaluation questions, target populations, and their use of project services can be more easily and rapidly analyzed. Although most project-monitoring data report only on activities and outputs, outcome indicators can sometimes be built into project-monitoring systems and records. Examples include the following:

- Records of use of services by project participants
- Changes in knowledge and attitudes of participants, as in a training course
- Access to and cost of services prior to the start of the project (information on this is often recorded in, for example, housing or **microcredit** projects and sometimes in health programs)
- Socioeconomic conditions of families at the start of the project

However, it is important to identify and evaluate any potential biases in these and all data sources, which may, for example, neglect some groups in the population or fail to include certain critical information. A frequent problem is that quality-control standards for completing administrative reports may be lower than for evaluation studies so that the risk of omitted data or careless recording may increase. Another approach is to ensure that information from existing records is organized and recorded in a way that can be easily analyzed. For example:

- Health clinic patient records should be filed by family so that it is possible to estimate how many families have used the clinic.
- Client information should be organized by type of service (e.g., type of training received, individual or communal water collection, type of loan, type of extension services).

- Ensure that client records include information on conditions prior to the project (e.g., type of water supply, whether women were already cultivating vegetables, whether farmers were already using fertilizers, student grades and test scores prior to state accountability).

10. Data-Collection and -Analysis Technology

The direct inputting of survey responses to handheld computers can greatly reduce the time required for data processing and analysis. Optical scanning of survey instruments is another time-saving device for data inputting. However, optical scanning sometimes works less well in remote field settings than in the office, so consultation with experts and pilot testing are advisable before relying on such technology. Mobile phones are now being used to directly input survey data, and GPS-enabled mobile phones can also be used to create GIS (geographic information system) maps.

A wide range of statistical packages for QUANT (see Chapter 12)[1] and QUAL data analysis are available[2]. Statistical packages can save considerable amounts of time during the analysis phase. However, it is not clear whether QUAL data-analysis packages can save time for QUAL studies because the coding schemes take a long time to set up and the purpose is usually to provide more comprehensive analysis rather than to save time. The use of handheld electronic data inputting devices has also created problems in many QUAL evaluation settings because it constrains the use of *emergent designs* when the set of key issues being studied will change (emerge) as the study progresses.

Web-based surveys[3] are now widely used and can save time and money, particularly for large populations or when subjects are widely dispersed. A number of Internet-based survey packages are available free. Concept mapping (discussed in Chapter 16) can also be conducted through Internet-based software and offers considerable time and cost saving (Kane and Trochim 2007).

11. Common Threats to Adequacy and Validity Relating to Time Constraints

The most common threats to validity and adequacy of evaluation conclusions that must be addressed when assessing the different approaches to time constraints discussed in this chapter are similar to those discussed in the previous chapter (Box 3.5). Readers who are not familiar with the concepts of threats to validity are recommended to read Chapter 7 and then to return to this section.

SUMMARY

- When identifying strategies to reduce time, it is important to determine whether there are also budget constraints or whether it is possible to increase expenditures to save time.
- Most of the cost-saving strategies discussed in the previous chapter can also be used to save time.

---

[1]See Bernard and Ryan, 2010 pp. 376–378, for a summary or resources for QUAL analysis.

[2]Salkind (2011) provides a useful introduction to the use of Microsoft Excel for basic statistical analysis.

[3]See Best and Harrison 2009 for a review of internet survey methods.

- Often, the main time pressure is on outside (often foreign) consultants who are available for only a short period of time. Their time can be used more efficiently by commissioning agency staff or a local consultant to prepare background studies or to do preparatory work for developing the methodology. Videoconferencing can also save outside consultant time (and often money). This also means that consultants can contribute to the evaluation design at the critical points when their input is most useful.
- Time can also be saved by increasing the number or raising the professional level of data collectors, field supervisors, and data analysts.
- In cases where the evaluator is involved at the start of the project, it may be possible to incorporate impact indicators into some of the administrative data forms used by the implementing agency to collect information that can later be used in the measurement of impacts.
- Modern handheld computers, mobile "smart" phones, and similar technology can sometimes be used to reduce the time required for data collection and analysis.

As discussed in the previous chapter with respect to cost-saving strategies, most of the time-saving strategies involve trade-offs because they pose threats to the validity of the evaluation findings and recommendations. The chapter concludes with a brief introduction to the assessment of threats to validity, which is discussed in more detail in Chapter 7.

FURTHER READING

Bamberger, M., ed. 2000. *Integrating Quantitative and Qualitative Research in Development Projects.* Washington, DC: World Bank.

Case studies on the use of mixed-method approaches to improve quality and often to reduce time.

Beebe, J. 2001. *Rapid Assessment Process: An Introduction.* Walnut Creek, CA: Altamira.

A clear overview of how to reduce the time required to conduct ethnographic studies of communities, programs, or organizations. Many of the most widely used qualitative evaluation methods are based on ethnography, so the approaches described in this book have a very wide application. However, while guidelines are presented for ensuring quality control during data collection, the issues concerning threats to validity of the findings and conclusions are not systematically discussed— which is a serious issue with these approaches given the very limited time spent in the field.

Bickman, L. and D. Rog. 2009. *The SAGE Handbook of Applied Social Research Methods. 2d ed.* Thousand Oaks, CA: Sage.

This is a useful general reference for the main evaluation research designs and data collection methods. Several chapters are particularly relevant with respect to potential time-saving data collection strategies, including: Internet Survey Methods (Chapter 13), Concept Mapping (Chapter 14), Mail Surveys (Chapter 15), and Telephone Surveys (Chapter 16).

Kumar, S. 2002. *Methods for Community Participation: A Complete Guide for Practitioners.* London: ITDG.

Detailed review of the main participatory data-collection and -analysis methods that can potentially be used as an alternative to sample survey data collection and that can save time (and money).

CHAPTER 5

Critical Information Is Missing or Difficult to Collect: Addressing Data Constraints

Step 4 of the RealWorld Evaluation (**RWE**) approach identifies strategies for making the best use of limited and sometimes biased or misleading data sources (see Figure 5.1). A common RWE scenario is that the evaluation does not begin until the **project** has been underway for some time and no baseline data have been collected. A number of strategies are discussed for recreating the conditions at the time the project began ("reconstructing" baseline data). A number of additional problems must often be addressed when reconstructing information on comparison groups. A different set of issues faces evaluators in the collection of data on sensitive topics and from groups that are difficult to reach. Addressing these questions, which are of vital importance to the purpose of many evaluations because they concern the most vulnerable groups or most intractable problems, is a particular challenge for the RealWorld evaluator: These kinds of information are often more time consuming and expensive to collect, so there are often pressures to ignore these groups or issues when time or money is scarce. We conclude by identifying important threats to validity of conclusions when working with limited and often unreliable data.

1. Data Issues Facing RealWorld Evaluators

Evaluators often face constraints in the real world of practice resulting from the limited availability and accuracy of critical data. Concerns may surface regarding, for example, the following:

- Lack of baseline data on the project population
- Selecting a comparison group and defining a counterfactual when conventional statistical matching is not possible

Figure 5.1   Step 4: Addressing Data Constraints

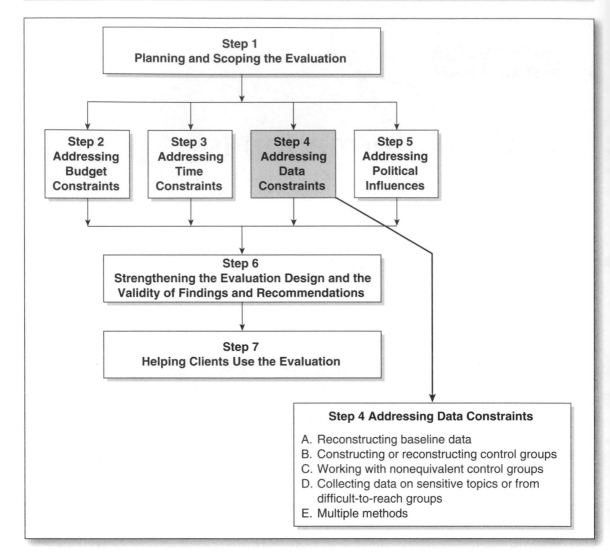

- Obtaining estimates of variables that might affect project outcomes that were not included in baseline surveys (**"omitted variables"** also known as "unobservables")
- Using incomplete or potentially biased sampling frames
- Collecting data on sensitive topics or where information is incomplete or potentially biased
- Identifying, locating, and interviewing difficult-to-reach subjects (e.g., members of illegal or clandestine groups, remote or voiceless groups, or participants who are unwilling to be interviewed)

In this chapter, we will propose approaches for addressing each kind of data constraint (see Tables 5.1 and 5.2). Let's consider four different data-collection scenarios, each with its own set of problems. The first relates to project participants from whom data are being collected on their present situation via a baseline survey, end-of-project survey, or other kind of quantitative (QUANT), qualitative (QUAL), or mixed-method data-collection method. In many ways, this is a straightforward situation, provided project participants are easy to identify. Unless the project is going badly, they are usually quite willing to give information. However, if they are involved in activities not authorized by the project (e.g., welfare beneficiaries using project benefits to set up a black market business, housing beneficiaries subletting part of the house provided to them by the project, teachers moonlighting as tutors) or think they might benefit from a misrepresentation of the project (e.g., because they want to create the impression that they are poorer than they really are in the hope that charges for water or other services may be reduced), there might be reasons for caution about the accuracy of data from them.

In a second situation, people in comparison groups, who will not receive any benefit from the project, have little incentive to cooperate by providing data. In many situations the challenge of finding subjects willing to respond may be considered so difficult that it is decided that a comparison-group design cannot be used. **Clients** or funding agencies might also discourage interviews of these people to avoid expectations of compensation, benefits, or political pressures to expand the coverage of the project. An additional challenge, which we will discuss later, will often be how to identify an appropriate comparison group that matches the project participants reasonably closely. In most cases, secondary data that could be used for statistical matching (using techniques such as propensity score matching that we discuss later) are not available, so matching will often have to be done judgmentally. This involves pooling information from local experts and rapid visits to possible comparison locations, with whatever secondary data might be available.

A third situation involves the *reconstruction* of baseline data on project participants or comparison groups through the use of existing data, key informants, or other indirect techniques. This is often a difficult situation for an evaluator who faces the problem of inaccurate recall (e.g., nostalgia, misremembering) and distorted representations either intentional or unintentional. For example, a community elder might tend to romanticize the "good old days" and underestimate the amount of crime or poverty in the community in the past, or a supporter of an opposition party might downplay the improvements that the current local government has produced. In the following section, we discuss some of the reasons baseline data may not be available—even in situations where the project design specified that a baseline survey would be conducted.

A fourth issue that can affect any of the above is the problem of ensuring that the sampling frame used to select subjects to be interviewed covers all of the intended target population. Often, the most convenient sampling frame is to use an existing register or map that was constructed for some other purpose but that may not include all of the target population. Examples might include a register of the internally displaced population, families eligible to receive Social Security or other welfare benefits, or a register of educational institutions or of commercial enterprises (see Box 5.1). As we will discuss later, there are reasons each of these sampling frames may not cover all of the target population, and when this happens, it is frequently the case that individuals, families, or institutions that are excluded are different in some important way from those that are included. This is a particular problem for the purposes of this chapter when using secondary data to reconstruct baseline data, as the evaluator has very little ability to correct for any exclusions or biases in the sample frame or even to estimate how important these exclusions may be for the purposes of the evaluation.

An issue when selecting the comparison group concerns sample bias. Often, project participants are either self-selected (interested individuals, families, or communities apply to participate in the project) or participants are selected by the implementing agency. In both cases, project participants are likely to have special characteristics that distinguish them from families or communities not in the project. This means that a random sample selected from the nonparticipant population is likely to differ from project participants in ways that might affect project outcomes. In most cases, participants are likely to have characteristics (education, income, prior experience in similar types of projects, strong community organization) making them more likely to succeed.

If the project and comparison-group samples are sufficiently large, it is often possible to improve the match between the project and comparison-group samples by using statistical matching techniques such as **propensity score** matching[1] (PSM; Khandker et al. 2010, chap. 4). PSM and other statistical matching techniques such as instrumental variables (Khandker, Koolwal, and Samad 2010 chap. 6) can significantly reduce the problem of sample bias.

BOX 5.1
EXAMPLES OF SAMPLING FRAMES THAT MAY EXCLUDE
SECTORS OF THE INTENDED TARGET POPULATION

The following are examples of sampling frames used to select samples for impact evaluations that often exclude or underrepresent certain sectors of the target population. Usually, the excluded groups are different in important ways from the sampled groups, frequently introducing a bias into the findings.

   i. Countries that have recently experienced civil war or major natural disasters that resulted in displacement of significant numbers of families or whole communities usually keep a register of internally displaced persons (IDPs). This register is often used to select samples for studies to evaluate the effectiveness of programs designed for IDPs. Often, significant numbers of IDPs do not appear in the register: in some cases through fear of being identified either by militant groups or a former spouse in cases where they have started a new family, in other cases through lack of awareness of the register, and in others because of lack of confidence in the agencies responsible for providing services.

   ii. Ministries of education often conduct censuses of schools that provide a useful sampling frame for many kinds of evaluation. However, the register may only include state-run schools, excluding religious and perhaps not-for-profit schools. In other cases, the register includes all legally registered schools but not the large number of schools that are not registered.

   iii. Ministries of labor or industry often conduct surveys of enterprises that provide a useful sampling frame for a range of topics relating to employment or work conditions. However, the surveys commonly only cover enterprises that employ more than, say, 10 people, so that the many smaller enterprises where most low-income groups work are not included.

---

[1]Propensity score matching (PSM) uses logistical regression to identify a set of around five subjects from the comparison group that most closely matches each subject in the project group with respect to the likelihood of participation (with the only difference being that the comparison group subjects did not participate, often for reasons of location or similar factors). These subjects are called the "nearest neighbors," and the difference in their pretest/posttest scores on the indicator of project impact are compared with the change in the project subject. The difference is defined as the "gain score" and is used to estimate the size and significance of project impact.

2. Reconstructing Baseline Data

When the evaluation does not begin until midway through or even toward the end of the project, evaluators all too often find that no baseline data have been collected on the project or on comparison groups or that information was not collected on the access of these groups to the types of services and benefits provided by the project. In most cases, at least some useful data will have been collected on the project population when the project began. Comparable data on potential comparison groups are usually more difficult to find. This section offers some ways to reconstruct baseline data for project participants and then discusses some of the additional challenges regarding comparable data on a comparison group.

There are a number of reasons baseline data might not be available—even when both donors and implementing agencies were interested in its being collected and when the project design might include plans and resources for the collection of baseline data. Sometimes the main reason is a lack of understanding of the value of baseline data or an unwillingness to spend money on its collection. In other cases, the organizational mechanisms are not in place for the collection and analysis of the data. Often, with a new project, it takes time to approve funds for consultants and hiring staff and installing M&E systems (purchasing computers etc.) and additional time for hiring and training staff and contracting consultants. So even with the best of intentions, it may take months or even years after the project launch before it is possible to collect or commission the collection of baseline data. A further delay is often that the M&E systems through which baseline data will be collected have teething problems, and it may take time before the required data are actually being collected. In other cases, when adequate coordination between data collectors and evaluators does not exist, the "baseline" information may not actually provide the required data for the evaluation. Sometimes the information is not collected or filed as required, the questions may not be asked in the right way, or the quality of information may be poor. This latter may be a problem if the project staff who should collect the information may not have been properly trained, they may not have the time or the incentive to collect it, or they do not believe it is useful, so they do not take the trouble to collect it properly. For example, it is much easier to guess how many people attended a meeting than to take the trouble to count.

A final issue that we will discuss later is the question of omitted variables *(unobservables)*. This is information that was not included in the baseline survey, either because it was difficult to collect or because the agency collecting the data had not focused on some of these issues. This is commonly an issue when secondary data collected for a different purpose are used to reconstruct the baseline for the evaluation.

2.1. Strategies for Reconstructing Baseline Data

When Should Baseline Data Be Collected?

Many impact evaluation designs implicitly assume that a project only starts to influence the target population once it officially begins, but in fact, changes may occur long before the project launch. For example, once it is known that roads, water supply, or other services are to be provided to certain communities, speculators may begin to buy land and families may start to make improvements to their houses or farms. Similarly, if a new school is to be built, families with school-age children may try to move to the communities eligible to attend the school. If the baseline is not conducted until the project officially begins, many of these important changes may not be captured in the data. Usually, it is not possible to advance the date of the baseline study, but the possibility of using qualitative techniques such as recall or key informant interviews to capture information on some of these early effects of the project should be considered. Figure 5.2 identifies four possible times that a baseline study could be conducted for a slum-upgrading project: 2003, when it became known that a project was being planned; 2004, when the project officially began (but when construction had not actually started); 2005, when construction of roads and water supply began; and 2006, when the construction of all roads had been completed and all houses had access to drinking water. The findings of the baseline study are likely to be quite different if it was conducted in 2003, 2004, 2005, or 2006.

Although baseline data normally cannot be collected until the project officially begins and funds are available for commissioning evaluations (i.e., 2004), it is important to appreciate that some important changes may already be taking place as soon as it is known that a project is planned. For example, in the case of road construction or slum upgrading, speculators may start to buy up land or properties with the expectation of making a capital gain. Sometimes poor residents are tricked into selling their property at a below-market price or sometimes they are forced to sell, even at gunpoint. Alternatively, residents may start to make improvements in their property to take advantage of the project. The evaluator is advised to use some of the techniques discussed in this section to try to understand these events, as they may significantly affect the interpretation of the evaluation findings.

Figure 5.2   When Should the Baseline Study Be Conducted for the Evaluation of a Slum-Upgrading Project?

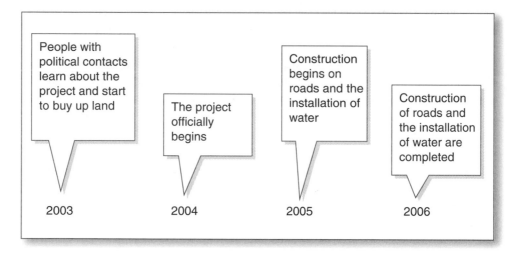

Using Administrative Data from the Project (and Sometimes from the Comparison Group)

Even when there is no baseline survey, many projects collect monitoring and other kinds of administrative data that could be used to estimate baseline conditions for the project population. For example: socioeconomic data included in the application forms of people, communities, or organizations applying to the project; planning studies (these may include data on socioeconomic conditions, social infrastructure, or access to services); regular project-monitoring reports; and administrative records providing information on, for example, changes in project eligibility criteria or in the package of services provided to beneficiaries. Sometimes the application forms for people who were not accepted can provide information on a comparison group of nonparticipants. However, except in the small number of cases in which excess demand results in participants being selected through a lottery or similar random selection process,[2] groups that are not selected are likely to differ from those who are selected, so issues of selection bias must be addressed. Box 5.2 provides examples of administrative data that have been used to reconstruct baseline data.

While administrative data are a potentially valuable source of baseline data, the data are often not collected or available in a convenient format for use in an impact evaluation. Data-collection procedures may not be clearly defined or consistently applied. Project application forms are often discarded or misplaced once selection has been completed, and monitoring records are often not organized in a manner conducive to selecting cases of interest. If project records are to be used as baseline data, the evaluator must work closely with project staff to ensure that data are recorded and filed in a way that will make them accessible for the future evaluation.

Documentary data not only come from officially published organizational reports but are also available from other sources within the organization such as computer-based monitoring, evaluation files, accounting records, websites, e-mail communications, brochures, personnel records, notice boards and signs, previous reports and evaluations, mission statements, procedures manuals, and policies.

BOX 5.2
USING ADMINISTRATIVE DATA FROM THE PROJECT TO RECONSTRUCT THE BASELINE

- A recent posttest multidonor evaluation of the Nepal Education for All project used the project's Education Management Information System (EMIS) to obtain sex-disaggregated data on school enrollment, repetition, and academic tests scores at the start of the program and at various key milestones during implementation.
- The evaluation of the poverty impacts of the World Bank–financed Viet Nam Rural Roads project used administrative data collected at the canton level to understand the selection criteria used to determine where roads would be built and to monitor the quality and speed of construction (van de Walle 1999).
- The evaluation of the feeder roads component of the Eritrea Community Development Fund used the planning and feasibility studies commissioned by the implementing agency to obtain baseline socioeconomic data on the communities affected by the roads.

The following are examples of questions that can be asked to learn about an organization from its own records and documentation:

- What can we infer from the fact that a national poverty-reduction strategy contains a detailed analysis of the linkages between economic growth and poverty reduction but only a few paragraphs on the impacts of poverty on women?

---

[2]One of the cases in which randomization is used in the selection of projects occurs when demand significantly exceeds supply and some kind of lottery or random selection is used. This sometimes occurs with social funds (see Baker 2000) or with community-supported schools (see Kim, Alderman, and Orazem 1999). Rural water supply programs in Bolivia and other countries have used lotteries as a transparent way to select communities to receive water, when demand significantly exceeds the capacity of local agencies to provide water.

- What can we infer from the fact that evaluation reports on the performance of government **programs** are automatically sent to members of Congress but are available to civil society only "on request"?
- Why was a baseline survey on the socioeconomic conditions of the target communities never conducted but financial reports were produced regularly from the start of the project?
- Why do planning documents for an integrated rural development program not discuss potential impacts on indigenous populations (even though indigenous groups represent a significant proportion of the population in the program areas)?
- Why does the project budget include a detailed analysis of project implementation costs but have little discussion (and less money) for expenditures concerning project **outcomes** and **sustainability**?
- What can we deduce from the fact that planning and evaluation reports from a country in South America are easily available in English, can be found with more difficulty in Spanish, but have never been translated into Aymara or Quechua (the main local languages)?

Using Secondary Survey Data

If the evaluator is fortunate, it may be possible to identify censuses or surveys that have been conducted by other organizations around the time the project began and that might provide all or at least some of the information required on the baseline conditions of the project and/or comparison group. Many countries conduct periodic income and expenditure surveys that include extensive social and economic data on households as well as information on access to services. As these surveys are conducted at least once a year, it is usually possible to find a survey that has been conducted close to the time of the project launch, thus providing a potentially strong baseline. Other useful surveys are conducted by central planning agencies, line ministries, or donors on education, health, or agricultural production. Many of these surveys include samples of several thousand households, so it is often possible to select a subsample of households with characteristics similar to the project population and that can provide a comparison group. However, the sample size of project households is often too small to use for the project group or, in some cases, the survey may not even include the information required to identify project participants. In these cases, it may be necessary to conduct a survey of project households while using the secondary data to generate the comparison-group sample.

- Whenever the use of secondary survey data is being considered, it is important to critically assess the data source to determine whether it satisfies the requirements of the evaluation. Some of the questions that must be asked include:
- Time differences between the start of the project (when data are required for the baseline) and the time when the secondary data were collected or reported: Time differences are particularly critical when general economic conditions may have changed between the date of the reports and the project launch.
- Differences in the population covered: For example, did the survey include employment in the informal as well as the formal sectors? Did it cover pedestrian as well as vehicular means of transport? Did it cover private as well as public schools?
- Was information collected on key project variables and potential impacts?

- Are the secondary data representative of the particular **target population** addressed by the project being evaluated?
- Does information cover both men and women, or was all information obtained from a single person (usually the "household head") and aggregated for all household members (see Box 5.3)?

Cautionary Tales—and Healthy Skepticism

There are many potential problems with documentary data. Documents may apply to different, perhaps not very comparable, time periods. Some sectors of the target population may be neglected. The accuracy of the data or the quality of the data-collection and reporting methods may reveal fundamental weaknesses. The skepticism appropriate for documentary sources is like that needed for other data sources; false survey data may be given or recorded, a sufficiently common occurrence in some Latin American countries to have earned the name "*entrevista de cafetería*," indicating that responses were fabricated while the data collector was sitting alone in the cafeteria. Interviewees may similarly be self-protective or less than fully forthcoming, and test scores can be manipulated by test takers or testing administrators. No data-collection method is free from the possibility—even likelihood—of inaccuracy, a main reason triangulation is so important. Box 5.4 gives three examples of seemingly straightforward secondary data on girls' education, each of which proved to be completely false.

BOX 5.3
EXAMPLES FROM DEVELOPING COUNTRIES OF DATABASES
THAT DO NOT ADEQUATELY REPRESENT BOTH SEXES

A common weakness of many secondary data sources that can potentially be used to reconstruct baseline conditions is that they do not provide separate information on both men and women. For example:

- Many household surveys interview only one respondent (usually the "head of household"), who either gives only his or her opinions or presents aggregate data for the whole family. Often, the household head, particularly male heads, do not have full information on all household members.
- Husbands and fathers tend to underestimate the seriousness of problems affecting women (such as the time spent collecting water and fuel and, sometimes, sexual harassment).
- Aggregate data on, for example, consumption and expenditures mask important differences in how food, medicine, and other goods are divided among different members of the household.
- Household interviews are often conducted in a situation in which other household members or neighbors can overhear the interview. This will often inhibit

(Continued)

(Continued)

spouses from giving information on their true earnings because they may not wish their partner to know how much they earn. It will also make it difficult for women to discuss sensitive topics such as domestic violence, the husband's (or mother-in-law's) control over her earnings, or harassment inside or outside the community.

- Women are reluctant to talk about sexual harassment, so many surveys under-estimate the seriousness of harassment in schools, on public transport, or walking around the village. In one survey on public transport, women mentioned "security" as a major problem. This was interpreted in the analysis as referring to problems of bad driving or poor maintenance of the vehicles, whereas in fact women were referring to sexual harassment but were unwilling to be more specific.
- In many cultures, women's participation in community decision making is very limited, so reports on community meetings, while purporting to reflect the views of all the community, in fact often reflect only the opinions of males. Many monitoring reports do not even break down attendance at meetings or community activities by gender.

Using Other Sources of Secondary Data

Many cultures and organizations are self-documenting. Governments, private enterprises, and many sectors of civil society keep extensive records on their activities. These records may be produced for planning purposes, administrative and financial control, assessing progress, or communicating with different groups, especially those whose authorization, financial support, or general approval is critical to the success of the organization and its activities. Project records, like other documentary sources, should not be considered simply factual representations of "reality," but something more like "social facts…produced, shared and used in socially organized ways" (Atkinson and Coffey 2004:58). Project records may provide helpful insights into how an organization operates, its priorities, and how it tries to present itself to stakeholders and external groups. How the records are organized, what they emphasize, what they omit, and to whom they are (and are not) distributed may tell a great deal about an organization in an efficient and unobtrusive manner.

Documentary data may also be available from sources external to the program, such as government statistics agencies, planning departments of ministries, national planning agencies, universities, health centers, schools, commercial banks and credit programs, accreditation agencies, professional and licensing agencies, the courts, and the mass media. Demographic data (e.g., enrollments, graduations, educational attainment, salary, births, deaths, marriages) may also be available from records maintained by government, community, or religious institutions.

BOX 5.4

GHOST SCHOOLS AND MISSING GIRLS: WHY THE VALIDITY OF SECONDARY DATA MUST ALWAYS BE CHECKED

- A donor agency was considering an educational loan to a West African country. One of its concerns was the anticipated difficulty of encouraging girls to continue with secondary education because it was believed that many families pulled their girls out of school once they reached puberty so that they could prepare for marriage. However, an analysis of school attendance reports showed, to the surprise of the donor, that there were no significant gender differences in school attendance rates. However, unannounced follow-up visits to a sample of schools found very few secondary school-age girls actually in the classrooms. It turned out that many traditional families did not wish to send their daughters to secondary school, and because school attendance was compulsory, they were bribing the teacher to report that their daughters were attending, even though they were actually at home.

- In one region of a South Asian country, there were almost no secondary schools for girls. However, exploratory studies funded by a donor had found many families expressing interest in having their daughters continue their education beyond primary school. The enrollment records of a sample of boys' secondary schools were checked to determine whether girls were in fact enrolling in boys' schools; however, the records showed that all the students were boys. A follow-up observation study found that, in fact, significant numbers of girls were attending the boys' secondary schools, but the headmasters, to avoid possible criticism from their superiors for allowing girls to attend boys' schools, had recorded all the students as being boys.

- Another South Asian country launched a nationwide program to increase girls' enrollment in secondary schools by giving scholarships to girls (but not to boys) and also authorizing special allowances to secondary schools according to the number of female students. Field inspections revealed that significant numbers of schools were claiming allowances for "ghost" girl students not actually attending the school. In a few cases, it was discovered that ghost schools were actually put up in anticipation of the inspector's visits and were then dismantled once the inspection was over.

Conducting Retrospective Surveys

Recall Techniques

Information on baseline conditions of the project and comparison groups is often collected by conducting a retrospective survey when the project has already been underway for some time or when it is nearing completion or has ended. The survey asks respondents to provide information on their situation, attitudes, or knowledge at the time the project began or at some other relevant point in the past.

Recall techniques are widely used in research areas such as poverty analysis, demography, and income and expenditure studies. Although it is always difficult to use recall to collect precise numerical data such as income, incidences of diarrhea, or farm prices (particularly in the absence of the kinds of systematic studies referred to in the previous paragraph), it can be used to obtain estimates of major changes in the welfare conditions of the household. For example, families can usually recall which children attended a school outside the community before the village school opened, how children traveled to school, and travel time and cost. Families can also often provide reliable information on access to health facilities, where they previously obtained water, how much water they used, and how much it cost. On the other hand, families might be reluctant to admit that their children had not been attending school or that they had been using traditional medicine. They might also wish to underestimate how much they had spent on water if they are trying to convince planners that they are too poor to pay the water charges proposed in a new project.

Two common sources of bias in recall of expenditure data have been identified. First, the under-estimation of small and routine expenditures increases as the recall period increases. Second, there is a "telescoping" of recall concerning major expenditures (such as the purchase of a cow, bicycle, home, car, or item of furniture), so that the time frame of expenditures may be misreported. Although most of the research on recall bias in income and expenditures comes from studies such as the Consumer Expenditure Surveys[3] conducted quarterly by the Bureau of Labor Statistics of the U.S. Department of Labor, the general results are potentially relevant to developing countries. The Living Standards Measurement Survey[4] (LSMS) program has conducted some assessments on the use of recall for esti-mating consumption in developing countries (Deaton and Grosh 2000), which are discussed below.

The most systematic assessments of the accuracy of recall data in developing countries probably come from demographic studies on the reliability of reported information on contraceptive usage and fertility. A number of large-scale comparative studies such as the World Fertility Survey[5] provide national surveys using comparable data-collection methods for different points in time. For example, similar surveys were conducted in the Republic of Korea in 1971, 1974, and 1976, each of which obtained detailed information on current contraceptive usage and fertility as well as obtaining detailed historical information based on recall for a number of specific points in the past. This per-mitted a comparison of recall in 1976 for contraceptive usage and fertility in 1974 and 1971, with exactly the same information collected from surveys in those two earlier years. It was found that recall produced a systematic underreporting, but that the underestimation could be significantly reduced through the careful design and administration of the surveys (Pebley et al. 1986). Similar **findings** are available from demographic analysis in other countries. The conclusion from these studies is that recall can be a useful estimating tool with predictable and, to some extent, controllable errors. Unfortunately, it is possible to estimate the errors only where large-scale comparative survey data are available, and there are few if any other fields for developing countries with a similar wealth of com-parative data to that available from demographic studies.

A major challenge in using recall is that estimates are very sensitive to changes in the research **design** methods, particularly the method used for data collection, the period over which estimates

---

[3]The Consumer Expenditure Surveys combine a quarterly survey of expenditures administered to a sample of U.S. households and the completion by a smaller sample of households of a diary in which all expenditures are recorded. The diary is used to check the reliability and sources of bias in the estimates, based on recall obtained from the quarterly surveys. For more information, go to www.bls.gov/cex/home.htm.

[4]The LSMS (Living Standards Measurement Survey) program was launched in the 1980s by the World Bank to develop standard survey methodologies and questionnaires for comparative analysis of poverty and welfare in developing countries (Grosh and Glewwe 2000).

[5]The World Fertility Survey is based on demographic and fertility surveys conducted in 41 developing countries in the 1970s and 1980s by many different agencies. For more information, go to http://www.healthmetricsand evaluation.org/data/series/world-fertility-survey-wfs

are obtained, and how the questions are formulated[6]. The following examples illustrate the design sensitivity. For example, a study in Latvia found that, on average, household expenditures were 46% higher when respondents were asked to keep a record of expenditures in a diary compared with when they were asked to recall expenditures (Scott and Okrasa 1998). In El Salvador, estimated expenditures were 31% higher when respondents were asked to provide detailed expenditure for 75 food categories and 25 nonfood categories compared with when they were asked to provide less detailed information covering 18 food items and 6 nonfood items (Jolliffe 2001). A study in Ghana found that average daily expenditure on a group of frequently purchased items fell by an average of 2.9% for every additional day over which respondents were asked to recall expenditures. The recall error leveled off at about 20% after two weeks (Scott and Amenuvegbe 1991). One of the best-known studies on the sensitivity of expenditure to the recall period comes from India. Between 1989 and 1998, the National Sample Survey in India experimented with different recall periods for measuring expenditure. It was found that when the 30-day recall period for food items was replaced with a 7-day period, the total estimated food expenditures increased by around 30%. When at the same time the 30-day recall period for infrequent expenditures was replaced with a one-year recall, the estimated total expenditure increased by about 17% (Deaton 2005).

Interestingly, a number of studies suggest that recall can provide better estimates of behavioral changes in areas such as primary prevention programs for child abuse, vocational guidance, and programs for delinquents than conventional pre- and posttest comparisons based on self-assessment (Pratt, McGuigan, and Katzev 2002). This is because before entering a program, subjects often overestimate their behavioral skills or knowledge through a lack of understanding of the nature of the tasks being studied and of the required skills. After completing the program, they may have a better understanding of these behaviors and may be able to provide a better assessment of their previous level of competency or knowledge and how much these have changed. Self-assessment of poverty, empowerment, or community organizational capacity in developing countries might all be areas in which the *response shift* concept could potentially be applied for reconstruction of baseline data (Schwarz and Oyserman 2001).

Another potentially useful approach concerns the use of calendars and time diaries to help respondents reconstruct past events or continuously changing activities. These methods are often referred to as life course research (Belli, Stafford, and Alwin 2009). Both of these methods encourage respondents to incorporate temporal changes as clues in reporting events such as their parental status, childhood experiences, schooling, marriages, residences, relationships, wealth, work, stressors, health conditions, levels of happiness, what they have taught others, and how they have spent their time during the past day. According to Belli et al. (2009), these methods have "shown the ability to provide data of remarkably high quality in fields as diverse as life cycle consumption, training, labor supply, psychological development and adaptation to the environment, age stratification and life course, evolutionary theories of aging, and demographic models."[7] Alwin (2009) shows how statistical models such as the Latent Markov Model can be used to assess the reliability of event data (for example, whether a person was or was not married or was or was not working at a particular point in time) and continuous variables.

---

[6]The references in this and the following paragraph are taken from a chapter by John Gibson (2006), "Statistical Tools and Estimation Methods for Poverty Measures Based on Cross-Sectional Household Surveys," in *Handbook on Poverty Statistics* (United Nations Department of Economic and Social Affairs). Available on-line at: http://unstats.un.org/unsd/methods/poverty/chapter5l.htm.

[7]For references to each of these areas of research, see Belli et al. 2009, page 2.

BOX 5.5
EXAMPLES OF RETROSPECTIVE SURVEYS USED TO RECONSTRUCT BASELINE DATA

1. In Bangalore, India, in 1999, a sample of households was asked to respond to a "citizen report card" in which they assessed the changes in the quality of delivery of public services (water, sanitation, public hospitals, public transport, electricity, phones, etc.) since the project started in 1993. Families reported that although the quality of services was still low, on average, there had been an improvement in most services with respect to helpfulness of staff and proportion of problems resolved. The use of recall was an economical substitute for a baseline study.

SOURCE: Paul (2002) and Operations Evaluation Department (2005).

2. At the time that an evaluation of the impact of social funds in Eritrea was commissioned, the program had already been underway for several years. Baseline conditions for access to health services were estimated by asking families how frequently they had used health services before the village clinic was built, how long it took to reach these facilities, the costs of travel, and the consequences of not having had better access. The information provided by the households was compared with information from health clinic records and key informants (nurses, community leaders, etc.) so as to strengthen the estimates through triangulation. While existing documents (secondary data) were useful, it was often found that the records were not organized in the way required to assess changes and impacts. For example, the village clinics kept records on each patient visit but did not keep files on each patient or each family, so it was difficult to determine how many different people used the clinic each month/year and also the proportion of village families who used the clinic. Similar methods were used to reconstruct baseline data on village water supply and rural roads and transport for the evaluation of the water supply and road construction components.

SOURCE: Based on unpublished local consultant impact evaluation report.

3. The Operations Evaluation Department (OED) of the World Bank conducted an ex-post evaluation of the social and economic impacts of a resettlement program in Maharashtra State, India. Baseline data had been collected by project administrators on all families eligible to receive financial compensation or new land, but information was not collected on the approximately 45% of families who had been forced to move but who were not entitled to compensation. A tracer study was conducted by OED in which families forced to relocate without compensation were identified through neighbors and relatives. A significant proportion of families were traced in this way, and these were found on average to be no worse off as a result of resettlement, but it was not possible to assess how representative they were of all families relocated without compensation.

SOURCE: World Bank (1993).

Working with Key Informants

Key informants such as community leaders, doctors, teachers, local government agencies, nongovernmental organizations (NGOs), and religious organizations may be able to provide useful reference data on baseline conditions. However, these informants, like all sources, have potential biases and their own particular agendas. Caldwell (1985), reviewing lessons from the World Fertility Survey, uses these considerations to express reservations about the use of key informants for retrospective analysis in fertility surveys. Box 5.6 illustrates the wide range of key informants that can be used in any given study (in this case, a study of crack cocaine users). When selecting informants, it is important to recognize that people have their own perspectives and often their own axes to grind. Consequently, the researcher should try to consult with people likely to have different sources of information (people who know prostitutes in their family setting or community, as commercial associates or clients), as well as different perspectives (e.g., the police, neighborhood associations trying to force the prostitutes out of the community, religious leaders). It is also important not to assume that all informants should be in positions of authority. The perspective of a child, neighbor, or friend is just as important.

BOX 5.6

SELECTING A WIDE RANGE OF INFORMANTS WHEN STUDYING SENSITIVE TOPICS: STUDYING CRACK COCAINE ADDICTS IN NEW YORK

"I spent hundreds of nights on the street and in crack houses observing dealers and addicts. . . . Perhaps more important, I also visited their families, attending parties, and intimate reunions. . . . I interviewed, and in many cases befriended the spouses, lovers, siblings, mothers, grandmothers and—where possible—the fathers and stepfathers of the crack dealers."

SOURCE: Bourgois (2002:16).

Using Participatory Evaluation Methods

Over the past 30 years, a broad range of participatory research and evaluation techniques has become widely used in developing countries. These were a reaction against *top-down planning*, in which surveys were designed, conducted, and interpreted by outside experts who then decided what a community needed. Participatory research methods—which have a number of different names, including PRA (participatory rural appraisal) and PLA (participatory learning and action)—are based on the principle of empowering the community to conduct its own analysis of its needs and priorities and to translate these into a plan of action. All the approaches have in common that they work through community groups rather than individuals and that they rely heavily on mapping and other graphical techniques, partly to work through group processes and partly because a high proportion of people in many rural communities is illiterate. These participatory evaluation approaches have two important attractions for RWE and the present discussion. First, they have placed a strong emphasis on rapid appraisals (often lasting a maximum of one week) and second, because they have developed a wide range of techniques for reconstructing the history of the community and for the identification and analysis of critical events in the life of the community. The following is a brief description of some of the techniques. For a fuller description, with extensive illustrations of the graphical and mapping techniques, the reader is referred to Somesh Kumar (2002) *Methods for Community Participation: A Complete Guide for Practitioners.*

BOX 5.7
CONSTRUCTING A PRA SEASONAL CALENDAR TO RECONSTRUCT PERIODS OF STRESS IN A RURAL COMMUNITY IN KENYA

Families were given small stones or seeds and asked to place them on the months of the year when the following incidents typically occur: light meals (survival foods) during periods of greatest hunger, begging, migration, unemployment, earned income, disease, and rainfall. The chart shows the critical relationships between rainfall and income on the one hand and disease, migration, begging, and light meals on the other.

Seasonal Calendar of Poverty Drawn by Villagers in Nyamira, Kenya

	Jan	Feb	Mar	Apr	May	June	July	Aug	Sept	Oct	Nov	Dec
Light meals	ooo	ooo	o	o								oo
Begging	ooo	ooo	o									ooo
Migration	ooo	ooo	o	o	oo							
Unemployment	ooo ooo	ooo ooo	oo									
Income			o	oo oo	oo oo	oo oo	ooo ooo	ooo ooo	poo ooo	o	o	o
Disease			o	oo oo	oo oo	oo	oo	ooo	o			
Rainfall			oo oo	oo oo					o	o	ooo	ooo

SOURCE: Rietberger-McCracken and Narayan (1997).

• *Seasonal calendars.* These are most frequently used in farming studies in which farmers report for each month factors such as rainfall, planting and harvesting of crops on different types of soil, labor demand, water sources, migration, market prices for agricultural products, and so on (Kumar 2002:148; Theis and Grady 1991). A chart is drawn on paper or on the ground marking the months. Participants are then asked to place stones or seeds to indicate the months with, for example, the highest incidence of famine, out-migration, or expenditures (see Box 5.7).

- *Time trends.* These can be used to study changes over time in farm yields; livestock population; prices; migration; time and distance to collect fuel, fodder, or water; population size and number of households; and malnutrition rates. In most cases, participants are asked to plot changes for each year, but sometimes longer periods may be used (Kumar 2002). A similar type of chart to the seasonal calendar is used, but this time, the spaces refer to years. In some cultures, the concept of a calendar year has no meaning, so reference points such as a major drought, the election of a new president, or the outbreak of a war may be used.

- *Historical profile.* This provides information on historical factors that are important for understanding the present situation in a community or region. This may cover, for example, building of infrastructure, introduction of new crops, epidemics, droughts and famines, foreign and civil war, and major political events (Kumar 2002; Theis and Grady 1991). Information can be collected from historical records as well as from informants. Another approach is to give a tape recorder to different people in the community and ask them to narrate their version of community history. In this case, triangulation is important to reconcile the major discrepancies of interpretation that are often found between the reports of different community members. Often, groups of community elders or senior citizens will be particularly important both because of their direct memory and their role as keepers of tradition.

- *Critical incidents:* This is similar to the historical profile except that the analysis is focused on the stressful events or periods. Sometimes the analysis covers one year (looking at seasonal variations in stress), or it may cover a longer period. Box 5.7 illustrates the application of this technique to the analysis of periods of greatest stress during the past year in a rural community in Kenya.

Using Geographical Information Systems (GIS) to Reconstruct Baseline Data

GIS systems create electronic maps (Clemmer 2010) that define the precise location of physical features (e.g., roads, rivers); services (e.g., hospitals, stores, public service facilities); populations classified by socioeconomic or other characteristics (income, ethnicity, number of children), or events (crime, high incidence of disease, infant mortality, etc.). In developed countries, increasing amounts of electronic information are available, much of it free, and this can be used to construct a baseline or to measure change over time. It is also possible to overlay different GIS maps to compare, for example, high infant mortality rates with socioeconomic data such as household income, education, ethnicity, or availability of public transport. GIS data are rapidly becoming available in many developing countries, although they are much less abundant than in countries such as the United States or Canada.

An exciting new development is that it is now possible with GPS-enabled mobile phones to create GIS maps. For example, the data collector can stand by a store or health clinic and the mobile will register the GPS coordinates.

3. Special Issues Reconstructing Baseline Data for Project Populations

We have already discussed a number of reasons baseline data are often not generated for the project population, either through special baseline studies or through the M&E system. This may be due to a lack of interest or understanding on the part of program (or donor agency) management, to compet-ing demands on management time, to political pressures (particularly important in explaining why baseline studies are often not conducted for comparison groups), to administrative difficulties and delays in setting up the financial and organizational arrangement to hire M&E staff, to implement new computerized data-collection and -analysis systems, or being able to contract consultants and commission studies. A lesson all of these experiences teach is that the evaluation team should not assume that baseline studies will actually be conducted simply because there is a project document stating that this will happen.

Another challenge is to identify and try to control for potential biases in the information gener-ated through the M&E system or other administrative reports. When program budgets or staff per-formance will be assessed on the basis of M&E reports, there may be incentives to present project performance in the most favorable possible light or to ignore or downplay problems identified during project implementation. In other cases, the problem may be related to the low quality of reporting. Overworked staff may be tempted to guess or report from memory data on, for example, the number of community residents attending meetings or communal workdays. A more subtle form of bias or poor quality of reporting often occurs when only quantitative indicators are reported, but no infor-mation is acquired on the process or quality of implementation. For example, the report may only indicate the number of women, landless, or ethnic minorities attending meetings, but without assess-ing their level of participation and involvement in decision making.

Another potential source of bias is that in many projects, there is no clear definition of the pro-gram beneficiaries (who uses the new road or village well or receives information on malaria or HIV/AIDS that is disseminated through posters, radio, opinion leaders, and perhaps community theatre). Consequently, there is a risk that if appropriate sampling procedures are not used, the survey may only include those beneficiaries who are easiest to identify or reach.

3.1. Special Issues in Reconstructing Comparison Groups

Comparison groups are communities, organizations, or groups selected to match the project communi-ties as closely as possible on social, economic, physical, historical, and other characteristics relevant to the study. The process of selecting well-matched comparison groups is often a challenging task. As dis-cussed earlier in this chapter, one of the major challenges in selecting the comparison group sample is that unless random selection is used, project beneficiaries are usually not a representative sample of the total target population. The most common beneficiary selection procedures are either self-selection or *administrative selection* by the implementing agency. When self-selection procedures are used, individu-als or communities who apply are likely to include a higher-than-average proportion of subjects likely to succeed (e.g., people with no business experience are less likely to apply for a microloan, and communi-ties with no organizational experience are less likely to apply for a community infrastructure project that requires the community to participate in implementation or maintenance). When *administrative selec-tion* procedures are used, with few exceptions, beneficiaries or beneficiary communities are selected *purposefully* to target, for example, the poorest areas or those with the greatest development potential rather than selected *randomly*, increasing the challenge of identifying matched local groups.

Given the fact that only a small minority of projects use random selection procedures, the evaluator will almost always be faced with the likelihood that there will be systematic differences between the characteristics of the project and comparison-group populations. This means that some of the post-project differences found between the two groups may be due to existing differences (business loan recipients already had experience in running a business, parents who enroll children in after-school activities may be better educated or more motivated, and communities that participate in infrastructure projects may have greater organizational capacity than those that do not). So the practical challenge for the evaluator is how to match the project and comparison groups as closely as possible to try to eliminate these differences, or at least to understand what the differences are and to take them into account in the analysis.

There are two main RWE scenarios concerning the selection of a comparison group. The first is where good secondary survey data are available (see earlier discussion) or where resources are available to conduct a sample survey with a sufficiently large sample (see Chapter 15 for a discussion of sample size). In these cases, it is possible to use *statistical matching* (see Chapters 11 and 12) of the project and comparison groups to adjust for the effect of all of the variables (income, education, household size, educational level of parents, plot size, distance from the nearest town, etc.). However, as we will discuss, it is never possible to match the two samples on all possible factors that might affect outcomes, so there is always the question of how much outcomes might be affected by the variables, known as *omitted variables* or *unobservables*,, that are not studied.

Be careful not to make the assumption that a comparison group is matched with the project groups in every respect except participation in the project. Rarely if ever in society are all factors equal between any two communities or groups. Many contextual and other factors must be considered in a holistic analysis of results, from which the evaluator should then try to determine the relative influence of the project's interventions compared with different internal and external factors in the project or the comparison group.

The second scenario is one in which well-matched comparison groups are not available, either from secondary data or sample surveys, and *judgmental matching* must be used. While research journals and quantitatively oriented textbooks tend to focus on cases in which statistical matching could be used (many journals do not publish studies where less rigorous procedures were used), unfortunately, in the real world, most evaluations probably use judgmental matching. Box 5.8 gives examples of relatively strong and relatively weak comparison groups.

Judgmental matching involves the pooling of all available sources of information to select a group of individuals, communities, or organizations (schools, health clinics, etc.) that match the project group as closely as possible. Often this will involve combining the opinion of experts and key informants, review of maps and secondary data on different communities, and, where possible, diagnostic studies or at least visits to possible communities. In Chapter 16, we discuss the use of *concept mapping* as a technique through which statistical procedures are used to synthesize the opinions of large numbers of experts or stakeholders to select the comparison group.

Statistical matching techniques (see also Chapter 12). Evaluations frequently compare the project population with comparison areas selected to match the project population as closely as possible. When, as is usually the case, subjects were not randomly assigned to the two groups, this is called a nonequivalent control group or comparison group. In some cases, the comparison group may seem to match the project group quite closely on most of the socioeconomic characteristics of the households or individuals, but in other cases, there may be important differences between the two groups (see Box 5.8). When relatively large and reasonably random samples have been interviewed in both groups, it is usually possible to strengthen the analysis by statistically matching subjects from two areas on a number of relevant characteristics such as education, income, and family size. The evaluations of the Ecuador cut flower export industry and the Bangladesh microcredit programs described in Box 5.8 are examples of this approach.

If differences in the dependent variables (the number of hours men and women spend on household tasks, men's and women's savings and expenditure on household consumption goods, etc.) between the project group and the comparison group are still statistically significant after controlling for these household characteristics, this provides preliminary indications that the differences may be due, at least in part, to the project interventions.

Although this type of multivariate analysis is a powerful analytical tool, one important weakness is that, without baseline studies of both groups, the evaluation design does not provide any information on the initial conditions or attributes of the two groups prior to the project intervention. For example, the higher savings rates of women in the communities receiving microcredit in Bangladesh might be due to their having previously received training in financial management or to the fact that they already had small business experience. These comparison-group designs can be strengthened by incorporating some of the methods discussed above for reconstructing baseline data. Using these methods, it is possible to assess the similarities and differences between the two groups at the time the project began. If the two groups are found to be relatively similar on key baseline indicators (socioeconomic characteristics, access to the kinds of services or benefits provided by the project), then this increases the likelihood that statistical differences found in the ex-post comparison are due at least in part to the project. If, on the other hand, there were important initial differences between the two groups in the reconstructed baselines, then it is harder to assume that the posttest differences are necessarily due to the project intervention. How effective the statistical controls are will depend on the adequacy of the control model and the reliability of the measurement of the control variables (Shadish, Cook, and Campbell 2002:esp.138, 249).

> ## BOX 5.8
> ## WORKING WITH COMPARISON GROUPS IN
> ## EX-POST EVALUATION DESIGNS
>
> 1. An evaluation was conducted in Guayaquil, Ecuador, to assess the impact of the cut flower export industry (which employs a high proportion of women and pays women well above average wages) on women's income and employment and on the division of domestic tasks between husband and wife. Families living in another valley about 100 miles away and without access to the cut flower industry were selected as a comparison group. This was a nonequivalent control group because families were not randomly assigned to the project and comparison groups. The project and comparison groups were interviewed after the flower industry had been operating for some time and, consequently, no baseline data were available. Multivariate analysis was used to determine whether there were differences in the dependent variables (women's employment and earnings and the number of hours spent by husband and wife on domestic chores) in the project and comparison areas after controlling for household attributes such as educational level of both spouses, family size, and so on. Significant differences were found between the two groups on each of these dependent variables, and it was concluded that there was evidence that access to higher-paid employment (in the flower industry) did affect the dependent variables (the distribution of domestic chores between men and women and the hours women and men devoted to paid and nonpaid work). Although

multivariate analysis matched the project and comparison groups more closely, it was not able to examine differences in the initial conditions of the two groups before the project began. For example, it is possible that the flower industry decided to locate in this particular valley because it was known that a high proportion of women already worked outside the home and that husbands were prepared to assume more household chores, thus allowing their wives to work longer hours. The analytical model used in the study was not able to examine this alternative explanation.

SOURCE: Newman (2001).

2. An ex post evaluation was conducted of the impact of microcredit on women's savings, household consumption and investment, and fertility behavior in Bangladesh. The evaluation used household survey data from communities that did not have access to credit programs as a nonequivalent control group (comparison group). Multivariate analysis was used to control for household attributes, and it was found that women's access to microcredit programs was significantly associated with most of the dependent variables. As in the case of the Ecuador study, this design did not control for existing differences between the project and comparison groups with respect to important explanatory variables such as women's participation in small business training programs or prior experience with microcredit.

SOURCE: Khandker (1998).

Judgmental Matching

The following are some of the strategies used for constructing comparison groups when statistical matching is not possible:

- It is sometimes possible to construct an *internal* comparison group within the project area. Households or individuals who did not participate in the project or who did not receive a particular service or benefit can be treated as the comparison for the project in general or for a particular service[8].
- When projects are implemented in phases, it is also possible to use households selected for the second or subsequent phases as the comparison group for the analysis of the impacts of the previous phase. This is sometimes called a pipeline comparison group. For example, the economic status of a new cohort of women about to receive their microfinance loans might serve as a comparison group to compare with the current economic status of women who received loans during the past year. The phased approach was used in the evaluation of the Tondo Foreshore Squatter Upgrading Project in Manila (see Box 5.9).
- The evaluation may be able to take advantage of *natural experiments*. For example, the start of the project in one area may be delayed due to administrative or other problems, so this can be used as

---

[8] For example, subjects may be categorized according to their distance from a road or water source, whether any family member attended literacy classes, the amount of food aid they received, and so on. This is sometimes called *intensity analysis*.

comparison for the areas where it did start on time. Sometimes resources do not permit all areas to receive all services (for example, there may not be sufficient textbooks or specially trained teachers, so some of the treatments may not be implemented in all areas; in malaria treatment programs, it is sometimes the case that supplies of tablets or bednets run out so that some families only receive the orientation talks, others receive tablets but not bednets, and some receive the complete treatment). In other cases, another agency might provide different services in some areas (for example, the project might provide school meals and, by chance, another agency might provide school transport to some of the schools but not to others). If the evaluation has the flexibility to adapt the design, and if information is available sufficiently quickly to know about the changes, it may be possible to conduct *natural experiments* to compare the intended evaluation model with these different situations. Care must be taken in the analysis of natural experiments, as it will often be the case that the communities or schools that do not receive the full treatment may be the poorest or most remote, or the areas where other donors provide additional services might be the better-off or more accessible areas. So the evaluation must always try to understand and correct for these differences.

BOX 5.9
POTENTIALLY STRONG AND WEAK COMPARISON GROUPS

The following three cases are examples of relatively strong comparison groups:

- In a community water-supply project in Bolivia, the number of communities that applied to obtain water far exceeded the resources available to construct water systems in that particular year. Successful communities were selected through a lottery so that the process could be seen to be transparent and unbiased.
- In the Tondo Foreshore Slum Upgrading Project in Manila, the project was designed to cover a population of more than 100,000 households in several phases over a period of 10 years. The areas to be included in Phase 2 were selected as a comparison group for Phase 1.
- In a low-cost housing project in El Salvador, all the project participants came from one of three distinct types of low-income settlements, and participants represented a relatively small proportion of the population in each of these areas. Although participants were self-selected, so that it was difficult to control for the effect of motivation, it was possible to randomly select a comparison sample from these three low-income settlements. Statistical analysis found the characteristics of the project and comparison groups were similar but not identical.

The following two cases describe situations in which it was more difficult to select a strong comparison group:

- An evaluation was conducted in Nairobi to evaluate the impacts of slum-upgrading programs that had been operating for a decade or longer. The programs had covered all the major slums that housed well over 75% of the low-income population. The slums not covered by these programs were very small, housing only a few hundred families (compared with some project areas with more than 50,000 households). All the potential comparison areas had special characteristics (such as a unique ethnic group) that distinguished them in potentially important ways from the project areas.

- The project sites to be included in an agricultural extension program in Ethiopia were selected to include the poorest and most remote rural communities and also to include only areas in which no other agencies were working. The selection process also meant that many of the project areas had unique ethnic characteristics. In addition to the difficulties of finding areas with similar characteristics, most other areas had at least one outside agency involved, making it very difficult to find suitable comparison areas.

3.2. The Challenge of Omitted Variables ("Unobservables")

While statistical techniques can control for differences between the project and comparison groups on the variables included in the survey (income, household size, educational level of the parents, types of agricultural equipment, or farm size), there may be important differences between the initial conditions of the two groups on which no information has been collected. In some cases, the evaluator is aware of key information that is not available (perhaps no information was collected on farm size or the education of parents), but in other cases, the evaluator may not even know what missing information might be critical. For example, women's success in using a microloan to start or expand a small business might be affected by factors such as: previous business experience, a husband or family who is more willing to allow her to start a business (and to travel outside the community, etc.) than is typical in this culture, self-confidence, greater fluency in reading or speaking the national language, being a member of an ethnic group that gives women greater property rights, or something as basic as the ability to ride a bicycle. As no information has been collected on these topics, how can the evaluator assess their potential importance?

Economic analysis distinguishes between initial differences that are *time invariant* (do not change over the life of the project) and those that do vary over the life of the project. When initial differences are time invariant, it is possible to control for their effects using double difference analysis (Khandker et al. 2010 chap. 5). Examples of unobservables that are not time invariant include situations in which public investment strategies change as a result of the project (e.g., additional investments are made in areas where the project is successful), governments divert resources intended for other areas into the project to increase its effectiveness so as to convince donors to fund a follow-on project, community organizational experience that lead to their selection of the project also enables them to attract additional resources or organize other activities that increase income or improve health. Time variance tends to be particularly problematic for large, multicomponent programs such as poverty-alleviation strategies.[9] Khandker (2010 chap. 5) reviews econometric strategies for adjusting for unobservables.

---

[9]Jalan and Ravallion (1998) showed that there was a large bias in double difference estimates of the impact of a poverty-alleviation program in China due to differences in area characteristics, agroclimatic conditions, and initial infrastructure development. These differences attracted initial investments to areas with more favorable conditions so that double difference analysis underestimated project impacts. After adjusting for these differences, the estimated project impact increased significantly (cited in Khandker 2010 p. 77).

It is also possible to use the qualitative techniques discussed earlier in this chapter to obtain information on unobservables. For example, in the example of microcredit programs to help women start small businesses, it would be possible to use focus groups, in-depth interviews, key informants, and PRA techniques to examine initial characteristics of borrowers and nonborrowers (prior experience in running small businesses, attitudes of the husband and other family members to women running businesses, attitudes of different ethnic groups). All of these techniques can be used, normally without requiring major time and budget to reconstruct conditions at the time of project launch.

4. Collecting Data on Sensitive Topics or from Groups Who Are Difficult to Reach

The collection of data on sensitive topics, such as domestic violence, contraceptive usage, or teenage gangs, or from difficult-to-reach groups, such as sex workers, drug users, ethnic minorities, or the homeless, raises special data-collection issues. These situations require the sensitive use of appropriate QUAL methods such as observation, individual interviews (more sensitive and ethically appropriate than group interviews in many cases), and key informants. These issues are particularly important for RWE because budget and time constraints may create pressures to ignore these sensitive topics or difficult-to-reach groups.

4.1. Addressing Sensitive Topics

At least three strategies are particularly useful for addressing sensitive topics: (1) identifying a wide range of informants who can provide different perspectives, (2) selecting a number of culturally appropriate strategies for studying sensitive topics, and (3) systematically triangulating. Whenever it is necessary to obtain sensitive information, try to identify and talk to as many people as possible who form part of the social network being studied (see Box 5.6 for an example of how this approach was applied in a study of crack cocaine users). This provides different perspectives, and some respondents may be more willing to discuss the issues than others, in addition to having different experiences and insights to offer.

Some of the culturally appropriate strategies that can be used include the following:

- *Observation.* In some cases, it is possible to use **participant observation,** whereas in other cases, such as a study of sex workers or drug users, this will not be possible, and a nonparticipant observation approach will be used. Box 5.10 describes the use of participant observation to observe sexual harassment on public transport in Lima, Peru, and to observe relations between spouses, particularly with respect to decisions about use of money in domestic situations in Bangladesh.
- *Focus groups.* Around eight participants are interviewed in a group, using a standard list of questions or topics to be addressed. Again, for sensitivity reasons, in some cases, individual interviews may be gentler and more likely to produce information.
- Single-subject or small-scale case studies
- Key informants

Box 5.10 presents three examples of techniques for collecting data on sensitive topics. Examples of sensitive topics include: (1) assessing the impacts of credit on women's empowerment in Bangladesh, (2) studying the incidence of sexual harassment on public transport in Lima, Peru, and (3) examining the informal operation of rural health clinics in Nepal. Each case demonstrates the need to recognize sensitive topics, the need for the development and use of culturally sensitive approaches, and the importance of mixed methods. In each of these cases, participant observation or discrete observation was an important way to compare observed behavior with what respondents reported and to collect data on natural rather than staged events.

4.2. Studying Difficult-to-Reach Groups

There are a wide variety of difficult-to-reach or relatively invisible groups, including: drug users, dropouts, criminals, informal and unregistered small businesses, squatters and illegal residents, ethnic or religious minorities, boyfriends or absent fathers, illegal aliens, indentured laborers and slaves, sex trade workers, informal water sellers, girls attending boys' schools, migrant workers, and persons with HIV/AIDS, particularly those who have not been tested. Initially, the evaluator may or may not be aware of the existence of these groups. Clients and funding agencies may also be ignorant of their presence vis-à-vis the program. The following are examples of situations in which the researcher was not initially aware of the existence of certain groups:

- In an evaluation of low-cost housing programs in Nairobi, the evaluator was surprised by how many female-headed households had no apparent source of income. A visit to the project early in the morning revealed that many of these women were brewing *buzaa,* the local beer. Because residents were not allowed to establish businesses in the community without special permission, the women were reluctant to tell the evaluator (and, of course, project management) about this source of revenue.
- During the planning of a squatter settlement-upgrading project in La Paz, Bolivia, project management was very pleased with the high turnout at community meetings when the willingness of families to pay for water and other services was discussed. Residents enthusiastically endorsed the closing of community hand pumps and wells and their replacement with more expensive individual water connections for each house. The project had been underway for some time before it was discovered (through participant observation) that the community contained a significant proportion of illegal squatters who were paying rent to landowners and who depended on the wells and hand pumps for their water supply. The squatters hid during community meetings with outside agencies, and the project staff members were not aware of their existence until they began finding that the wells that had been sealed because of cholera contamination were being forcibly reopened. The discovery of the large numbers of squatters required a dramatic reassessment of the project's impact, because instead of showing that all families were better off because of the improved water supply, it was now realized that a significant number of the poorest families were probably worse off because their access to water for drinking and hygiene had been severely curtailed.

- In a housing project in Guayaquil, Ecuador, it was discovered, again through participant observation, that a clandestine opposition group was pressuring residents not to vote in favor of providing household water connections—arguing that providing water was a trick by the capitalist government and donor agency to deprive the poor of their full rights.

BOX 5.10
EXAMPLES OF COLLECTING DATA ON SENSITIVE TOPICS

1. In a study in Bangladesh to assess the impact of microcredit on women's empowerment, experience showed that conventional household survey methods would not allow women to speak freely about sensitive issues concerning control of household resources and male authority. Participant observation in subjects' houses and elsewhere was used to observe women's behavior and intra-household dynamics over a period of years to study changes in household power relations before and after women had obtained loans from a village bank. Observation was combined with the administration of an empowerment scale based on items identified by the women themselves in group discussions.

SOURCE: Hashemi, Schuler, and Riley (1996).

2. In Lima, Peru, it was believed that one of the reasons women did not use public transport was because of the fear of sexual harassment. However, women were unwilling to mention this in conventional transport surveys. Participant observation, in which researchers spent days traveling on public transport, was able to document the high incidence of harassment. This was confirmed and quantified in focus groups with women, men, and mixed groups stratified by age, conducted by a market research firm in their office in the center of town (i.e., away from the community).

SOURCE: Gomez (2000).

3. Visits by representatives of donor agencies to rural health clinics in Nepal found that all the health diagnosis and prescription of medicines was done by the resident doctors, most of whom had been transferred (against their will) from large towns to the villages. The untrained "peon" recruited from the local community kept the clinic clean, made tea, and the like. However, an anthropologist observed the clinics during normal periods when there were no outside visitors. She found that the doctors were absent for long periods of time and that the peon, who, unlike the doctors, spoke the local language, regularly advised patients and even prescribed medicines during the long absences of the doctor. The donor agency was unwilling to accept this finding because during their visits, only the doctor treated patients and the humble peon was very much in the background.

SOURCE: Justice (1986).

The following are useful techniques for the identification and analysis of difficult-to-reach groups:

- *Participant observation.* This is one of the most common ways to become familiar with and accepted into the milieu in which the groups operate or are believed to operate. Often, initial contacts or introductions will be made through friends, family, clients, or, in some cases, the official organizations with whom the groups interact. Salmen (1987) lived in low-income housing projects and slum-upgrading areas in Guayaquil, Ecuador, and La Paz, Bolivia, for several months until he had sufficiently gained the confidence of the communities that he began to be aware of the presence of illegal squatters and similar difficult-to-reach groups. He made a point of renting rooms in houses of families with children rather than having his own self-contained house so that families could help provide him with different entry points to the community.
- *Key informants:* These are identified and used in the ways discussed earlier.
- *Tracer studies:* Neighbors, friends, work colleagues, and so on are used to help locate people who have moved, sometimes a decade or longer ago. Former neighbors and tribal members were used to help locate families in India who had lost their land and been forced to relocate without any compensation more than a decade earlier (World Bank 1993). Because of the close family and tribal networks, it was possible to locate a significant proportion of these households. A study in Brazil used a similar technique to trace the origins of poor Brazilian families who had migrated to the South and who had lost contact with their regions of origin (Perlman 1976, 2002). Carol Stack, an American anthropologist, used an interesting method in one of her early studies to locate African American men who had moved back to the South after having migrated to the North. She rented a stall in state fairs in some of the Southern States and put up a sign offering a free beer to anyone who had arrived from the North within the past few years (Stack 1996).
- *Snowball samples:* With this technique, efforts are made to locate a few members of the difficult-to-locate group by whatever means available. These members are then asked to identify other members of the group so that if the approach is successful, the size of the sample will increase. This technique is often used in the study of sexually transmitted diseases.
- *Sociometric techniques:* Respondents are asked to identify who they go to for advice or help on particular topics (e.g., advice on family planning, traditional medicine, or for the purchase of illegal substances). A sociometric map is then drawn with arrows linking informants to the opinion leaders, informants, or resource persons.

5. Common Threats to Adequacy and Validity of an Evaluation Relating to Data Constraints

The threats to validity that must be assessed when using the different approaches to reconstructing baseline data and recollecting information on sensitive topics and from difficult-to-reach groups are similar to those discussed in Chapter 3 (see Table 3.5). Readers who are not familiar with the concepts of threats to validity and adequacy may wish to read Chapter 7 and then return to this section.

Table 5.1   Summary of Strategies for Addressing Data Constraints

Approaches	Sources/Methods	Comments/Issues
Using existing documents (secondary data) and assessing their reliability and validity (see Chapter 7 for a discussion of these concepts)	<ul><li>Project records</li><li>Data from public service agencies (health, education, etc.)</li><li>Government household and related surveys</li><li>School enrollment and attendance records</li><li>Patient records in local health centers</li><li>Savings and loans cooperatives records of loans and repayment</li><li>Vehicle registrations (to estimate changes in the volume of traffic)</li><li>Records of local farmers markets (prices and volume of sales)</li></ul>	All data must be assessed to determine their adequacy in terms of <ul><li>Reference period</li><li>Population coverage</li><li>Inclusion of required indicators</li><li>Documentation on methodologies used</li><li>Completeness</li><li>Accuracy</li><li>Freedom from bias</li></ul>
Using recall: asking people to provide numerical (income, crop production, how many hours a day they spent traveling, school fees) or qualitative data (the level of violence in the community, the level of consultation of local government officials with the community) at the time the project was beginning	<ul><li>Key informants</li><li>PRA (participatory rural appraisal) and other participatory methods</li></ul>	Recall can be used for <ul><li>School attendance</li><li>Sickness/use of health facilities</li><li>Income/earnings</li><li>Community/individual knowledge and skills</li><li>Social cohesion and conflict</li><li>Water usage and cost</li><li>Major or routine household expenditures</li><li>Periods of stress</li><li>Travel patterns and transport of produce</li></ul>
Key informants	<ul><li>Community leaders</li><li>Religious leaders</li><li>Teachers</li><li>Doctors and nurses</li><li>Store owners</li><li>Police</li><li>Journalists</li></ul>	Use to triangulate (test for consistency) data from other sources
Improving the reliability and validity of recall	<ul><li>Conduct small pretest–posttest studies to compare recall with original information</li><li>Identify and try to control for potential bias (underestimation of small expenditures, truncating large expenditures by including some expenditures made before the recall period, distortion to conform to accepted behavior, intention to mislead)</li><li>Clarifying the context (time period, specific types of behavior, reasons for collecting the information)</li><li>Link recall to important reference points in community or personal history</li><li>Triangulation (key informants, secondary sources, PRA)</li></ul>	

Table 5.2 Special Issues and Challenges When Working with Comparison Groups

Approach	Sources	Comments/Issues
Identifying and reconstructing comparison groups	Government statistics, earlier surveys, records of schools, health centers, and other public service agencies	Challenges and issues include • Political pressures • Ethical issues in using comparison groups • Using previous surveys as sampling frame • Rapid pilot studies to test variance, etc. • Judgmental matching • Use later phase of project as "pipeline" comparison • Internal comparison groups when different participants receive different combinations of services • Appropriateness of potential comparison groups • Statistical matching of samples (e.g., propensity scores)
Special issues in reconstructing data on comparison groups; Collecting sensitive data (e.g., domestic violence, fertility behavior, household decision making and resource control, information from or about women, and information on the physically or mentally handicapped)	• Econometric analysis posttest project and control groups (this design cannot control for historical differences between the two groups—see Chapter 11)	Methodological issues • Self-selection of participants (issues: difficult to match a comparison group on factors such as motivation) • Projects selected to represent either groups with the greatest potential to succeed or the groups facing the greatest challenge (issues: in both cases, difficult to find comparison group with similar characteristics)
Collecting data on difficult-to-reach groups (e.g., sex workers, drug or alcohol users, criminals, informal small businesses, squatters and illegal residents, ethnic or religious minorities, and, in some cultures, women)	• Participant observation • Focus groups • Unstructured interviews • Observation • PRA techniques • Case studies • Key informants • Observation (participant and nonparticipant) • Informants from the groups • Self-reporting • Tracer studies and snowball samples • Key informants • Existing documents (secondary data) • Symbols of group identification (clothing, tattoos, graffiti)	These issues also exist with project participants, but they tend to be more difficult to address with comparison groups because the researcher does not have the same contacts or access to the community

SUMMARY

- When evaluations do not begin until after the project has been underway for some time, the evaluator will often find that no baseline data have been collected and that no comparison group has been identified or studied.
- A number of strategies can be used to try to reconstruct the baseline conditions that existed at the time the project began. These include the use of documentary (secondary) data sources, interviews with key informants, using participatory methods such as PRA to help the community to recreate historical data and timelines, and the use of recall.
- While documentary (secondary) data are a valuable source of information, they were normally collected for a purpose other than evaluation of a particular project, and it is necessary to identify any biases or other factors that might limit the utility of some secondary sources.
- Additional challenges exist when reconstructing comparison groups because it is necessary to identify a group or community that is comparable to the project population as well as collecting information from this group.
- Many evaluations require the collection of sensitive data or collecting information from difficult-to-reach groups. This is a particular challenge for RWE because this information is often expensive and time consuming to collect, so there are often pressures to ignore these questions or groups. Some of the techniques for reaching difficult-to-locate groups include participant observation, use of key informants, tracer studies, snowball samples, and sociometric techniques.
- Like the two previous chapters, the present chapter ends with a discussion of some threats to validity arising from the innovative approaches that have to be used to reconstruct or obtain difficult and sensitive information.

FURTHER READING

Belli, F., F. Stafford, and D. Alwin. 2009. *Calendar and Time Diary Methods in Life Course Research*. Thousand Oaks, CA. Sage.

Readings on a wide range of techniques that are specifically designed to reconstruct past events and processes. The readings include sections on data collection through calendars, diaries, and time-use analysis; assessing the quality of data; and methodological issues affecting reliability and validity of time-based data.

Clemmer, G. 2010. *The GIS: 20 Essential Skills*. Redlands, CA. ESRI Press.

A good introduction to GIS with detailed maps and data charts illustrating how to collect and interpret GIS data.

Khandker, R. S, G. B. Koolwal, and H. A. Samad. 2010. *Handbook on Impact Evaluation: Quantitative Methods and Practices*. Washington, DC: World Bank.

Explanation of quantitative and particularly econometric methods for statistical matching of project and comparison groups and for addressing issues of unobservable variables.

Kumar, S. 2002. *Methods for Community Participation: A Complete Guide for Practitioners*. London: ITDG.

Detailed description of all the main PRA techniques that can be used for reconstructing baseline conditions of a community or group or for collecting sensitive data. Case studies are included illustrating how each technique has been used in the field.

Pretty, J., I. Guijt, J. Thompson, and I. Scoones. 1995. *Participatory Learning and Action*. London: International Institute for Environment and Development.

Useful training and reference manual on how to use and teach PRA techniques, including for reconstruction of baseline data.

Silverman, D. 2004. *Qualitative Research: Theory, Method and Practice*. 2d ed. Thousand Oaks, CA: Sage.

Part III ("Textual Analysis") presents a thorough discussion of ethnographic approaches to the use and assessment of secondary data.

CHAPTER 6

Political Constraints

While the politics that affect evaluations can be disturbing, they are a fact of life, and—to take a positive view—indicate the importance of the work and the interests of the stakeholders. This chapter addresses political issues that commonly arise at the start of an evaluation, during the conduct of the evaluation, or during reporting and use of the evaluation findings and recommendations. An issue many evaluators need to address is balancing stakeholders' "right to know" about the progress and findings of an evaluation with the desire of a client to restrict access to potentially sensitive findings.

1. Values, Ethics, and Politics

Although the term *evaluation* includes *value* at its etymological core, many evaluation users expect evaluation to be value free so as to be unbiased. They expect programs to be appraised in terms of external standards or progress toward their own goals and objectives and to avoid political maneuvering or pressure; they expect evaluators to adhere to high ethical standards (see Chapter 9). But in evaluation, values and politics are inescapable. Program goals manifest values, and implementing programs are ways of pursuing these values. Pursuit of goals through programs is an inherently political enterprise. Programs are part of a political agenda. The result of such activity is that values and politics affect and sometimes constrain the work of the evaluator (see Table 6.1).

"This is a good program (or not) because . . ." Any ending to this sentence implies values. For example, "This is a good program because it has improved the nutrition of poor children in this community" suggests that proper care of children, including the impoverished, is valued by members of a community working to ensure that funds are allocated to feeding poor children. "This is not a good program because administrative costs divert a large proportion of public funds from job training" suggests that economic capacity building, efficiency, and stewardship are valued and pursued. The following examples illustrate different kinds of political influences on evaluations:

Table 6.1 Points at Which Political Influences May Affect an Evaluation

Evaluation stages	Potential Political Influences
Commissioning an evaluation	Evaluators may be selected: • For their impartiality or their professional expertise • For their sympathy toward the program • For their known criticisms of the program (in cases where the client wishes to use the evaluation to terminate the program) • For the ease with which they can be controlled • Because of their citizenship in the country or state of the program's funding agency
Designing an evaluation	Exclusion of some stakeholders from design discussions can limit attention to some issues and groups. The decision to use either a quantitative or qualitative approach can predetermine which issues the evaluation will and will not address. Methods may be chosen to exclude full stakeholder participation in the evaluation or to give an illusion of rigor. Time and resources may be deliberately limited to discourage critical attention of certain issues or stakeholders.
Conducting an evaluation	Internal and external evaluators tend to face different types of political pressures and to have different resistance capabilities. The evaluator may have to negotiate between the roles of guide, publicist, advocate, confidante, hanging judge, and critical friend. Cordial relations at the start of an evaluation may sour if negative findings emerge or if the evaluator does not follow the client's wishes. Access to data may be obstructed.
Reporting	Feedback on drafts is more likely to be positive if critics of the program are missing from among the reviewers. Short deadlines, innocent or not, may leave insufficient time for some groups to comment and introduce systematic bias against them. Few evaluation reports are translated into all of the languages spoken by a diverse array of stakeholders. Budget is usually given as the reason, suggesting that informing stakeholders is not valued by the client. Often, an effective way to avoid criticism is to tailor reports for different audiences, perhaps excluding some. Public interest may be at stake when clients attempt to manipulate dissemination.

- Public funding for Head Start programs, which provide early childhood education to impoverished children and their families in the United States, comes with a requirement for regular local evaluations and occasional system-wide evaluations. During economic downturns, Head Start's substantial funding generates political debate about the long-term impact of the program, initiated by Democratic president Lyndon Johnson, and whether tax dollars should be used for this or other educational initiatives such as the No Child Left Behind Act (NCLB, 2002), initiated by Republican president George W. Bush.

- As part of NCLB, the U.S. Department of Education proposed, then enacted, a "priority [that] makes it possible for any office in the Department to encourage or to require appropriate projects to use scientifically based evaluation strategies" (2003, see also 2005) defined as (and in order of priority) experimental design involving random assignment of subjects to treatment and control groups, quasi-experimental design with matched comparison groups,

Figure 6.1 Step 5: Addressing Political Influences

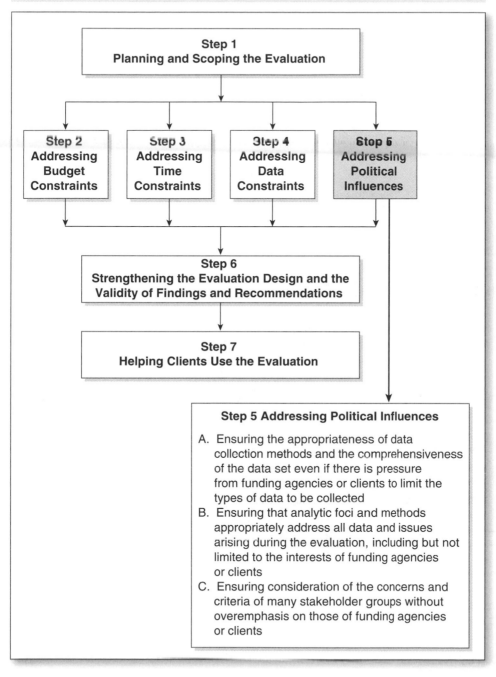

and regression discontinuity designs. Debate on the appropriateness of requiring particular evaluation designs subsequently went far beyond the technical merits of different evaluation methodologies to concerns about the political motivations underlying the choice of these particular methods (see Julnes and Rog 2007).

- Evaluators are sometimes told not to collect baseline data on comparison groups to avoid creating expectations regarding rights to services or compensation. In developing countries, examples might include irrigation, urban renewal, or power projects that involve forced resettlement of large numbers of families or communities. Less common in the United States, examples might include job retraining, allocating limited quantities of influenza vaccine, or providing laptop computers or enrichment programs to students in designated schools.

- In programs involving specific interventions such as new teaching methods, the provision of drinking water, or the introduction of an improved medical treatment, randomly assigning subjects or communities to treatment and control groups is often not possible for ethical or political reasons. For example, a politician might not favor an evaluation design that included selection of his or her constituents for a comparison group because the voters might subsequently clamor for extension of services.

Evaluation is the most challenging of all approaches to inquiry because it often confirms or confronts programs, their underlying values, and their political supporters and opponents. Findings have ramifications for individuals and economic, political, and ethical implications. Throughout the course of a project, evaluators should exercise sharp alertness regarding political and ethical issues.

2. Societal Politics and Evaluation

Society has a stake in evaluation, so politics writ large sometimes influence evaluation. As discussed in Chapter 9, the *Standards for Program Evaluation* (Yarbrough, Shulha, Hopson, and Caruthers 2011) and the *Guiding Principles for Evaluators* (AEA, 2004) urge evaluators to consider the public good, the societal good—to think in terms of broad stakeholder groups and right-to-know and need-to-know audiences. But, often, the interests of the immediate client (to whom the evaluator reports) take precedence as evaluators are reluctant to bite the hand that feeds them. Evaluators should avoid the assumptions that political influence is either bad or avoidable and that measures should be taken to insulate the evaluation from these pressures. Rather, political maneuvering is natural, inevitable, and a sign that evaluation results matter to stakeholders.

Societal politics have proved critical at times in the history of evaluation. The modern period in evaluation is often dated to the U.S. response to the former U.S.S.R.'s successful launch of the first spacecraft, *Sputnik I*, in 1957, when the Kennedy administration funded new educational programs and evaluations to determine which programs worked best. The Great Society programs of the 1960s and 1970s (e.g., Head Start, urban housing programs) also gave an impetus to program evaluation in the United States. Evaluations were undertaken to study which attempts to improve education and to eradicate poverty merited continued government funding. During the Reagan presidency, 1981 to 1989, evaluation findings were cited as rationales to cut and close social programs (e.g., Stake, 1986). During the first term of George W. Bush, the U.S. Department of Education instituted a policy preference for certain quantitative evaluation designs over all other quantitative and qualitative approaches to program evaluation in determining which programs to fund (U.S. Department of Education, 2005).

Since the 1980s, evaluation has also grown in the European Union (EU), where evaluation activity is overwhelmingly located in the European Commission, the executive arm of the EU. There, evaluation is aligned to public management and governance and intended for use primarily by decision makers and policy makers. While there has been some diversification of evaluation practice across the EU, the Commission expects to specify evaluation questions and for these questions to be used in impact evaluations to analyze the logic of interventions (Stern, 2009).

Clearly, then, national, regional, and international policy can either catalyze or constrain evaluation. When a program draws from public funds, all members of society are stakeholders in its evaluation. Some people are directly affected and constitute right-to-know or need-to-know audiences, while others are distant stakeholders. In some cases, public reporting is appropriate, even over the objections of the clients who are financing the program and the evaluation. For example, in 1990, evaluators publicly reported that the standards-setting procedures for the National Assessment of Educational Progress (NAEP) were flawed despite strong governmental efforts to suppress and contradict this finding, which was upheld in subsequent evaluations (Mabry et al., 2000). This instance illustrates how a national government can act to obstruct, discontinue, or discredit an evaluation.

3. Stakeholder Politics

Diverse stakeholder values ensure that politics writ small always plays a role in evaluation. *The Program Evaluation Standards* (Yarbrough et al., 2011) assert that evaluations should be designed to address the needs of the full range of stakeholders, but it is not easy to identify the multiplicity of stakeholder values and much more difficult to prioritize their interests appropriately.

Some stakeholders wield more influence than others and are in a stronger position to affect an evaluation's focus, criteria, and methods and to ease or obstruct access to data. Other stakeholders may be harder to identify, harder to contact, and harder to understand for cultural or other reasons, and their interests may be harder to incorporate in the political swirls of an evaluation. Although developing consensus among stakeholders is often urged on evaluators— for example, during the process of determining evaluation focus and criteria for judging program quality—dissension among diverse stakeholder groups may be more natural and more common. These differences are often intractable and appropriate for representation in the design and report, although it may be neither feasible nor appropriate for the evaluator to try to resolve them.

BOX 6.1
EXAMPLE OF DIFFICULTY IN OBTAINING STAKEHOLDER INPUT

When public transportation programs (e.g., road construction, a new subway station) are being planned, many states in the U.S. require that all affected groups be identified and that public hearings be held in which these groups are invited to express their views. While agreeing with the principle of democratic participation, some agencies feel that public hearings may not be the most equitable way to obtain stakeholder feedback, since it is relatively easy for a small, well-organized group to manipulate the public meetings to their advantage.

Program managers are generally an evaluator's main contacts. Clients are almost always what Patton (1997) has called "primary users." These stakeholders make program decisions, formalize procedures, and allocate resources. To promote use of evaluation for program improvement, some approaches explicitly prioritize the provision of data and findings to assist these stakeholders with programmatic decision making (e.g., Stufflebeam 1987). Although other approaches to evaluation explicitly prioritize either a broader spectrum of stakeholders or the historically underserved, the interests of managers, who are often concerned with financial bottom lines and outcome statistics, often dominate. Their values are not easily melded with the values of beneficiaries, who are more likely to be concerned with the availability and quality of the medical, social, or educational services to which they are (or feel) entitled. In actuality, the interests of client-managers often supersede those of other stakeholders.

Such *managerial bias* is compounded by **clientism**, evaluators' desires to please their clients and to secure future contracts (Scriven 1991). It has been suggested that, as more women become evaluators, their inclination toward relational ethics may promote a *positive bias* toward increasing a broader range of stakeholders in evaluations compared with the male inclination toward utilitarian ethics. The manner in which evaluators should respond to clients and other stakeholders is not a settled issue but, rather, contributes to yet another type of evaluation politics—professional politics.

4. Professional Politics

Just as there are a variety of approaches to inquiry in general, there are a variety of approaches to evaluation as a specialized form of inquiry (e.g., Madaus, Scriven, and Stufflebeam 1987; Stufflebeam 2001a). Individual evaluators have not only developed approaches that resonate with their personal views as to what constitutes competent, appropriate practice but have also publicly argued for their own approaches and against the approaches of others (e.g., Scriven 1998; Stufflebeam 1994; Stufflebeam et al., 2001). These arguments indicate the presence of diverse professional values in the field of evaluation, as in society, and professional politics among evaluators based on the pursuit of values.

Evaluators who continue their work beyond delivery of findings to assist with utilization of results (Patton 1997) or the empowerment of stakeholders (Fetterman 1996), for example, have been described by other evaluators as *consultants* rather than *evaluators* for exceeding the scope and purpose of evaluation (Scriven 1998). Ideologues pressing for evaluation in the service of social justice (House 1993; Mertens 2010) or for evaluation focused on improving working relationships within programs (Greene 1997) can find themselves at odds with colleagues who urge rational, dispassionate efforts (Chelimsky and Shadish 1997; Scriven 1997). At times, the differing values that underlie differing evaluation approaches have created arenas of heated professional politics.

Divergent views about professional practice have obstructed sporadic initiatives in the United States to ensure competence through accreditation or licensing. After consideration, many evaluators have realized that trying to resolve some of the unresolved and probably irresolvable differences of approach and philosophy within an evaluation code of practice would further politicize evaluation.

On a smaller scale, within an evaluation team, as within the professional field, different opinions may arise when questions such as these must be collectively considered:

- We were contracted to evaluate the cost effectiveness of the program's service delivery, but should we also consider the quality of the services?

- Should we check to see why Native Americans are underrepresented among the program's beneficiaries even though we were not asked to do so?
- Should we follow up our suspicion that the agency funding the evaluation is merely a front for a corporation manipulating its regulatory agency at the expense of the public?
- Should we release our findings to the media?

Different evaluators, even those who have chosen to work together on a project, may naturally take different stances regarding their public and ethical responsibilities. In vigorous exercise of their differing opinions regarding professional responsibilities, an evaluation can become subject to acrimonious team politics.

5. Individual Advocacy

Evaluators charged with making determinations of program merit or quality, have, like everyone else, their own personal values. However, for many evaluators, it may be more comfortable to think of the work of evaluation not as an imposition of the evaluator's values but, rather, as a data-based judgment about program merit, shortcoming, effectiveness, efficiency, and goal achievement. That individual values are influential in evaluation has been recognized in the *Guiding Principles for Evaluators* (AEA 2004).

Even what the evaluator regards as data is influenced by perspective and values. This was demonstrated in a volume in which several prominent evaluators each authored a chapter reporting their various methods and wildly different findings for the same program (Brandt 1981). Best (2004), in his discussion of how politicians, the media, and advocates for particular causes misunderstand or deliberately distort statistics, points out that "all statistics are products of social activity, the process sociologists call social construction" (p. xiii), adding this:

> We usually envision statistics as a branch of mathematics, a view reinforced by high school and college statistics courses, which begin by introducing probability theory as a foundation for statistical thinking, a foundation on which is assembled a structure of increasingly sophisticated statistical measures.

Many people have similar faith in the findings of what are believed to be rigorous, scientific evaluations. Many evaluation users fail to appreciate how much personal judgment, which always involves bias, inevitably goes into the formulation of evaluation questions and design. Whether or not evaluators explicitly advocate for their own values in their professional endeavors, their values— those they recognize and those they do not—inevitably affect what they see and interpret. All these intrusions might be considered advocacies of a sort, sometimes subtle and unrecognized, other times clear; sometimes unintentional and other times deliberate and proactive.

Is advocacy an improper intrusion of the evaluator's individual values? For those who seek to make evaluation a tool of social improvement and who treasure values they consider pro-social, the answer to this question may be an unequivocal "no" (see Freeman, 2010). For those who seek to improve social conditions through just-the-facts evaluation, the answer to this question may be an unequivocal "yes"—at least, in the abstract. But those who object to advocacy may find that, in the political contexts of practice, their answers may depend on contingencies such as who or what is threatened, the magnitude of the threat, and the consequences of an evaluator's failure to speak up.

6. Political Issues at the Outset

Just as programs reflect values advanced through policy and politics, program evaluations are often commissioned with political motives. These motives may or may not be clear to an evaluator at the outset. Even if political intent is clear, how best to respond may not be (see Table 6.1).

6.1. Hidden Agendae and Pseudoevaluation

A client, sure that the findings of an evaluation of his or her program will be strongly positive, may commission an evaluation in hopes that it will serve a public relations function. She or he may mount strong opposition to any other result and may insist that the evaluation consider that the evaluation look only at the aspects of the program that are likely to be judged positive. When evaluators capitulate to these demands, they may be said to conduct **pseudoevaluations** (Scriven 1991; Stufflebeam 2001a). Other political agendae, often hidden, can be even more problematic. When elections alter the composition of government and the enforcement of policies, evaluations may be commissioned for the purpose of obtaining data-based judgments of the inadequacies of previous initiatives to fuel their termination or the ouster of lingering personnel committed to different social ideologies. Evaluations may also be used as delaying tactics to stall changes in policy, to reallocate funding, to downsize personnel, or for many other politically charged motives.

Clients may be influenced by political intentions when they select evaluators. Evaluators may be selected because their reputation for uncompromising honesty ensures the credibility and acceptance of findings, because they have taken ideological stances in agreement with the client, or because the client expects they can be persuaded. These manipulations, too, may be so understated as to go unnoticed initially in friendly negotiations, generous travel allowances, and enthusiastic statements about the importance of getting the word out.

Sometimes political constraints can be avoided by being selective about the work an evaluator agrees to perform or diminished through negotiation. For example, where there is a suggestion of conflict of interest because of a preexisting relationship, an evaluation contract can be refused. In developing a contract, an evaluator might specify the client's obligation to ensure access to crucial or sensitive data as a condition of performance. In discussions or in the response to a sample of previous reports, an evaluator might attempt to judge the client's openness to methodological comprehensiveness and findings, both positive and negative. Questions about previous evaluations of the program and management's reaction, about how the program is responding to the legal and regulatory requirements to which it may be subject, about the existence of internal and external conflicts, about personnel cohesiveness or divisiveness, and about management style and its impact may be revealing and helpful.

Unfortunately, the obvious benefits of avoiding difficulty by refusing work with heated political implications or by negotiating them away are not matched by opportunity to do so. Political entrenchments or obstacles may not be clear initially, although later pressure may make them all too obvious—threats to cancel the contract or to deny future work, or bringing in other analysts likely to reach contrary conclusions and to discredit the work. Learning enough in advance of contractual agreements to identify difficulties and to estimate the degree to which they might obstruct the work may require background research tantamount to conducting the evaluation—or luck!

In international evaluations, understanding is often further complicated by subcontracting that leaves the evaluator hierarchically as well as geographically remote from clients and program managers. There may even be a series of subcontracts—for example, an evaluation managed by the country office of an international aid agency on the other side of the world may be working with a government agency to evaluate a program being implemented by another international aid agency. Other complications may arise when the evaluation is cofinanced by two or more agencies, each with its own agenda. When an evaluator is on site for only a few weeks, she or he may never meet some of the key stakeholders. The evaluation may be almost completed before some of the hidden agendae of the key agencies start to be revealed.

In the design phase, evaluation clients have a strong voice in determining the focus of the evaluation, the program aspects to be scrutinized, and even the methods to be used. Their efforts may represent diligence in ensuring that they obtain the information they need or crass self-protection. Sometimes their narrow focus constrains the comprehensiveness of an evaluation as, for example, when an agency such as the World Bank requires an econometric rather than an educational emphasis in evaluations of schooling or training in developing countries. Professional ethics suggest that where clients adamantly stipulate inappropriate or improperly constrained designs and methods, contracts should be refused.

6.2. Consideration of Differences among Stakeholders

Preexisting differences among stakeholders can immerse evaluations in political turmoil. Policymakers, managers, or implementation personnel may be at odds about the value of or approach to implementing a program, rendering some of them naturally opposed to an evaluation. Affected communities or members of communities may hold strongly divergent opinions about a program, its execution, its motives, its leaders, and its evaluation. Evaluation opponents may be able to preempt an evaluation or obstruct access to data, acceptance of evaluation results, or continuation of an evaluation contract.

Where time and budgets permit, reconnoitering in advance to try to identify sources of support and opposition may be useful. However, in the RealWorld, time and budgets often do not make this practical, at least not as thoroughly as may be needed.

The many dimensions of political positions—economic, institutional, environmental, and sociocultural—influence the way that politically concerned groups will view a program and its evaluation. Evaluation may create pressure for job creation, welfare support, alternative program delivery, protection against deforestation and water contamination, and protection of programs by (or from) government. Working to understand stakeholder concerns may help an evaluator identify ways to address political pressures. To identify the priorities, concerns, and constraints of different players, an initial stakeholder analysis may help identify political realities by asking such questions as:

- What helps the program work well (or not)? Which of these things are most important?
- What are some of the accomplishments of the program? What are the key problems and challenges?
- What helps or hinders access to program benefits? Do some stakeholders enjoy easier access than others?
- What questions or issues should the evaluation address (or not address at this time)? Which might be politically sensitive?
- How should information be gathered? How should evaluators assure that all of the needed information is obtained?
- What should evaluators keep in mind as they try to understand this information?
- Is there anyone likely to try to bias or manipulate the evaluation? If so, who and how?

As the concerns of stakeholders are discussed and potential areas of disagreement identified, a shared investment in the evaluation may help to establish common ground.

7. Political Issues in the Conduct of an Evaluation

Evaluations can make explicit a variety of underlying assumptions and perspectives held by a variety of stakeholders. The increased visibility of potentially divisive issues can raise pressure on evaluators and the stakes associated with evaluation findings.

7.1. Shifting Roles: The Evaluator as Guide, Publicist, Friend, Critic

The function of the evaluator, from the perspective of clients and other stakeholders, often tends to shift and overlap—guide, publicist, critical friend, therapist, hanging judge. Clients who initially see evaluators as partners helping them identify areas for potential improvement may feel betrayed when midcourse formative reporting is shared, as may be required by funding agencies. Cooperation may decline as project managers and personnel realize that evaluators might endanger their programs.

7.2. Data Access

Ensuring access to data by maintaining rapport and good working relationships can be challenging. Observers may be suspected as management spies and interviewers as interrogators, complicit or unwitting pawns in power plays orchestrated by clients. Maintaining professional neutrality visible to all parties is advisable but not always easy, not always possible, not always ethical. Some grievances are real and should be strongly investigated and reported. In some instances, evaluators may feel that action as well as reporting is required to discharge their public responsibilities fully or appropriately. While the mere presence of evaluators may intensify the political swirl, evaluators' proactive engagement in it will certainly raise the stakes.

Because evaluation can threaten programs and personnel, some people who are important data sources may take protective measures by limiting or denying access to information. Documents and records can be delivered slowly, partially, illegibly, or not at all. Observable events can be staged (see Box 6.2) or unannounced until after they have happened. Interviewees can be less than forthcoming. Survey instruments can be ignored or their distribution and collection by program personnel can be faulty.

BOX 6.2
OBSERVING STAGED EVENTS AND EXEMPLARY SITES

Site Visits by External Evaluators

Site visitors may be provided easy access to atypical model projects where everything is going well and everyone seems happy. For example, many international funding agencies want to ensure that women are actively involved in project planning, and their participation may be a condition for continued funding. When given advance warning, most agencies are able to arrange for a sufficient number of women to attend the meeting during a site visit by the funding agency visit—even if none of the women participate in discussion. Similarly, site visitors may find themselves at model projects where everything is going well and everyone is happy (Chambers 1983).

Limited access sometimes results from cultural barriers rather than deliberate obstructionism. For example, in paternalistic societies, where outside visitors are expected to meet only with male community leaders and male household heads, determining whether women or girls are benefiting from initiatives undertaken on their behalf can be difficult. Where the evaluator does not share the language, dialect, or street vernacular of interviewees, dependence on a translator and the extrapolation of meanings can be problematic. For these and for ethical reasons, there have been increasing calls for cultural competence in evaluation in recent years (see AEA, 2011).

7.3. Maintaining Access

Keeping stakeholders informed of evaluation progress can sometimes maintain access to needed data, particularly if it can be shown that the evaluation is less negative than had been feared or that useful information is being produced. Politicians and managers concerned about negative community reaction may be relieved by data summaries indicating that attitudes are mixed and that stakeholders have constructive suggestions. Feedback can also demonstrate the practical utility of methods about which stakeholders may have had reservations.

8. Political Issues in Evaluation Reporting and Use

Most—perhaps all—competent evaluations end with mixed results to report because programs, like all human endeavors, are imperfect. Consensus is often needed to implement results and recommendations, but evaluations sometimes clarify and intensify disagreement or reveal discord more deeply entrenched than stakeholders previously realized, and the revelation may serve to entrench disagreement.

8.1. Evaluation Reporting: Clientism and Positive Bias

The professional evaluation community has often expressed concern that evaluators may be tempted to provide overly positive findings to avoid conflict with clients and to ensure future work. The temptations toward clientism and positive bias may fall heavily on private evaluation firms and independent consultants, whose livelihoods may depend on continuing and future contracts, and also on internal evaluators, whose jobs may be threatened by their immediate superiors. Developing a reputation for unswerving honesty and competence as a long-term professional goal, which may ultimately ensure future work, may be threatened by the need to maintain short-term relationships with current clients and stakeholders.

Maintaining focus on the interests of stakeholder groups may be needed to preserve the opportunity to conduct good evaluation. Timely provisions of data to support program decisions through focused discussions, for example, can help to build confidence in the work and its usefulness. Appropriate assistance to clients, consistent care regarding confidentiality, and professional demeanor can also help. Perhaps most important are the accuracy and comprehensiveness of data and the validity of findings. Where evaluators have earned reputations for competence and honesty under pressure, stakeholders may feel confident about an evaluation and the implementation of its results (see Chelimsky, 1994).

8.2. Evaluation Use: Neglect, Suppression, Distortion, and Misuse

The possibilities for disagreement related to evaluation results and their dissemination are limitless. Members of an evaluation team may disagree about findings and recommendations, or even whether they should make recommendations at all, and either find consensus or dissociate themselves from the evaluation (see Box 6.3). Meta-evaluators may disagree with evaluators. Stakeholders, faced with a combination of positive and negative findings, may hold quite different ideas regarding what constitutes an appropriate response to an evaluation report.

BOX 6.3
SPINNING THE FINDINGS: AN OLD ART FORM

Due to increasing concerns about the alleged atrocities in the Belgian Congo in the late 19th and early 20th centuries, King Leopold of Belgium found himself forced to create an independent commission to assess his policies in the Congo. The commission produced a long and very damning report on Belgian policies. However, before the report was issued, Leopold was able to circulate a so-called "summary" report exonerating his policies while the full report vanished quietly into the archives. The "summary" was largely accepted by the public, and Leopold received awards as a protector of Africans from Arab slave traders (Hochschild 1998).

Powerful stakeholders are not helpless. In the field of evaluation, enduring issues across time include failure to utilize evaluation results and, more ominously, misuse of evaluation results. Clients can and do neglect evaluation reports, relegating them to shelf space among unused volumes. Clients can and do suppress distribution by circulating only to carefully selected readers, by circulating only abbreviated and softened summaries, and by taking responsibility for presenting reports to funding agencies and then acting on that responsibility in manipulative ways. Clients can and do give oral presentations and even testimony that distorts evaluation findings. Clients can and do cite evaluation reports to engage in follow-up activities not suggested and even contraindicated by evaluation reports. Clients can and do attempt to discredit evaluations and evaluators who threaten their programs and prestige. When clients choose to employ this formidable arsenal, evaluators often find themselves blindsided and their response options weaker than the clients' offensives.

Although *The Program Evaluation Standards* require comprehensive reporting to all interested parties (Yarbrough et al. 2011), doing so may pit evaluators against defensive clients. If evaluators perceive that their responsibility also requires that they argue for the data or attempt to set the record straight, they may find themselves engaged in advocacy, labeled political instigators, and in other ways embroiled in politics they did not seek.

In a series of programs and evaluations, evaluators may detect a larger agenda. If this agenda opposes prevailing social values or their own values, evaluators may face the decision of whether or not to speak out. For example, if they see that evaluation is being used to undermine social programs or to foist unfamiliar Western values and cultural institutions on poor countries, evaluators may consider it ethically and professionally obligatory to notify the media and the public. In these circumstances, evaluators may find themselves in uncomfortable positions on grand policy stages.

8.3. Strategizing for Use

When evaluators encounter clients who do not intend to publish or use findings, they will need to determine whether and how to ensure that findings are made available to the public or to right-to-know stakeholder groups. Conflicts between the evaluator's professional responsibilities to the client, which would normally preclude independent actions to disseminate the findings, and the evaluator's values and commitments to broader social concerns are not easily decided. The situation may be eased if findings are of direct practical utility and by:

- The timing of the evaluation
- Noting that the evaluation is only one of several sources of information for decision makers
- Maintaining positive relationships with key stakeholders and keeping them informed of the progress of the evaluation

SUMMARY

In evaluation, values and politics are inescapable, and no evaluation can ever be value free or completely objective. Decisions as to what to study, which methods to prefer, and whose criteria to use in determining program success all involve human judgment. Issues include maintaining access to data if political snags arise or if some groups are difficult to reach, respecting the values of various stakeholders, prioritizing conflicting interests appropriately, balancing stakeholders' and the public's "right to know" with client interests. Evaluators may encounter pressures to produce overly positive findings or to manipulate dissemination of reports.

FURTHER READING

American Evaluation Association. 2003. "Response to U.S. Department of Education Notice of Proposed Priority, 'Scientifically Based Evaluation Methods.'" *Federal Register*, November 4, RIN 1890-ZA00. Retrieved October 3, 2005 from www.eval.org/doestatement.htm An example of political intrusion into the practice of evaluation by government plus an organizational response.

American Evaluation Association. 2004. *Guiding Principles for Evaluators*. Retrieved from www.eval.org/Publications/GuidingPrinciples.asp

Best, J. 2001. *Damned Lies and Statistics: Untangling Numbers from the Media, Politicians and Activists*. Los Angeles: University of California Press. Discussion of how statistics—and, by extrapolation, evaluation statistics and findings—can be misleading and politically manipulated.

Best, J. 2004. *More Damned Lies and Statistics: How Numbers Confuse Public Issues*. Los Angeles: University of California Press.

Brandt, R. S., ed. 1981. *Applied Strategies for Curriculum Evaluation*. Alexandria, VA: Association for Supervision and Curriculum Development.

Chelimsky, E. 1994. "Evaluation: Where We Are." *Evaluation Practice* 15(3):339–45.

Chelimsky, E. and W. R. Shadish, eds. 1997. *Evaluation for the 21st Century: A Handbook*. Thousand Oaks, CA: Sage.

Chelimsky, E. 2007. Factors Influencing the Choice of Methods in Federal Evaluation Practice. In G. Julnes & D. Rog (Eds.), Informing Federal Policies on Evaluation Methodology: Building the Evidence Base for Method Choice in Government Sponsored Evaluation (pp. 13–33). *New Directions for Evaluation* (no. 113). San Francisco: Jossey-Bass.

Discussion of evaluation in U.S. policy making.

Datta, L. 2007. Looking at the Evidence: What variations in practice might indicate. In G. Julnes & D. Rog (Eds.), Informing federal policies on evaluation methodology:

Building the evidence base for method choice in government sponsored evaluation (pp. 35–54). *New Directions for Evaluation* (no. 113). San Francisco: Jossey-Bass.
  Discussion of evaluation in U.S. policy making.

Datta, L. 2011. Politics and Evaluation: More Than Methodology. *American Journal of Evaluation*, 32 (2), 273–294.
  Discussion of evaluation in U.S. policy making.

Fetterman, D. M. 1996. *Empowerment Evaluation: Knowledge and Tools for Self-Assessment and Accountability.* Thousand Oaks, CA: Sage.

Freeman, M., ed. 2010. "Critical Social Theory and Evaluation Practice." New Directions for Evaluation No. 127. San Francisco: Jossey-Bass.

Greene, J. C. 1997. "Participatory Evaluation." Pp. 171–89 in *Evaluation and the Postmodern Dilemma*, edited by L. Mabry. Greenwich, CT: JAI Press.

Hochschild, A. 1998. *King Leopold's Ghost.* Boston: Houghton Mifflin.

House, E. R. 1993. *Professional Evaluation: Social Impact and Political Consequences.* Newbury Park, CA: Sage.

Julnes, G. and D. Rog, eds. 2007. *Informing Federal Policies on Evaluation Methodology: Building the Evidence Base for Method Choice in Government-sponsored Evaluations.* In New Directions for Evaluation No. 113. San Francisco: Jossey-Bass.

Mabry, L., D. Stufflebeam, R. Hambleton, C. Ovando, R. O'Sullivan, B. Page, M. Wakely, and C. Swartz. 2000. "Both Sides Now: Perspectives of Evaluators and Stakeholders in Educational Evaluations." Paper presented at the annual meeting of the American Educational Research Association. New Orleans.

Madaus, G. F., M. S. Scriven, and D. L. Stufflebeam, eds. 1987. *Evaluation Models: Viewpoints on Educational and Human Services Evaluation.* Boston: Kluwer-Nijhoff.

No Child Left Behind Act (2002). Public Law No. 107-110. 107th Congress, 110 Congressional Record 1425, 115 Stat.

Patton, M. Q. 1997. *Utilization-Focused Evaluation.* 3d ed. Thousand Oaks, CA: Sage.

Scriven, M. 1991. *Evaluation Thesaurus.* 4th ed. Newbury Park, CA: Sage.

Scriven, M. 1997. "Truth and Objectivity in Evaluation." Pp. 477–500 in *Evaluation for the 21st Century: A Handbook*, edited by E. Chelimsky and W. R. Shadish. Thousand Oaks, CA: Sage.

Scriven, M. 1998. "An Evaluation Dilemma: Change Agent vs. Analyst." Paper presented at the annual meeting of the American Evaluation Association, November 6, Chicago.

Stake, R. E. 1986. *Quieting Reform: Social Science and Social Action in an Urban Youth Program.* Urbana: University of Illinois Press.

Stufflebeam, D. L. 1987. "The CIPP Model for Program Evaluation." Pp. 117–41 in *Evaluation Models: Viewpoints on Educational and Human Services Evaluation*, edited by G. F. Madaus, M. S. Scriven, and D. L Stufflebeam. Boston: Kluwer-Nijhoff.

Stufflebeam, D. L. 1994. "Empowerment Evaluation, Objectivist Evaluation, and Evaluation Standards: Where the Future of Evaluation Should Not Go and Where It Needs to Go." *Evaluation Practice* 15(3):321–38.

Stufflebeam, D. L., ed. *Evaluation Models.* New Directions in Evaluation No. 89. San Francisco: Jossey-Bass.

Stufflebeam, D. L., M. Q. Patton, D. Fetterman, J. G. Greene, M. S. Scriven, and L. Mabry. 2001. "Theories of Action in Program Evaluation." Panel presentation at the annual meeting of the American Evaluation Association, November 9, St. Louis, MO.

U.S. Department of Education. (2003, November 4). "Notice of Proposed Priority: Scientifically Based Evaluation Methods (RIN 1890-ZA00)." *Federal Register* 68(213): 62445–47.

U.S. Department of Education. (2005, January 25). "Scientifically Based Evaluation Methods (RIN 1890-ZA00)." *Federal Register* 70(15):3586–89.

Yarbrough, D. B., L. M. Shulha, R. K. Hopson, and F. A. Caruthers. 2011. *The Program Evaluation Standards: A Guide for Evaluators and Evaluation Users.* 3d ed. Thousand Oaks, CA: Sage.

CHAPTER 7

Strengthening the Evaluation Design and the Validity of the Conclusions

Step 6 of the RWE approach concerns ways to strengthen the evaluation design and the validity of conclusions and recommendations (see Figure 7.1). We begin by discussing the analysis of threats to validity affecting the findings and recommendations of the evaluation and how these can be addressed once they have been identified. The concepts of validity as used in quantitative (**QUANT**), qualitative (**QUAL**), and mixed-method evaluation traditions are compared, and factors affecting validity are discussed. We then discuss ways to assess threats to the validity of QUANT evaluation **designs** and strategies for correcting the threats once they have been identified. The subsequent sections cover the same ground for QUAL and mixed-method evaluation designs. We discuss worksheets that have been developed for assessing the validity of QUANT, QUAL, and mixed-method designs respectively and for communicating the assessment and the recommended follow-up to managers and policymakers (see Appendixes A–E). The final section identifies points in the evaluation cycle at which corrective measures can be taken.

1. Validity in Evaluation

In common terms, *validity* has a meaning roughly similar to *accuracy*. Evaluation data may be described as *valid* if actual conditions are accurately represented. For example, survey or interview data recording that teachers are satisfied with a new curriculum but parents are not could be described as valid only if a majority of teachers are, in fact, satisfied with a new curriculum and a majority of parents are not. Data that recorded that borrowers from a microcredit program established small businesses lasting more than two years would be less than entirely valid if, in fact, only the better-off borrowers who were able to take out larger loans established small businesses that lasted more than two years. In QUANT methodology, the accuracy of the data is referred to as *internal validity* (Shadish, Cook, and Campbell 2002) and, in QUAL methodology, as *descriptive validity* (Maxwell 1992) or *credibility* (Lincoln and Guba 1985).

Figure 7.1 Step 6: Strengthening the Evaluation Design and the Validity of Conclusions

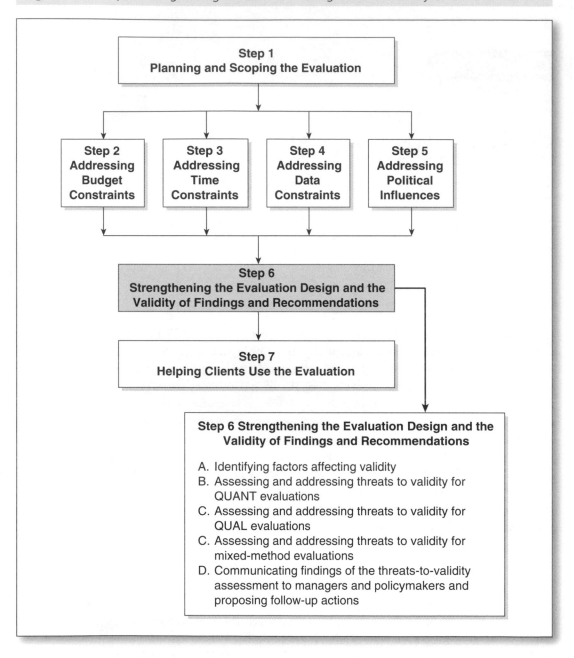

Findings as well as data need to be valid. Findings are judgments, interpretations, and inferences of program quality. To be valid, findings need to be adequately and appropriately based on valid and comprehensive data. Findings based on hopelessly limited, inaccurate, or falsified data are certain to be *invalid*. Invalid data obstruct the validity of the findings based on the data.

Invalid findings may also result from failure to understand the meaning of the data. For example, data from a criminal justice program indicated that recidivism rates (i.e., repeated offenses by convicted criminals) were identical for serious offenders sentenced to 10 years in prison and for those sentenced to 10 days in the local jail. But it would have been erroneous to infer that the enormous public expense of prison could be dramatically reduced by incarcerating serious offenders for 10 days rather than 10 years. What the data do not show is whether offenders "went straight" after 10 days because of the threat that, if they were convicted a second time, they would probably be sentenced to 10 years. If an evaluator had recommended the establishment of a 10-day jail time program for these offenders, failing to attribute its success to the potent implications of longer sentencing, public safety might well have been undermined.

The sensitivity of the methods to define and measure actual program **outcomes** is crucial for ensuring the validity of findings. For example, in the 1980s, in the United States, an evaluation of a multistate program to meld school and social services for at risk urban youth reported the program had no substantial **impact**, a finding that led to funding cuts for many federally supported social programs. This occurred despite a **meta-evaluation** (evaluation of the technical quality and adequacy of the evaluation design) indicating that the data were collected at too broad a level to detect impacts that were well known to program personnel and beneficiaries—a failure of the evaluation rather than of the program.

2. Factors Affecting Adequacy and Validity

In evaluation, validity and feasibility often demand different courses of action. For validity, the most skillful team operating with unlimited time, budget, and access to data is desirable. Rarely, if ever, are such perfect conditions available. Budget is limited; time is limited; personnel are limited; not all the data needed may be available or, if available, easily accessed. For feasibility, evaluators must consider what can be competently done within such limitations. To avoid having to refuse potential clients, evaluators have sometimes overestimated whether good evaluations could be accomplished. Sometimes designs and methods have been so minimized that it becomes impossible to produce valid findings. Methodological weaknesses owing to real-world constraints can threaten the validity of evaluation findings.

Box 7.1 illustrates how the concept of threats to validity is used in the field to assess factors affecting the validity of evaluation conclusions. The case is extracted from a meta-evaluation of CARE International evaluation methodologies that identified four main factors affecting the validity of the evaluations. It is emphasized that the evaluations were conducted under very difficult circumstances, often at great personal risk to the evaluators, and the threats to validity were largely due to factors beyond the control of the evaluation team.

BOX 7.1

FACTORS AFFECTING THE VALIDITY OF CARE INTERNATIONAL'S PROGRAM EVALUATION METHODOLOGY

A meta-evaluation of evaluations of CARE International projects and programs identified four common threats to validity of the evaluation findings and conclusions. *Historical factors* (changes to an area's security status between evaluator visits, civil

(Continued)

(Continued)

unrest, invasions, de-escalation of conflicts, weather, changes in a country's economic status, elections, and international terrorism) affected the validity of more than half of the evaluations, and problems with the *measurement instruments* (testing) (changing evaluation questionnaires in mid-project, changing indicators between baseline and final surveys, delays in establishing a baseline, poor record keeping, and badly formed questions), bias in terms of who was interviewed (in Muslim countries, male evaluators did not have access to female translators, so they were unable to interview female subjects, and the unavailability of some subject groups) both affected nearly half of the evaluations. Problems of experimental mortality (CARE and government staff turn-over, out-migration in response to crises, sites being replaced because wells went dry, and budget cuts that closed project sites) affected nearly 20%. The report commented, "CARE evaluators conduct their work under very difficult circumstances and sometimes at great personal risk. Considering all of these challenges, it is often amazing that any evaluation could be conducted at all."

Threat to validity	Responses	% of evaluations affected
History	17	53.1%
Testing	15	46.9%
Bias	13	40.6%
Experimental mortality	6	18.8%
Total	51	

SOURCE: Russon (2005).

The adequacy of an evaluation design and of the findings based on subsequent data collection is contingent on a number of important factors (see Table 7.1), including:

- How well suited the evaluation focus, approach, and methods are for obtaining the types of information needed, for example:
  - Information needs regarding managerial decision making. Does the evaluation focus on program procedures, personnel, and product quality? Does the evaluation design take into consideration infrastructure, resources, training, safety, and access as well as outcomes?
  - Information needs regarding stakeholder perspectives of program adequacy. Does the evaluation design include procedures for understanding the experiences and perceptions of intended beneficiaries? Are the methods to be used sensitive to the gender, cultural, and linguistic characteristics of stakeholders?

- Availability of data and data sources, for example:
  - Whether appropriate data exist or can be generated to address information needs. Do records provide accurate information about how, when, and to whom program services and benefits are delivered? Are financial records available and accurate, and have they been audited?
  - Are stakeholders accessible to evaluators? Can stakeholders be identified and located? Are they willing and able to provide data? Are there language, cultural, political, or other barriers to their provision of information?
- How well the data collected will support valid interpretations about the program, for example:
  - The achievement of program goals. Which program objectives were accomplished, and how well? Did some intended beneficiaries fare better than others? Which factors, if any, proved critical to program success? What, if anything, hindered or undermined goal attainment?
  - Cost-effectiveness of the program. How accurate and comprehensive are the program's financial records? What was the cost of program delivery per beneficiary (or other unit of analysis)? Did benefits justify the cost of the program? How do the costs and benefits of this program compare with similar programs?
  - The extent of delivery of program benefits. Did all intended beneficiaries benefit as planned? Did all appropriate stakeholders enjoy sufficient and equal access to program benefits or services? Should benefits or services have been accessible to a larger group than those defined by the program? Was there any significant "leakage" of benefits to groups not entitled to receive them? Were the benefits readily available or hard to obtain?
  - The adequacy of resources affecting goal attainment. Were funding, personnel, and other resources sufficient for satisfactory program implementation? Where funding was authorized, were needed resources actually available within the program's context?
  - Unintended consequences. Were there unexpected benefits resulting because of the program? How important were they? Were there negative side effects? To what extent did they undermine or counteract benefits?
- The adequacy of professional expertise and knowledge of the evaluation team in terms of both evaluation methodology and the specific sector or field of the program, for example:
  - Expertise in terms of evaluation methodology. If content analysis of QUAL data is part of the design, does the team include specialists in QUAL methodology? If a cost-effectiveness analysis is part of the design, does the team include financial analysts?
  - Expertise in terms of the specific field of the program. If evaluating a well-child program, does the team include medical and public health specialists? If evaluating an adult literacy program, does the team include specialists in reading curriculum and pedagogy for adult education?
  - Capacity of evaluation resources for the scope of the program. Are there enough interviewers to collect the interview data? Are they sufficiently trained, or are there sufficient resources (expertise and budget) to provide training? Is there sufficient evaluation capacity in terms of database development and capacity, statistical analysis of QUANT data? Are there adequate logistical resources for communication, transportation, and other needs?

Table 7.1   Factors Determining the Adequacy of the Evaluation Design and of the Findings

1. **How well suited are the evaluation focus, approach, and methods for obtaining the information needed regarding, for example:**

   a. Managerial decisions

   b. Stakeholder perspectives on program adequacy

2. **How available are data and data sources? For example:**

   a. Whether appropriate data exist or can be generated to address information needs

   b. Whether stakeholders and documentary data sources are accessible to evaluators

3. **How well the data will support valid interpretations about the program regarding, for example:**

   a. Achievement of program goals, extent of delivery of program benefits

   b. Cost-effectiveness of the program

   c. The adequacy of resources affecting goal attainment

   e. Unintended consequences

4. **How adequate is the evaluation team? For example in terms of:**

   a. Evaluation methodology

   b. The specific field of the program

   c. Sufficiency of evaluation resources for the scope of the program

3. A Framework for Assessing the Validity and Adequacy of QUANT, QUAL, and Mixed-Methods Designs

While most evaluators agree on the importance of ensuring methodological rigor (although they may not agree on how to define *rigor*), relatively few evaluations include clearly defined procedures for assessing the quality and rigor of the evaluation design and implementation and for assessing the consequences of any design weaknesses on the validity of the evaluation findings and the recommendations. Even fewer include procedures for addressing weaknesses once they are identified. Although many evaluations are subjected to peer reviews, often these do not include clearly defined guidelines for assessing all aspects of the design and implementation, and the focus of the review will often depend on the particular interests or concerns of each reviewer.

Threats-to-validity analysis assesses the extent to which the conclusions and recommendations of an evaluation are supported by the available evidence and asks whether any qualifications concerning findings and recommendations are required due to limitations of the evaluation design or what happened during implementation. In some cases, the limitations may be due to things the evaluators could have avoided, but frequently they are due to factors beyond their control—most commonly the budget, time, data, and political constraints under which the evaluation was conducted.

One of the most common ways that evaluators assess validity is through the use of *triangulation* whereby estimates from different methods of data collection (including data collected at different times, in different locations, and by different researchers) and data analysis are compared. However, many evaluations that claim to use triangulation do not in fact include a clearly defined strategy for comparing estimates from different sources. If inconsistencies are found, it is quite unusual, particularly for QUANT evaluations, for time and resources to have been allocated to return to the field or to conduct further data analysis to determine the reasons for the discrepancies. Often, the only reference to triangulation in the final evaluation report will be a footnote pointing out any inconsistencies and recommending that these should be addressed in a future study!

Why does the assessment of evaluation validity matter? If the conclusions of the evaluations are not methodologically sound, there is a risk that:

- Programs that do not work, or that are not efficient and cost effective, may continue or be expanded.
- Good programs may be discontinued.
- Priority target groups may not have access to project benefits.
- Important lessons concerning which aspects of a program do and do not work and under what circumstances may be missed.

Even where methodologically rigorous QUANT, QUAL, or mixed-method evaluation designs are used, there are always factors that pose threats to the validity of the evaluation findings and recommendations (see Bamberger and White 2007). Unfortunately, in the real world of development evaluation, it is frequently not possible to use strong evaluation designs, so the risks of arriving at wrong conclusions and providing wrong or misleading policy advice are much greater.

3.1. The Categories of Validity (Adequacy, Trustworthiness)

Evaluators distinguish between *internal validity* (reasons conclusions about the contribution of project and program interventions to explaining observed changes in the beneficiary population may not be valid) and *external validity* (reasons conclusions about the replicability of the project in other contexts may not be valid). Some QUAL evaluators prefer to use terms such as *adequacy* and *trustworthiness* (Guba and Lincoln 1989). Miles and Huberman (1994) also proposed a third category of *utilization validity.* These authors argue that if the findings and recommendations of an evaluation are not used and do not have any influence on future policy or operational decisions, then questions must be asked about the validity of how the evaluation design was formulated and how the key questions were identified. Utilization as a dimension of validity is particularly important for evaluations that have used stakeholder analysis and participatory planning.

Internal validity, which is the main focus of most validity assessments, can be broken down into several components. As we will see in the following sections, these categories are often defined and used in different ways by QUANT, QUAL, and mixed-method evaluations—although a number of authors have proposed parallel terminology for QUANT and QUAL evaluations (Guba and Lincoln 1989). Figure 7.2 indicates the different terminology used by QUANT and QUAL evaluators to describe these components (frequently used QUAL terminology is in parentheses). We will see later that while some mixed-method evaluators draw on both conventional QUAL and QUANT terminology for the different strands of the mixed-method approach, many are now developing their own terminology (see Figure 7.3). The four most widely used components of internal validity are the following:

Objectivity (*confirmability*): Are the conclusions drawn from the available evidence and are they relatively free of researcher bias? For example, if the report uses terms like "*most* participants had a positive opinion concerning . . .", or "*many* respondents were critical of . . . ," do the data support these statements or was the evaluator generalizing from a few comments in, for example, a focus group, and then generalizing to the total study population? It is good practice to require the consultants/evaluators to indicate the source for each of their conclusions and recommendations and to only cite sources that the reader can check. It is also important to ensure that assessments of qualitative data are based on verifiable sources and do not just rely on the opinion of the researcher. A good criterion is to use data-collection and -analysis procedures that ensure that different members of the research team would all report and interpret the findings in the same way.

a. *Internal design validity (dependability/credibility)*: Could the way the project is designed and implemented, or the evaluation is designed, lead to wrong conclusions about the extent to which the project has contributed to the observed outcomes? For example, the areas or communities to be included in pilot projects are often selected by the implementing agency, and in many cases the agency will try to select target populations that are likely to respond well to the project. So if the pilot project is in fact successful, this may be due to some extent to the way the target population was selected. So there could be potential questions concerning internal design validity.

    QUAL researchers often ask whether the descriptions, findings, and recommendations seem *credible* to the populations studied, to other research colleagues, and to clients and stakeholders. While peer reviews are widely used for ensuring the methodological rigor of QUANT evaluations, it is much less common for QUANT researchers to seek the opinion of the populations studied on the credibility of the findings.

b. *Statistical conclusion validity:* While many QUAL researchers use statistical tests to assess the statistical significance of differences between groups, and there is a wide range of statistical procedures for small-sample research (many based on the t-test), statistical conclusion validity does not usually appear as a separate validity component in QUAL approaches to validity. For QUANT evaluations, statistical validity concerns the risk that inappropriate statistical design and analysis procedures may result in wrong conclusions about the presence or absence of a statistical association between program interventions and changes in outcome and impact indicators. For example, there are many challenging project contexts such as areas of extreme poverty or postconflict situations in which even a well-designed and -implemented project is likely to only produce a small (but often extremely important) improvement. In many instances, time and budget pressures mean that only a relatively small sample is studied and, consequently, a numerically small improvement may not be found to be statistically significant (due to the low power of the test) and it may be wrongly concluded that the project did not have an effect. This is a typical example in which there were issues concerning the statistical validity of the conclusions.

Figure 7.2   Dimensions of Threats to Validity used to Assess Quantitative and Qualitative Evaluation Designs (Terms in **bold** indicate QUANT terminology and terms in ***bold italics*** indicate QUAL terminology)

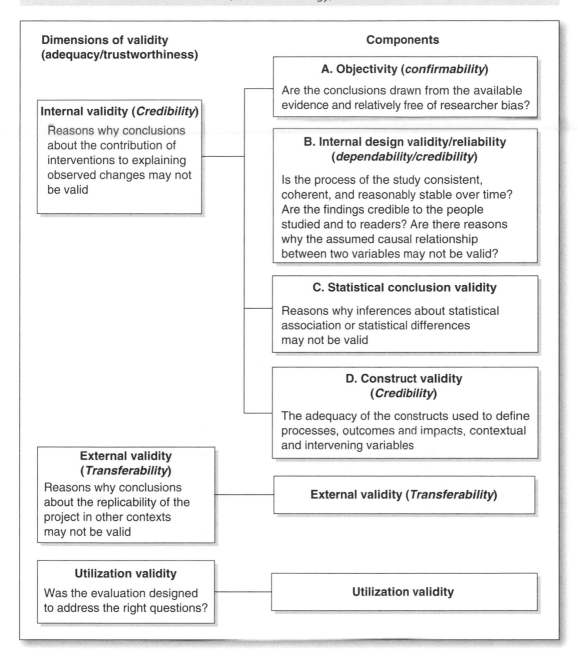

c. *Construct validity (credibility)*: The indicators of outputs, impacts, and contextual variables may not adequately describe and measure the constructs (hypotheses about the process of change or how processes, outcomes, and impacts are defined) on which the program theory is based. For example, in many development projects the changes that they are hoped to produce are complex and combine economic changes with behavioral changes on the part of the target population and organization changes on the part of the implementing agencies. Consequently the constructs used to define and measure intended project outcomes are multidimensional and frequently combine both quantitative and qualitative indicators. However, in order to conduct statistical analysis of the evaluation findings, the outcome indicators will often be reduced to a small number of quantitative measures. So even when statistically significant findings are found, they may be misleading if the key outcome constructs are not in fact being measured.

4. Assessing and Addressing Threats to Validity for Quantitative Impact Evaluations

There is consensus among most QUANT evaluators both about the importance of assessing validity and concerning the categories of validity that must be assessed. Shadish, Cook, and Campbell (2002), building on the seminal works of Campbell and Stanley (1963), propose assessing threats to conclusion validity for QUANT evaluations in terms of four of the components discussed in the previous section:

- *Threats to statistical conclusion validity*: reasons inferences about the statistical association or covariation between two variables may be incorrect. In program evaluation, we are most interested with determining whether there is a statistically significant difference in the observed changes in outcome or impact indicators between the project and comparison groups or, in the case of more complex designs, between the outcomes of different treatments or combinations of treatments. The analysis may also assess the statistical significance of moderator or mediator variables, such as household characteristics or contextual variables, in explaining variations in outcomes.
- *Threats to internal validity*: reasons inferences that the relationship between two variables is causal may be incorrect. In program evaluation, we are normally assessing whether and by how much the program interventions have contributed to the observed changes in the project group.
- *Threats to construct validity*: reasons inferences about the constructs used to define project implementation processes, outputs, outcomes, and impacts may be incorrect. Examples include: defining complex concepts such as household welfare, employment (or unemployment), or empowerment in terms of one or a small number of oversimplified indicators; or defining project implementation only in terms of the procedures described in the operations manual and ignoring the social and cultural context within which implementation takes place.
- *Threats to external validity*: reasons inferences about how study results would hold over variations in persons, settings, treatments, and outcomes may be incorrect. For example, pilot projects are often launched in geographic areas, economic settings, or with groups of subjects whose characteristics increase the likelihood of success. Consequently, it is dangerous to assume that similar outcomes would be achieved if the project were replicated on a larger scale and in more "normal" or typical settings.

4.1. A Threats-to-Validity Worksheet for QUANT Evaluations

Appendix A presents a worksheet for assessing the validity of findings and recommendations of QUANT evaluations. This has three parts:

- Part 1 is a one-page summary of the findings and recommendations of the theats-to-validity assessment intended for senior management and sometimes for partner funding and implementing agencies.
- Part 2 presents a half page assessment for each of the four components (see Part 3). This is intended for evaluation managers and others who require a slightly more detailed explanation of the conclusions and recommendations presented in Part 1 but who do not need to receive the more technical assessment presented in Part 3.
- Part 3 presents a set of technical indicators for identifying and rating methodological weaknesses of each of the four components (1: threats to internal design validity, 2: threats to statistical conclusion validity, 3: threats to construct validity, and 4: threats to external validity). Each of the checklists includes two columns that can be used for rating each indicator. **Column A** is used to check which of the indicators identify methodological weaknesses of the evaluation design, and **Column B** is used to check which of these issues represent serious problems for the purposes of the evaluation being assessed. The distinction between these two columns is that for evaluations intended to provide an overall assessment of performance and to indicate whether a project has the potential to achieve its objectives, some of the more technical threats to validity may not be very important. For example, checklist 2 item 9 (incorrect effect size estimations due to outliers) may be an important statistical issue, but it may not have great operational significance for an exploratory study designed to learn whether the program theory seems to "work" and if there is evidence that the intended outputs were produced, and whether the target communities are willing to participate. In another scenario, where the cost-effectiveness of the program is being compared with alternative programs that are competing for funding, being able to demonstrate a large effect-size may be very important to policymakers.

These two columns can be used in two ways. The first is simply to check whether a particular methodological issue exists (Column A) or is important for the client (Column B). The second alternative is to apply a rating scale (for example where 1= "not serious" or "not of concern to the client" and 5 = "very serious" or "very important for the client"). With this second option, a summary score can be produced either as an arithmetic average or by noting how many boxes are rated 1, 2, 3, 4, and 5. If a mean value is computed, care must be taken to recognize the dangers of manipulating ordinal scales as if the values were interval.

Many textbooks only give Part C of the worksheet (the list of technical indicators for each component). However, the drawback is that the analysis will be too technical for nonspecialist managers and clients; hence the inclusion of Parts A and B. A later section of this chapter discusses how this and the following worksheets for QUAL and mixed-method evaluations can be used at different stages of the evaluation.

4.2. Strengthening Validity in Quantitative Evaluations: Strengthening the Evaluation Design

Random Sampling

QUANT evaluators are concerned to ensure that the sample of subjects to be surveyed or tested is randomly selected and sufficiently large to permit the use of statistical analysis and significance testing procedures. One of the key questions in sample design is, "Was the sample selected in such a way as to permit statistically valid generalizations to be drawn from the analysis of the data?" For readers who are interested in sample design, Chapter 15 identifies key design and analysis decisions that must be made before the sample is designed, during the process of sample selection, and after the survey has been administered. If the right decisions are not made before the sample is designed and selected, there is little that can be done to rectify the problems during the post survey analysis phase.

One of the main messages is that management and administration of the actual sample-selection process in the field is as important as the theoretical sampling design in ensuring the validity of the findings. For example, the sample design may include precise instructions as to what procedure to follow if the person to be interviewed is not at home when the interviewer comes to the house. Perhaps the instruction is that the interviewer must return once more to try to locate this person before selecting a replacement family. However, if the interviewer ignores this instruction and either interviews a different member of the family (who happens to be present) or immediately selects another family, then the theoretical sample design will not actually have been implemented. In a well-managed survey, a supervisor would detect most of these selection errors either by debriefing the interviewer at the end of the day or by randomly revisiting a sample of households to check that the correct procedures were followed. These issues are particularly critical for the RealWorld evaluator because decisions often have to be made as to how to invest limited budget resources to ensure the quality of the sample and of the survey data. Is it more important to invest resources to improve the sample frame (e.g., by preparing community maps locating all houses—if such a map does not exist), to increase the sample size, or to carefully monitor the implementation of the survey? Unfortunately, the answer is usually that all these are important, so careful thought must be given as to how to use the limited budget.

A critical issue for **statistical conclusion validity** is sample size. The sample needs to be large enough to detect whether the project has contributed to producing the intended effects (impacts) without wasting resources by having a sample larger than necessary. Reducing sample size is often an important option for reducing costs, so it is essential to strike the right balance between saving money and ensuring that the sample is large enough to detect project impacts. The factors determining the appropriate sample size for a given evaluation are discussed in Chapter 15.

Triangulation

One of the advantages of mixed-method approaches is that they provide two or more independent measures of key variables (e.g., household income, school enrollment and absentee rates, main sources of economic activity—particularly in the informal sector—changes in crime rates, and community violence over time). This makes it possible to use data **triangulation,** to collect data at different points in time and from different sources to compare information from different sources to check whether the information is consistent. See Chapter 14 for an example in which three different sources are used to obtain independent estimates of changes in household income.

An important aspect of triangulation is to plan ahead what will be done if triangulation reveals inconsistencies among measures made by different methods. While many QUAL approaches expect that inconsistencies will be revealed and consider this as adding to the richness of the data and something that will be addressed during the interpretation phase, most QUANT approaches try to obtain consistent and uniform responses. Ideally, the QUANT evaluation design should allow time and resources to return to the field (as is common practice in much QUAL research using, for example, constant comparative methods) to follow up when inconsistencies are discovered, either during the interview supervision phase or during the analysis phase (when the discrepancies tend to be discovered). Unfortunately, this is usually not possible, particularly on the RWE budget, so other options should be considered. These include the following:

- Those who conduct evaluator-administered surveys should be instructed to note inconsistencies between interviewee-reported information and their direct observation. They should indicate how they interpret the discrepancies and possibly what they think is the best estimate of the truth. They may also be instructed to ask some follow-up questions such as, "Why do you think that so many residents say they are dissatisfied with the health clinic?" "Could you explain what you mean by that?"
- Identify as many as possible of the inconsistencies during the interview supervision phase and follow up through post interview discussion with interviewers and possibly revisits to a sample of respondents. The purpose is to understand the reasons for the discrepancies and to provide guidance to the interviewers on what to do when similar discrepancies are detected in future interviews.
- Define rules for interview coding and analysis of how to address inconsistencies (e.g., whether more weight should be given to one source of data, whether QUANT estimates should be adjusted in a certain defined way—when, for example, one family in the community is reported as having an income far in excess of any other family or when reported expenditures are far greater than reported income). These rules should take into account feedback received during the interview process (another reason for the importance of the post interview debriefing sessions). However, such rules rarely anticipate all the judgments that were made in the field, which is one of the major benefits of mixed-method designs, where QUANT analysis can be combined with emergent QUAL designs that can help interpret these kinds of questions.
- For critical indicators in QUANT analysis, it is possible to create during the analysis phase two different variables giving upper and lower estimates (e.g., income, school enrollment, unemployment). One estimate is derived from the survey information and is not adjusted, whereas the other is adjusted up or down to take into account the estimates obtained from other data-collection methods (e.g., observation, key informants). Statistical tests can then be used to examine whether the two estimates are associated in a consistent way and also how each is affected by household attributes (e.g., income, size, education) and by **contextual variables**. This is an example of the practical utility of mixed-method approaches allowing a number of different explanations of the discrepancies to be compared.

Selection of Statistical Procedures

One important aspect of statistical procedures for RWEs is the decision on sample size. A trade-off often has to be made between the level of **precision** that is required and the available resources. A common threat to statistical validity is the lower **power of the test** and the resulting inability to test for small **effect sizes** when the sample is too small. This important question is discussed in Chapter 15, in which guidelines are given for determining the appropriate sample size for typical RWE contexts where the budget is tight. When mixed-method evaluations are used, it will usually be necessary to select different statistical procedures for the analysis of interval variables (such as weight, age, and number of children), ordinal variables (e.g., satisfaction with school, level of agreement or disagreement with statements concerning local health facilities), and nominal variables (e.g., economic sector in which a person works, region of origin, reasons for migrating to the city). As we will see later in this chapter, several of the factors affecting statistical conclusion validity are related to the use of an inappropriate statistical test.

Peer Review and Meta-Evaluation

The evaluator's peers and professional colleagues are often the group best qualified for assessing the strengths and weaknesses of the evaluation design. An effort should always be made to solicit either formal or informal peer review of the evaluation design and later the analysis.

If resources permit, it is also extremely useful to commission a meta-evaluation in which an evaluation specialist is hired to critique the evaluation methodology. The meta-evaluation will often address most of the questions included in the checklists in Appendix A Part 3 Checklist 1 and should include an assessment of the potential threats to validity and adequacy of the evaluation design, data analysis, and presentation of findings.

4.3. Taking Corrective Actions
When Threats to Validity Have Been Identified

Earlier in this chapter, we discussed the worksheet that can be used to identify and assess the importance of threats to validity for QUANT evaluations (Appendix A). Once threats to validity have been identified and assessed, it is important to have a management plan either to take corrective actions or, if this is not possible, to ensure that the implications of these threats are fully discussed in the evaluation report. Readers who are interested might like to refer to the example of a completed Project Evaluation Worksheet in Appendix D. While this example refers to a mixed-method evaluation, the worksheet is used in the same way to identify issues and propose corrective measures for QUANT (and also for QUAL) evaluations. This illustrates how threats to validity are identified and their importance assessed in a typical evaluation (the impacts of a low-cost housing program on family income). Several common threats to validity are discussed in this example and are summarized for evaluation managers in Part II and for senior management in Part I. In the following paragraphs, we present one example to illustrate the process of identifying potential threats to validity, deciding how important they are, and then deciding what actions to take to try to correct or reduce the threat.

We take the example of one of the most common threats to internal validity—namely, history (Checklist 2 threat 16 in Part III of Appendix D). *History* refers to the fact that external events unrelated to the project but that affect outcomes might have occurred during the period in which the project is being implemented. For example, drought, changes in the demand for agricultural produce, or the construction of a new road might all have affected farm income, or a school-feeding program started by a nongovernmental organization (**NGO**) might have affected school enrollment or attendance rates. Box 7.1 (this chapter) illustrates the effect of historical factors on the implementation of CARE International projects. If the effects of these external events are not taken into account, it may be wrongly assumed that the observed changes in farmers' income or school enrollment are due to the projects when, in fact, they may be at least partly due to these external history factors.

In the example in Appendix D, it was found that household income had increased by an average of 70% over the three years since the start of the housing project. The evaluation report assumed that the increase in income could be attributed to the benefits of improved housing. However, the lack of a comparison group meant that the analysis did not take into account general changes in wage levels and income that might have affected all the low-income population. This threat was considered very serious because it could lead to completely wrong conclusions about the impacts of the project.

Several possible actions are proposed to rectify the problem. The first option was to reconstruct a comparison group through the use of secondary data or through information provided by key informants such as the Chamber of Commerce, Ministry of Planning, local industries, community leaders, or NGOs. The second option was to identify areas of the city with similar characteristics that could be used as a comparison group. Ideally, a rapid survey would be conducted to obtain information on current and past economic conditions or, if this is not possible, qualitative interviews could be conducted with people who have lived in the comparison areas for a number of years and who can provide information on the changes that have occurred. The cheapest option would be to use direct observation to compare the physical and economic conditions of the project and comparison areas.

It was concluded that the proposed actions could identify potentially important external factors and provide a rough estimate of their importance. This could significantly reduce but not eliminate the problem.

Box 7.2 provides additional examples of how to identify and address typical problems affecting each of the four types of threat to validity of QUANT evaluation designs.

5. Assessing Adequacy and Validity for Qualitative Impact Evaluations

While there is a high degree of consensus on how to assess the validity of QUANT evaluations, this consensus does not exist for QUAL evaluations. Some QUAL researchers prefer to talk about *adequacy*, where the emphasis is on the appropriateness of the methodology and the analysis within a particular context. Many QUAL researchers argue that, given the wide range of QUAL evaluation methodologies, different criteria must be used for assessing different methodologies (Frick 2007 chap 2). However, despite the greater difficulty in reaching consensus on the approach, most QUAL evaluators would agree that it is necessary to address many of the same fundamental questions as their QUANT colleagues, namely: Are the conclusions and recommendations presented in the evaluation report supported by the available evidence and what, if any, qualifications are required due to limitations of the evaluation design or what happened during implementation?

The inductive, intuitive nature of QUAL evaluation places enormous demands on the judgment capacity of the QUAL evaluator. While QUANT evaluators are also required to make judgments in the interpretation of their findings, there are methodological guidelines that they can often rely on to determine, for example, the adequacy of the sample size and design or the statistical significance of associations found between different variables. The QUAL evaluator, on the other hand is rarely, if ever, able to draw on such precise guidelines.

BOX 7.2
EXAMPLES OF THE IDENTIFICATION AND WAYS TO ADDRESS TYPICAL THREATS TO STATISTICAL, INTERNAL DESIGN, AND CONSTRUCT AND EXTERNAL VALIDITY FOR A MIXED-METHOD EVALUATION (THE EXAMPLES REFER TO APPENDIX C)

- **Unreliability of measures of change of outcome indicators** (threats to statistical conclusion validity—Checklist 3 Threat 4): Unreliable measures of the rate of change in, for example, income, literacy, or infant mortality reduce the likelihood of finding a statistically significant effect. The problem may be that the concepts are multidimensional (such as income) so that a single indicator can never fully capture all the dimensions, or it may be that different organizations use different definitions (e.g., literacy).

  ○ **Possible corrective measures:** Two approaches can be considered to address this threat. First, ensure that sufficient time and resources are allocated to develop and field-test the data-collection instruments; second, incorporate multimethod data-collection approaches so that at least two independent measures are used for all key variables, and use triangulation to check on the reliability and consistency of the different estimates. Where estimates are convergent (consistent), the evaluator can feel more confident of the findings. However, when estimates are divergent (not consistent), a decision must be made as to how to interpret the inconsistencies. A first step is to consult with the team members who have been using QUAL methods to discuss what these studies have to say. Resources permitting, it may be possible to explore these issues further, either through the ongoing QUAL studies or by conducting a rapid follow-up survey.

- **Project selection bias** (threats to internal conclusion validity—Checklist 2 Threat 15): Project participants are often different from comparison groups in important ways. Participants may be self-selected, as when people apply to participate in the program, or the project may deliberately target groups with special characteristics, such as the poorest communities or those with the most dynamic community organizations. In either case, it is difficult to find comparison groups that match these characteristics.

  ○ **Possible corrective measures:** Four possible measures are proposed. First, compare characteristics of participants and comparison groups, and identify important differences. Try to find ways to produce a better match, but even if this is not possible, it is useful to understand what the differences are so these can be taken into account in the analysis and preparation of recommendations. Second, statistically control for differences in participant characteristics in the two groups (see Chapters 11 and 12 for a discussion of the use of multivariate analysis for this purpose). Third, use key informants (particularly if no comparison group is used) to compare participants with the total population. Fourth, use focus groups or direct observation of other group settings to assess psychological characteristics such as self-confidence and motivation.

- **Reactivity to the experimental situation** (threats to construct validity—Checklist 4 Threat 8): Often, project participants try to interpret the project situation, and this may affect their behavior. For example, if participants think the program is being run by a religious group, they may react differently than if they think it is organized by a political organization.
  - o **Possible corrective measures:** Use exploratory studies and observations to understand respondent expectations and to identify potential response bias. Of course, these studies, too, would have observer effects.

- **The attitude of policymakers and politicians to the program (and how this may affect the success of the program and estimates of its replicability in other locations)** (threats to external validity—Checklist 5 Threat 6): Identical programs may have different outcomes depending on the level and type of support or opposition of policymakers and politicians.
  - o **Possible corrective measures:** If a project is implemented in different locations, identify differences in the attitudes of policymakers and politicians in each location (through interviews, secondary sources such as newspapers and radio, or key informants) and assess how these differences appear to affect the project.

The implications for accuracy and bias have often generated concerns among QUANT evaluators about the potential mischief of the subjective judgments of their QUAL colleagues (Bamberger, Rugh, and Mabry 2006:145). How can the reader be assured that the findings and conclusions, many of which are drawn from material compiled by one or more researchers often working independently, present a fair and unbiased interpretation of the situation being studied? How do we know that another researcher studying the same situation would not have arrived at a different set of conclusions because of a different set of preconceptions? QUAL practitioners have sometimes responded that all human ways of knowing are necessarily subjective, including QUANT ways, that subjective minds are all evaluators have, and that what is important in evaluation in *trustworthiness* (Guba and Lincoln 1989) or *adequacy*.

In Chapter 13, we argue that QUAL researchers recognize that subjectivity is inevitable (whereas many QUANT researchers believe that they can separate themselves from what is being studied and achieve a considerable degree of objectivity). Subjective judgment is involved not only in developing findings but also in the process of identifying what should be counted or measured, how data should be categorized or recorded, what the critical data sources are, which features of a program contribute to its outcomes, or which criteria are appropriate for judging program quality. QUAL researchers discipline their acknowledged subjectivity through (pp. 297–300):

- Triangulation: deliberate attempts to confirm, elaborate, and disconfirm facts and interpretations through multiple data sources, multiple methods of data collection, repeated data collection over time, and achieving multiple perspectives through involving/consulting multiple researchers
- Validation: checking with informants about the accuracy of the recorded data and the reasonableness of the interpretations drawn from them

- Peer review: critical review by colleagues and external experts may bolster validity and credibility
- Meta-evaluation: the evaluation of the evaluation by experienced individuals or professional panels

Appendix B presents a similar worksheet to that described in the previous section for QUANT evaluations. The checklist draws on the work of Guba and Lincoln (1989), Miles and Huberman (1994), Yin (2003), and Teddlie and Tashakkori (2009) to develop indicators that can be used to assess the adequacy, trustworthiness, or validity of qualitative evaluation designs.

Recently Frick (2007) has proposed an approach to quality assessment for QUAL evaluations that focuses on different aspects of the evaluation process. The first step assesses the appropriateness of the evaluation decisions, or the decision-making process, for addressing the research questions.[1] The second step involves the introduction of a quality-management system. This begins with the definition of an audit trail for tracking the different stages in the collection and analysis of data. Box 7.3 presents Frick's guidelines for quality management.

BOX 7.3
FRICK'S PROCESS-ORIENTED APPROACH TO ASSESSING
THE QUALITY OF QUALITATIVE EVALUATIONS

Step 1. The appropriateness of the evaluation design for addressing priority evaluation questions

Step 2. Introducing a quality-management system, beginning with an audit trail

Step 3. Assessing the quality of the decision-making process throughout the evaluation

Step 4. Quality of transparency, documentation, and dissemination

SOURCE: Frick (2007) Chapter 10, Adapted from Tables 10.2 and 10.3.

5.1. Strengthening Validity in Qualitative Evaluations: Strengthening the Evaluation Design

Purposeful (Purposive) Sampling

The sampling strategies useful and appropriate for QUAL evaluation differ markedly from those appropriate for QUANT evaluation. QUAL methods, concentrating on depth rather than breadth, require understanding at the level of the individual participant—phenomenological understanding, or understanding from the participant's insider perspective. Because it takes longer to interview a person and to transcribe or write up the interview data, for example, than it does to hand him or her a self-administered survey or even to administer a closed-question questionnaire, fewer persons can be interviewed than can be surveyed. When

---

[1]Frick 2007, Tables 10.2 and 10.3, provide guidelines for selecting the appropriate design.

relatively few participants in a program can be interviewed, selection of interviewees must be very careful—not random, but purposive or purposeful.

Chapter 15 Section 2 presents a variety of selection criteria in determining a sample. Determinations as to which of these sampling strategies (or others) is appropriate depend on the evaluation questions and the information needs of stakeholders.

Triangulation

Program quality should not, of course, be based on unsubstantiated opinion or a few site visits where the evaluator may observe nonrepresentative interactions, either innocent or planned. Triangulation, crucial to protecting against invalidity, involves deliberate attempts to confirm, elaborate, and disconfirm facts and interpretations through reference to the following:

- Multiple data sources
- Multiple methods of data collection
- Multiple evaluators or data collectors
- Repeated observations over time
- Multiple analytic perspectives

For example, the evaluator will need to confirm the information from an interview through direct observation of the events described by the interviewee, through interviews of others, through documentary evidence of the events, and through patterns of their occurrence. In this way, the *descriptive validity* of the interview data can be assessed, answering the question, Is the program fully and accurately represented by the data? Through consideration of the events' meaning and implications from perspectives other than those of the interviewee—including those from other program participants, different members of the evaluation team, and relevant literature—the *interpretive validity* can also be strengthened, answering the question, Are the interpretations of program aspects or program quality overall warranted (supported) by the data?

Validation

Validation is also used to strengthen the accuracy of the data set and the reasonableness of interpretations. Validation involves checking with informants about the accuracy of the recorded data and the reasonableness of the interpretations drawn from them. The best-known validation techniques are these:

- *Member checking*—the review of data and interpretations by a gathering of persons representing relevant stakeholders (Lincoln and Guba 1985)
- *Comprehensive individual validation*—individual validation of data and findings, with each informant provided an opportunity to review, first, the relatively uninterpreted data that he or she provided (such as an interview transcript or an observation write-up) and, later, a draft of the report that includes the selected presentation and interpretation of data, for validation of both data and interpretations (Mabry 1998)

In addition, drafts of reports may be submitted to diverse audiences, selected on the bases of expertise and confidentiality, to try to ensure "getting it right" (Geertz 1973:29). The scope of distribution of the draft should reflect sensitivity to ethics and politics, including matters such as possible need to protect informants' identities or to avoid premature distribution of tentative interpretations that might be either wrong or damaging. Also, validation may occur informally by opening conversational opportunities for participants to react to some data or to ideas about its meaning.

Meta-Evaluation and Peer Review

Meta-evaluation, the evaluation of an evaluation, is advisable, especially for expensive and high-impact evaluations. Where full-scale meta-evaluation would strain fiscal resources, less formal collegial review may help to discipline the subjectivity of the evaluator, enhance analysis, and bolster the validity of findings.

Critical review by evaluation colleagues and external substantive experts, either individually or as professional panels, may promote both validity and credibility. Technical advisory panels may monitor and assess an evaluation's quality, providing ongoing checks and critique during report drafting. Informally, too, colleagues may listen, read, comment, argue, suggest, and advise. In addition to review by program participants and other stakeholders, internal review by the evaluation team may be either informal and ongoing, formal and undertaken at critical junctures, or both.

5.2. Addressing Threats to Validity in Qualitative Evaluations

To help ensure the validity of findings in QUAL evaluations, the following suggestions regarding comprehensiveness of data, sensitivity to informants, opportunity for analysis, and observer effects are offered.

Collecting Data across the Full Range of Appropriate Settings, Times, and Respondents

Consider whether a sufficient number and type of observations and interviews have been planned or conducted to ensure thorough understanding and the validity of findings. If not, and if the study has not yet been conducted, discuss ways to revise the evaluation design. If data collection has already been undertaken, consider the possibility of re-interviewing key informants or others or revisiting a site to fill in some of the gaps.

If stakeholders engaged in review of data and findings consider the report's representation of the program faulty, consider seeking out key informants or organizing meetings to determine whether the problems concern missing information (e.g., only men were interviewed), whether there are factual errors, or whether the problem concerns how the material was interpreted by the evaluator. Based on the types of problems identified, consider revising the report or returning to the field for further interviews, observations, or review of documents.

Inappropriate Subject Selection

If important program participants have inadvertently been neglected and if the fieldwork has not yet been completed, include them in the sample to make the evaluation data more representative of the total population. If fieldwork has already been conducted, consider individual or group interviews with some members of the missing population groups. In areas where subjects have access to these technologies, telephone or e-mail interviews may be needed if the evaluator is not able to return to the program site. If this is not possible, try to identify and review information about the missing groups or to observe them (or arrange for them to be observed by local team members) to obtain missing information.

Insufficient Language or Cultural Skills to Ensure Sensitivity to Informants

If, in negotiating the evaluation design, it becomes apparent that specific cultural competencies are needed to collect valid data, consider hiring experts in the competencies needed or hiring (and perhaps training) local persons for additional data collection. If the need for specific skills has become apparent as data have been collected, consider bringing in experts or representatives of the community to help with the analysis to ensure appropriate cultural and linguistic sensitivity.

Insufficient Opportunity for Ongoing Analysis by the Team

If periodic analytic discussion by evaluation team members is precluded by the timeline of the evaluation or the geographic remoteness of program sites, consider electronic means of sharing. For example, debriefing updates may be faxed or e-mailed to all team members, or report-and-respond forms may be adapted for internal use to spur interpretation toward collective preliminary findings.

Minimizing Observer Effects

Threats to validity from observer effects can be minimized by building triangulation and validation into the design—checking impressions from observations by interviewing those observed or by conferring with other observers, checking the validity of data from interviews against first-hand observations and documents. Validation of data write-ups through requests for additions and corrections from those observed and interviewed can guard against misinterpretation. Discussions within the evaluation team, with selected clients, review panels, or technical advisory panels or meta-evaluators, can also bring balance to individual impressions.

Supporting Future Action

Interpretive findings do not necessarily imply specific corrective actions. Many well-known evaluators advise against making recommendations or consider the program personnel better able than evaluators to devise action plans because of their more intimate knowledge of their program and participants. Evaluators could meet with key stakeholders to discuss or brainstorm plans for program improvement, although some evaluators would consider this a threatening move beyond evaluation into consultancy.

6. Assessing Validity for Mixed-Method (MM) Evaluations

6.1. The Standard Mixed-Method Worksheet

Appendix C presents a worksheet for what we call the "standard version" of the mixed-methods validity assessment. This combines the main elements of the checklists for QUANT (Appendix A) and QUAL

(Appendix B) evaluations. Each of the six checklists uses italics to indicate the items that are normally used in QUANT validity analysis and normal text for the items that are normally used in QUAL validity analysis. The worksheet has the same format and the same system of rating as for the two previous worksheets. This worksheet can be considered the default worksheet that can be used for most validity assessments, as in practice, most evaluations combine some elements of both QUANT and QUAL approaches.

Appendix D presents a completed version of Worksheet 3 that has been applied to a hypothetical but fairly typical project evaluation. This illustrates how the detailed technical assessments in Part 3 are summarized through the ratings and then presented in a condensed form in Part 2, which is intended for evaluation managers who are often not research specialists but who require a paragraph to explain the main findings for each of the six checklists. The findings are further summarized in Part 1 to provide for senior management and partner funding agencies a brief assessment of the strengths and weaknesses of the evaluation methodology and what this means for the interpretation of the findings and recommendations. In this example, due to the lack of baseline data on the comparison group, it is recommended that the evaluation's findings concerning the positive project impacts are not fully supported by the interpretation of the data.

6.2. A More Advanced Approach to the Assessment of Mixed-Method Evaluations (Appendix E)

Over the past few years, mixed-method (MM) evaluation has emerged as a distinct approach to evaluation that is much more than simply a combination of different methods of data collection. Appendix E presents a worksheet that tries to capture and assess the complexities of an integrated MM evaluation approach. MM combine QUANT and QUAL conceptual frameworks, methods of hypothesis generation, data collection, analysis, and interpretation. This means that a two-stage assessment of validity is required. In Stage 1, each element of the evaluation design and implementation must be assessed using the appropriate QUANT or QUAL validity criterion. Then, in Stage 2, the overall evaluation design must be assessed to determine how well the QUANT and QUAL components have been integrated into the MM design. The validity analysis is further complicated by the fact that evaluation designs form a continuum from mainly QUANT designs to mainly QUAL designs (see Chapter 14), so there is an element of judgment in deciding which components of a MM evaluation design should be assessed in terms of QUANT threats to validity, which in terms of QUAL dimensions of adequacy and trustworthiness, and which may require the application of both QUANT and QUAL criteria.

Appendix E presents a worksheet with a set of five components for assessing the validity of MM designs. The MM validity analysis is based on the three dimensions (internal, external, and utilization validity), but a number of additional indicators have been added to reflect the unique nature of the mixed-method approach (see Figure 7.3):

    a. During the process of data analysis, MM will sometimes *quantitize* QUAL variables by transforming them into QUANT variables and *qualitize* QUANT variables by transforming them into QUAL variables (see Teddlie and Tashakkori 2009 chap 11). This is defined as a *conversion mixed-method design.* Consequently, for these designs, in addition to assessing QUANT and QUAL data collection, it is also necessary to assess the adequacy of the process of transformation of the variables.

    b. One of the strengths of MM approaches is that they permit multilevel analysis, for example, to examine the interactions between the project-implementation process and individuals, households, communities, and organizations and to model how these interactions affect project implementation and outcomes. This requires an assessment of the whole modeling process as well as the adequacy of the data collection and analysis at each of the levels (see Teddlie and Tashakkori 2009 chap 11).

c. Most MM designs combine the use of separate QUANT and QUAL techniques for data collection, analysis, and interpretation, and these must be examined separately using the appropriate QUANT and QUAL assessment criteria (see Appendix E, Checklist 2).

d. The overall evaluation design must then be reviewed to assess how well the QUANT and QUAL components have been integrated to produce a true MM design as opposed to the separate use of QUANT and QUAL techniques that are used separately and not integrated into a true MM design (see Appendix E, Checklist 1).

e. Finally, a new element must be introduced to assess the overall interpretative rigor with which the MM framework has been applied. This is required because MM designs are required to integrate both QUANT and QUAL approaches to the development of conceptual frameworks and the definition and testing of hypotheses. It is quite possible for an evaluation to include methodologically sound interpretations of both QUANT and QUAL data but fail to ensure their integration into a fully integrated MM interpretation of all aspects of the evaluation (see Appendix E, Checklist 5).

7. Using the Threats-to-Validity Worksheet

The worksheets for assessing validity for QUANT, QUAL, and mixed-method designs all have three parts, each of which is targeted to a different audience (see Figure 7.3):

- **Part 1**. The cover sheet provides a one-page summary for senior management and for partner agencies. This explains the purpose of the evaluation and the reason for conducting the threats-to-validity assessment. It also summarizes the main conclusions of the validity assessment and the recommended follow-up actions.
- **Part 2**. The summary assessment for each component is intended for middle-level management. It presents a half-page text summary of the validity assessment of each of the five components and a summary numerical rating (1 = very strong to 5 = serious problems). This provides sufficient detail for middle-level management to understand the main strengths and weaknesses of the evaluation and how these affect the validity of the findings and recommendations. In cases where only a general assessment of the evaluation quality is required, only Parts 1 and 2 of the worksheet may be used. However, when a more rigorous and comprehensive validity assessment is required, Part 3 can also be used.
- **Part 3**. Between four and six checklists are included that permit a comprehensive technical analysis by an evaluation specialist of each of the components. Each indicator can be rated on a scale of 1 to 5 (Column A), where 1 indicates that the methodology is sound and 5 indicates there are significant methodological problems. A summary score can then be calculated for each checklist, indicating the overall strength or weaknesses of the methodology for each component. Column B can then be used to check how many of the methodological problems (i.e., those with a rating or 4 or 5) have important operational or policy issues for the purposes of this evaluation. The distinction between Column A and Column B is important because, depending on the purpose for which the evaluation was commissioned, and the

Figure 7.3   Dimensions of Threats to Validity for the Assessment of Mixed-Method Evaluation Designs [QUAN terms are in **bold** and parallel QUAL terms are in ***bold italics***]

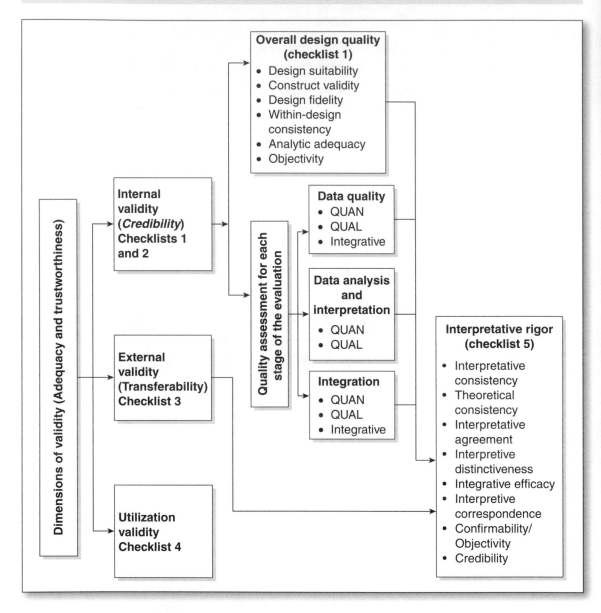

types of decisions that will be based on its findings, there will often be a number of methodological weaknesses that may not have important implications for the intended users.

The worksheet can be used at various points in an evaluation:

- During the evaluation design phase to identify potential threats to validity or adequacy. When important problems or threats are identified, it may be possible to modify the design to address them. In other cases, if some of the potential threats could seriously compromise the purpose of the evaluation, further consultations may be required with the client or funding agency to consider either increasing the budget or the duration of the evaluation (where this would mitigate some of the problems) or agreeing to modify the objectives of the evaluation to reflect these limitations. In some extreme cases, the evaluability assessment may conclude that the proposed evaluation is not feasible and all parties may agree to cancel or postpone the evaluation.

- During the implementation of the evaluation (for example, a midterm review). If the checklist had also been administered at the start of the evaluation, it is possible to assess if progress has been made in addressing the problems. Where serious problems are identified, it may be possible to adjust the evaluation design (for example, to broaden the sample coverage or to refine or expand some of the questions or survey instruments).

- Toward the end of the evaluation—perhaps when the draft final report is being prepared. This may still allow time to correct some (but obviously not all) of the problems identified.

- When the evaluation has been completed. While it is now too late to make any corrections, a summary of the checklist findings can be attached to the final report to provide a perspective for readers on how to interpret the evaluation findings and recommendations and to understand what caveats are required.

- For organizations that regularly commission or conduct evaluations, a very useful exercise is to conduct a meta-analysis to compare the ratings for different evaluations to determine whether there is a consistent pattern of methodological weaknesses in all evaluations (or all evaluations in a particular country, region, or sector). We discussed earlier how the checklist can be used at different points in the evaluation—for example, at the evaluation design stage, during implementation, and when the draft final report is being prepared. When the checklist is applied at these different points, it is possible to detect whether any of the threats are corrected or mitigated over time or whether, on the other hand, some of them get worse. Differential sample attrition (between the project and control groups) is a familiar example in which a problem may get worse over time, as differences between the characteristics of subjects remaining in the project and the control samples may increase.

7.1. Other Checklists

In addition to the checklists developed by Shadish et al. (2002), Guba and Lincoln (1989), and Miles and Huberman (1994) referred to earlier in this chapter, a number of other checklists have been developed for assessing the quality of evaluations or the validity of their conclusions (see also Chapter 9 for a discussion of evaluation guidelines and standards). The following are some widely used examples:

A. *The Western Michigan University Evaluation Checklist Project*[2] provides refereed checklists for designing, budgeting, contracting, staffing, managing, and assessing evaluations of programs, personnel, students, and other evaluands; collecting, analyzing, and reporting evaluation information; and determining merit, worth, and significance. Each checklist is a distillation of valuable lessons learned from practice. The site's stated purpose is to improve the quality and consistency of evaluations and enhance evaluation capacity through the promotion and use of high-quality checklists targeted to specific evaluation tasks and approaches. The checklists are classified into the following groups: evaluation

---

[2]For information on the Western Michigan University Evaluation Center Checklist Project, see http://www .wmich.edu/evalctr/checklists/checklist_topics

management, evaluation models, evaluation values and criteria, meta-evaluation and evaluation capacity development, and institutionalization. Many but not all of the checklists focus on the education sector.

The site includes a number of widely cited checklists, among which are Michael Scriven's *Key Evaluation Checklist* (2007); Daniel Stufflebeam's *Program Evaluations Metaevaluation Checklist* (1999); Daniel Stufflebeam's *CIPP Model* (2007); and Michael Patton's *Qualitative Evaluation Checklist* (2003) and *Utilization Focused Evaluation Checklist* (2002c).

B. The American Evaluation Association's *Guiding Principles for Evaluators* (2004), which provides guidance to evaluators on five areas: systematic enquiry, competence, integrity/honesty, respect for people, and responsibilities for general and public welfare.

C. The OECD/DAC *Quality Standards for Development Evaluation* (2010b). This provides standards for (1) the rationale, purpose, and objectives of an evaluation; (2) evaluation topic; (3) context; (4) evaluation methodology; (5) information sources; (6) independence; (7) evaluation ethics; (8) quality assurance; (9) relevance of the evaluation results; and (10) completeness.

While these three sources are extremely valuable resources, they focus mainly on ensuring quality in the design and implementation of the evaluation and ensuring that evaluators follow appropriate professional standards. There is little direct discussion of threats to validity and how they can be addressed.

Figure 7.4   Structure, Audience, and Responsibility for the Different Parts of the Threats-to-Validity Worksheet

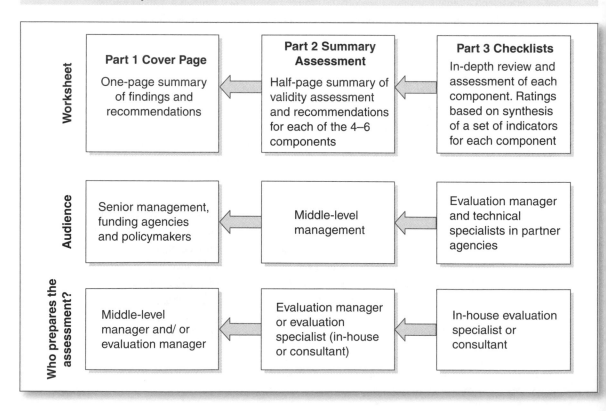

7.2. Points During the RWE Cycle at Which Corrective Measures Can Be Taken

The RWE **Integrated Checklist** and other similar checklists can help identify threats to validity and adequacy of designs, as well as strategies for addressing the threats once they have been identified. Threats can be addressed at three points in the evaluation: during design, during implementation, and during report preparation. Some of the questions to be addressed when assessing the adequacy and validity of evaluation designs include the following:

- Are methods appropriate for information needs? For example, is the evaluation question to be addressed in data collection one of meaning, understanding, or process? Will the methods generate data that will help the client and other stakeholders address their information needs?
- Is there a clear, positive relationship of the methodology to the evaluation focus or questions?
- Are the evaluation team's expertise and capacity sufficient for the approach and methods?
- Are strategies to ensure validity, trustworthiness, and confirmability adequate and appropriate?
- Using this design, are the data to be collected likely to be relevant, comprehensive, and representative of the program?
- Are adequate and appropriate technical and ethical safeguards in place?
- Are there procedures to ensure cultural sensitivity, competence, and capacity?

Increasing the comprehensiveness of the methods would improve many evaluations—for example, increasing the period and number of observations or increasing the number of stakeholders and stakeholder groups interviewed or surveyed. Adding experts in the application of these methods (e.g., sociologists, statisticians) or in the type of program to be evaluated (e.g., economists to study a microcredit program, civil engineers to study a clean-water program) can also strengthen evaluation designs. However, in many RWE contexts, budget and time constraints limit the ability of the evaluation team to take these additions.

Strengthening the Evaluation Design

The Integrated Checklist (see Appendix C) can be used to review a proposed evaluation design and make corrections before the evaluation begins. If analysis by an evaluator, evaluation team, or technical advisory panel determines that an evaluation design is weak, steps may be taken to improve the design, protecting the quality of the evaluation before data collection begins. The specific improvements needed vary from design to design, of course, but some general advice may be helpful.

Strengthening Data-Collection Methods

As the evaluation focus, questions, and information needs are considered with reference to the planned methods, it may become clear that the methods may not elicit adequate or strong enough data to provide sufficient evidence of program quality. The substitution of more appropriate methods or addition of complementary methods may be needed.

For example, in an evaluation of state assessment programs in education, an examination of methods may suggest that the evaluation will generate data describing the types of achievement testing used by the state, the types of items on the tests, whether the tests are standards based or norm referenced, how they are scored, how scores are reported, and the proportions of students across time who are passing and failing the tests. Such information can be obtained from state documents and online sources, perhaps supplemented by interviews with state education agency personnel. The combined use of several or all of these methods would provide extremely useful data for judging the quality of the state assessment system.

But these data would not be sufficient to determine how much measurement error is included in the tests, whether the tests are well aligned with state content standards and state curriculum guides such that teaching is likely to provide appropriate preparation for test takers, and whether failure rates impose inappropriate negative consequences on students and educators. For information of this type, more detailed study of the test content, content standards, and standards-based curricula are needed. Interviews with a representative sample of teachers, school administrators, students, and parents are needed to provide the perspectives of critical stakeholders regarding whether the state testing program is strengthening or corrupting educational practices and outcomes—and these interviews need to be followed up with surveys to determine how widespread the experiences of those interviewed are in the affected population. Observations in classrooms are needed to determine whether standards-based curricula are integral to learning opportunities and, therefore, aligned to standards-based tests. The design needs to expand from review of documents and state-level interviews to classroom-level observation, interviews of a variety of stakeholder groups, and general surveys.

In such a case, a wider range of methods and data sources would often provide triangulation, strengthening the validity protections in the evaluation design. More carefully focused methods—in this case, getting into the details of test content, measurement soundness, and the appropriateness of score-based consequences—allow for the refinement and validity of findings. Such findings would be more informative, better supported by the data, and more useful for state assessment directors who may be hoping to improve their systems on the basis of evaluation data and findings.

Strengthening Capacity of the Evaluation Team

So that the benefits of different types of methodological approaches and techniques can help protect the soundness of the evaluation and the validity of its interpretations, specialized types of methodological expertise may be needed on the evaluation team. QUANT team members may be needed to ensure appropriate sample sizes for data to be used in representing populations or determining statistical significance, comparable experimental groupings, and selection and use of statistical tests and procedures. QUAL team members may be needed to ensure fine-grained focus on individually and socially constructed meaning, the human implications of program effects, and the identification and magnitude of unintended consequences.

The complementarity of these approaches—that is, using mixed methods—can be extraordinarily useful in producing high-quality evaluation. It takes considerable open-mindedness and managerial expertise, however, to find working consensus among disparate points of view. A positional stance that privileges macro-level descriptors of the program, the population overall, or aggregated results and costs may be dismissive of micro-level effects on individuals, their experiences, and their perspectives of program quality. From an opposing positional stance, macro-level indicators and trends may be accorded little meaning if intended beneficiaries disagree with numbers that suggest they should be satisfied with program outcomes they may actually find unsatisfactory.

Working consensus, rather than melding or integration, may be useful for preserving the benefits of different methodological perspectives and expertise.

Often, an evaluation benefits from more than a variety of methodological specialties. Professionals in the field of the program who are familiar with relevant theory, professional literature, and best practices are as critical to the strength of data analysis as evaluators trained and experienced with inquiry procedures, including different strategies of data analysis. The situation is analogous to that in critical thinking: General critical-thinking strategies can be taught, but one must be able to think critically within a content area, where general strategies may be greatly differentiated and augmented. Analysis attentive to the literature in the field of the program (e.g., the field of epidemiology in programs intended to combat HIV/AIDS or the field of early childhood education in programs intended to reduce school dropout rates through early intervention) is as important as methodological strength.

For example, survey data in an evaluation of a state grant program to support the inclusion of children with disabilities suggested that all the 150 or so grantees had included, as intended, children with disabilities in prekindergarten, kindergarten, and first-grade classrooms of typically developing peers. Telephone interview data, however, suggested that some of the grant programs provided more inclusion than others. Observations and interviews at daylong site visits and a few weeklong case studies indicated that, at some sites, no inclusion was practiced. While all members of the evaluation team were able to recognize when programs segregated special-education from regular-education classrooms, initially, only the special-education members of the evaluation team were able to distinguish whether classrooms with mixed populations met the definition of *inclusion* or segregated regular-education from special-education students within the same physical spaces. Only the trained special-education eyes perceived whether instruction was differentiated and developmentally appropriate.

Determining the point of entry of such content specialists in the evaluation of a program and the scope of the role they might play is a consideration in strengthening evaluation design and conclusions. In an ideal world, of course, such resources would be abundant for an evaluation. However, in the real world, balancing the costs of differentiated expertise (feasibility) with the value to the evaluation (quality, validity, credibility) is almost always necessary.

Strengthening the Implementation of the Evaluation

The RealWorld evaluator is always encouraged to consider the use of mixed-method approaches. One of the strengths of these approaches is that QUAL methods can be used in parallel with QUANT data-collection methods in a compensatory manner. For example, in the evaluation of a community water-supply project, surveys may not reveal that residents have to pay bribes to local leaders to obtain water, information more likely to be revealed through ethnographic observation.

Strengthening Data-Analysis Procedures

Too often, data analysis progresses no farther than trends or correlations, sometimes in combination with calculations of statistical significance. Consider a trend toward increased numbers of children from an indigenous population in the highlands of Papua New Guinea in English-speaking primary schools. The trend itself is not a finding; it must be interpreted. Should the interpretation be that education is improving for indigenous children living in the highlands of Papua New Guinea? If analysis ventures no further than enrollment figures, using easy-to-analyze simple QUANT procedures, important underlying explanations may be missed.

On the other hand, analysis complicated by both QUANT and QUAL data, including ethnographic observations and systematic interviews, requires more complex analysis. Content analysis may, for example, make it much less clear whether education in English-language primary schools is beneficial for children in Papua New Guinea. While English-language primary schools may improve children's chances to succeed in higher education, those chances may come at the risk of extinguishing the indigenous language and culture. Records kept by state officials are unlikely to include such data and important stakeholder considerations, while sensitive inquiry—in this case, such as that by Malone (1997)—can offer more comprehensive and informative analysis.

Strengthening the Evaluation When Preparing to Report

Many evaluators submit draft reports to clients for review, comment, and correction prior to finalization. This practice is sometimes referred to as *negotiation drafts.* Feedback from clients may identify issues or gaps needing attention. Some time and budget should be reserved to permit additional fieldwork or analysis, if called for. These may include follow-up clarification interviews with key informants, focus group interviews with newly identified groups of stakeholders, or site visits to newly identified natural comparison groups.

SUMMARY

- When referring to data, the term *validity* is roughly similar to *accuracy.* It is a criterion used to assess whether data adequately and accurately represent actual conditions.
- The validity and adequacy of an evaluation are affected by (a) the appropriateness of the evaluation focus, approach, and methods, (b) the availability of data, (c) how well the data support valid findings, and (d) the adequacy of the evaluation team in terms of methodology, the specific field of the program, and the available resources.
- The validity of QUANT evaluations is usually assessed in terms of statistical conclusion validity, internal validity, construct validity, and external validity.
- QUANT evaluation designs can often be strengthened by (a) ensuring that random sample selection has been properly applied, (b) using triangulation to obtain independent estimates of key indicators, (c) correct selection of statistical procedures, and (d) using peer review and meta-evaluation.
- Once threats to QUANT validity have been detected, measures can be taken to correct or reduce their effects.
- The capacity of a QUAL design to support valid conclusions can be considered in terms of descriptive validity, interpretive validity, and evaluative validity.
- The Integrated Checklist for assessing evaluation validity and adequacy assesses mixed-method evaluations in terms of confirmability, reliability, and **dependability**; credibility and **authenticity**; **transferability** and fittingness; and use, application, and action orientation.
- QUAL evaluation designs are strengthened through triangulation, validation, meta-evaluation, and peer review.
- Once threats to the validity of QUAL, QUANT, or mixed-method evaluations have been identified, measures can be taken to correct or reduce their effects.
- Measures can be taken to improve the validity of evaluations during the design stage, during implementation, or when preparing and reviewing the report on evaluation findings and conclusions.

FURTHER READING

Campbell, D. T. and J. C. Stanley. 1963. *Experimental and Quasi-Experimental Designs for Research.* Boston: Houghton Mifflin.

The classic reference for explaining different types and advantages of quantitative designs and for terms such as internal and external validity.

Denzin, N. K. 1989. *The Research Act. A Theoretical Introduction to Sociological Methods.* 3d ed. Englewood Cliffs, NJ: Prentice Hall.

Thorough and classic reference for the types and purposes of triangulation.

Lincoln, Y. S. and E. G. Guba. 1985. *Naturalistic Inquiry.* Beverly Hills, CA: Sage.

A classic reference across fields and the source for the most common terms and explanations of validity and reliability in qualitative work. This is also the source for member checking as a validation technique.

Shadish, W., T. Cook, and D. Campbell. 2002. *Experimental and Quasi-Experimental Designs for Generalized Causal Inference.* Boston: Houghton Mifflin.

Probably the most comprehensive reference on threats to validity in quantitative evaluation designs. Quite technical and long, but provides an excellent overview of the philosophy, theory, and methodology of quasi-experimental designs.

Teddlie, C. and A. Tashakkori. 2009. *Foundations of Mixed Methods Research: Integrating Quantitative and Qualitative Approaches in the Social and Behavioral Sciences.* Thousand Oaks, CA. Sage.

Discussion of the assessment of validity for mixed method evaluations.

Frick, U. 2007. *Managing Quality in Qualitative Evaluation.* Thousand Oaks, CA: Sage.

Discussion of how to build quality into qualitative evaluations. Includes a chapter on standards, criteria, checklists, and guidelines.

CHAPTER 8

Making It Useful: Helping Clients and Other Stakeholders Utilize the Evaluation

Thisis chapter presents the final step of the RealWorld Evaluation (RWE) approach, in which guidelines are presented for increasing the likelihood that the evaluation findings will be used (see Figure 8.1). We begin by discussing what we mean by *influential* or *useful* evaluation and show that evaluations can be used in many different ways. We then consider some of the reasons evaluation findings are frequently underused and stress the importance of the scoping phase in ensuring that the evaluation is focusing on the right issues and is involving clients and stakeholders. We then describe formative evaluation strategies that provide constant feedback of findings to managers and planners so they can be used to improve performance of the ongoing project, and we suggest ways to ensure constant communication with clients and stakeholders. We then discuss building evaluation capacity as a way to strengthen use and provide pointers on effective communication of evaluation findings. Finally, we suggest ways to develop a follow-up action plan to ensure that evaluation findings are put into practice.

1. What Do We Mean by Influential Evaluations and Useful Evaluations?

How do we know if an evaluation has been "influential" or that it was "useful"? One definition is that an evaluation is considered useful if clients agree with the findings and recommendations and if they intended to use them. Many useful evaluations will be well designed and methodologically rigorous. However, there are also many examples of poorly designed evaluations in which the methodology is very weak and the findings have a (usually positive) bias but where the client finds the evaluation useful (Bamberger 2009d). There are also other cases in which the client's initial reaction to the

Figure 8.1 Step 7: Helping Clients Use the Evaluation

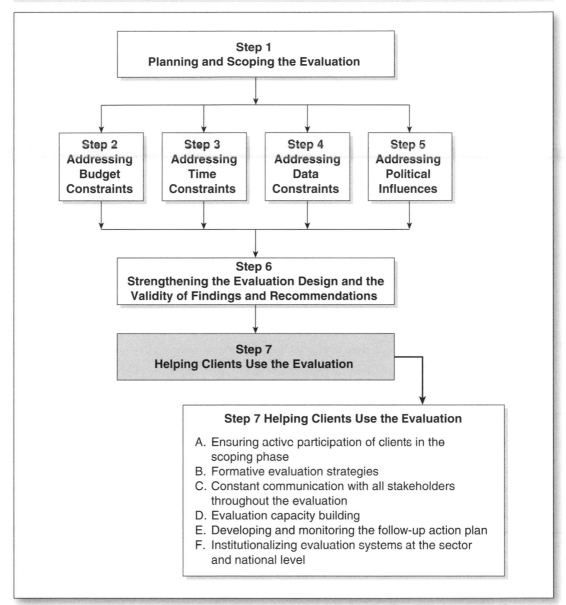

evaluation findings and recommendations is negative and in which the client disagrees with the findings. It is a common reaction to reject findings with which one does not agree. However, there are many cases in which the client may gradually come to accept some of the findings and recommendations and may use them in a later project. This is known as "the sleeper effect." Some evaluation reports will be targeted for a number of different audiences, and while some might reject the evaluation findings, others might find them useful.

Many evaluators, particularly those new to the profession, might expect that their evaluation report will have a major influence on clients and dramatically change how they think about the issues being studied ("the evaluation that changed the world"). Evaluators who start with this high level of expectations will normally be disappointed. Experience will teach them that even a very well designed evaluation will be only one of many sources of guidance available to decision makers, and many evaluations that are considered useful will only reinforce what managers or policymakers were already intending to do or will only add one additional insight. Vaughan and Buss (1998) point out that on major policy and planning decisions, there is rarely a single decision but "rather a complex process of consensus building between legislature, executive and administrative agencies" (page 56). There are also large numbers of actors at different levels, and there are many lower-level gatekeepers who can prevent evaluations and other kinds of information from ever reaching the higher-level decision makers.

When assessing usefulness of an evaluation, we also need to ask, "Useful to whom?" An evaluation can be found useful by any combination of the following audiences: the primary client, primary stakeholders, secondary stakeholders, public opinion, the mass media, or, in some cases, groups who did not have access to project benefits or where negatively affected. This latter group, although often overlooked, is considered important by agencies whose motto is "Do no harm," so it is important to inform policymakers about groups who have not benefited or who are worse off as well as to inform the members of these groups. This relates to the often sensitive issue of transparency of evaluation findings.

Box 8.1 provides examples from a recent World Bank evaluation of "Influential Evaluations" on the many different ways that evaluations can be influential and can be used.

So the first message is that evaluations can influence or be useful to many different groups in many different ways, some of which are not expected or intended. The second message is that the process of policy change or the selection or revision of new programs is a long process, usually involving many different decision makers, so that even the best designed evaluation will normally be only one of many sources of information and advice that are used by the decision makers.

2. The Underutilization of Evaluation Studies

There is widespread concern that, despite the significant resources devoted to program evaluation and its importance in the United States and for development programs, the **utilization** of evaluation findings is disappointingly low (Patton, 1997 chap 1). This holds true even for evaluations that are methodologically sound. In 1995, the U.S. General Accounting Office conducted follow-up case studies on three major federal program evaluations: the Comprehensive Child Development Program, the Community Health Centers program, and Title 1 Elementary and Secondary Education Act aimed at providing compensatory education services to low-income students and found:

> Lack of information does not appear to be the main problem. Rather, the problem seems to be that available information is not organized and communicated effectively. Much of the available information did not reach the [appropriate Senate] Committee, or reached it in a form that was too highly aggregated to be useful or that was difficult to digest. (GAO 1995:39)

BOX 8.1
HOW ARE EVALUATIONS USED?
WHEN ARE THEY INFLUENTIAL?

The following examples, taken from a review of evaluations that were considered to have been useful, illustrate the many different ways in which evaluations are used:

- Evaluations are only one piece of the puzzle, and the information will normally complement and reinforce information and opinions from many different sources.
- An evaluation, particularly if it is conducted by an independent and prestigious research or consulting agency, can provide political cover for agencies that need to make politically difficult decisions.
- Evaluations that identify both likely winners and losers from proposed policy changes will often have more influence. While many evaluations focus on who benefits, politicians are always anxious to identify influential groups who will be losers, and recommendations on how to mitigate the negative consequences for these groups will always gain the attention of politicians and policymakers.
- Evaluations can provide clients with the "big picture," helping them to understand the influence of the social, economic, and political context within which programs operate. Many clients operate within and tend to only focus on a particular sector, and this broader perspective can be very helpful.
- The evaluation can also help managers understand how political and other pressures can limit access of certain groups to project benefits.
- The evaluation can provide new knowledge or understanding (for example, explaining procedures or policies for external agencies with whom the client has not previously worked).
- Evaluations can also have a catalytic function: bringing people together or forcing action.

SOURCE: Bamberger, Mackay, and Ooi (2004 and 2005). Influential Evaluations: Evaluations That Improved Performance and Impacts of Development Programs. Operations Evaluation Department. Washington, DC: World Bank.

The GAO's report helped to explain why "the recent literature is unanimous in announcing the general failure of evaluation to affect decision-making in a significant way" (Wholey et al. 1970:46) and confirmed that "producing data is one thing. Getting it used is quite another" (House 1972:412)[1]. Evaluators are also concerned about the related issue of *misuse* of evaluation findings. House (1990) observed, "Results from poorly conceived studies have frequently been given wide publicity, and findings from good studies have been improperly used" (p. 26). In some cases, the misuse might be intentional, but in other cases it results from a lack of understanding of how to interpret and use evaluation findings (Best 2001, 2004).

---

[1]Several of the examples and citations in this paragraph are taken from Patton 1997, chapter 1.

Regarding evaluations of development programs, the World Bank Operations Evaluation Department (OED) recently concluded that "for all development agencies, monitoring and evaluation remains the weakest link in the risk management chain."[2] The Swedish International Development Agency (SIDA), in a recent assessment of its evaluation practices, found disappointingly that most stakeholders never even saw the findings and that most of those who did found nothing very new or useful.[3] They concluded that "for the majority of stakeholders evaluation could just as well have been left undone." A former director general of OED observed that the "prerequisite of credibility is missing in the evaluation systems used by most governments, companies and development agencies" (Picciotto 2002:14).

2.1. Why Are Evaluation Findings Underutilized?

Lack of ownership or investment in evaluation may be an inevitable result when, as is often the case, many stakeholders are never consulted about the objectives or design of the evaluation, are not involved in the implementation, and have no opportunity to comment on the findings. This is as true in the United States as in many developing countries. Many stakeholders never even get to see the report. For evaluations in developing countries, access and use are further limited because relatively few reports are translated into the national language of the country studied, and even fewer are available in the local languages spoken by many stakeholders. Civil society also frequently shows its frustration at the lack of involvement in the evaluation process.

There are a number of reasons why evaluation findings are underutilized:

- *Bad timing*: The findings are often not available when they are needed, making them largely irrelevant by the time they are available. At the other end of the project cycle, evaluators often wish to discuss baseline studies and evaluation design at the start of the project at a time when program management is still struggling to launch the project and when it is far too early for them to have any interest in thinking about results that will not become available for perhaps five years.
- *Lack of flexibility and responsiveness to the information needs of key stakeholders:* Evaluations are normally conducted according to their own administrative logic and frequently cannot respond to the information needs and deadlines of the stakeholders.
- *Wrong questions and irrelevant findings:* Many evaluations do not ask the questions of concern to stakeholders and provide information on topics that are of little interest.
- *Difficulties of attributing causality from complex programs:* The difficulties of attributing causality for complex programs operating in a context with many other actors and many exogenous factors, combined with time and budget pressures and a lack of comparative data, frequently make it impossible to produce very precise and conclusive evaluation findings.
- *Many evaluations are expensive and make too many demands on overtaxed program staff:* Even many potential supporters of evaluation may complain that the exercise requires more

---

[2]OED. Memorandum to the Executive Directors and the President on the Annual Report on Operations Evaluation, June 10, 2002.

[3]SIDA. 1999. *Are Evaluations Useful? Cases from Swedish Development Cooperation.* Department for Evaluation and Internal Audit.

resources in terms of funds, staff time, and effort than they feel are justified in terms of added value.

- *Lack of local expertise to conduct, review, and use evaluations:* The lack of familiarity with evaluation methods on the part of client agencies also limits their potential usefulness.

Wholey, Hatry, and Newcomer (2010 chap 27) identify nine sets of political and bureaucratic challenges that affect the use of evaluation (See Table 8.1). They are referring specifically to the U.S. government system, but all of the challenges probably apply in most other countries.

Table 8.1 Political and Bureaucratic Challenges Affecting Use of Evaluations

1. Institutional challenges: fragmentation among the Congress, the executive branch, and the courts; among congressional committees; and among federal, state, and local governments; legal and regulatory requirements; legislative and budget processes

2. Political challenges (narrowly defined): constituency, interest group, and advocacy group pressure; partisan politics; intraparty rivalries; individual legislators' pride of authorship of specific policies or programs

3. Competing ideologies, values, and goals

4. Organizational cultures, structures, policies, systems, and procedures

5. Changes in the organizational environment

6. Changes in organizational leadership

7. Lack of coordination and cooperation within agencies; overlapping accountability frameworks

8. Lack of interagency coordination and collaboration; overlapping accountability frameworks

9. Lack of willingness to use evaluation findings

SOURCE: Wholey, Hatry, and Newcomer (2010), Chapter 27, Exhibit 27.1.

2.2. The Challenges of Utilization for RWE

Ensuring that the findings of RWE evaluations are utilized offers additional challenges. First, many of the time and budget constraints that affect the conducting of the evaluation also affect the ability of the program staff to use the findings. The implementing agency is often understaffed, and clients often do not have time to attend briefing meetings on the evaluation or even to read the report. Funds may also not be available to bring key staff together for briefing meetings, and budget constraints limit the organization's ability to follow up on many of the recommendations. Time constraints may also make it particularly difficult to deliver the report in time for it to contribute to the decision-making process. The loss of even a few days can be critical in situations in which the evaluation team is only given a few weeks to conduct the evaluation and present the findings.

Many of the political constraints discussed in Chapter 6 affect the acceptance or implementation of RWE recommendations. As any experienced evaluator will tell you, if stakeholders agree with the findings, there are rarely any questions about the methodology, but if the findings are negative, claiming that the evaluation methodology was unscientific can be a convenient excuse for ignoring findings. RWE constraints may also affect the quality of the evaluation and, consequently, its credibility. Even if the mixed-method approach is able to provide reliable answers to the key questions of concern to the client, the lack of large sample surveys may affect the credibility of the findings in the eyes of some important stakeholders such as project management, the donor agency, or the Ministry of Planning or Finance. Consequently, it is very important to encourage the active involvement of the client right from the start to ensure that she or he understands and accepts the strengths and the limitations of the proposed methodology.

3. Strategies for Promoting the Utilization of Evaluation Findings and Recommendations

Ensuring the utilization of evaluation findings and recommendations requires a proactive utilization-focused strategy from the beginning of the evaluation. Box 8.2 identifies eight sets of actions for promoting utilization:

BOX 8.2
EIGHT ACTIONS TO PROMOTE EVALUATION UTILIZATION

A. Scoping the evaluation to ensure that it is based on a full understanding of the client's information needs, the program setting, and the context within which the evaluation will be implemented

B. Using a formative evaluation strategy

C. Constant communication with the client throughout the evaluation

D. An active evaluation-capacity development program

E. Strategies for overcoming political and bureaucratic challenges

F. Using "carrots, sticks, and sermons" to encourage utilization

G. Communicating the findings of the evaluation

H. Developing a follow-up action plan

3.1. The Importance of the Scoping Phase

One of the determinants of whether the evaluation will be useful and whether the findings will be used is the extent to which the clients are involved in the evaluation process (see Chapter 2 for a discussion of Step 1: Scoping the Evaluation). Do the clients feel that they "own" the evaluation, or do they not really know what the evaluation will produce until they receive the final report? How many evaluators have felt the frustration of a client reacting to an evaluation report by saying, "This is not what we wanted or expected"? The following guidelines for the scoping phase will help increase the likelihood that the evaluation will be useful:

Understand the Client's Information Needs (See Chapter 2)

Some of the critical questions to determine include:

- *What do the clients need to know and what would they simply like to know?* This distinction is critical when deciding whether the data-collection instruments can be simplified and information cut.
- *How will the evaluation findings be used?* To defend the program from its critics? As an initial exploration of whether a new approach seems to work? To present statistically precise estimates of whether the program has achieved quantitative goals? To estimate the cost-effectiveness of the program compared to competing programs?
- *How precise and rigorous do the findings need to be?* As we have emphasized earlier, some digging may be required to determine this. Sometimes the client will state that "a rigorous scientific evaluation" is required. The evaluator may assume this means that a large sample survey is needed to support pretest/posttest evaluation design with a comparison group, when in fact the client only means that the report must be considered by Congress, Parliament, or the funding agency to have been professionally conducted.

Box 8.3 offers guidelines for helping clients enhance the utilization of evaluation findings and recommendations; Box 8.4 lists lessons learned from a study on ways to enhance evaluation utilization.

BOX 8.3
GUIDELINES FOR HELPING CLIENTS USE THE EVALUATION

1. Scoping the evaluation
   a. Understand the client's information needs.
   b. Understand the dynamics and timetable of the decision-making process.
   c. Define the program theory on which the program is based in close collaboration with key stakeholders.
   d. Identify budget, time, and data constraints and prioritize their importance.
   e. Understand the political context.
   f. Prepare a set of RWE options to address the constraints and strategize with the client to assess which option is most acceptable.

2. Formative evaluation strategies
   a. Try to incorporate **process evaluation** and other methods that provide periodic feedback to clients on ways to improve project implementation.

3. **Constant communication with clients throughout the evaluation**
   a. Keep clients informed about the progress of the evaluation and the preliminary findings and hypotheses.
   b. Ensure there are no surprises for clients in the main evaluation reports.

(Continued)

(Continued)

4. **Strategies for overcoming political and bureaucratic challenges**

   a. Redesign management systems to focus on results.

   b. Create incentives for higher program performance.

   c. Develop agreement on key national, state, or community indicators.

   d. Develop performance partnerships.

5. **"Carrots, sticks, and sermons"**

   a. Provide rewards for individuals, departments, and agencies that are committed to the implementation and use of evaluations.

   b. Provide sanctions for those who do not implement or use evaluations.

   c. Provide indications of support from high-level and prestigious figures.

6. **Evaluation capacity building**

   a. Actively involve clients and users in the scoping phase.

   b. Ensure the program theory model is developed in a participatory way.

   c. Ensure users understand the trade-offs in the choice between RWE designs.

   d. Invite users to participate in the evaluation training programs for practitioners.

   e. Encourage users to participate in the periodic progress briefings on the evaluation.

   f. Involve users as resource people in briefings for other organizations that are planning evaluations.

7. **Communicating the findings of the evaluation**

   a. Understand what users want to know.

   b. Understand how different users like to receive information.

   c. Understand the kinds of evidence users want (statistics, case studies, photos, etc.).

   d. Ensure presentations are pitched at the right technical level.

   e. Consider separate customized presentations targeted for different audiences.

   f. Ensure reports are available in the user's language.

8. **Developing a follow-up action plan**

   a. Ensure there is user buy-in to the evaluation so users are prepared to consider using relevant findings and recommendations.

   b. Identify options but, where possible, let users decide the actions to be taken.

   c. Keep the role of the evaluation in the preparation of the action plan to that of low-key technical resource and facilitator. Sometimes it is better not to attend all action planning meetings to allow more freedom to the users.

   d. Ensure an action plan is prepared. The content should be left to the users to define as far as possible.

Understand the Dynamics of the Decision-Making Process and the Timing of the Different Steps

Many evaluations had little practical utility because they missed some critical deadlines or did not understand who the key actors in the decision-making process were. A report delivered on March 4 may be of no practical use if the Ministry of Finance had already made decisions on future funding on March 3! Similarly, utility will be reduced if the preliminary findings did not reach some of the key decision makers on time (or at all).

Define the Program Theory on Which the Program Is Based in Close Collaboration with Key Stakeholders (See Chapter 10)

It is essential to ensure that the clients and stakeholders and the evaluator are "on the same page" with respect to the understanding of the problem the program is addressing, what its objectives are, how it is expected to achieve these objectives, and what criteria the clients will use in assessing success. In some cases, it is necessary to formulate two or more program theory models to reflect the views of different stakeholder groups. This can be particularly important if the evaluation needs to recognize the views of important critics of the program. Even when conducting an evaluation under extreme time pressure, it is essential to find time to involve clients in this process so as to give them ownership and so they have a stake in the evaluation outcomes. Evaluators who prepare a model describing their understanding of the program would be well advised not to take the client's silence or unenthusiastic nods of the head as signals of full understanding and agreement.

Identify Budget, Time, and Data Constraints and Prioritize Their Importance and the Client's Flexibility to Adjust Budget or Time if Required to Improve the Quality of the Evaluation (See Chapter 2)

The constraints will be assessed by the evaluator, but their importance and the client's flexibility (e.g., to delay submission of the report or obtain additional funds) must be discussed and agreed to with the client. It will sometimes be found, for example, that the "deadline" for presenting the report is in fact only a deadline for the preparation of an informal status report. Similarly, there may be some

---

BOX 8.4
ENHANCING EVALUATION UTILIZATION—LESSONS LEARNED

The Operations Evaluation Department of the World Bank prepared case studies on evaluations in seven different countries that had a significant influence on the client agencies and on the design or implementation of future policies or programs. The following factors affected the likelihood that evaluation findings would be used:

- *The importance of a conducive policy environment*: The findings of the evaluation are much more likely to be used if they address current policy concerns and if policymakers are committed to accepting the political consequences of implementing the findings.

(Continued)

(Continued)

- *The timing of the evaluation*: The evaluation should be launched when decision makers have clearly defined information needs. The findings must be delivered in time to affect decisions, and key results must often be communicated informally before the final report is completed.
- *The role of the evaluation:* The evaluation is rarely the only or even the most important source of information or influence for policymakers and managers. A successful evaluation must adapt to the context within which it will be used, and the evaluator must understand when and how the findings can most effectively be used.
- *Building a relationship with the client and effective communication of the evaluation findings*: It is essential to establish a good relationship with key stakeholders, listen carefully to their needs, understand their perception of the political context, and keep them informed of the progress of the evaluation. There should be no surprises when the evaluation findings are presented.
- *Defining who should conduct the evaluation*: There are pros and cons of conducting an evaluation internally or of commissioning an independent external evaluation. It is important to determine the most appropriate arrangement for each evaluation. Sometimes a combination of internal and external evaluators can be a good compromise.
- *Adapting the scope and methodology of the evaluation to the client's needs and local context:* Sometimes utilization can be enhanced if the scope of the evaluation can be broadened or the methodology modified in response to a better understanding of client needs.

SOURCE: Operations Evaluation Department. World Bank 2004.

flexibility in the evaluation budget. However, these constraints and priorities must be fully discussed in a strategy session with the client, and the evaluator must never assume that, for example, "the client would not mind waiting a few more weeks to get a better report."

Understand the Political Context (See Chapter 6)

It is essential for the evaluator to understand as fully as possible the political context of the evaluation. The evaluation may often address sensitive or even confidential issues, so a great deal of sensitivity and tact is required. Some of the questions include:

- Who are the key stakeholders and what is their interest in the evaluation?
- Who are the main critics of the program, what are their concerns/criticisms, and what would they like to happen? What kinds of evidence would they find most convincing? How can each of them influence the future direction of the program (or even its continuance)?
- What are the main concerns of different stakeholders with respect to the methodology? Are there sensitivities concerning the choice of QUANT or QUAL methodologies? How important are large sample surveys to the credibility of the evaluation?

In addition to the sensitivity of the questions, the relationship with the client on these issues must also be treated carefully. While it is important to gain the confidence of the client, it is essential for the evaluator to maintain objectivity and not to be seen as an ally of program management against their critics.

Prepare a Set of RWE Design Options to Address the Constraints and Strategize with the Client to Assess Which Option Is Most Acceptable

A chart or similar format should be prepared describing several possible design options that can address the budget, time, and other constraints and highlighting the strengths and weaknesses of each one. It is particularly important that the client understands the trade-offs and how the validity of the conclusions can be affected by the different options. It is essential that clients see this as a strategy session in which they have a major role in making the final decision on the option to choose. The role of the evaluator is to advise on the consequences of each option and *not* to tell the client which is the "best" or the "correct" option. This is usually the most critical stage at which the client either buys into the evaluation or abdicates responsibility and ownership.

3.2. Formative Evaluation Strategies

An evaluation intended to furnish information for guiding program improvement is called a formative evaluation because its purpose is to help form or shape the program to perform better (Rossi, Lipsey, and Freeman 2004:34). A central element of the RWE approach, particularly for QUANT evaluations, is that, even when the primary objective is to assess program outcomes and impacts, it is important to open up the black box and to study the process of program implementation[4]. This is important for the following reasons:

- To explain why certain expected outcomes have or have not been achieved.
- To explain why certain groups may have benefited from the program while others have not.
- To identify and assess the *causes* of outcomes and impacts. These may be planned or unanticipated, positive or negative.

BOX 8.5

USING FEEDBACK FROM PROCESS ANALYSIS TO IMPROVE PROJECT PERFORMANCE (FORMATIVE EVALUATION)

The following are examples of feedback for process evaluations:

- The material supply stores (for a self-help housing program) need to stay open later in the evening so that people can go there after work.

(Continued)

---

[4]The issue of the "black box" (a term widely used in economic analysis) only concerns QUANT pretest/posttest evaluation designs in which data are only collected at the start and the end of the project and the project-implementation process is not studied. Many authors, including Stufflebeam's CIPP, Greene's participatory, Stake's responsive, Patton's utilization, Fetterman's empowerment, Scriven's goal-free, House's democratic approaches, do not treat implementation or process as a black box.

> (Continued)
>
> - Less educated people are discouraged from applying for small loans because the forms are too difficult for them.
> - There are frequent complaints that bribes must be paid to staff in the health clinics.
> - Absentee rates for girls in high school increase because many girls are teased when they walk through the village to school.

- To provide a framework for assessing whether a program that has not achieved its objectives is fundamentally sound and should be continued or expanded (with certain modifications) or whether the program model has proved not to work—at least not in the contexts where it has been tried so far.

In addition, the analysis of the program-implementation process also means that the evaluation can contribute formatively to improving the performance of the ongoing program. Positive contributions can be made by providing regular feedback and suggestions to program management and other key stakeholders or by involving program staff and other stakeholders in the evaluation so that they learn for themselves what is working and what is not.

Many but not all formative evaluation strategies help promote evaluation utilization as stakeholders start to use the findings of the process evaluation long before even the draft final evaluation reports have been produced. Involving the clients at this early stage also means they are more likely to review the final reports and consider how to use the recommendations.

Box 8.5 gives examples of feedback from process analysis can be used as formative evaluation to improve project implementation.

3.3. Communication with Clients Throughout the Evaluation

Promoting a positive attitude toward evaluation findings often involves ensuring that clients face no surprises. The client should be kept informed of the progress of the evaluation and of preliminary findings as they emerge. In particular, the client should be fully briefed on and should have a chance to react to the final conclusions and recommendations before they are presented or made available to others. Clients tend to react more defensively to negative findings if they are sprung on them in a formal meeting with other agencies or, even worse, if they learn the findings from the press or another agency.

As always, there is the need to involve clients while maintaining neutrality. This is particularly the case where some negative or sensitive results are coming out that the client may wish to suppress.

The communication strategy should be developed before the evaluation begins and should identify:

- Who needs to receive information
- What information they need at what phase
- What format of information should be used
- When/how frequently should the information be provided
- Who is responsible for providing the information

3.4. Evaluation Capacity Building

A commitment to evaluation capacity building is a key factor in promoting evaluation (see Chapter 18).

3.5. Strategies for Overcoming Political and Bureaucratic Challenges

Wholey and colleagues (2010), drawing on experience with the U.S. public sector, proposes four strategies for overcoming political and bureaucratic challenges:

- *Redesigning management systems to focus on results.* Agency cultures and management systems typically focus on process and give little attention to the results of the agency programs. The recent focus on management for results and results-based monitoring and evaluation (Morra-Imas and Rist 2009 and Kusek and Rist 2004 require agencies to focus on results/ achieving their stated outcomes) increases interest in and demand for M&E systems that provide feedback on progress toward results.
- *Creating incentives for higher program performance.* "If evaluators seek to have their work used in government, they should look for ways to alter the individual and organizational incentives systems that drive behavior" (Wholey, Hatry, and Newcomer, 2010, chap 27). Wholey lists a range of intangible and financial incentives targeted to both managers and staff and to organizations. For example, intangible incentives for managers and staff could include: performance-focused meetings with senior managers, honor awards, public recognition, favorable publicity, increased responsibility, more interesting work, removal of constraints, delegation of authority, better office space or better parking, more flexible hours, additional leave, and performance agreements. Mackay (2007), referring to the strengthening of M&E systems in developing countries, proposes a combination of "carrots" (positive incentives), "sticks" (negative sanctions), and "sermons" (public displays of support from high-level officials). These are discussed in Chapter 18.
- *Developing agreement on key national, state, or community indicators.* In the United States, a number of states (e.g., Oregon Benchmarks and Virginia Performs) and foundations (e.g., the Casey Foundation's Kids Count) have developed benchmarks to inform members of the public, advocacy groups, legislators, and public and nonprofit agencies about trends in health, education, social, economic, and environmental conditions (Wholey et al. 2010). Wholey and colleagues (2010:663–4) cite United Way of America as saying that community indicators "can present a compelling snapshot of a community's status [and] may serve as powerful catalysts to ... fostering collaboration and mobilizing resources" (United Way 1999:1). "The use of key indicators increases the demand for reliable performance measurement systems and evaluation studies, and can stimulate the use of evaluation findings among many actors who may wish to learn about approaches that have been effective in improving conditions and who can influence legislation."
- *Developing performance partnerships.* Often, the achievement of benefits for the target population will require changes or improvements in how several agencies operate and how they cooperate among each other. With performance partnerships, two or more agencies agree to take joint responsibility for achieving specific outcomes. These partnerships will usually require the development and use of a performance measurement system to monitor progress on the areas of collaboration.

3.6. Communicating Findings

Many potentially useful evaluations have little impact because the findings are not communicated to potential users in a way that they find useful or comprehensible—or, even worse, because the findings never ever reached important sections of the user community. The following are some guidelines for communicating evaluation findings to enhance utilization:

- Clarify what each user wants to know and the amount of detail required. Do specific users want a long report with lots of tables and charts or a brief overview? Do they want many details on each project site, school, and region or just a summary of the general findings?
- Understand how different users like to receive information. In a written report? In a group meeting with slides or PowerPoint? In an informal personal briefing?
- Clarify whether users want hard facts (statistics) or whether they prefer photos and narratives. Do they want a global overview, or do they want to understand how the program affects individual people and communities?
- Be prepared to use different communication strategies for different users. One size usually does not fit all.
- Ensure presentations are pitched on the right level of detail or technicality. Do not overwhelm managers with statistical analysis or detailed discussion of sample design, but do not insult professional audiences by implying that they could not understand the technicalities.
- Ascertain what the preferred medium is for presenting the findings. A written report is not the only way to communicate findings. Other options include: verbal presentations to groups, video, photographs, and meetings with program beneficiaries or visits to program locations. Sometimes attending a meeting in the community in which residents talk about the program can have much more impact than a written report.
- Make sure the communication is in the right language(s) when conducting evaluation in multilingual communities or countries.

3.7. Developing a Follow-Up Action Plan

Many evaluations present detailed recommendations with very little practical utility because the recommendations are never implemented—even though all groups might have indicated their agreement with the proposals. What is needed is an agreed-upon action plan with specific, time-bound actions, clear definition of responsibility, and procedures for monitoring compliance. Many government and international agencies have standard procedures to monitor the implementation of evaluation recommendations, but such systems are used much less frequently for RWE-type evaluations. For example, many agencies keep a log of all recommendations included in their evaluations, management response to these recommendations and the agreed-upon actions, and periodic follow-ups to report on the status of the agreed actions.

SUMMARY

In order to ensure that the findings and recommendations of RWEs are fully utilized, it is essential to have a clearly defined strategy to promote utilization. Some of the steps include:

- As we have stressed above, a key strategy involves ensuring client and stakeholder buy-in to the evaluation process so that there is willingness to review, and where there is agreement, implement the evaluation findings.

- The evaluation report must identify the key issues on which decisions must be taken and follow-up actions agreed upon. However, the external evaluator needs to be cautious about presenting specific recommendations so as to not discourage users from taking ownership of the action plan. In preparing the report, the evaluator, in consultation with the clients, must decide whether it is better to:
  - Present a list of issues but not propose specific actions
  - Present a number of follow-up options but not recommend which one is best
  - Present specific recommendations on follow-up actions. This may be appropriate when discussing technical issues (for example, which financial management package is compatible with the computer systems used by the agency).
- The action plan must be developed by the interested organizations with the evaluator as a technical resource and, possibly, facilitator. It is sometimes better for the evaluator not to participate in the action planning meetings so as to give more feeling of ownership and freedom of action to the agencies themselves.
- Often, the evaluator can help develop measurable indicators and timetables to monitor progress. One of the evaluator's key contributions is to ensure that the action plan is actually developed before she or he leaves.

FURTHER READING

Bamberger, M. and A. Kirk, eds. 2009. *Making Smart Policy: Using Impact Evaluation for Policy Making. Case Studies on Evaluations That Influenced Policy.* Doing Impact Evaluation Series No. 14. Thematic Group on Poverty Analysis, Monitoring and Impact Evaluation. Poverty Reduction and Economic Management. The World Bank.

The report describes 12 evaluations of education, health, antipoverty, and sustainable development programs that we considered to have been influential. The methodology and findings of each evaluation are described together with an assessment of how they were influential and the factors that contributed to their usefulness.

Operations Evaluation Department. 2004, 2005. *Influential Evaluations: Evaluations That Improved Performance and Impacts of Development Programs.* Washington, DC: World Bank. Available at www.worldbank.org/oed/ecd

This describes eight evaluations from countries in Africa, South and East Asia, and Eastern Europe that had a significant impact on the future directions of the programs or policies evaluated. A set of criteria is applied for determining whether observed changes could be attributed to the evaluation and where possible cost-effectiveness analysis was applied to demonstrate that evaluation can be an effective management tool. The final chapter includes lessons on how to design and implement useful evaluations. The summary (2004) report is available in English, Spanish, French, Portuguese, Arabic, and Russian. The 2005 report provides more detailed information on each case study.

Patton, M. Q. 1997. *Utilization-Focused Evaluation.* 3d ed. Thousand Oaks, CA: Sage.

This is one of the most comprehensive and widely used texts on evaluation utilization.

Rossi, P., M. Lipsey, and H. Freeman. 2004. *Evaluation: A Systematic Approach.* 7th ed. Thousand Oaks, CA: Sage.

Chapters 2 and 12 (pp. 411–18) are particularly useful with respect to stakeholder analysis and the social and political context of evaluation.

Thomas, A. and G. Mohan. 2007. *Research Skills for Policy and Development: How to Find Out Fast.* London. Sage/The Open University.

This collection of readings is aimed at development managers and others who are involved in policy investigation for international development and other development fields. It distinguishes clearly between academic research and research designed to help formulate policy and development planning. The different sections discuss how to conceptualize policy-related investigation, the logic of using documents, interviews with people, and collecting and presenting data.

Wholey, J., H. Hatry, and K. Newcomer, eds. 2010. *Handbook of Practical Program Evaluation.* San Francisco: Jossey-Bass.

The *Handbook* draws on the extensive experience of the authors in how program evaluation is used by the federal and state governments in the United States. It has a very practical focus and includes extensive illustrations of the political and organizational constraints on the implementation and use of evaluations. The six chapters of Part 4 discuss the use of evaluation.

PART II

A Review of Evaluation Methods and Approaches and their Application in RealWorld Evaluation

*For those who would like to
dig deeper on particular evaluation topics*

CHAPTER 9

Standards and Ethics

I n order to minimize the negative consequences of social science to persons and to societies, governments and organizations have formalized expectations in law and in professional codes of conduct. Addressing issues of competence and ethics, these formalities offer protections but also suffer limitations. Evaluators, subject to legally binding regulations incumbent on all social scientists, have developed more specific voluntary guidelines. Both legal restraints and nonbinding professional expectations impact the practice of evaluation in the real world. This chapter discusses codes of competent and ethical practice for evaluation with attention to The Program Evaluation Standards (Yarbrough et al. 2011) in the context of RealWorld constraints.

1. Responsible Professional Practice

As applied social scientists, evaluators serve society by collecting, analyzing, and conveying information intended to improve programs, policies, institutions, products, and the functioning of personnel. Although "contributing to organizational or social value" (Yarbrough et al. 2011) is the aim, the effort can go awry. Not only can clients ignore or misuse results, as evaluators have long lamented (Chelimsky 1999; Fitzpatrick and Morris 1999; Morris and Cohn 1993), but evaluators can be irresponsible in either of two ways: *insensitivity*, which has an obvious ethical dimension, and *incompetence*, which has a less obvious ethical dimension. Insensitive evaluators can ignore or misrepresent groups of stakeholders, lack cultural competence, and create unnecessary risks for vulnerable respondents. Incompetent evaluators can produce faulty designs, gather useless or inaccurate data, analyze it clumsily, or submit ill-timed or misleading reports with erroneous findings that lead to social and organizational harm.

History shows all too well that promising programs can be closed or threatened because of evaluations (DeStefano 1992; House et al. 1978; Stevens and Dial 1994) and that research subjects or participants can be abused rather than respected. For example, in the infamous Tuskegee experiments, the course of syphilis in impoverished African-American men was *studied* rather than *treated*, contrary to what the subjects were told (Jones 1993), the government apologizing to the few surviving research participants 65 years later (Hunter-Gault 1997). In Stanley Milgram's obedience research, subjects thought they were *to compel* obedience by administering (fake) electric shocks to unseen others but were actually *being compelled* to obey against their wishes (Milgram 1963, 1974). In Laud Humphreys's study of clandestine homosexual encounters, subjects were observed without realizing that they would be individually (and illegally) identified or that their behaviors were being recorded for publication (Humphreys 1970). Such egregious practices have necessitated efforts to ensure ethical conduct in social science, including evaluation.

1.1. International Standards

In the pursuit of information for human advancement, the benefits of research have never been equally available to all persons. The record includes instances in which some have paid dearly for potential benefits to others. For example, the first heart transplants were performed on unwilling victims in Nazi concentration camps—"experiments" that, when they became known after World War II, led to promulgation of the Nuremberg Code to protect human beings worldwide (International Military Tribunals 1949). Other international standards were developed by the United Nations (1948, 1966, 1990, 2005) and the World Medical Association (1964/1996).

Compliance to international codes and standards has proven difficult to compel without recourse to national laws and enforcement. Even then, individuals, entire societal sectors, or even national self-determination may be at risk where social scientists (or their sponsoring agencies) in one country can evade protective laws in another. For example, exploitation of the citizens of poor countries has been documented in biomedical research (Macklin 2004) where the rights of research subjects or participants have been effectively trumped by the financial interests of pharmaceutical corporations (or other research sponsors) to advance their own proprietary or financial interests.

In evaluation, a continuing example highlights the conflicting interests of the World Bank as opposed to those of financially strapped borrower countries. The Bank has established an evaluation department and has also commissioned external evaluations of its projects in developing countries, evaluations that have overemphasized the Bank's financial interests by prioritizing "economic analysis of investment choices" (Psacharopoulos and Woodhall 1991:10). The misfocusing, sometimes acknowledged even by the Bank (World Bank Independent Evaluation Group 2006), runs counter to the *Program Evaluation Standards'* admonition against "favoring a specific evaluation method or approach without proper regard for the needs of the actual stakeholders" (Yarbrough et al. 2011:116) and also to the *Guiding Principles* of the American Evaluation Association (2004):

> Evaluators should explore with the client the shortcomings and strengths both of the various evaluation questions and the various approaches that might be used for answering those questions . . . [and should use] appropriate evaluation strategies and skills in working with culturally different groups. (p. 2)

The overemphasis on outcomes desired by the Bank also runs counter to the multi-organization *Program Evaluation Standards'* stipulation that "[e]valuation conclusions and decisions should be explicitly justified in the cultures and contexts where they have consequences" (Yarbrough et al. 2011:165).

The relative over-prioritization of the client and disregard of other stakeholders has had "harmful impact on poor people, increasing their poverty, not reducing it" (Kovach and Lansman 2006:3) rather than "guarding against unintended negative consequences" as the *Standards* require (Yarbrough et al. 2011:65). The *Guiding Principles* further stipulate that evaluators include relevant perspectives and interests of the full range of stakeholders. . . . consider not only the immediate operations and outcomes of whatever is being evaluated, but also its broad assumptions, implications and potential side effects. . . . [and] maintain a balance between client needs and other needs. . . . [C]lear threats to the public good should never be ignored in any evaluation. . . . [E]valuators will usually have to go beyond analysis of particular stakeholder interests and consider the welfare of society as a whole. (p. 4)

Yet, the societal consequences of Bank evaluations in the Education sector have included prohibitive educational fees (Kovach and Lansman 2006), overreliance on standardized testing without regard to "educational quality and outcomes" (World Bank Independent Evaluation Group 2006:26) and the "jeopardising [of] public commitments to educational quality" (Jones 1992:249), and the privatization of schooling (Kovach and Lansman 2006).

1.2. Government Regulation

International guidelines, not easy to enforce, were followed by the enactment of national laws to regulate ethical behavior by social scientists. For example, in 1974, based on the Nuremberg Code, the United States adopted the *Belmont Report* (National Commission for the Protection of Human Subjects of Biomedical and Behavioral Research 1979) and, five years later, legalized protections for the human subjects of research. Current U.S. statute requires that potential research subjects be invited to participate in a study, be informed about the methods and potential risks, consent in advance to participate, and retain the right to withdraw at any time. Going beyond the Nuremberg Code, U.S. law also provides that research and evaluation designs be approved in advance by panels referred to as Institutional Review Boards (IRBs). IRBs, however, do not interpret the law uniformly (Stair et al. 2001), indicating just one limitation of government regulation.

Another problem: No government is equally interested in protecting all its citizens. Some ethnic groups or economic classes tend to be routinely denied privileges, including protections from legal, economic, and other risks. Nor do all governments subscribe to the same concepts of ethics or justice. Self-governing societies are more likely than totalitarian regimes to try to ensure the safety of citizens, but not necessarily on the same basis—and some ethical approaches are more protective than others. For example, *utilitarian* ethics (Mill, 1863/1891) tolerates harm to a few for the good of the many. By contrast, Rawls's (1971/1999) widely accepted theory of justice accepts no casualties, founded on the notion of commensurate rights and opportunities for all. Beyond even that, *transformative* ethics (Mertens 1999, 2001) deliberately tips the scales in favor of the disenfranchised to empower them toward full participation and rights.

Governments are rarely inclined to go so far; a more typical approach follows **deontological** ethics (see Flinders 1992), delineating expectations formally as a matter of policy, which governments can back up with regulatory or statutory penalties. This approach reduces ethical practice to compliance with rules, which governments have the power to enforce. Thus, some protection to subjects and stakeholders is provided, but not without complications. For example, governments may favor certain research topics, methods, or researchers, and they may control social science inquiry through approval requirements or funding preferences. These powers can exacerbate the differential privileges of citizens that accrue from variations in wealth, class, gender, age, tradition, or other bases. For example, in comparison to women's health issues, men's health issues have long benefited from disproportionate research funding in the U.S., a situation that has only recently been redressed.

Governments certainly have the obligation to safeguard their citizenries, and the need for some degree of protective oversight of social science is historically evident. However, appropriate balancing of independence and oversight in policy has proven elusive, and many researchers and evaluators chafe at governmental regulations (Begley 2002; Denzin 2003; Oakes 2002). The distress has been particularly evident where government policies have targeted not only *ethics* but also research and evaluation *designs* and *methods* (AEA 2003; Berliner 2002; Chelimsky 2007; Datta 2007; Eisenhart and Towne 2003; Erickson and Gutierrez 2002; Feuer, Towne, and Shavelson 2002; Mabry 2008b; men's health issues have long benefited from disproportionate research funding in the United States, Pellegrino and Goldman 2002; Viadero 2007).

1.3. Professional Codes of Conduct

Professional associations whose members engage in social science have developed their own codes of conduct, sometimes in the service of ethics, sometimes in the service of competent practice, sometimes both. By identifying practices and risks specific to each field, these codes can be more nuanced and detailed than generalizable national or international standards.

However, the standards of professional organizations tend to be aspirational and "voluntary, consensus statements . . . approved by the members" (Yarbrough et al. 2011:xxii) lacking enforceability. As is the case for many such groups, membership in the American Sociological Association (1997) implies voluntary conformity to its code of conduct, while the American Psychological Association explicitly decouples its *Ethical Principles of Psychologists and Code of Conduct* (2007) from civil liability. In contrast to the general trend, the National Association of Social Workers exhorts members "who believe that a colleague has acted unethically" to report suspected violations to a committee of the association or to an external "state licensing board or regulatory body" (1996/1999, n.p.).

Although more specific than laws that cover the entire range of social science, professional codes nevertheless fail to anticipate the myriad situations inevitable in practice where "many factors influence how standards are applied " (Yarbrough et al. 2011:xxx). Consequently, a practitioner's application of standards requires balancing and prioritizing among various provisions (House 1995), and some conflicts among standards that are unapparent in the abstract but manifest in practice inevitably prove irreconcilable (Mabry 1999). Recognition of the complexities of application is evidenced by the practical scenarios provided in *The Program Evaluation Standards* (Yarbrough et al. 2011).

The difficulty of balancing among standards is exacerbated by the proliferation of professional codes to which an individual social scientist may be subject as a result of membership in more than one professional organization. In explicitly recognizing that its members may engage in multidisciplinary studies falling under the aegis of several professional organizations' codes, the American Anthropological Association (1998) implicitly recognizes that what is forbidden by one organization but unaddressed (or allowed) by another may offer spurious justification for opportunistic exploitation of the gap. The Joint Committee on Standards for Educational Evaluation has tried to bridge the gap for evaluators by offering itself "as a contact point facilitating comparisons and contrasts" (Yarbrough et al. 2011:xxxix), but comparison falls short of resolution.

Moreover, professional codes do not encumber practitioners who are not members of professional organizations. The standards of the National Council on Measurement in Education (1995) make this painfully clear by encouraging nonmembers to follow its guidelines. Yet, NCME does not so much as monitor compliance by its members.

2. Evaluation Codes of Conduct

As in other fields, codes of conduct have been developed in evaluation that address both ethics and competence but, in program evaluation there are particular risks related to the potential termination of programs, which can jeopardize jobs, needed benefits, and the public good. While there has been worry that "incompetent evaluators, charlatans, and crooks may well pass as seasoned professionals" (Stevahn et al. 2005:45; see also Stufflebeam 1997), reflecting badly on the field as a whole, perhaps more serious is the persistence of the question, "What does ethics have to do with evaluation?" (Newman and Brown 1996:89). Longstanding ethical concerns have included impartiality (House 1993); the effects of funding pressures and political conflicts (Chelimsky 1999, 2007; Sheinfeld and Lord 1981); misunderstanding, misrepresentation, and depersonalization of stakeholders (Walker 1997; Mabry 1997, 1999, 2001); and reinforcement of unequal power relationships (Abma 1997).

Evaluation professional codes of practice in evaluation were established, notably including *The Standards for Program Evaluation* (Yarbrough et al. 2011) and *The Guiding Principles for Evaluators* (AEA 2004). However, nearly a decade after the initial effort (Joint Committee on Standards for Educational Evaluation 1988), it was reported that "evaluation principles are violated both frequently and seriously" (Newman and Brown 1996:87).

While additional efforts have been made to establish *evaluator competencies* (King et al. 2001; Stevahn et al. 2005) and to formalize checklists "to improve the quality and consistency of evaluations" (Evaluation Center, undated, n.p.), professional organizations have declined to ratify them officially. Even when described as "refereed" (The Evaluation Center, undated, n.p.), the checklists are subject to a further caveat: "It is not always helpful to simply list . . . what allegedly needs to be done . . . especially when the issues are highly controversial" (Scriven 2007:1; see also Scriven 2005).

2.1. The Guiding Principles for Evaluators

The professional code formulated by the American Evaluation Association (2004) indexes *Guiding Principles for Evaluators* according to five overlapping categories: *systematic inquiry, competence, integrity or honesty, respect for people,* and *responsibilities for general and public welfare* (see Box 9.1). While the first three categories essentially address technical competence, the final two focus specifically on ethical practice, encouraging evaluators to "respect the security, dignity and self-worth of respondents, program participants, clients, and other evaluation stakeholders" (p. 3).

BOX 9.1
THE GUIDING PRINCIPLES FOR EVALUATORS (AMERICAN EVALUATION ASSOCIATION 2004)

Systematic inquiry

Competence

Integrity or honesty

Respect for people

Responsibilities for general and public welfare

Not only individuals but also societies are encompassed by the *Principles*. As the AEA has increasingly recognized the importance of cultural competence and the globalization of evaluation, it has taken pains to note that:

> These principles were developed in the context of Western cultures, particularly the United States, and so may reflect the experiences of that context. The relevance of these principles may vary across other cultures, and across subcultures within the United States. (p. 6)

Despite urging sensitivity to individuals and cultural contexts, the *Guiding Principles* are an example of deontological ethics (see Flinders 1992) in admonishing evaluators to "abide by current professional ethics, standards, and regulations regarding risks, harms, and burdens that might befall those participating in the evaluation" (AEA 2004:3). The implication is that adherence to the *Principles* will assure (or help assure) ethical practice, with the caveat that

> it is impossible to write guiding principles that neatly fit every context in which evaluators work, and some evaluators will work in contexts in which following a guideline cannot be done for good reason (p. 1)

> at which point evaluators "should consult colleagues about how to proceed" (p. 1).

The necessity of interpretation is the Achilles heel of a deontological approach to evaluation ethics. More than a matter of conformity to principles, judgment is needed for applying principles in highly contextualized circumstances (Mabry 1999). Yet evaluator judgment is susceptible. Clientism, the positive bias injected into evaluations, deliberately or not, in order to preserve contracts and future work (Scriven 1991) is just one pervasive threat. Another is limited imagination and reasoning to interpret, for example, which harms are "unnecessary," or to determine "when the benefits from doing the evaluation . . . should be foregone because of the risks," or to "balance between client needs and other needs," or to "foster social equity" (pp. 3–4). How is an evaluator to be sure of having identified all of the "relevant perspectives and interests of the full range of stakeholders" (p. 4)?

2.2. The Standards for Program Evaluation

Such questions are not answered even by the more voluminously explained *Program Evaluation Standards* (see Box 9.2). Long organized under the designations *utility, feasibility, propriety*, and *accuracy* (Joint Committee on Standards for Educational Evaluation 1988, 1994), *evaluation accountability* has been added in the most recent revision of the *Standards* (Yarbrough et al. 2011) but without provision for actually holding evaluators accountable for competent practice. The *evaluation accountability* standards also lack a clear statement related to protecting from harm individuals or groups of stakeholders; the statements do not even reference IRB oversight.

BOX 9.2
THE PROGRAM EVALUATION STANDARDS
(YARBROUGH ET AL. 2011)

Utility

Feasibility

Propriety

Accuracy

Evaluation accountability

By contrast, the *utility* standards promote inclusiveness in advocating "attention to the full range of individuals and groups invested in the program and affected by its evaluation" (p. 23) and to the "needs of stakeholders" (pp. 29, 45). The *feasibility* standards also require attention to social contexts, urging evaluators to "recognize, monitor, and balance the cultural and political interests and needs of individuals and groups" (p. 93). The *accuracy* standards similarly encourage evaluators to "document programs and their contexts with appropriate detail" (p. 185) and stipulate that "[e]valuation conclusions and decisions should be explicitly justified in the cultures and contexts where they have consequences" (p. 165). The *utility* standards further urge evaluators to guard "against unintended negative consequences and misuse" (p. 65).

Ethical Implications

It is the *propriety standards* that have the most obvious connection to ethics. They emphasize fairness, inclusion and transparency, attention to the cultural contexts of stakeholders, and protection of human and legal rights as "an integral part of evaluation" (p. 125). They admonish evaluators to practice in a manner "consistent with local, state, and federal laws. . . . [even] when laws in one stakeholder jurisdiction conflict with those in another . . . [and] may require legal counsel" (p. 107).

Note that strict adherence requires evaluators to develop, for *each* evaluation, familiarity with an array of legal and regulatory provisions—a considerable demand but also a mere minimum. Beyond legal compliance in context, evaluators "should be knowledgeable about stakeholders' *experienced* rights" (p. 106, emphasis added), which may differ from their statutory rights. Moreover, evaluators should "inform stakeholders of their rights" (p. 127) as needed and respect them "from the design through dissemination" (p. 106).

Cultural competence, the admonition that "evaluators should be knowledgeable about social manners and mores" (p. 126) moves the profession from deontological ethics to *ecological ethics* (see Flinders 1992) and practice that supports rather than intrudes upon settings. Consider that anthropologists and ethnographers hold that the acquisition of cultural knowledge takes very extended periods of time, longer than the timeframe of most evaluations. Even working in one's own context, as internal evaluators do, calls for "making the familiar strange" (Erickson 1986:121) in an anthropological or ethnographical sense so that the ordinary can be seen from a new and revealing perspective. Nevertheless, the *propriety standards* advise that "attending to stakeholders and their contexts is . . . a moral and professional duty" (p. 114).

The moral implications of methodological choices is implied in the *propriety standards*, which recommend that evaluators "[d]evelop culturally sensitive and congruent methods that support the well-being of communities and participants" (p. 127). Qualitative methods are generally recognized as more culturally congruent than quantitative methods, largely because qualitative methods require *in situ* study, much more contact with research subjects or stakeholders, and the development of rapport with individuals. While this contact has the potential to disturb privacy and confidentiality, it also permits deeper understanding of individuals and their ethos. Qualitative methods also tend toward the *standards*-required "inclusive orientation [that] helps stakeholders make their own judgments and interpretations" (p. 115) and toward "culturally appropriate ways . . . to disseminate information to stakeholders" (p. 141).

Political Implications

The urging of inclusiveness and "fair and equitable relationships with stakeholders . . . [to] lessen the danger that powerful stakeholders' questions and interest will dominate while the perspectives, needs, or interest of others are ignored" (p. 114) takes evaluators beyond ecological ethics and into the explosive arena of political advocacy (House 1991; House and Howe 1998; Mabry 1997; Patton 2002a; Scriven 1998). The *propriety standards* reason:

> [T]o be fair, evaluations must justify any differential valuing of any stakeholders' evaluation needs over the needs of other stakeholders ... [although] in some contexts the existing political and cultural rules are designed to benefit some groups ... [U]nfairness is often created when the wants of individuals in more powerful groups receive greater attention than the needs of those in less-empowered groups. (pp. 131–32)

This reasoning leads to an explicitly political stance in which "[e]valuations should be as inclusive as possible because it is one of the basic values of a democratic society" (p. 114) and evaluators are cast in the role of "public stewards ... [who] respect and promote the dignity of diverse groups, cultures, and traditionally underserved populations" (p. 126). The obligations of this role are spelled out:

> [E]valuators should be able to understand and address the needs of the least powerful in society without jeopardizing their safety and well-being ... where evaluation can be a method for democratizing. (p. 109)

In urging inclusiveness of all stakeholders, the first of the *propriety standards*:

> presumes a social justice perspective ... [the] empower[ment of] stakeholders to function as skilled participants in democratic institutions even beyond the action evaluation ... [as] a moral good.... [and that evaluators] do not exacerbate oppression, discrimination, power differences or other imbalances. Instead, whenever possible, they attempt to interrupt such forces so as to contribute to improved democratic functioning and social betterment. (pp. 114–15)

Values Implications

An obvious complication here is that neither all evaluators nor "all stakeholders have the same values or conceptions of social justice" (p. xxviii). A more imposing but unaddressed complication is that neither all evaluators nor all clients favor a radical approach to practice. While some evaluators already work toward social change (Freeman 2010), others are extremely unlikely to forsake a technical role for a political one (Mabry 2009). Adherence to technical responsibilities can result from training focused on technical skills and the predispositions and habits of mind that ensue or from an assumption that only value-free, technical information will be credible. Good arguments for the latter have been advanced (Scriven 1997, 1998). However, focus on the technical might also stem from lack of imagination, lack of courage to tackle value laden issues with political implications, or unwillingness.

This aspect of the *Standards* make clear that an evaluator's personal values matter in practice (see also Mabry 1997, 1999). They cannot be set aside as the evaluator crosses a boundary between personal and professional life. An inescapable component of identity, personal values survive attempts at compartmentalization and manage nonetheless to influence all behavior, either consciously or unconsciously.

But the *Standards* are too optimistic in stating that "evaluators should make explicit their own moral principles and codes of conduct" (p. 126). Evaluators, like everyone, honor tacit values, moral principles so deeply held that they are inarticulable, presumed rather than recognized. Their values, at least some of them, may not be explicit even to themselves. Also, like everyone, evaluators discover and refine their values in everyday experiences. Dynamic, they are not amenable to being pinned down but, rather, may change during the course of an evaluation. This is especially likely where evaluators follow the *Standards'* many prescriptions to understand and honor diverse interests, populations, and contexts.

3. Ethics in the RealWorld of Evaluation

Although the *Standards* recognize that "most evaluations are designed and implemented with restricted resources" (Yarbrough et al. 2011:xxvi), they nevertheless impose demands that will, in many cases, strain an evaluation to bursting. Of particular interest here is the intensification of time and political constraints.

3.1. Time Constraints

A serious attempt to comply with the *Standards* will necessarily consume time. In the service of ethics, competence, and professionalism, the time may be well-spent, but it may be hard to find enough time to address ethics expectations alone.

Time will inevitably be required to abide by stipulations calling for sensitive attention to "the full range of stakeholders" (p. 4) in evaluations that are "as inclusive as possible" (p. 114). Considerable resources may be needed even to identify all those who may be affected by an evaluation, much less to become familiar with their needs, interests, and values. The *Standards* identify evaluators as "public stewards" (p. 126) but also hint at other roles vis-à-vis stakeholders: therapists regarding their "dignity and self-worth" (p. 3), guards of their "security" (p. 3), advocates and legal representatives protecting them from infractions of their rights (pp. 125, 127) and from potential negative consequences of evaluation (p. 65).

Cultural competence sufficient to meet the *Standards* will also require time but is so important as to be delineated as "a moral and professional duty" (p. 114). Time will be needed to learn about local "manners and mores" (p. 126); to "document programs and their contexts with appropriate detail" (p. 185); to justify findings, especially if they involve "differential valuing of any stakeholders' evaluation needs over the needs of other stakeholders" (p. 131) "in the cultures and contexts where they have consequences" (p. 165); and to find " culturally appropriate ways . . . to disseminate information" (p. 141).

Part of the expected response to context involves the *Standards'* requirements that evaluators be familiar with the federal, state, and local laws and regulations relevant for each evaluation setting and even with "stakeholders' *experienced* rights" (p. 106, emphasis added). Outsourcing or designating a team member to acquire legal and regulatory familiarity, if funding allows, would shift the onus from time to budget constraints.

3.2. Political Constraints

In RealWorld Evaluation, the *Standards* may open new prospects for values-informed practice, create daunting challenges, or foreclose on opportunities altogether. Exciting as the more optimistic visions may be, in the real world of evaluation, clients rarely (if ever) request evaluations focused on those *Standards* that imply or demand upheaval of social hierarchies or political rights. Evaluators who trumpet the more politically inflammatory of *Standards* may lose contracts or encounter strains with clients, strains that can have spill-over effects regarding access to data.

A likely source of stress will involve making sure that the client's needs do not "receive greater attention than the needs of those in less-empowered groups" (p. 132), groups not directly paying the costs of the evaluation. The *Standards* require this kind of evenhandedness as a matter of fairness, urging evaluators allocate time to "recognize, monitor, and balance the cultural and political interests and needs of individuals and groups" (p. 93).

The choice of methods for data collection and analysis are not to be simply negotiated with the client (or predetermined in a Request for Proposals) but, rather, designed to "support the well-being of communities and participants" (p. 127). The *Standards* call for dissemination to be similarly handled, and seem to imply time-consuming qualitative methods and narrative reporting, whether or not clients approve.

Beyond this level of relative disregard, clients are even less likely to appreciate the *Standards'* avowed "social justice perspective" (p. 114) or an evaluator's efforts to "interrupt" power differentials in the service of "improved democratic functioning" (p. 115). Clients hiring evaluators are not generally looking for political activists or restructurers of personnel hierarchies, and the *Standards* do not encourage surreptitious efforts in this regard (p. 126).

Bringing the *Standards* into RealWorld Evaluations complicates already highly complex practical considerations. The challenges are great, so practitioners may need to remind themselves that evaluation is an applied social science that is meaningless unless it serves people—whatever their politico-cultural circumstances—and that is counterproductive unless it serves them well.

SUMMARY

As their potential for harm to persons became manifest, researchers and evaluators became subject to restrictions from national, international, and professional organizations. Professional codes of conduct suffer from the enforceability available with statutory guidelines but offer more specific guidance to practitioners in each of the various fields of social science. These guidelines typically target competent and ethical practice.

In evaluation, the *Guiding Principles for Evaluators* of the American Evaluation Association (2004) and the more detailed and multi-organization *Program Evaluation Standards* (Yarbrough et al. 2011) call for ethical treatment of all stakeholders and stakeholder groups, sensitivity regarding cultural contexts, and actions that promote fairness and social justice. Challenges regarding time and political constraints ensue for evaluators in the real world.

FURTHER READING

American Association of University Professors. 2001. "Protecting Human Beings: Institutional Review Boards and Social Science Research." *Academe* 87(3):55–67.

Australasian Evaluation Society. 2006. *Guidelines for Ethical Conduct of Evaluations.* Retrieved from www.aes.asn.au

Australian Institute of Aboriginal and Torres Strait Islander Studies. 2000. *Guidelines for Ethical Research in Indigenous Studies.* Canberra, AU: Author.

British Educational Research Association. 2004. *Revised Ethical Guidelines for Educational Research.* Notts, UK: Author.

Centre for Social Research and Evaluation. 2004. *Guidelines for Research and Evaluation with Maori.* Ministry of Social Development, NZ: Author.

Coryn, C. L. S. 2009. "The Fundamental Characteristics of International Models and Mechanisms for Evaluating Government-Funded Research." *Access: Critical Perspectives on Communication, Cultural & Policy Studies* 27(1/2):9–25.

Coryn, C. L. S., and M. Scriven. 2007. "Are National-Level Research Evaluation Models Valid, Credible, Useful, Cost-Effective, and Ethical?" *Journal of Multidisciplinary Evaluation* 4(8):92–96.

Dewey, J. D., B. E. Montrosse, D. C Schröter, C. D. Sullins, and J. R. Mattox. 2008. "Evaluator Competencies: What's Taught versus What's Sought." *American Journal of Evaluation* 29(3):268–87.

Evergreen, S. D. H. and A. Cullen. 2010. "Moving to Genuine: Credible Cultural Competence." *Journal of Multidisciplinary Evaluation* 6(13):130–139.

Fisher, C. B. 2003. *Decoding the Ethics Code: A Practical Guide for Psychologists.* Thousand Oaks, CA: Sage.

Hood, S., R. K. Hopson, and H. Frierson, eds. 2005. *The Role of Culture and Cultural Context in Evaluation: A Mandate for Inclusion, the Discovery of Truth, and Understanding in Evaluative Theory and Practice.* Greenwich, CT: Information Age.

Morris, M., ed. 2008. *Evaluation Ethics for Best Practice: Cases and Commentaries.* New York, NY: Guilford.

Picciotto, R. 2005. "The Value of Evaluation Standards: A Comparative Assessment." *Journal of Multidisciplinary Evaluation* 3:30–59.

Posavac, E. J. and R. J. Carey. 2003. *Program Evaluation: Methods and Case Studies.* 6th ed. Upper Saddle River, NJ: Prentice Hall.

Russon, C. and G. Russon, eds. 2004. *International Perspectives on Evaluation Standards.* New Directions for Evaluation, No. 104. San Francisco: Jossey-Bass.

Shaw, I. F. 2003. "Ethics in Qualitative Research and Evaluation." *Journal of Social Work* 3(1):9–29.

Thurston, P. W., J. C. Ory, P. W. Mayberry, and L. A. Braskamp. 1984. "Legal and Professional Standards in Program Evaluation." *Educational Evaluation and Policy Analysis* 6:(1):15–26.

Collections of evaluation standards adopted by national and international bodies are posted online at www.european evaluation.org/library/evaluation-standards

CHAPTER 10

Applications of Program Theory in RealWorld Evaluation

I n this chapter, we discuss the use of program theory in evaluation and some of its main applications. Program theory is particularly useful for RealWorld Evaluation (RWE) because it helps identify the critical issues on which scarce evaluation resources should focus, and where possible a program theory model should be developed during Step 1 (scoping) of the evaluation. Although the term program theory[1] is used, at least until recently the approach has mainly been used at the project level, frequently to provide a summary of the framework (typically referred to as a theory of change or logical framework, or logframe) for an M&E system. When the approach is used at the program level to model multicomponent and often multilevel interventions that often do not have clearly defined start and end points, more complicated models are required. However, although more complicated to model, program theory models have also proved to be a valuable tool at this level as well. Two submodels are frequently combined in program theory: the impact model (sometimes called the theory of change model) and the implementation model (sometimes called the logic or action model).[2] The construction of these two submodels and their main components are discussed together with the ways in which each is used. Although all programs are based on a set of ideas and assumptions about the problems being addressed, how the program will work, and what it will achieve, in too many cases these assumptions have not been made explicit. Often one of the tasks of the evaluator is to work with the client and other stakeholders to elicit and formulate the underlying program theory or logic model. Logical framework analysis (logframe) is one form of logic model used by many agencies to monitor program performance. Results-Based Management is another model commonly used. The chapter concludes with a review of some of the different perspectives on the extent to which program theory can help explain causality.

---

[1] We will follow the convention of using the term *program theory* even when it is applied at the project level.

[2] There is often overlap and confusion between the terms *model* and *design*. We define *model* as "different approaches to evaluation" (see note 4) and *design* as the methodologies used to determine whether a project or program has produced the desired outcomes and impacts. Although there are differences between the various forms of theory models, we use the terms rather interchangeably in this book.

1. Defining Program Theory Evaluation

Program theory evaluation "consists of an explicit theory or model of how the program causes the intended or observed outcomes and an evaluation that is at least partly guided by this model" (Rogers, Petrosino et al. 2000:5). Program theory "identifies program resources, program activities, and intended program outcomes, and specifies a chain of causal assumptions linking program resources, activities and intermediate outcomes and ultimate program goals" (Wholey 1987:78). Also known as program theory (Bickman 1987), theory-based evaluation (Weiss 1995, 1997), program theory-driven evaluation (Donaldson 2007), and program logic (Funnell 1997, 2000; Lenne and Cleland 1987), program theory evaluation has been gaining in popularity due to the recognition that a program's success or failure can be assessed only with a clear understanding of the problem it was intended to address, the rationale for choosing a particular approach, and how the program was expected to operate.

Program theory can significantly strengthen quantitative pretest–posttest evaluation designs. Critics of these designs often refer to them as "**black box**" evaluations (see Figure 10.1) because no information is collected on what actually happens inside the **project** while it is being implemented. If the degree of change of measured indicators between the pretest and posttest is not significant, at least compared to a control group, it is not possible to judge whether the failure was due to a weakness in the analysis and theory on which the project was based ("design failure"); weaknesses in how the project was implemented ("implementation failure"); or the effects of a particular set of contextual factors such as a weak economy, political opposition, lack of support from partner agencies, or environmental and climatic factors ("contextual constraints").

Figure 10.1 Weaknesses of the "Black Box" Approach to Evaluation

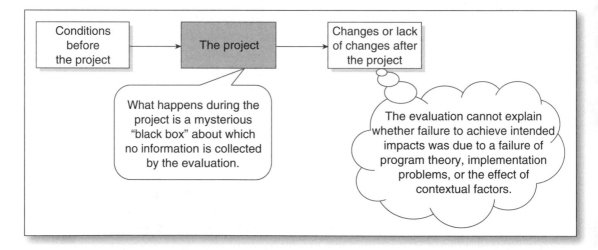

The purpose of program theory evaluation is to help explain why expected impacts were or were not achieved by assessing the following:

- The strengths and weaknesses of logic of the program theory underlying the project or program design
- The strengths and weaknesses of how the project or program was implemented
- How contextual factors contributed to, or militated against, the achievement of intended impacts
- How the project or program affects, and is affected by, different groups

In this way, program theory can contribute to improving the design and implementation of ongoing projects or programs (**formative evaluation**); assess how any impact was achieved (**summative evaluation**); and also recommend whether, where, and how the program could be scaled up or applied in other settings.

2. Applications of Program Theory in Evaluation

2.1. The Increasing Use of Program Theory in Evaluation

Program theory in evaluation is now used extensively by government agencies, not-for-profit organizations, and discipline-specific research journals in many fields including education, criminology, and sociology (Rogers, Petrosino et al. 2000). For example, the U.S. National Institutes of Health now require the discussion of program theory in all research proposals, and the Centers for Disease Control and Prevention (CDC) has developed extensive training material to assist the organizations with which it works to strengthen their capacity in the use of logic models (Centers for Disease Control 1999). Three separate volumes of *New Directions for Evaluation,* a periodical published by the American Evaluation Association (AEA), have been devoted to program theory evaluation, and many evaluation textbooks (e.g., Chen 2005; Creswell 2003; Rossi, Lipsey, and Freeman 2004) include chapters on program theory. In the United States, many nongovernmental organizations (NGOs) and the organizations that fund them (e.g., W. K. Kellogg Foundation 1998) also provide extensive guidance on the use of logic models. The Community Tool Box (2005) is one example.[3]

Logical framework analysis ("logframe") or one of its variants (see later in this chapter), in spite of its limitations, has until recently been one of the most common ways to translate program theory into performance indicators that can be monitored and evaluated, and was required by many national and international development agencies, including the World Bank, the U.S. Agency for International Development, and the U.K. Department for International Development. Most international development agencies and many governments and NGOs have now replaced logframes with Results-Based Management (RBM) as the framework on which their M&E and program evaluation systems are based. RBM is a refinement of the logframe approach, but with more emphasis on the measurement of results (see later in this chapter).

By identifying critical assumptions and issues in program design, program theory can contribute to improving the way in which the program is managed and implemented by ensuring that the monitoring system provides feedback on issues affecting performance (see Box 10.1).

BOX 10.1
APPLYING PROGRAM THEORY TO EVALUATE THE FAMILY EMPOWERMENT PROJECT

Bickman and his colleagues conducted an experimental test of the effects of a program that trained parents to be stronger advocates for children in the mental health system. They articulated a model of how the program was assumed to work. First, parent training would increase the parent's knowledge, self-efficacy, and advocacy skills. Second, parents would then become more involved in their child's mental health care.

(Continued)

---

[3]The Community Tool Box provides detailed guidelines and case studies on how to plan and assess the participation of community-level organizations in the United States. See, for example, Chapter 36 of the tool box (available free online at http://ctb.ku.edu/tools/en/chapter_1036.htm).

(Continued)

Finally, this collaboration would lead to the child's improved mental health outcomes. They also constructed measures, collected data, and then analyzed them to test these underlying assumptions. The program was able to achieve statistically significant effects on parental knowledge and self-efficacy, but no useful measures for testing advocacy skills could be found. Based on this model, it was found that the intervention had no apparent effect on caregiver involvement in treatment or service use and ultimately had no impact on the eventual mental health status of the children.

SOURCE: Bickman (1987).

By pointing out where to look, a program theory can increase the practical utility of monitoring and rapid assessment studies. For example, a program theory that anticipates different ways that men and women are likely to participate in and be affected by the project or program can help ensure that relevant sex-disaggregated monitoring and performance indicators are used.

Developing a program theory can assist evaluation design in the following ways (see also Chen 2005:74):

- *Defining the project or program rationale.* What problem is the project or program trying to alleviate or resolve? On which target groups does it focus? Which interventions are used to affect implementation and outcomes? On which determinants should the evaluation focus? What goals or outcomes are to be achieved?
- *Clarifying stakeholders' implicit program theories.* Program planners and implementers almost always have assumptions about why this program approach is better than other options and how it is expected to work and produce the desired results. Frequently, these assumptions or hypotheses have not been written down or clearly articulated in a manner that can be used for developing the program theory. Sometimes different staff members or stakeholders have different assumptions that may be tested. For example, some staff members may feel that the inculcation of moral values is a key factor in determining success of programs for youth, whereas others may feel that the organization of sports and other group activities is more important.
- *Articulating program rationale.* Programs are often based on explicit or implicit assumptions about the needs that should be addressed. It could be helpful to conduct a social and economic study or needs assessment for answering such questions as these: What are the most important social, economic, cultural, psychological, and security problems affecting the community? How could the program address them? This information might be obtained through interviews with community leaders and other key informants, focus groups, and rapid socioeconomic surveys.
- *Choosing interventions/treatments that affect the problems the project or program is designed to address.* Usually a number of different interventions can be used to address the problems on which the program is focused. These options should be identified (e.g., a review of the literature, experience from earlier programs and evaluation reports, consultation with specialists in the field) and the strengths and weaknesses of each approach assessed.

- *Identification and analysis of unintended effects.* Many programs have unanticipated effects, some of which may be positive (e.g., when the experience gained in this project encourages a community council to launch other projects) or negative (e.g., if the project creates conflicts between different groups in the community or the construction of a road leads to an increase in robberies and violence by outsiders who can now more easily visit the community). Sometimes the program theory will be able to specify some of the effects. (See Figure 10.2 for an example of how potential negative effects were identified for a **microcredit** program for women.) In many cases, a program theory will be able to alert evaluators and staff to some of the areas where such effects might occur.

- *Identifying the critical areas or linkages of the program to evaluate.* Figure 10.2 also illustrates how program theory (in this case in the form of a **results chain**) can identify critical areas or linkages. For example, once new businesses established by women drawing on a microcredit program begin to generate profits, it is possible that these profits will not be reinvested in the business (as intended in the program design), but instead be taken by the husband or used by the woman to provide her daughter with a dowry or to pay off debts. A program theory might be helpful in identifying this as one of the critical issues to be assessed in an evaluation.

- *Using program theory to help scale up successful programs.* By identifying and then assessing the critical assumptions on which the program was based, program theory can help assess the likely success of expanding the program to benefit larger numbers of stakeholders. It can also help identify the elements of program design that will require particular attention if it is expanded.

2.2. Utility of Program Theory for RealWorld Evaluation

Program theory can be particularly valuable for RWE in helping to identify priority issues on which to concentrate when working under time, budget, and possibly data constraints. For example:

- What are the critical links and assumptions on which the success of the program depends? Do the key issues address whether the program will be able to reach all the target groups (e.g., ethnic minorities, landless laborers)? Will the program's inputs (e.g., training, technical assistance, mentoring) be sufficient to produce the desired effects? Will the effects be sustainable over time?

- What are the critical links and assumptions for which additional information is needed? An analysis of the literature, consultation with experts, or a review of earlier project evaluations may be able to help determine which links in the program theory model are supported by existing data and which might be dubious or require investigation.

- Which are the key issues or areas of concern to program managers and other key stakeholders? Consultations with managers and stakeholders as the program theory is developed during the scoping phase (see Chapter 2) will help identify priority issues for management. Often the realization that there is no firm **evidence** to support some assumptions may also highlight the importance of new questions.

- Which links or assumptions are most critical for assessing the potential expansion of the program? When evaluation resources are tight, program theory can help identify the questions that are critical. For example, a pilot job-training program to help young men move from welfare to work may include subsidies (e.g., travel vouchers, help with car payments) that would not be included in a large-scale replication of the program. Consequently, a critical question for replicability might be whether the kinds of jobs that the young men are able to get pay enough for them to stay at work without these subsidies.

Figure 10.2   A Results Chain Model of a Women's Microcredit Project

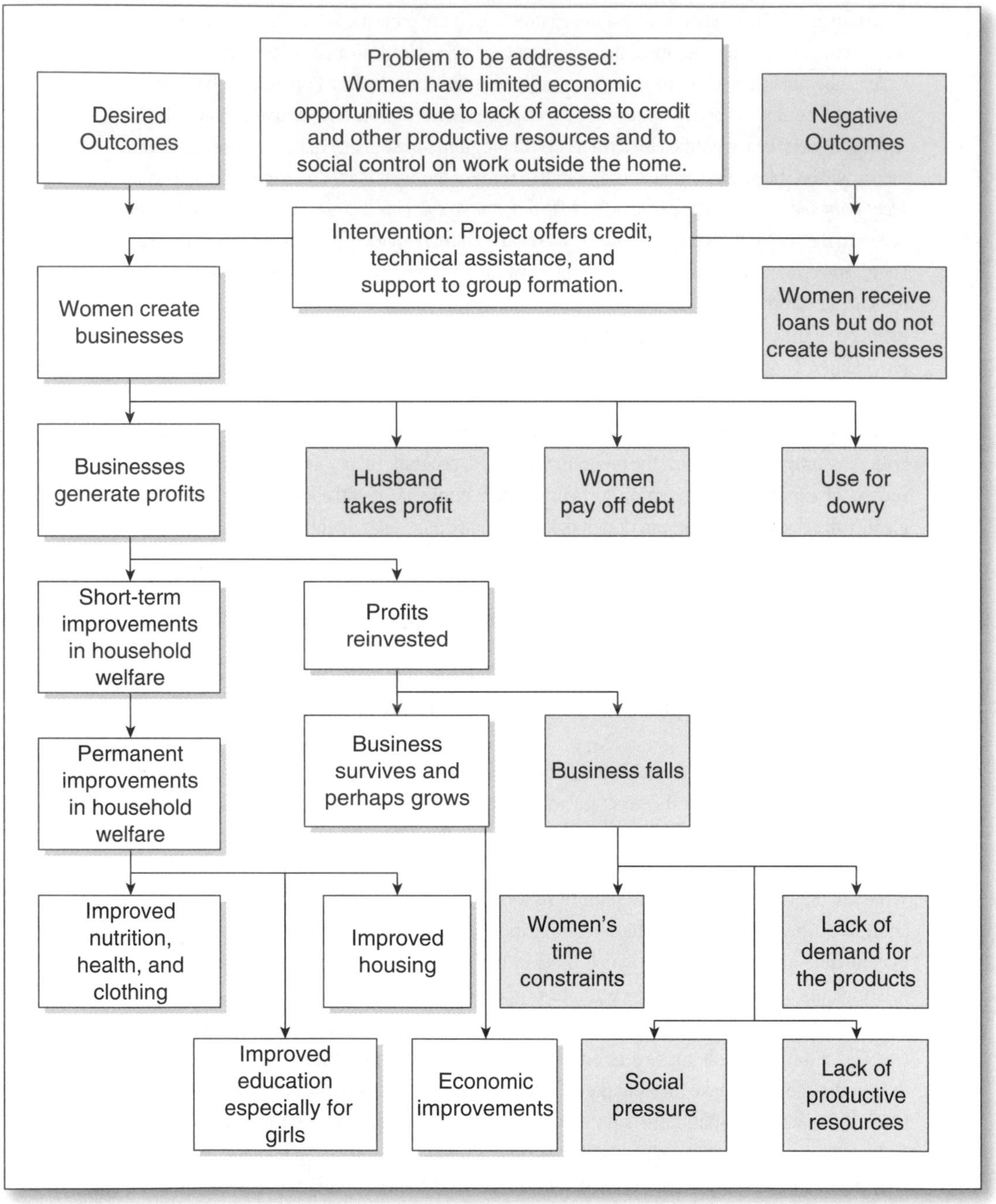

- What initial indicators of program success can be used? Using a results chain model similar to the one in Figure 10.2 can often identify economical and easy-to-measure indicators showing that the program is on the right track. These can be very useful for RWE if resources are not available to conduct a full evaluation covering all stages of the program (i.e., long-term economic impact or effects on girls' education).

- Can program theory suggest some simple and economic ways to determine program impact? Our view is that, when used with the appropriate caveats, program theory can suggest some useful tentative indications of potential impacts. However, readers should read Section 5.1 of this chapter presenting both sides of the argument and decide for themselves.
- Can program theory help distinguish between theory failure and implementation failure (Chen 2005; Lipsey 1993)? In cases where the intended program effects have not been achieved, program theory can help determine whether the program model (underlying hypothesis) does not work or whether it is a potentially good model requiring fine-tuning for effective implementation.

3. Constructing Program Theory Models

Figure 10.3 summarizes the possible stages in the development of a program theory model. Not all theory models include all of these stages.

Figure 10.3 The Stages in the Development of the a Program Theory Model

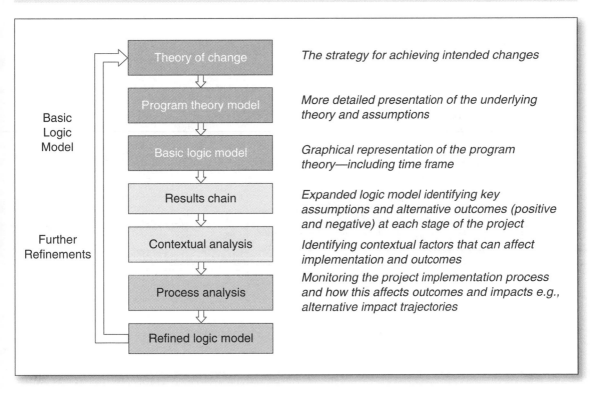

There are three steps in the development of the basic logic model:

Step 1: Definition of the theory of change underlying the model. Morra-Imas and Rist (2009) quote ActKnowledge and Aspen Institute (2003) as defining a theory of change as "an innovative tool to design and evaluate social change initiatives," a kind of "blueprint of the building blocks" needed to achieve the long-term goals of a social change initiative. While some theories of change present a very detailed and often complex model of how an intervention is intended to achieve its objectives, other approaches try to keep the model as simple as possible so that all stakeholders, including community organizations with no previous exposure to models, can understand the basic logic of what the intervention is intended to achieve (results) and what the key strategies are that will be used to achieve the results. This latter approach is important because many program theories and logic models (e.g., Steps 2 and 3 below) are too complicated for many stakeholders to understand. Keep in mind that different forms of logic models may be useful for different audiences.

Figure 10.4 presents an example of a very simple theory of change that was used in a workshop with the Ministry of Environment in Brazil to help identify the intended short-, medium-, and long-term results of an antipoverty program designed to increase environmental awareness of low-income urban and rural communities. Workshop participants reported that they had found this simple model to be very helpful, as they had previously been exposed to very detailed and complicated logical frameworks identifying all of the inputs, activities, outputs, and outcomes of their programs. So while everyone was able to describe the activities for which they were responsible and the outputs the activities were intended to produce, many staff did not have a clear understanding of the ultimate purpose of their programs and the results to be achieved.

Figure 10.4   A Theory of Change for Minas Gerais, Brazil, Antipoverty Program

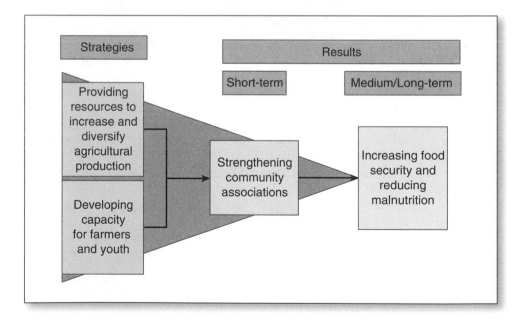

Step 2: Articulation of the theory of change in a program theory model. This provides the underlying rationale on which the theory is based. These can include review of the literature including evaluations of similar projects in the past, experience from previous projects, exploratory studies, planning workshops, and consultations with different stakeholder groups and experts.

Step 3: Graphical representation of the program theory (logic model). Sometimes a single model is used (see the example in Figure 10.5 discussed below), while other authors (e.g., Chen 2005) propose the use of two models, one to describe how the program plans to achieve its intended results (impact model) and a second to describe the different agencies involved in the process of project implementation and the relationships between them (implementation model).

A number of refinements can be made to the basic model, as described in the following steps:

Step 4: A results chain to identify the expected results and the possible constraints or negative effects at each stage (see Figure 10.2).

Step 5: Contextual analysis to quantify and assess the importance of the contextual factors (discussed below).

Step 6: Process analysis to monitor how the project is actually implemented and how this compares with the project design and assess how any deviations from the plan affected outcomes or impacts on the basis of new information obtain from M&E and other studies.

Step 7: Refinements to the initial logic model. As new information is obtained from the M&E system and other sources, the initial logic model should be periodically revised to reflect the more complete understanding of the project/program and how it operates, as well as the external context and how it may have changed over time. It is also possible to include additional refinements such as the expected trajectory of project outcomes and impacts (discussed below).

3.1. Program Impact and Implementation Models[4]

A program theory includes both descriptive assumptions about the causal processes, explaining the social problems a program is trying to address, and prescriptive assumptions about the components and activities that program designers and other stakeholders consider necessary to a program's success. As we mentioned above, some authors propose a single logic model while others use two separate models to describe the program impact model (based on the theory of change) and the program implementation model.

Figure 10.5 illustrates a somewhat enhanced version of a single logic model. This includes the seven stages of a typical project, including design, inputs, implementation processes, outputs, outcomes (short- and medium-term impacts), long-term impacts, and sustainability. It also identifies five sets of contextual factors (economic, political, policy, institutional and organizational, environmental and socioeconomic characteristics of the affected populations) that can affect implementation and outcomes and that help explain why projects that are implemented in the same way can have very different outcomes in different project locations. Importantly, this logic model also includes a projected timeline over which the different

---

[4]Evaluation models are different approaches to evaluation. Stufflebeam (2001a) identifies 22 evaluation models that he categorizes into four groups: pseudo-evaluation, quasi-evaluation studies, improvement or accountability-oriented, and social agenda or advocacy. Various other classifications describe models in terms of purpose, assumptions, organization, questions asked, strengths and weaknesses, intended users, primary methodology, proponents of the model, epistemology, and ethics (Mathison 2005:256–68). In this book, we distinguish between quantitative, qualitative, and mixed-method models or approaches.

stages of the model are expected to be achieved. As we will see later, the timeline describing when (usually in years) the different stages of the project are scheduled to start and to produce their respect outputs, outcomes, and impact can be critical in the design of the impact evaluation. When the timeline is not included, there is a risk that outcome or impact evaluations will be scheduled when it is too early in the **project cycle** for them to have been achieved and to be measurable.

Descriptive assumptions are generally based, at least in part, on an analysis of available research and evidence from other programs, and often include a needs assessment or rapid diagnostic study of the social, economic, cultural, security, and other characteristics of the subjects or communities that the program is intended to affect. *Prescriptive assumptions,* on the other hand, are based on judgments and values about which intervention strategy should be selected. These assumptions may be based on a review of earlier projects or consultation with specialists, or they may be largely based on personal values concerning what is the "right" way to address the problems.

The descriptive assumptions are translated into a *program impact model* (Donaldson 2003) articulating the assumptions about the causal processes underlying the decisions to use certain program strategies. Some program theories also develop a *program implementation model* describing how the program will be organized to achieve the intended outcomes and impacts. Depending on the focus of the evaluation, it may be that only one of these two models will suffice, often the case for RWE operating with budget and time constraints. If the purpose of the evaluation is to assess the achievement of goals and impacts, then the impact model will probably be sufficient. If, on the other hand, the purpose is to assess effective implementation and the production of outputs in order to help improve performance (formative evaluation), then the implementation model may be preferred. In some cases, and resources permitting, it may be useful to use both models.

3.2. Program Impact Model

Different terminology has been used to describe the components of an *impact model* (Bamberger et al. 2004; Chen 2005; Creswell et al. 2003; Donaldson 2003; Rossi et al. 2004), sometimes indicated by terms such as *change model.*[5] Figure 10.5 illustrates a program impact model for a women's microcredit project. This model integrates the following components:

Contextual Variables (the Setting).[6] A contextual analysis is conducted to identify and understand the social, economic, psychological, security, and environmental setting within which the project operates and the problems, needs, priorities, and constraints of the intended project beneficiaries and the different stakeholders. Projects implemented in the same way in different communities, schools, or regions can have very different outcomes because of differences in these **contextual variables**. This analysis may cover the following:

- *The economic climate.* Are economic conditions getting better, remaining constant, or getting worse? This will influence the decisions of families as to whether or not they want to participate in any project that either requires payments or that promotes present or future income-generating activities.

---

[5]Chen (2005) uses the term *change model.*

[6]This component is not included in the Chen (2005) and Donaldson (2003) models. However, conceptual factors are similar to what Donaldson (2003) defines as *moderators.*

Figure 10.5 An Impact Model for a Women's Small Business Development Program

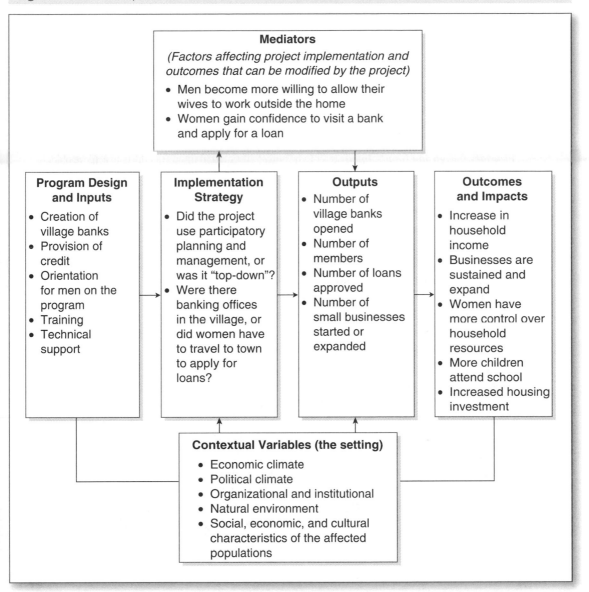

Mediators

(Factors affecting project implementation and outcomes that can be modified by the project)
- Men become more willing to allow their wives to work outside the home
- Women gain confidence to visit a bank and apply for a loan

Program Design and Inputs
- Creation of village banks
- Provision of credit
- Orientation for men on the program
- Training
- Technical support

Implementation Strategy
- Did the project use participatory planning and management, or was it "top-down"?
- Were there banking offices in the village, or did women have to travel to town to apply for loans?

Outputs
- Number of village banks opened
- Number of members
- Number of loans approved
- Number of small businesses started or expanded

Outcomes and Impacts
- Increase in household income
- Businesses are sustained and expand
- Women have more control over household resources
- More children attend school
- Increased housing investment

Contextual Variables (the setting)
- Economic climate
- Political climate
- Organizational and institutional
- Natural environment
- Social, economic, and cultural characteristics of the affected populations

- *The political climate.* Is the local political climate likely to support or undermine the project?
- *Organizational and institutional factors.* To what extent do local organizations (government, NGOs, and private sector) support or hinder the project?
- *Natural environmental factors.* In what ways do environmental factors influence the project?
- *The characteristics of the communities affected by the project.* How do social, cultural, economic, and other characteristics influence how different groups respond to the project or are affected by it? How might the needs, problems, constraints, and expectations of the different groups affect the project?

The contextual analysis can be derived from a review of the literature, the opinions of stakeholders, a rapid assessment study, or a needs assessment during which the target group is consulted. The needs assessment might use a market research approach in which a target group is surveyed and asked to select among a set of options relating to the planned program strategies, or it might use a participatory assessment method in which families identify their concerns, needs, and proposed solutions. (See, for example, Dayal, van Wijk, and Mukherjee [2000]; Rietberger-McCracken and Narayan [1997]; Theis and Grady [1991]). In a microcredit example (see Figure 10.2), a contextual analysis identified a number of constraints on women's access to economic opportunities, including labor laws, labor union protection of male workers, and women's difficulties in obtaining bank loans.

Program Design and Inputs. Inputs refer to resources allocated to program efforts to achieve objectives and goals (e.g., money, staff, materials, trainers, vehicles, teaching materials).[7] This includes what some authors call *interventions.* Although some interventions are intended to directly achieve program goals (for example, emergency food or medical supplies), in most cases, programs are designed to influence **mediators** (see below) through changing knowledge, attitudes, or practices. In the case of a women's small-business development project, interventions might include the organization of women's savings and loans groups, orientation sessions to reduce the opposition of men to their wives starting their own businesses, in addition to the provision of credit.

Implementation Strategy. The implementation strategy refers to the way in which inputs are used to produce the planned outputs and achieve the desired effects. Many agencies refer to these as *activities.* Two programs using the same inputs might achieve different results depending on their implementation strategies and the quality of how their activities are carried out. For example, one project may use participatory planning and management in which stakeholders were actively involved in program design, implementation, and monitoring, while another uses top-down planning with design and management by the client or funding agency. Similarly, one microcredit project might open an office in a community, while another might require women to travel to the nearest town to apply for loans.

Mediators.[8] Mediators are **intervening variables** potentially affecting project performance that the project may be able to influence (Donaldson 2003). Most programs are influenced by many factors that exert influence on program outcomes. There are, of course, many external, contextual variables that are outside the direct control of an intervention program. What we are referring to here are those factors that are essential to motivating people to participate in a program, or potential barriers to such participation. For example, in the case of a health program, mediators might include how a person's course of action is influenced by his or her perceived susceptibility to illness, perceived seriousness of the problem's consequences, perceived benefits of a specific action, and perceived barriers to taking action (Strecher and Rosenstock 1997, cited in Chen 2005:21). For a microcredit program, mediators could be the willingness of husbands to allow their wives to work outside the home following an orientation session on the program, or poor rural women gaining sufficient confidence, after joining a village banking group, to visit the local bank to apply for a loan.

---

[7]Some authors, for example Chen (2005), use the term *interventions* to cover both the resources (what we call *inputs*) and the way the resources are used (what we call the *implementation strategy*, or *activities*). However, we consider it helpful to distinguish between the two because the same inputs can have very different effects depending on the implementation strategy and how well the activities are carried out.

[8]Chen (2005) combines moderators and mediators into a single category, *determinants*, but the present authors consider it better to separate the two because they operate in different ways (see Donaldson 2003).

Outputs. Outputs are the immediate results that a project seeks to achieve, and over which it has direct control. In the case of a small-business development project, these might include the creation of a certain number of village banks with a certain number of members and the authorization and repayment of a certain number of loans.

Outcomes and Impacts. These are the short-, medium-, and long-term changes in behaviors or conditions or systems that the project hopes to affect, the achievement of which it may influence but does not have direct control. Again referring to the microcredit example, outcomes and impacts might include the number of businesses started or expanded; the additional income earned; the increase in women's control over family resources and role in family decision making; and the improvements in family living conditions, such as increased school attendance, better health, and increased investment in housing. A project's implementations will hopefully make significant contributions to such impacts, but there are many other factors that affect such changes, positively or negatively.

3.3. Applying Program Theory at the Level of Sector-Wide and Multicomponent Programs and Complex Country-Level Interventions

We indicated earlier in this chapter that program theories and their articulation through logic models are easier to use at the level of a simple project that involves relatively few components or services, is time-bound (has a clear start and end date), has a defined and often relatively small and geographically concentrated target population, and often has a defined budget. Another advantage of projects is that they are often linear, in that there is a sequence of events with inputs and activities clearly preceding the production of outputs and outcomes. However, even at the project level the above considerations often apply better to projects funded by an external donor agency or by a government department. Many projects managed by NGOs are not necessarily that straightforward.

With respect to programs, the situation becomes more complicated. Many programs involve a wide range of services, including capacity development and institution building; they have a larger but not clearly defined target population; and they may not have a defined start and end dates. They may also operate at different levels (e.g., classroom, school, education district, and the national ministry of education) and may involve a larger number of actors. In addition, many programs are not linear, as feedback from different levels (classrooms, schools, etc.) may lead to modifications in how the program operates and even to the incorporation of new components. This will often require the development of a number of different logic models describing how the program operates at different levels, and the interactions among different subcomponents. In spite of those challenges, many agencies have been able to develop logic models that work at the program level. Figure 16.5 (Chapter 16) presents a relatively simple multilevel logic model that could be applied to the evaluation of programs such as the education example described above.

When we move to the level of complex, often national-level interventions, the situation becomes more challenging (see Chapter 16). These complex interventions, with names like country assistance strategy, will often comprise a quite large number of different programs working with different agencies, and often with very little direct connection between the different components. Often there will be a number of different donor agencies funding and managing different parts of the program, each with their own objectives and management style (see Wood et al. 2011). A further complication is that increasingly donors are providing general budget support where the recipient country has considerable flexibility with respect to how the funds are used, often merging them with other sources of funding so that it even becomes difficult to track how the funds are used. Rogers (2008) cites a number of examples of how program theory can be applied to complex programs. She concludes that a much more flexible and less formulaic approach is required often involving emergent designs, and with a strong reliance on participatory and other qualitative methods. She also points out that one of the challenges is that the uncertainty and ambiguity involved in many complex interventions are very stressful for public sector managers. "The anxiety provoked by uncertainty and ambiguity can lead managers and evaluator to seek the reassurance of a simple logic model, even when this is not appropriate," she says. Rogers suggests that a "better way to contain this anxiety might be to identify instead the particular elements of complication or complexity that need to be addressed, and to address them in ways that are useful, using the examples in this article as an initial guide" (Rogers 2008:45).

3.4. Articulating Program Theory

Social science literature relevant to the type of program to be evaluated and the beliefs of stakeholders concerning the nature, causes, and possible remedies for the problems the program should address are important sources of information for developing a theory of the program. A literature review may help in developing a *theory-driven evaluation* approach focused on the problems facing the target population and the causal chains through which impacts are expected to be achieved. One of the challenges of theory-driven evaluation is identifying and accounting for unanticipated effects not specified in the model. Especially when programs are based on the beliefs of stakeholders or the lessons drawn from experience, the theoretical basis for a program may not be clearly articulated. In these cases, theory-driven evaluation design will require articulating the theory. For developing program theory, evaluators may review material produced by the program (e.g., funding proposal, program implementation plan, reports, publicity materials, brochures, posters) and interview program staff members and other key stakeholders, individually or through focus group discussions.

Different people may hold significantly different opinions about the problems to be addressed and how they should be approached. Evaluations done without agreement on the program definition are likely to be of limited use (Centers for Disease Control 1999:3). Different models reflecting these different views can be presented, discussed, compared, and perhaps tested. Weiss (2000) recommends that three or four is realistically the maximum number of models that can be compared. Sometimes, negotiating with stakeholders to formulate a clear and logical description of the program will bring benefits before data are even available to evaluate program effectiveness (Centers for Disease Control 1999:3). Box 10.2 illustrates an example of two alternative theories formulated to evaluate the outcomes and impacts of **social funds** in developing countries.

There are at least three ways to reconstruct a program's theory. The *strategic approach* identifies, through group discussions with key stakeholders, the means through which the program is expected to achieve its goals. In an *elicitation approach*, strategic documents are reviewed, managers are consulted, and

---

BOX 10.2
FORMULATING AND TESTING TWO RIVAL PROGRAM THEORIES

Social funds are widely used programs in developing countries in which local communities are invited to identify social infrastructure projects (water supply, schools, roads, health centers, etc.). The projects are then funded and usually constructed by local government agencies with a high level of community involvement. In their evaluation of more than 50 social funds, Carvalho and White (2004) identified two alternative theories of potential outcomes and impacts of the social funds. Critics argued that the social funds would be captured by the local elites and would also undermine local government by creating parallel social service–implementing agencies. In contrast, supporters argued that the social funds would strengthen community-level institutions while at the same time providing a cost-effective delivery system for the provision of social services. Two social program models were formulated to test these two alternative theories.

decision-making processes are observed, from which the program theory is derived (Leeuw 2003). Field studies can also provide information used to construct program theories with, for example, the evaluator observing how the program is explained to clients and other stakeholders by program staff and whether staff members encourage or discourage different groups of potential beneficiaries.

A *conceptualization facilitation* approach to formulating program theories (Chen 2005) draws on program planners and stakeholders, who often have plenty of ideas about their program's rationale but often do not know how to clarify their thoughts and connect them systematically. An evaluator may facilitate this process by helping them either through *forward reasoning* (working from a prospective intervention to predicting its outcomes) or *backward reasoning* (starting from the desired outcomes and working backward to identify determinants and intervening factors). In intensive interviews or working groups, they may identify the problem, target population, final goals and measurable outcomes, and critical influences on outcomes. Backward reasoning may permit greater flexibility, but whether or not the group has already decided on the program's intervention may determine whether forward or backward reasoning is appropriate.

Weiss (2000) argues that there are two main sources of ideas and hypotheses on which the program theory can be based. The first source is the research literature and the findings of earlier programs, and the second source involves ascertaining the beliefs of implementers, sponsors, and other people associated with the program. What these people deeply believe to be critical is likely to determine their actions with respect to the program. One also needs to assess the plausibility of any logic model. Can the program actually do the things the theory assumes? Some indicators of plausibility include the following:

- *How funds have been allocated.* If people talk a lot about the importance of something but no funds have been allocated, this is an indication that the program component or process is not a high priority, at least to those who control the funds.
- *The topics on which information is and is not available.* A lack of available information often (but not always) suggests an aspect that is not a high priority.
- *What staff members actually do.* How people spend their time is another good indicator of priorities.

Another factor is the centrality of the theory to program activities. Some theories are interesting but not essential to a program's effectiveness, whereas others address critical issues that affect program success. This distinction is particularly important for RWE because the evaluator must decide which critical theories to test when resources are limited. If a program provides resources to community groups to allow them to select from an array of available services, then understanding how the provision of funds works and how well communities use them is likely to be critical to the program theory and success. In another example, if the program makes very little use of the mass media as a way of informing community groups about available options, a theory of how mass media would affect program outcomes may be of little importance.

Weiss (2000) also points out that cost and time constraints usually make it impossible or unnecessary to study all aspects of program change, as might be articulated in theories of change or theories of action, and proposes the following guidelines for selecting the critical program links on which an evaluation should focus:

- *When in the program timeline the evaluator is engaged.* Some kinds of issues are important to study at the start of a program (e.g., the criteria for defining the target group and participant selection) but less important at a later point in the project. When an evaluation begins long after the start of the program, early documents may no longer represent actual components on which the evaluation should focus its attention and resources.
- *Funds and time available for the evaluation.* Some issues may be important but be so expensive and time-consuming to study that they may have to be excluded from the evaluation.
- *How easy it is to collect different kinds of information.* Some kinds of information are more difficult to collect than others; importance and availability need to be balanced.
- *Priority concerns of program staff.* Special attention must usually be given to the issues of concern to staff. However, this is not the only criterion for determining evaluation priority; there may be issues that staff members do not consider important but might nevertheless appreciate after valuable information has been collected.
- *Psychosocial linkages (the "why?" of social change) underlying the program.* Why should developing countries give priority to getting more girls into school? Why do trainees remain in programs (or not)? Understanding the justification for the beliefs that underlie program goals and strategies often helps identify critical issues and assumptions that an evaluation might usefully address.
- *The links most critical to program success.* Some assumptions about linkages between inputs, implementation strategies, mediators, contextual factors, and outcomes may be critical to the success of the program and receive priority. Other links, i.e., where the correlation between outputs and outcomes has been well established, may not need to be tested.
- *The degree of uncertainty.* Some information is likely to be already known reasonably well (e.g., the proportion of children enrolled in school), whereas information on other topics may be scarce (e.g., the reasons why certain groups of children drop out of school or perform poorly). Often (but not always) there is a higher payoff on collecting data to fill bigger information gaps than to add small details.

4. Logical Framework Analysis, Results-Based Management, and Results Chains

Logical framework analysis (LFA, or logframe) and Results-Based Management (RBM) translate program theory into sets of measurable indicators so that progress can be tracked and factors determining achievement or nonachievement of outputs and impacts can be assessed. As we mentioned earlier in this chapter, logframes or variants thereof have been widely used as program monitoring and evaluation tools by international development agencies. Over the past decade, most international development agencies and many governments and NGOs moved from a logframe-based approach to a RBM approach. RBM, and the related Results-Based M&E, builds on the logframe (what Morra-Imas and Rist call the "traditional" approach to M&E) but places the emphasis on defining and measuring results rather than monitoring outputs. The reason for the change is the concern of development agencies to better understand whether the resources they provide and the initiatives they support have contributed to achieving their development objectives. This is seen as contrasting with the primary concern that the logframe approach was too often used to monitor the provision of the planned outputs (schools built, loans approved, children vaccinated, etc.). In addition, many RBM models include multiple cause-effect chains in a pyramid-type graphic, not just one linear chain that fits neatly in the classical 4×4 logframe matrix.

According to Morra-Imas and Rist (2009), there are 10 steps in the design and implementation of a Results-Based M&E system:

Step 1: Conducting a readiness assessment to determine an agency's or a government's organizational capacity and political willingness to monitor and evaluate progress toward the achievement of its development goals.

Step 2: Agreeing on a set of outcomes to monitor and evaluate.

Step 3: Selecting key indicators to monitor outcomes.

Step 4: Generating baseline data on indicators.

Step 5: Planning for improvements: selecting results targets. These are defined as outcomes.

Step 6: Monitoring for results: implementing the M&E system with a clear focus on the measurement of results.

Step 7: Using evaluation to support a Results-Based Management system: designing impact evaluation studies to assess attribution and causality. While the monitoring system can track the production of outputs and can measure changes between the baseline and the end-of-project values of results indicators, monitoring systems cannot, on their own, determine the extent to which the measured changes can be attributed to the project intervention. Hence, evaluation is an essential component of the RBM system. *It is noted below that there are still probably very few instances in which impact evaluation studies are actually conducted as part of RBM systems.*

Step 8: Reporting findings.

Step 9: Using findings.

Step 10: Sustaining the M&E system within the organization.

A logframe and other types of program theory models identify for monitoring and evaluation of the critical assumptions on which the choice of inputs, the selection of **implementation processes**, and the expected linkages between the different stages of the program cycle are based. One of the important and very useful elements of the logframe is that it identifies some of the critical assumptions about the linkages between the different stages of the model. Table 10.1 illustrates critical assumptions that might be included at each stage of a logframe of a project to strengthen women's economic and social empowerment through microcredit. For example, the use of credit as the major input is based on two assumptions: First, that lack of access to credit is one of the main constraints on women's ability to start a small business; second, that if women have access to credit, this will significantly increase the number and **sustainability** of small businesses they start. Both of these assumptions can be tested, and their correctness will be an important determinant of the project's success. Similar assumptions can be identified and tested for each stage of the model.

Table 10.1 Testing Critical Assumptions in a Logic Model of a Project to Strengthen Women's Economic Empowerment through Microcredit

Stage of Project	Critical Assumptions to Be Tested
Design	• Poor women have the skills needed to operate viable income-generating projects but lack only capital. • Women are able to decide what business to start/expand. • Women will be able to control how the loan is used, and the money will not be appropriated by the husband.
Inputs	• Access to credit, in a form that the woman can control, is critical to enhance women's access to economic opportunities.
Implementation process	• The creation of solidarity groups through which loans are approved and technical support provided is essential to enable women to control their use of their loans and to manage their small businesses. • Solidarity groups must select their own members without any outside pressures.
Outputs	• Women will use loans to invest in small businesses (not just to pay off debts or pay for consumption or ceremonial activities). • Women will be able to control the use of the loan (despite cultural traditions that economic resources are controlled by male household members).
Outcomes	• If women produce goods, they will be able to market them. • Their businesses will be profitable. • Women will control, or share in the control of, the profits.
Impact	• Profits will increase household consumption, women's savings, and quality of life of members of their households.
Sustainability	• The women's solidarity groups will be able to continue providing loans after the project's external credit and support has ended. • Their businesses will continue to operate and to grow.

Table 10.2 presents a typical format for a project completion results report. This is adapted from an implementation completion report for a World Bank–funded protection of basic services project in Ethiopia. For reasons of space, only selected indicators are presented. The project had 10 project development objectives, each of which was defined as an outcome. These outcomes are defined as the results included in this results framework. For each outcome, a verifiable indicator was defined, a baseline measurement was given together with the target to be achieved at the end of the project or at milestones during implementation, and the actual value at the time of completion. A comments row indicates whether the target was achieved. Four of the 10 outcomes are included to illustrate

different kinds of indicators. Some indicators give precise quantitative measurements (for example, the percentage of children immunized, and contraceptive acceptor rates), while others only provide more general and often more qualitative indicators. For example, the indicator for citizen access to public budget information gives the percentage of *woredas* (districts) posting budgets and providing budget literacy training where there may be considerable variations in the amount or quality of information posted or the quality of training. Similarly, the indicator for *woreda* adoption of new planning systems is partly based on a qualitative assessment and covers variations in the degree of adoption.

The outcomes also illustrate cases where there were precisely defined targets (e.g., the percentage of children to be immunized) and others where the target is to achieve an increase without providing a specific target (e.g., the number of citizens informed about how to access public budget information). Similarly, there are some outcomes where a precise baseline is given (immunization rates and contraceptive acceptance) and others where the baseline is zero (use of new planning systems and knowledge of how to access public budget information).

The results framework also included 14 intermediate outcome indicators, most of which were process indicators measuring intermediary steps toward the achievement of the outcome targets.

As is normally the case with RBM and M&E, results are defined in terms of changes in the outcomes between the baseline measurement and the end-of-project measurement. There is no attribution analysis and no systematic impact assessment. The report acknowledges that it was not possible to assess poverty impacts, gender aspects, and social development, stating: "No direct data-driven evidence on poverty or gender impacts was available to assess the impact of PBS (the protection of basic services), largely due to absence of recent household or other data that could measure poverty. However, indirectly PBS almost certainly contributed to the long-run reduction of poverty through sustaining and expanding coverage of basic health, education, clean water and rural agricultural services. PBS may also have contributed to the narrowing of the gender gap observed in primary education." While the authors are not aware of any study that has been conducted to assess the frequency with which RBM systems include impact evaluation or attribution analysis, it is our impression that this is not done for the great majority of RBM-based projects and programs. So developing RealWorld strategies that permit the incorporation of attribution analysis and impact remains a challenge for RBM.

Table 10.2 Example of a Results Report: The World Bank Ethiopia Basic Services Project

Project Development Objectives (PDO) Indicators				
Outputs and Outcomes (Results)	**Verifiable Indicator**	**Baseline**	**Target (at End of Project or at Some Intermediary Point)**	**Actual Value Achieved at End of Project**
Citizens have improved access to public budget information	(a) percentage of *woredas* (districts) posting budgets in public places (b) number of people participating in budget literacy training	Zero	Increasing number of citizens informed about how to access public budget and expenditure information	(a) 90% of districts posted budgets (b) budget literacy training conducted for 1,500 citizens

(Continued)

Table 10.2   (Continued)

Project Development Objectives (PDO) Indicators				
Outputs and Outcomes (Results)	Verifiable Indicator	Baseline	Target (at End of Project or at Some Intermediary Point)	Actual Value Achieved at End of Project
Comments: Target achieved. Follow-up survey to gauge likely changes in citizens' understanding of and engagement in public budget process will provide more in-depth understanding of the impacts of the information.				
Immunization of children	% of children under 1 year of age receiving (a) DPTs and (b) Penta vaccine	(a) 70.1% DPTs (b) 61.3% Penta	(a) 83.3% (b) 73.0%	(a) 81.6% (b) 76.6%
Comments: Target surpassed by 3.6 point of a percent in the case of Penta vaccines and almost reached in the case of DPT (diphtheria, pertussis (whooping cough), tetanus) vaccinations.				
Increased contraceptive use	Contraceptive acceptor rate for women in the 15–49 age group	25.2%	57%	56.2%
Comments: Target almost achieved, falling short by less than one percent point.				
Pilot *woredas* adopt new planning systems	Pilot *woredas* (receiving local investment grants) adopt and implement new national standards and systems in the areas of planning and budgeting, procurement, environmental screening, and resettlement	Zero	40%	Based on visits to 10 out of 51 pilot *woredas*, all had adopted and were implementing the national standards/systems on planning and budgeting, procurement, and financial management. However, environmental screening is still at a preliminary stage.
Comments: Targets largely achieved.				
Intermediary outcomes	This monitors indicators assessing progress toward the outcomes at milestones during the project life. These are mainly process indicators. For example: number of *woredas* that disclose public budget information; number of *woredas* that post "laypersons" budget templates; improved dialogue between government and civil society organizations on social accountability and basic service delivery issues; number of health extension workers employed per rural district.				

NOTES:

1. This table is adapted from the World Bank's "Implementation Completion and Results Report" on the Ethiopia Protection of Basic Services Project, dated June 30, 2010. This is a publicly disclosed document. The results analysis framework included project development objectives with results indicators defined for each one. The four presented in this table were selected to represent different kinds of indicators. Some are outputs, others are outcomes; some with precise quantitative measures and others with more general qualitative assessments.

2. The framework also included 14 intermediary outcome indicators that have not been presented due to length.

3. The "verifiable indicator" column was not included in the original table, but was added by the present authors (based on information included in the table) because this column is included in many results frameworks (Kusek and Rist 2004, Chapter 2).

4. Original report available electronically at: www-wds.worldbank.org/external/default/WDSContentServer/WDSP/IB/2010/07/08/000333037_20100708010130/Rendered/PDF/ICR15690P074011IC0disclosed07161101.pdf

5. Program Theory Evaluation and Causality

5.1. Arguments for and against the Use of Program Theory to Help Explain Causality

Some qualitative evaluators have argued that a carefully designed program theory can provide *operationally useful* estimates of program impacts in situations in which it is not possible to implement one or more of the quantitative (QUANT) evaluation designs discussed in Chapter 11. As noted earlier in this chapter, many QUANT pretest-posttest evaluation designs do not address one of the key questions of interest to many stakeholders—namely, do disappointing statistical results mean that the underlying theory is wrong and the program should be scrapped, or is the theory potentially sound but with some weaknesses in its design or implementation? Both program theory impact models and implementation models provide frameworks for assessing the effectiveness of project implementation that can help address this question.

Davidson (2000) identifies nine potential types of evidence for inferring causality (see Box 10.3) that can be obtained from program theory models. These are based on different kinds of logical inference. For example, the first type of evidence (causal list inference) states that if a number of different causes of an Event B have been hypothesized, but if A is the only one that is systematically present when B occurs, then this is evidence for inferring that A may have caused B. Similarly, Type 3 (temporal precedence) states that if A is always observed to occur before B, then this (in conjunction with other evidence) supports the possibility that A is a cause of B. None of these types of evidence in isolation is very convincing as an explanation of causality, but if several of the types are all found to be present, then the case for a causal relationship becomes more plausible.

BOX 10.3
NINE POTENTIAL TYPES OF EVIDENCE
FOR INFERRING CAUSALITY

1. Causal list inference: Almost all Bs are caused by As. If there is a list of possible causes (As) and only one is systematically present when B occurs, this can infer that this A is the cause.

2. Modus operandi influence: Establish causal chain/modus operandi and use all available sources of evidence to systematically eliminate other possible causes.

3. Temporal precedence: A happens before B is seen.

4. Constant conjunction: When A is present, there is always B.

5. Contiguity of influence: A plausible mechanism links A and B.

6. Strength of association: Much more B with A than other possible causes.

7. Biological gradient: If more A, then more B.

8. Coherence: The A–B relationship fits with what else we know about A and B.

9. Analogy: The relationship between A and B resembles the well-established pattern documented between C and D.

SOURCE: Adapted from Davidson (2000:21–22).

Other writers argue that there are a number of fundamental methodological reasons why program theory is not able to provide sound estimates of causality and cannot be considered a satisfactory alternative to randomized experiments. Cook (2000) argues that program theory is often used as an excuse for not conducting appropriate experimentation and that the design of a program theory can be manipulated and the findings interpreted to justify a program or protect it from criticism. Disappointing results may also be dismissed by arguing that it was too early to expect results or that the indicators did not adequately capture many important program outcomes. The following are Cook's main criticisms of program theory as a tool for assessing program impact and causality:

- The formulation of program theory is not sufficiently explicit to permit testing or refutation.
- The formulation of most program theories is linear (i.e., if *A*, then *B*) and does not capture feedback loops or the effects of external contingencies.
- Most program theories do not specify time periods over which effects are expected to be achieved. Consequently, it is not possible to assess whether negative results show a program does not work or that it is too early to judge.[9]
- Program theory often does not provide sufficient guidance on what to measure and how.
- Most program theories do not identify alternative models for examination. Consequently, even if observed outcomes fit the theory, it is impossible to know whether there are other theories that might equally well explain the facts.
- Another major weakness is the lack of a **counterfactual,** a comparison that provides a way to know whether the observed changes might have been caused by other factors unrelated to the project (Cook 2000:29–32).

For qualitative evaluations, even without strong supporting quantitative data, some of the program theory approaches discussed earlier can provide useful preliminary indicators of possible program effects. Defenders of program theory can also point out that the explanatory value of most experimental and quasi-experimental designs is limited to estimating a statistical association, but they do not help clients to understand why the association exists. Also, as we indicated earlier in this section, experimental designs are particularly limited in their ability to provide guidance to clients on how to interpret negative results that did not find any statistical association between project interventions and intended outcomes and impacts. (See more on this topic in Chapter 11.)

5.2. Using Program Theory to Help Explain Causality in Mixed-Method Evaluations

While program theory cannot provide the precise statistical estimates of causality that can be obtained from experimental and strong quasi-experimental designs, theory models can provide a useful way to support or challenge evidence of causality obtained through mixed-method evaluation designs. A program theory model can sometimes provide useful indicators of *plausible causal linkages.* The following guidelines can be applied:

---

[9]For a discussion of the importance of defining how effects are expected to evolve over time, see Lipsey's *Design Sensitivity* (1990, chap. 7).

Step 1: Construct an impact model (see Figure 10.5). This should include a contextual analysis of the underlying rationale of the program based on the analysis of the situation and a review of the literature, definition of the proposed interventions and intended outputs, and an identification of potentially important **moderators** and **mediators**. The model should also recognize the likelihood of multiple causality and that different people may respond differently to the same set of program services. The model should also include the feedback loops found in interactions between the project and its environment.

Step 2: Identify some of the alternative hypotheses/explanations concerning the causes of change and the expected outcomes/impacts. Obtain alternative explanations for causal links through, for example, a review of the research literature, evaluations of similar programs, discussions with program staff and other stakeholders, soliciting the views of program critics, and exploratory fieldwork. Defining at least one alternative model to test alternative outcomes, perhaps using qualitative approaches, can be useful for understanding actual effects.

Step 3: Define operationally measurable input, process and outcome indicators. Define indicators with sufficient **precision** to permit them to be measured and quantified.

Step 4: Define the time period over which outcomes and impacts are expected to occur and the intensity of inputs required to achieve outcomes. The time period selected to measure project effects can make a significant difference on the estimated magnitude of the effects. Table 10.3 and Figure 10.6 illustrate three ways in which the effects of a project could vary over time. In Scenario 1, the maximum effects could be achieved immediately; for example, all the health benefits (e.g., reduced intestinal infections) could be achieved as soon as drinking water is available, and could be sustained with no decrease over time. In Scenario 2, the effects gradually increase, not reaching their maximum level for about nine years. In Scenario 3, the effects gradually increase until about Year 5, after which they steadily decrease. It can be seen from this example that a posttest measurement taken in Year 3 would find a high level of effect in the first scenario, a low level in the second, and a medium level in the third. On the other hand, observations in Year 5 would find high effects in the first and third scenarios, with medium effects for the second. These variations show that the program theory model should specify the expected time period for producing effects and whether the effects are expected to be sustained or to decrease over time. If the time dimension is not specified, then it is impossible to tell whether low effects show that the program theory model is invalid or whether the measurements were taken at the wrong time.

Table 10.3   Variations in the Estimated Level of Effects Depending on the Year in Which the Posttest Study Is Conducted

Scenario	Year 3	Year 5	Year 8
1	High	High	High
2	Low	Medium	High
3	Low	High	Low

Figure 10.6   Different Scenarios for the Variation of Project Effects over Time

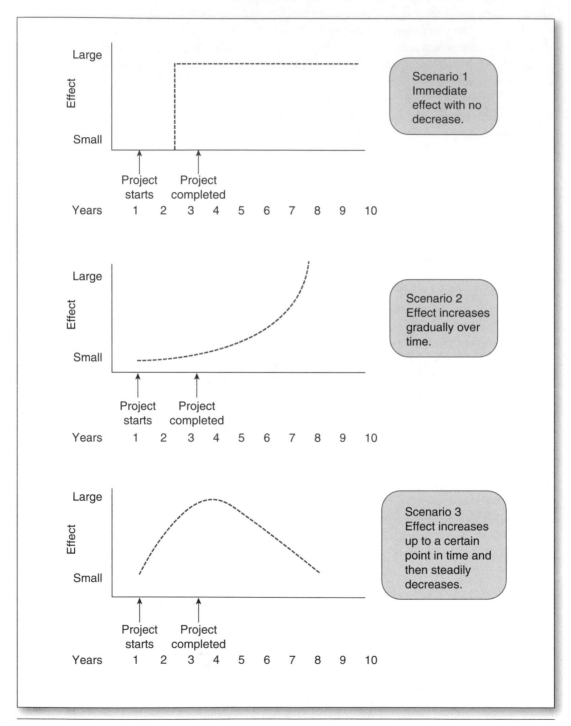

SOURCE: Adapted by authors with permission from Upsey (1990:149).

Step 5: Using PRA and other qualitative methods to identify causality. Those promoting participatory appraisal methods (variously known as PRA, RRA, and PLA), which were discussed in Chapter 5, have developed a variety of tools for working with community groups to identify causality.

Some of the *time-related methods* include timelines, trend analysis, historical transects (used to explore and represent the temporal dimension of people's reality), and seasonal diagrams. R*elational methods* include cause-effect diagrams, impact diagrams, systems diagrams, network diagrams, and process maps. All these techniques are based on working with stakeholders in facilitated discussions and exercises to construct maps, timelines, or causal chains defining the natural, political, and socio-cultural factors relevant to the program. (See Kumar 2002 for a detailed explanation of these techniques.) For example, in a recent evaluation in the Philippines using PRA techniques, facilitated community meetings identified the impacts of constructing a water supply system, and **triangulation** through site visits, observations, and interviews confirmed the identified impacts.

Step 6: Define and combine all available evidence for inferring causality. When operating with budget, time, and data constraints, the evaluator will often collect a number of different types of data that provide evidence on how the project has performed, what types of effects it has produced, and which groups have benefited most and least. Often, none of these sources of information is completely convincing when taken in isolation, but when they are combined and their consistency checked through triangulation, the evidence base becomes stronger.

SUMMARY

- A program theory is an explicit theory or model of how a program is intended to produce the intended outputs, outcomes, and impacts and the factors affecting or determining its success.
- A program theory is particularly helpful in planning an evaluation under RWE constraints because it helps identify the critical issues or hypotheses on which scarce evaluation resources should focus.
- Evaluators often have to work with clients and stakeholders to construct the implicit program theory because it has often not been formally articulated in project documents.
- Program theories often combine an impact model and an implementation model.
- The impact (change) model describes the linkages between project inputs, the implementation strategy, and the intended outputs, outcomes, and impacts. It also examines how performance is affected by *mediators*—factors affecting performance that can be modified by the project (e.g., willingness of different groups to support the project or to change their behavior)—and by *contextual factors* (such as the economic, political, organizational, natural environment, and characteristics of the affected populations) that affect performance but over which project managers have little control.
- The implementation (action) model describes how staff and resources are to be used to deliver the program services to the target population.
- Logical framework analysis (logframe) or Results-Based Management (RBM) are forms of program theory or modeling used by many agencies to monitor program performance against a set of measurable indicators. Such logic models can also be used to identify and test critical assumptions about conditions that will affect program success (e.g., actions that the government must take, the stability of the local and national economy, the willingness of communities or individuals to change traditional forms of behavior).
- Some, but not all, program theory practitioners believe that program theory can be used to help explain causality in situations where it is not possible to use randomized control trials or quasi-experimental designs.

FURTHER READING

Carvalho, S. and H. White. 2004. "Theory-Based Evaluation: The Case of Social Funds." *American Journal of Evaluation* 25(2):141–60.

An example of the application of program theory to the evaluation of social investment funds (a widely used model for providing health, education, water supply, and other local infrastructure in developing countries). The article illustrates how program theory can be reconstructed during the evaluation when it was not defined in the project documents. The article is also interesting because it presents the concept of an "antitheory" based on the views of critics as to the potential negative outcomes of the project interventions.

Centers for Disease Control and Prevention. *Manuals/ Assistance with Specific Evaluation Steps—Logic Models.* Retrieved August 5, 2011 (http://www.cdc.gov/ eval/resources/#logicmodels).

Extensive reference material on logic models presented in user-friendly formats and including material prepared for use by community groups. The portal leads to many other guidelines on evaluation. See especially *Logic Model Development Guide* developed by the W. K. Kellogg Foundation.

Chen, H. T. 2005. *Practical Program Evaluation: Assessing and Improving Planning, Implementation, and Effectiveness.* Thousand Oaks, CA: Sage.

A thorough, clear introduction to the design and use of program theory evaluation.

Donaldson, S. 2007. *Program Theory–Driven Evaluation Science: Strategies and Applications.* Thousand Oaks, CA: Sage.

Recent overview of program theory. Includes eight case studies illustrating diverse applications of program theory.

Mercy Corps. 2005. *Design, Monitoring and Evaluation Guidebook.* Portland, OR: Mercy Corps.

Includes chapters on project design and criteria for useful evaluations.

Morra-Imas, L. G. and R. C. Rist. 2009. *The Road to Results: Designing and Conducting Effective Development Evaluations.* Washington, DC: World Bank.

Very practical guidance for the evaluation of international development programs. Includes understanding the

context, developing the program theory of change, considering the evaluation approach and design, developing evaluation questions, and much more.

Patton, M. Q. 2008. *Utilization-Focused Evaluation.* 4th ed. Thousand Oaks, CA: Sage.

Probably the most widely cited text on how to ensure that evaluations respond to the needs of stakeholders and that the findings will be used.

Pawson, R., and N. Tilley. 2006. *Realist Evaluation.* Available electronically at http://www.evidence-basedmanagement .com/research_practice/articles/nick_tilley.pdf or http:// www.sociology.leeds.ac.uk/about/staff/pawson.php

An update to the authors' influential 1997 "Realist Evaluation," in which they argue for the need for a better understanding of the intervention, what happens during implementation, who benefits, and why.

Rogers, P., T. Hacsi, A. Petrosino, and T. Huebner, eds. 2000. *Program Theory in Evaluation: Challenges and Opportunities.* New Directions for Evaluation No. 87. San Francisco: Jossey-Bass.

One of the most comprehensive overviews of recent developments in program theory evaluation.

Rossi, P., M. Lipsey, and H. Freeman. 2004. *Evaluation: A Systematic Approach.* 7th ed. Thousand Oaks, CA: Sage.

A thorough presentation of the design and use of program theory evaluations.

Weiss, C. 2001. "Theory-Based Evaluation: Theories of Change for Poverty Based Programs." Pp. 103–114 in *Evaluation and Poverty Reduction,* edited by O. Feinstein and R. Picciotto. New Brunswick, NJ: Transaction.

A discussion of how program theory models can be applied to the evaluation of poverty reduction programs.

CHAPTER 11

Evaluation Designs

The RWE Strategy for Selecting the Appropriate Evaluation Design to Respond to the Purpose and Context of Each Evaluation

We begin by introducing the reader to eight steps involved in selecting an **evaluation design** *appropriate for a given purpose and* **evaluand** *(program being evaluated), or even possible given a particular circumstance, e.g., not having been planned until the end of a project, with no comparable baseline, much less a* **counterfactual**. *These evaluation design steps are summarized in Figure 11.1. A range of purposes and contexts is identified in Table 11.1, and the major evaluation designs are summarized in Table 11.2. We then consider a variety of tools and techniques for strengthening any evaluation design. That section is followed by discussions of some of the more common impact evaluation designs, including* **randomized control trials** *(RCTs), and how they are suitable (or not) to RealWorld evaluation. Realizing that some readers might be interested in more detailed coverage of these and other designs, the subject of evaluation designs is continued in greater depth in Appendix F.*

1. Different Approaches to the Classification of Evaluation Designs

There are many ways to classify different types of evaluations. Before presenting the RWE approach (see Box 11.1 and the following section) we discuss some of the approaches used by other authors. Some authors distinguish evaluations by purpose or scope, or by methodological paradigm. Though many definitions of evaluation **design** are linked to predominantly either quantitative (QUANT), qualitative (QUAL), or mixed-method approaches, in this book we are proposing a framework that is equally applicable to QUANT, QUAL, and mixed-method approaches.

Patton (2008:300–305) presents a 79-item list of alternative ways of focusing evaluations. In his more recent book, he provides a 26-item list of characteristics divided into: (a) purpose and situation, (b) focus and target of evaluation, (c) modeling and methods, (d) roles and relationships, (e) evaluation results and impacts, (f) approaches to complexity, and (g) professional qualities, and contrasts these between what he calls "traditional evaluation tendencies" with "complexity-sensitive developmental evaluation" (Patton 2011:23–26).

Some sources characterize different types of evaluation using very basic categories. The "Basic Guide to Program Evaluation" (McNamara 2002) contains a fairly typical list of types of evaluations: goal-based, process-based, and outcomes-based evaluations. Stufflebeam (2001a, 2007) proposed a much more comprehensive classification of evaluation models or approaches, breaking them into: (a) pseudo evaluations, (b) questions and methods-oriented evaluations, (c) improvement and accountability-oriented evaluations, (d) social agenda and advocacy approaches, and (e) eclectic evaluation approaches. In Chapter 13 we discuss a variety of approaches used in qualitative evaluations. Teddlie and Tashakkori (2009) and Tashakkori and Teddlie (2010) list a similarly wide range of options for mixed-method evaluations (discussed in Chapter 14). Quantitative researchers have often followed the typology for experimental and quasi-experimental designs first proposed by Campbell and Stanley in the 1960s (Campbell and Stanley 1963) and updated more recently (Shadish, Cook, and Campbell 2002). Their approach identifies four sets of threats to validity (internal validity, statistical conclusion validity, construct validity, and external validity), and proposes evaluation designs that can address each of these threats. Almost all quantitative evaluation texts distinguish between internal and external validity, but not all use the other two categories. The threats-to-validity checklists for statistical evaluation designs presented in Appendix A of this book are based upon the Campbell and Stanley framework.

One other example of how other authors have classified evaluations is the set of seven evaluation designs identified by Paul Duignan (2011). This classification is based on the type of methodology and does not discuss the purpose of the evaluation:

1. True experimental design
2. Regression-discontinuity design
3. Time-series design
4. Constructed matched comparison group design
5. Exhaustive alternative causal identification and elimination design
6. Expert opinion summary judgment design
7. Key informants' summary judgment design

2. The RWE Approach to the Selection of the Appropriate Impact Evaluation Design

Our point of mentioning these varieties of ways to classify evaluations (and there are many other classifications proposed by other authors) is simply to recognize that there are many purposes and kinds of evaluations and also acknowledge that there is much more to evaluation design than when the data are collected or whether there is a comparison group. In this chapter, we identify a set of factors that describe the **evaluation scenario** within which an evaluation design is selected and an **evaluation design framework** that narrows the range of design options that can be considered within a given scenario (see Box 11.1). We point out that under each particular scenario and within each particular framework there is a range of options for how information can be obtained and analyzed. Indeed, one of the main objectives of the RWE approach is to promote a wise mix of methods to provide more holistic, valid, credible, and useful findings, given the purpose of the evaluation, and no matter what the constraints are, what designs are feasible and in consideration of the methodological preferences of **clients** and **stakeholders**.

Figure 11.1 summarizes the eight steps for the selection of the appropriate design. We describe them in more detail in the text that follows.

BOX 11.1
THE RWE APPROACH TO THE
CLASSIFICATION OF EVALUATION DESIGNS

The RWE approach distinguishes between:

- The *evaluation purpose and context.* These are the kinds of programs being evaluated, the basic reason(s) an evaluation is called for, and the internal and external context within which the evaluation will be designed and implemented (see Table 11.1).
- The *evaluation design framework.* These are scenarios, many of which contain factors beyond the control of the evaluator, that narrow down the range of possible evaluation designs that could be used. These factors include: when the evaluation is commissioned, whether or not there will be (or was) a baseline, midterm, endline, and/or ex-post assessment; the kinds of secondary data that are available and whether or not and when it will be necessary or possible to select a comparison group. In Table 11.2 we show seven design frameworks. In Table 11.4 we identify some of the strengths and weaknesses of these designs. They are covered in more detail in Appendix F.
- *The evaluation design options.* Within each of the evaluation frameworks there are a number of design options that can be considered. The design options include the procedures for selecting the comparison group (e.g., randomized control trials, regression discontinuity, quasi-experimental designs with statistical or judgmental matching of the project and comparison groups), and the choice between quantitative, qualitative, or mixed-method approaches. Within a particular evaluation framework the choice of methods will also vary according to the point in the project/program cycle when the evaluation is commissioned. In Table 11.3 we list a total of 19 more nuanced evaluation designs. These include options for evaluations designs that are commissioned at the start of the project (Option A) and at the end of the project (Option B). They also identify different ways that the comparison group can be selected for experimental and quasi-experimental designs. Each of these design options is discussed in more detail in Appendix F, which also includes cases illustrating most of the designs.
- *Tools and techniques to strengthen any evaluation design:* Though the experimental and quasi-experimental evaluation designs can address statistical sampling issues such as controlling for selection bias, they frequently do not address the many other threats to validity of the evaluation design (see Table 11.5). Similarly qualitative and mixed-method designs face different sets of threats to validity. The techniques described in that table can be used to strengthen all evaluation designs.

NOTE: The seven basic evaluation design frameworks or scenarios are applicable to any approach and data collection method, whether it be QUANT, QUAL, mixed-method, developmental, extractive, empowering, or any other approach. But there are major differences in *how* data (or evidence) are obtained and processed.

Figure 11.1 Eight Steps for the Selection of the Appropriate Evaluation Design to Address Different Evaluation Contexts, Purposes, and Scenarios

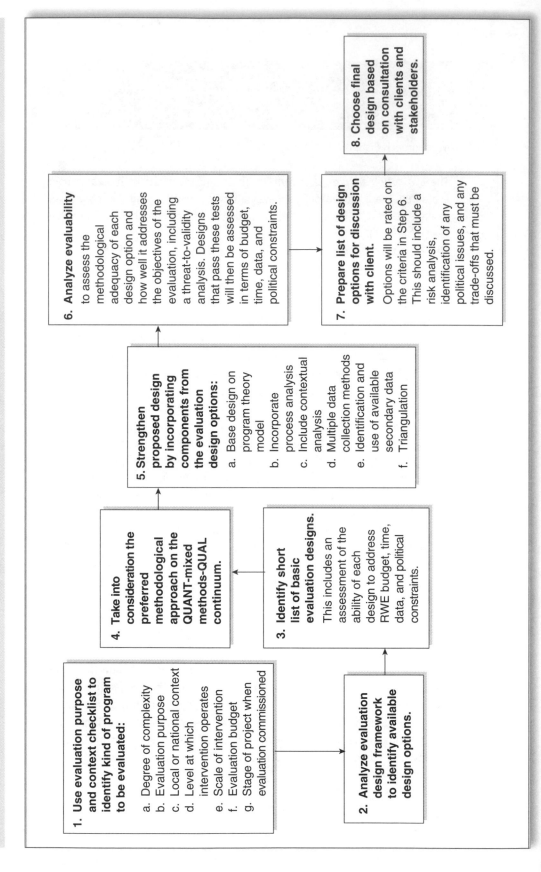

2.1. Design Step 1

*Using the Evaluation Purpose and Context
Checklist to Describe the Evaluand, the Purpose(s)
of the Evaluation, and the Context Within Which
It Will Be Designed, Implemented, and Used*

In order to select the most appropriate evaluation design it is essential to understand the characteristics of the intervention being evaluated (the *evaluand*) and the political, economic, and organizational context within which the evaluation is being implemented. And, of course, it is important to understand the purpose for which the evaluation is being called and to define the evaluation questions that must be addressed. Evaluations are conducted for a number of different purposes, each of which may require a different evaluation design.

The following are some of the common purposes for which evaluations are used. Items 1–5 have been adapted from Patton's *Developmental Evaluation* (2011:44–45, 308–12) and items 8–10 from Morra-Imas and Rist's *The Road to Results* (2009:14):

1. *Developmental.* Developing and testing innovative approaches for addressing problems. Often this will be used to assess whether a pilot program has the potential for replication on a larger scale.

2. *Formative evaluation.* Helping managers and planners to improve the design and implementation of an ongoing intervention or to learn lessons that can improve future interventions. Stabilize and standardize the model to prepare for a summative evaluation.

3. *Summative evaluation.* Assessing the overall merit, worth, and significance of a program. This will often include estimates of the quantitative impacts at the program level as well as at a broader sector or societal level. Summative evaluation is often used to help decide whether an intervention should be replicated in other settings or on a larger scale.

4. *Adapting the intervention to a new context.* The new context may be local, regional, national, or even another country.

5. *Adapting an existing program to a major change.* The change may be a crisis, new legislation, or a systems change.

6. *To promote accountability.* This could be seen as overlapping with summative evaluation, but it refers to any requirements to report to donors or other stakeholders on whether or not "results" are being obtained. In many cases it refers to compliance evaluation, i.e., how well the process is being implemented according to plan.

7. *To promote learning* Although too often in discussions about evaluation the purpose of learning is contrasted with the purpose of accountability, surely learning should be based on accountability. For example, "Let's see how well our program is doing, learn from that feedback, and then use that information to improve performance."

8. *To help make resource allocation decisions on competing or best alternatives.* In addition to assessing whether the intervention achieved its objectives, donors, planners, and

Table 11.1   Evaluation Purpose and Context

This table identifies some of the characteristics and dimensions of the evaluand and methodological considerations that need to be taken into consideration as decisions about the design of the evaluation are made.

I. Characteristics Related to the Evaluand (Program to Be Evaluated)

1. Basic purpose of evaluation[1]	a. Developmental, i.e., support innovative exploration of evolving approaches for addressing problems
	b. Formative, i.e., learning and improvement of planned intervention during process in order to improve the process itself
	c. Summative, i.e., accountability and judgment of the overall merit, worth, value, and significance of completed program. (Though this can feel like a postmortem, summative evaluation can inform major decisions about future programming.)
2. Other purposes of evaluation	a. Compliance with stated program plan
	b. Impact: existing or potential achievement of higher level outcomes, e.g., improved quality of life of intended beneficiaries
	c. Adapting an intervention to a new context
	d. Adapting an existing program to a major change
	e. Helping make resource allocation decisions on competing or best alternatives
	f. Helping identify emerging problems and building consensus on the causes of a problem and how to respond
	g. Supporting public sector reform and innovation
3. Complexity of the evaluand[2]	a. *Simple project*: few intervention components, defined timeline
	b. *Complicated program*: sector program with various components, often combining several individual projects
	c. *Complex interventions*: e.g., general budget support or multiprogram interventions often involving several funding agencies and operating at the national or cross-country level
4. Local and national context within which the evaluation will be implemented	a. Economic context
	b. Political context
	c. Policy, legal, and administrative context
	d. Organizations and agencies involved in the project
	e. Natural environment
	f. Characteristics and culture of the target population, politics, history, socioeconomic context, values, relative peace or conflict, needs and interests of stakeholders
5. Geographic level	a. Program or sector level (which could involve multiple countries)
	b. Multinational/regional (several countries)
	c. National (one country)
	d. Subnational region (e.g., district or province)
	e. One or a few local communities
6. Scale of intervention[3]	a. Small (e.g., less than 5,000 individuals or households)
	b. Medium (e.g., up to 50,000 units)
	c. Large (e.g., over 50,000 units)

7. Size of the evaluation budget[4]	a. Small (e.g., less than 5% of program budget)
	b. Moderate (e.g., up to 15% of program budget)
	c. Generous (e.g., over 15%—for example, a major purpose is research, to test a new intervention)
8. When evaluation commissioned	a. Start of intervention (baseline/pretest)
	b. Midterm
	c. End of intervention (posttest)
	d. After intervention completed (ex-post)
9. Duration of the evaluation	a. Continues throughout intervention cycle
	b. Evaluation commissioned late in the intervention cycle but sufficient time is budgeted to conduct required data collection and analysis
	c. Great time pressure (the evaluation must be completed in weeks or a few months)
10. Client	a. Donor agency
	b. Planning ministry
	c. Implementing agency
	d. Civil society or other
11. Who conducts the evaluation	a. Internal evaluator (or evaluation team)
	b. External consultant(s) (individual or team)
	c. Mixed team combining external and internal members
II. Methodological Dimensions	
12. Statistical rigor (client preference and what is feasible)	a. Statistically strong evaluation design
	b. Statistically weaker design
	c. Nonexperimental design with alternative definition of the counterfactual
	d. Nonexperimental design without clearly defined counterfactual
13. Location on the QUANT/QUAL continuum (client preference)	a. Predominantly quantitative design
	b. Mixed-method design
	c. Predominantly qualitative design
14. Primary source of data (client preference and what is feasible)	a. Primary data collection
	b. Mainly primary data collection combined with secondary data
	c. Mainly secondary data complemented by some primary data
	d. Only secondary data

[1]Adapted from Patton (2011, as summarized in Exhibit 2.2, pp. 44–46, and Exhibit 10.1, pp. 308–13) and Morra-Imas and Rist 2009 (Box 1.1, p. 15), with additional categories added by the present authors to reflect other purposes of funding agencies and clients.

[2]The concept of *complexity* is discussed in Chapter 16.

[3]The concepts of *large* and *small* with respect to cost and scale are relative. What might be considered small-scale or low-cost by a major donor might be considered very large by an NGO.

[4]Though we give relative budget percentages for illustrative purposes, obviously the actual amount available for evaluation makes a significant difference on the kind of evaluation that can be undertaken.

implementers need to know whether the results were achieved in a cost-effective way, and the relative cost-effectiveness compared with alternative interventions that could achieve the same objectives. (For this and the remaining objectives see Morra-Imas and Rist [2009:14].)

9. *To help identify emerging problems and build consensus on the causes and how to respond.*

10. *To support public sector reform and innovation.*

Other aspects of the program that need to be assessed include the following:

Complexity of the intervention. In recent years the evaluation literature has begun to focus on the complexity of an intervention and how this affects the analysis of causality and the type of evaluation design that can be used. (See, for example, Patton 2011.) In Chapter 16 we discuss the difference in approach to the evaluation of simple projects, complicated programs, and complex interventions.

The local and national context within which the program operates and the evaluation will be implemented. Factors that may need to be assessed include the economic context (when most people are employed and incomes are rising the response to a program may be quite different than when the economy is declining); the political context (do local and national politicians and parties support or oppose the program? what is their attitude to the evaluation?); the policy, legal, and administrative context (can women own property and can a woman use property to obtain a bank loan? do small farmers have access to legal process in the case of disputes over land titles?); organizations and agencies involved in the project (how effective are they in supporting the program?); the natural environment (are there problems of flooding, drought, deforestation, or soil erosion?); and the socioeconomic characteristics of communities affected by the program.

The level at which the program operates. The evaluation design for a small, local project operating in only a few communities will be quite different than that required for a regional or sector-wide program or for a national program operating in all parts of the country.

The scale of the intervention. The number of individuals, groups, or communities affected by the intervention will influence the evaluation design. While there is considerable overlap between level and scale of an intervention, it is sometimes useful to distinguish between the two. Some programs may be operated at the national level but actually benefit a limited number of institutions or individuals, while other programs may affect large numbers of individuals but only operate at the local level. For example, a slum-upgrading program may affect several hundred thousand people but only operate in one area of a large city.

Evaluation budget. The size of the evaluation budget is often a major constraint on the type of evaluation design that can be used. In many organizations the flexibility of the budget and the ease with which funds can be accessed can also be important. For example, in Chapter 5 we point out that one reason why baseline studies are often not conducted is due to administrative difficulties and delays in accessing funds to contract consultants or to cover other evaluation-related costs, even when the funds had been approved.

The stage of the program at which the evaluation was commissioned. If an evaluation is not commissioned until a program has been underway for some time, or may even be nearing completion, the range of evaluation design options is more limited than when the evaluation is commissioned at the start of the program. Also, if an evaluation is only conducted at the time of the midterm review, any assessment of outcomes or impacts must be based on projections of how the program will develop in the future; and the perspective will be quite different than if the evaluation were conducted at the time of program completion or when the program had already been operating for several years.

Duration of the evaluation. The duration of an evaluation concerns not only the start and end date but also how much time the evaluators have to plan the evaluation and collect and analyze the data at each stage that data are collected. Many, but certainly not all, evaluations that use a pretest–posttest design are conducted under time constraints that limit the amount of time allocated for fieldwork at each stage, making it very difficult to conduct initial diagnostic studies or to adequately test the data collection instruments.

Who is the client? An evaluation of a program that is commissioned by the funding agency may ask different questions and use a different methodology than an evaluation of the same program that is commissioned by the implementing agency, a national planning or finance agency, or a public interest or advocacy group.

Who conducts the evaluation? We discuss in Chapter 17 the implications of having an evaluation conducted in-house or contracted to an outside research or consulting group. The kind of external consultant can also affect the focus and methodology. A professor from an economics department may wish to use a rigorous econometric design, hoping to publish an article in an economics journal, whereas a professor from a sociology or political science department might try to give the evaluation a different focus. Similarly, an NGO might focus more on the impacts of the program on women or ethnic minorities, or may be interested in critically assessing the performance of government agencies. When cost is a factor the client might look for an agency that can conduct the evaluation more economically (for example, a university professor using her students to give them field experience, or the use of teachers or student nurses), and this may have consequences for the quality of the evaluation.

2.2. Design Step 2

Analysis of the Evaluation Design Framework

There are at least three factors that always have a major influence on the available design options for a particular impact evaluation:

1. The point in the program cycle at which the evaluation is commissioned (the later the evaluation is commissioned the narrower the range of design options). Basically, this refers to whether or not there was or will be a baseline study conducted at the beginning of

program implementation that will be comparable to later measurement of the same indicators, e.g., during the endline evaluation study.

2. The number and timing of other planned data collection events as part of this or complementary evaluations, e.g., an ex-post evaluation some time after the program's interventions have ended (to assess sustainability of any impact).

3. Whether a reasonably well-matched control (comparison) group is feasible or available.

NOTE: *For the purpose of the design frameworks depicted in Table 11.2 and discussed here, we only refer to primary data collection by those commissioned to undertake a particular impact evaluation. In the following section we discuss the important distinction between: (1) evaluation designs that are commissioned at the start of the project, and which can use primary data collection (surveys, etc.) to construct the baseline; and (2) evaluations that are not commissioned until late in the project and where baseline data must be estimated from either secondary surveys conducted by other organizations around the time of project launch or from the use of the techniques for reconstructing baselines that were discussed in Chapter 5.*

When the three factors identified in Design Step 2 (Figure 11.1) are combined, they form the *evaluation design framework* that defines the range of evaluation design options that are available in any given scenario. These are summarized in Table 11.2. Designs 1–5 all include a control or comparison group so that it is possible to define a statistical counterfactual. However, only Designs 1 and 2 include the comparison group for both the pretest and posttest observations. In Design 3 data are collected on both groups at the time of the midterm assessment. Only Designs 1, 2, 4, and 6 include primary baseline data for the project group.

The final two design frameworks do not include a comparison group at all, so it is not possible to define a statistical counterfactual, and consequently these are called nonexperimental designs. (As we will see in Chapter 16, there are other ways to determine counterfactuals.)

An important element of the framework is the identification of the type of data that is used to estimate the baseline conditions of the project and comparison groups. When the evaluation begins at the start of the project the baseline data can be collected by conducting a survey or other primary data collection. (In Table 11.3 we call this Option A.) However, if the evaluation is not commissioned until late in the program, then baseline data can only be obtained through the use of secondary survey data (in cases where it is available) or through the techniques for reconstructing baseline data that are discussed in Chapter 5. We refer to this as Option B. This distinction is important because many discussions of evaluation designs implicitly assume that that baseline data can only be obtained through primary data collection and consequently that Designs 2, 4, and 6 can only be used when the evaluation is commissioned at the start of the program. With the distinction between Options A and B the important point is made that there are many situations in which these designs can be used even when the evaluation is not commissioned until late in the program cycle (see Table 11.3).

While Option B is often a viable option, it will frequently be the case that reconstructed baseline data are statistically weaker than primary and secondary data, so this should be kept in mind when assessing this option. Even when good-quality secondary data are available it will often be the case that there are problems because the period when the data were collected does not coincide exactly with the start of the project, the sample may not correspond exactly to the target population, and some important information is not included (i.e., whether respondents received any of the project services). Another problem is that important information on the characteristics of the project beneficiaries (such as their prior experience, or unusual household characteristics that might make them

Table 11.2 Seven Basic Impact Evaluation Design Frameworks

Key:
T = Time period
P = Project participants
C = Control/comparison group (Note 1)
P_1 P_2 C_1 C_2 = First and second and any subsequent observations
X = Project intervention

Time Period (Evaluation Event)	Start of Project (Baseline / pretest) (Note 2)	Project Intervention (Note 3)	Midterm Evaluation	End of Project Evaluation (endline)	Post-project Evaluation (Some Time after Intervention Ended) (Ex-post)
	T_1	X	T_2	T_3	T_4
1. *Longitudinal design* with pretest (baseline), midterm, posttest (endline), and ex-post observations of both project and comparison groups (Note 4)	P_1 C_1	X	P_2 C_2	P_3 C_3	P_4 C_4
2. *Pretest + posttest project and comparison group design*, i.e., before-and-after plus with-and-without comparisons	P_1 C_1	X		P_2 C_2	
3. *Truncated pretest + posttest of project and comparison groups* where the initial study is not conducted until the project has been underway for some time (most commonly at the midterm evaluation)		X	P_1 C_1	P_2 C_2	
4. *Pretest + posttest comparison of project group combined with posttest (only) of comparison group*	P_1	X		P_2 C_1	
5. *Posttest (only) comparison of project and comparison groups*		X		P_1 C_1	
6. *Pretest + posttest of project group* (no counterfactual comparison group)	P_1	X		P_2	
7. *Posttest (only) analysis of project group* (no baseline or statistical comparison group)		X		P_1	

NOTES:

(1) Technically a *control group* is only used in an experimental design (as randomization supposedly ensures there is no systematic difference in the distribution of subject characteristics between the two groups, i.e., selection *controls* for differences), and a *comparison group* is used in quasi-experimental designs where different selection procedures are used for the nontreatment group (sometimes called a "nonequivalent control group"). However, we will follow the common practice of using *comparison group* as shorthand for all kinds of matched groups, except when we wish to specifically indicate that randomization *was* used, in which case we will use the term *control group*.

(2) In this simplified table the point at which data are first collected on the project group (P_1) is also the time at which the evaluation begins. In Table 11.3 we distinguish between evaluations that start at the beginning of the project (and where baseline data are collected through primary data collection), and evaluations that start late in the project but where baseline data are obtained from secondary sources or through the baseline reconstruction techniques discussed in Chapter 5.

(3) The project intervention is usually a process that occurs over time, i.e., past the midterm to the end of the life of the project.

(4) Though these designs call for direct collection of baseline data through surveys or other data collection instruments, there may be alternative ways for obtaining baseline data, e.g., from secondary census or survey data, or it may be reconstructed (see Chapter 5).

more likely to be successful) are not included in the secondary data. This is referred to as the omitted variable problem or the issue of unobservables.

2.3. Design Step 3

Identify a Short List of Potential Evaluation Designs

The analysis of the desired or available frameworks in Step 2 narrows down the range of possible design options. The list can be further narrowed by assessing each of the possible designs in terms of the RWE budget, time, data, and political constraints. Designs can also be prioritized in terms of how well they address the purposes of the evaluation and reflect the dimensions of the evaluation scenario.

Within each of the evaluation design frameworks there are a number of different design options that could be considered. For each of the design frameworks that permit the use of a comparison group (design frameworks 1 through 5) there are a number of different ways that the comparison group can be selected (see Table 11.3). There are also the options of using a purely quantitative or a purely qualitative approach, or a combination of methodologies (mixed methods). For many frameworks the options will vary depending on whether the evaluation is commissioned at the start of the project, while it is being implemented, or at the end. Thus there are variants of each of those seven basic design frameworks that deal with a variety of ways to deal with Option A (where the evaluation is commissioned at the start of the program) or Option B (where the evaluation does not start until near or at the end of the life of the program).

The following descriptions refer to the seven basic design frameworks in Table 11.2. See Table 11.3 for 19 nuanced evaluation design options. All of these designs can be strengthened by including some of the techniques described in Table 11.5. These are introduced briefly below, and discussed in more detail in Appendix F.

Design Framework 1: Longitudinal design with data collected at the start of the project (pretest), during implementation, at project completion (posttest), and some time after the project has been completed (ex-post). While this is a powerful design, and really the ideal for rigorous assessment of sustainable impact, it is not used very frequently due to the cost of data collection (at least four points in time) and the long period of time covered by the study. The methodology for selecting the comparison group could use most of the design options discussed under Design Framework 2.

Design Framework 2: Pretest–posttest comparison group design. Among the options for selecting the comparison group are:

- *Randomized control trial:* Subjects are randomly assigned to the project (treatment) and control groups.[1]
- *Other statistical techniques* such as propensity score matching are used to ensure a close match of the project and comparison groups.
  - o *Regression discontinuity:* A clearly defined cut-off point is used to define eligibility for the project. Subjects above the cut-off are assigned to the project and subjects below the

---

[1]Econometric analysis often makes assumptions about whether initial differences will remain constant over the life of the project (time invariant) or will vary. If initial differences are time invariant, then their effect can be cancelled out using double difference analysis. However, there are many situations in which little is known about the nature of omitted variables, so it is not possible to assume that they are time invariant and that their effect can be ignored.

cut-off are assigned to the comparison group. When the cut-off point is strictly adhered to, regression discontinuity designs can provide unbiased estimates of project impact.

○ *Pipeline comparison group design:* When projects are implemented in phases, subjects in the second and sometimes subsequent phases are used as the comparison group for subjects entering in phase 1.

○ *Pretest–posttest comparison group design with judgmental matching:* When statistical matching is not possible, the comparison group is selected by combining interviews with experts, stakeholders, and key informants; review of available maps and documents; and rapid reconnaissance studies.

Design Framework 3: The evaluation does not begin until the project is already under way (most commonly, the evaluation is commissioned at the time of the midterm review).

- Theoretically, any of the five designs described for Framework 2 could be used, but in practice, judgmental matching is the most commonly used.

Design Framework 4: Pretest + posttest comparison of project group combined with posttest only of the comparison group.

- Posttest comparison group design combined with baseline data collection for the project participants but not for the comparison group.

Design Framework 5: Posttest comparison group design.

- In cases where secondary survey data are available, it may be possible to use a robust statistical design using techniques such as propensity score matching. But in other cases only judgmental matching may be possible. A weakness of even strong statistical designs is that it is difficult to determine whether statistically significant posttest differences between the project and comparison groups are due to the project intervention or to pre-existing differences between the two populations.

Design Framework 6: Pretest–posttest project group comparisons with no external comparison group.

- *Pretest–posttest single case project group design.* This design involves a pretreatment/posttreatment comparison in which the baseline condition serves as the comparison group (counterfactual). The design requires that the test be repeated at least three times, either using the same subject (group) in each test or using different groups each time. If the test is carefully administered and significant differences are found in each test, then these are considered methodologically credible evidence of a treatment effect (Kratchowill et al. 2010). To date, this design has mainly been used in educational evaluations and the health sciences (Morgan and Morgan 2009); there is still very limited evidence on how effectively the approach can be applied in development evaluation contexts.
- *Longitudinal design with no comparison group.* Data are collected on the project group throughout the life of the project so that the process and trajectory of change can be assessed as well as the difference between the start and end points. Data can be collected through

Table 11.3 List of Experimental, Quasi-Experimental, and Nonexperimental Evaluation Design Options, With a Focus on How the Counterfactual Is Determined

Design	Start of Project	Intervention	Midterm	End of Project	Post-Project	Stage of Project When Evaluation Commissioned
	T_1		T_2	T_3	T_4	
I. Experimental (Randomized) Designs						
1.1[2] Longitudinal design starting with randomized selection of intervention and control group	P_1 C_1	X	P_2 C_2	P_3 C_3	P_4 C_4	Start
2.1 Randomized control trial with only pretest and posttest	P_1 C_1	X		P_3 C_3		Start
II. Quasi-Experimental Designs						
1.2 Longitudinal design (without randomized selection)	P_1 C_1	X	P_2 C_2	P_3 C_3	P_4 C_4	Start
2.2 Option A. Pretest-posttest comparison group design with statistical matching of samples. Evaluation commissioned at start of project.	P_1 C_1	X		P_2 C_2		Start
2.2 Option B. Pretest-posttest comparison group design with statistical matching of samples. Evaluation commissioned at end of project.[3]	(P_1) (C_1)	X		P_2 C_2		End
2.3 Regression discontinuity	P_1 C_1	X		P_2 C_2		Start

	Phase	Start of Project	Intervention	Midterm	End of Project	Post-Project	Stage of Project When Evaluation Commissioned
2.4. Pipeline comparison group design. Can be used when projects are implemented in phases. Individuals, households or communities entering in Phase 2 (P2), and later phases, can be used as the comparison group for those entering in Phase 1 (P1). Note that $C1_2$ becomes $P2_1$, $C2_2$ becomes $P3_1$, etc.	Phase 1	$P1_1$ $C1_1$	X_1	$P1_2$ $C1_2$			Start
	Phase 2			$P2_1$ $C2_1$	X_2	$P2_2$ $C2_2$	
	Phase 3					$P3_1$	
2.5 Option A. Pretest–posttest comparison group design with judgmental matching. Evaluation commissioned at start of project.		P_1 C_1	X		P_2 C_2		Start
2.5 Option B. Pretest–posttest comparison group design with judgmental matching. Evaluation commissioned at end of project. Recall or secondary data used to reconstruct initial status of both project and comparison groups.		(P_1) (C_1)	X		P_2 C_2		End
3.1 Pretest–posttest comparison group design in which initial data collection (delayed baseline) is not conducted until project has been underway for some time.			X	P_1 C_1	P_2 C_2		During implementation.
4.1 Option A. Posttest comparison group design combined with collection of baseline data on project. Evaluation commissioned at start of project.		P_1	X		P_2 C_1		Start
4.1 Option B. Posttest comparison group design combined with collection of baseline data on project. Evaluation commissioned at end of project. Recall or secondary data used to reconstruct initial status of project group.		(P_1)	X		P_2 C_1		End
5.1 Posttest-only comparison group design.			X		P_1 C_1		End

(Continued)

(Continued)

	Start of Project	Intervention	Midterm	End of Project	Post-Project	Stage of Project When Evaluation Commissioned
6.1 Pretest–posttest single case project group design with no external comparison group. *Note:* Though it looks similar to the pipeline design, it is based on single cases, not group observations. This design is complicated to represent because the methodology requires that the treatment is applied sequentially in three separate cases, so more cells are required to represent all three phases.	$C1 ([P1_1])$	X_1	$C1 [P1_2]$ $C2 [P2_1]$ X_2	$C2 [P2_2]$ $C3 [P3_1]$ X_3	$C3 [P3_2]$	Start
6.2 Longitudinal design with no comparison group.	P_1	X	P_2	P_3	P_4	Start
6.3 Interrupted time series: This is a special case of Design 6.2, where more frequent observation points are available.	$P_1 P_2 P_3 P_4 P_5$	X	$P_6 P_7 P_8$	$P_9 P_{10} P_{11}$	$P_{12} P_{13} P_{14}$	Before start
6.4 Option A. Pretest–posttest project group design without comparison group. Evaluation commissioned at start of project.	P_1	X		P_2		Start
6.4 Option B. Pretest–posttest project group design without comparison group. Evaluation commissioned at end of project.	(P_1)	X		P_2		End
7.1 Posttest analysis of project group without a baseline or comparison group.		X		P_1		End

[2]Initial number refers to design frameworks in Table 11.2; second digit refers to a variant of the basic design.

[3]The parentheses, e.g. (P_1) and (C_1), indicate designs in which the evaluation was not commissioned until late in the project cycle and baseline conditions of participants and comparison groups need to be estimated either through the use of secondary data from surveys conducted by other agencies or through the baseline reconstruction techniques discussed in Chapter 5.

continued visits to a small (panel) sample of individuals, households, or communities; from periodic sample surveys; or from in-depth anthropological techniques.

- *Interrupted time series.* This is a special case of the longitudinal design in which a longer series of observation points is available before the project starts, while it is being implemented, and after it is completed. This permits the use of a cut-off point at the time the project intervention takes place. If the project has had an effect, there will be a break in the series (with frequency of outcomes increasing or decreasing significantly). Examples of how these designs have been used include analysis of the impacts of legislation on the number of traffic deaths from drunk driving, or changes in school enrollment or attendance after the introduction of a treatment (e.g., school meals).

Design Framework 7: Posttest analysis of the project group with no baseline data and no comparison group.

- While this design is frequently used for rapid evaluations that must be completed within a few weeks and with very limited resources, it can also be used for more rigorous mixed-method or qualitative evaluation designs. In most cases, that might include some method for using recall or secondary data to estimate what changes occurred during the life of the project, and some indirect means for obtaining counterfactual comparisons. Although this design is obviously the weakest of those we have identified, in the real world it is by far the most common scenario.

It is important to distinguish between situations in which nonexperimental designs are used because they are the only options available when working under severe budget and time constraints, and situations in which these designs are selected because they are considered to be the most appropriate for a particular design scenario and purpose. While evaluations conducted under the pressure of limited time and budget tend to be methodologically weak and to include significant biases, many of the designs, even those conducted under the limitations implied in the scenario of Design Framework 7, could, with the use of sound qualitative techniques, be considered to be as or even more methodologically rigorous than any experimental or quasi-experimental design. Box 11.2 lists some of the potentially strong nonexperimental designs.

BOX 11.2
EXAMPLES OF METHODOLOGICALLY STRONG
NONEXPERIMENTAL DESIGNS

- Single-case evaluation designs: With these designs the pretest situation provides the counterfactual. If the treatment is repeated three times under controlled conditions and if significant changes (often assessed judgmentally by experts) are found in each case, it is argued that this provides strong evidence of treatment effects.
- Longitudinal designs in which subjects are observed over a long period of time (sometimes years) to observe the process of change. These are effective designs

(Continued)

(Continued)

when complex behavioral changes must be assessed. These designs have been applied to assess the impacts on women's empowerment through access to microcredit.

- The preparation of in-depth case studies on a carefully selected sample of subjects.
- Concept mapping in which a group of experts identifies dimensions for assessing program performance and then rates programs on these dimensions. These techniques can be used to reconstruct baselines or to identify a counterfactual.
- Multiple-case study designs where cases are selected to ensure their representativity using mixed-method sampling.

Table 11.4 summarizes some of the strengths and weaknesses of each of these evaluation design frameworks.

Table 11.4   A Summary of the Strengths and Weaknesses of the Seven RWE Design Frameworks

Design	Advantages	Disadvantages
1. Comprehensive longitudinal design with pre-, mid-, post-, and ex-post observations on the project and comparison groups	This is the strongest design framework, studying both the implementation process and sustainability. May be required for research testing new project innovation that, if sustainable impact can be proven, will be expanded to a much greater scale.	• Requiring multiple evaluation events or observations during and after the life of a program, it is the most expensive, the most time-consuming, and the most difficult to implement.
2. Pretest-posttest project and comparison groups	This is a strong, general-purpose experimental or quasi-experimental design. With a well-selected comparison group, it provides good estimates of project impacts.	• Assumes the comparison group is reasonably similar to the project group and willing to participate in two surveys even though they receive no benefits. • Does not assess project implementation or sustainability.
3. Truncated pretest–posttest project and comparison group design (beginning at midterm, no pre-project baseline)	• Observes implementation process as well as impacts. Reasonably robust model, particularly for projects in which implementation begins slowly, so that not too much is missed by starting the evaluation late.	• Does not begin until around project midterm, so the project startup and initial implementation period are not captured.
4. Pretest–posttest project group combined with posttest analysis of project and comparison groups	• Assesses if the project model works and produces the intended outputs. • Assesses similarities and differences between project and comparison groups, at least at the end of the project. • Assesses the extent to which the project could potentially be replicated.	• Does not assess whether observed end-of-project differences between the project and comparison groups are due to the project or to preexisting differences between the two groups. • Does not control for local history that might affect outcomes.

Design	Advantages	Disadvantages
5. Posttest project and comparison groups	• Evaluates projects that implement well-tested interventions or that operate in isolated areas where there is no interference from other outside interventions.	• Does not measure the exact magnitude of project impacts or even changes over time. • Does not control for local history. • Does not assess potential for replication on a larger scale. • Does not study project implementation process.
6. Pretest-posttest project group	• Provides an approximate estimate of project impacts, or at least changes in outcome indicators during the life of a program.	• Does not compare changes in project population with other communities (i.e., counterfactual). • Does not control for local history. • Does not control for the effect of intervening variables through the use of multivariate analysis.
7. Posttest only, only on project group	• Useful for exploratory studies to get a general idea of how well the project model works. • Provides a first, approximate estimate of results, particularly for small or isolated projects.	• Though recall or other methods could be used, this scenario or framework does not directly measure change occurring during the life of the project. • Hard to feel confident that any purported changes are due to the project and not to other factors or interventions. • Does not directly control for external events; nor does it obtain comparative data to estimate attributable impact.

NOTE: The strength of all of these models can be increased by combining them with the impact evaluation framework and analysis of contextual factors discussed in Chapter 10 and with some of the RWE techniques discussed later in this chapter and in Appendix F. For Designs 1, 2, 3, 4, and 5, which use comparison groups, the analysis can be greatly strengthened by using multiple regression analysis to statistically control for differences in the characteristics of the project and control groups. Where appropriate secondary data are available, these designs can also be strengthened through statistical matching techniques such as **propensity scores** and **instrumental variables**.

2.4. Design Step 4

Take into Consideration the Preferred Methodological Approach on the QUANT/Mixed Methods/QUAL Continuum

The choice of evaluation design is also partly determined by the methodological preferences of the clients, stakeholders, and evaluators. While certain scenarios might seem to lend themselves more naturally to a more QUANT or a more QUAL approach, in most situations there is a choice of approaches. The present authors believe that a mixed-method approach brings many advantages (see Chapter 14), but even then most mixed-method designs tend to have a predominant methodological preference leaning more to either QUANT or QUAL approaches. When mixed methods are used with a predominantly QUANT approach the designs tend to be quite different than in cases where the evaluator has a predominantly QUAL preference. The situation will often arise in which the client has a strong preference for either a QUANT or QUAL approach, and the evaluator may sometimes find it necessary to point out some of the potential limitations of designs that are too strongly oriented toward one or the other methodological approach.

2.5. Design Step 5

Strategies for Strengthening the Basic Evaluation Designs

In Appendix F we discuss in more detail the most common basic impact evaluation designs. However, it is important to understand that while some of these are experimental and quasi-experimental designs that are able to address statistical issues such as selection bias, the designs do not address a wide range of other threats to validity (see Appendixes A through E), which is why we call them *basic evaluation designs*. A few of the issues that the basic designs do not (automatically) address include:

- Problems concerning the reliability and/or validity of measurement of key indicators, particularly when these relate to sensitive issues such as household income, control of household resources, domestic violence, and social constraints on women's economic activities or mobility.
- Variations in the way the project is implemented, in the quality of services, and in the differential access of different groups to the services and benefits.
- Contextual factors affecting the outcomes and impacts of the project even when it is implemented in exactly the same way in each community/site.
- Differences (nonequivalency) between the project and comparison groups, particularly those that are difficult to quantify (e.g., motivation, community organization, etc.). This includes the omitted variable problem (see example of the Kenya flip chart evaluation in Box 11.5 on page 236).

The RWE approach proposes a number of strategies that can be used to enhance the strength of all the basic impact evaluation designs, including those that are considered to be statistically robust. The strategies are discussed in the next section, and summarized in Table 11.5 on page 229.

2.6. Design Step 6

Evaluability Analysis to Assess the Technical, Resource, and Political Feasibility of Each Design

Each of the shortlisted designs will be assessed to determine its methodological soundness, the threats to validity (see Chapter 7 and Appendixes A through E), and how well they can be addressed. Each of the options that is considered methodologically sound will then be assessed in terms of budget, time, access to data, political acceptability, and how well each one responds to the objectives of the evaluation. If necessary, a chart will be prepared comparing options on each of these criteria.

2.7. Design Step 7

Preparation of Short List of Evaluation Design Options for Discussion with Clients and (Possibly) Other Stakeholders

The design options developed through these steps will then be presented to the client and possibly other key stakeholders for a decision on which design to select. A note should be prepared explaining the strengths and weaknesses of each design and the potential trade-offs. This may include a risk analysis as well as a discussion (where appropriate) of any political or policy issues that should be taken into consideration. It is important to stress that there is no single "best" evaluation design, and that while the evaluation consultants can provide guidance on technical issues and trade-offs, the final decision must be made by the client. The following are examples of some of the trade-offs and issues that might be discussed: A randomized control trial may have statistical advantages, but there may be political opposition or ethical concerns. Of course, if the evaluation is being commissioned late in the life of the program it is too late to randomize participants and control groups.

Higher levels of statistical precision or more detailed disaggregation of the findings will usually increase the required sample size and therefore the cost. On the other hand, reducing the sample size to save money will reduce the power of the test and increase the danger of a false negative (rejecting a potential project effect when it really does exist). The role of the consultant is to help the client understand the issues and to arrive at a satisfactory compromise.

When operating under budget constraints there may be a trade-off between statistical precision (larger sample size) and a more in-depth understanding of the process of project implementation and the experience and opinions of different sectors of the target group. Often the consultant will propose a mixed-method design as a compromise between the QUANT and QUAL objectives.

2.8. Design Step 8

Agreement on the Final Evaluation Design

Based on the above discussions an agreement will be reached on the evaluation design. Sometimes if there is concern about how well the design will work, it may be agreed that the design will be reviewed at a certain point. This is often the case where a program is being implemented in phases and the evaluation design may be assessed at the end of Phase 1. However, to repeat our oft-stated caveat: The later in the life of a project an evaluation is planned, the more limited the options are for what kind of evaluation design framework is possible.

3. Tools and Techniques for Strengthening the Basic Evaluation Designs

3.1. Basing the Evaluation on a Theory of Change and a Program Theory Model

A **program theory model** defines the cause-effect relationships through which a program is intended to achieve its objectives and identifies and tests some of the critical assumptions on which the success of the program will depend (see Chapters 2 and 10). Program theory also helps identify the contextual factors (economic, political, organizational, environmental, and sociocultural) likely to affect implementation and outcomes of the project, and that can help explain why the same project implemented in the same way can have very different outcomes in different locations. The formulation of this model helps identify the concepts and issues that should be examined by the evaluation and the hypotheses that should be tested. The theory model is also very helpful in the interpretation of the findings and in the assessment of whether or not a project should continue or be replicated. Program theory is particularly valuable in many RWE settings because it helps identify the key assumptions and hypotheses on which the limited evaluation resources should focus.

Box 11.3 illustrates how program theory could be used to strengthen two case studies to illustrate the different evaluation designs:

BOX 11.3
EXAMPLE OF HOW PROGRAM THEORY CAN
STRENGTHEN EVALUATION DESIGNS

The impacts of housing on family income. The pretest–posttest evaluation design could have been strengthened by using program theory to formulate the processes through which the intended outputs were expected to be produced. This could have identified and tested some of the key assumptions about how improved housing was expected to increase employment and household income. **Contextual analysis** would also have helped identify local political, economic, institutional, environmental, and cultural factors explaining why the same housing designs, implemented in the same way, had different outcomes in different locations. The example indicates that local economic conditions might have contributed as much as improved housing to influence changes in household income.

- *The effects of resettlement on project beneficiaries and nonbeneficiaries in an irrigation project in India.* The evaluation found that the differences in the social and economic conditions of families who had received land and support to resettle and those who were forced to resettle without any compensation were much less than expected. The evaluation was not able to explain why the differences were so small and why the project seemed to have produced so little benefit for participants. A program theory model could have helped define the process of resettlement and could have identified and suggested ways to test hypotheses about how project beneficiaries were expected to benefit from the provision of land and other services. Designing the evaluation to test these hypotheses would probably have helped to explain why these benefits did not occur.

3.2. Process Analysis

Many QUANT evaluations use a pretest–posttest design to assess the QUANT effects of the project by measuring the change in a key indicator (**summative evaluation**). With many of these designs, data are only collected at the start and end of the project (and no information is obtained during the process of project implementation). These designs do not study how well the project was implemented, or how the implementation process affected outcomes, or the accessibility of the project to different sectors of the target population. Without an understanding of what happened during project implementation it is difficult to know whether the lack of observed impacts is because the program is not a good model for achieving the intended impacts or whether the program is potentially good but that there were problems with the way it was implemented.

As we saw in Chapter 10, the incorporation of process analysis strengthens the ability of the evaluation to provide guidance on ways to improve program effectiveness (**formative evaluation**). Process analysis can assess, for example, whether participatory planning did in fact involve all the intended sectors of the community and whether the benefits reached all the intended groups. Depending on the scale of the project and the types of questions being addressed, process analysis can use QUANT, QUAL, or mixed-method designs.

Table 11.5 Tools and Techniques to Strengthen Any of the Basic Impact Evaluation Designs

Some of the evaluation designs depicted in Tables 11.3 and 11.4 and further elaborated in Appendix F might address problems of selection bias, but they are still vulnerable to a wide range of additional threats to validity. The tools and techniques described in this table can enhance the methodological rigor of all of these designs, including the designs that are considered to be statistically rigorous.

Essential Tools and Techniques	Why Required	How to Implement
1. Basing the evaluation on a theory of change and a program logic model	The purpose of an evaluation is not just to estimate "how much" change has occurred but also to explain "why" and "how" the changes were produced. Clients also wish to know to what extent the changes were due to the intervention and whether similar changes would be likely to occur if the program is replicated in other contexts. In order to achieve these objectives it is necessary to explain the underlying theory and the key assumptions on which the program is based, and to identify how they can be tested in the evaluation.	The design and use of program theory is discussed in Chapter 10. That chapter also illustrates how the theory can be articulated graphically through a logic model.
2. Process analysis	Project outcomes are affected by how well a project is implemented and by what happens during implementation. Without process analysis it is not possible to assess whether failure to achieve outcomes is due to design failure or to implementation failure.	See Chapters 10, 11, and 17.
3. Contextual analysis	Projects implemented in an identical way in different locations will often have different outcomes due to different local economic, political, or organizational contexts or different socioeconomic characteristics of target communities. This can result in wrong estimations of project impact, often leading to underestimation of impacts (due to increased variance of the estimations).	See Chapters 10 and 11.
4. Using mixed-method approaches to strengthen evaluation design, data collection, and analysis	Most evaluation designs can be strengthened by combining QUANT techniques that ensure the statistical representativity of the data with QUAL methods that permit in-depth analysis and assessment of the quality of implementation, outputs, and outcomes.	See Chapters 13 and 14.
5. Identification and use of available secondary data	Many evaluations do not identify and use all of the available secondary data. Secondary data can often reduce the costs of primary data collection and provide independent estimates of key variables.	See Chapter 5.
6. Triangulation	The validity of data and the quality and depth of interpretation of findings is enhanced when two or more independent estimates can be compared.	See Chapters 13 and 14.

3.3. Incorporating Contextual Analysis

While contextual analysis is a standard part of many QUAL evaluations, it is frequently not included in QUANT evaluations. However, because an understanding of the influence of contextual factors can greatly enrich the interpretation of QUANT analysis, RWE evaluators are always encouraged to consider the utility and feasibility of incorporating contextual analysis into their evaluation design. Contextual analysis assesses the influence of economic, political, organizational, and environmental factors on the implementation and outcome of projects. Contextual analysis also examines the influence of the preexisting sociocultural characteristics of the target populations on how different groups respond to the project. These are described in some program theory models as *moderators*.

Most contextual analysis is descriptive—for example, using interviews with key informants, review of project and nonproject documents for context, and **participant observation**. However, contextual variables can be quantified, either by using survey data on, for example, households, students, factory workers, or farmers; or by transforming ratings into **dummy variables** that can be included in regression analysis.[4]

3.4. Complementing Quantitative Data Collection and Analysis with Mixed-Method Designs

Quasi-experimental designs (QED) can be strengthened by incorporating mixed-method approaches in the evaluation design, data collection, or analysis stages (see Chapter 14). The following are examples of the use of mixed methods:

- Exploratory studies to understand the context and to identify key issues and hypotheses to be tested. This is particularly important in the construction of the program theory model.
- Analysis of the quality of the services provided by the project and the accessibility of these services to different sectors of the target population.
- Analysis of the contextual factors (the economic, political, organizational, and natural environmental conditions) within which each project site operates.
- Understanding the cultural characteristics of the affected populations and how these affect project implementation and outcomes.

3.5. Ensuring That Full Use Is Made of Available Secondary Data

It is always good practice to check to see what sources of secondary data might be available (from previous surveys, project documents, school attendance records, use of health centers, etc.). In some cases secondary data can eliminate the need to conduct new surveys or can provide an independent estimate to check information collected during the evaluation. Chapter 5 describes the many sources of secondary data that can be used to reconstruct baseline data, and most of those sources can also be used for other purposes.

---

[4]For example, the attitudes of the municipal government to the project could be rated as positive or negative, and these could be transformed into dummy variables (for example, positive = 1 and not positive = 0).

3.6. Triangulation: Using Two or More Independent Estimates for Key Indicators and Using Data Sources and Analytical Methods to Explain Findings

Estimates obtained from a single data collection method can often be strengthened if they can be independently confirmed from two or more independent sources. This can be done in any of the following ways:

- Getting independent estimates of the magnitude or direction of change in variables (such as income, school enrollment and absentee rates, proportion of households using the village health center) obtained from surveys, observation, **focus groups,** secondary data, and so on.
- Comparing the estimates through triangulation. If estimates using different methods are consistent, there can be greater confidence in the findings.
- If estimates are inconsistent, follow up to determine the reasons and make adjustments to the estimates.

4. Developing Designs Suitable for RealWorld Evaluation Conditions

We now address a very important decision that needs to be made by those commissioning and those responsible for conducting an evaluation: What evaluation design would be most appropriate for responding to the priority questions determined during the assessment of client needs, and which design options are even possible, given the constraints and the stage the project has reached? As we saw in Tables 11.2 and 11.3, the earlier in the life of the project this decision is made, the more options there are.

Table 11.2 proposes a classification of seven basic evaluation design frameworks. This narrows down the set of possible evaluation designs that could be used in a particular scenario. They are classified in terms of when the evaluation began or will begin, whether baseline (or only midterm or posttest) data were or can be collected, and whether or not a comparison group was or can be used. These frameworks define the skeleton of the evaluation design and a wide range of different methodologies (quantitative, qualitative, and mixed-method) can be used within each scenario. Given the ongoing debates concerning whether there is a "best" evaluation design, it is important to stress that we do not believe there is a single best design and that the choice of the appropriate design must be made on the basis of the review of evaluation purposes and scenarios presented earlier.

It is useful at this point to recall the distinction we made earlier between designs that are *statistically* strong and those that are *methodologically* sound. Many of the "strong designs" referred to in the evaluation literature are in fact only strong in their ability to address statistical threats to selection bias, but they are potentially weak with respect to other important methodological issues, or at the very least they do not automatically include sound methodology for addressing other challenges.

The range of evaluation designs can be divided into three categories depending on whether there is a control/comparison group, and if so, how it is selected:

Experimental designs (randomized control trials or RCTs) in which subjects are randomly assigned to the project and treatment groups: This is a strong statistical design in terms of control for selection bias, but these designs have a number of potential methodological weaknesses when used in isolation. Also, RCTs typically are not longitudinal, thus missing out on trends during the life of a project or measuring long-term impacts through ex-post evaluations. Thus in terms of scenario (when data are collected), we consider longitudinal scenarios the most comprehensive.

Quasi-experimental designs in which a comparison group is used but is selected separately from the project group so that there are potential problems of selection bias: When large samples are used, or good secondary data are available, it is possible to use statistical matching procedures such as propensity score matching. When this is not possible, judgmental matching procedures can be used, though they are statistically weaker. While these designs can reduce the effects of statistical selection bias, as in the case of experimental designs, when used in isolation they are subject to a range of methodological challenges.

Nonexperimental designs that do not use a statistical comparison group: While these designs are often used when an evaluation must be conducted under time and budget constraints and where as a consequence the methodology is often weak, many other evaluations use methodologically strong qualitative and mixed-method designs to compensate for the weaknesses in statistical design (see Chapters 13 and 14).

Thus the framework structures or scenarios presented in Table 11.2 should be considered as a starting point for identifying the most appropriate evaluation design and not as a comprehensive list of evaluation designs, and certainly not as a ranking of "strong" and "weak" designs.

Whichever design is selected, the RWE approach strongly recommends that the basic statistical design be complemented by a number of tools and techniques that address some of the weaknesses of the statistical designs discussed in Table 11.5.

While these scenarios have often been discussed within the context of QUANT evaluation designs, the scenarios (e.g., whether or not the evaluation begins with a baseline assessment, makes before-and-after comparisons, or whether or not there is some form of counterfactual analysis) apply equally to QUAL and mixed-method evaluations. Most QUANT evaluations are based on either an experimental or a quasi-experimental design in that they seek to directly measure changes in a set of QUANT variables and to assess whether the changes are associated with the project interventions. Even if using QUAL methods to determine people's perspectives of changes that have taken place, there will be discussion of what things were like before the intervention started, what changes might be attributed to the project, and how these might compare with what has happened in other communities. These considerations make it possible to identify a limited number of evaluation designs that cover most RWE scenarios. Table 2.4 (p. 35) provides a decision tree matrix to help decide which design is possible under different scenarios.

We conclude this chapter with more in-depth discussion of experimental and quasi-experimental designs. See Appendix F for further discussion of these and other designs.

5. Experimental and Quasi-Experimental Designs

Although for many evaluation design purposes it could be preferable to use one of the more statistically robust designs described in this chapter, under RealWorld budget and time constraints, it is often necessary to use a design without a direct before-and-after comparison or without a control or comparison group.

(We follow the practice of using the term *comparison* group to refer to any kind of nontreatment group and only use *control* group to indicate that the matched group was selected through random assignment.) We begin by describing **randomized** control evaluation designs, considered by many if not most QUANT evaluators to be the strongest statistical designs for assessing project **impacts**, and then discuss the reasons why these designs are not more widely used under RealWorld conditions.

It should be noted that while the RWE approaches can be relevant to almost any kind of evaluation, in this book we mainly focus on impact evaluations, i.e., evaluations whose main purpose is to determine whether or not (and how much) an intervention achieved its higher-level goals, which hopefully means that it contributed to significant and sustainable changes in the quality of life of its intended beneficiaries.

5.1. Randomized Control Trials

In a true randomized experimental design (often referred to as randomized control trials, or RCTs), subjects or units (e.g., individuals, rats, agricultural plots) are randomly assigned to the experimental (treatment) or **control** (no treatment) groups.[5] If the sample is reasonably large,[6] the attributes of the subjects (age, sex, previous experience with similar programs, etc.) should be randomly distributed between the project (treatment) and control groups, and there should be no systematic selection bias. However, there are often a number of practical difficulties in ensuring randomization. For example, the treatment may not be administered in a completely uniform way, there may be political or personal pressures to allow certain people or communities to participate, or the procedures for treating individuals or communities identified after the initial selection may not be clearly defined or uniformly implemented. Khandker, Koolwal, and Samad (2010, chap. 3) propose a two-stage randomization procedure. In Stage 1, a sample of potential participants is randomly selected from the relevant population. This stage seeks to ensure *external validity*. In the second stage, individuals are randomly assigned to the treatment and control groups, ensuring internal validity (in that changes in outcomes are due to the project intervention and not to other factors). The two groups are measured on indicators of the **output** or **outcome** that the experiment is seeking to produce.

After baseline measurements are taken, the treatment (e.g., teaching method, drug, fertilizer) is administered to the experimental group and not to the control group, but otherwise the conditions of the two groups are kept (or assumed to be kept) as much the same as possible until the posttest measurements are taken. If there is a significant difference in the posttest measures for the two groups (after controlling for any pretest differences[7]), this is taken as an indication that the experimental treatment had an effect. Ideally, the experiment should be repeated several times under slightly different conditions (such as duration or intensity of the treatment and how it is administered) before any conclusions are drawn about a causal relation between the treatment and the observed outcomes.

Box 11.4 gives examples of randomized evaluation designs from the MIT (Massachusetts Institute of Technology) Poverty Action Lab and the World Bank. The examples cover education, nutrition, labor market, health, microcredit, poverty reduction, and conditional cash transfer projects

---

[5]See Shadish et al. (2002, chap. 1) for a discussion of experiments and the analysis of causation.

[6]The required sample size should be determined based on the acceptable standard error of the estimated effect size (see Chapter 15).

[7]Even with relatively large samples, sampling variation will normally produce differences between the project and control groups with respect to, for example, average weight, crop yield, family demographic characteristics, or pretest performance scores.

in India, Kenya, South Africa, Mexico, Morocco, Cambodia, and the United States. These examples show that it is possible to conduct randomized evaluation designs in developing countries as well as in countries such as the United States. Box 11.5 describes in more detail the procedures used for designing an RCT to evaluate the impacts of flip charts on test score performance in Kenya.

The Cambodia lower-secondary-school scholarship program presents an example in which it was proposed to use randomization to select low-income girls to receive the scholarships. However, the government objected to the use of randomization on political and ethical grounds, and the proposed RCT design was replaced with a regression discontinuity design. In recent years there has been a revival of interest in regression discontinuity designs (which were popular in the 1960s and 1970s but were afterwards little used[8]) partly because they avoid the ethical and political concerns about randomization while still permitting unbiased estimates of project effects. (For further discussion see Chapter 12.) One of the situations in which randomization is used, particularly in developing countries, is when demand for a particular service (e.g., improved water supply, sanitation, or self-help housing) exceeds the supply of the service that an agency can provide in a given year. Under these circumstances, a lottery is sometimes used to select the families or communities who will receive the services, and the unsuccessful applicants can be used as a control group (Carvalho and White 2004).[9] Many agencies feel more comfortable using randomization in situations in which demand exceeds supply, both because many of the ethical issues are resolved and also because a lottery provides a public and transparent way to select beneficiaries. Hopefully there will be a subsequent phase when the "control" people will have their opportunity to receive the benefits of the intervention.

BOX 11.4
EXAMPLES OF RANDOMIZED CONTROL TRIALS

In June 2003 the Massachusetts Institute of Technology (MIT) launched a program of **randomized trials** *to assess the impacts of development programs in developing countries and the United States. The main justification for doing this was the belief that nonrandomized, quasi-experimental evaluation designs can often come to erroneous conclusions about program effectiveness because of the "omitted variable" problem (important factors that might explain apparent program effects have been excluded from the analysis). Some of the randomized control trials reported by the MIT Abdul Latif Jameel Poverty Action Lab (J-PAL) include:*

- Women as policymakers—the impact of female political leaders on policy decisions
- The Balsakhi (Mumbai, India) program—charting the effects of remedial education programs on school quality and test scores
- Measuring the impacts of school inputs in Kenya—the case of flip charts (see Box 11.5)

---

[8]Shadish et al. (2002:208) suggest that these deigns were used more than 200 times under the 1965 Title 1 of the Elementary and Secondary Education Act, but that the limited use in later years may have been due to the practical problems in administering this design that we discuss later in this chapter.

[9]This does not, of course, mean that ethical issues are not important, but it does show that a number of research institutions and development agencies have felt that there are acceptable ways to address these issues.

- Primary school deworming project (Kenya)—the impacts of child health gains due to preschool health and nutrition projects on preschool participation
- Incentives to learn—the impacts of scholarships for girls in Kenya
- School choice in Colombia—measuring the impacts of vouchers for private schooling
- Peer effects, alcohol, and college roommates in the United States—the impact of randomly assigned college roommates on drinking behavior
- A study of racial discrimination in the job market in Chicago and Boston
- The Balwadi health program (New Delhi, India)—the impacts of child health gains due to a preschool health and nutrition project on preschool participation
- Interest rate and consumer credit in South Africa—the effect of changing interest rates on loan acceptance
- Understanding technology adoption—fertilizers in Western Kenya: Why do farmers not use fertilizer even though it appears to have the potential to increase yields considerably?

SOURCE: Adapted by the authors from the MIT Poverty Action Lab Web site (www.povertyactionlab.org).

In 2009 the World Bank produced a volume of case studies on evaluations that influenced policy. The following are some examples in which randomized designs were used:

- The Progresa/Oportunidades conditional cash transfer program in Mexico used randomized selection of communities for each phase of the project. A pipeline design (see Appendix F) with subjects who would not receive benefits until the next phase was used as the comparison group for beneficiaries of the first phase.
- In Kenya an evaluation was designed to assess the effects of charging for insecticide-treated bednets for malaria prevention compared to providing them at no cost. Randomization was used to determine which clinics would provide bednets free and which would charge.
- In Kenya a deworming program for schools was to be introduced in three phases to accommodate financial and administrative constraints. Schools were randomly assigned to the three phases with the schools not yet phased-in acting as a control group.
- In Morocco a rural microfinance program developed a national RCT to evaluate the effects of microfinance on agricultural and nonagricultural activities, and on income, expenditures, and household security. The RCT was introduced in the second phase of the project to increase the credibility of the evaluation findings.

SOURCE: Bamberger, M., and A. Kirk, eds. (2009), "Making Smart Policy: Using Impact Evaluation for Policy Making. Case Studies on Evaluations That Influenced Policy." Washington, DC: World Bank.

NOTE: For additional examples, see evaluations conducted by the International Initiative for Impact Evaluation (3ie) at www.3ieimpact.org

There are serious questions related to the ethics of using randomized designs under real-world conditions, and also concerns that the lack of control over the process of project implementation makes it difficult to isolate project effects from extraneous factors. However, there are those who feel that in situations where only a subset of the population can be reached by a planned intervention anyway, randomized trials to test the efficacy of a specific experimental intervention may be justified.

BOX 11.5
COMPARING THE FINDINGS OF A RANDOMIZED CONTROL TRIAL AND A RETROSPECTIVE EVALUATION OF THE IMPACTS OF FLIP CHARTS ON SCHOOL TEST PERFORMANCE IN KENYA

One of the examples of the MIT J-PAL approach was an evaluation in Kenya to assess the impacts of flip charts (i.e., hand-drawn or preprinted charts that can be presented on an easel) on student test scores on various school subjects. Of a total of 178 schools, 89 were randomly assigned to receive the flip charts (by listing schools alphabetically and then randomly allocating alternate schools to the project and comparison groups), and the other 89 schools formed the comparison group. Test scores were measured at the start of the school year (before the flip charts were introduced) and again at the end of the year. A statistical analysis found no significant differences between the two groups (Glewwe et al. 2004). This example is interesting because an earlier *retrospective evaluation,* in which test scores were compared for the project and comparison groups after the flip charts had been introduced into the schools, found a significant test score improvement in the project scores. Glewwe and his colleagues argued that this apparent project effect was due to the **omitted variable problem**—in this case, that the analysis did not control for the level of parental participation in their children's education. The authors argue that schools with a higher level of parental involvement showed significant improvements in test scores, and that when the analysis controls for the level of parental involvement, flip charts are no longer positively associated with test score improvement. This example shows that the omitted variable problem is one of the reasons for preferring randomized designs and one of the potentially serious threats to validity presented by *omitted variables* in QEDs.

SOURCE: Glewwe et al. (2004).

Although the promotion and use of RCTs has rapidly increased in recent years, the implementation of randomized designs in real-world field settings offers many challenges. Even where it is possible to achieve a randomized allocation of communities, schools, individuals, or other units to project and control groups, it is more difficult to ensure a standardized implementation of the project in all sites or to control for differences between the project and control sites during the **implementation process**. In the case of an education project, for example, there will often be differences in the extent to which different schools are able to comply with the proposed project design. The quality of teachers may vary; the ability of schools to provide the required administrative and other support may also vary, as well as the physical conditions of the schools and the class sizes. In the case of health programs, not all health centers may have adequate supplies of the medicines, or pressures on staff may mean that not all patients receive advice on how to use the medicines or the necessary follow-up support. In many cases, these variations will not be well monitored, so the extent of the variations in the treatment may not be known.

Another set of issues has to do with differences that will often develop between the project and control groups during the implementation period. The fact that an international donor agency is supporting a project may raise the profile of the project and draw in other sources of support (particularly when the implementing ministry or agency wants the project to work well in the hope that additional funding will be received for a future expansion). On the other hand, staff members working on similar projects in control areas may become discouraged, or they may begin lobbying local politicians hoping that their communities will also receive some of the same benefits.

Another criticism of RCTs is that, all too often, they are based on the quest for a "silver bullet"— one fairly simple (and inexpensive) intervention that will (presumably by itself) directly produce the desired impact. In fact, in the RealWorld multiple conditions and factors are usually needed in order to achieve higher-level impact. Thus a rigorous impact evaluation should really be based on a multi-layered logic model, recognizing the contributions of multiple actors.

Given the complex interactions among all these factors, if a randomized design does not find statistically significant project impacts, it is often difficult to determine to what extent this is due to weaknesses in the project design concept (*design failure*) or to problems that arose during implementation (*implementation failure*). Similarly, it may also be difficult to assess to what extent statistically significant project impacts are due to the project and not to the effect of these other factors. The lack of attention to process analysis (*implementation monitoring*) in many randomized designs makes it even more difficult to address these questions.

Although randomized evaluation designs offer many QUANT methodological advantages, in most evaluations conducted in the field it is not feasible or advisable to use these designs due to a combination of cost, logistical, ethical, and methodological issues. Even if budget is not an issue, there are a number of methodological reasons why random assignment is not feasible or even possible in most RealWorld situations. One of the most common situations for RWE is that the evaluation does not begin until the project has already been implemented, so there is obviously no way to influence who does and who does not participate in the project. Even when the evaluation begins at the start of the project, in many cases the choice of project locations is based on political considerations (e.g., one school must be included in each district) or technical factors (e.g., it must be possible to link the water and sanitation system or the feeder roads to the main infrastructure). In other cases the project is designed to cover communities or groups with certain unique characteristics (e.g., the largest or the poorest urban slums or the communities with the most dynamic community leadership) that make it difficult to use a random allocation of subjects to a control group. In yet other cases, participants are self-selected (e.g., communities apply to participate in a water supply project or entrepreneurs decide to apply for small-business loans).

There are also important ethical concerns about withholding services and benefits from people in the control group. These are particularly critical with respect to drugs or other medical services that can potentially save lives or protect people from serious illness, but there are also important concerns if improved educational opportunities or better housing or infrastructure are being withheld. These are important issues that must be seriously addressed, in consultation with all major stakeholders, whenever the possibility of using a randomized design is being considered. In many cases political pressures—some of which reflect the ethical concerns discussed above, others of which are less idealistic—may make it impossible to ensure that services are provided to the constituents of local politicians, whether or not they were in the control group. However, while ethical issues should always be considered with respect to every evaluation, their importance for RCTs is sometimes exaggerated. There are many instances in which resource constraints require that some criteria be applied for deciding how the scarce resources are applied. In many situations a lottery or other random assignment procedure may be the fairest and most transparent way to be in the allocation. Plans for offering to include control groups in subsequent phases of a project can also help (assuming the intervention proves to be effective and future funding will be secured).

BOX 11.6
POTENTIAL METHODOLOGICAL WEAKNESSES IN MANY
STATISTICALLY STRONG EVALUATION DESIGNS

Many evaluation designs that are commonly referred to in the evaluation literature as experimental design are in fact only strong with respect to their ability to control for sources of statistical selection bias. The reasons that they are statistically strong (e.g., randomization or statistical matching of samples, strict and inflexible rules concerning how data are collected, and administration of the same survey instrument to the same or equivalent samples before and after the project implementation) makes these quantitative designs potentially weak in other respects, including:

- *Weak construct validity*: Many statistical designs are not based on a program theory model (although it is perfectly possible to incorporate a program theory model).
- *No analysis of the project implementation process.*
- *No consideration of contextual variables* that can explain differences in outcomes in different project locations.
- *Mono-method bias*: Many quantitative designs collect all of their data from a single instrument, most commonly a structured questionnaire. This increases the risk of bias or incomplete information, as it is not possible to compare estimates obtained from different independent sources.
- *Difficulties in collecting information on sensitive topics*: Many quantitative data collection methods use structured questionnaires and a sampling protocol that requires a predetermined sample frame.
- *Inflexibility and difficulty in adapting the design to changes in the project design or the context in which it is implemented*. Two conclusions result from these potential methodological weaknesses in strong statistical designs. First, it is important when discussing the merits of different evaluation designs to always distinguish between "strong statistical designs" and "methodologically strong designs." While statistical evaluations can be designed to ensure all-round methodological strength, this is frequently not done, leaving many statistically strong designs to be vulnerable in other ways. Similarly, it is possible to have qualitative or mixed-method designs that might be considered weak in terms of conventional quantitative terms but that may use designs that are methodologically sound in other ways. Second, it is almost always possible to strengthen the methodology of all evaluation designs—quantitative, qualitative, and mixed method—by incorporating the "tools and techniques to strengthen any of the basic impact evaluation designs" discussed in this chapter (see Table 11.5).

5.2. Quasi-Experimental Designs: Adapting the Most Robust Evaluation Designs to RealWorld Program Evaluation

When using designs to evaluate the impacts of development projects and service provision (e.g., water supply, road construction, microcredit, teacher training, and teaching materials), there are, as mentioned above, very few situations in which randomized control trials can be applied. As we will see in Chapter 13, for qualitative (QUAL) practitioners, laboratory settings and controlled randomization, even if they were possible, are not as helpful as naturalistic settings. Just because something has a certain effect in controlled conditions does not mean the effect can be achieved in natural settings.

Quasi-experimental designs (QEDs) seek to match as closely as possible the characteristics of the project and comparison groups to eliminate as far as possible the different causes of selection bias and to accomplish the following:

- Make the best possible estimate of the extent to which a project, program, or policy has produced its intended impacts.
- Identify the factors that positively or negatively influence the magnitude and direction of the impacts.

In the RealWorld, evaluators trying to approximate the most robust designs typically face one or more of the following problems.

It is rarely possible to randomly assign subjects to experimental and control groups. For logistical, administrative, political, and sometimes ethical reasons, most projects are accessible to or affect everyone in a given community or area. For example, a school, water supply system, or road will usually be accessible to all families in the community, and it is difficult to tell some families they cannot send their children to the school or use the water (assuming they are willing to pay or that they have participated in the construction of the water system).

Some projects use a self-selection process when, for example, people decide if they wish to apply for microcredits, enroll in a literacy class, or plant new varieties of seed. In these cases, it is likely that the people who do decide to participate will be different in important ways from those who do not participate. Typically, people who take the initiative to participate are economically better off, better educated, and have more self-confidence. Consequently, it is difficult to know whether observed changes in income, reading skills, health, and so on are due to the effects of the project or to the differences in initial conditions and capabilities of participants and nonparticipants.

It is very difficult to find a comparison group closely matching the experimental group on the key indicators. Project communities are often selected because of special characteristics. In some cases, project planners choose the poorest communities; in other cases, they choose communities that have the greatest likelihood of success. In either case, it will be difficult to find a comparison group that closely matches the project population.

- In many cases, it is difficult to use any kind of comparison group at all for political or ethical reasons. Frequently, politicians and community leaders in a designated comparison group area will pressure for their community to be included in the project. From the ethical perspective, one would not want to withhold a service (such as oral rehydration treatment for severely malnourished children) just to prove the efficacy of the treatment. Another ethical (or practical) consideration is that it is often considered inappropriate to ask families in comparison communities to spend a long time responding to surveys if they will not receive any benefit. In some cases, the fact that families are being interviewed creates false expectations that they will be eligible to participate in this or a later phase of the project.

- It is also difficult to ensure that treatments (services) are administered in exactly the same way to all project sites and families. Sometimes the delivery of materials and equipment is delayed; in other cases, there are major differences with respect to the organization of the project and delivery of services in different sites. In one microcredit program, the local administrator may speak the local language and may create a welcoming atmosphere that encourages families to visit the project to discuss loans. In another site, the administrator may not speak the local language and the project may be seen as hostile to the community, causing fewer people to visit the center. For all these reasons, it is difficult to determine whether differences in project performance are due to differences in the responsiveness of different communities or whether the differences are due to the way the project was administered in different sites.

- Finally, each project operates within a unique economic and political context and must interact with a number of government or nongovernmental organizations (**NGOs**), each of which has its own particular characteristics. Also the social, economic, and cultural characteristics of the **target population** may vary significantly among project sites. All these **contextual factors** can have an important influence on the outcome of the project. Consequently, even when a project is administered in exactly the same way in each site, there may be significant differences in the outcomes as a result of these contextual factors.

BOX 11.7
USAID'S POLICY ON IMPACT EVALUATION

This is the definition of *impact evaluation* as it appears in the evaluation policy adopted by the United States Agency for International Development:

"*Impact evaluations* measure the change in a development outcome that is attributable to a defined intervention; impact evaluations are based on models of cause and effect and require a credible and rigorously defined counterfactual to control for factors other than the intervention that might account for the observed change. Impact evaluations in which comparisons are made between beneficiaries that are randomly assigned to either a treatment or a control group provide the strongest evidence of a relationship between the intervention under study and the outcome measured."

It has been noted that the first sentence could be interpreted as the more important principle, allowing for "credible and rigorously defined counterfactual," while the second sentence should be seen as just giving one (not exclusive) example of a methodology for doing so. Such an interpretation leaves open possibilities for well-developed QED evaluation designs that are much more feasible for evaluating the majority of kinds of programs USAID (and other development agencies) operate.

SOURCES: USAID Evaluation Policy, USAID, Washington, DC, January 2011; editorial comment by authors of this book based on conversations with senior USAID staff.

These issues stress the need to understand fully the problems facing a particular evaluation and to select the methodologically strongest design possible under the particular circumstances. The strengths and weaknesses of each evaluation design should be carefully analyzed and the implications for the interpretation of **findings** and the presentation of conclusions assessed. In some cases, the methodological weaknesses may not seriously affect the kinds of recommendations to be prepared, whereas in other cases they may be very serious. For example:

- The lack of a comparison group may not be very important if the purpose of the evaluation is to assess whether indigenous communities participating in pilot projects are able to manage and sustain community water supply projects or whether women will apply for small loans if a loan office, staffed by local-language speakers, is established in the community.
- On the other hand, if the purpose of the evaluation is to estimate whether a pilot project could be replicated on a national scale and if it would offer a more cost-effective way to deliver a particular service, then the lack of a comparison group might be a serious problem.
- In addition, keep in mind that if the correlation between particular outputs and outcomes has been acceptably established by previous research or evaluations in very similar contexts, it should not be necessary to retest them in every project.
- Many if not most experimental research designs strive to fit reality into the experiment, rather than the other way around. For example, they tend to focus on one or a few quantitatively measurable indicators of intermediary-level outcomes that can be achieved and measured within a relatively short time, rather than higher-level indicators of long-term impact (sustainable changes in human conditions).

6. Determining Appropriate Methods

A key decision is whether the evaluation will use QUANT, QUAL, or a combination of methodologies (mixed methods). We emphasize throughout this book that although we see certain advantages to using a purposeful mix of methods, both to address RWE constraints and to gain multiple perspectives, there is no "best" evaluation methodology. The choice of research methods is determined by a number of different factors that, in addition to the types of questions to be addressed, include the professional orientation of the client and also that of the evaluation practitioner. The list of questions in the next section can help determine which methods are most suitable for the purposes of an evaluation and the conditions under which it is to be conducted.

BOX 11.8
A PERSPECTIVE ON EVALUATION DESIGNS USED BY
INTERNATIONAL NONGOVERNMENTAL ORGANIZATIONS

Over a period of eight years CARE International conducted biannual meta-evaluations of evaluations conducted on its relief and development projects in many countries over the previous two years. An analysis of a combined total of 339 evaluation reports found that 59% of them used an evaluation design in which information was collected

(Continued)

(Continued)

only at the end of the project and only from the project communities. Twenty-seven percent of them used a before-after (baseline + endline) design, 15% a with-without (counterfactual) design, and 0.6% some other form of counterfactual. This is just one example of what is probably fairly representative of many international development agencies. In other words, in a majority of cases no baseline data were collected before project startup (at least not using a methodology and rigor comparable to the endline evaluation), and no information was collected on a comparison group. This is Design number 7 of the RWE evaluation design frameworks that we describe in Table 11.2. From the methodological point of view, this is the weakest design and the one most open to a wide range of threats to validity of the conclusions of the evaluation. In many situations, the evaluation design could have been strengthened had project management begun the evaluation process from the beginning of the project and conducted a baseline study on at least the target population. However, in many RealWorld situations, this is the only design possible within the time and budget constraints and within the local political and security context in which the evaluation must be conducted.

Consultations with colleagues who are familiar with evaluations by other agencies confirm that this is very typical. In fact, some say that considerably more than 59% of their evaluations are conducted only at the end of a project.

SOURCE: Author's previous unpublished work; however, CARE meta-evaluations and many individual evaluation reports are publicly accessible at www.careevaluations.org

The main points we hope we have made in this chapter on evaluation design are: (a) if evaluation plans are made at the beginning of a program it is possible to preselect an appropriate evaluation design framework; (b) if not (i.e., donors and implementers do not "think evaluatively" until near the end of the project), there are methods for strengthening a weak design with alternative means for obtaining the missing data. The objective is for those responsible for evaluation to use the best means possible to conduct it as rigorously as feasible and as required by the purposes for which the evaluation was called.

SUMMARY

- There are those who consider experimental research designs (or randomized control trials, RCTs) the methodologically strongest QUANT (statistical) designs for impact assessment. However, the appropriate role for randomized designs for the evaluation of complex social development programs is hotly debated in the United States as well as in the field of international development. Even without these debates, the application of randomized designs—particularly for RWE scenarios—is limited by the technical, budgetary, ethical, and political difficulties in using a randomly selected control group that will be excluded from receiving the services being offered to the project group.

- One of the limitations of the typical RCT or experimental design is that it only measures quantitative indicators before and after, and with and without the intervention being tested. Typically, it does not provide a perspective over time, including an ex-post evaluation of the sustainability of any impact. A longitudinal design that combines pre- and posttest observations with data collected during project implementation and data collected after the project has been completed offers a more powerful design. However, longitudinal designs are used infrequently due to the additional cost and time requirements.

- Quasi-experimental designs (QEDs) seek to approximate the experimental design as closely as possible while adapting to realities of the RealWorld social context. One of the most robust QEDs involves pretest-posttest comparisons of the project group and a comparison group selected to approximate as closely as possible relevant characteristics of the project group.

- Even under the most favorable conditions, experimental designs or even QEDs, when used in isolation, have a number of limitations for impact assessment. A purely QUANT pretest–posttest design does not examine the project implementation process or the contextual factors (economic, political, organizational, environmental, and the characteristics of the affected populations) affecting project performance and results. It is also difficult to quantify many important input, process, and outcome indicators, and the rigidity of the design makes it difficult to adapt to changes in the project design and/or the evolution of the internal and external contexts over time.

- Seven variations of the basic QEDs are described that can be applied in RWE contexts. The different designs adapt to cost and time constraints and to the fact that many evaluations do not start until the project has been underway for some time and, consequently, no relevant baseline data were collected. Some of these designs save cost or time by eliminating one or more of the four major data collection points (pretest–posttest of project and comparison groups).

- The less robust designs involve trade-offs, as the elimination of data collection points increases vulnerability to different threats to validity of the conclusions. A number of strategies can be used to strengthen all these designs, including (a) the use of mixed-method designs, (b) using a program theory model, (c) incorporating process analysis, (d) making judicious use of secondary data and recall, and (e) using multivariate analysis to more closely match the project and comparison groups.

FURTHER READING

Baker, J. 2000. *Evaluating the Impacts of Development Projects on Poverty: A Handbook for Practitioners.* Directions in Development. Washington, DC: World Bank.

Duignan, P. 2011. *Impact/Outcome Evaluation Design Types: An Outcomes Theory Knowledge Basic Topic.* March 10. Version 65. Knol. Available from http://knol.google .com/k/paul-duignan-phd/impact-outcome-evalua-tion-design-types/2m7zd68aaz774/10

On his Web site Duignan presents a series of very useful graphics depicting what he classifies as the seven types of evaluation design.

Gray, D. 2004. *Doing Research in the Real World.* Thousand Oaks, CA: Sage.

Chapter 4 provides a simple introduction to quasi-experimental designs.

Khandker, S. 1998. *Fighting Poverty with MicroCredit: Experience in Bangladesh.* Oxford, UK: Oxford University Press.

Kratchowill, T. R. et al. 2010. *Single-case design technical documentation.* What Works Clearinghouse. Retrieved August 9, 2011 (http://ies.ed.gov/ncee/wwc/pdf/wwc_scd.pdf).

A panel of experts commissioned by the U.S. Department of Education explains the justification for considering single-case evaluations as a rigorous impact evaluation methodology. The documentation presents detailed criteria for assessing the methodological validity of the design.

McNamara, C. 2000. *Basic Guide to Program Evaluation.* Free Management Library. Retrieved August 9, 2011 (www .managementhelp.org/evaluatn/fnl_eval.htm).

Morgan, D. and R. Morgan. 2009. *Single-Case Research Methods for the Behavioral and Health Sciences.* Thousand Oaks, CA: Sage.

A clear and comprehensive explanation of the single-case approach and a comparison of some areas of advantage over the conventional group-based evaluation designs.

Patton, M. Q. 2011. *Developmental Evaluation: Applying Complexity Concepts to Enhance Innovation and Use.* New York: Guilford Press.

Reichardt, C. 2005. "Quasi-Experimental Designs." Pp. 351–55 in *Encyclopedia of Evaluation,* edited by S. Mathison. Thousand Oaks, CA: Sage.

Provides a five-page overview of the principles of quasi-experimental designs.

Rossi, P., M. Lipsey, and H. Freeman. 2004. *Evaluation: A Systematic Approach.* 7th ed. Thousand Oaks, CA: Sage.

Chapters 8 and 9 review randomized field experiments and quasi-experimental designs and also discuss limitations of quasi-experimental designs for impact assessment.

Shadish, W., T. Cook, and D. Campbell. 2002. *Experimental and Quasi-Experimental Designs for Generalized Causal Inference.* Boston: Houghton Mifflin.

The most comprehensive reference on quasi-experimental designs and threats to validity. However, many readers may find this too detailed and technical for their needs.

Stufflebeam, D. 2001a. *Evaluation Models.* New Directions for Evaluation No. 89. San Francisco: Jossey-Bass.

Characterizes 22 evaluation approaches.

Stufflebeam, D. and A. Shinkfield. 2007. *Evaluation Theory, Models and Applications.* San Francisco. Jossey-Bass.

CHAPTER 12

Quantitative Evaluation Methods

T his chapter discusses quantitative (QUANT) data collection and analysis methods, and the following two chapters cover similar ground for qualitative (QUAL) and mixed-method evaluations. We begin with a review of QUANT data collection methods and then discuss the management of data collection for QUANT studies, with emphasis on the data management challenges for **RealWorld Evaluation (RWE).** The chapter concludes with a discussion of QUANT data analysis.

1. Quantitative Evaluation Methodologies

A key characteristic of most QUANT methodologies is that standardized indicators are defined and standardized data collection procedures are used throughout the evaluation to ensure comparability. Most QUANT program evaluation is based on one of two types of experiments to estimate the effects of treatments and interventions: randomized experiments and quasi-experiments (Reichardt 2005:351). Both designs involve the collection of quantitative data that can be represented in numerical form (e.g., age, number of people living in the household, income, percentage of students passing a standardized test) and that can be analyzed with statistics, both descriptive and inferential. The data can be used to test hypotheses or to determine the statistical difference between observations made at two points in time (e.g., student test scores before and after the introduction of new teaching methods) or between two or more groups (e.g., individuals or businesses who received technical assistance and small-business loans and a comparable group who did not). Many QUANT methodologies are *deductive* in that they begin with a theory or hypothesis and then develop a research design to test it. In this section, we describe some of the features of QUANT methodologies.

1.1. The Importance of Program Theory in the Design and Analysis of QUANT Evaluations

We argue that program theory plays an important role in the design of QUANT (as well as QUAL and mixed-method) evaluations (see Chapters 10 and 11). A program theory is an explicit theory or model of how the program causes the intended or observed outcomes. A central element of many QUANT methodologies is the specification of hypotheses that can be tested through experimental or quasi-experimental designs. Sometimes an evaluation will test a single hypothesis, such as, "School attendance rates will be higher for children who receive free school meals." However, in many cases, a program theory model is developed in which a causal chain of interlinked hypotheses is specified and tested. For example, Carvalho and White (2004) develop a program theory model to describe the process through which social investment funds[1] are intended to improve the welfare of low-income populations in developing countries, and how the participatory mechanisms built into these programs help ensure the sustainability of the programs. Waddington et al. (2009) develop separate theory models to explain the causal chain through which water, sanitation, and hygiene interventions are expected to reduce childhood diarrhea. Theory models help define the input, process, outcome, impact, and contextual indicators to be measured in QUANT evaluations as well as help identify the hypotheses to be tested and the key assumptions underlying the hypotheses that should be assessed. These models also strengthen the analysis and interpretation of findings by testing whether observed processes and outcomes are consistent with the stages of the impact and implementation theories built into the model.

1.2. Quantitative Sampling

Sampling procedures for QUANT surveys are intended to ensure (a) that the subjects sampled are representative of the whole population so that generalizations about the population may be made confidently and (b) that the sample is sufficiently large that statistical differences between groups can be estimated. Much of the discussion of QUANT sampling focuses on the estimation of sample size, although, as we will see in Chapter 15, the effectiveness of the sample also depends on the adequacy of the sampling frame, policies for addressing nonresponse, and how carefully the implementation of the sample design is managed. Sampling procedures, discussed in Chapter 15 (Sections 1, 2, and 3), are particularly important for RWE because one of the most common ways to save cost and time is by reducing the size of samples. When reducing sample size, it becomes critical to ensure that samples are still sufficiently large to allow for statistical analysis and appropriate generalizations.

2. Experimental and Quasi-Experimental Designs

2.1. Randomized Control Trials (RCTs)

In this book we distinguish between three kinds of impact evaluation designs: experimental designs, where subjects are randomly assigned to the treatment and control groups; quasi-experimental designs, which use a comparison group but in which random assignment is not used and the evaluator defines a selection procedure for the comparison group; and nonexperimental designs, in which there is no statistical comparison group (see Chapter 11). Consequently, our use of the term *experimental design* corresponds to what some authors call *randomized control trials* (Boruch et al. 2009; Dane 2011; Fink 2008) and others call randomized experiments (Shadish, Cook, and Campbell 2002,

---

[1]More than 60 social investment funds are now operating in South America, Africa, Asia, and the independent states of the former Soviet Union. A basic principle of social funds is that communities are able to select from among a menu of public services such as water supply, health, schools, or roads. The social fund is usually managed by an autonomous government agency, and the community is required to contribute a certain percentage of the cost in the form of labor, materials, or cash.

chap. 8) or randomization (Khandker, Koolwal, and Samad 2010, chap. 3). This clarification is important because other writers use the term *experimental design* to include a broader range of evaluation
designs that include a comparison group but which do not necessarily use random assignment.

Randomized designs offer a number of important statistical advantages, as they control for *selection
bias*, which is a major challenge facing quasi-experimental designs (see Box 12.1). A randomized or
experimental evaluation design involves the random assignment of subjects (e.g., individuals, families,
schools, communities) to the treatment (project) group and to a control group that does not receive the
treatment. In practice, randomized assignment typically follows a two-stage process. In the first stage a
sample of subjects (individuals, communities, etc.) is randomly selected from the target population, ensuring that the sample is large enough to permit statistical estimates to be made at the required level of significance (Khandker et al. 2010, chap. 3). This ensures *external validity* of the design. In the second phase
subjects are randomly assigned to the treatment and nontreatment groups, ensuring *internal validity*.
Khandker et al. (2010) distinguishes between pure randomization, in which the treatment and nontreatment groups are drawn directly from the phase 1 sample, and partial randomization, in which the two
groups are selected using a proxy variable representing a program eligibility criterion such as land-holding
or income. In practice, most randomization designs use the latter option, which can introduce a potential

---

BOX 12.1
THE BENEFITS OF RANDOMIZED DESIGNS

Randomized designs, when properly implemented, offer a number of important advantages over most other evaluation designs.

- They eliminate selection bias that can distort the estimates of potential project
  impacts when:
  - participants are self-selected (and those *most likely to be successful* are the
    individuals or groups most likely to apply);
  - participants are selected by the project agency that will often try to select the
    individuals or communities *most likely to succeed*. On the other hand, in a few
    cases they may select the most needy communities, who are perhaps *least
    likely to succeed.*
- They eliminate the problem of not knowing whether variables not included in
  the survey ("unobservables") that might influence program outcomes are
  disproportionately more represented in the project population. Randomization
  ensures that unobservables will be equally distributed among control and project participants.
- The transparency of the selection process is an important advantage in communities where there is suspicion of political interference in the distribution of
  public services.
- The randomization process automatically selects the control group at the same
  time as the project group, which is an important practical, as well as theoretical,
  advantage. In contrast, when using quasi-experimental designs the process of
  selecting the control group can be both time-consuming and difficult.

sampling bias if the data on proxy variables are not completely reliable. Randomization is most commonly used at the project design stage, but modified versions of randomization can be introduced at a later stage—for example, when subjects who are already in the project may be selected to receive some additional treatment.

The random assignment can be done in several ways (see Box 12.2). Sometimes the evaluators will be involved in the decision to use a randomized participant selection process, but in many cases the decision to use randomization is determined by political rather than methodological considerations, and often the evaluator is not consulted. The two groups are compared at the start of the experiment on the variables that will be used to estimate outcomes or impacts (school test scores, agricultural productivity, small-business profits, etc.) and on individual or group characteristics (income, education level, farm size, etc.) that might affect outcomes. The experimental treatment (e.g., drugs, nutritional supplements, new teaching methods) is then administered to the treatment group but not to the control group. The two groups are again compared at an appropriate point in time after the treatment has had time to take effect. If a statistically significant posttest difference is found between the two groups, this is considered evidence of a potential project effect. Ideally, the experiment would be repeated a number of times to determine how the effect varies with different intensity of the treatment (dosage), or when and how it is administered.

Although precisely controlled randomized **experimental designs** are often used in areas such as medical research, animal behavior, and some areas of psychological investigation, it is never possible to ensure the same degree of control when randomized experiments are used in field settings. Although randomized allocation of subjects to treatment (project) and control groups can be used in program evaluation, it is rarely possible to control the conditions of the two groups over the period when the project (treatment) is being implemented (which can be several months or even several years). Consequently, there is always the problem of determining how much of any observed difference is due to the effect of the project and how much is due to other differences, unrelated to the project, in the situation of the two groups during the project implementation period.

BOX 12.2
METHODS FOR RANDOMLY ASSIGNING SUBJECTS TO THE PROJECT AND CONTROL GROUPS

Random assignment is most commonly used at the start of a project to select beneficiaries from among the eligible target population. However, it can also be used at a later stage to select participants who will receive some additional benefits. A two-stage selection process is commonly used: In stage 1 a sample is randomly drawn from the target population, and in stage 2 subjects in the sample are randomly assigned to the treatment and control groups.

1. A widely used selection method in development evaluations is through a public lottery in which names or numbers are drawn from a box or from the kind of rotating cylinder often used in television quiz shows. This is done in a public event to ensure that the process is seen to be transparent. This is particularly important in situations where communities are suspicious of manipulation by politicians or government officials.

2. Another method—used, for example, in the selection of schools to receive special services—is to list all schools (or other institutions) alphabetically and then to select every other school to receive the treatment.

3. Another widely used method in experimental research is the use of random numbers.

Box 12.3 gives some of the sources providing compilations of RCTs. In Chapter 11 we gave a number of examples of randomized control trial (RCT) evaluations in the fields of education, primary health, and agricultural extension in developing countries such as Kenya, India, Colombia, and the United States (see Box 11.1, p. 209). A high proportion of the reported randomized experiments in developing countries is in the field of education and involves the random assignment of school classes to receive educational TV programs or special textbooks, or to have teachers who have received special training. Many of these designs provide different classes with different combinations of treatments so that interactions can be studied. Other areas where RCTs have been widely used are conditional cash transfers (Bamberger and Kirk 2009) and health and education (Waddington et al. 2009 and Box 12.3). It should be noted that despite the increasing application of RCTs, the majority are in a relatively narrow range of fields, and there are many major development areas where RCTs have rarely been applied.

Shadish, Cook, and Campbell identify the following conditions most favorable to random assignment (Shadish et al. 2002:269–75):

- When demand outstrips supply
- When an innovation cannot be delivered to all units at once
- When experimental units can be temporally isolated
- When experimental units are spatially separated or communication among units is low
- When change is mandated and solutions are acknowledged to be unknown
- When some persons express no preference among alternatives
- When you can create your own organization
- When you have control over experimental units
- When lotteries are expected or there is a pressure to ensure transparency

An example where demand outstrips supply is **social investment funds** (Carvalho and White 2004) that allow poor communities in many developing countries to select to receive one service (e.g., water, sanitation, health centers) from a menu of services. The demand for services is often very high, and the lottery system has been used in a number of countries such as Bolivia to select the communities that will receive the service. This example of randomized assignment has worked well, both because it is completely transparent and because communities that are not selected have accepted the procedure knowing they will have the opportunity to apply again in future years.

There are, however, a number of practical, ethical, and political problems that limit the use of randomization. Some relate to costs or to the logistical difficulties of administering a random allocation (including problems relating to how participants are recruited), and others are ethical (e.g., withholding medicines or beneficial services from the control groups) or political (pressures from local politicians to extend coverage to the whole population or to exercise more control over the selection process). Many educators and evaluators of educational programs would object on ethical grounds to depriving some students—those who might be assigned to control groups—of promising educational TV programs, special textbooks, or teachers who have received special training. Ethical issues in evaluation design, including the question of randomization, are discussed in Chapters 6 and 9.

Another set of problems concerns the difficulties of ensuring that the project is administered uniformly so that all subjects receive the same set of services delivered in the same way. A final set of problems relates to participant attrition as when, for example, the poorer, less educated, or less motivated participants drop out of the project more rapidly. The combination of these factors often makes it extremely difficult to approximate an experimental design even when it is initially possible to use random assignment of subjects to the treatment and control groups.

BOX 12.3
LARGE-SCALE COMPILATIONS OF THE FINDINGS OF
RANDOMIZED CONTROL TRIALS

The **Cochrane Collaboration** is an international, independent, not-for-profit organization of over 28,000 contributors from more than 100 countries, dedicated to making up-to-date, accurate information about the effects of health care readily available worldwide. Contributors work together to produce systematic reviews of health care interventions, known as Cochrane Reviews, which are published online in the Cochrane Library. Cochrane Reviews are intended to help providers, practitioners, and patients make informed decisions about health care, and are the most comprehensive, reliable, and relevant source of evidence on which to base these decisions. The reviews seek to achieve the highest possible level of evidence-based findings, in most cases using randomized control trials (www.thecochranelibrary.com/view/0/index.html).

The **Campbell Collaboration** (C2) helps people make well-informed decisions by preparing, maintaining, and disseminating systematic reviews in education, crime and justice, and social welfare. The Campbell Collaboration is an international research network that produces systematic reviews of the effects of social interventions. Again, most are based on randomized control trials (www.campbellcollaboration.org/system atic_reviews/index.php).

The **Abdul Latif Jameel Poverty Action Lab** (J-PAL) is a network of 44 affiliated professors around the world who are united by their use of randomized evaluations (REs) to answer questions critical to poverty alleviation. There are more than 170 evaluations that have been either completed or are ongoing (www.povertyactionlab.org).

The **World Bank Poverty Web site** includes various catalogues of impact evaluations. The following is one source where most but not all of the evaluations use RCTs (http://econ.worldbank.org/external/default/main?pagePK=64166018&piPK=6416 7664&menuPK=477165&theSitePK=469372&docTY=620265&colTitle=impact%25 20evaluation%2520series).

Although there are examples in which a specific intervention needs to be tested using a randomized experimental design to test the correlation between intervention and effect, in most development programs we are evaluating much more complex and multifaceted phenomena so that there are limitations on the utility of randomized designs, even when resources are available.

For all of the above reasons, the merits of RCTs continue to be hotly debated in the evaluation and development communities. While many proponents of RCTs claim that randomized designs are the gold standard for evaluation and should be used whenever possible (Center for Global Development 2006; Poverty Action Lab 2005), critics question the appropriateness of these designs on both methodological and ethical grounds (Patton 2011:290);[2] some even argue that these designs are rarely if ever appropriate (see Box 12.4). The majority of evaluators probably fall between these two extremes, recognizing the methodological benefits of RCTs while at the same time acknowledging the many practical challenges of applying these designs in RealWorld contexts. One important piece of information usually lacking from these debates is a reliable estimate of the proportion of impact evaluations where these designs have been successfully applied, as well as some information on the frequency with which attempts to apply these designs have failed or have had only limited success. As most of the information on the use of RCTs is presented by advocates of these approaches, the uninformed reader could get the impression that attempts to use these approaches are almost always successful, and that it is self-evident that they should be used wherever possible. Most of these sources provide no information at all on the frequency with which attempts to use these approaches have resulted in (often costly) failures. At the other end of the spectrum, while critics of RCTs have claimed that there are equally valid alternative approaches that can provide methodologically valid assessments of project impact, it is difficult to find well-documented examples of the methodologies and findings from these alternative approaches.

BOX 12.4
CHALLENGES IN USING RANDOMIZED CONTROL TRIALS

- Randomization is not possible in the majority of programs that use self-selection or administrative selection of beneficiaries.
- There are ethical and political constraints on their acceptance and use.
- They are difficult to administer because of lack of accurate administrative data (e.g., on farm size or income) or because of pressures to relax the process to allow favored candidates to be accepted.
- The choice of programs to evaluate can be "methods driven" (selected on the basis of whether randomized designs can be used) rather than on the operational or policy priority of different programs.
- Randomization only controls for selection bias and does not ensure that the design addresses other threats to validity.
- RCTs are potentially vulnerable to several important threats to validity (see Box 11.6, p. 238). Some reasons:
    o Difficulty in adapting to changes in project design or implementation or to changes in the control group

(Continued)

---

[2]Patton (2011:290) states, "I am not hostile to RCTs. I am hostile to their being treated as the gold standard, which connotes, among other distortions, that every other design is inferior."

(Continued)

o Inability to capture changes in the context within which the project is implemented
o Mono-method bias
o Potential issues of construct validity
o Do not "unpack the black box" and assess what happens during project implementation
o Surveys and other QUANT data collection techniques are not well suited to capture sensitive information or to identify and interview difficult-to-reach groups

2.2. Quasi-Experimental Designs (QEDs)[3]

Much more commonly, the evaluator has no control over the individuals or groups who participate in programs or receive services. In many cases, the individuals, families, communities, organizations, or regions who will receive services such as educational programs, roads, water supply, soil conservation, or public transportation are selected on the basis of administrative or political criteria, and the evaluator has no influence over the allocation process. In other cases, beneficiaries are self-selected, as when individuals apply for small-business loans or mothers enroll children in an education or health program. In both cases, if the evaluator wishes to compare project beneficiaries to a group that did not receive these services, the evaluator must attempt to identify a comparison or matched group in which the individuals resemble the beneficiary group as closely as possible. Box 12.5 clarifies that, technically, the term *control group* should be used only when subjects have been randomly assigned to the treatment (project) and no-treatment groups. When the no-treatment group has to be selected independently, then this should be referred to as the comparison group.

Comparison groups may be selected in one of the following ways:

- An external comparison group may be selected from, for example, different communities or schools.
- An internal comparison group can be used where projects are implemented in phases. For example, families who will receive the services in phase 2 can be used as a comparison to assess the **impacts** of the program on phase 1 families. This is sometimes referred to as a "rolling baseline," or a "pipeline" comparison group, where the baseline for the second cohort can be used to serve as the comparison group for the achievements of the first cohort.
- Both QUANT and QUAL evaluations make use of naturally occurring comparison groups. For example, one of the authors was involved in an evaluation of the impacts of a program to improve access to infrastructure and public service of communities living on islands (*chars*) in the main rivers in Bangladesh. These islands are flooded every monsoon season, and

---

[3]Quasi-experimental designs are discussed in more detail in Chapter 11. See also Reichardt (2005) for a brief overview of alternative approaches to quasi-experimental designs, and Shadish et al. (2002) for a more in-depth discussion.

many of them completely vanish each year while new islands constantly emerge from the river. The variable duration of the islands provides (unfortunately, for the inhabitants) a natural experiment in which the conditions of communities on islands that have survived for different periods of time can be compared.

- Surveys already conducted or that are being planned can be used to create a comparison group. High-quality survey data that are available on a sufficiently large sample can be used to statistically match the two samples through the use of techniques such as propensity score matching, producing potentially stronger and more reliable estimates.
- When secondary data are only available from a small sample it may only be possible to use judgmental selection of the comparison group.
- Documentary data (e.g., census data, household surveys, records of agricultural sales, and *data* from local health centers) can be used to compare the project group with the larger population of which it is a part.

BOX 12.5
CONTROL GROUPS AND COMPARISON GROUPS

Although the term *control group* is often used quite broadly, we follow the widely accepted practice of using *control group* to refer only to the group in a randomized experimental design that does not receive the experimental treatment. We use the term *comparison group* to refer to a group that is selected independently and by a different procedure in a quasi-experimental design to match as closely as possible some important characteristics of the project group. The distinction is important because the comparison group will often differ from the project group in ways that can significantly affect the interpretation of the evaluation findings. For example, if families enrolled in a children's nutrition program turn out to be on average better educated and to have higher incomes, some of the differences in **outcomes** between the project and comparison groups may be due to these initial differences—rather than to the effects of the program, *per se.*

A common methodological problem occurs when secondary data sets do not include information on factors that potentially might affect project outcomes (known as "omitted variables" or "unobservables"). When secondary data sets are used to estimate baseline conditions, these missing variables usually refer to characteristics of the project population that might affect the likelihood of successful project outcomes. For example, in the case of an evaluation of the impacts of a village bank on women's economic empowerment discussed earlier, some important missing information might refer to borrowers' prior experience in managing a small business, the support received from the woman's husband or family (particularly important in cultures where there are cultural constraints on a woman's ability run a business—or even to travel outside of the family compound), or the woman's role in household decision making. If these potential determinants of project outcomes are not measured, and if they may be unequally distributed between project and comparison groups, these may introduce a bias into the interpretation of the evaluation findings—often leading to an overestimation of project impacts.

A widely used econometric technique is to control for the effect of unobservables by arguing that if they are "time invariant" (do not change over the life of the project) their effect can be controlled for (eliminated) through the use of double-difference analysis (Khandker et al. 2010:73), discussed later in this chapter. However, the nature of the potential unobservables is often not known, so it is difficult to assume away their effect by arguing that they are time-invariant (Khandker et al. 2010:76). As we will see in Chapter 14, mixed-method designs provide valuable tools for improving our understanding of unobservables.

One of the biggest challenges for **QEDs** is to understand how differences between the project and comparison groups might affect the interpretation of findings and the assessment of project impacts. For example, when participants are self-selected, it is likely that the individuals or groups that decide to participate will differ in some important ways from those who do not. Participants may differ from nonparticipants in terms of their economic status, political or religious affiliation, education, or household composition. While some of these characteristics may be relatively easy to identify, other potentially important factors such as motivation, self-confidence, teaching styles, or a woman's role in control over household resources are much more difficult to identify and assess.

On the other hand, when beneficiaries are selected on administrative grounds, it is likely that selection criteria will be used that will be difficult to match in the selection of a comparison group. For example, project groups may be selected because they are the poorest or the largest communities, because they are considered to have the highest probability of success, or because of their political affiliation or ethnic characteristics. These criteria are also difficult to match when the criteria are not made explicit or when the project includes most of the individuals or communities in a given category. For example, when a retrospective assessment was being made of the effects of donor interventions in slum communities in Nairobi, it was found that significant interventions had been made in all of the largest slums so the only possible comparison communities would be slums with small populations—usually only a few hundred families. It was concluded that the differences between the large slums affected by donor interventions and the small slums that had not been affected were so great that the latter would not have a practical benefit as a comparison group.

3. Strengths and Weaknesses of Quantitative Evaluation Methodologies

Table 12.1 summarizes some of the strengths and weaknesses of QUANT evaluation methods. A well-selected sample is representative of the total population so that findings can be generalized to a broader population, such as all program beneficiaries or members of a community, city, country, or particular socioeconomic group of interest (e.g., the poor, agricultural laborers, secondary school students). Another advantage is that systematic statistical comparisons can be made among groups. QUANT evaluations also offer means to statistically control for the influence of household or community characteristics such as age, sex, class, or type of school (different authors call these *control* or *intervening* variables[4]) on program outcomes. The QUANT approach also allows the specification and testing of hypotheses. Standardized research instruments and methods also mean that if the study is

---

[4]A *control variable* is often defined as a preexisting attribute of the project or comparison group population that affects project outcomes. The analysis will often use techniques such as multiple regression to match subjects on these variables so as to control for their effect on the outcome variable. *Intervening variables* are often defined as variables that "surface between the time the independent variables start operating to influence the dependent variable and the time their influence is felt on it." However, other authors use a more general definition such as "an intervening variable facilitates a better understanding of the relationship between the independent and dependent variables when the variables appear to not have a definite connection." (These are two of many definitions given on Wikipedia.)

replicated in other areas, it will be possible to compare the findings. Finally, QUANT approaches require that the study instruments and procedures are carefully documented so that other researchers can assess the methodology, the analytical procedures, and the validity of the findings.

On the other hand, many of the criticisms of the QUANT approach concern the reduction of detailed data into numbers, inattention to **contextual variables,** and the rigidity of procedures that prevent refinements of focus based on increasingly sophisticated understanding of the program. The standardized categories found, for example, in questionnaires and QUANT data coding schemes often fail to capture variations and nuances within the groups or communities studied, and the analysis often lacks the depth and detail of QUAL methods. QUANT evaluation risks becoming *decontextualized,* ignoring how programs are affected by the economic, political, institutional, and sociocultural characteristics of the populations studied. The RWE approach fully recognizes all the strengths and weaknesses of QUANT and QUAL approaches, which is why mixed-method designs are frequently preferable.

Table 12.1 Strengths and Weaknesses of QUANT Evaluation Approaches

Strengths	Weaknesses
• Study findings can be generalized to the population about which information is required. • Samples of individuals, communities, or organizations can be selected to ensure that the results will be representative of the population studied. • Structural factors that determine how inequalities (such as gender inequalities) are produced and reproduced (perpetuated) can be analyzed. • QUANT estimates can be obtained of the magnitude and distribution of impacts. • QUANT estimates can be obtained of the costs and benefits of interventions. • Clear documentation can be provided regarding the content and application of the survey instruments so that other researchers can assess the validity of the findings. • Standardized approaches permit the study to be replicated in different areas or over time with the production of comparable findings. • It is possible to control for the effects of extraneous variables that might result in misleading interpretations of causality (although this can be challenging in the natural settings of evaluations).	• Many kinds of information are difficult to obtain through structured data collection instruments, particularly on sensitive topics such as domestic violence or income. • Many groups such as sex workers, drug users, illegal immigrants, or squatters and ethnic minorities are always difficult to reach, but the problems are often greater for QUANT data collection methods. • Self-reported information obtained from questionnaires may be inaccurate or incomplete. • There is often no information on contextual factors to help interpret the results or to explain variations in behavior between households with similar economic and demographic characteristics. • The administration of a structured questionnaire creates an unnatural situation that may alienate respondents. • Studies are expensive and time-consuming, and even the preliminary results are usually not available for a long period of time. • Research methods are inflexible because the instruments cannot be modified once the study begins. • Reduction of data to numbers results in lost information. • The correlations produced (e.g., between costs and benefits, gender, and access to services or benefits) may mask or ignore underlying causes or realities. • Untested variables may account for program impacts. • Errors in the hypotheses tested may yield misimpressions of program quality or influential factors. • Errors in the selection of procedures for determining statistical significance can result in erroneous findings regarding impact.

4. Applications of Quantitative Methodologies in Program Evaluation

4.1. Analysis of Population Characteristics

QUANT methods can be used to produce descriptive analysis of the characteristics of the project and comparison populations. Understanding the size and characteristics of a population is often an important preparatory stage in evaluation design and also for sample strategies. For example, if a population is made up of a number of different or widely dispersed subgroups (e.g., communities producing different types of crops, or urban communities of different economic levels), *stratified sampling* may be needed to ensure that all the different kinds of communities or groups are adequately represented in the sample. This will make it possible to conduct **disaggregated analysis**, in which the characteristics of the different groups or strata are compared. However, disaggregation can significantly increase the size and cost of the sample, so a preliminary analysis can help decide whether disaggregated analysis and a larger sample are really necessary.

4.2. Hypothesis Testing and the Analysis of Causality

QUANT evaluations often use a deductive approach based on a set of hypotheses about how the project communities or groups are likely to respond to the program treatments (e.g., new varieties of seed, access to microcredit, new teaching materials, or teaching methods). Hypotheses may also link treatments and implementation methods with a program's goals and the intermediate steps and intervening variables expected to influence the magnitude and direction of change and which groups benefit least and most.

Programs often begin with a hypothesis about how a desired outcome might be achieved—for example, that education in rural areas might be improved by the use of interactive video programs. Among the intervening variables influencing whether an educational video outreach program might actually improve rural education might be the availability of video technology at the project sites, personnel with sufficient technological expertise, the quality and relevance of the programs made available to rural schools, and the willingness and ability of teachers to embed the programs usefully in their curricula. Deductive analysis would involve discovery of whether the data do, in fact, indicate that these intervening variables are important to achieving the desired outcome—that is, whether having technology, technology personnel, good programs, and capable, willing teachers is associated with an improvement in rural education. When a study begins with the hypothesis of such a *causal chain* and data are collected and analyzed in order to confirm or disconfirm it, then the analysis is said to be deductive.

While the purpose of an evaluation is normally to test whether a program or intervention has had an effect, the statistical analysis tests the **null hypothesis** (see Chapter 15) reflecting that an evaluation cannot prove causality but can only assess the probability that the observed relationship between the treatment and outcome could occur by chance if there was no association. The simplest form of a null hypothesis is to state that outcomes (change between T_1 and T_2) for an experimental group (those participating in the program) will not differ significantly from the observed change in the comparison group. If there is a statistically significant difference between the two groups, then the null hypotheses will be rejected "beyond any reasonable doubt." The null hypothesis can be formulated in terms of mean scores or other appropriate measures. Following the example above, the change in state test scores of students in rural schools participating in the educational video outreach program might be compared with the state test scores of students in nonparticipating rural schools at the end of the academic year in which the treatments were introduced. In that case, P_1 might be the average test score of students in participating schools, and C_1 might be the average test score of students in nonparticipating rural schools. If P_1 were higher than C_1 to a statistically significant degree, this could be considered as supporting the hypothesis that the video outreach program had a positive educational impact and the null hypothesis would be rejected.

In the world of the policymaker, the quantitative and qualitative findings of evaluations are combined with other sources of evidence (including the opinions of respected advisors, experience from other programs, and anecdotal evidence). Decision makers, in consultation with other stakeholders, will then decide whether they find the cumulative evidence provides credible support for the effectiveness of the treatments in contributing to the desired outcomes.

4.3. Cost-Benefit Analysis and the Economic Rate of Return (ERR)

Many agencies use cost-benefit analysis to determine whether funding a particular project would be economically justified. The economic rate of return (ERR) is an estimate of the economic return on the investment. Many agencies use a discount rate that reflects the *opportunity cost of capital* (the average interest rate that could be obtained by investing the funds in a different project). Many agencies define the minimum ERR that must be obtained before a project could be approved. The calculation and use of the ERR is often a two-step process:

- Step 1: Ensuring that the estimated ERR reaches the minimum threshold. This is typically between 10 and 12%.
- Step 2: Using the expected ERR as one of the criteria for evaluating project effectiveness. For a large and complex project, separate ERR may be estimated for each major component and the success of the project in achieving each of these ERR may be evaluated separately.

While many agencies use ERR as one evaluation criterion, some use this as their principal performance evaluation criterion. The calculation of ERR is often based on a logic model that defines a causal chain of intermediary outputs and short-term outcomes. While many implementation completion reports (ICRs) focus only on the overall ERR, it is possible and sometimes useful to assess the logic of the program theory model. This can be particularly useful in a midterm review to assess the extent to which project implementation has conformed to the steps of the logic model, whether any adjustments to assumptions or design are required, and whether the project is on track to achieve the projected ERR.

4.4. Cost-Effectiveness Analysis

QUANT methods may be used to estimate program costs, outputs, and benefits, including the cost of delivering each program service. Comparison of costs against outputs or benefits is the approach taken in a cost-effectiveness analysis. While it is important to policymakers to know whether a program had a significant effect on outputs or benefits, it is also necessary to know the cost of achieving the outputs or benefits. This may include an estimation of the cost per participant of providing the service (the unit cost) or how the unit cost compares with that of alternative (and often competing) programs. In contrast to cost-benefit analysis, cost-effectiveness does not (necessarily) attach a monetary value to the outputs or benefits achieved, which is hard to do in social contexts—for example, the value of a healthier child or lives saved.

5. Quantitative Methods for Data Collection

This section describes some of the most common QUANT methods for data collection. We also discuss some areas of overlap with QUAL data collection methods, although QUAL and QUANT researchers tend to use different methods for recording data. QUANT evaluations record information into precoded categories that can be converted to numerical form, whereas QUAL approaches favor open-ended and less structured formats.

A distinguishing characteristic of QUANT data collection methods is that data are collected in the form of numbers that can be manipulated statistically. A second is that indicators and data collection methods are standardized throughout the evaluation to permit comparability between, for example, pretest and posttest or between project and comparison groups. A consequence of these requirements is that complex phenomena must be broken down into a set of simpler numerical indicators. Another characteristic is that while rigorous QUANT techniques such as opinion research and psychometric and sociometric analysis are widely used for the analysis of opinions, meanings, and social interactions, many kinds of QUANT studies, particularly in the field of international development, tend to ignore or oversimplify many of these dimensions. For example, many of the studies commissioned by bilateral and multilateral agencies to evaluate the impacts of poverty reduction, microcredit, water supply and sanitation, and road construction tend to focus on socioeconomic characteristics of the target population and outcomes such as school enrollment, household income and consumption, and investments in social infrastructure, and to largely ignore dimensions such as opinions, meanings, and social interaction. The following chapter shows that QUAL evaluators adopt a very different approach to all these questions.

Later in this chapter, we describe the most widely used methods for QUANT data collection, including questionnaires and other closed or semiclosed survey instruments, structured observation, **focus groups,** self-reporting methods, unobtrusive measures, tests, anthropometric measures, and other physical tests. Several of these methods, such as observation and focus groups, are generally considered to be QUAL data collection methods, and they are discussed in more detail in the following chapter, but there are also a number of QUANT applications.

5.1. Questionnaires[5]

Questionnaires are research instruments through which all respondents answer the same set of questions in a predetermined order. The potential advantages are that comparable data can often be collected from large numbers of people much more quickly than if they were interviewed or observed

---

[5]For a comprehensive review of issues concerning questionnaire design and, particularly, question wording, see Presser et al. (2004a, 2004b). This book demonstrates the importance of careful choice and testing of question wording; seemingly small changes can have a major influence on how people respond.

using in-depth QUAL methods; responses to closed items can be obtained in numerical form so that statistical analysis is possible, and the sample can be selected to avoid selection bias and to permit calculations of the statistical significance of the association between the program intervention and the desired outcomes. The order in which questions are asked, and the way in which they are asked, can also be controlled.

Although most researchers have some familiarity with questionnaires, skill is needed to design a questionnaire that produces reliable responses that support valid findings. There are many ways in which questionnaires can produce misleading responses. For example, the meaning of questions may be unclear, or the way in which the question is phrased may influence how people respond. For example, "Do you agree that school fees should be increased?" may incline people to respond affirmatively, whereas the wording, "Do you think that school fees should be increased, stay the same, or be reduced?" is more neutral.

One of the disadvantages of a questionnaire is that this is not a natural way for people to communicate. Many people would rather talk informally than answer survey questions—particularly when they feel the questions are forcing them to give answers that do not fully capture how they feel or what they did. Also, the longer the questionnaire, the less reliable the information becomes as people either become fatigued or annoyed or try to answer as quickly as possible to get rid of the **interviewer**.

Types of Questions

The following are commonly used types of question (adapted from Gray 2004:191–98). Some of the categories, such as open questions, are normally considered qualitative approaches, but questions of this type are also frequently included in QUANT surveys as probes or for clarification.

- *Classification questions* collect information on questions such as age, sex, education, whether attending school, type of housing, access to services, amount of land owned, ecological characteristics of the land and types of crops produced, and other relevant characteristics of individuals, communities, or groups. In household surveys, a *household roster* will often compile information on each household member. This information serves two main purposes for the evaluation. First, it is used to select people who are involved in different ways in the project being evaluated. For example, an irrigation project will have different effects depending on the amount and type of land and the crops produced, and evaluating the effects of different kinds of programs to increase school enrollment and reduce dropouts will have different effects on children attending school and their regularity of attendance. Second, the information is used to select control variables to include in the statistical analysis (see Section 7 of this chapter).
- *Open questions* do not present a predefined menu or list of options. The responses should be recorded in full. Examples include, "Why did you move to this community?" "How do you feel about . . . ?" "What do parents think about the new teaching programs introduced into the school this year?"[6]
- *Closed questions* can ask for Yes/No answers or can ask respondents to choose one answer from a multiple-choice menu.

---

[6]Although open-ended questions should technically be considered QUAL, a few such questions are often included in structured questionnaires (e.g., as follow-up in case of people responding "Other"), so they are mentioned.

- *Lists* allow respondents to select as many responses as they wish.
- *Category (ordinal) questions* are a variety of closed questions where numerical information is put into a series of categories. Instead of asking an open question such as, "How much did you earn last month?" or "How frequently do you and your spouse go out together?" the question is asked in the form:

  - Several times a week

  - Once a week

  - Once a month

  - At least once a year

  - Never

Although category (ordinal) questions can simplify the analysis, they require careful field testing. If there is insufficient pretesting the wrong range of categories may be selected and everyone may select the same response category (e.g., all spouses go out together several times a week, or everyone falls into the lowest or highest income category), making the information of very little use. The range of categories can also influence the response. For example, if the question asks, "How many times did you and your husband have an argument during the past week?" some respondents will consider this includes minor arguments, such as which TV program to watch. However, if the question uses the same wording but includes "during the past year," many respondents will only report on major family disputes, perhaps mentioning only one or two.

- *Ranking questions* ask respondents to rank a set of options in order of their importance, seriousness, and the like. Questions may cover what they like or do not like about the local school or a community organization, the main causes of worker absenteeism, important features of a public transport system, and so on.
- *Scales* are designed to measure the degree or intensity of opinion or experience on a particular topic. The following example illustrates one of the many ways in which scales can be presented. Respondents are asked to indicate how strongly they agree or disagree with a statement such as, "The community has become a much safer place since the police post was opened last year."

  - Agree strongly (or very satisfied)

  - Agree (or satisfied)

  - Neither agree nor disagree (or neither satisfied nor dissatisfied)

  - Disagree (or dissatisfied)

  - Strongly disagree (or very dissatisfied)

A common form of a scaled question asks the respondent to rate his or her judgment or opinion on something on an ordinal scale that typically has between 5 and 10 points. Some scales ask respondents to indicate how strongly they "agree" or "disagree," while others may range from, for example, *poor or not at all* (1) to *excellent or always* (5). Some scales may use simple computation of the average ratings (Fink 2008 and Fink 2009), while others may use more complex forms of analysis, such as multidimensional scaling where different items are combined (e.g., Kane and Trochim 2007, chaps. 4–6;

Litwin 2003; Spector 1991). Wikipedia provides an excellent overview of widely used scales such as Lickert, Thurstone, and Guttman. Although scales are a useful way to measure how people feel about, for example, community organizations or public service agencies that affect their lives, the development and testing of scale items and the structure of the whole scale is a time-consuming and specialized skill. Consequently, when scales are constructed rapidly and items are not carefully selected or pretested, there is a danger that the results will be either meaningless or misleading. Even when scales are carefully designed, there is still the danger that they may provide distorted or misleading information that leads to invalid findings.

Most scales are based on the assumption (sometimes not explicitly stated) that attitudes are unidimensional. Respondents either like everything about the school or they don't like anything about it. They find that everyone in the government agency is helpful or that everyone is unhelpful. Unfortunately, life is rarely so simple. If, instead of using a scale, respondents had been asked an open question—"What do you like and dislike about the school?"—it would probably have been found that there are some aspects of the new programs that they like and other aspects that they do not like, some teachers and administrators that they like, and others that they do not.

Useful sources for a further discussion of ways to ask questions include the following: Fink (2009), *How to Conduct Surveys*; Fowler and Cosenza (2009), *Design and Evaluation of Survey Questions*; Presser et al. (2004a, 2004b), *Methods for Testing and Evaluating Survey Questionnaires;* and Sudman and Bradburn (1982), *Asking Questions* (still worth reading). For international development evaluations, particularly those focusing on the evaluation of poverty reduction programs, two of the most comprehensive sources are Grosh and Glewwe (2000), *Designing Household Survey Questionnaires for Developing Countries: Lessons from 15 years of the Living Standards Measurement Study* (3 vols.); and Klugman (2002), *A Sourcebook for Poverty Reduction Strategies* (2 vols.).

5.2. Interviewing

An interview is a focused conversation between people in which one person has the role of researcher. Interviews can be effectively combined with QUANT evaluations through the use of the mixed-method approaches discussed in Chapter 14. For example, follow-up questions can be included in a closed interview to clarify answers or to ask for details. Closed questions often include an "Other" category, and when respondents use this category, the survey administrator is often asked to write in the answer. Interviewing techniques are discussed in the next chapter.

5.3. Observation

Observation is normally considered a QUAL technique (see Chapter 13), but there are a number of QUANT applications. Observation in QUANT evaluations can be used as a principal data collection method and also as a complement to other methods as part of a triangulation strategy to check the reliability of data. For example, when informants are asked about their economic status, it is useful to observe the quality of house construction, the type of furniture, and the possession of durable consumer goods to determine whether these seem consistent with what the respondent has reported about household income and expenditure. Observation can also be used to check the accuracy of a respondent's survey response that no one in the family is working and that the family is very poor, which may be contradicted by the presence of a sewing machine or more food cooking on the stove than a poor family would normally have to eat. These may suggest sources of income from dressmaking or selling food that the respondent did not mention. In such cases, the observer should find a tactful way to check whether, for example, the qualities of food are related to a source of income or signs of an upcoming family reunion.

Observational Protocols

Observational protocols provide a list of relevant aspects to be observed. When used in QUANT evaluations, the observations must be structured into categories so that they can be quantified. Here are some examples:

- *Using community stores as an indicator of the economic status of a community.* The range and quality of goods on sale in local stores are good indicators of the economic status of a community. For example, in many parts of Latin America, the sale of whisky (compared with beer) is usually an indicator that at least a few families are doing well. The number and types of electrical appliances such as radios, video players, and TVs are another good indicator. The types of vegetables on offer and the types of footwear are other indicators. An exploratory study is required to identify the types of products that are the best indicators, and once they have been identified a checklist can be developed to record the presence or absence of different products in the local stores in different communities. These indicators are particularly useful for observing changes in the economic status of the community as storekeepers rapidly respond to changes in the purchasing power of their customers.
- *Families subletting part of their house.* In many low-income communities, subletting is one of the few possibilities for earning money. Families are often reluctant to admit they are subletting, and in some housing projects this is also forbidden. In some developing countries, an easily observable indicator is the number of doors that have numbers or letters painted on them; this usually indicates there are tenants.
- *Time use.* The amount of time that different categories of people spend on different activities (collecting water and fuel, preparing food, nonpaid agricultural work, self-employment, etc.) can be an indicator of constraints on the ability of different groups to participate in community activities or to seek new sources of income, and changes in time use can be an indicator of the impacts of certain types of projects.

Unobtrusive Measures in Observation

It is sometimes possible to collect data using unobtrusive measures that have little or no effect on the situation being observed. Unobtrusiveness is a continuum, with some methods producing almost no effect on the situation being observed, but with other relatively unobtrusive methods producing some effects on the situation being observed. The degree of unobtrusiveness also depends on how conspicuous the observer is in a particular setting. Following are some examples of unobtrusive methods:

- Automatic counters to record the number of people entering or leaving a building or the number of drivers using a road
- Natural accretion, such as the volume of waste accumulating in certain parts of a community or city

- Observation of types of housing materials (as an indicator of the wealth of the household), physical condition of roads and pathways, and maintenance of projects such as drainage channels or minor irrigation
- Observation of the types of goods on sale in community stores as an indicator of the economic conditions of the community
- Taking photographs every year from the same locations in a community as a way to measure changes in the conditions of buildings or other infrastructure
- Secondary sources (discussed later in this chapter). Requesting documents from public agencies, registrars of births and deaths, or libraries offers opportunities for introducing observer effects, so these are not always unobtrusive.
- With the rapid increase in electronic communication, it is now possible to use the number of "hits" on a Web site as a measure of use. It is also possible to monitor chat rooms and e-mail traffic to identify issues and attitudes of a particular group.

5.4. Focus Groups

A focus group is "a small group of people involved in a research interviewing process specifically designed to uncover insights regarding the research focus. The group interview is distinctive in that it uses a set of questions deliberately sequenced or focused to move the discussion toward concepts of interest to the researcher" (Krueger 2005:158). Focus groups are discussed in Chapter 13 because they are normally considered a qualitative data collection method. However, it is possible to conduct QUANT analysis of the findings, particularly if a number of focus groups representing the different categories covered in a sample survey are selected as an in-depth follow-up to a QUANT method such as a structured questionnaire. For example, in a study of factors affecting women's use of public transport in Lima, Peru, 10 focus groups were organized with men and women of different age groups and different economic levels. Responses to questions such as mode of transport used to travel to school or work and the reasons for using or not using public transport were recorded into precoded categories and compared for different groups (Gomez 2000).

5.5. Self-Reporting Methods

Subjects can be asked to keep records of income and expenditures, time use, or travel patterns. Diaries have been widely used for collecting data on household consumption and, when adequately supervised, can significantly reduce the costs of data collection. Even in countries where adult literacy rates are low, it may be possible to arrange for one of the children in a household to record the data (Deaton and Grosh 2000:119–22). Although there are sometimes problems with increasing non-response rates when families are requested to continue reporting over a long period of time, when families are motivated to participate, it has sometimes proved possible to achieve almost 100% response rates for daily reports over periods as long as one year (Valadez and Bamberger 1994:256–58). Participant self-reporting using standardized psychological and attitudinal assessments can also be used to measure needs and to assess outcomes (W. K. Kellogg Foundation 1998:82).

5.6. Knowledge and Achievement Tests

These can be used to test knowledge and behavior with respect to the effects the project seeks to achieve. Tests can also be used to measure intervening (mediator) variables that explain variations in project effects. For example, people with more knowledge of business practices might use small-business loans more effectively. Knowledge or achievement can also be tested through observation—for example, observing how well a mother follows instructions for giving her child medicine, or improvements in an elderly person's mobility (W. K. Kellogg Foundation 1998:81–82). When tests are used to compare changes over the life of a project, standardized indices must be used (see Klugman 2002, vol. 2, chaps. 18 and 19, for a discussion of indicators in the fields of health, nutrition, and education).

Standardized test scores are sometimes considered an objective and easily analyzed way to measure changes in performance associated with different kinds of educational programming. However, many argue that standardized tests are not, in fact, objective. Every step in the process of creating and scoring tests involves subjective judgments and the intrusion of measurement error. While test scores are increasingly used in education research and evaluation as impact indicators, they are highly controversial types of data. Michael Kane (1994) has analyzed standard-setting procedure in current use and has found them all to be seriously flawed. The quality of the test, the reliability of scores, and the validity of inferences and decisions based on the scores should be scrutinized rather than accepted as objective and precise indicators of outcomes.

5.7. Anthropometric and Other Physiological Health Status Measures

Anthropometric measures of the height and weight of children under the age of five are regularly used to assess the frequency and severity of malnutrition as well as to evaluate the impacts of poverty and health-related interventions, since many accept nutritional status as a proxy of poverty in a community (Alderman 2000). In countries with effective maternal and child health care programs, anthropometric measurements are relatively economical and easy to administer, and the data are usually reliable. Norms for average weights for height and age have been developed for most countries, so it is also possible to estimate and assess effect sizes produced by different interventions.

A number of basic medical tests are also widely used in program evaluation. Probably the cheapest and most common are stool tests used for evaluating the effects of improved water quality and sanitation, and of the incidence of infectious diseases. Blood tests, although more expensive and difficult to administer, are also used to assess the incidence of malaria and, of course, more recently for HIV/AIDS testing. Simpler cognitive tests can also be used to assess the cognitive functioning of adults and the cognitive development of children (Glewwe 2000).[7]

5.8. Using Secondary Data

Secondary data can be classified into documentary data and secondary survey data. *Documentary data* comprise a wide range of sources including reports, monitoring data and other sources produced by the implementing agency, publications produced by government and donor agencies, and mass media (TV, radio, and newspapers). In recent years electronic sources such as blogs, social media, and e-mail have become increasingly important documentary sources. While documentary analysis is a major QUAL data collection technique with a well-developed methodology (see Chapter 13), QUANT evaluators often only

---

[7]Glewwe's (2000) research was conducted in very poor parts of Africa and recommended the following, based on the correlation of these factors with test scores: feeding poor children snacks but not meals, teacher-pupil ratios of greater than 1:40+, and shared rather than individual textbooks. Clearly, this was a setting very different from those normally found in most U.S. education research.

use documentary data either to fill in gaps or as a consistency check of data already collected to ascertain their accuracy. The analysis of many kinds of documentary data is a potentially important, but often underutilized, source of information for QUANT evaluations.

Secondary survey data comprise surveys that have already been conducted by other agencies. The types of secondary data most widely employed in QUANT research are household surveys and national census data that are used extensively for impact evaluations, particularly posttest comparisons of project and comparison groups (see, for example, Box 5.5, p. 90). Ideally the evaluator will have access to the original data so that these can be used to match project and comparison group samples (e.g., propensity score matching), but sometimes only the published report will be available. GIS (geographical information systems) (DeMers 2009) is a relatively recent secondary data source that offers many applications for evaluation research.

Table 12.2 summarizes some of the main types of secondary data used in QUANT evaluations. Sources include national surveys, including household and longitudinal student surveys; data from social sector ministries and governmental departments; records from institutions and facilities (e.g., schools, health centers); reports from international development agencies (e.g., UNICEF, U.S. Agency for International Development, the World Bank); reports from studies and evaluations conducted by universities, research institutions, and governmental and other agencies; and administrative records and monitoring data from the project itself. Care is needed in the interpretation and use of these data sources; most were not designed for evaluation purposes, and the quality of the data collection may be poor. The reader is referred to Chapter 5, pp. 84-87, for a discussion of how to assess the strengths and weaknesses for evaluation purposes of different types of secondary data.

Secondary data can be used both in an exploratory stage of the evaluation and also, where appropriate, as a substitute for primary data collection. For example, if all schools or local health facilities keep good records on students or patients, it may not be necessary to conduct new surveys to obtain information on how many children attend school or how many patients use local health services. It is, of course, necessary to check the quality and completeness of the records, for example, by visits to a sample of schools or health clinics. Similarly, periodic household socioeconomic surveys conducted by a central statistics bureau may provide required information on household expenditures or labor force participation rates.

Many of the following ways in which secondary data can be used are equally applicable to both QUANT and QUAL evaluation studies:

- In exploratory studies, to obtain initial estimates of the magnitude and characteristics of the program population and how they compare with the overall characteristics of the broader population
- To obtain information on comparison areas when surveys do not cover these areas
- To reconstruct baseline data and obtain information on different points in time
- As a substitute for collection of primary data
- To reduce the costs and time of data collection
- As a form of triangulation to compare evaluation survey estimates with other independent estimates

Common Problems with Secondary Data for Evaluation Purposes

Because most secondary data sources were collected for purposes quite distinct from those of a project evaluation, data may have serious limitations for evaluation purposes. Where data are collected for administrative purposes, quality control may have had relatively low priority. The following are some of the common problems of using secondary data for evaluation purposes:

- The data may cover a different population (e.g., farmers producing for export but not those producing for local markets; only government or only private schools).
- The data may ask different questions (e.g., data may cover income but not expenditures, whereas the evaluation is measuring expenditures).
- Even if the same questions are addressed, different definitions and measurement techniques may be used. Concepts or variables such as poverty, vulnerability, well-being, sickness/health, and employment/unemployment can be defined and measured in many different ways.
- The data may cover a time period not relevant for the evaluation.
- The data may include intentional or unintentional biases (e.g., they may highlight the positive features of a program and downplay criticism).
- Coverage may not be complete.
- The quality of the data collection and reporting may be poor (e.g., coding instructions often get lost; old data on cards or tape may be difficult to access; and marginal notes on photocopied questionnaires may be difficult to read).
- The data may be recorded in a way that is difficult to analyze.
- Certain sectors of the target population may be underrepresented (e.g., only the "household head" may have been surveyed, leaving out women and other household members. In the United States and other countries, groups such as illegal immigrants may be insufficiently represented).
- Data may have been falsified, incomplete, inaccurate, or reflective of the perspective of the person producing the document (e.g., test scores inflated by a teacher paid per successful examinee).

Table 12.2   Useful Sources of Secondary Data

Source	Types of Data	Comments
National household surveys	<ul><li>Income, expenditure, and consumption data</li><li>Access to public services (education, health)</li><li>Educational enrollment and performance</li><li>Poverty</li><li>Household demographic characteristics</li></ul>	<ul><li>In some countries, these have been conducted several times a year for a number of years.</li><li>The National Center for Education Statistics (NCES) in the United States has been surveying and making longitudinal data available for decades.</li><li>These normally use sound sampling techniques but may not cover all the informal sector population (which often represents an important part of the project population), or may not be disaggregated to the population targeted by a particular project.</li></ul>
Social sector ministries and departments (health, education, water, transport) in developed countries such as in North America and Europe, and in some developing countries	<ul><li>Use of services (school attendance, use of health facilities)</li><li>Amount paid by users</li></ul>	<ul><li>Some data sources are comprehensive and well designed, but the reliability and coverage of some studies, particularly in some developing countries, can vary.</li><li>Many surveys focus only on quantitative indicators such as access to services (e.g., water, education, and health) but do not include much information on the quality of these services.</li></ul>

Source	Types of Data	Comments
Social service facilities (schools, health centers)	• Attendance and utilization rates • Common diseases and their incidence	• Data can be good and comprehensive, but quality varies greatly. • May be problems of under- or misreporting.
Bilateral and multilateral donor agencies (U.S. Agency for International Development, World Bank, U.S. foundations)	• Extensive information on the programs and geographical areas where they operate	• Donors have promoted some of the most comprehensive socioeconomic databases (examples include the World Bank's Living Standards Measurement Studies and USAID's Demographic and Health Surveys). • Data sometimes criticized for being too narrowly quantitative (e.g., the definition of poverty). • Samples often drawn for national statistics; not statistically significant for a smaller target population.
Universities and research institutions	• In many countries, these are the technically best studies available • Often include both QUANT and QUAL approaches	• Although some university studies, particularly in the United States and Europe, may cover large populations, in developing countries many such studies cover only relatively small areas and samples. For example, many graduate dissertations contain valuable information on the topics of interest to an evaluation, but often they study only relatively small populations.
Government-, donor-, and foundations-supported programs and reports	• Detailed information on the characteristics of the target population, their access to the program, and program performance	• Many studies cover only program beneficiaries and do not include a comparison group. • In other cases, the target population is not clearly defined.
Nongovernment organizations (NGOs)	• In-depth information on populations covered by the agency	• Often cover only relatively small populations and may be more qualitative. • There may be questions on the representativity of the data, particularly for organizations conducting studies on a small budget.
Cooperatives and microfinance programs	• Information on the size and use of loans and repayment rates • Sometimes information on the socioeconomic characteristics of program participants	• Quality of the data is quite variable.
Geographical information systems (GIS)	GIS identifies the physical location of, for example: • Public services, commercial establishments • Areas with particular characteristics such as high crime, traffic accidents, information mortality Infrastructure (roads, waterpipes, etc.); the information is provided in the form of electronic maps that permit different kinds of information to be overlaid	• Extensive GIS data, much of them free, are now available in the United States, and the data are starting to become available in many developing countries. • Mobile phones with GPS capacity now provide a cost-effective way to develop GIS maps in developing countries.

Chapter 5 gives a number of criteria for assessing the quality and utility for evaluation of secondary data available within the organization and from outside sources. In both cases, it is important to understand why the information was collected, by whom, and by what methods. Also try to determine whether there were procedures to check the accuracy of the data (e.g., was there any quality control or follow-up?) and what organizational incentive may there have been to distort or conceal the findings. The fact that an organization claimed to place a high value on accuracy does not guarantee that this was necessarily achieved. For example, a police department may have a greater incentive to report crimes that have been solved than those that have not. On the other hand, an agency that is trying to convince funding sources of the magnitude of a problem (e.g., prostitution, homelessness, drug abuse) might have an incentive to overestimate the number of potential clients (Best 2001, 2004).

6. The Management of Data Collection for Quantitative Studies

The management of the data collection process is often as critical to the success of an evaluation as the research design. Table 12.3 summarizes the requirements for a well-designed QUANT evaluation and also indicates the chapter in this volume where each requirement is discussed. Points 1 through 8 of this table (planning and design, implementation and management of data collection, and data analysis) are discussed in this chapter; reporting and communication of findings are discussed in Chapters 8 and 17.

Table 12.3   Features of Well-Designed Quantitative Evaluations

	Chapters in This Volume Where These Aspects Are Discussed
Planning and Design	
1. Clear definition of objectives	2, 3, and 10
2. Definition in consultation with clients of a program theory model	2 and 10
3. Measurable indicators	2, 10, and 11
4. Sound research design	3–5 and 11
Implementation and Management of Data Collection	
5. Sound sampling	15
6. Recruitment, training, and supervision of interviewers	15 and 17
7. Reliable and valid instruments that have been tested in the field	2, 11–13
Data Analysis and Communication of Findings	
8. Appropriate analysis	11–14
9. Accurate reporting	17
10. Effective communication of findings to all key audiences	8 and 17

SOURCE: Adapted from Fink (2003a).

6.1. Survey Planning and Design

Planning should begin with a clear definition of objectives: Is this an exploratory study? Is the purpose to define and test quantitative hypotheses? Will the evaluation report be used by decision makers to decide whether the project should continue or be replicated on a much larger scale? The definition of *objectives* often has significant implications for the evaluation design and the required level of precision—which, in turn, can affect the sample size and design. For example, if the purpose is to provide the implementing agency with an initial assessment of whether the program has been successful in attracting and retaining the different sectors of the target population, a simpler and more economical design can probably be used than if outcomes and impacts have to be compared with competing programs. The objectives will also determine whether or not a comparison group is required (see Chapters 2 and 11). In the previous example, the second alternative—to compare outcomes with competing programs—might justify the selection of a comparison group, whereas the first option probably would not.

The incorporation of a program theory model can also contribute to the evaluation design (see Chapter 10). Once the objectives and the program theory are defined, it is then possible to identify and define the indicators that will be used to measure **inputs**, processes, **outputs**, outcomes, and impacts, as well as contextual factors. For RWE, the budget, time, data, and political constraints affecting data collection must be identified and their implications assessed. Based on all the above, a draft evaluation design is developed and the appropriate data collection methods are selected and tested, and the evaluation design is then finalized.

It should be noted that although all these steps are presented sequentially, the development of the evaluation design is actually an iterative process. For example, the constraints on data collection may lead the evaluator and the client to reconsider the evaluation objectives, state less ambitious objectives in the light of the types of information available, adjust data collection methods, and refocus analysis or reporting.

6.2. Implementation and Management of Data Collection

Once the evaluation design and the data collection methods have been defined, a data collection management plan is developed together with a plan to ensure the sound implementation of the proposed sample design. Even when the sample design is theoretically sound, problems often arise during implementation because of lack of attention to the construction of the sampling frame or inadequate monitoring and treatment of nonresponse in the sample selection. It is also critical to ensure that data collection instruments have been well formulated and adequately tested in the field. Investment of time and resources in interviewer selection, training, and supervision usually pays dividends. Training should include field experience for interviewers in the administration of the survey instrument. Insufficient or poor-quality supervision or training will often result in a significant proportion of the surveys being incomplete, wrongly completed, or in some cases falsified. If the survey instrument has to be translated into the local language, it is also necessary to conduct a separate field test in the local language to be sure that people in the community understand what is being asked and that the evaluation team knows how to interpret possible answers in the way people are likely to express them.

RealWorld Constraints on the Management of Data Collection

Many evaluations have rigorous design, clearly defined data collection procedures, and significant resources and effort to support data analysis, but the quality of the final product can be seriously affected by lack of attention to the management of data collection. The following are examples of common problems that can be addressed through careful management of the data collection process:

- The sampling frame (the list or map that includes all units—individuals, schools, communities—in the population) does not adequately cover the target population. For example, if the sample of schools does not include private or religious schools, a well-managed survey will detect this and take measures to include these two categories of schools in the sample.
- The actual sample selected does not conform to the sample design because of lack of supervision of the interviewers. For example, in cases where the person who should be interviewed is not at home, the interviewer may be instructed to return at a time when the intended respondent is likely to be at home. However, some interviewers, to save time, may proceed directly to interview another family member, thus changing the composition of the selected sample. A well-managed survey should monitor the respondent selection process and take appropriate actions if there are deviations from the planned selection procedure.
- There is an unnecessarily high nonresponse rate and lack of supervision of how nonrespondents are replaced.
- The interviewers do not have the necessary qualifications or experience to administer the data collection instruments.
- The interviewers are not well trained.
- The interviewers do not speak the local language or do not speak it well.
- The age, sex, ethnicity, and other characteristics of the interview team are not appropriate. A frequent problem is that only male interviewers are used, and there may be cultural constraints on their ability to interview female respondents.
- The data may be falsified by some interviewers who fill out the questionnaire without ever visiting the selected household.
- Interviews are conducted in the presence of other people (other family members, neighbors, community leaders, supervisors, or employers) who may inhibit respondents' ability to talk freely.
- There is no immediate checking of completed interviews, and there is no standard procedure for returning incomplete surveys to the **enumerators.**[8]

While some of these problems can be attributed to poor team management and could be corrected, in the real world a number of factors are difficult to control. In some cultural contexts, it may be difficult to contract female enumerators to conduct interviews in remote rural areas, or to ensure that interviews are conducted without the presence of other people. Leaving aside cultural

---

[8]We use the term *enumerator* to refer to people who are administering structured questionnaires, and *interviewer* to those conducting qualitative, unstructured, or semistructured interviews. The distinction is important because interviewers normally have a higher level of research experience.

constraints, in crowded or confined spaces such as a one- or two-room house or a bustling and brimming hospital, there may be no private place to talk.

Other issues concern the relationship with the client and program sponsors. Clients may expect to influence the selection or assignment of evaluation team members—believing, for example, that top program administrators will be interviewed by the evaluation director. In some developing countries, enumerators are provided or recommended by the client or a government agency, and the evaluator may have little choice over the selection of the team. When enumerators are paid, the client agency may be particularly interested in deciding who should be provided the additional income, which may be quite substantial compared with government salaries. The political dynamics of enumerator selection may also limit the possibilities for close supervision, also making it impossible to dismiss enumerators who do not perform.

The following guidelines can help improve the efficiency and quality of the management of data collection in the real world:

- *Anticipate client concerns or constraints that might affect data collection.* The scoping exercise (RWE Step 1) can be used to identify client concerns or constraints that might potentially affect data collection. Sometimes clients may indicate a preference for certain data collection methods or reluctance to use other kinds of data collection, or the client may be reluctant to allocate scarce budget resources to rigorous enumerator selection, training, and supervision. The evaluator should anticipate potential issues and should make sure that questions such as data collection methods, enumerator selection, training, and supervision are brought up early on. Some of the possible strategies that can be used to address the issues mentioned in this section include the following:
  - Set up a national steering committee to oversee the evaluation—but don't have too high expectations of the extent to which the committee will wish to get involved in sensitive management issues.
  - Consider the option of contracting a professional research agency to conduct the data collection rather than selecting and training a new interview team. This option may not in fact be more expensive than the selection and training of a new team. However, if **evaluation capacity building** is an objective, then it may be necessary to invest the time and resources in developing the new research team.
  - Be aware when working on a tight budget that there are trade-offs between the costs of selection, training, and supervision of enumerators and investment in other quality improvement activities, such as improving the sampling frame or trying to reduce nonresponse rates. There is no point in having a brilliant interview team if the sampling frame excludes major sections of the target population or if the nonresponse rate is extremely high.

- *Recruit the best available supervision/training team.* Even if resources are scarce, it is always a good idea to invest in the best available supervisors. The performance of even the best enumerators will seriously decline if there is not good supervision, whereas a good supervision team can do a great deal to improve the performance of inexperienced enumerators. Ensure also that there are sufficient numbers of supervisors. Particularly during the early stages of interviewing, there should be enough supervisors to be able to review all the completed surveys and to meet on a daily basis with the enumerators to detect problems and *to send them back to correct the interviews the next day.*

- *Develop a strategy for enumerator recruitment.* Define the type of enumerators required, including the sex, age, and other characteristics, and develop a strategy for contacting potential enumerators. Prepare a checklist that will be used in the selection.
- *Conduct pilot interviews.* This is a critical part of enumerator training and also provides feedback on any unanticipated issues concerning the selection of respondents or how to complete the different sections of the questionnaire.
- *Prepare interview supervision guidelines and make sure that the enumerators fully understand them.* This strategy should include careful monitoring of how the sampling strategy is actually applied in the field and documentation of the procedures to follow when the desired subject (e.g., "household head") is not available or when the target family/individual cannot be identified or interviewed. In many cases, the enumerator will not receive part of his or her payment until the interview is satisfactorily completed, and it may be useful to get the enumerators to sign a document stating that they fully understand this procedure. Evaluators who have participated in heated meetings with enumerators late into the night about how this strict supervision shows a lack of trust or professional respect will appreciate the need to clarify the rules of the game well in advance.
- *Hold periodic debriefing meetings with the interview teams.* The only people who really know what happened during the interviews are the enumerators. Much of their experience and impressions will not be captured in the interview report, so it is important to have regular debriefing meetings to capture these impressions. Their impressions may cover questions that subjects did not understand or that were ambiguous, additional questions that should have been asked, significant information from observations or things respondents said that were not in the questionnaire, information that people were reluctant to provide, or factors inhibiting the respondent's ability to talk freely.
- *Prepare a report on the interview process.* This should identify issues affecting the quality of the data as well as the insights obtained from the enumerator debriefings.

7. Data Analysis

An important part of data analysis is the design of a data management plan spelling out the objectives of the analysis, the key questions to be addressed, and the hypotheses to be tested. The plan should refer to the scoping phase during which the client's information needs were defined. The analysis plan is particularly important for RWE to ensure that the limited resources and time are focused on the critical issues and questions of concern to clients. The data analysis plan involves the following stages:

- *Drafting an analysis plan* (see Table 12.4).
- *Developing and testing the codebook.* If there are open-ended questions, the responses must be reviewed in the preliminary stage of the analysis to define the categories that will be used in the final analysis. If any of the numerical data have been classified into categories ("More than once a week," "Once a week," etc.), the responses should be reviewed to identify any problems or inconsistencies and to ensure responses are distributed across all categories and not just concentrated in one or two.

- *Ensuring reliable coding.* This involves both ensuring that the codebook is comprehensive and logically consistent, and monitoring the data coding process to ensure accuracy and consistency between coders.
- *Reviewing surveys for missing data and deciding how to treat missing data.* In some cases it will be possible to return to the field or mail the questionnaires back to respondents, but in most cases this will not be practical. Missing data are often not random, so the treatment of these cases is important to avoid bias in the analysis. For example, there may be differences between sexes, age, economic status, or levels of education of respondents in their willingness to respond to certain questions. There may also be differences between ethnic or religious groups or between landowners and squatters. One of the first steps in the analysis should be to prepare frequency distributions to determine the frequency of missing data for key variables. For variables with significant levels of missing data, an exploratory analysis should be conducted to determine whether there are significant differences in missing data rates for the key population groups mentioned above.

Table 12.4 Example of an Analysis Plan for an Evaluation of the Impacts of Microcredit on Female Borrowers

Evaluation Objective 1: To assess the impacts of the program on women's earned income

Hypothesis: Women who participate in the program will have higher earned income than those who do not.

Variables: These might include women who have received loans and women who have not, earned income, age, education, and prior experience in running a business.

Analysis Stage 1: Comparing the mean earned income of women who have and have not received loans through the project (t-test for difference of means).

Analysis Stage 2: Multiple regression analysis testing whether there is a difference in earned income for participants and nonparticipants after controlling for age, education, and prior experience in running a business.

Evaluation Objective 2: To assess the impact of the program on women's feeling of personal empowerment

Hypothesis: Women who have participated in the program will have a stronger feeling of personal empowerment than women who have not participated.

Variables: Women who have participated in the program and those who have not (*Note:* Participation will be defined both as dichotomous Yes/No variables and also in terms of the number of different services received—loans, training courses, technical support, group meetings, etc.), scale of personal empowerment.

Analysis 1: Two-way table comparing participation/nonparticipation with the score on a 5-point empowerment scale. Chi-square or similar contingency tests will be used.

Analysis 2: Two-way table comparing two ordinal variables: the score on the 5-point empowerment scale and the number of services (between 1 and 5) received from the program. A contingency test for comparing two ordinal variables (e.g., Goodman and Kruksal's Gamma)[9] will be used.

SOURCE: Adapted from Fink (2003c, ex. 1.1).

[9]The Goodman and Kruksal Gamma is an example of a nonparametric statistical test, which is used to test the correlation between two variables, such as rankings, where the variables are not interval. The test compares the number of pairs that are "concordant" (both have the same ranking) with the number that are "discordant" (the number of pairs in which the rankings are different). See Sirkin (1999:358–62).

- Entering the data into the computer or manual data analysis system.
- *Cleaning the data.* This involves the following:
  - Doing exploratory data analysis to identify missing data and to identify potential problems such as outliers
  - Deciding how to treat missing data and the application of missing data policies
  - Identifying any variables that may require recoding
- Full documentation of how data were cleaned, how missing data were treated, and how any indices were created.

7.1. Descriptive Data Analysis

Descriptive data analysis describes important characteristics of the populations studied through measures of central tendency—means, modes, and medians—or the distribution (spread) of the data. The purpose is to obtain an initial understanding of the characteristics of the population studied and to identify similarities and differences among different sectors of the population. These kinds of analysis are almost always conducted before planning more detailed analysis. The types of analysis to be conducted and the statistics to be used will depend on what kind of variable is appropriate:

- *Nominal variables.* For these types of variables, the frequencies of each category can be counted, but the categories do not have any numerical order (i.e., one category is not greater or lesser than another on a scale). Examples: economic sectors in which persons work, regions of birth, reasons for migrating to a city, favorite subjects in school. While the distribution of responses among the different categories can be described, it is not possible with a nominal variable to calculate, for example, a mean or average.
- *Ordinal variables.* The values of these variables have an inherent order and can be ranked from lesser to greater. For example, relative satisfaction with local schools or health facilities can be ranked by asking respondents to indicate their satisfaction levels on a Likert scale (i.e., one that offers response choices such as *strongly agree, agree, disagree,* or *strongly disagree*). However, because the intervals between the different categories (e.g., strongly agree and agree compared with disagree and strongly disagree) cannot be assumed to be equal, it is not possible to calculate the means and **standard deviations** (see below). Sometimes, to simplify the analysis, interval variables such as income or age may be transformed into ordinal variables by creating categories such as "under 5 years of age," "5–10 years," "11–20 years," or "over 20 years." This reclassification results in a considerable loss of data but may be justified due to budget and time constraints and in order to make the findings easier to understand for readers with no background in statistics.
- *Interval (numerical) variables.* These are variables such as weight, age, income, time traveling to work, and number of children that can be measured on a scale where the distance between each category is equal. Numerical ordering from largest, most frequent, or longest, for example, to smallest, rarest, or shortest is possible—and the distances between each two numbers is the same on an arithmetic number line. With interval variables, a much wider range of statistical indicators and tests can be used (e.g., mean, standard deviation, statistical significance tests).

The analysis will often begin by presenting measures of central tendency and distribution and will then compare these values for different groups to identify similarities and differences. Let us take the example of household income. The analysis might begin by presenting one or more of the following indicators of central tendency:

- *The mean (average) income of all households.* For example, the mean household income may be 350 pesos per month.
- *A frequency distribution in which income is classified into groups.* The preliminary frequency distribution would give the frequency of each value, for example: "less than 50 pesos," "51–100 pesos," "101–150 pesos," and so on, and the number of families in each category is shown in a table.
- *The mode.* This is the category with the highest frequency. For example: "150–200 pesos."
- *The median.* Assume there were 150 interviews. If these are arranged in a frequency distribution from lowest to highest, the median with is the 75th value, for example, 175 pesos. In most distributions, the mode and the median will be fairly close to each other. However, there are some distributions where they can be quite different. For example, a bimodal distribution may have many values concentrated at the lower end of the distribution (many poor households) and many near the top of the distribution (relatively wealthy households) and relatively few in the middle. In this case, the mode (or modes) would be quite different from the median.

The next stage will often be the analysis of dispersion—whether values are similar for most subjects (e.g., most families have similar incomes) or widely dispersed (e.g., some families have very low incomes and others have much higher incomes). The following are indicators of dispersion:

- *Range.* This is the difference between the highest and lowest value. For example, the lowest income may be 75 pesos and the highest may be 1,025 pesos (range = 950).
- *Standard deviation.* This is based on the average difference between each value and the mean. This average is divided by the mean, and the square root is calculated. One of the great advantages of the standard deviation for many kinds of statistical analysis (such as the statistical significance tests discussed in Chapter 15) is that approximately 65% of the scores in any approximately normal population will be within one standard deviation of the mean and 95% will fall within two standard deviations. In our earlier example, the mean income was 350. If the standard deviation were 25, then we would expect that approximately two-thirds of families (65%) would have incomes between 325 pesos (one standard deviation below the mean) and 375 pesos (one standard deviation above the mean). Similarly, around 95% of families would have incomes between 300 and 400 pesos.
- *Standardized z score.* The standard deviation can be transformed into a standardized (z) score by subtracting the mean and dividing by the standard deviation, so that the value of the standard deviation can be compared for populations with different means.[10]

7.2. Comparisons and Relationships between Groups

Once the characteristics of the population have been studied, the next stage will usually be to examine similarities and differences between groups on the variables of interest to the evaluation. For example, boys and girls might be compared on school enrollment rates or school test scores, or fishermen and farmers may be compared on income.

---

[10]Statistical significance tests and the calculation of the standard deviation are discussed in Chapter 15.

The simplest comparisons involve two-way tables. Table 12.5 shows a hypothetical two-way table comparing the frequency with which men and women attend community meetings. From the table, it appears that women attend meetings more frequently than men: 71.1% of women attend either once a week or at least once a month compared with only 27.3% of men. However, when the number of observations is small, a large-percentage difference may not be statistically significant. As will be discussed in Chapter 15, a statistical significance test calculates the probability that the difference between the two groups (71.1% and 27.3%) could occur by chance if the two groups actually came from the same population. This is often expressed by saying there is a statistically significant difference between the two groups "beyond a reasonable doubt." A number of statistical tests (such as Chi-square and the *t*-test) are available to assess the statistical significance of differences. It is important to ensure that the correct statistical test is used to avoid incorrect conclusions about statistically significant differences between groups. In our discussion of threats to validity in Chapter 7, the incorrect application of statistical tests was given as one of the main threats to **statistical conclusion validity**. It is always a good idea to consult with a statistical specialist if there is any doubt.

Comparisons between more than two variables may use more sophisticated statistical tests of association such as analysis of variance (ANOVA), simple and multiple correlation, and multiple regression.

Table 12.5   Example of a Tallying Chart of the Frequency with Which Men and Women Attend Community Meetings

Frequency of attending community meetings	Men		Women		All Adults	
	Number	% All Men	Number	% All Women	Number	% All Adults
1. Every week	25	11.3	60	38.8	85	22.7
2. At least once a month	35	16.0	50	32.3	85	22.7
3. Several times a year	80	36.3	25	16.1	105	28.0
4. Once a year	70	31.9	10	6.4	80	21.3
5. Never	10	4.5	10	6.4	20	5.3
Total	220	100	155	100	375	100

7.3. Statistical Procedures for Assessing Program Effects

The Logic of Hypothesis Testing

Most QUANT evaluations involve the testing of hypotheses to determine whether the predicted or desired program effects have been achieved and whether the magnitude of the observed change (effect size) shows beyond a reasonable doubt that the program intervention is associated with this outcome (effect). In some cases, the hypotheses to be tested are derived from a program theory model (see Chapter 10). In other cases, the *null hypothesis* (often represented as H_0)—that there is no difference between project and comparison groups—is tested. The reason for using a null hypothesis is that it is never possible to prove that a program has produced a certain effect. What a statistical significance test does is to indicate the probability that the observed difference between the project and comparison groups could have occurred if the project participants and comparison groups are drawn from the same population. For example, let us assume that the study finds that the average household income of farmers who have used the new seed varieties is 8% higher than the income of farmers who have not used the new seeds, and let us also assume that the analysis finds that there is only a 4 in 100 (4%) chance of a difference as large as 8% occurring if there really is no difference between the two groups. The conventional practice is to assume that if the probability is less than 5 in 100 (5%), then there is a statistically significant difference between the two groups. In situations in which it is important to avoid wrongly assuming that treatments are effective (e.g., the testing of new drugs), a higher level of precision (e.g., 1 in 100 or 1 in 1,000) may be used. These issues are discussed further in Chapter 15 (Section 5). For readers interested in statistical analysis, Table 12.9 summarizes some of the common statistical procedures for testing different types of hypotheses and models with nominal, ordinal, and interval variables.

The comparison to be tested is most commonly between samples selected from the project and comparison groups. In this case the null hypothesis would state that there is no significant difference between the project group and the comparison group with respect to the outcome measure (aptitude test score, household income, proportion of girls attending secondary schools, etc.). The null hypothesis (H_0) is specified as follows:

$$H_0: x_0 = x_1$$

Where:

x_0 = mean or other outcome measure for the total population or for the comparison group.

x_1 = mean or other outcome measure for the project population.

Chapter 15 discusses the use and interpretation of significance tests and the concept of Type I (false positive) and Type II (false negative) errors in the interpretation of significance tests.

7.4. Tests Involving the Comparison of Two Means (the T-test)

Most statistical analyses of project impacts compare the mean value of an outcome indicator for the project group with the corresponding mean value for the comparison group. If there is found to be a statistically significant difference between the two means this will be considered evidence of a potential project effect. The comparison group could be:

- *T-test for a single sample*: The total population of interest (for example, all children attending secondary school in a particular region).
- *T-test for dependent means*: A comparison of the mean score for the project group at two points in time (usually before and after the project treatment has been implemented).

- *T-test for independent means*: A comparison group selected to be representative of the total population of interest (e.g., a sample selected from all high school students not selected for the project).
- *Double-difference analysis*: A comparison of the mean score of the project group before and after the project implementation with the mean score for the comparison group before and after the project. The analysis actually compares two means by calculating the *change score* for the project and comparison groups and then applying the t-test to compare the means of the two change score.
- *T-test for independent means*: A comparison group that represents an alternative treatment with which the project is being compared (for example, the project may be introducing innovative teaching methods while another program may reduce class size).

The statistical significance of the difference between the mean for the project group and each of these different kinds of comparison groups can be tested by using a t-test. While the exact application of the t-test will vary slightly for each of these comparisons (see Aron and Aron 2002, chaps. 8 and 9), the basic logic of the test and the stages of the analysis are similar in each case. We assume in the following example that the t-test is being used to compare two independent samples, such as the project group and an independently selected comparison group, so that the form of the test we use is for the comparison of independent means. The key steps are the following:

Step 1. Formulate the research hypothesis. For example: "Scores on the end-of-year math test for 6th graders will be higher for the project group than for the comparison group." When formulating the hypothesis it is essential to decide whether the research question is to determine *whether there has been an increase in test scores* for the project group or whether the purpose is to test *whether there is a difference between the two groups*. In this latter case the test must be able to determine whether the mean score for the project group is either significantly higher or significantly lower than for the comparison group. As we will see in the following step, this decision will determine whether a one- or a two-tailed t-test will be required.

Step 2. Determine whether to use a one- or two-tailed test of significance. While most evaluations are interested in measuring a particular direction of change (increased test scores, reduced incidence of waterborne disease), there are cases where the project could produce either a positive or a negative change. For example, an increase in school fees might reduce enrollment if poor families are unable to pay; on the other hand, it could increase enrollment if the fees were used to improve the quality of buildings and equipment or to hire more staff. If the research hypothesis only wishes to test whether change occurred in the predicted direction, a one-tailed test will be used, but if there is interest in studying the direction of change, then a two-tailed test will be used. Clarifying whether a one- or two-tailed test will be used is very important, as it will significantly affect the size of change that has to be produced for it to be found statistically significant. For example, using a one-tailed test, it might be found that a 5% greater increase in enrollment in the project schools might be found statistically significant, whereas for a two-tailed test it might be found that a larger difference would be required for it to be statistically significant.

Step 3. Reformulate the research hypothesis as a null hypothesis that can be tested. Decide whether this should be specified as a one- or two-tailed test.

Step 4: Interpret the t-score. Normally the t-score will be calculated using one of the many statistical packages such as SPSS or SAS. We assume for the purpose of this example that the estimated t-score is 1.75. When using the t-test to determine whether there is a statistically significant difference between the two independent sample means, use the following procedure:

- Determine the degrees of freedom (df). This is $N_1 - 1 + N_2 - 1$ where N_1 and N_2 represent the respective sample sizes for the project and comparison group samples. We will assume in this example that samples of 26 were used for both samples so that df $= (26 - 1) + 26 - 1) = 50$.
- Determine whether a one- or two-tailed test will be used. We will assume in this example that a one-tailed test is used.
- Define the significance level that will be used (0.01 where a high level of precision is required, 0.05 as the most generally accepted level, or 0.1 where a low level of significance is considered acceptable). We will assume that the 0.05 level is chosen.
- Define the cut-off point in the t-table for determining if there is a statistically significant difference between the two samples. This is determined by selecting the column for the one-tailed test and finding the row for df = 50. We then choose the column for the 0.05 significance level and find that the cut-off t-score is 1.67 for a one-tailed test with df = 50. In our example we have assumed that the t-score = 1.75, and as this is higher than the cut-off score of 1.67 there is a statistically significant difference at the 0.05 level between the project and comparison group.
- If the evaluation were using a two-tailed test the cut-off value for t would be 2.009 and our t-score of 1.75 would not be significant. This illustrates the importance of deciding whether a one- or two-tailed test should be used.

Applying the T-test for Other Types of Comparison between Means

In the previous example we showed how the t-test would be applied to the comparison of independent means. However, the t-test can also be used to compare a single sample mean (normally the project mean) with the true population mean, to compare two dependent means or for double-difference analysis. The t-test can be used to test differences between means for each of these types of comparison, and while the logic remains the same, there are certain differences in how the t-test is applied. Aron and Aron (2002, chaps. 8 and 9) explain and provide examples for each of these applications.

7.5. Comparisons among Three or More Means (Analysis of Variance)

Sometimes an evaluation requires a comparison of means of three or more groups to determine whether there are differences among them with respect to the project outcome indicator. While it would be possible to conduct separate comparisons between each pair of means using the t-test, analysis of variance (ANOVA) has the advantage that it can compare all of the means at the same time to determine whether there are differences.

For example, low-income families selected to participate in a self-help housing project were all previously living in one of three types of low-income housing: slums, low-income tenement housing, and traditional Spanish-type housing with a large patio that had been converted into a multifamily dwelling with shared toilets and washing facilities. The housing authority wants to know whether there are any differences among families coming from these three types of settlement with respect to the average amount they invest in the construction of their new homes. Analysis of variance is designed to address this type of question.

The basic logic of ANOVA is to define a null hypothesis stating that there are no significant differences between the means of each population. The hypothesis is tested by comparing the variance of the total population with the variance within each group. The population variance is normally not known, so it is calculated by comparing two estimates: the within-group variance and the between-group variance.

If there are no significant differences between the group means, then there will be no significant difference between the estimates of the population variance obtained from the within-group and between-group estimates. If the research hypothesis is true, then the *within-group* variance should be greater than the *between-group* variance. However, if the null hypothesis is true, then the size of the within- and between-group variances should be similar (but never exactly the same, as they are both estimates). The significance of the difference between the two variances is calculated through the F ratio, which is defined as the within-group variances divided by the between-group variance.

The following example illustrates how to find the appropriate F in the F distribution table. Assume that three groups are being compared and that there are five subjects in each group (total 15 subjects).

- The *numerator* column in the table is the number of groups minus 1. In this example, 3 − 1 = 2.
- The *denominator* column in the table is the total number of cases minus the total number of groups. In this example, 15 − 3 = 12.
- In this example, we select the 0.05 significance level.
- Table 12.6 illustrates the rows of the F distribution table for denominator = 11 and 12. Select the row for denominator degrees of freedom = 12 and significance level = 0.05, then find the column for numerator degrees of freedom = 2. The critical F value = 3.89. So if the F ratio is greater than 3.89, then there is a statistically significant difference between the means of the three groups.

Table 12.6 An Extract from the F Distribution Illustrating for Denominator Degrees of Freedom from 10 to 13

Denominator Degrees of Freedom	Significance Level	Numerator Degrees of Freedom					
		1	2	3	3	5	6
11	0.01	9.65	7.21	6.22	5.67	5.32	5.07
	0.05	4.85	3.98	3.59	3.36	3.20	3.10
	0.10	3.23	2.86	2.66	2.54	2.45	2.39
12	0.01	9.33	6.93	5.95	5.41	5.07	4.82
	0.05	4.75	**3.89**	3.49	3.26	3.11	3.00
	0.10	3.18	2.81	2.61	2.48	2.40	2.33

SOURCE: Salkind (2008: 336–38, Table B-3).

7.6. Analysis of Cross-Tabulations for Interval, Ordinal, and Nominal Variables (Chi-Square Tests)

The tests used in the previous sections are used for the comparison of means. However, in some evaluations it is necessary to compare differences between groups on *categorical* (also called *nominal*) outcomes such as the type of housing that people currently living in different kinds of urban settlements select in a low-cost housing project; the different ways that children from different types of family structure (female-headed household, male-headed household, single-parent household, etc.) respond to a school feeding program (they eat the meals at school as was intended by the project, they try to take the food home to share with their siblings, or they bring their siblings to school and try to ensure that they also get fed). In these cases the Chi-square test is widely used. Chi-square tests can in fact be used for any kind of cross-tabulations, including for interval and ordinal data.

The Chi-square test compares the expected distribution of a particular group among the different outcome categories if there was no association between a particular group and the outcomes, with the observed frequencies of outcomes. It then tests for the "goodness of fit" and how closely the actual and expected frequencies match. The Chi-square table shows the cut-off points for each significance level and a given number of degrees of freedom above which there is a statistically significant difference between how each group is distributed among the outcome categories.

In the following example the sex of household head is compared with three types of response to students with respect to school breakfasts: they eat the breakfast themselves, they try to take it home to share with siblings, or they bring their siblings to school and try to get them breakfast even though they are not enrolled in school. The research question is whether the sex of household head affects the response of students to school breakfasts. The underlying assumption is that households headed by women are on average likely to be poorer, with children knowing from experience the importance of sharing food; therefore, students from female-headed households may be more likely to try to share their school breakfast with their siblings. The Chi-square test assesses the "goodness of fit" of the results to the null hypothesis that there is no association between sex of household head and attitudes to school breakfast (see Table 12.7). It does not directly test the research hypothesis but only determines whether there are differences among the groups.

Table 12.7 Hypothetical Illustration of a Cross-Tabulation That Could Be Analyzed Using Chi-Square

Sex of household head	Student Attitude to Sharing Breakfast with Siblings			Total
	Students eat breakfast	Students try to take food home to share with siblings	Students bring siblings to school and try to get them breakfast	
Female-headed households	20	25	35	80
Male-headed households	80	15	25	120
Total	100	40	60	200

The Chi-square test involves the following steps:

- Step 1: Determine the observed frequencies in each group.
- Step 2: Determine the expected frequencies in each group if there was no association between groups and outcomes categories.
- Step 3: Compute for each group observed minus expected categories.
- Step 4: Square the differences and divide by the expected group frequency.
- Step 6: Sum the results for each group.
- Step 7: Refer to the Chi-square table to determine the cut-off point for rejecting the null hypothesis for the given degrees of freedom and required significance level.

In this example the value of Chi-square = approximately 62. The degrees of freedom = (no. of columns − 1) × (no. of rows 1 − 1). In this example df = 2 [(3 − 1) × (2 − 1)]. Table 11.9 shows a section of a table of cut-off scores for df = 1, 2, and 3. In our example, df = 2 and for the 0.05 significance level the cut-off score is 5.99. The calculated Chi-square score of 62 is clearly much higher than the cut-off, so we can conclude there is a statistically significant difference between the groups with respect to their attitudes to sharing school breakfasts.

Table 12.8   Section of Table of Cut-off Scores for the Chi-Square Test

df	Significance Level		
	.01	.05	.10
1	6.64	3.84	2.71
2	9.21	**5.99**	4.60
3	11.34	7.81	6.25

SOURCE: Sirken (1999:547, app. 4).

7.7. Controlling for the Effects of Independent Variables That Might Affect the Outcomes Being Studied (Uses of Multiple Regression in Program Evaluation)

The kinds of statistical analysis that we have been discussing so far test for differences between the means of two groups or differences between the distribution of outcomes in different groups. They indicate the probability of finding a particular t-test, F-test, or Chi-square score of all groups that come from the same population. One of the limitations of these tests for the purposes of program evaluation is that they are not able to determine the extent to which these differences are due to the effects of the project intervention or to characteristics of the two groups that might affect outcomes. For example, assume that an evaluation is being conducted of the social and economic effects of providing low-income families with better housing. A pretest–posttest comparison is made of the change in household income of project participants and a matched control group over the first three years of the project. Assume that a t-test for independent means compared the change scores for the project and comparison groups (double-difference analysis) and found that there had been a significantly great increase in household for the project than for the comparison group. Based solely on this analysis, we only know that the rate of increase was higher for the project group, but we do not know whether the difference was due solely to the project intervention or whether project households had certain attributes not shared by the comparison group that might have made it more likely that their incomes would have increased more rapidly even if they had not moved to the project. For example, the project group might have had a higher education level, greater household assets, or fewer dependent children (and therefore fewer health and education expenses), all of which might have increased their ability to increase their income.

Questions such as these can be addressed through multiple regression. When the evaluation survey includes information on household characteristics such as education, number of children, income, employment, and household assets (and other characteristics relevant to a particular survey), multiple regression is able to statistically match households in the project and comparison group so as to determine whether differences between the two groups with respect to the project outcomes still exist after controlling for the effect of these households' characteristics. Sometimes the analysis will show that the rate of increase in income is closely associated with education, household assets, or types of employment, and that when the effects of these characteristics are accounted for the differences in outcome indicators are significantly reduced. In other words, much of the difference between the project and comparison group is due to these characteristics and not to the project effect. In other cases it will be found that after controlling for these characteristics there is a still a significant difference between the two groups with respect to project outcomes, suggesting that the project intervention seems to have been a major contributor to the observed differences in outcomes.

The following paragraphs indicate some of the ways that multiple regression can be used to reduce sample bias by strengthening the match of the project and comparison group samples.

Strengthening the Matching of the Project and Comparison Groups at the Stage of Sample Design (Propensity Score Matching and Instrumental Variables)

Propensity Score Matching

Sometimes the evaluation will be fortunate enough to have access to sample survey data that had already been collected by another agency around the time that the project had begun and that covered the project and comparison group population, used a relatively large sample, included the key information of interest to the evaluation, and interviewed the right people. Examples of such surveys include household income and expenditures; living standard measurement surveys that are conducted periodically in a number of countries; or more specialized surveys or censuses that are conducted by government or international agencies on topics such as health and nutrition, education, or employment.

A logistical regression is run to determine the household characteristics that predict participation in the project. A sample of project households is then selected and each household is then matched with a set of (usually around five) "nearest neighbors" that closely match a particular household with respect to the probability of participation but who are not in the project. So each project household in the sample is matched by its own set of "nearest neighbors."

Data are obtained from the secondary data set of the score of each household at the start of the project on the outcome variable being tested (for example, household income). Both project and comparison households are re-interviewed at the end of the project and a *change score* is then computed for each set of households by calculating the change for the project household and then subtracting from this the average change for the set of "nearest neighbors." The average change score is then computed for the total sample as the mean of the change scores for each set of households. A statistical significance test is then conducted to determine if the average change score is sufficiently large to reject the null hypothesis.

Instead of using secondary data for the baseline survey it is also possible to conduct a sample survey covering a random sample of project and comparison group households at the start of the project and to use this sample to conduct the propensity score matching.

Instrumental Variables

This is a regression technique to control for sources of bias in estimating outcomes due to factors affecting program participation. When these biases are not addressed the outcome estimates are based on intended participation rather than actual participation. The instrumental variable (IV) approach identifies a variable that is correlated with program participation but not with program outcomes for subjects once they are in the program. The IV approach, by adjusting for factors affecting the likelihood of participation, improves the validity of the analysis of determinants of project outcomes.

Regression Discontinuity

This is a form of multiple regression that provides an unbiased estimate of project impact. The approach requires the definition of an *assignment variable* that is used to determine a cut-off point for determining whether subjects are assigned to the project or the control group. The assignment variable must be either an interval or an ordinal scale. It can be an interval variable such as size of farm, education of the household head, or hours of vocational training received while in jail. It can also be a scale constructed by experts or program managers that either defines the need to participate in the program or the likelihood of success. Examples of such constructed scales, all of which must be ordinal, are scores on a scale of clinical depression based on ratings by psychiatrists, likelihood of success in developing a small business, or a scale of economic and social vulnerability that combines various dimensions. A cut-off point is defined on the scale, and all subjects above the cut-off point will be selected for the project and all below will form part of the control group.

The evaluation design compares subjects just above the cut-off point (who are in the project group) with those just below (who are in the control group). The logic is that by comparing groups just below and just above the cut-off point the two groups are likely to be similar to each other in all respects other than that one group participates in the project and the other does not. After the project treatment a multiple regression analysis is conducted and a regression trend line is computed. If the project had an effect, then the line will jump at the cut-off point. Figure 12.1 presents an example of a regression discontinuity analysis where there is a clear discontinuity ("jump") in the regression line. It is, of course, necessary to conduct a multiple regression analysis to determine whether the discontinuity is large enough to be statistically significant.

Figure 12.1 Hypothetical Example of a Regression Discontinuity Design

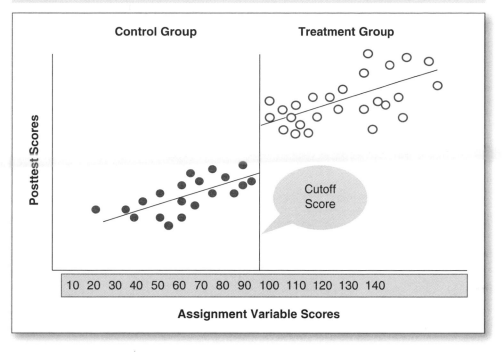

SOURCE: Prepared by the present authors.

Using Multiple Regression during the Analysis of Project and Comparison Group Data

Often the data analysis will begin by using the t-test to determine whether there are statistically significant differences between the means of the project and comparison groups on key outcome indicators. Multiple regression can then be used to assess whether there is still a significant difference after controlling for key household characteristics. The following is an example of a multiple regression analysis to determine whether there are differences in the change in household incomes between the project and comparison groups over the first three years of the project. The analysis controls for the years of education of the household head, the amount of land owned by the household at the start of the project (a proxy for wealth), and the number of dependent children.

$$Y = f(D_1, x_1, x_2, x_3)$$

Where:

Y = the change in household income over the first three years of the project

D_1 = dummy variable indicating if the household is in the project ($D_1 = 1$) or in the comparison group ($D_1 = 0$)

x_1 = years of education of the household head

x_2 = hectares of land owned by the household at the start of the project

x_3 = number of children in the household under the age of 15

If the regression coefficient of D_1 is statistically significant this shows that there is a difference in the average change in household income over the first three years of the project between the project and comparison groups. If the coefficient is positive this shows that the project income has increased faster, while if it is negative this shows the comparison group income grew faster.

If a statistically significant t-test score was found but at the same time the coefficient of D in this regression equation was not significant, that would show that the apparent project effect revealed by the t-test was in fact due to the difference in household characteristics of the two groups and not to the project effect.

Table 12.9   Examples of Statistical Procedures for Testing the Main Types of Evaluation Hypotheses[11]

Test	Type of Variable	Type of Data	Reference
Contingency tables: Chi-square	Nominal	Two-way tables comparing the distribution of two nominal variables. *Example:* comparing male and female frequency of attending meetings	Frankfort-Nachmias and Leon-Guerrero (2011, chap. 11); Salkind (2008, chap. 16)
Contingency tables: for example, Goodman and Kruskal's Gamma	Ordinal	Two-way tables comparing the distribution of two ordinal variables. *Example*: comparing high, medium, and low levels of income with high, medium, and low levels of participation	Sirkin (1999:358–62)
T-test and z-test	Interval	Comparing two means. *Example*: comparing the average income of two groups	Frankfort-Nachmias and Leon-Guerrero (2011, chap. 9); Salkind (2008, chaps. 10–11); Moore and McCabe (1999, chap. 8)
Analysis of variance	Interval	Comparing differences between three or more means. *Example*: comparing the average income of farmers, self-employed, and wage earners	Frankfort-Frankfort-Nachmias and Leon-Guerrero (2011, chap. 14); Salkind (2008, chap. 13)
Multiple regression	Interval sometimes including dichotomous or nominal (dummy) variables	Estimating the magnitude (proportion of the variance) and statistical significance of the association between two variables after controlling for intervening variables	Brief introduction: Aron and Aron (2002, chap. 12) fuller discussion in Sirkin (1999, chaps. 13 and 14); Khandker et al. (2010: various chaps.)
Econometric methods for impact evaluation	Nominal, ordinal, and interval	Covers randomization, propensity score matching, double-difference analysis, instrumental variables, regression discontinuity	Khandker et al. (2010)

---

[11]The reader is referred to the recommended readings at the end of this chapter, which provide both brief introductory texts and more advanced discussions of statistical analysis.

SUMMARY

- QUANT and QUAL methodologies represent two distinct social science traditions. It is important for evaluation practitioners, clients, and users to have a basic understanding of the two approaches; most social scientists have a professional or personal preference for one or the other of the two traditions, and this will often affect their approach to evaluation research.

- It is also useful for clients to understand these differences because QUANT- and QUAL-oriented evaluators may adopt quite different approaches to the same evaluation.

- Some of the advantages of QUANT approaches are that findings can be generalized to broader populations, subjects are selected to ensure their statistical representativity, quantitative estimates can be obtained of project impacts, and the quantitative contribution of intervening variables can be assessed. The combination of clearly documented procedures and standard instruments means that the research can be replicated in other settings.

- Some of the limitations of QUANT approaches are (a) many types of information are difficult to express numerically, (b) some groups are particularly difficult to reach using structured data collection instruments, (c) contextual factors are often ignored, (d) research methods are expensive and difficult to adapt to changing circumstances, and (e) statistical associations may be misleading if important explanatory variables are not included in the analysis.

- QUANT evaluators tend to use experimental (randomized) or quasi-experimental designs that rely on the application of structured data collection instruments that must be administered in exactly the same way at different points in the project to ensure comparability.

- Some of the principal data collection instruments include structured questionnaires, structured observation, physical measurements (height, weight), and knowledge and aptitude tests.

- Secondary data are an important, but often underutilized, source of data for QUANT evaluations.

- The management of the process of data collection is often as critical to the success of evaluation as the research design. Some of the common data management problems for RWE are (a) the best available sampling frame may not cover all the target population; (b) the actual sample selected may not correspond exactly to the sampling plan due to lack of enumerator supervision; (c) there may be high nonresponse rates; (d) enumerators may lack experience, may not speak the local language, or the team may not have the right ethnic, sex, or age composition; or (e) interviews may have to be conducted in the presence of other people, which may have affected the responses.

- QUANT data analysis may include descriptive data analysis, comparisons and relationships between groups, hypothesis testing, and analytical models.

FURTHER READING

Aron, A. and E. Aron. 2002. *Statistics for the Behavioral and Social Sciences.* 2d ed. Upper Saddle River, NJ: Prentice Hall.

A thorough and clearly presented introduction to data analysis and hypothesis testing.

Dane, F. 2011. *Evaluating Research: Methodology for People Who Need to Read Research.* Thousand Oaks, CA: Sage.

Chapter 6 ("Measurement") discusses the principles of levels of measurement and validity and guides readers on how to understand the underlying principles of measurement.

Fink, A. 2003c. *How to Manage, Analyze, and Interpret Survey Data.* Vol. 9, *The Survey Kit.* Thousand Oaks, CA: Sage.

A simple and well-documented introduction to the management and analysis of surveys, with a brief description of the main methods of data analysis and hypothesis testing. Chapter 1 presents an overview of data management.

Fink, A. 2003d. *How to Report on Surveys.* Vol. 10, *The Survey Kit.* Thousand Oaks, CA: Sage.

Chapter 1 presents some useful guidelines for the preparation of visual material for group presentations.

Frankfort-Nachmias, C. and A. Leon-Guerreo. 2011. *Social Statistics for a Diverse Society*. 6th ed. Thousand Oaks, CA: Sage

A comprehensive coverage of statistical methods with the introduction of many worked examples drawn from current social, economic, and political policy issues.

Gray, D. 2004. *Doing Research in the Real World*. Thousand Oaks, CA: Sage.

A very thorough explanation and critique of all the main QUALitative data collection and analysis methods. Chapter 10 reviews observational techniques, and Chapter 12 presents an overview of data management.

Grosh, M. and P. Glewwe, eds. 2000. *Designing Household Survey Questionnaires for Developing Countries: Lessons from 15 Years of the Living Standards Measurement Study*. 3 vols. Washington, DC: World Bank.

Probably the most comprehensive reference work on the design of household surveys in developing countries. The three volumes report on a 15-year program of Living Standards Measurement Studies supported by the World Bank. The chapter by Deaton and Grosh (2000) presents a detailed discussion of the use of diaries to report on household consumption, and the chapter by Harvey and Taylor (2000) describes self-reporting methods for recording time use.

Khandker, S., G. Koolwal, and H. Samad. 2010. *Handbook on Impact Evaluation: Quantitative Methods and Practices*. Washington, DC: World Bank.

An easy-to-understand introduction to econometric approaches to impact evaluation.

Patton, M. Q. 2002. *Qualitative Research and Evaluation Methods*. Thousand Oaks, CA: Sage.

A comprehensive review of a wide range of qualitative data collection and analysis techniques, including interviewing and observational techniques and challenges and the use of focus groups.

Presser, P., M. Couper, J. Lessler, M. Martin, J. Martin, J. Rothgeb, and E. Singer. 2004a. *Methods for Testing and Evaluating Survey Questionnaires*. New York: John Wiley.

Presser, P., M. Couper, J. Lessler, M. Martin, J. Martin, J. Rothgeb, and E. Singer. 2004b. "Methods for Testing and Evaluating Survey Questions." *Public Opinion Quarterly* 68(1):109–30.

Explains how the choice of items and the way questions are asked can influence responses. The second reference is a summary of the book.

Shadish, W. R., D. Newman, M. Scheirer, and C. Wye. 1995. *Guiding Principles for Evaluators*. New Directions for Program Evaluation No. 66. San Francisco: Jossey-Bass.

One of the most widely used reference sources on the recommended principles for the design, implementation, presentation, and use of evaluations.

Thomas, A. and G. Mohan, eds. 2007. *Research Skills for Policy and Development: How to find Out fast*. London: Sage/The Open University.

Chapter 10, "Thinking with Quantitative Data," helps the reader understand the logic of statistical data use and interpretation.

CHAPTER 13

Qualitative Evaluation Methods

T his chapter discusses qualitative methodology in terms of history and tradition, design, data collection and analysis, reporting, and RealWorld constraints. Although interpretivism *is the term preferred by many researchers and evaluators who practice what is more generally called* qualitative inquiry, *the term* qualitative (QUAL) *will be used here because it helpfully distinguishes this approach from its* quantitative (QUANT) *counterpart. As a descriptive term,* qualitative *signals that, unlike numerical QUANT data, QUAL data are typically nonnumeric and are therefore gathered, analyzed, and reported differently. The term* interpretivism *suggests that, rather than correlational and statistical analysis, QUAL data require complex, content-centered analysis to recognize and understand patterns, relationships, and conditionalities that affect the interpretation of findings. Although QUAL data tend to be minutely descriptive of programs and phenomena, the goal is not merely description but deep understanding.*

1. Introduction

Shaped over time in the fields of anthropology, sociology, and philosophy, QUAL methodology has been elaborated into an array of approaches with shared characteristics. The "family resemblance" (Brown and Palincsar 1989) among members of this array readily distinguishes them as a group but does not offer a precise way to distinguish among specific members of the "family" that include:

- *naturalistic inquiry*—study in natural settings, not laboratories, where contexts and conditionalities can be documented and analyzed (Guba 1978; Lincoln and Guba 1985)
- *ethnography*—sustained field studies to understand and document the ethos or culture of a group or society (Denzin 1997; Smith 1978)
- *case study*—study of a particular case because of its intrinsic interest or because it is an instance of a phenomenon of interest (Mabry 1998, 2008a; Yin 1994; Yin and Davis 2007)
- *phenomenology*—study of things as they are perceived, without regard for whether they are objectively real, to understand people's perceptions and experiences and the meanings they

give to events and concepts (Barritt, Beekman, Bleeker, and Mulderij 1985; Holstein and Gubrium 1994; Schutz 1970)

- *hermeneutics*—study of human meaning-making including how experiences, conscious and unconscious purposes, and multiple contexts affect meanings as they are locally perceived and expressed (Dilthey, 1883/1976; Gadamer 1960; Heidegger 1927/1996; Weber 1904/1949)
- *semiotics*—study of signs and symbols, what they denote, and what effects they have within cultural settings (Peirce 1931–58).
- *ethnomethodology*—study of human perceptions, meanings, interactions, and how they maintain social structure (Holstein and Gubrium 1994)
- *critical ethnography*—ethnographic study focused on power structures and the cultural assumptions, institutions, and relationships that contribute to the disenfranchisement or oppression of dominated groups (Anderson 1989; Habermas 1975, 1981/1987, 1987)

This family of related approaches shows that QUAL researchers and evaluators share a view of social phenomena as dynamic composites of many participants' or stakeholders' perceptions and experiences, strongly influenced by the contexts in which their experiences occur. Seeking an insider's (or **emic**) rather than an outsider's (or **etic**) understanding, QUAL researchers and evaluators share a commitment to staying on site long enough to appreciate and document multiple perspectives, contexts, circumstances, and experiences. While the time involved is a significant issue for RealWorld Evaluation, prolonged engagement in the field is necessary to recognize the patterns of behavior, themes and variations, nuances and subtleties, conditionalities and complications, and articulated and inarticulable meanings that enable deep understanding.

Coming to understand the local meanings of experiences within a culture or case or program requires not only time but also open-mindedness. Analytic discipline is needed to restrain the human impulse to jump to premature conclusions. Using **emergent design** or progressive focusing, QUAL practitioners are expected to revise their plans and methods during data collection as they better understand the phenomena and programs under study and as they encounter unanticipated data sources, rather than to rigidly adhere to an original focus or plan. This marks a sharp contrast: QUANT studies are likely to be judged on the basis of fidelity to the research or evaluation design, but QUAL studies are likely to be judged on the basis of how insightful, well-warranted, and useful the interpretations are—their *catalytic validity* (Lather 1993).

QUAL evaluation offers an array of methodological approaches and often involves mixed methods (both QUAL and QUANT):

- *fourth-generation evaluation*—evaluation involving sensitive, systematic attention to context and to stakeholders' perceptions and meanings, verifiable by audit trails and by member-checking with groups of stakeholders to assure the validity of data and findings (Guba and Lincoln 1989)
- *utilization-focused evaluation*—evaluation responsive to the information needs of "primary intended users," facilitating their use of evaluation results or catalytic validity (Patton 1997)
- *developmental evaluation*—evaluation conducted side-by-side with program development to provide formative feedback as a program is designed and revised during implementation (Patton 2011)
- *participatory evaluation*—evaluation intended not only to improve program understanding but also to transform program-related working relationships through broad local participation in evaluation processes (Greene 1997)

- *empowerment evaluation*—evaluation intended to improve not only program understanding but also the effectiveness of participant involvement in program development and decision making (Fetterman 1996)
- *connoisseurship evaluation*—evaluation relying on the enlightened eye of the expert to recognize program quality, including subtleties not easily discerned by nonexperts (Eisner 1991)
- *responsive evaluation*—evaluation more attentive to emerging issues than to an initial design (Stake 1975)
- *ideological evaluation*—evaluation intended to promote identified ideologies or values, such as social justice or deliberative democracy (House 1993; Mertens 1999, 2001, 2010).

2. History, Development, and Traditions

Although QUAL-QUANT differences are most readily visible in design and methodology, the distinction between them is essentially *epistemological*, a contrast about what is thought to constitute knowledge and reality. Interpretivism's historical and philosophical roots lie in 18th-century German understandings of *natural science* and *social science*. Focusing on disciplined, systematic human meaning-making, interpretive inquiry was intended to discover the meanings people give to what they see and experience and, reciprocally, how their meanings and experiences create their social realities. This thinking foreshadowed Fred Erickson's (1986) 20th-century admonition to researchers to "put *mind* back in the picture, in the central place it now occupies in cognitive psychology" (p. 127, emphasis original), rather than to try to eliminate subjectivity in futile attempts to achieve objectivity—all types of research and evaluation being filtered through subjective human minds.

Egon Guba and Yvonna Lincoln (Lincoln and Guba 1985; Guba and Lincoln 1989, 2005) articulated these ideas as a new research paradigm, "an integrated set of theoretical presuppositions that lead the researcher to see the world of one's research interest in a particular way" (Erickson 1986:120, after Kuhn 1962). This framework for understanding the nature and pursuit of knowledge features a vision of truth as individually constructed and a concept of social inquiry as a quest to understand the multiple meanings people construct regarding social phenomena.

The QUAL, interpretive, or **constructivist** paradigm (see Piaget 1955) stands in stark contrast to the QUANT, objectivist, or positivist paradigm, leading to very different views of reality—and to very different views of the tasks and responsibilities of the researcher and evaluator. Although some have considered these differences "incommensurable" (Lincoln and Guba 1985), mixed methods have nevertheless emerged from useful debates regarding such fundamental issues as:

- What makes a good design? Should designs specify pre-post (or experimental group-control group) comparisons to detect quality, or should designs attend to contexts, conditions, and experiences as well as measurable effects? Should designs be flexible enough to facilitate attention to unexpected sources, occurrences, and influences?
- What constitutes data? Can only information that can be enumerated be considered data? What about personal observations of ordinary events by participants or by researchers or evaluators? Can unplanned conversations among participants be considered data, or insiders' statements that include obvious bias?
- How should data be collected and analyzed? Are numerical indicators sufficient to determine effects, or should human experiences be recorded and analyzed to discover local meanings ascribed to outcomes and consequences? What types of data should be considered accurate

enough to support findings—for example, should easily quantifiable survey data be considered more accurate than less quantifiable interview data?

- What constitutes an appropriate research or evaluation product? Is it more (or less) effective to offer deep, site-specific understanding in a narrative QUAL report than it is to provide charts, correlations, and broad generalizations in a QUANT report?
- How should the quality of an inquiry be judged? Do validity or credibility depend on fidelity to the design and on standard bias reduction procedures—or on flexibility and careful management and acknowledgement of subjectivity?

In the 1980s and 1990s, disagreements within professional research and evaluation communities erupted into the so-called "paradigm wars" (Guba 1990; Reichardt and Rallis 1994) until calls for a truce allowed differences to be seen as points along a continuum of inquiry. However, the underlying differences have not been universally reconciled. Lingering tensions were evidenced by the U.S. Department of Education's policies (2003, 2005) to prefer funding for "scientifically based" QUANT research and evaluation and by the objections of researchers (see Shavelson and Towne 2002; Viadero 2007) and evaluators (see American Evaluation Association 2003).

Evaluators may have been quicker than researchers to recognize the benefits of combining QUAL and QUANT approaches in mixed-methods designs that allowed more comprehensive data sets and better warranted findings. Still, personal preferences (or greater familiarity with one or the other approach) make effective use of mixed methods a challenge. Often, mixed-methods work suffers from imbalance, the dominance of one paradigm inappropriately limiting the usefulness of the other. For example, a QUANT evaluator professing to use mixed methods might constrain interviewing by using an inflexible structured protocol (essentially an oral survey), might be uncertain about how to analyze nonnumeric or nonaggregable data, or might limit the reporting of qualitative data to a mere sprinkling of colorful interview excerpts. On the other hand, an evaluator trying to incorporate QUANT methods into a design that is essentially QUAL might tack on a table or two of survey results to suggest context or frequency without taking the survey data as seriously as the qualitative data. The full advantages of mixed methods can be gained only if both are well understood and appreciated, which sometimes requires teaming methodologists of different persuasions.

3. Characteristics of Qualitative Inquiry

3.1. Naturalistic Inquiry

Qualitative study occurs *in situ*, data collected at sites where relevant events naturally or ordinarily occur. Early educational evaluations in the United States concentrated on QUANT data, often collected remotely, and were heavily criticized by educators who complained that evaluators were judging them without having set foot in their schools. Now, it is often considered insufficiently comprehensive to examine demographic or statistical information, test scores, or tallied survey data (including oral surveys) without attention to processes and contexts and to stakeholders' experiences and understandings.

The importance of observing in natural settings where stakeholders engage in program activities makes qualitative evaluation *naturalistic*. Naturalistic inquiry involves trying to make data collection unobtrusive enough to minimize interference with ordinary events and interactions (Lincoln and Guba 1985). Ethnographic data collection—observations, interviews, collection of documents and artifacts onsite—is repeated until patterns emerge from which analytic **thick description** (Geertz 1973) can be developed, facilitating deep understanding.

Contextualized Meaning. Qualitative inquirers work toward detailed, contextual, holistic portrayals of naturally occurring events and experiences. QUAL evaluators recognize that unique contexts shape each program and its outcomes, for example:

- the *macrosystem*—the ideological environment, including whether or not people value the program and its intended outcomes
- the *exosystem*—the policy and regulations (and the politics involved in enacting and maintaining them) that govern program implementation and its organization and procedures
- the *mesosystem*—the working relationships such as those among service providers and beneficiaries, including whether personnel are accessible, supportive, isolated, or antagonistic
- the *microsystem*—the daily interactions, communications, and practices within the program (Bronfenbrenner 1979).

Within these systems, many types of contexts affect programs—physical, social, economic, legal, ethical, psychological, emotional, intellectual, and more. Contextual effects may be obvious or subtle, and they may originate locally or remotely. Investigation of the particular contexts of a program promotes understanding of what the program is able to accomplish, under what circumstances, and why.

Particularities of context obstruct large-scale program replication and also the **sample- or case-to-population generalizations** (Firestone 1993) generally desired of QUANT studies. More appropriate and justifiable in QUAL work are **petite generalizations** (Erickson 1986) limited to the program at hand, or **case-to-case generalizations** made by readers to cases of personal interest to themselves (Firestone 1993). Experimental conditions utilized to advance broad generalizations are often unavailable in naturalistic qualitative studies, although *natural experiments* may be possible where two similar programs naturally coexist and may be studied and compared.

Since social programs do not occur under controlled, laboratory-like conditions, decontextualized findings offer little information about either real-life program quality or how it might be generalized (or replicated) in other circumstances. By contrast, deep experiential understanding of one program promotes a level of comprehension that can promote successful adaptations or can inform analysis of other programs.

Understanding versus Explanation. Interpretation of qualitative data for the purpose of *understanding* has been distinguished from analysis of quantitative data for the purpose of *explanation* (von Wright 1971). The distinction involves the difference between *explicit knowledge* in the form of declarative or expository statements such as general principles or theories as contrasted with implicit or **tacit knowledge** that is less easily articulated but more influential on behavior (Polanyi 1958).

With deep, contextual understanding of the particular as the goal of QUAL inquiry, narrative reporting of program events promotes vicarious experience so that understanding is not merely abstract but deeply, personally felt. Narratives can convey a complexity not easily attained in numerical and correlational presentations (Carter 1993; Holley and Colyar 2009), and they can be more effective in promoting utilization of findings.

3.2. Multiple Perspectives

Qualitative evaluators see a program as created by human perceptions and actions in an ongoing, dynamic process in which stakeholders' understandings of a program affect their behavior, and their behavior influences the evolving nature and meaning of the program. In QUAL evaluation, program impact and quality cannot be determined without understanding the diverse, local experiences of stakeholders. The perceptions of many must be searched out—managers, personnel, beneficiaries, supporters, proponents, adversaries—and program representation must take into account multiple vantage points.

As an illustration of the importance of multiple perspectives for full understanding, imagine that a school district implements a sex education program in its middle schools. A comprehensive evaluation would involve not only the opinions of district administrators about the quality of the program—just as it would involve not only the number of students enrolled or the number of students exempted by their parents. The experiences and perspectives of pro-program and anti-program teachers, students, parents, and school board members would all be needed—as well as analysis of curriculum content and observations of its delivery.

Data Complexity and Conflicts. Because stakeholders in different positions vis-à-vis the program experience, perceive, and value it differently, their multiple perspectives tend to diverge rather than converge. Conflicts in the data are inevitable, and they do not easily resolve into clear, unequivocal findings. Continuing with the example of a sex education program, consider these possibilities: How can it be that stakeholders at Alba School report satisfaction when stakeholders at Bardo School report dissatisfaction? Why do district administrators describe the program as effective when many students report feeling uncomfortable or distracted? What level of parent complaints to the school board would indicate whether program modification or termination is appropriate?

QUAL researchers and evaluators struggle to comprehend the implications of disparities in viewpoints, but complexity in data sets needs to mirror the complexity of social phenomena. A program cannot be fully evaluated if data from only a few stakeholders becomes a narrow focus or priority. QUAL researchers and evaluators must go beyond readily available data sources to seek out the marginalized, the silent, the remote, and the powerless and to record and consider their perspectives and experiences. Outliers that contradict general trends in the data are not considered *noise*, as QUANT evaluators might see them, but integral to a full representation of reality.

The different ways that outliers and divergent data are handled in QUAL and QUANT inquiry highlight another important distinction between the two. Inquiry in the QUANT paradigm has been described as *reductionist*, reducing data to numbers in order to measure outcomes and support correlations, comparisons, trends, and probabilities. But, for QUAL inquiry, data generally cannot be reduced to numbers without unacceptable loss of meaning. Rather, as new data reveal ever more complexity, the inquiry is *expansionist* in its appreciation of the complexity and diversity in the real world. The expansionist tendency requires continuous judgment regarding the relevance and productiveness of each emerging issue or focus.

Ethical Considerations. In comparison to QUANT, QUAL research and evaluation involve different risks to participants and stakeholders. While reductionist QUANT strategies, translating perceptions and experiences into numbers, runs the risk of objectifying and subjugating participants (see Foucault 1980), QUAL methods involve closer personal contact with participants and stakeholders who, consequently, may be more affected and exposed as individuals. Participants and stakeholders may experience discomfort when they are observed or interviewed for a variety of reasons involving cultural, linguistic, age-related, gender-related, and political factors. Those observed or interviewed may be more identifiable in a QUAL report's detailed representation of a program or phenomenon, and their candor could result in negative personal consequences.

QUAL researchers and evaluators need to maintain rapport with participants and stakeholders so that informants will be willing to be observed and interviewed and so that they will respond honestly and fully to questions. While close contact enables understanding of intricate nuances and implications, participants and stakeholders may become too trusting and treat interviewers and observers too much like friends and fail to be appropriately self-protective.

Consequently, QUAL inquirers are obliged to make determined efforts to avoid unnecessary risk to respondents—for example, asking interview questions respectful of privacy or culture, avoiding technological data recording equipment that confuses or discomfits, or working from assumptions which imply that stakeholders' beliefs or customs are primitive or wrong. Care is needed regarding differences in language, dialect, and colloquialisms that might lead to irritation, offense, and inaccuracy. Some suggestions:

- *Conditions for collecting data* from observees and interviewees should correspond to their comfort and willingness to participate. For example, especially where tensions are high, teachers might be interviewed away from schools, microbank clients away from lenders, irrigation workers out of sight of their supervisors. Discomfort cannot always be dispelled, but sensitivity to reticence and unease may help in framing respectful questions or in recognizing when to offer to turn off a recording device.

- *Appreciation of cultural norms* is needed both to develop the rapport necessary to obtain information and to respect the local ethos. Because of the need to be immersed in program settings so as to understand local experiences and meanings, QUAL researchers and evaluators benefit from precontact study of the cultures they enter and from refinement of their understandings when on site. Not only exotic cultures require such attention but also settings that may be considered well known, following Erickson's advice to "make the familiar strange" (1986:121) so as to avoid implicit preconceptions.

- *Interpreters, translators, or guides* who are members of the local community may help access and comprehend data. Training local or native-speaking persons to conduct interviews may save time in collecting data and may help avoid external bias in the data set. However, it may inject internal bias resulting from their ties to particular participants or community groups whom they do not (or do) want to present in a negative light, a possibility to which the researcher or evaluator should be alert.

- *Authority figures*, including program or funding officers, may facilitate access to data by requiring stakeholders to participate. However, top-down directives may also be coercive and may produce reluctance, inaccuracy, and passive resistance. Especially informants who have something to lose from negative findings may subtly obstruct comprehensive data collection. Alertness and diplomacy may be needed.

- *Repeated observations* may reduce the perceived threat of the observer and provide opportunity to document the ordinary scene, not a version staged to look good. Obtaining permission for unannounced, drop-in observations helps to minimize observer effects that can otherwise cloud data and findings.

The cultural sensitivity that may be needed to minimize potential risk to individuals may also be needed to protect cultures (see Flinders 1992). In some evaluation approaches, impact on the culture of the site is intended; for example, empowerment evaluations (Fetterman 1996) and pro-democracy evaluations (House 1993) are designed to change perceptions and behaviors. These changes may be unwelcome to some participants—for example, outsiders may not consider the empowerment and enfranchisement of women in patriarchal cultures undesirable. Consideration is needed regarding the potential cultural impact of a study and its specific data collection methods.

Cultural sensitivity is also needed to show how programs may honor or violate the ethos of stakeholders. Not only evaluators but also program designers may think their plans culture-neutral when they are not. Evaluations that focus on intended program effects while neglecting cultural impact or implications are necessarily incomplete, a point which underscores the importance of contextual QUAL methods.

3.3. Generalizability

One QUAL-QUANT contrast that exhibits the value of mixed-methods approaches to research and evaluation involves the depth and breadth of inquiry. QUANT inquiry tends to involve data from large numbers of participants to facilitate *broad* or *sample-to-population* generalizations—taking what was learned and applying it to unstudied populations and contexts (Campbell and Stanley 1963; Firestone 1993). QUAL inquiry tends to require ethnographic methods that promote *deep* under-standing and that allow a reader to make an *analytic* or *case-to-case generalization* (Firestone 1993), adjusting what was learned about the reported case to a different case of personal interest to the reader. Put another way, QUANT data gathered from a *breadth* of participants support *grand general-izations* for large-scale explanations, while QUAL data gathered in *depth* from a smaller number of participants document particularities of experience and context which facilitate *petite generalizations* for understanding unique instances (Erickson 1986).

Combining QUAL and QUANT in mixed-methods studies offers opportunity for binocular vision that includes breadth to explain trends, factors, and correlations—and depth to understand why trends occur, how factors operate, and what meanings may be attributed to correlations. For example, in a mixed-methods evaluation of a policy requiring motorcyclists to wear helmets, statistical quantitative data might indicate how many people own motorcycles, purchase helmets, are ticketed for not wearing them, and die annually in accidents—while qualitative data collected through observations while riding with motorcyclists and interviews of riders might reveal why some choose not to wear helmets and the impact of accidents on them, their families and friends, and emergency medical facilities. Together, the QUAL and QUANT data would be more informative than either in isolation.

While QUANT studies are generally designed for the purpose of broad applicability of findings, QUAL practitioners focused on deep understanding of particularities tend to consider context so influential on a program's implementation and outcomes as to render doubtful generalizations to unstudied populations and settings. However, if program personnel expect their efforts to be judged partly on generalizability, they may feel pressed to neglect the local context and thereby imperil the success of their own programs (DeStefano 1992).

These differences have contributed to methodological clashes. For example, Campbell and Stanley (1963) famously disapproved of research in which "a single group is studied" by means of "tedious collection of specific detail, careful observation, testing, and the like," claiming that "such studies have such a total absence of control as to be of almost no scientific value" (pp. 6–7). On the other hand, QUAL inquirers are inclined to think QUANT studies inattentive to the detail needed for comprehensiveness and accuracy, not going quite so far as William Blake (c. 1798–1809) who said that "to generalize is to be an idiot; to particularize is the alone distinction of merit."

Reconsiderations of extreme positions (e.g., by Campbell 1978) and the emergence of mixed methods softened the clash until recently. QUAL researchers were rankled by wording of a U.S. National Research Council report (Shavelson and Towne 2002) in which "almost all of the qualitative research mentioned in the report is treated as 'descriptive,' . . . identified as a lower category . . . [and] described as appropriate only when theory is weak" (Maxwell 2004:8). Worse, as already mentioned, the so-called "paradigm wars" were reignited by the U.S. Department of Education's preference to fund generalizable QUANT research and evaluations, which they called "scientifically based." Preferential funding was adopted despite strong professional objections from researchers (e.g., Berliner 2002; Eisenhart and Towne 2003) and from evaluators (e.g., American Evaluation Association 2003; Mabry 2008b). The resurgence of debate suggests that generalizability remains at issue between the two approaches to social science.

3.4. Validity

In an important sense, quality in research and evaluation rests on validity—whether findings are well-warranted and whether they support adequate and appropriate inferences and actions (from Messick 1989). While researchers' and evaluators' interpretations are based on systematic inquiry, nothing can guarantee that findings will be valid—and, even when evaluation findings do promote valid inferences of program quality, they may not be credible to diverse stakeholder audiences. Nevertheless, both validity and credibility are needed to promote use of findings.

Disciplining Subjective Judgment. Is science a search for value-free objective knowledge? QUANT practitioners are more inclined to think so than QUAL practitioners, who are likely to raise a follow-up question: If science is a search for objective knowledge, is science possible? The reasoning behind this question: Thinking occurs within subjective minds, and the history of even the "hard" sciences involves paradigm shifts which reveal that things once considered "facts" may have merely been consensual opinions.

Subjectivity is inevitable. Subjective judgment is involved not only in developing findings but also in the process of identifying what should be counted or measured, how data should be categorized or recorded, what the critical data sources are, which features of a program contribute to its outcomes, or which criteria are appropriate for judging program quality. It is less subjectivity itself and more its implications for accuracy and validity that generate concern about potential bias.

Both QUAL and QUANT evaluations are susceptible to **clientism**, the positive skewing of evaluation results in order to secure the professional and financial rewards bestowed by happy clients. In addition, all methods of inquiry are susceptible to inaccuracies because "there are no procedures that will regularly (or always) yield either sound data or true conclusions" (Phillips 1987:21). However, the vulnerability is more obvious in QUAL than in QUANT work (Johnson and Onwuegbuzie 2004) because subjectivity is more obvious.

QUAL and QUANT methodologies have evolved different means of handling the challenge of subjectivity. Qualitative practitioners accept that human ways of knowing are necessarily subjective, that the mind of any researcher or evaluator is subjective, and that what is important in research and evaluation is **trustworthiness** (Lincoln and Guba 1985). To help assure that readers truly understand their reports, they discipline their acknowledged subjectivity through triangulation, validation, peer review, and **meta-evaluation** and may also explicitly acknowledge their ideological commitments. These strategies help to assure descriptive validity, interpretive validity, and evaluative validity (Maxwell 1992).

Triangulation. Of these strategies, triangulation begins with design. Program quality should not, of course, be based on unsubstantiated opinion or on a few site visits where the evaluator may observe nonrepresentative events or interactions. Triangulation, which involves deliberate attempts to confirm, elaborate, and disconfirm facts and interpretations, is built into good QUAL research and evaluation designs by including:

- multiple data sources
- multiple methods of data collection
- repeated data collection over time
- multiple perspectives including, where possible, multiple researchers or evaluators or data collectors who may notice different things during observations and interviews.

Originating in navigation on the open seas, the term triangulation implies three of something but, actually, as many relevant sources or methods as possible and practicable are sought. The purpose is to check the accuracy and completeness of information gathered from each source, by each method, and from each perspective. For example, information in the data from one interview needs to be compared with what other interviewees had to say (triangulation by data source) and with data from observations and documents (triangulation by data collection method). Data from an observation on one occasion needs to be compared with a series of other observations to determine which events occur regularly, how they vary, and why (triangulation by time). In this way, the **descriptive validity** of data—how well the data describe or represent actualities—may be determined (Maxwell 1992), a QUAL concept roughly corresponding to the QUANT notion of **internal validity** (Campbell and Stanley 1963).

Triangulation is not limited to data collection. In the interpretive process, members of a research or evaluation team are encouraged to note and to offer multiple analytic perspectives—their own and those drawn from informants, scholarly literature, or other sources. **Theoretical triangulation** refers to analytic consideration of data from different theoretical perspectives (Denzin 1989) and can involve recourse to *a priori* social theories that offer different interpretations of the data. The theoretical lens through which the data are analyzed may include *program theory*, also called *theory of change* or *logic model*.

As an example of theoretical triangulation, consider different theoretical perspectives used in evaluating a program to promote schooling in remote areas of a country. If program success is conceptualized *architecturally*, positive evaluation results might depend on whether buildings are efficiently erected—but fail to consider whether these facilities are used for educational purposes (Jones 1992). If program success is conceptualized in terms of *achievement indicators*, positive evaluation results might depend on rising test scores—but fail to consider whether the scores reflect achievement or drill-and-kill test preparation (Linn 2000). If program success is conceptualized in terms of *human capital*, positive evaluation results might depend on the ultimate employability of students—but fail to consider whether school attendance alienates indigenous students from their local language communities (Malone 1997). Considering the data from multiple conceptual or theoretical viewpoints encourages thorough analysis, consideration of rival explanations, and **interpretive** and **evaluative validity** (Maxwell 1992).

Validation. Validation involves checking with informants about the accuracy of the recorded data and the reasonableness of the interpretations drawn from them. Validation of data can take either of two forms: member checking or comprehensive individual validation. **Member-checking** of data involves review by a selected group of persons representing relevant informants and stakeholders (Lincoln and Guba 1985). These participants are charged with confirming or disconfirming the accuracy and sufficiency of the data from the selections they review. A more **comprehensive validation process** (Mabry 1998, 2003) involves review by each informant of the data collected from him or her—for example, the review of his or her interview transcript, or of the write-up of an observation in which his or her behaviors were documented (see Box 13.1).

BOX 13.1
EXAMPLES OF REQUESTS IN COMPREHENSIVE VALIDATION

Example 1: Interview validation – a request included at the beginning of an interview data write-up sent to each interviewee:

Thank you for your participation in the evaluation. Please review for completeness and accuracy this write-up of your interview. Pseudonyms have been substituted for real names. If this narrative is used in future reports, additional care will be taken to avoid identification of you or anyone you may have named. Suggested corrections and additions would be welcome. Please contact (*telephone and e-mail listed here*).

Example 2: Validation of state profile and narrative – a cover letter sent to each state official who provided interview and documentary data:

Greetings! As you know, we have been working for three years to learn about state-mandated performance assessments from across the country. We are now requesting your review of two brief summaries of your state's testing system. We fully understand that state personnel are very busy, and we are working hard to limit to bare bones the amount of time needed for your review. Enclosed please find an assessment profile and a narrative about your state. Please check these for accuracy. If the profile and narrative are accurate, please confirm via e-mail. If any corrections or updates are needed, please e-mail, fax, or mail corrections. A response is respectfully requested by May 13, at which time follow-up telephone calls will begin.

Not only *data* but also *interpretations* can be validated through review by informants or stakeholders. Validation of interpretations focuses on the potential findings—that is, on interpretive validity or evaluative validity (Maxwell 1992). Again, member checking will involve review of preliminary interpretations by selected informants or stakeholders, while comprehensive validation will involve review of draft findings by each informant or stakeholder.

With a focus on "getting it right" (Geertz 1973:29), validation of interpretations may involve read-and-respond forms (Stronach, Allan, and Morris 1996) in which a summary of preliminary findings is succinctly stated and presented to informants with a request that they edit the statements for accuracy from their own perspectives. Another approach is to request review of a draft of the report, taking care that the scope of distribution avoids violation of confidentiality agreements or political misinterpretation and incitement.

Peer Review and Meta-Evaluation. In addition to review by participants and internal review by the research or evaluation team, critical review by colleagues and external experts may bolster validity and credibility. Meta-evaluation, the evaluation of an evaluation by experienced individuals or professional panels, is advisable especially where findings may have substantial public impact or face predictable challenge. Technical advisory panels may serve in an ongoing capacity to monitor and assess an evaluation's quality, providing feedback at planned checkpoints. In situations where full-scale meta-evaluation would strain fiscal resources, even small-scale collegial review may invigorate analysis and counterbalance the subjectivity of the evaluator. Informally, colleagues may serve as critical friends who listen, read, comment, argue, suggest, advise.

4. Emergent Design

Qualitative designs emerge as researchers and evaluators gradually learn about the phenomena and programs they examine. An evaluation client's information needs and available data sources may serve for initial planning of the focus and methods of an evaluation. From this somewhat tentative beginning, as critical features and issues come more clearly into view, early questions and methods are to be refined, a process called *progressive focusing* that is useful for both QUAL and mixed-methods designs.

Keeping initial designs purposefully open allows for flexible, strategic adjustment as information is gathered, maximizing opportunity to learn about critical aspects that may not have been apprehensible initially. The gradual shaping of the study helps to ensure attention to matters that are actually important, not just those which appeared important during an introductory phase. Refinements of data collection methods may involve incremental extensions or adaptations, or more sweeping changes of focus or plans.

Constant-comparative method, a term introduced by Glaser and Strauss (1967; Strauss and Corbin 1990, 1994), captures the essence of emergent design as a dialogic process involving the plan, data collection, and analysis—a cycle of collecting information, subjecting it to interpretation, then using the preliminary interpretations to sharpen the focus for subsequent data collection. Thus, incoming data and ongoing analysis continuously shape each other in a reciprocal interplay, an unbroken feedback loop, a conversation that hones information-gathering, understanding, and the evolving design.

Glaser and Strauss (1967) describe constant-comparative as generating **grounded theory**, inductively derived explanation of how and why a program or social phenomenon functions—in contrast to the deductive or *a priori* theories more common to QUANT studies. Grounded theories are more likely to be localized than broadly generalizable—if a qualitative inquiry involves theory development at all. While constant-comparative method is common to QUAL work, the findings are much more likely to take the form of *petite generalizations* (Erickson 1986) than theories.

The characteristic of emergence in designs requires that practitioners continuously revisit the design task and exercise ongoing judgment; the design cannot be checked off early on as a completed task. In evaluation, this characteristic presents a challenge for contracting with evaluation clients. Potential clients may prove less than enthusiastic about allocating resources for work that can be only tentatively outlined in an evaluation proposal; they may consider the tentativeness to be uncertainty rather than flexibility. For a RealWorld Evaluation, a second difficulty is the limited time that can be devoted to reiterations of the design.

5. Data Collection

Qualitative research and evaluation involve three hallmark data collection methods: (a) observation, (b) interview, and (c) the review or analysis of documents or artifacts. Essentially, these methods systematize ordinary human ways of learning or knowing. There are many variations and adaptations of these three methods, allowing sensitivity to particular contexts and circumstances; to information needs; and to specific programs, populations, and data sources.

5.1. Observation

Often, QUAL data collection begins with systematic observation of ordinary events, then continues until enough redundancy in the data set is achieved to facilitate identification of themes, patterns, and issues. Observations are also needed so that researchers and evaluators can triangulate data collected using other methods. Observations allow them to obtain direct evidence that confirms, disconfirms, or elaborates statements recorded in interviews or evidence found in documents or artifacts collected at or about a site.

Structure of Observations. Observations vary according to how much they are structured or focused in advance. Most qualitative observation is unstructured, with the observer taking detailed notes initially on everything observed and gradually becoming more focused, for example:

- Moving from general observations to focus on how personnel determine which applicants are granted and which are denied program benefits, a basis for analyzing whether these determinations are fair
- Moving from general observations of how students are selected for high-expectation and low-expectation academic tracks to focusing on individuals and whether the tracking produces appropriate results.

Unstructured observation avoids instrumentation bias, the misdirection of attention based on advance focusing. Consistent with the purpose of emergent design, QUAL observations are nearly always open-ended, unencumbered by tally sheets or pre-set categories. The resultant flexibility allows whatever is observed to be recorded without overemphasis on *a priori* categories. Unstructured viewing and recording of human interactions are key to understanding what happens and where, when, by whom, for whom, how, under what conditions, and why.

Unstructured observation notes are typically taken by hand, often hurriedly to keep up with the dynamic flow of events. Notes need to capture detail for analysis and for narrative reporting.

Subsequent write-ups must transform pages of scribbling into storylike experiential vignettes with evocative word choice, sensory details, word-for-word conversations where relevant and summaries where less relevant, sequences of action and dialogue, tones, gestures, attitudes, and contexts—a level of detail difficult to capture in real time.

After struggling to capture experiential details, qualitative practitioners often yearn for surer and more efficient ways to record all they see. Photography and, even more, videography offer visual means of recording observation data. Whether such means are advisable and appropriate requires consideration of the possibility of intrusive observer effects: Will program participants behave differently than they otherwise would if they are being photographed or videorecorded? Videotaping may improve the fidelity of the observation record to actual events but simultaneously undermine accuracy by causing nervousness or nonnatural behaviors, introducing observer effects and inaccuracy. Where natural behavior cannot be assured (for example, by observations over a long term), QUAL researchers and evaluators must take the artificiality into account when analyzing and presenting data.

If, however, photography and videography are available, not too intrusive in the naturalistic setting and not complicating ethical practice, then video offers the observer formidable assistance in capturing experiential detail. If photographs or videorecordings may be made but, because of confidentiality, not reported or published, the observer may review videorecordings as a way to capture details in subsequent text. If permission is granted to publish or present photographs or videorecordings, the experientiality of reports can be enormously enhanced.

Rarely does audiotaping produce useful documentation of observations. In natural settings, conversations are often overlapping and simultaneous, obscuring parts of the dialogue and the identity of speakers. The words of those who speak softly or are far from the recorder, for example, may be indecipherable. However, audiotaping may work when there are only one or two participants if the presence of the recording equipment does not interfere with natural behavior. Hand-held devices into which a few words can be unobtrusively spoken and laptop computers may also help capture detail, especially if observation notes are written up very soon after data collection.

Structured observations typically involve the use of protocols or instruments that direct the observer to tally or record certain behaviors. For example, specific types of activities may need to be counted to show their frequency. Focusing observations in this way can help to answer such evaluation questions as, "Are ethnic minorities excluded from program benefits?" (see Figure 13.1) or "Are low ability–tracked students inappropriately prevented from moving to high tracks?" (see Figure 13.2).

Figure 13.1   Observation Protocol: Are Ethnic Minorities Excluded from Program Benefits?

Date and time	Applicant	Applicant's Ethnicity	Application Examiner	Determination of Eligibility

Figure 13.2 Observation Protocol: Are Low Ability–Tracked Students Inappropriately Prevented from Moving to High Tracks?

Student	Student's Original Ability Track	Length of Time in Original Track	Evidence of Achievement or Progress	Highest Track Student Reached

The protocol in Figure 13.1 could be used to record observations of the application process, noting who applied for program benefits, their ethnicity, and determinations of their eligibility. Such data would support interpretations of which, if any, ethnic groups were disproportionally obtaining program benefits and would also help identify which, if any, application examiners were exercising preference based on the ethnicity of applicants. Systematic recording of such data, tallied over time, would allow an observer to interpret the influence of ethnicity and prejudice in delivery of program benefits. The protocol in Figure 13.2 could be used to observe and document how long students remain in different tracks and whether evidence of achievement or progress was used or ignored to justify promotion to a higher track.

Observation structure varies by the detail specified in an observation protocol. A detailed observation protocol (see Figure 13.3) was developed for the second year of data collection in a study of the educational benefits of providing laptop computers to high-risk elementary students (Mabry and Snow 2006). This protocol was developed based on the categories of interest that emerged in the first year of an evaluation when unstructured observations were conducted.

Perception and interpretation are entwined. It is impossible to see and recognize without interpreting what one sees, and it is regularly necessary to make judgments when conducting observations. The collection of both observable facts and judgments about their meaning may be desirable. The observation protocol in Figure 13.3 requires both collecting and categorizing—not only counting the number of students present but also judging such things as whether the classroom atmosphere is relaxed or tense, whether students seem motivated or unengaged in learning, or whether their work is demanding or unchallenging.

The availability of multiple observers may serve as a helpful check on the subjective bias of each (triangulation by observer). However, assurance will be needed as to whether all team members record data according to the protocol's categories consistently, since disagreement among team members regarding what should be recorded as evidence would obstruct sound data analysis. So, **reliability checking** is needed to ensure that all observers record information similarly. For example, with protocol shown in Figure 13.2, reliability checking would determine whether all observers were similarly recognizing evidence of students' achievements or progress; with the protocol shown in Figure 13.3, reliability checking would determine whether all observers were similarly recognizing evidence of "rigorous" instructional activities or the criticality of teachers' use of technology.

Figure 13.3 Observation Protocol: Does Provision of Laptop Computers to Students Improve Achievement, Personalization or Rigor of Their Educations, or Classroom Community?

School: __Anthony __Hillside __Treetop   *Observer*: __L. Mabry __J. Snow

Teacher: _____   *Date and time of observation*: ____

Grade level: __ *Challenge*: __yes __no   *Number of students present*: _____

Classroom layout: __Rows of separate desks __Rows/lines of adjacent desks

                         __Desks grouped as tables __Desks in pairs __Other:

Teacher-student interaction:

__Teacher working 1:1 with students __Teacher working with small groups __Whole-class

Subject: __Literacy __Math __Science __Social Studies __Other: _____

Check if clear to students: __directions __lesson purpose __assessment criteria, standards, process

Brief description of content/subject/activity observed:

Number of computers in use by students: __   *In use by teacher*: __yes __no

Student use of personal computers: __none __individual __pairs __small groups

Technology in evidence as part of the culture of the learning environment __yes __no

Other technology in use, if any, and its purpose:

Criticality of computers (yes/no)   *Motivational effect of computers (yes/no)*

__Necessary for this activity to occur   __Enhances student motivation/on-taskness

__Enhances learning/the activity   __Distraction from content learning

__Not needed for this activity

Computers as support (check all that apply)

__Transparency/skill/automaticity in use of technology *as a tool*

__Computer as information source/provider

__Computer as logistical support, e.g., word-processing, spreadsheets, PowerPoint

Rigor	Above Grade level	Grade-Appropriate	Below Grade Level	Babysitting	Not Applicable/ Not Appropriate
Discourse—content					
Discourse—vocab.					
Test/Assgmt.—content					
Test/Assgmt.—vocab.					
Describe:					

(Continued)

Engagement	Consistently/ Strongly/Most Students	Often/ Moderately/ About Half of Students	Seldom/ Little/ Few Students	None/No Evidence/ No Students	Not Applicable/ Not Appropriate
Motivation					
Time on task					
Smoothness of operations					
Efficiency of transitions					

Describe:

Personalization	Teacher- Directed	Student- Chosen	None/Can't tell
Learning goals			
Learning activity (e.g., research report)			
Topics or tasks (e.g., report subject, report format)			
Modifications to assignments in progress			

Describe:

Observation protocols with fewer categories tend to require more judgment calls. As a case in point, in Figure 13.1, there may be many gradations of "ethnicity," such as the many variations within the category "Hispanic," each of which may come with distinguishable patterns of prejudice. Instruments with more categories, such as the protocol in Figure 13.3, may complicate quick, consistent decisions in real time.

For most qualitative observation, unstructured observation is practiced for two important reasons. First, the need for fuller, experiential data generally outweighs the need for tallies related to inquiry subquestions. Second, advance construction of categories works against emergent design, foreclosing on opportunities for improving focus along the way. Nevertheless, structured observation is sometimes a useful application of observation methods.

Participant Observation. Another way that data collection by observation varies is according the role of the data collector. A continuum of possibilities is anchored by these two points: an external *observer* who behaves something like the proverbial fly on the wall and, its opposite, a program *participant* who documents activities while being fully engaged in them. In between is the

participant-observer (Atkinson and Hammersley 1994), someone who both observes and participates to greater or lesser degree in the activities being documented (see Box 13.2 for an example). The task undertaken by participant-observers is more difficult than that of external observers because simultaneous participation and observation compete for attention.

BOX 13.2
PARTICIPANT OBSERVATION IN A PEER MEDIATION PROGRAM

Hoping to decrease the incidence of harassment and violence on school grounds, a school district in Indiana approved pilot implementation of a peer mediation program at one of its elementary schools. Student volunteers were trained to listen to complainants accuse their alleged tormentors and to facilitate discussion and resolution of altercations to the satisfaction of each party. Peer mediators were trained in facilitation techniques, all students were directed to turn to the mediators (rather than to adults) when they encountered difficulties, and teachers and other adults were trained regarding the support and expectations of mediators.

A doctoral student at Indiana University was engaged to study the peer mediation program from its outset and to provide formative feedback. Presentations of data served essentially as formative feedback and, on the basis of the data and interpretations shared with stakeholders, targets for the program and for the study were revised. In addition, observation data revealed where additional or refresher training was needed for peer mediators and for adults involved with the program and the type of information—often data—needed in the additional training.

In the study of the program, the doctoral student was an observer (and interviewer and documents analyst) and, in providing feedback, participating in decisions about next steps for the program, and assisting with additional training, she was also a participant. Because of her dual role in the study of the program and also in its implementation, evolving design, and delivery, she was fully both a participant and an observer.

SOURCE: Mahoney (1999).

These role variations have implications for sensitivity and credibility. If program participants are asked to serve as participant-observers, their lived experience of the program will enhance their understanding of what they see and their ability to record and analyze activities, although training may be needed to promote data quality. An external observer lacks, at least initially, the insider's community awareness and, consequently, may need to conduct many observations in order to focus appropriately and to understand the implications of what is seen.

Credibility trade-offs accompany these different roles. An external observer is likely to be more ignorant about the cultural and local meanings of what they observe but more impartial—and therefore more credible to some audiences. On the other hand, the credibility of internal observers may be suspect because of their own interests and allegiances or enhanced by their richer historical and contextual knowledge. For some audiences, a participant-observer will be more credible than a "hired gun" who spends limited time on site; for other audiences, a disinterested external observer will be more credible.

Experiential Narratives. Experiential narratives are the products of most qualitative observations, the way that observations are recorded and included in the data set. Narratives that take a storylike quality promote vicarious experience for the reader, giving him or her the impression almost of having been there. The reader's personalization of information aids his or her ability to grasp its full meaning, to understand the complexities of the scene. So the qualitative observer should be skilled at portrayal, detailing what was done, in response to what, with what implications; what was said, in what tone or manner, with what accompanying nonverbal communication. Crafting experiential texts requires sensitivity, skill, and time.

Time, of course, can be in short supply—time to arrange, time to conduct, time to write up observations, and time to validate them. Time requirements are intensified by the need to repeat observations often enough to be sure that the observer is witnessing ordinary events, not behaviors intended to impress an outsider. That is, repetition is needed to protect the descriptive validity of observation data and the interpretive or evaluative validity of findings based partly on observations. Also, observations must be sufficient in number and conducted over a long enough period of time to surface meaningful patterns of behavior. Collecting only a few observational "snapshots" risks misrepresenting and misunderstanding the program—a validity issue and also an issue of credibility and ethics.

Representation of events and experiences presents several challenges simultaneously, of which data accuracy is just one. Cultural insensitivity is another, as alertness and skill are needed to portray interactions in a manner that reveals, rather than neglects or obscures, the norms and expectations of the culture. Accurate, respectful representation may be especially challenging where cultural nuances are subtle.

Observation is not an unobtrusive method of collecting data; being observed tends to create anxiety for participants, who may alter their behavior, introducing inaccuracies in the data set in the form of observer effects. Perceived power differentials between observers and those observed (common in evaluation) and videotaping (increasing feelings of exposure and challenges to privacy and confidentiality) can intensify discomfort.

5.2. Interview

Interviews can help explain why participants act as they have been observed to do, and observations can confirm the extent to which interviewees' statements of intent and beliefs actually inform their behavior. Observations can also support later interviewing by promoting the development of specific interview questions that probe for explanations of what was seen. QUAL interviews tend to offer exceptional opportunities to reach deep understanding based on the multiple perspectives of participants or stakeholders.

Structure of Interviews. Interviews are often characterized as structured, semistructured, or unstructured. In **structured interviewing**, each informant is asked the same prepared questions, with the same wording, in the same order. In **semistructured interviewing**, the interviewer varies the questions in order to obtain the maximum information from each interviewee. In **unstructured interviewing**, there is no **interview protocol**—or list of prepared questions.

QUAL interviewing is typically semistructured for flexible use of prepared questions, maximizing opportunity for both focused and emergent information gathering. Structured interviews are generally too limiting for progressive focusing, and unstructured interviews can be so haphazard that they are usually reserved for situations where preparation of a protocol in advance is not possible. While semistructured interviewing is the most useful because it offers both focus and flexibility, it may also be the most demanding. The semistructured interviewer must record data while adjusting the wording and order of questions, maintaining rapport, preserving focus, and assessing and following up on conversational leads that may yield unexpected information by developing new questions on the spot.

Questions on interview protocols should elicit explanations rather than simple answers (see Figure 13.4). Questions should be clearly worded, focused, and brief rather than complicated or ambiguous. Wording should encourage interviewees to respond with their actual thoughts, rather than with responses that may seem correct or socially appropriate. To be sure that questions are comprehensible and answerable, protocols need to be carefully developed and field-tested in advance by trying out interview questions with groups similar to the intended interviewees, then refined before interviewing begins in earnest.

Figure 13.4 Guidelines for Developing Questions for Interview Protocols

- Use clear, unambiguous wording, as simple and jargon-free as possible.
- Prepare follow-up questions to ask if the initial query fails to elicit a relevant or fulsome response.
- Ask easy and less sensitive questions, including demographic questions, first in order to facilitate building rapport. Reserve complex and sensitive questions to later in the interview when respondents may feel more comfortable about answering them.
- Ask questions that call for descriptions and explanations, rather than questions that can be answered yes or no. Questions should stimulate free-flowing conversation and allow interviewees opportunity to move in unanticipated directions.
- Ask questions relevant to the purpose of the interview but that allow for productive digressions.
- Avoid leading questions that imply correct or appropriate or desired answers. For example, ask "Did the program increase your opportunity to do X, limit your opportunity, or have no effect in your own case?" rather than "Did the program increase your opportunity to do X?"
- Avoid double-barreled questions that ask for related bits of information simultaneously without allowing interviewees to indicate whether they consider the bits to be related. For example, separate this question: "Did the program change your understanding of whether you could pursue your interests regarding Y and help you succeed at it?"
- Be sure questions are answerable by intended interviewees and that they capitalize on the opportunity to learn about the respondents' particular perspectives and experiences. For example, do not ask beneficiaries questions that only program managers could reasonably be expected to answer.
- Avoid creating unnecessary discomfort or unjustifiable invasions of privacy. If a respondent appears uneasy, be prepared to offer to turn off recording devices, to move to a more neutral location, or to discontinue the interview.

Armed with a well-developed protocol, the interviewer then focuses on obtaining information that addresses the research or evaluation questions and also probes for the information each interviewee can uniquely provide. Probing requires follow-up questions responsive to what interviewees have said, follow-up questions that provide flexibility to pursue information uniquely available from each interview. The interviewer must exercise judgment about which leads to follow—which will offer promising but unexpected information related to the research or evaluation question. Because on-the-spot development of follow-up questions can be challenging, the interviewer may find it useful to word in advance some possible follow-ups—questions that might help to expand the conversation and explore the topic—and to have in mind some general follow-ups such as, "Can you tell me more about that (or help me understand what you mean)?" or "Why would that be the case (or did it happen that way)?"

For maximum informational value, different interview protocols are needed for different interviewee positions or groups. For example, different questions should be asked of program managers and program beneficiaries in order to maximize what can be learned about the perspectives and experiences of each. Questions should not be asked of road engineers that can only be answered by homeowners displaced by highway construction, or of students that only teachers can answer.

Individual and Group Interviews. Interviews may be conducted as individual or group sessions (Fontana and Frey 1994), the latter sometimes borrowing the term **focus groups** from marketing. More information may be gained in a shorter time with **group interviews**, especially when members of the group respond to each other's comments as well as to an interviewer's questions. Interactive conversation may take the focus in highly informative and unanticipated directions, deepening the discussion, adding useful detail, and providing some in-the-moment triangulation as interviewees elaborate, explain, and correct information as it is provided.

However, group interviews are more difficult to arrange and manage (see Box 13.3). In some cases, the intended focus may be lost unless the interviewer is insistently directive, which can undermine rapport. Candor may be more difficult to elicit or assess with group interviews than with individual interviews, as there may be social status or power issues (unknown to the interviewer but clear to the interviewees) that inhibit some speakers and encourage others. Loquacious participants may monopolize discussion, while others are silenced. Reticence is difficult to decipher; it may suggest restrained personalities, cultural conditions, the sensitivity of the issues being discussed, or status differentials.

BOX 13.3
GROUP INTERVIEWS ABOUT WOMEN'S
USE OF PUBLIC TRANSPORTATION

As part of an international program to promote women's access to public transportation, an evaluation was conducted in Lima, Peru, focused on women's experiences with buses, taxis, bicycles, and the like. A series of focus groups was combined with observation in buses and taxis. In some group interviews, all participants were of the same sex

(Continued)

(Continued)

and age range. Interviews with women only revealed that sexual harassment on buses was a main reason why they did not like to use them and why some parents would not allow their daughters to attend a local university. Young men participating in an all-male group tended to downplay sexual harassment but, in mixed groups, they recognized the seriousness of the issue. Observation data proved effective for stimulating group discussions.

SOURCE: http://siteresources.worldbank.org/INTGENDERTRANSPORT/Resources/G_T_ ReportMain.pdf

As with observation, detailed data are needed from interviews. Exact quotations must be recorded to support experientiality and exactness in reports. An interviewer may choose to take notes and write them up immediately afterward or to audiotape an interview and transcribe the tape. Both audiotaping and note-taking can interfere with interviewer-interviewee rapport and can introduce artificiality into a conversation; videorecording tends to be even more intrusive. For ethical reasons, interviewees should be offered opportunity to decline electronic recording.

Transcribing recorded group interview data is demanding, whether interview data are recorded by hand or by machine. If audiotaping, the transcriber may have difficulty hearing every comment and matching words to their speakers because verbal interchanges often overlap. Moreover, technology glitches can occur—batteries can fail, the wrong buttons on a machine can be pushed, volume settings can be faulty. Transcribing interview notes taken by hand presents different challenges, especially because of the speed and overlapping nature of interviewees' comments. An evaluator may find it helpful both to take notes and also to tape-record group interviews. It may be even more helpful to have a colleague take notes and operate a tape-recorder as the interviewer asks questions from the protocol and devises follow-ups.

Interviewing may require more cultural sensitivity and competence than observations because interviewers must interact with participants without giving offense and undermining rapport. Cultural differences may prevent him or her from fully comprehending the nuances and implications of interview information. Access to reliable key informants or teaming with a local participant, with whom the evaluator can later debrief, can help ensure (but not guarantee) accuracy. Where language is a significant barrier, translators may be required—and there may be no way to ensure exact translations from one language to another, no way to know whether the data are clouded by the translator's judgment about phrasing or about what is appropriate to convey.

5.3. Analysis of Documents and Artifacts

Documentary and artifactual data include texts, photographs, and other tangible items from the site that are collected and analyzed. Review of documents and other artifacts of material culture provides a relatively unobtrusive method for gaining information and may offer information unavailable from other types of data sources (Hodder 1994). For example, documents such as curricula or meeting minutes and artifacts such as artworks or historic photographs (see Figure 13.5) may provide

Figure 13.5   Documents and Artifacts that May Be Available from Evaluation Sites

In Education

- Content and performance standards
- Curricula, guidelines, lesson plans, textbooks, instructional materials and modules
- Samples of student work, both academic and artistic
- Test scores, grades, and other indicators of achievement and progress
- Individualized Education Plans (IEPs) or learning contracts
- Statistics regarding student ethnicity, gender, socioeconomic status, disciplinary measures
- Qualifications and performance evaluations of personnel
- Records regarding school accreditation, funding and other resources, expenditures, allocations of resources
- Legal and regulatory requirements

In Social Science

- Statements of program purpose, mission, goals, objectives
- Reports to funders and government agencies, stakeholders and communities
- Databases, records, minutes of meetings
- Documentation of program changes over time
- Indicators of program accessibility, use, processes, progress, success
- Regulatory guidelines, procedures, requirements
- Resources, budgets, expenditures
- Personnel standards, credentials, records, training, allocation, compensation

information about occurrences prior to the arrival of the researcher or evaluator. In some instances, documents and artifacts may offer better or more data than other sources or may do so more easily, unobtrusively, quickly, or cheaply.

Not all documents and artifacts are equally accessible, and the existence of some may be unknown at the outset. A growing list of items requested, obtained, and reviewed may be needed to keep track. Once obtained, not every document or artifact should be allocated equal attention; some may not be sufficiently relevant or useful for more than a quick scan. Each item should be considered for its informativeness, accuracy, and authenticity and analyzed accordingly.

For some items, relevance, accuracy, or authenticity may be uncertain enough that an evaluator might wonder, for example: Was the vote at this meeting recorded accurately in the minutes, and did it have any actual effect on the program? Did the summary provided to the funders by the program manager underemphasize complaints from beneficiaries? What is the "plan B" mentioned in this document?

As do other types of QUAL data, documents and artifacts require both careful analysis and interrogation since they, too, embed the perspectives of participants. An effort to detect naturally occurring perceptual bias is needed, as participants naturally want to present themselves and their work favorably. Their self-presentations and their choices of what to share should be checked against other data (triangulation) to take into account any inaccurate rosiness. Because most documents and artifacts are obtained on the basis of requests, there can be a double-dose of inherent bias in documents and artifacts—the stakeholders who provide them might make available the most positive or favorable.

Although all data should be analyzed critically, self-report data (such as QUAL interview and QUANT survey data) require such healthy skepticism. Caution applies both to self-initiated records and those that an evaluator may request participants to keep and submit. Evaluators might, for example, ask stakeholders to create documents and artifacts specifically for the evaluation—for example, timelines of their educational and work histories or food journals recording details of their diets during a period of interest. Analysts need to be alert for the potential of stakeholders to exaggerate or underplay the facts.

Privacy-Protected and Self-Report Documents. Some documents are legally protected against invasions of privacy, and others are restricted because they are classified or proprietary. Documents such as students' Individualized Educational Plans (IEPs) are legally protected in the United States to ensure privacy.

In addition, some documents require special sensitivity because they may contain personal or confidential information. Participants sharing documents such as personal expense accounts, travel records, and training logs are not always aware that their cooperativeness may expose them to risk. Diaries and personal journals are particularly likely to expose vulnerabilities. It is sometimes ethically necessary for an evaluator to be more protective of participants than they themselves are.

5.4. Hybrid Qualitative Data Collection Methods

Qualitative data collection methods allow for an endless variety of adaptations to particular data and information needs. Purposeful modifications suited to specific circumstances help ensure the completeness and accuracy of the data. For example, the analysis of documents and artifacts may include **bibliometrics** to indicate a program's scholarly impact by documenting the number of citations and publications arising from it. Technology also opens new data collection opportunities, as do hybrid amalgams of familiar methods.

Visually Stimulated Interviews. Videotapes and photographs can document observations and, with permission to share them, promote deep and experiential understanding. For example, videos and photos of activities at different program sites might inform program managers about consistencies (or inconsistencies) in procedures and the impact of different program contexts; before-and-after videos and photos might clarify program progress and accomplishment for managers and other stakeholders. In addition, these observation data can be used to stimulate interviews.

With the permission of those observed, a montage of photos or video clips may stimulate group interviews about critical, typical, or ambiguous events (see Tobin, Wu, and Davidson 1989). Development of protocols for semistructured interviewing, at least as backup conversation starters, may enhance the usefulness of the photos or videos for eliciting discussion. As participants are asked to describe or interpret the activities they can see in pictures, differences in their reactions can surface a diversity of responses and perspectives and, in group interviews, deep thinking about different perspectives and meanings.

Video-stimulated interviews blur the distinction between observation and interview methods, as interviewees become co-observers. Video-stimulated interviews also blur the distinction between data collection and analysis. While the comments and responses of interviewees constitute interview data, they also constitute participants' analyses of the interactions they observe on video.

Adaptations might include other types of visual stimulation to spur discussion with interviewees. For example, a group of interviewees might be provided an array of photographs taken during data collection, and each might be asked to select one and tell what it represents to him or her about the program. Or visual data or other images that might serve as program metaphors (e.g., a roller coaster, an umbrella on a rainy day, a circle of happy children at play) could be offered to participants as conversation-starters. Or participants might be asked to sketch representations of their experiences in the program, then explain them.

Think-Aloud Interviews. **Think-aloud** or **cognitive interviews** also blend observation and interview. This technique calls for a subject to vocalize his or her thoughts while engaged in a task (such as reading or using a computer) and for these vocalizations to be documented by a data collector. The evaluator could be seen as conducting an observation focused on a participant at task, or as conducting an interview with one question: "Can you tell me what you are thinking as you do that?"

Think-aloud interviews provide insight into an individual's cognitive and metacognitive processing, decision making, and rationales. However, a caution is needed: Vocalizing while at task is not natural, ordinary behavior, so analysis of think-aloud data should take this into account.

Arts-Based Research Methods. Qualitative methodology is useful for penetrating the tacit knowledge drawn from experience and existing at a subliminal level, things participants know but find difficult to articulate. Arts activities also elicit and manifest personal understandings not easily shared otherwise. This conceptual linkage between qualitative methods and the arts suggests opportunities for adaptations of data collection, even those involving non-arts activities or programs.

Arts-based data collection procedures include use of images, drawings, music, or other expressive modes to capture experiential and tacit knowledge. Participants might be asked to draw, mime, or mold clay and then to explain the meaning of their creations relative to the research question or program being evaluated. For example:

- Students might be asked to act out taking a high-stakes test (e.g., drinking coffee to stay alert, cramming).
- Personnel might be asked to sing a song that describes working relationships (e.g., "I get by with a little help from my friends" by the Beatles, "I can't get no satisfaction" by the Rolling Stones).
- Beneficiaries might be asked to select pictures or cartoons that indicate relative access to program goods or services (e.g., a long queue extending from a doorway, a whites-only drinking fountain).
- Managers might be asked to represent their experiences by drawing (e.g., a dripping faucet, an unscalable castle).

Subsequent discussion may surface experiences and perceptions not otherwise available to researchers and may reveal deep personal meanings relevant to the program.

Technology in Data Collection. Technology opens new data collection opportunities such as observation of interactions in virtual space, online surveys and documents and asynchronous discussion, interviews by phone or videoconference or e-mail. As more devices and applications become available, the possibilities will continue to expand.

This type of data collection may be especially important when the programs to be evaluated are online, such as distance education, webinars, and electronic diagnostic or referral services. As such programs proliferate, especially where potential participants are geographically dispersed but have access to computers, program managers and consumers increasingly want to know about their quality.

Observations in virtual reality require technology for access. In contrast to observation of ordinary events, interactions in virtual space may occur on camera or by typing messages on a computer keyboard and transmitting them electronically. Messages in discussion threads document word-for-word the conversations among participants. Observing on screen, the online observer simultaneously captures the activities as they happen.

Electronic Interviews. Where face-to-face interviews cannot be conducted and electronic means are available, interviews by telephone, e-mail, or other electronic means may be needed—but they come with caveats. Telephone interviews, in contrast to in-person interviews, lower the interviewer's opportunity to develop rapport, critical for gaining enough trust to ensure honest answers, and eliminate opportunities to observe nonverbal indications of meaning.

E-mail interviews, convenient because the data are written up by the interviewee at the time they are collected, lack spontaneity. Because interviewees may more carefully craft and revise their responses, the data may be skewed by overediting, "political correctness," or posturing than might be the case with a spontaneous oral response.

6. Data Analysis

Qualitative findings are developed inductively. The process is essentially substantive, driven by content, rather than procedural. It involves identification of patterns in the data from which understandings must be developed and interpretations constructed. The interpretive process is not a clear series of steps but, rather, has been compared with reading and interpreting a complicated text—an intuitive process of searching for meaning among a tapestry of interwoven threads, strands that are too many and too embedded to isolate meaningfully. Inductive analysis can be a dialogic effort to understand both details and the "big pictures" to which they contribute.

Thematic analysis involves macro- and micro-examination of the data and identification of emergent patterns and themes, both broad-brush and fine-grained. Micro-review of data promotes recognition of important details that may have been barely noticed during data collection, identification of relationships between data and themes, and discovery of patterns and consistencies. As patterns emerge, the important themes can be identified. These themes can focus reorganization of the data set, allowing the details related to each theme to be examined closely. The process of thematic analysis often involves reading and rereading the entire data set several times, each time marking points of interest and gradually grouping them into themes.

Identifying which themes are important and which data are relevant to them involves judgments that "often involve multidimensional criteria and conflicting interests. . . . The evaluator should strive to reduce biases in making such judgments" (House 1994:15). But one's own biases can be difficult to recognize, much less reduce. Having accepted that objectivity is unattainable, QUAL practitioners use their subjective capacities proactively to understand while simultaneously trying to discipline their subjectivity so that it does not undermine the trustworthiness of their work. In this effort, triangulation, validation, and meta-evaluation are strong allies.

Theoretical Triangulation. Qualitative inquiry is not generally undertaken for the purpose of developing theory, but theory may emerge inductively or existing theory may be referenced, extended, or challenged. Theoretical triangulation, or the analysis of data from different theoretical or conceptual vantage points (Denzin 1989), may spur deeper understanding and may surface an array of potential interpretations. Rival explanations of data allow critical consideration of the validity of different potential findings.

For example, consider an educational program viewed from different theoretical frames. Rising test scores might suggest evidence of success from a measurement perspective. However, rising scores might suggest the distortion of curriculum into mere test preparation which, from a progressive education perspective (Dewey 1916), could indicate educational failure. Other frames from which the same program might be viewed include Stufflebeam's (1987) CIPP model to examine context, input, process, and product; and Bronfenbrenner's (1979) levels of ecological analysis to examine the reciprocal effects of ideology, policy, working relationships, and interactions. Analysis from each perspective would emphasize and reveal different aspects and different interpretations that, when juxtaposed, could deepen understanding.

Although in general, external theories are not the *a priori* impetus for qualitative study, QUAL data collection and analysis can be focused (at least initially) on a program theory or logic model describing how a programs is expected to produce intended outcomes. A program theory might be developed collaboratively with stakeholders or developed (and refined) during data collection.

Criteriality. In some evaluations, programs are judged against criteria. Criteria may be pre-specified externally by a funding agency, professional organization, or accrediting body, or criteria may be pre-specified internally by clients or by evaluators in consultation with clients who may create criteria specifically for the program to be evaluated. In other cases of criterial evaluation, criteria may emerge during the course of the evaluation. This is likely to be the case as factors and outcomes gradually become clear during QUAL evaluations.

Objectivity (or reduction of potential subjective bias) is an oft-stated purpose for criterial analyses referencing explicit external standards. However, since the standards and criteria manifest the subjective biases of their developers, the objectivity is illusory. Recognizing this, QUAL practitioners tend to be skeptical that criteria are objective, that all relevant criteria can be identified in advance, and that preordinate criteria will focus data collection and analysis appropriately. There is the danger that pre-specified criteria will ensure attention to some program aspects at the expense of others and inject systematic bias rather than eliminate it.

The qualitative perspective is that each program is complex, too unique and contextual to be judged comprehensively by comparison to a set of criteria intended for all programs of its kind. Superimposing common criteria can amount to fitting square pegs into round holes. Emphasis on the program as a specific case predisposes QUAL evaluators toward limited, rather than total, reference to external or preordinate criteria in judging quality and effectiveness.

Electronic Data Analysis. Use of electronic tools marketed for analysis of QUAL data need to be approached with caution. While the promise of time-saving strategies is attractive, especially in the face of RealWorld constraints, so-called qualitative data analysis programs tend to offer little more than retrieval of data by categories. Consequently, these programs tend to undermine validity in two ways.

First, data must be entered into a computer using categories or codes during the data collection process. This task occurs prior to the emergence of patterns and themes, so the initial codes and categories may be off-target. Premature coding suggests that retrieval will be based on inappropriate categories, thus undermining the quality of data analysis. Re-coding after data collection—in accordance with the concepts of emergent design and constant-comparative method (Glaser and Strauss 1967; Strauss and Corbin 1990)—would eliminate any savings of time.

Second, reliance on electronics undercuts QUAL analysis's minds-on, content-oriented approach. Dependence on mechanistic data retrieval decreases opportunity to confront and consider the data, to read and reread for understanding, to develop and test preliminary themes and interpretations—that is, to analyze the data. So, electronic "data analysis" actually lessens the depth of analysis expected of QUAL researchers and evaluators, suggesting detriments to validity.

7. Reporting

Reports based on QUAL data should portray the complexity of the phenomenon or program studied—the multiple perspectives, overlapping contexts, and various conditionalities, criteria, and values. Such things are not easily or fully represented by numbers, charts, or tables. Multifaceted descriptions are needed to present enough data to show the evidentiary basis for findings, to avoid oversimplification in representations of phenomena or programs, and to promote valid findings. So, QUAL reports tend to be somewhat narrative in style.

Avoiding oversimplification and presenting enough data to show the evidentiary basis for findings, especially detailed observation narratives, tends to lengthen QUAL reports. However, succinct summaries of events tend to offer opinions or interpretations more than the data on which they are based. Presentation of interview excerpts sufficient to represent multiple perspectives also tends to require more space than, for example, a tally of survey responses.

Narratives have long been recognized as having the capacity to convey a complexity not easily attained in numerical and correlational presentations (Carter 1993; Holley and Colyar 2009) and, consequently, they can be more effective in promoting utilization of findings. Narrative reporting can help readers or stakeholders *understand* the particular, rather than merely *explain* the general (von Wright 1971), providing understanding so deep that it may be difficult to articulate otherwise (Polanyi 1958). Such deep understanding enhances the validity of inferences about a phenomenon or the quality of a program.

The effectiveness of narratives for influencing behavior can be seen in the power of fables and parables and stories from history, of legends preserved over centuries, of the ease with which people remember a character in a novel longer than their own experiences at the time they were reading it. For example, we may have drawn important personal lessons and vividly remember *Don Quixote* by Miguel de Cervantes Saavedra (1615/1964), or Scout in *To Kill a Mockingbird* by Harper Lee (1960), or *Anna Karenina* by Leo Tolstoy (1889) but remember little or nothing of our lives as we read the book. Don't we all try to remember not to tilt at windmills, not to overexpose the shy or vulnerable, not to ruin our lives over an infatuation? Narratives, then, suggest a significant strategy for addressing utility.

8. RealWorld Constraints

In the real world, the time required for high-quality QUAL methods may be difficult to find. Compensating for time by hiring skillful QUAL practitioners may shift the problem from time to budget. Shortcuts in the interest of feasibility tend to undermine validity—not an advisable trade-off—but balancing resources and evaluation quality are always necessary. Such balancing requires as much knowledge and judgment as the practice of qualitative methods, and must always address the specifics of a particular project. That is, consistent with the foundational concepts of qualitative methods, how to balance project resources and needs involves careful attention to particulars and contexts.

The particulars for a given project include the amount, type, and availability or accessibility of data. Less time will be needed if data collection is built-in to a program such as the archiving of enrollment information, budgets, plans and materials, and the like. More time will be needed if translation is necessary, if transportation to sites is difficult, or if facts are inseparable from opinions in the data available. To ensure full access, it is often important for data collectors to maintain a positive interface with data providers to minimize the possibility that some data sources may prove unwilling to provide needed information.

Ensuring the willingness of critical data sources to share their recollections may prove important if documents are insufficient or unavailable for needed historical timelines or perspective. Recall data must be analyzed with special care not only because of the self-report nature of such data but also because memory can be faulty and different persons may remember the same events in very different ways.

QUAL data tend to offer more personal experience and perspective than QUANT data—and the more personal the data the more likely the risk of exposure to political repercussions. Program-related politics that can, in effect, block access to information may arise among stakeholders, emerge between program personnel and funding agencies, or emanate from governmental or regulatory sources. Politics among research or evaluation players can also take time to work out or can otherwise constrain data collection and analysis—politics between evaluators and clients, among members of an inquiry team, or between evaluators and stakeholders (see Chapter 6).

If time is available, it may be able to compensate for budget, data, or political constraints—for example, providing time on site without repetitive travel costs, repeated or alternative attempts to obtain data not initially made available, opportunity to work out obstructive relationships. If money is available, it may be able to compensate for time constraints—for example, paying experts (or training and paying locals) to gather needed data over a shorter period of time. If data are available, there may be reduced need for collecting more and, consequently, less time and budget required. The specifics encountered in a project determine how real-world constraints may be balanced and managed.

SUMMARY

Qualitative data collection, analysis, and reporting make heavy demands on real-world evaluations, but failure to attend to these demands compromises the validity of findings. QUAL designs are emergent, offering flexibility and increasingly well-targeted foci. Analysis and reporting are complex—attentive to many perspectives, diverse experiences, contrasting theoretical frameworks and criteria—and tend to offer site-specific (rather than broad) findings. The personal nature of much QUAL data raises challenging ethical issues. Yet, QUAL methods offer insights otherwise unavailable and lead to deep understanding. These insights and understandings facilitate constructive application and use of findings.

FURTHER READING

Guba, E. G. and Y. S. Lincoln. 1989. *Fourth Generation Evaluation.* Newbury Park, CA: Sage.

General (and seminal) reference for use of qualitative methods in evaluation.

Strauss, A. and J. Corbin. 1990. *Basics of Qualitative Research: Grounded Theory Procedures and Techniques.* Newbury Park, CA: Sage.

Original source for grounded theory and constant-comparative method.

Tobin, J. J., D. Y. H. Wu, and D. H. Davidson. 1989. *Preschool in Three Cultures: Japan, China, and the United States.* New Haven, CT: Yale University Press.

Published example of using qualitative methods, including video-stimulated interviewing, in an international comparison.

CHAPTER 14

Mixed-Method Evaluation

T his chapter reviews mixed-method designs *that combine quantitative (QUANT) and qualitative (QUAL) approaches and methods to take advantage of the strengths of each approach and overcome their respective weaknesses when applied separately. We begin by describing the essential characteristics of mixed-method designs and consider when and why they are used. The main mixed-method designs are then discussed. These include sequential, the most widely used, where QUANT and QUAL approaches are applied one after the other; concurrent, where both approaches are applied at the same time; and multilevel, where analysis may be conducted at the level of, for example, the school district, the school, the classroom, and the individual teacher or student. Distinctions are also made between (a) mixed-method designs in which either a QUAL or QUANT approach is dominant and the other approach is used to complement it, and (b) designs in which both QUANT and QUAL approaches are given equal weight. The chapter concludes with a discussion of strategies for using mixed-method designs, emphasizing that this requires an integrated approach at all stages of the evaluation, one that is more complex than simply mixing and matching QUANT and QUAL data collection methods.*

1. The Mixed-Method Approach

Mixed-method evaluation involves the use of a multidisciplinary team so the evaluation design and hypothesis formulation, as well as data collection, analysis, dissemination, and use, all draw on the theories and methods of two or more relevant disciplines. Normally, the term is used to refer to designs that combine elements of both QUANT and QUAL approaches. Although many evaluators now routinely use a variety of methods because the field has come to accept the legitimacy of various methodological traditions, "What distinguishes mixed-method evaluation is the intentional or planned use of diverse methods for particular mixed-method purposes using particular mixed-method designs" (Greene 2005:255). While many so-called mixed-method approaches rely heavily on one particular discipline (for example, economics, demography, or rural development), only drawing on alternative disciplines for one particular phase (such as exploratory ethnographic studies before a survey instrument is designed, or data collection), a fully integrated mixed-method approach will use a multidisciplinary approach at all stages of the evaluation design, implementation, and use. Most commonly, what are combined are methods of data collection, but it is also possible to combine conceptual frameworks, hypotheses, methods of data analysis, or frameworks for the interpretation of the evaluation **findings**.

Because both QUANT and QUAL methodologies, when used alone (*monomethod* approach), are prone to "methods-induced bias" (Johnson and Onwuegbuzie 2004:15), evaluators recognize that mixed-method designs generally produce more comprehensive coverage and more valid findings than either QUANT or QUAL alone. In evaluation, an applied social science, appreciation of mixed methods came early, even before formal articulation and documentation of the methodology. Now, "It is time that methodologists catch up with practicing researchers" (Johnson and Onwuegbuzie 2004:22) and evaluators.

However, a number of writers have questioned the possibility of integrating QUANT and QUAL approaches that are based on different philosophical orientations and reflect historically different traditions in the social sciences. Lincoln and Guba (1985) introduced the notion of **incommensurability,** which has influenced subsequent discussion of the difficulties of trying to integrate different research methods. A number of other authors (e.g., Creswell et al. 2003; Morse 2003) have also cautioned against trying to work with two different evaluation approaches simultaneously:

> Recall that methodological strategies are tools for enquiry and that methods are cohesive collections of strategies that fit a particular perspective. To incorporate a different strategy into a study is risky and should be done with care, lest the core assumptions of the project be violated. Maintaining balance between respecting these assumptions and respecting the assumptions underlying your supplementary strategies is delicate, for they may often clash. (Morse 2003:192)

While we argue in this chapter and throughout the book that mixed-method approaches usually enhance the quality and utility of an evaluation, it is important to recognize and address the practical and theoretical issues involved in working together as a multidisciplinary team to implement a mixed-method strategy.

2. Rationale for Mixed-Method Approaches

In Chapter 12 (Table 12.1) we mentioned what are frequently considered to be the main strengths and weaknesses of QUANT approaches. Table 14.1 presents a similar summary for QUAL evaluations. One of the main reasons for using mixed-method designs is to combine the strengths of QUANT and QUAL while at the same time addressing some of the inherent weaknesses of either monomethod approach. Mixed methods can be applied at any stage of the design, implementation, or analysis of an evaluation.

Let us take the example of an evaluation of the effectiveness of rural health centers in reaching low-income and minority sectors of the community, and let us assume that the evaluation will adopt a predominantly QUAL approach. The evaluation team wishes their evaluation to influence national health policies by identifying some of the reasons why poor and minority families do not use the health centers, and they are aware that the Ministry of Health has criticized earlier evaluations for having focused on communities known to have particular problems so that the findings are not representative of the whole country. The evaluators are aware that the ministry has sometimes found

Table 14.1 Strengths and Weaknesses of Qualitative Evaluation Approaches

QUAL Features	Strengths	Weaknesses
Emergent design and progressive focusing	Evaluators are not bound by initial designs but, rather, are expected to improve them as they learn more about the program.	Designs cannot be fully articulated at the outset, which can be off-putting for clients who want to know what they are getting. QUAL evaluations are not usually replicable, partly because of continuous adjustments.
Purposeful sampling	Stakeholders with experience or information related to specific aspects of the program are identified as data sources.	Samples are not random or large enough for reliability or generalizability in the quantitative sense.
Contextuality and generalizations	Qualitative evaluations support understanding of the program in its actual setting and also case-to-case generalizations by readers to settings relevant to them.	Qualitative evaluations do not usually support case-to-population generalizations or wide applicability to other populations and settings.
Stakeholder orientation	Emphasis on the experiences and perceptions of multiple stakeholders helps reveal program processes as experienced and their human impact.	Revealing many points of view tends not to lead to easy consensus, including consensus about use of findings for program decisions.
Holism	Big-picture views that include many aspects and influences help convey the actual dynamics and complexity of programs.	Specific factors are not isolated, measured, and correlated, although their relationships and effects are documented and portrayed.
Expansionism	Proliferation of data and meanings contributes to complex understanding and improves the validity of program representations and findings.	Qualitative reports tend to be lengthy. Most findings are contextualized and conditional rather than clear and absolute.
Narrative reporting	Narrative reports are accessible to nontechnical audiences, including many evaluation stakeholders and users. Narratives promote readers' deep understanding through vicarious experience, which enhances use of findings.	Narrative reports tend to be lengthy and may not offer clear, bottom-line results.
Validity of findings	Detailed data and triangulation support valid findings.	Some consider interpretivist methods too subjective to be credible.

the lack of statistical representativity to be a convenient excuse for ignoring valid criticisms, and they want to ensure that their study will not be dismissed on these grounds. Consequently, the evaluation team meets with the National Institute of Statistics and uses their national household sample frame to ensure that the sample of communities they select is broadly representative of the whole country (or the region where the study is conducted). The evaluation uses the same QUAL methods, but it is now possible to indicate that the sample of communities was selected in consultation with the National Institute of Statistics and is considered broadly representative of all communities in the regions studied (see Figure 14.1).

Figure 14.1   Using a National Household Sample Frame to Ensure the Representativity and Credibility of a QUANT Case Study Evaluation Design Assessing the Access of Women to Rural Health Centers

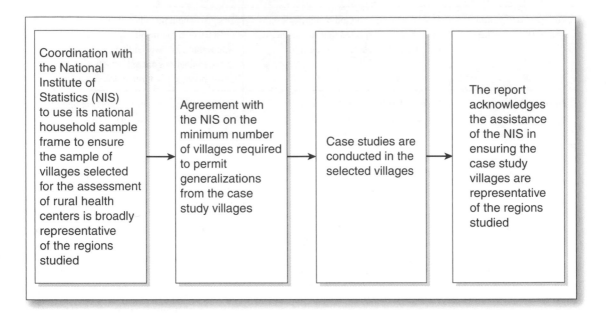

Let us now assume that the same evaluation was to be conducted by a different team planning to use a QUANT approach based on a nationally representative household sample survey. They are concerned that although a well-designed survey may obtain reasonably reliable estimates of the proportion of the population using the health centers (although even then there is a potential problem of misreporting), they are fully aware that the survey will not provide a good understanding of why some groups use the health centers and others do not. Consequently, they invite an ethnographer to join their team and conduct in-depth studies in a small number of communities. The ethnographic studies will explore health-related attitudes and beliefs of different ethnographic groups and the factors influencing their decision to use or not use the health centers. The studies will also examine the economic, political, organizational, cultural, and ecological factors affecting the operation of the health centers in different communities. The first part of the analysis will address broad cultural differences likely to affect all health centers, and the latter part (the contextual analysis) will help to explain factors affecting the performance of different centers (see Figure 14.2). The evaluation director is aware that mixed-method designs work well only when there is respect and understanding and a feeling of equality among team members from different professions, so the ethnographer was invited to join the team from the time of the first planning meeting. The following are some of the ways in which the QUANT and QUAL approaches will be integrated into this evaluation:

- Rapid ethnographic studies will be conducted in a small number of communities to identify some of the issues that must be addressed in the study and to help identify the best way to phrase the questions to be included in the questionnaire.

- Once the sample has been selected for the household survey, a number of communities will be selected from the same sample frame for conducting ethnographic studies of families and health services and for preparing contextual analysis.
- To compare information obtained by different methods, QUAL interviews and case studies may be conducted with a small number of families included in the sample survey.
- **Triangulation** procedures will be built into the evaluation design so that independent QUANT and QUAL estimates can be obtained for key variables (such as use of health facilities and attitudes toward these facilities).
- Separate QUANT and QUAL reports will be prepared, and the team will then meet to compare the two and to identify areas where the findings support each other as well as questions on which there are apparent differences of facts or interpretation.
- Follow-up fieldwork will be conducted to check on inconsistencies and also to prepare additional cases to illustrate and explain some of the key issues and conclusions.

Figure 14.2 Using QUAL Ethnographic Village Studies to Help Interpret the Findings of a National QUANT Sample Survey Estimating Women's Utilization Rates of Rural Health Centers

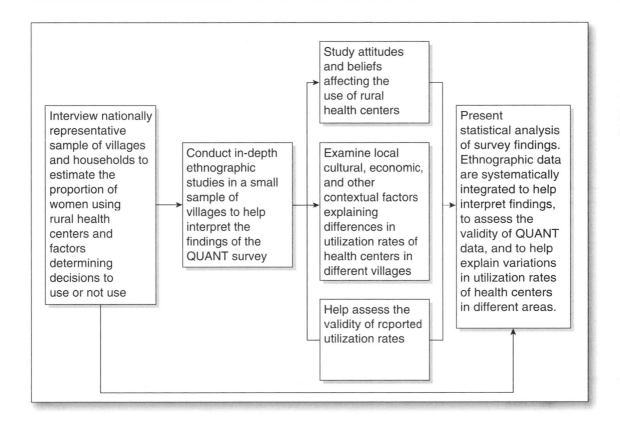

In both of these cases mixed methods can strengthen the evaluation, but the focus is quite different when mixed methods are used to strengthen predominantly QUAL designs (Figure 14.1) than when they strengthen a predominantly QUANT design (Figure 14.2).

Greene (2005:255–56) suggests five reasons for using mixed-method designs:

- Triangulation, or enhancing the validity or credibility of evaluation findings through results from the different methods that converge and agree, one with the other.
- Development, or using the results of one method to help develop the sample or instrumentation for another.
- Complementarity, or extending the comprehensiveness of evaluation findings through results from different methods that broaden and deepen the understanding reached.
- Initiation, or generating new insights into evaluation findings through results from the different methods that diverge and thus call for reconciliation via further analysis, reframing, or some other shift in perspective.
- Value diversity, or incorporating a wider diversity of values and thus greater consciousness about the value dimensions of evaluation through the use of different methods that themselves advance difference values.

From an operational perspective, mixed methods can offer the following advantages:

- Understanding how local contextual factors help explain variations in program implementation and outcomes.
- Reconstructing baseline data to strengthen the database for QUANT evaluations.
- Strengthening the representativity of in-depth QUAL studies so they can make a greater continuation to QUANT evaluations.

3. Approaches to the Use of Mixed Methods

Often, mixed-method evaluation designs have exhibited a dominant QUANT or QUAL orientation, with methods or approaches from the other orientation used to complement, strengthen, or corroborate data and findings. However, mixed-method designs need not feature a dominant and a secondary or subservient approach. The most powerful application of an integrated, mixed-method approach may well occur when both QUAL and QUANT approaches are used fully and appropriately (Bamberger 2000b; Greene and Caracelli 2003; Mertens 2003). Figure 14.3 shows that mixed-method approaches can be considered as a continuum ranging from exclusively QUANT approaches, through mainly QUANT approaches that incorporate some QUAL elements, through approaches that give equal weight to both approaches, through mainly QUAL approaches with some QUANT elements, and finally exclusively QUAL approaches. Examples of evaluation designs at different points on this continuum include (see Table 14.2):

- *Dominant QUANT designs*. The evaluation is based on the application of a structured questionnaire to a randomly selected sample of individuals, households, groups, institutions, or communities, and the analysis mainly relies on econometric or other quantitative methods. Ethnographic techniques such as in-depth interviews, observation, and group interviews are only used to help develop and test the questionnaire; they are not used in the analysis and interpretation of the findings.

- *Designs that give equal weight to QUANT and QUAL approaches.* QUANT surveys are combined with a range of different QUAL techniques. Sometimes the latter focus on the process and contextual analysis, other times the focus is on the same unit of analysis as the surveys (e.g., individuals, households, communities, organizations) but different data collection methods are used.
- *Dominant QUAL designs.* A rapid QUANT survey is used either to identify the issues or groups to be covered in the in-depth QUAL studies or to show that the QUAL sample is reasonably representative of the total population.

Figure 14.3 The QUANT-QUAL Research Design Continuum

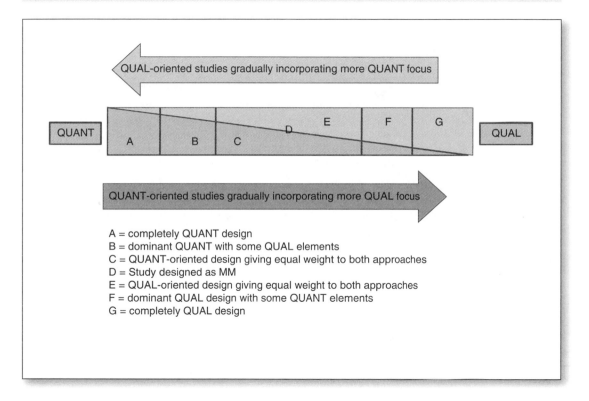

A = completely QUANT design
B = dominant QUANT with some QUAL elements
C = QUANT-oriented design giving equal weight to both approaches
D = Study designed as MM
E = QUAL-oriented design giving equal weight to both approaches
F = dominant QUAL design with some QUANT elements
G = completely QUAL design

Table 14.2 Examples of Evaluation Designs at Each Point on the QUANT-QUAL Continuum

Design	Some Applications
A. Completely QUANT design	Evaluation is based on the analysis of secondary survey data that cover both project and control areas. Where the samples are sufficiently large it may be possible to use techniques such as propensity score matching.

(Continued)

(Continued)

Design	Some Applications
B. Dominant QUANT design	Evaluation is mainly based on the application of a structured questionnaire to a randomly selected sample of individuals or households. QUAL techniques are only used to develop, validate, or illustrate the QUANT data collection and analysis. Exploratory QUAL interviews and observations used to test the survey instrument and a small number of case studies may be used to illustrate the main groups identified in the QUANT analysis. The case studies are only used for illustrative purposes.
DESIGN STRATEGIES THAT GIVE EQUAL WEIGHT TO QUANT AND QUAL APPROACHES. The program theory model draws on hypotheses, constructs, and research findings from both QUANT and QUAL disciplines.	
C. Designs originating with a QUANT orientation that give equal weight to QUANT and QUAL components	Usually a large-scale QUANT sample survey (e.g., households, communities, organizations) is used. QUAL techniques are used to conduct exploratory studies to identify issues and to formulate questions to help develop this instrument. The QUANT survey is complemented by process and/or contextual analysis to understand factors explaining differences in outcome in different project sites. Follow-up case studies or focus groups may be conducted to explore and illustrate in more depth some of the key issues arising from the survey analysis.
D. Designs that originate as MM without either a QUANT or QUAL orientation	QUANT surveys are combined with a range of different QUAL techniques. Sometimes the latter focus on process and contextual analysis, in other cases the focus is on the same unit of analysis as the surveys (e.g., individuals, households) but different data collection methods are used.
E. Designs originating with a QUAL orientation that give equal weight to QUANT and QUAL components	QUANT surveys may be used to identify key issues or key groups to be explored in more depth using QUAL methods. Selection procedures are used to ensure that units selected for in-depth study are at least broadly representative of the total population. Rapid follow-up QUANT surveys may be conducted to assess the generalizability of the QUAL findings.
F. Predominantly QUAL design	A rapid QUANT survey is used either to identify the issues or groups to be covered in the in-depth QUAL studies or to show that the QUAL sample is reasonably representative of the total population.
G. Completely QUAL design	The evaluation is based exclusively on QUAL techniques. In many cases data will be collected from a small number of individuals or groups complemented by general description of the setting. In other cases the study may have a broader focus, using artifacts and other kinds of secondary data to study a community or broader culture.

Table 14.3 describes some of the typical ways that QUANT and QUAL approaches are used in the different stages of an evaluation. Mixed methods seek to strengthen some or all stages of the evaluation by combining these different approaches.

- *Conceptual framework and formulation of hypotheses.* QUANT evaluations often derive hypotheses deductively from existing theories or literature reviews. In contrast, many QUAL evaluations emphasize the uniqueness of each situation and frequently do not identify hypotheses. When hypotheses are used by QUAL evaluators, they will often be developed inductively as the study evolves. Mixed methods can combine both approaches. For example, a QUANT evaluator may develop hypotheses deductively from a review of the literature, and the QUAL colleague can then explore and refine the ideas through, for example, interviews or observation. In contrast, the initial stages of QUAL data collection may identify and describe processes and issues that the QUANT team members may then define in such a way that they can be tested through data collected in a sample survey.

- *Selection of subjects or units of analysis.* QUAL evaluations typically, but not always, use a relatively small number of subjects, and a variety of procedures is used for selecting the sample. Often, subjects are selected purposively (theoretical sampling) to ensure that all important groups are included in the relatively small number of cases to be studied. In contrast, QUANT evaluations normally use a relatively large, randomly selected sample. The aim is to permit generalizability to larger populations and also to have a large enough sample to permit the statistical comparison of differences between groups (e.g., the **project** and **comparison groups**). The previous example of the health center evaluation illustrates how the QUANT and QUAL approaches to sampling can complement each other.

- *Evaluation design.* Most QUANT evaluations use one of a small number of clearly defined randomized or quasi-experimental designs (see Chapter 11). Where possible, representative samples of the project and comparison groups will be interviewed at two or more points during the life of the project to measure relative changes in **outcome** or impact indicators. In contrast, the QUAL evaluator normally becomes immersed in the community over a long period of time and seeks to understand the **program** through holistic analysis of the interrelationships among many different elements of the community and of the social, economic, political, and cultural setting in which the program operates. Normally, QUAL evaluations do not seek to establish a direct cause and effect or linear relationship between project interventions and outcomes, and the study may or may not involve a comparison group. One of the many ways in which the two approaches can be combined is to use QUAL methods to study the project **implementation process** and the influence of **contextual variables** (**contextuality**) on project performance in some of the communities in which a QUANT survey of project participants is being conducted.

- *Data collection and recording methods.* Whereas QUANT evaluations seek the collection of standardized, numerical data (see Chapter 12), QUAL evaluations usually use less structured data collection methods that provide greater flexibility and that seek to describe and understand the complexities and holistic nature of a situation (see Chapter 13). QUAL evaluators draw on a wide range of data collection and recording methods. Semistructured data collection instruments are often used in interviews or observation. The instruments will often be modified as the evaluation progresses. Data from the interview may be recorded in the form of notes or with audio- or videotapes. Group interviews are also commonly used. These may involve unstructured or semistructured conversations with small groups, such as families, gangs, school staff, or police, or in more structured group meetings such as **focus groups** or community meetings. Participant and nonparticipant observations are also used to collect data on individuals, groups, communities, or organizations. Document analysis (e.g., organization documents, different kinds of records, meeting reports) is also widely used. Photography is another common method. In contrast, QUANT evaluations rely heavily on structured questionnaires applied in exactly the same way throughout the study and where most of the information is recorded in numerical form or precoded categories. Precoded checklists, performance tests, and physical measurements such as anthropometric tests are also used.

- *Triangulation.* Both QUAL and QUANT evaluators use triangulation to obtain two or more independent estimates of key variables concerning program outcomes and the factors affecting these outcomes. QUANT evaluators combine consistency checks built into the

Table 14.3 Characteristics of Quantitative and Qualitative Approaches to Different Stages of the Evaluation Process

Evaluation Activity	Quantitative Approach	Qualitative Approach
The conceptual framework and the formulation of hypotheses	• Evaluations are usually, but not always, based on a theoretical framework derived from a review of the literature and usually involve testable hypotheses. • Hypotheses are often deductive (based on testable hypotheses derived from theory). • Hypotheses are usually quantitative and can be evaluated with statistical significance tests. • The framework often starts from the macro rather than the micro level.	• While some evaluations define and test hypotheses, many do not. • Many evaluations emphasize the uniqueness of each situation, and the conceptual framework may be defined through a process of iteration, with the framework being continuously updated as new information is obtained. • Hypotheses, if used, are often inductive (derived from information gathered during the course of the study).
Selection of subjects or units of analysis	• Random sampling so that findings can be generalized, and to permit statistical testing of differences between groups. • Requires a sampling frame that lists all the members of the target population(s) to be studied. • Selection methods are usually defined in advance, clearly documented, and unchanging throughout the study. • Typically a fairly large sample is selected from which to collect a finite set of quantitative data.	• Choice of selection procedures varies according to the purpose of the study. • Purposive sampling is used to collect the most useful and interesting data related to the purpose of the study. • While this is not usually done for QUAL evaluations, sometimes for mixed-method approaches the sample may be selected using the same master sampling frame as for the QUANT component of the research. For example, a subsample of the villages in which samples of households (or other units) are selected for the QUANT survey may be selected for the QUAL analysis (although the types of data collection and the subjects, groups, or organizations to be studied in the QUAL analysis will usually be different). • Usually a smaller number of people are interviewed in more depth.
Evaluation design	• Normally one of the quasi-experimental designs described in Chapter 11 is used. A randomly selected sample that represents the project participants, and possibly a control or comparison group, is interviewed at one or more points of time during the project. • Where possible, outcomes and impacts are estimated by comparing data collected before and after (and possibly during) the implementation of the project.	• The researcher(s) become immersed in the community over a long period of time. • The effects of the program are studied through collecting information on the many different elements of the community and its economic, political, cultural, ecological, and psychological setting. • Normally the evaluation does not try to establish a direct cause and effect or linear relationship.

Evaluation Activity	Quantitative Approach	Qualitative Approach
Data collection and recording methods	• Data are usually recorded in structured questionnaires that are administered consistently throughout the study. There is extensive use of precoded, closed-ended questions. • The study mainly uses numerical values (integer variables) or closed-ended (ordinal or nominal) variables that can be subjected to statistical analysis. • Observational checklists with precoded responses may be used.	• Interview protocols are the most common instrument, often semistructured. • The data collection instrument may be modified during the course of the study as understanding grows. • Interview data are sometimes recorded verbatim (audiotape, videotape) and sometimes in written notes. • Study may use analysis of existing documents. Textual data from documents are often highlighted in a copy of the original, which is kept as part of the data set. • Study may use focus groups (usually fewer than 10 people) and meetings with larger community groups. • Study may use participant and nonparticipant observation. • Study may use photography. • Several qualitative methods are used for multiple perspectives and triangulation.
Triangulation	• Consistency checks are built into questionnaires to provide independent estimates of key variables (e.g., data on income may be compared with data on expenditures). • Direct observation (a QUAL technique) can be used as a consistency check on answers given by the respondent (e.g., information on income can be compared with evidence of the number and quality of consumer durables in evidence inside or outside the house). • Information from earlier surveys with the same respondents is sometimes used as a consistency check on information given in a later survey. • Secondary data (census data, national household surveys, information from government agencies) can be used to check estimates from the evaluation survey.	• Triangulation by observation: A monitor can observe a focus group or group meeting both to identify any potential bias resulting from how the session was conducted and also to provide an independent perspective (e.g., reporting on the interactions between group members, observing how certain people respond to the comments or behavior of others). • Triangulation of findings from different researchers, data collection, times and location of data collection, and methods of interpretation; are a central element of the QUAL approach.

survey instruments with the use of secondary data (previous surveys and published reports) and the use of direct observation to compare with information provided by survey respondents. QUAL evaluations are often less concerned with consistency checks than with deepening and broadening understanding through multiple perspectives obtained from different sources of information. Triangulation is one of the most frequently used mixed-method approaches. For example, different methods of data collection can be used to validate data and to provide different perspectives and interpretations.

- *Data analysis.* QUAL evaluators use a wide range of data analysis methods. The purpose of many of these methods is to identify broad patterns and interrelations and to obtain a holistic overview of the complex interactions between a project and the setting within which it is embedded. The purpose of QUANT analysis, on the other hand, is to describe the statistical characteristics of the key variables, to determine statistical differences between project and comparison groups, and to identify factors contributing to the magnitude and direction of change. QUAL analysis can be used to help understand the meaning that different subjects or groups give to the statistical associations found in the QUANT analysis and to provide cases and examples to illuminate the findings. On the other hand, QUANT analysis can be used to assess how well the cases included in the QUAL studies represent the total population of interest and which if any sectors have not been covered. This complementarity is an important feature of mixed methods in situations where the evaluators are asked to generalize their findings.

While the methods, foci, and areas of concern of QUAL and QUANT approaches may seem to be heading in different directions, and while adherents of each camp often criticize what they perceive as methodological or philosophical weakness of the other, the two in fact can potentially complement each other. The purpose of mixed-method approaches is to draw on the strengths of each approach to overcome the weaknesses of the other when used in isolation. The rest of this chapter is devoted to discussing how the mixed-method approaches have developed and how they can be used to help evaluators mitigate the budget, time, data, and possibly political constraints under which RealWorld Evaluations (**RWE**) must be conducted.

3.1. Applying Mixed Methods When the Dominant Design Is Quantitative or Qualitative

Mixed-method designs are used differently, and produce different benefits, depending on whether the dominant design is QUANT or QUAL. For example, when the predominant design is QUANT, incorporating QUAL methods can provide the contextual analysis to help explain how project implementation and outcomes are affected by the economic, political, institutional, environmental, cultural, and other unique aspects of the project setting. Mixed methods also help QUANT evaluators use triangulation to provide independent estimates of key information collected through surveys and help provide a broader framework for the interpretation of the statistical data. Methods can also be triangulated so that different approaches to data collection and analysis can also be compared. Table 14.4 summarizes some of the potential weaknesses of statistical evaluation designs with respect to design, data collection, and analysis and shows how mixed-method designs can help address these issues and strengthen the designs. For example:

- Many quantitative evaluation designs do not systematically examine how local contextual factors (the local political, economic, institutional, and sociocultural context) affect program implementation and outcomes. QUAL techniques such as ethnographic studies, key informant interviews, participatory group interviews, and participant observation can analyze these contextual factors and show how they can affect the program. It is also possible to "quantize" this information, for example, by transforming descriptive analysis into a set of dummy variables that can be incorporated into regression analysis.
- The kinds of structured questionnaires used as the primary data collection instrument in most quantitative evaluations are frequently not able to capture information on sensitive topics such

as domestic violence, drug use, criminal activities, and social attitudes to people who are HIV positive. Case studies, in-depth interviews, focus groups, and participant observation are some of the qualitative techniques that are well suited to study these sensitive topics.

- Many QUANT evaluations are based on posttest comparisons of project and control groups often complemented by secondary data that are used to estimate baseline conditions of the two groups. Frequently, no information is available on important initial characteristics of the project population ("unobservables") that might explain some of the outcomes assumed to have been produced by the project. For example, many of the women who apply for microbusiness loans may have had previous experience running a business, or had unusually supportive husbands—both of which factors might increase their likelihood of being successful in their new businesses. There are a number of mixed-method techniques that could assess whether loan beneficiaries had special characteristics that might account for the business successes that were assumed to have been due to their having obtained a village bank loan. Techniques include in-depth interviews, key informants, recall, and participatory group interviews.

In contrast, when the predominant design is QUAL, a mixed-method design can potentially strengthen the evaluation in a number of different ways. For example, what can the in-depth evaluation findings from a small number of schools, agricultural extension centers, village banks, or community development groups tell policymakers about the potential of these programs? How and why the programs work or don't work is often more important to planners and policymakers than the statistical significance of the findings. QUANT approaches can contribute either by helping with the selection of the sample (see earlier discussion) or by using secondary data from censuses and surveys to contextualize the sample against the wider population. One of the areas of strength of QUAL evaluations is the presentation of a holistic analysis of the many contextual factors affecting the performance of a program. This helps explain variations in outcomes among different project sites found in the QUANT analysis. When the program being evaluated is operating on a large scale (throughout a city or state, or at the national level), it may be necessary to assess how these different contextual factors (e.g., economic, social, political, institutional, cultural) interact and how they affect program performance. Contextual factors can be analyzed either qualitatively through cross-case analysis (see Miles and Huberman 1994), or quantitatively by incorporating contextual variables into multiple regression and other forms of statistical analysis.[1] Rapid QUANT surveys can also be used to provide a project-wide backdrop for the interpretation of QUAL data by indicating the representativeness of the subjects or units studied within the project (cf. Erickson 1986, "petite generalizations").

Finally, statistical analysis can be used to present a broader context for assessing possible explanations of a phenomenon. For example, statistical analysis might identify household characteristics (e.g., household composition, educational level, economic status) associated with project outcomes, and this might identify some issues to be explored through in-depth QUAL analysis.

---

[1]One of the ways to do this is through the transformation of contextual variables into a set of dummy variables that can then be incorporated into the regression analysis (see Chapter 12). For example, if the activities of a particular government agency support the project in a particular location, this could be coded "1"; if they do not, this could be coded "0." If the economy is growing, this could be coded "1," and if it is static or declining, this could be coded "0." Assume that a regression analysis is conducted with "proportion of farmers adopting the new type of seed" as the dependent variable. If the analysis finds that the regression coefficient of some of the dummy variables is statistically significant, this suggests that the particular factor (e.g., support of a particular government agency) contributes to the program outcome. This is a highly simplified example, and it would often be necessary to include a number of dummy variables to describe each contextual factor; also, a number of exploratory analyses would be conducted to refine the definition of the contextual variables—often, to combine several into a composite index.

Table 14.4   Common Issues Affecting the Validity of Statistical Impact Evaluation Designs and How Mixed-Method (MM) Designs Can Help Address Them

Issue	Potential Contribution of Mixed Methods
Evaluation Design Issues	
1. **Limited construct validity.** Many strong evaluations use secondary data sources and must rely on proxy variables that may not adequately capture what is being studied, so findings can be misleading.	• Exploratory qualitative studies can strengthen understanding of the key concepts being studied. • Focus groups and PRA can provide beneficiary perspective on concepts and constructs.
2. **Decontextualizing the evaluation.** Conventional IE designs ignore the effect of the local political, economic, institutional, sociocultural, historical, and natural environmental context. These factors will often mean that the same project will have different outcomes in different communities or local settings.	• Ethnographers, key informants, and other qualitative techniques can provide information on the local context. Contextual analysis can be incorporated into regression analysis through the creation of dummy variables.
3. **Ignores the process of project implementation— the problem of the "black box."** Most IEs use a pretest-posttest comparison and do not study how the project is actually implemented. If a project does not achieve its objectives it is not possible to determine if this is due to *design failure* or *implementation failure*.	• Qualitative techniques such as participant and nonparticipant observation and key informants can be combined with program monitoring to integrate quantitative and qualitative information on implementation and other project processes.
4. **Designs are inflexible and cannot capture or adapt to changes in project design and implementation and in the local contexts.** IEs repeat the application of the same data collection instrument, asking the same questions and using the same definitions of inputs, outputs, outcomes, and impacts. It is very difficult for these designs to adapt to the changes, which frequently occur in the project setting or implementation policy.	• Panel studies, participant observation, key informants, etc., have the flexibility to detect and observe changes in the project or its setting.
5. **Hard to assess the adequacy of the sampling frame.** Evaluations frequently use the client list of a government agency as the sampling frame. This is easy and cheap to use, but frequently the evaluation ignores the fact that significant numbers of eligible families or communities are left out—and these are usually the poorest or most inaccessible.	• Small-scale, rapid studies of selected areas can be used to assess the adequacy of sampling frames.
6. **No clear definition of the time frame over which outcomes and impacts can be measured.** The posttest measurement is frequently administered at a time defined by administrative rather than theoretical considerations. Very often the measurement is made when it is too early for impacts to have been achieved, and it may be concluded that the project did not have an impact.	• Program theory models can be used to define the time frame over which outcomes and short-, medium-, and long-term impacts can be expected to occur. This can both help define when the impact evaluation should be conducted and also the initial indicators that a project is on track to achieving its outcomes/impacts.

Issue	Potential Contribution of Mixed Methods
7. **Difficult to identify and measure unexpected outcomes.** Structured surveys can also measure the expected outcomes and effects and are not able to detect unanticipated outcomes and impacts (positive and negative).	• Program theory models can identify preliminary indicators that can be measured early in the project and that provide evidence that the project is on track. • Qualitative methods such as key informants, participant observation, and focus groups can provide early indicators whether the project is on track.
Data Collection Issues	
8. **Reliability and validity of indicators.** Many statistical designs only use a limited number of indicators of outcomes and impacts, almost all of which are quantitative.	• MM can combine multiple quantitative and qualitative indicators that in combination can enhance validity and capture different dimensions of what is being studied. • MM makes extensive use of triangulation through which estimates obtained from different indicators are systematically compared and refined, and understanding is enhanced by comparing different perspectives.
9. **Inability to identify and interview difficult-to-reach groups.** Most QUANT data collection methods are not well suited to identify and gain the confidence of sex workers, drug users, illegal immigrants, and other difficult-to-reach groups.	• Ethnographers and other qualitative researchers have extensive experience in reaching inaccessible groups.
10. **Difficult to obtain valid information on sensitive topics.** Structured surveys are not well suited to collect information on sensitive topics such as domestic violence, control of household resources, and corruption.	• Case studies, in-depth interviews, focus groups, and participant observation are some of the many qualitative techniques available to study sensitive topics.
11. **Lack of attention to contextual clues.** Survey enumerators are trained to record what the respondent says and not to look for clues such as household possessions, evidence of wealth, interaction among household members, or the evidence of power relations to validate what is said.	• Observation and key informants are two of the many useful techniques.
12. **Often difficult to obtain a good comparison group match.** Adequate secondary data for using propensity score matching are only infrequently available, and often control groups must be selected on the basis of judgment and usually very rapid visits to possible control areas.	• Judgmental comparison group selection can be strengthened through rapid diagnostic studies, consultations with key informants, etc.
13. **The vanishing control group.** Control groups get integrated into the project, or they may be eradicated through migration, flooding, or urban renewal.	• Panel studies and observation techniques can monitor changes in the size and composition of the comparison group, can help explain the dynamic of the changes, and can provide early warning when corrective actions must be taken.

(Continued)

(Continued)

Issue	Potential Contribution of Mixed Methods
14. **Lack of adequate baseline data.** A high proportion of evaluations are commissioned late in the project and do not have access to baseline data. Many IEs collect baseline data but usually only collect QUANT information.	• There are a range of qualitative techniques that can be used to help "reconstruct" baseline data.
Analysis and Utilization Issues	
15. **Long delay in producing findings and recommendations that can be used by policymakers and other stakeholders.** Conventional IEs do not produce a report or recommendations until the posttest survey has been completed late in the project cycle or when the project has ended. By the time the report is produced it is often too late for the information to have any practical utility.	• Formative evaluation can provide periodic feedback to stakeholders throughout the life of a project. Some of this information can be generated by the planning and initial data collection phases of the impact studies, building up a constituency for the later findings of the quantitative studies.
16. **Difficult to generalize to other settings and populations.** This is a particular challenge for RCTs and similar designs that estimate average effects by controlling for individual and local variations.	• Techniques such as quota sampling can use small samples to study variations in the population studied, providing a stronger basis for assessing the populations for which program replication is most and least likely to be successful.
17. **Identifying and estimating influence of unobservables.** Participants who are self-selected, or who are selected by an agency interested in ensuring success, are likely to have unique characteristics that affect, and usually increase, the likelihood of success. Many of these are not captured in structured surveys, and consequently positive outcomes may be due to these preexisting characteristics rather than to the success of the project.	• PRA techniques, in-depth interviews, and key informants can help identify and study "unobservables" that could not be easily addressed through formal surveys.

3.2. Using Mixed Methods When Working under Budget, Time, and Data Constraints

The following are examples of some of the ways in which mixed-method approaches can potentially strengthen evaluations conducted with budget, time, and data constraints:

- Judicious combinations of QUAL and QUANT methods enhance triangulation, helping confirm and elaborate the information in data.
- Different perspectives can be obtained by combining in-depth analysis of a small number of cases, holistic analysis of the project context, and broader QUANT analysis of relationships between, say, household characteristics and project outcomes. For example, a QUANT evaluation may have initially assumed income or consumption to be the key indicators of

household welfare. However, ethnographic studies may reveal that women are more concerned about vulnerability (defined as the lack of access to social support systems in times of crises), powerlessness, or exposure to violence. This may encourage the QUANT evaluators either to include additional indicators in the survey or to commission case studies to help readers understand the multidimensionality of poverty. Similarly, a QUAL evaluation that had studied the impacts of government budget cuts on access to health services in a number of villages might benefit from the findings of a longitudinal statistical analysis showing that many of the reductions in health services had already started before the current rounds of budget cuts. Comprehensive data of both types help pinpoint and explain critical aspects of a program.

QUAL and QUANT methods typically adopt different approaches to multilevel analysis, and both can benefit from combining or sharing their approaches. For example, QUAL method-by-method analysis (e.g., analyze all the surveys first, then all the observations) combined with cross-method thematic analysis provides a useful framework for the interpretation of data from a range of mixed-method approaches. QUANT analysis can also contribute different approaches to multilevel analysis. For example, the analysis of surveys conducted at the level of the household, school, or farm can identify statistically significant differences in behavior or outcomes in different locations that cannot be fully explained in terms of the subject's socioeconomic characteristics (e.g., household members, students, or teachers). These differences can then be explored at a higher aggregate level (e.g., community, school district, local district of the ministry of agriculture). These higher levels of analysis can combine QUANT and QUAL approaches in ways that can contribute new perspectives to both.

- Preliminary evaluation reports frequently identify apparent inconsistencies in findings or interesting differences between communities or groups that cannot be explained by the currently available data. Mixed methods can widen the range of approaches available to understand these questions. In the case of QUANT evaluations, it is often the case that once the data collection phase is completed, it is not possible to return to the field to check on such questions. However, if planned ahead of time, it is sometimes possible to conduct a rapid QUAL follow-up to help understand some of these questions. For example, in a QUANT evaluation of village water supply programs in Indonesia, the survey found that in all villages except one, the women were responsible for water management. In the case of the single village where it was reported that men managed the water supply, the researchers were not certain if this was a reporting error or if this was an example of a different pattern of social organization that should be investigated. A rapid follow-up QUAL study found that, in fact, water was managed by men in this village because in this area women were involved in dairy farming and because this was a very profitable activity that in this culture could only be managed by women, the men were willing to take over water management to free up time for their wives to manage the dairy cattle (Brown 2000). In the case of a QUAL study, a mixed-method approach might permit a QUANT analysis of secondary data sources to compare the characteristics of the sample subjects or communities with the broader population, hence contributing to an assessment of the generalizability of the evaluation findings.

4. Mixed-Method Strategies

Mixed-method designs can be categorized along three key dimensions. One is whether the different methods are used concurrently or sequentially. A second is whether the different methods are considered to have relatively equal importance or one methodology is considered dominant and the others are used to complement it. A third dimension deals with the stages of the evaluation at which the methods are integrated. The options range from integration during a single stage to complete integration throughout all stages of the evaluation. In the next two sections, we discuss various sequential and concurrent mixed-method designs (see also Creswell et al. 2003).

4.1. Sequential Mixed-Method Designs

In sequential designs, the QUANT and QUAL data collection and/or analysis are conducted sequentially (in either order), with one method being used to identify issues or hypotheses to be studied in depth (often by the other method) to assess how findings can be generalized or to help interpret the findings. One method (either QUANT or QUAL) is generally, perhaps always, dominant (see Creswell et al. 2003). To the best of our knowledge, no analysis has been conducted on this point.

The advantage of sequential designs compared with concurrent designs (discussed in the next section) is that the logistics of sequential designs are often easier to organize. Data collection through structured questionnaires often involves having a relatively large team of **enumerators** in the field at the same time and following a precisely defined schedule of household selection and number of interviews to be conducted each day. The field supervisors need to know where all the enumerators are working each day because quality control often involves repeat visits to a subsample of subjects; also, the supervisor must be on hand to answer questions from any of the enumerators. In contrast, ethnographic and many other kinds of QUAL methods often have a much more flexible schedule both in terms of duration and where the researchers will be at any given time. For this and other reasons, concurrent mixed-method designs can often be more difficult to manage, particularly for evaluation teams with only a few experienced supervisors. On the other hand, a potential disadvantage of sequential designs for RWE evaluations is that the duration of the evaluation is likely to increase if one stage cannot begin until the previous stage is completed and analyzed.

Figure 14.4 presents an example of a sequential design with a dominant QUANT approach. This is a study of interhousehold transfers of money and goods among poor urban households in Colombia (Wansbrough, Jones, and Kappaz 2000). A common coping strategy among poor families is the transfer of money and goods from households that are doing relatively well at a particular point in time to their poorer and more needy relatives and friends. It is expected that when fortunes change, the transfer will be reciprocated or that other forms of assistance may be provided (e.g., labor to help build a house or having a child coming to live while attending high school). The purpose of the study was to describe the patterns of transfers and to estimate whether the transfers were sufficiently large to act as an informal social safety net to help the poorest sectors of the community in times of need. These kinds of interhousehold transfers are difficult to identify and measure, so an anthropologist spent a month living in the community prior to the design of the sample survey to study the patterns of transfers and to help design the questionnaire. A QUANT survey was then administered to several hundred households. The data were analyzed using QUANT economic analysis (econometrics).

Figure 14.4 Sequential Mixed-Method Design with a Dominant Quantitative Approach: Studying Interhousehold Transfers of Money and Goods in Cartagena, Colombia

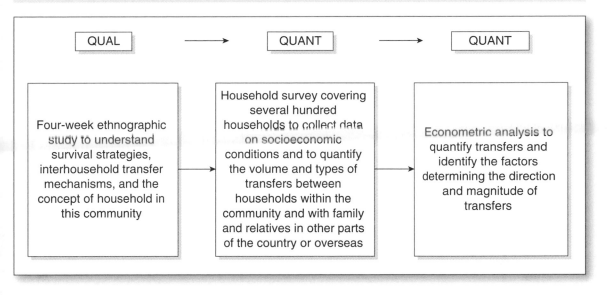

Figure 14.5 illustrates a sequential design with a dominant QUAL approach. This describes a hypothetical evaluation to assess the adoption of new varieties of seed by different types of rural families. The principal data collection methods are qualitative: interviews, focus groups, observation, and case studies of individual households and small farming communities. The principal methods of analysis are also qualitative: within- and cross-case analysis and the constant comparative method. However, to obtain information on the ethnic distribution of households, household economic conditions, and agricultural production, the evaluation begins with a rapid QUANT household survey covering a sample of households in all the villages covered by the agricultural extension project. The findings of this study were used to help identify the types of households to be studied in more depth through the QUAL data collection methods.

Either of the two evaluation designs described above could have been modified to give equal weight to both QUANT and QUAL approaches with neither being dominant. In the case of the inter-household transfer study, it would have been possible to complement the household survey with QUAL case studies on families or informal transfer networks. These could then have been integrated into the analysis to compare the description and interpretation of the functions and operation of the transfer networks obtained from the QUAL studies with the findings of the econometric analysis. In the second example, the QUANT data collection could have been complemented by an exploratory ethnographic study conducted in the planning phase to help design the structured questionnaire to be administered to a sample of families in all project communities to obtain more detailed QUANT data on the impacts of the seed distribution program. A QUAL or QUANT study of marketing outlets could also have been conducted to estimate the changes in sales of agricultural produce from the project areas and, possibly, the changes in the purchase of consumer goods by project area families.

Figure 14.5   Sequential Mixed-Method Design with a Dominant Qualitative Approach: Evaluating the Adoption of New Seed Varieties by Different Types of Rural Families

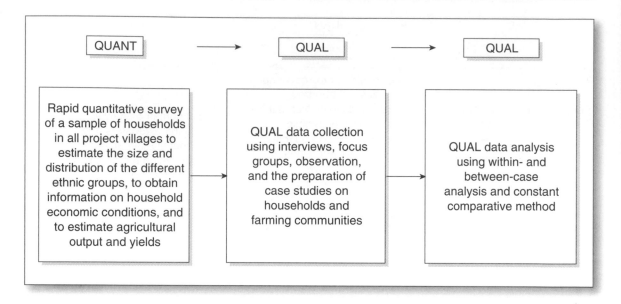

4.2. Concurrent Designs

In concurrent designs, the QUANT and QUAL approaches are used at the same time. An example of a concurrent design is where QUANT and QUAL data are collected simultaneously, using triangulation to compare information on outcomes, impacts, and other key indicators from different independent sources. Another example is when QUAL methods are used to conduct a contextual analysis of a project site (or the surrounding areas) at the same time that a QUANT sample survey of households or individuals is being carried out. This provides the opportunity for a very rich but more complicated analysis in which the interactions between the setting (context) and the project implementation process are analyzed.

Concurrent methods have the advantage for RWE in that data collection and analysis can be completed more quickly than for sequential designs. However, concurrent designs tend to be more difficult to manage, both because there are two sets of activities going on simultaneously and because QUANT and QUAL data collection methods typically have a different dynamic and timing, so that they can be difficult to conduct at the same time. This can be a particular problem in areas where logistical planning (e.g., travel to sites, places to stay, security) can become difficult to coordinate. Concurrent methods also make it more difficult to handle feedback from one method that may suggest changes required in other parts of the study. Decisions and actions will often have to be taken under greater time pressure than for sequential designs. For example, QUANT data collection has to be planned with a tight timetable so that a team of enumerators can be managed and perhaps transported to and from data collection sites. If QUAL observers, **interviewers**, and case study specialists are at a variety of different sites at the same time, this greatly complicates coordination of data and preliminary findings. It is sometimes easier to absorb incoming information with a sequential design, but this must be balanced against the longer period over which data are collected—a concern for most RWE evaluations.

Concurrent Triangulation Design

Two or more methods are used to confirm, cross-validate, or corroborate findings within a single study. Either the QUANT or QUAL design may be dominant or the two may be fully integrated and given equal weight. Figure 14.6 illustrates how this design could be used to obtain and triangulate different estimates of poverty and household income. The QUANT study uses household income as the primary indicator of poverty. A household questionnaire is administered to a sample of households, and a number of questions are included on household income and expenditures. Statistical analysis is conducted to calculate means, frequency distributions, and **standard deviations** of household income. Internal consistency checks are also used in which income is compared with expenditures. At the same time, a number of QUAL data collection techniques, including interviews with household members and key informants and observation, are used.

Figure 14.6 Concurrent Triangulation Design: Comparing and Integrating Different Data Sources on Poverty and Household Income

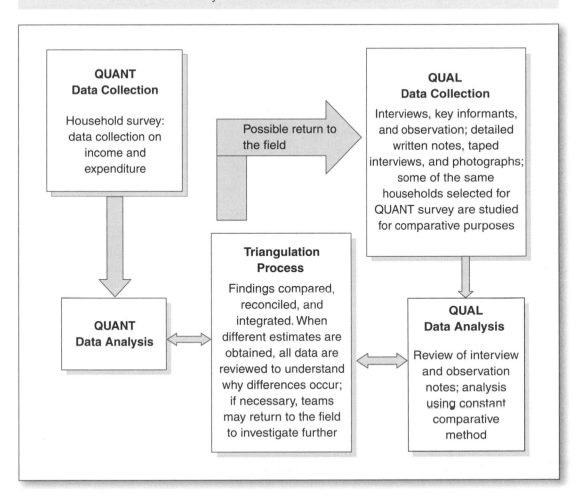

SOURCE: Model adapted from Creswell et al. (2005, Figure 8.5a). Example developed by present authors.

While the QUAL researchers look at household income and expenditures, they also try to understand how people in the community think about poverty, well-being, and security. Detailed notes are
taken on the interviews and observation, and some interviews are taped. Photographs are also taken
to illustrate the economic conditions of individual households and the community in general. A few
of the households included in the QUANT household sample survey are also covered in the QUAL
survey to permit direct comparisons. The notes are analyzed using the constant-comparative method,
and some preliminary conclusions are drawn on how families think about well-being and economic
security as well as describing their income and expenditure patterns.

The QUANT and QUAL teams then meet to present and compare their findings. For example, the
QUAL team reports that although it may be true (from the QUANT data coming in) that many families
have very low incomes and very modest consumption, there are some families (it is hard to know how
many)—particularly female-headed households—that are equally concerned about *vulnerability* and
how well families will be able to survive crises such as unemployment, illness, or death. Crime and
physical security are also major concerns expressed by those whom the QUAL team interviewed. The
two teams also compare information obtained on the families that were included in both the QUANT
household survey and interviewed and observed by the QUAL team. If specific inconsistencies arise,
such as different estimates of income or expenditures for particular families, the two teams compare
their notes to try to explain the differences. In some cases, resources and time permitting, one or more
researchers might return to the field to check on some of these issues. The final report will integrate
findings from all the different sources of QUAL and QUANT data collection and analysis.

Concurrent Nested Design

In this design, one method is dominant and the other method is nested within it (Creswell et al. 2003).
The less dominant method may be used to explore a particular aspect in more detail, to provide
illustrative material, or to quantify different findings or processes. The following are examples of how
this design can be used:

- *Different methods can be used to study different groups.* For example, if the dominant design is
  quantitative, a structured questionnaire may be used to interview all household heads, but a more
  open interview may be used to interview a subset of the population, such as spouses, children, and
  other household members. Similarly, a structured questionnaire may be used with a sample of
  employees, and focus groups may be used for more in-depth analysis of groups of particular interest, such as members of work groups with a particularly low or high level of work satisfaction.
- *QUAL methods may be used to prepare in-depth case studies to describe the behavior, attitudes,
  or social and economic conditions of typical members of different subgroups covered by a
  QUANT survey.*
- *Rapid QUANT surveys can be used to estimate the prevalence of some of the behavior revealed
  in the QUAL studies.* For example, if case studies reveal that the poorest families depend for
  their survival on money or food from relatives living outside the community, a rapid survey
  could try to assess what proportion of poor families receives these kinds of support.

4.3. Using Mixed Methods at Different Stages of the Evaluation

Mixed methods can be used at any stage of the evaluation. Although a fully integrated mixed-method
design would require full integration of QUAL and QUANT approaches at all stages of the evaluation,

in practice, mixed-method designs are usually applied at only one or two stages of an evaluation. This is usually the case for RWE where time and cost are likely to be constraints. The following are some of the ways in which mixed methods can be used at different stages of the evaluation:

- *During the formulation of hypotheses and research questions.* Exploratory QUAL studies can be used to better understand and refine the hypothesis to be tested in the dominant QUANT evaluation design. Similarly, rapid QUANT studies can be conducted to help refine the evaluation question by indicating some population characteristics, such as ethnic composition or principal economic activities that should be explored.

- *During data collection.* Mixed data collection methods are often used as a component of triangulation to confirm, elaborate, or disconfirm data collected from various sources, by various methods, and by various evaluation team members. Mixed methods are also used to simultaneously collect information in different ways. For example, a QUANT-structured questionnaire may be administered to a sample of schoolchildren and their parents while QUAL methods are used to document the culture and quality of schools and the behavior of teachers.

- *During data analysis and follow-up.* If triangulation has been used to obtain two or more independent sources of data on important indicators or topics, a key part of the analysis phase is to compare and reconcile the different sources. In many QUAL studies, much of this reconciliation and follow-up will be done during the data collection phase, but when QUANT and QUAL approaches are combined, the comparison and reconciliation will often not occur until after the preliminary analysis of the QUANT data has been conducted. Sometimes the reasons for inconsistencies among the different data sources are clear, as when observation indicates that families have informal sources of income such as dressmaking and beer brewing that were not captured by the structured questionnaire. However, in other cases, the explanation may not be evident, and if resources and time permit, follow-up fieldwork can greatly enhance the quality and depth of the analysis.

- *Presentation and dissemination of the findings.* The findings of QUANT evaluations are often presented in the form of written reports, including tables of QUANT data, supported by briefings of key **stakeholders** in which PowerPoint or other forms of graphical presentations are used. Often, there is very little feedback to the communities studied. In contrast, findings of QUAL evaluations are more likely to include presentations to a wider range of stakeholders, but the written reports may be more qualitative and descriptive. The presentation of mixed-method evaluations can draw on both approaches, both broadening the range of presentation techniques and reaching out to a wider range of stakeholders.

5. Implementing a Mixed-Method Design

Although some applications of mixed-method designs involve only adding additional data collection methods to a dominant QUANT or QUAL design, a fully integrated mixed-method evaluation strategy involves much more than this. To enjoy the full benefit of combining QUANT and QUAL orientations, methodologies, and methods, it is necessary to implement from the first day of the evaluation a mixed-method evaluation strategy involving the following aspects (see Box 14.1):

Composition of the Research Team. The effective design and application of fully integrated designs often require that the research team include principal researchers from two or more disciplines (e.g., anthropology, medicine, law, sociology, economics). It is important to allow time and opportunities for each researcher to become familiar with the methodology of the others and to develop mutual respect and trust among the members of the team. Allowing sufficient time is even more important when the evaluation team is comprised of specialists from different countries as well as from different disciplines.

Integrated Approaches during the Evaluation Design. It is important to develop an evaluation framework that draws on all the involved disciplines and to ensure that the research questions and issues incorporate each of these methodologies. This will encourage the development of an evaluation design that draws on the literature and skills/benefits of each methodology. Integration will require careful sharing and joint planning by equal partners.

As discussed earlier in this chapter, project outcomes are affected significantly by the social, economic, political, institutional, and cultural contexts within which the project is implemented. One very valuable contribution that QUAL research can make to strengthen QUANT designs is to help understand these different contexts or processes, to evaluate which elements are likely to influence project outcomes, and to propose ways to study them. Hentschel (1999) discusses how contextual variables can be built into the research design, and how they can be used to interpret findings. On the other hand, there are cases in which QUANT sampling procedures and numerical analysis can contribute to QUAL designs by helping assess how widely opinions or behavior of the individuals or groups that have been studied in depth are shared by other sectors of the community or to assess the relative quantitative importance of different problems and issues identified in focus groups. Many evaluation **clients** want to know whether the groups studied are broadly representative of the total population or in what ways they differ. For example, if people who attend community meetings or focus groups differ in some important ways from the groups who do not attend, it is important to know this and, possibly, to conduct some follow-up interviews with the underrepresented groups.[2]

BOX 14.1
ELEMENTS OF AN INTEGRATED, MULTIDISCIPLINARY RESEARCH APPROACH

Composition of the Research Team

- Include primary researchers from different disciplines. Allow time for researchers to develop an understanding and respect for one another's disciplines and work. Each should be familiar with the basic literature and current debates in the other field.
- Ensure similar linkages between local researchers from the city, state, country, or region where the project is being implemented.

---

[2] In some university or market research studies, it may be possible to carefully select and monitor participants in focus groups, but in many RealWorld contexts, the evaluator may have only a limited degree of control over who attends the groups.

Integrated Approaches during the Evaluation Design

- Ensure that the evaluation framework draws on theories and approaches from all the disciplinary teams involved in the evaluation (e.g., anthropology, medicine, law, sociology, economics, demography) and frameworks from predominantly qualitative and quantitative perspectives, with each being used to enrich and broaden the other.
- Ensure that hypotheses and research approaches draw from all disciplines.
- The research framework should formulate linkages between different levels of analysis (e.g., both quantitative survey and qualitative interviews of households, students, farmers; qualitative holistic analysis of the program setting).
- Ensure that concepts and methods are not taken out of context but draw on the intellectual debates and approaches within the respective disciplines.
- Consider using behavioral models that combine economic and other quantitative modeling with in-depth understanding of the cultural context within which the study is being conducted.

Data Collection and the Use of Triangulation

- Conduct exploratory analysis to assist in hypothesis development and definition of indicators.
- Select quantitative and qualitative data collection methods designed to complement each other, and specify the complementarities and how they will be used in the fieldwork and analysis.
- Select at least two independent estimating methods for key indicators and hypotheses.
- Ensure full documentation of all sample selection, data collection, and analysis methods.

Data Analysis and Interpretation and Possible Field Follow-Up

- Conduct and present separate analyses of quantitative and qualitative findings to highlight different interpretations and findings from different methods and then prepare an integrated report drawing on all of the data.
- Use systematic triangulation procedures to check on inconsistencies or differing interpretations. Follow up on differences, where necessary, with a return to the field.
- Budget resources and time for follow-up visits to the field.
- Highlight different interpretations and findings from different methods and discuss how these enrich the interpretation of the study. Different, and seemingly contradictory, outcomes should be considered a major strength of the integrated approach rather than an annoyance.
- Present cases and qualitative material to illustrate or test quantitative findings.

(Continued)

(Continued)

Presentation and Dissemination of Findings

- Combine conventional forms of presentation with written reports complemented by PowerPoint presentations with some of the more participatory presentation methods used in some qualitative evaluations. Recognizing lack of receptivity by many stakeholders to long technical reports, the team may also develop more innovative and user-friendly reports.
- Broaden the range of stakeholders invited to the presentation and review of findings to include some of the community and civil society groups that qualitative evaluators often work with but many of whom may not be consulted in many quantitative evaluations.

Integrated Approaches during Data Collection. Although many QUAL data collection methods are designed to study and document in depth a limited number of individuals, cases, or settings and to provide a holistic understanding of the setting, QUANT data collection methods are designed to obtain precisely defined, comparable measures of a limited number of questions from a large and representative sample. Consequently, the goal of mixed methods is to combine depth and a holistic focus with quantification and generalizability. This is particularly important when a large, complex, and geographically dispersed program is being evaluated. The triangulation of data from a number of different QUAL and QUANT sources, as well as the triangulation of different methods, are both goals of using mixed methods. Mixed methods can be used both as a consistency check on key estimates or information and to provide different perspectives for interpreting and understanding a complex phenomenon.

Integrated Approaches during Data Analysis and Interpretation. With a dominant QUANT design, data analysis normally does not begin until all, or most, of the data have been collected. The preliminary stages of the analysis will normally try to determine whether there are statistically significant associations between participation in the project and the **outputs** or effects that the project is trying to achieve. Multivariate analysis may then be used to identify socioeconomic characteristics of the subjects, groups, or communities that contribute to variations in the project outcomes (see Chapter 12). QUAL analysis may then be used to enrich the interpretation of the findings, to examine some of the contextual factors that affect outcomes, or to help explain some of the unexpected statistical results.

In contrast, with a dominant QUAL design, analysis is an iterative process continuing throughout the data collection process. Consequently, the preliminary analysis and interpretation of findings will already be well advanced by the end of the data collection period. Data analysis can combine both descriptive textual analysis as well as matrices, tables, and charts (Miles and Huberman 1994). If survey data were collected, they can be used to generalize the findings to the population of concern to the evaluation. Because many QUAL evaluations do not seek to generalize their findings, or only do so to a limited extent, this is one of the areas in which QUANT analytical methods can contribute.

When both approaches are given equal weight, the general methods for integrating QUANT and QUAL analysis are similar to the above discussion. The main difference is that more complete integration offers more opportunities to enrich and deepen the analysis.

6. Using Mixed Methods to Tell a More Compelling Story of What a Program Has Achieved

One of the weak points of many evaluations is that the reports produced during and at the end of the evaluation are not able to capture the richness of the information generated and the lessons learned in a way that will be compelling to the different stakeholders and audiences. Some reports present rigorous statistical analysis, but the narrative on the lived experiences of the affected groups is less compelling or not well integrated. In other cases the report may present compelling narrative based on case studies, observation, and in-depth interviews, but may not include QUANT data to show how representative the findings are, to present QUANT estimates of the distribution and magnitude of outcomes and impacts, and to assess to what extent and how the project could be replicated in other contexts.

Mixed-method approaches offer possible frameworks for presenting a more compelling story that can integrate QUANT and QUAL data in a way that can appeal to a wider range of audiences. One example of an approach designed to achieve these objectives is Collaborative Outcome Reporting Technique (CORT) (Dart 2010). CORT combines a collaborative participatory approach for the collection, analysis, interpretation, and use of QUAL and QUANT evaluation findings with the preparation of a report that combines a summary of QUANT findings with QUAL analysis of what stakeholders consider to be the most significant changes in outcomes and impacts and the areas for action. Figure 14.7 shows the six stages in the planning, collection, and interpretation of data and recommendations on areas for action:

- *Scoping:* Agreeing on the objectives and coverage (geographical, temporal, and substantive) of the report.
- *Data trawling:* Identification and review of relevant data from the project and other sources.
- *Interview process:* Where possible, different stakeholder groups are encouraged to conduct some of the interviews so as to become more familiar with the realities of the project and the lived experiences of participants. Depending on resources and the importance of statistically representative data, interviewers (volunteer or contracted) may also be used.
- *Data analysis and integration:* This can either be done by one or more analysts (from the consultant team and/or the project) or on a larger and more participatory scale.
- *Outcome panel:* Stakeholders meet to review the findings and to identify the most significant changes (positive and negative, expected and unanticipated) that the project has produced. In some cases methodologies such as Most Significant Change will be used, while in others the process will be less formal.
- *Summit workshop:* The draft report will be reviewed by an independent group of experts to assess the validity and credibility of the analysis.

Figure 14.7 also describes the main components of the report that will be produced in parallel to the planning and analysis stage:

- *Scope:* The content and purpose of the report and the context of the project, including its history.

- *Results chart:* The relevant QUANT data are summarized in one or a small number of easy-to-understand tables or charts.
- *Implications:* The key findings are summarized in narrative form and the implications for improving performance or designing future programs are discussed.
- *Instances of significant change:* This section includes summaries of case studies and descriptions of major impacts on different groups.
- *Index:* Every piece of data in the results chart and in the significant findings is referenced to a source that is listed in the index. This is an important way to ensure the credibility and validity of the findings.

Figure 14.7   Collaborative Outcome Reporting Technique (CORT): Data Collection, Analysis, and Report Structure

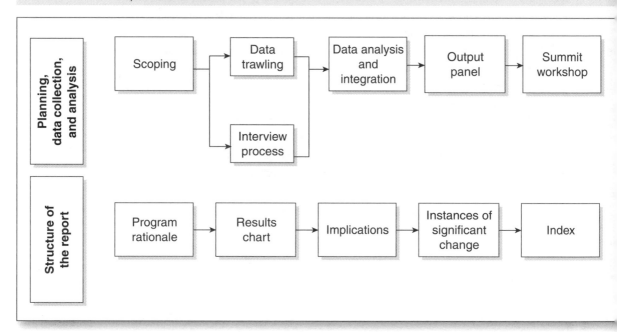

7. Case Studies Illustrating the Use of Mixed Methods

This section describes three case studies illustrating different ways in which mixed-method designs have been used for the evaluation of development projects. The first case is an evaluation of the effectiveness of a program in Indonesia for targeting small-scale development assistance projects to poor rural communities, the second is a program in India for promoting democratic decentralization, and the third is an evaluation of a program in Eritrea concerning the social and economic impacts of feeder road construction. All three evaluations use sequential mixed-method designs.

7.1. Indonesia: The Kecamatan Development Project

The Kecamatan Development Project (KDP) in Indonesia is one of the world's largest social development projects. Implemented in the aftermath of the Suharto era and the East Asian financial crisis in 1998, KDP was primarily intended as a more efficient and effective mechanism for getting targeted, small-scale development assistance to poor rural communities, but it was also envisioned as a project that could help to nurture the proto-democratic state at the local level. KDP requires villagers to submit proposals for funding to a committee of their peers, thereby establishing a new (and, by design, inclusive) community forum for decision making on development issues (Guggenheim 2006). Given the salience of conflict as a political and developmental issue in Indonesia, a key evaluation question is whether these forums are in fact able to complement existing local-level institutions for conflict resolution and in the process help villagers acquire a more diverse, peaceful, and effective set of civic skills for mediating local conflict. Such a question does not lend itself to an orthodox stand-alone quantitative or qualitative evaluation, but rather to an innovative mixed-method approach.

In this instance, the team decided to begin with qualitative work, as there was relatively little quantitative data on conflict in Indonesia and even less on the mechanisms (or local processes) by which conflict is initiated, intensified, or resolved. Selecting a small number of appropriate sites from across Indonesia's 3,500 islands and 350 language groups was not an easy task, but the team decided that work should be done in two provinces that were very different (demographically and economically), in regions within those provinces that (according to local experts) demonstrated both a high and low capacity for conflict resolution, and in villages within those regions that were otherwise comparable (as determined by propensity-score matching methods) but that either did or did not participate in KDP. Such a design enabled researchers to be confident that any common themes emerging from across either the program or nonprogram sites was not wholly a product of idiosyncratic regional or institutional capacity factors. Thus quantitative methods were used to help select the appropriate sites for qualitative investigation, which then entailed three months of intensive fieldwork in each of the eight selected villages (two demographically different regions by two high- or low-capacity provinces by two program or nonprogram villages). The evaluation design is summarized in Figure 14.8.

The results from the qualitative work—useful in themselves for understanding process issues and the mechanisms by which local conflicts are created and addressed (see Gibson and Woolcock 2008)—fed into the design of a new quantitative survey instrument that would be administered to a large sample of households from the two provinces and used to test the generality of the hypotheses and propositions emerging from the qualitative work. A data set on local conflict was also assembled from local newspapers. Together, the qualitative research (case studies of local conflict, interviews, and observation), the newspaper evidence, data on conflict from national level surveys, and key informant questionnaires provided a broad range of evidence that was used to assess the veracity of (and, where necessary, qualify and contextualize) the general hypotheses regarding the conditions under which KDP could and could not be part of the problem and/or solution to local conflict.

7.2. India: Panchayat Reform

A recent project evaluating the impact of *panchayat* (village government) reform—democratic decentralization in rural India—combines qualitative and quantitative data with a randomized trial. In 1992 the Indian government passed the 73rd amendment to the Indian constitution to give more power to

Figure 14.8   The Mixed-Method Design for the Evaluation of the Kecamatan Development Project in Indonesia

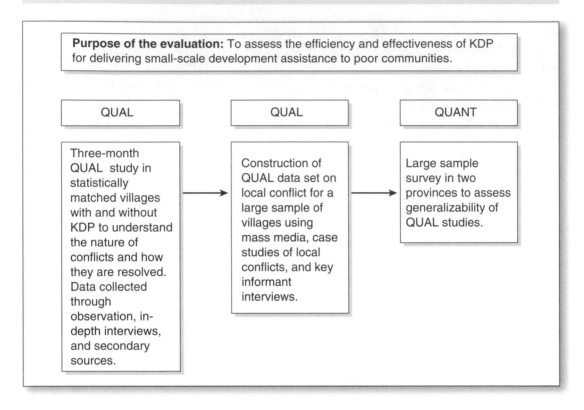

Purpose of the evaluation: To assess the efficiency and effectiveness of KDP for delivering small-scale development assistance to poor communities.

QUAL

Three-month QUAL study in statistically matched villages with and without KDP to understand the nature of conflicts and how they are resolved. Data collected through observation, in-depth interviews, and secondary sources.

QUAL

Construction of QUAL data set on local conflict for a large sample of villages using mass media, case studies of local conflicts, and key informant interviews.

QUANT

Large sample survey in two provinces to assess generalizability of QUAL studies.

democratically elected village governments (*gram panchayats*—henceforth GPs) by mandating that more funds be transferred to their control and that regular elections be held, with one third of the seats in the village council reserved for women and another third for "scheduled castes and tribes" (groups who have traditionally been targets of discrimination). It was also mandated that a deliberative space— village meetings (*gram sabhas*)—be held at least two times a year to make important decisions such as the selection of beneficiaries for antipoverty programs and discussing village budgets.

It is widely acknowledged that the state of Kerala has been by far the most effective in implementing the 73rd amendment. There were two elements that contributed to this success. The first was that the state government devolved significant resources to the GPs with 40% of the state's expenditures allocated to them; the second was the "people's campaign," a grassroots training and awareness-raising effort to energize citizens to participate, with knowledge, in the panchayat system. This led to better village plans, widespread and more informed participation, and more accountable government. Kerala is, of course, a special case, with very literate and politically aware citizens (literacy rates are close to 100%). The crucial policy question is whether the Kerala experiment can be replicated in much more challenging and more representative settings.

The northern districts of the neighboring state of Karnataka represent such settings. The literacy rate is about 40%, with high levels of poverty and a feudal social environment with high land inequality. These districts are also known to be beset by corruption and extremely poor governance. If a people's campaign could work in these districts, it could provide an important tool to transform the nature of village democracy in the country by sharply increasing the quality and quantity of citizen participation in the panchayat system and, in turn, have a significant effect on the standard of living. Also, these districts have access to two large national schemes that have substantially increased the funding of GPs, raising the budget of GPs from about 200,000 Indian rupees a year to approximately 4,000,000 rupees. Thus GPs in these districts have fulfilled the first element of the Kerala program—high levels of funding. The evaluation focuses on assessing the impact of the people's campaign. It randomly assigns 50 GPs as "treatment." Another set of GPs, matched to belong to the same county as the treatment GPs and with similar levels of literacy and low-caste populations and randomly chosen within this subset, is selected as "control" GPs. (They are also chosen to be at least one GP away from treatment GPs to avoid treatment spillover problems.)

The "treatment" consists, initially, of a two-week program conducted by the Karnataka State Institute of Rural Development, which is responsible for all panchayat training in the state and has extensive experience in the field. The program trains citizens in participatory planning processes and deliberative decision making, and disseminates information about the programs and procedures of the panchayat. At the end of two weeks, a village meeting is held where priorities are finalized and presented to local bureaucrats. At a meeting with the bureaucrats, an implementation agreement is reached wherein the bureaucrats commit to providing funding and technical support for the selected projects over the course of the year. Following this initial training, the GP is monitored with monthly two-day visits over a period of two years in order to ensure the program's progress.

An extensive quantitative baseline survey was implemented in the 200 treatment and control villages randomly selected from the 100 selected GPs and completed a month prior to the intervention. The survey instruments, developed after several weeks of investigative fieldwork and pretesting, included village-level modules measuring the quality and quantity of public goods, caste and land inequality in the village, and in-depth interviews with village politicians and local officials. Twenty households from each village were also randomly chosen for a household questionnaire assessing socioeconomic status, preferences for public goods, political participation, social networks, and other relevant variables. Two years later, the same sample of villages and households was re-interviewed with identical survey instruments. These pretest and posttest quantitative data provide a gold-standard quantitative assessment of impact using a randomized trial. The design is summarized in Figure 14.9.

Figure 14.9 The Mixed-Method Design for the Evaluation of the Gram Panchayat Program in India

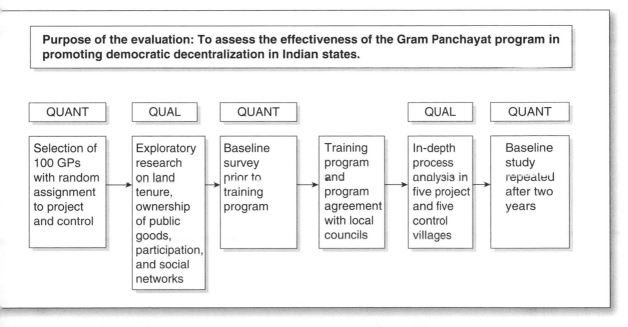

Purpose of the evaluation: To assess the effectiveness of the Gram Panchayat program in promoting democratic decentralization in Indian states.

QUANT	QUAL	QUANT		QUAL	QUANT
Selection of 100 GPs with random assignment to project and control	Exploratory research on land tenure, ownership of public goods, participation, and social networks	Baseline survey prior to training program	Training program and program agreement with local councils	In-depth process analysis in five project and five control villages	Baseline study repeated after two years

To understand "process" issues, however, equal attention was given to in-depth qualitative work. A subset of five treatment and five control GPs from the quantitative sample was selected purposively for the qualitative investigation. They were selected to compare areas with low and high literacy and different types of administrative variation. A team of qualitative investigators visited these villages for a day or two every week over a two-year period investigating important dimensions of change: political and social dynamics, corruption, economic changes, and network affiliation, among other things. Under the supervision of two sociologists, the investigators wrote monthly reports assessing these dimensions of change. These reports provide a valuable in-depth look at month-to-month changes in the treatment and control areas that allow the assessment of the quality of the treatment, changes introduced by the treatment, and other changes that have taken place that are unrelated to the treatment. Thus the qualitative work provides an independent qualitative evaluation of the people's campaign but also supplements findings of the quantitative data.

An important challenge in understanding the nature of the 73rd amendment is to study participation in public village meetings (*gram sabhas*) held to discuss the problems faced by villagers with members of the governing committee. Increases in the quality of this form of village democracy would be a successful indicator of improvements in participation and accountability. To analyze this, a separate study was conducted on a sample of 300 randomly chosen villages across four South Indian states, including Kerala and Karnataka. Retrospective quantitative data on participation in the meetings are very unreliable, however, because people's memories are limited about what may have transpired at a meeting they may have attended. To address this issue, the team decided to record and transcribe village meetings directly. This tactic provided textual information that was analyzed to observe directly changes in participation (see Ban and Rao 2009). Another challenge was in collecting information on inequality at the village level. Some recent work has found that sample-based measures of inequality typically have standard errors that are too high to provide reliable estimates. PRAs were therefore held with one or two groups in the village to obtain measures of land distribution within the village. This approach proved to generate excellent measures of land inequality, and since these are primarily agrarian economies, measures of land inequality should be highly correlated with income inequality. Similar methods were used to collect data on the social heterogeneity of the village. All this PRA information has been quantitatively coded, thus demonstrating that qualitative tools can be used to collect quantitative data. In this example, the fundamental impact assessment design was kept intact, and both qualitative and quantitative data were combined to provide insights into different aspects of interest in the evaluation of the intervention.

7.3. Eritrea: The Community Development Fund

The Eritrean Community Development Fund (CDF) was launched soon after Eritrea gained independence in the early 1990s, and it had two objectives: developing cost-effective models for the provision of community infrastructure (schools, health care centers, water, environmental protection, veterinary clinics, and feeder roads) and strengthening the participation of the local communities in the selection, implementation, and maintenance of the projects. Separate evaluations were conducted to assess the implementation and impacts of each of the six components. This case describes how mixed methods were used to strengthen the evaluation of the feeder roads component (similar approaches were used to assess the health and education components). Three feeder roads were being constructed, each between 50 and 100 kilometers in length and each serving many small villages that currently had no access to roads suitable for vehicular traffic.

The evaluation was not commissioned until work had already begun on each of the three roads, but none of which had yet been completed (planning and construction took on average around one year, with work often interrupted during the rainy season). The evaluation had a relatively modest budget, and no baseline data had been collected prior to the start of road construction. However, the CDF was intended as a pilot project to assess the efficiency and socioeconomic outcomes of each of the six project components, with the view to considering replication in a follow-up project. Consequently, policymakers were very interested in obtaining initial estimates, albeit only tentative, of the quantitative impacts of each component. Given the rapidly changing economic and social environment during the first decade of independence, it was recognized that the changes observed over the life of the different project components could not be assumed to be due to the project intervention. The need for some kind of simple attribution analysis was recognized, despite the absence of a conventional comparison group.

The possibility that was first considered was to try to identify areas with similar socioeconomic characteristics but that did not have access to a feeder road and that could serve as a comparison group. However, it was concluded, as is often the case with the evaluation of the social and economic impact of roads, that it would be methodologically difficult to identify comparable areas and, in any case, extremely expensive to conduct interviews in these areas, even if they could be found. Consequently, the evaluation used a mixed-method design that combined a number of different data sources and that used triangulation to assess the validity and consistency of information obtained from different sources. The evaluation combined the following elements (see also Figure 14.10):

- The evaluation was based on a program theory model that described the steps and processes through which the project was expected to achieve its economic and social impacts and that identified contextual factors that might affect implementation and outcomes.
- The theory model also strengthened construct validity by explaining more fully the wide range of changes that road construction was expected to achieve so that impacts could be assessed on a set of quantitative and qualitative indicators.
- Some of the unanticipated outcomes that were identified in this way included strengthened social relations among relatives and friends living in areas that were previously difficult to reach, and strengthened and widened informal support networks as people were able to draw on financial, in-kind, and other support from a geographically broader network.
- Quantitative survey data were obtained from a stratified sample of households along the road who were interviewed three times during and after the road construction (the evaluation started too late for a pretest measure).
- The baseline conditions of the project population prior to road construction were reconstructed by combining recall of the time and cost to travel to school, reach a health center, transport produce to markets, and visit government agencies in the nearest towns with information from key informants (teachers, health workers, community leaders, etc.) and from secondary sources. Estimates from different sources were triangulated to test for consistency and to strengthen the reliability of the estimates.
- Data on comparison groups before, during, and after road construction were obtained from a number of secondary sources. Information on school attendance by sex and age was obtained from the records of a sample of local schools. In some cases, the data also included the villages from which children came so that it was possible to compare this information with recall from the interviews in project villages. Records from local health clinics were obtained on the number of patients who attended and the medical services that were provided. Unfortunately, the records did not permit an analysis of the frequency of visits of individual patients, so it was not possible to

estimate whether there was a relatively small number of patients making frequent use of the clinics or a much larger number making occasional visits. Most of the local agricultural markets were cooperatives that kept records on the volume of sales (by type of produce and price) for each village, so this provided a valuable comparison group. It was planned to use vehicle registration records to estimate the increase in the number and types of vehicles before and after road construction. However, qualitative observations revealed that many drivers "forgot" to register their vehicles, so this source was not very useful.

- Process analysis was used to document the changes that occurred as road construction progressed. This combined periodic observation of the number of small businesses along the road; changes in the numbers of people traveling; and the proportions of people traveling on foot or using animal traction, bicycles, and different kinds of vehicles.

- Country-level data on agricultural production and prices, available over a number of years, provided a broader picture and were used to correct for seasonal variations in temperature and rainfall (both between different regions and over time). This was important in order to avoid the error of measuring trends from only two points in time.

Figure 14.10   Mixed-Method Design for the Evaluation of the Eritrea Feeder Roads Project

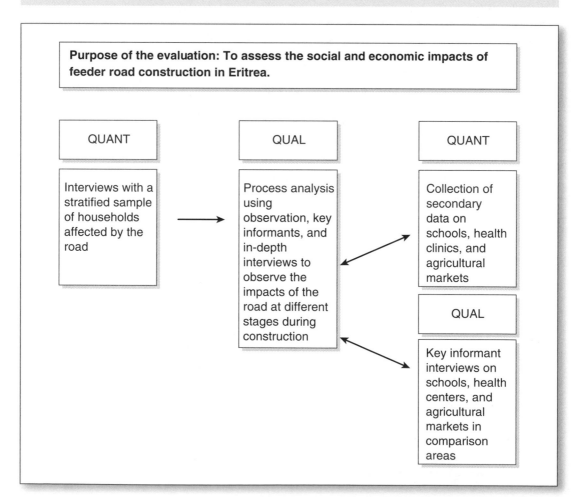

All of the data sources were combined to develop relatively robust estimates of a set of social and economic changes in the project areas over the life of the project and to compare these changes with a counterfactual (what would have been the condition of the project areas absent the project) constructed through combining data from a number of secondary sources. The credibility of the estimates of changes that could be (at least partially) attributed to the project intervention was then tested through focus groups with project participants, discussions with key informants, and direct observation of the changes that occurred during project implementation.

This evaluation, conducted with a relatively modest budget and drawing on the kinds of secondary data and recall information that are often available, illustrates how mixed-method designs can offer a promising approach to developing an alternative to the conventional statistical counterfactual, thus strengthening our understanding of the potential impacts of the majority of projects where the conventional counterfactual cannot be applied.

SUMMARY

- Mixed-method designs involve the planned use of two or more QUANT and QUAL methods of data collection and analysis.
- Building on the strengths of both QUANT and QUAL approaches, mixed methods can combine more comprehensive coverage with in-depth analysis of individual cases and a holistic understanding of the context within which each project is implemented.
- There are at least five reasons for using mixed-method designs: (a) strengthening validity through triangulation, (b) using the results of one method to help develop the sample or instrumentation of the other, (c) extending the comprehensiveness of findings, (d) generating new insights, and (e) incorporating a wider diversity of values.
- Mixed methods can be used at any stage of an evaluation.
- Mixed methods can either be used where one approach (either QUANT or QUAL) is *dominant* and the other approach is used as a complement, or both approaches can have equal weight. Mixed methods are used differently and bring different benefits depending on which approach is dominant.
- Mixed methods can be used either *sequentially,* when one approach is used after the other, or *concurrently,* when both approaches are used at the same time. The sequential approach is more widely used because it is simpler to manage.
- Although mixed-method approaches can be used at just one stage of the evaluation, a fully integrated mixed-method design involves more than simply combining data collection methods. A fully integrated approach involves (a) attention to the composition of the research team and allowing sufficient time to build relations between members from different professions; (b) integrating different conceptual frameworks and planning approaches during the design phase; (c) integrated data collection methods; (d) systematic use of triangulation during data collection; (e) integrating different approaches during data analysis, including the possibility of returning to the field to verify or elaborate on initial findings; and (f) combining different methods for the presentation of findings.

FURTHER READING

Bamberger, M., ed. 2000b. *Integrating Quantitative and Qualitative Research in Development Projects.* Directions in Development. Washington, DC: World Bank.

Case studies on how integrated mixed-method evaluations have been conducted on education, health, poverty, and water supply projects in different parts of the world.

Bamberger, M., V. Rao, and M. Woolcock. 2010. "Using Mixed Methods in Monitoring and Evaluation: Experiences from International Development." Pp. 613–41 in *SAGE Handbook of Mixed Methods in Social and Behavioral Research.* 2d ed., edited by A. Tashakorri and C. Teddlie. Thousand Oaks, CA: Sage.

Creswell, J. 2003. *Research Design: Qualitative, Quantitative and Mixed-Methods Approaches.* Thousand Oaks, CA: Sage.

Chapter 11 provides an overview of the main stages in the design and implementation of a mixed-method evaluation and of six mixed-method designs.

Greene, J. C. 2007. *Mixed Methods in Social Enquiry.* San Francisco. John Wiley.

In addition to a discussion of the methodology of mixed methods, Greene examines the rationale, purposes, and potentialities of mixed methods as a particular way of thinking. She argues that an important contribution of mixed methods is to generate new and more insightful understanding of complex social phenomena.

Greene, J. C. and V. J. Caracelli. 2003. "Making Paradigmatic Sense of Mixed Methods Practice." Pp. 91–110 in *Handbook of Mixed Methods in Social & Behavioral Research,* edited by A. Tashakkori and C. Teddlie. Thousand Oaks, CA: Sage.

The authors argue that research decisions are rarely consciously rooted in philosophical assumptions or beliefs. They recommend that more attention should be paid to understanding the philosophical and methodological distinctions between QUANT and QUAL while at the same time balancing this with practical and political considerations relevant to the context of each study.

Mertens, D. M. 2003. "Mixed Methods and the Politics of Human Research: The Transformatory-Emancipatory Perspective." Pp. 135–66 in *Handbook of Mixed Methods in Social & Behavioral Research,* edited by A. Tashakkori and C. Teddlie. Thousand Oaks, CA: Sage.

The author argues that mixed methods are a powerful tool for contributing to the transformatory-emanicipatory perspective that recommends the adoption of an explicit goal for research to serve the ends of creating a more just and democratic society that permeates the entire research process, from the problem formulation to the drawing of conclusions and the use of results. Readers will find this provides a very different perspective than do some of the other, more methodologically focused references.

Tashakkori, A., and C. Teddlie, eds. 2010. *SAGE Handbook of Mixed Methods in Social and Behavioral Research.* 2d ed. Thousand Oaks, CA: Sage.

Provides a comprehensive but technically more difficult selection of readings on these questions. Chapter 24 discusses how mixed methods have been applied in the evaluation of international development projects and presents three detailed case studies—two of which have a more quantitative focus while the third is more qualitative.

Teddlie, C., and A. Tashakkori. 2009. *Foundations of Mixed Methods Research: Integrating Quantitative and Qualitative Approaches in the Social and Behavioral Sciences.* Thousand Oaks, CA: Sage.

This is probably the more complete and systematic presentation of all of the stages of the formulation, design, implementation, analysis, and interpretation of mixed-method designs.

CHAPTER 15

Sampling Strategies and Sample Size Estimation for RealWorld Evaluation

T his chapter discusses the application of sample **design** principles to RealWorld Evaluation **(RWE)**. *It begins by emphasizing the importance of sampling for both qualitative* **(QUAL)** *and quantitative* **(QUANT)** *evaluations while showing that the approach to sampling is quite different in each case. Most QUAL evaluations use* **purposive sampling,** *in which a small number of carefully selected cases or individuals are studied in depth, and these sampling strategies are described. The next section discusses the use of* **probability** *(random)* **sampling** *for QUANT evaluations. Different sample selection procedures are discussed, and some of the key decisions at the presampling, sample design, and postsampling stages are considered. The concepts of power analysis and effect size are introduced, and their importance for estimating sample size is explained. The concept of* **Type I** *(wrongly concluding that a program has a significant effect) and* **Type II errors** *(wrongly concluding that a program does not have a significant effect) are introduced. A worked example is given to illustrate the different steps in estimating sample size. We then show how meta-analysis can be used to help estimate in advance the likely effect size that can be expected from any new program. The chapter ends with a discussion of sampling design issues for RWE.*

1. The Importance of Sampling for RealWorld Evaluation

The approach to sampling varies according to the evaluation methodology and the purposes of a particular evaluation. Two concerns of most QUANT evaluations are to ensure that the selected sample is representative of the total population and to determine whether the **findings** can be generalized to a wider population (e.g., other school districts, other rural communities in the province or surrounding area). In QUANT evaluations, a *representative* sample is defined in statistical terms and has to do with whether the sample was selected randomly and is large enough to test for the statistical significance of differences between, for example, the project population and a **comparison group** or between the project group before and after the project has been implemented. It is, of course, possible to have an evaluation that uses a large and randomly selected sample but that produces misleading conclusions because the data collection instruments were poorly designed, respondents did not wish to provide some of the information, or the study design ignored important contextual factors affecting program **outcomes**.

Although most QUANT evaluators broadly agree on the principles and uses of sampling in research and evaluation, QUAL evaluators have different approaches to sampling. QUAL evaluators often, but not always, work with a smaller number of organizations or communities (e.g., schools, factories, drug treatment centers, villages) or subjects (e.g., families, individuals, gangs). The relevant sample categories will often be determined and refined through a process of iteration. In most cases, the selection does not use **random sampling**, both because this will not work well for a very small sample (the sampling error would be too large to produce reliable estimates) and because most QUAL evaluators think about *representation* in terms of the care taken to ensure that the sample covers all important issues and types of subjects, not in terms of statistical procedures. The purpose of many evaluations is to understand a particular program rather than to make generalizations to broader populations. Some evaluators would also argue that each situation is so unique that it is very difficult (or even inappropriate) to try to generalize.

While some evaluations are looking at programs affecting only a few districts, communities, or subjects, others are undertaken to determine the **impacts** of a **project** or **program** on hundreds or sometimes thousands of subjects (e.g., individuals, families, schools, water user associations). The numbers become even larger for evaluations—usually, but not always, quantitative—that include a comparison group. For all but the smallest program populations, it is not possible to interview all the affected subjects and **stakeholders** and, consequently, evaluation findings are normally based on generalizations from a sample of subjects.

Sampling is critical to evaluation for two reasons. First, the way in which the sample is designed and implemented is an important determinant of the validity of the conclusions. Second, decisions about the type and size of the sample (the number of subjects to be interviewed or studied) is one of the major determinants of the cost and duration of the evaluation. The issue is how to ensure that the sample is appropriate for the type of findings based on it. Addressing this issue takes different forms in QUANT and QUAL evaluation.

Crystallizing the issue for QUANT evaluation, where *probabilistic sampling* is based on large numbers, Henry (1990) states:

> The sampling dilemma is simple. Time and cost prohibit a researcher from collecting data on the entire group or population that is of interest to a particular study. However, researchers and the consumers of research are usually interested in the population rather than a subset of the population. Extending the study findings from a subset of the population, or "sample," to the entire population is critically important to overcome the dilemma between cost and time on the one hand and information needs on the other. Knowledge of basic sampling logic and methods is fundamental to ascertain if study findings reasonably apply to the population represented by the study participants or the study respondents. (p. 9)

For QUAL evaluation, where time-intensive methods decree smaller numbers of subjects, groups, or organizations, the issue of appropriate selection is addressed through subject-by-subject

choices according to specified criteria. Selecting subjects to be maximally informative about evaluation questions is called **purposive** or **purposeful sampling**.

An understanding of the basic principles of sampling is particularly critical for RWE because
the size of the sample has a major impact on the cost and duration of the evaluation. If the size of the
sample is reduced without serious danger to the validity of the findings, a significant saving in cost
and time may be gained. The key question is, How can the size of the sample be reduced without
affecting the validity of the conclusions and recommendations? On the one hand, if the sample is
larger than necessary, money and time are wasted; on the other hand, if the sample is too small, or
otherwise inappropriate, the validity of the conclusions and recommendations will be compromised
(see Box 15.1).

**BOX 15.1
SMALL SAMPLES MAY OVERLOOK IMPORTANT REAL EFFECTS**

In a meta-analysis assessing the findings of large numbers of evaluations of programs
to reduce juvenile delinquency, Lipsey estimated that when programs had small but
operationally important effects (when the effect size is less than 0.3), perhaps as many
as 75% of the evaluations were not able to detect the effects because the sample was
too small (the power of the test was too low) and it was wrongly concluded that the
program had no effect.

SOURCES: Lipsey (1990, chap. 3) and Rossi, Lipsey, and Freeman (2004, chap. 10).

---

2. Purposive Sampling

Because the QUAL methods used to obtain data from human subjects—observation and interview—
take time, there is almost always a limit to the number of persons who can be observed or interviewed
during the data collection period. Appropriate selection of persons to observe and interview helps to
ensure the richest and most meaningful information and understanding of the program and its
impact. What is learned about some individuals will support findings about the program and stakeholders as a whole. These *petite generalizations* (Erickson 1986), like any findings, need to be warranted by adequate and appropriate data. Questions of concern include the following: What kinds of
findings will be made from the data? Will the subjects selected be able to provide adequate and
appropriate information to support these findings?

When the number of subjects to be sampled is very small, random sampling will often not be
appropriate. A small random sample increases the risk of a skewed or distorted data set and in the
findings based on it. For example, random selection with a very small sample might by chance result
in a lopsided sample of all or mostly men, mostly advocates of a particular cause, or residents of
mostly one region served by the program. However, the t-test was created for working with small
samples, where the sample size is less than 30, and the t-test is frequently applied to samples of this
size in medicine, industry, and agriculture. But the use of random selection with small samples

becomes more problematic in many kinds of development evaluation where the population is heterogeneous with many different ethnic or sociocultural groups. In these cases, alternative sample selection procedures may be needed that ensure the inclusion of participants who can inform understanding of the program. So with small samples it will often be better to select each subject carefully and deliberately, based on criteria related to the purpose and questions of the evaluation. This type of sampling is purposeful or purposive. With small sample sizes, the choice between random and purposive sampling will be decided based on the purposes of the particular study as well as the characteristics of the population to be studied.

2.1. Purposive Sampling Strategies

Many strategies or selection criteria may be used for purposive sampling. Defining the selection criteria is as important as selecting the respondents. The goal is identifying persons with knowledge and experience relevant to and sufficient for the evaluation purpose(s) or question(s) to be addressed. Except for a census (*comprehensive sample)* in which every member of the population is selected, to some extent, all samples (both purposive and probabilistic, and in both qualitative and quantitative evaluations) are *convenience samples.* In this context, convenience is a broad concept and includes not only persons who are readily at hand and agreeable to interviewing or surveying, for example, but also persons who are willing to provide information. No survey or interview schedule can obtain information from persons who refuse to respond.[1] Still, some of the willing are easier to reach than others, who may be so remote that evaluation resources exclude them on feasibility grounds.

However, there is a difference between purposive and probability sampling in this respect. Probability sampling strategies select a random sample, and even though it will normally not be possible to interview all selected subjects, for the reasons mentioned above, there are procedures for identifying the characteristics of the nonrespondents (for example, noting the location of the house or farm, observing the quality of housing or the area of land owned, or obtaining information from neighbors on household composition or economic activities). This information can then be used to compare the characteristics of nonrespondents and respondents so that, if necessary, adjustments can be made in the final estimates (see Lohr 1999, chap. 8, for a discussion of procedures for addressing the problems of nonresponse).

Among the willing, researchers or evaluators may define what is convenient in a given project and, within the boundaries of their definition, find a convenience sample. *Typical case samples* are drawn when it is important to know how the program has affected typical stakeholders. *Representative samples* are drawn when it is important for the sample to reflect or represent an entire group of stakeholders. Either of these types of samples might be used in pursuit of evaluation questions like these: How does this program affect participants? If an average person accesses this program, what will he or she experience? In general, are most participants satisfied or dissatisfied with this program (or an aspect of it)?

---

[1]Although this is true to some extent, many QUANT samples do aim to cover all the population and not only those persons willing to be interviewed. In these cases, procedures are used to obtain information on subjects who cannot be located or who are not willing to respond so that their characteristics can be compared with people willing to be interviewed. A well-known example is voting surveys where it is important to cover all the electorate, not only those willing to be interviewed. When face-to-face interviews are conducted, it is possible to note the sex, age, and ethnicity of nonrespondents. If the interviewer visits homes, it is also possible to note characteristics of the house and the neighborhood.

Quota samples and *range samples* involve identifying characteristics of interest and some or all the variations found in the population of interest; respondents are then selected to ensure that each characteristic is represented in the sample. A *quota sample* is one in which each group of interest is allocated proportional representation in the sample. An example: It may be important to include a number or proportion (exact or approximate) of men and women, young and old, working and unemployed, and different ethnic groups in order to understand the impact across a range of stakeholders and the perspectives and experiences of each. A range sample is intended to be representative of the range of variations within a population rather than to focus on the typical or average cases. While a quota sample is intended to achieve proportional representation, the range sample will often only include examples of the highest and lowest cases, but usually without ensuring proportionality.

Unique case samples are sometimes as informative or more informative than typical case samples. Many programs will have some program personnel or beneficiaries who differ in unique ways from the group as a whole. Understanding their experiences and perspectives may be particularly helpful. For example: An efficiency expert might choose to watch the fastest bricklayer in order to understand how he or she approaches the process of laying brick and to train others. The different or unique cases, the *outliers* if graphed, may offer special insights unavailable in typical, range, or quota samples.

Snowball samples involve the identification of likely sources of information by the evaluators, perhaps in collaboration with **clients**, followed by the identification of other sources of information by the contacted informants themselves. For example: The final question to an interviewee might be, "Who else knows about this subject and might be willing to speak with me?" This strategy has the characteristic of capitalizing on insiders' knowledge of local sources of information and may identify data sources the evaluator might otherwise neglect. Snowball samples are often used to locate subjects who are particularly hard to identify, such as families who have left the community, illegal immigrants, or people engaging in high-risk behavior (such as multiple sex partners).

Critical case samples are drawn when there is a particularly challenging subgroup within a program's stakeholders—for example, the chronically homeless, the lowest academic achievers, or the intended beneficiaries who live farthest from service delivery outlets. When evaluators feel that if these groups are well served all groups are likely to be well served, their interest in such critical cases suggests special attention to them during data collection. Critical case sampling may also be the selection criterion of choice when particularly challenging subgroups claim disproportionate program services or benefits, create the greatest disruption to program processes, or are the most likely to be overlooked. Learning from these groups may be recognized as particularly informative for program decision makers and other personnel.

Extreme case samples, negative case samples, and *deviant case samples* help evaluators and clients understand atypical experiences, some of which may be especially important. Among the atypical samples that might be drawn, extreme case samples obtain information about cases or members of the target population at one end or another of the continuum of program experiences—for example, the most positive or negative or those receiving the most or fewest benefits. Negative case samples are not samples of those whose experiences are negative but of those whose experiences, like the negative of a photograph, are very different—even opposite—from those of most program participants. Finding out why their experiences or outcomes are so different from the mainstream can be helpful for understanding and improving a program. Deviant case samples are not samples of those whose behavior is legally or socially deviant but of those whose experiences deviate from the norm in the program, a concept similar to negative case samples.

Reputational samples are drawn from those who are recognized as having perspectives that might provide especially helpful information. For example: The *American Journal of Evaluation* has begun publishing a series of interviews with nationally recognized evaluators, chosen on the basis of their reputations. In a program, stakeholders who might be known by reputation might be the most outspoken proponents or opponents of the program, the personnel most or least successful at dispensing services at the lowest cost, the community in the program that has improved the most or least, or the school with the highest or lowest test scores. As some of these examples show, some reputational samples are also extreme case samples.

Comparable case samples are drawn in order to allow for a comparison of some type. For example, a sample of men might be compared with a sample of women; a sample of urban beneficiaries might be compared with a sample of rural beneficiaries; a sample of teachers of high-risk students might be compared with a sample of teachers of college-bound students. Following the logic (but not the size) of samples common to experimental and quasi-experimental designs, a sample of nonparticipants might be drawn to compare with participants in a program. Thus both within-program comparisons and a small-scale variation of treatment and comparison group comparisons can be purposefully included in a qualitative evaluation.

2.2. Purposive Sampling for Different Types of Qualitative Data Collection and Use

Sampling for Data Collection

Sampling is often a decision point for more than one type of data collection. An evaluator must consider who and how many to sample in interviewing, which and how many sites and events to observe, and which and how many program documents and records to review when it is not possible to collect and study each potential datum. The different types or strategies for purposive sampling described above apply to each of these data collection types. For example:

Sampling interviewees (individual or **focus group** interviews):

- *Range sample,* including a member of each ethnic subgroup
- *Extreme case sample* of participants receiving the fewest benefits
- *Reputational sample* of local activists promoting the program

Sampling observations:

- *Typical sample* of day-to-day program operations
- *Comparable case sample* of day-to-day activities outside the program
- *Critical case sample* of activities personnel find most difficult

Sampling documents:

- *Quota sample* with a proportion of each of several types of documents
- *Comprehensive sample* of all prior evaluations of the program
- *Negative case sample* of all applications that were denied

More than one purposeful sampling strategy is often useful in an evaluation in which many things must be understood—for example, both typical cases and extreme cases, both ordinary events and periodic ceremonies, both program plans and working documents such as benefi-ciary records.

Some evaluations (qualitative, quantitative, or mixed-method) include case studies in their designs. Although each evaluation could be considered a case study, with the program constituting the case, mini-case studies within an evaluation might be employed to illuminate specific aspects of the program. For example, in a multisite study, evaluators might include a case study of each of three program implementa-tion sites, perhaps choosing a thriving site, a failing site, and a struggling site. This selection of sites could be considered a range sample, showing a range of implementation success, or it could be considered a typical case sample and two extreme case samples. This shows how the selection criteria can be applied to case selection and site selection, as well as to specific data collection choices.

Sampling from Data for Reporting

Related to the concept and strategies of sampling for data collection is the sampling of data for qualitative reporting. For example, from the many observation vignettes and interviews recorded, which should be included in a report to provide a reader with a vicarious experience of the program to deepen his or her understanding of its workings and effects? Not merely the most interesting or most vivid snippets should be chosen; the point is not the entertainment of the reader. For under-standing, a typical sample might be juxtaposed against a deviant case sample or a range sample to illustrate different patterns of interaction between project personnel and beneficiaries. The sample of data included in the report should be as purposeful as the sampling itself, revealing the basis on which findings were generated and warranting them. The purpose of sharing the selected samples should be explained along with the data presentation so the reader understands, for example, that an extreme case is not typical.

2.3. Considerations in Planning Purposive Sampling

Sampling can support or undermine the validity of evaluation findings about a program's merits and shortcomings, depending on the appropriateness of the sampling criteria for the purpose of the evaluation. An insufficient or skewed sample, one in which some aspect is exaggerated, is unlikely to lead to valid find-ings or real program improvement. Planning a sample larger than can be accomplished with evaluation resources (time, personnel, funds) may lead to truncation at the end, with no assurance that the data col-lected early would have been confirmed by the data lost. The particular question to be addressed may suggest the type of sample or samples that would be most appropriate. For example:

For interviewing (individual and focus group): Are new students benefiting from the school's peer-mentoring program?

- *Range sample* of mentees matching each ethnic group in the school
- *Extreme case samples* of mentees succeeding (and not) academically
- *Typical sample* of peer mentors
- *Reputational sample* of supportive and nonsupportive teachers

Is the new **microcredit** program helping beneficiaries establish sustainable businesses?

- *Quota sample* of each type of business begun by borrowers
- *Snowball sample* of the clients of (and identified by) these borrowers

- *Comprehensive sample* of the managers of the program
- *Negative case sample* of applicants denied loans

Again, these considerations hold not only for developing a sampling plan for data collection but also for sampling data to support findings in reports, where the sampling criteria should be documented and justified.

3. Probability (Random) Sampling

3.1. Key Questions in Designing a Random Sample for Program Evaluation

The focus of this section is on the use of random sampling in the design of a program evaluation. While different methods for the selection of random samples are discussed, the main focus is on guidelines for determining the appropriate sample size. For evaluations that are designed under budget constraints, one of the main options for cutting costs is to reduce the sample size, as data collection is always a major part of the total evaluation cost. Consequently, the question of how to determine the appropriate sample size is critical. For QUANT evaluation, one of the most serious dangers of too small a sample is that the program may appear not to have produced its desired effects when, in fact, it had but the sample was too small to detect the effects (see Box 15.1). An understanding of the concepts of effect size and the power of the test and their influence on the determination of sample size is critical for all evaluation designs,[2] but particularly for RWE. In addition to questions of sample size, the following questions must usually be addressed for policy evaluations:

- Is the **target population** of concern to policymakers defined in the same way as the population in the study?
- Have the sampling procedures biased the estimates of project effects?
- Are the estimates of project effects and the influence of **intervening variables** on these effects precise enough for the policy purpose?

Although the estimation of sample size is important, it is only one of the factors affecting the choice of the appropriate sample design. Kraemer and Thiemann (1987, chap. 10) warn that quantitative researchers often become so involved with the statistical refinements of sample design and analysis that they tend to overlook some basic principles of sample planning. Making a mistake in planning a study as to what data to collect and how many subjects to study is irrevocable in quantitative studies. No amount of statistical analysis can overcome, for example, the use of a sampling plan that excludes critical parts of the target population. Box 15.2 points out that when consulting with statisticians on questions such as sample size, it is important to try to find a statistician who also has some familiarity with the specific subject area.

---

[2]Effect size and the statistical power of the test do not only apply to randomly selected samples. For example, most clinical trials in medicine and public health are based on studies in which subjects are either recruited voluntarily or in which advantage is taken of data collected on a nonrepresentative sample. The analysis of these kinds of quasi-experimental designs is discussed in Chapters 11 and 12. In the present chapter we are only discussing the importance of effect size and power of the test in determining the size of a random sample selected for the purpose of estimating program outcomes.

BOX 15.2

BE CAUTIOUS ABOUT ADVICE FROM STATISTICIANS NOT FAMILIAR WITH THE FIELD OF EVALUATION

When seeking statistical consultation, issues of particular and specific relevance in their own fields of research may never be brought to the attention of the consulting statistician. A consulting statistician (not versed in a particular field) may not know that there are several extant valid and reliable scales. . . . The researcher is then informed that 500 patients might be needed and never realizes that 50 might otherwise have sufficed. As a result, the most cost-effective decisions are not necessarily the ones made, even with expert advice.

SOURCE: Kraemer and Thiemann (1987:99).

Initial exploratory studies and careful review of the literature will often be required before finalizing the sample design and administering the data collection instrument. Statistical tests based on poorly prepared sample plans can often be misleading. For example, in the previously mentioned study of survival strategies of low-income families in Colombia (see Chapter 14), the exploratory participant observer study found that poor families relied heavily on the transfers of money, food, and even household members between family groups living in different parts of the country or even overseas. This preliminary observation modified the sample design because it became clear that it would be misleading to define the basic economic and social unit as people living in one particular house.

Researchers should think in terms of cost-efficiency to a much greater extent when defining the sampling strategy. For example, it probably does not make sense to invest too many resources in refining the **sampling frame** (the list or map from which the sample is to be selected) if this means that there is not enough money to hire a sufficient number of supervisors to ensure that **interviewers** follow the sample selection procedures.

There are at least five critical choices in sample design:

1. *Deciding whether a sample should be used.* In quantitative evaluation, when the population is large there is often no choice but to select a sample, but there are several circumstances in which it may be better to cover the whole population. When the population is small, it is possible to consider collecting data on the whole population, and sometimes the **credibility** of the conclusions may require that all the population is studied. The concept of sampling is not universally understood or accepted, and where it is important to convince key decision makers as to the validity of the findings, it may be necessary to go beyond normal sampling procedures (e.g., by surveying all the population, even though this may not be considered necessary by the evaluation team).

2. *Defining the population from which the sample will be drawn.* Frequently, the quantitative evaluator does not have access to a sampling frame (e.g., directory, list, or map including all schools, households, or communities to be covered by the sample) that corresponds exactly to the target population. For example, the directory of schools may not include certain types of small private

schools, or the map of urban communities may not include houses built within the past three years. An assessment must be made of the magnitude and importance of the discrepancies between the sampling frame and the program population, how these might affect the validity of the conclusions, and what if anything could be done to improve the coverage of the sampling frame. Assuming that the sampling frame could be improved (e.g., by finding ways to include small private schools excluded from the schools directory or updating community maps to include houses constructed since the map was prepared three years ago), a decision must be made on the potential trade-offs between investing resources to make these improvements versus, for example, increasing the size of the sample or reducing the nonresponse rate.

For example, in communities where all adults have two or three different jobs, it may be very difficult to find people at home to interview. To get a representative sample, it may be necessary to revisit many houses two or three times. On the other hand, if the decision is made to interview any adult found at home on the first visit (rather than the household head, for example), the sample would be biased toward people who are unemployed or who are elderly or otherwise not working. Thus, ensuring a representative sample would significantly increase the costs of data collection (if on average two or three visits were required to complete each interview). In this case, the evaluator might have to decide whether it would be more useful to invest scarce resources to improve the sample frame or to increase the time and budget for data collection (to permit revisits to reduce the nonresponse rate).

3. *Choice of sampling methods.* Often, a number of different sampling methods are available, and a decision must be made as to which method will be most reliable and at the same time cost-effective for the purposes of this evaluation.

4. *Defining the precision of the estimates.* It is essential to agree with the client on the required level of precision and then to determine the size and type of sample that can best approximate this level within the available resources. We continually remind evaluators that decisions on precision must be made in consultation with the client—this is a policy decision and not just a "technical" issue that is better left to the experts, as many clients assume.

5. *Purposive or probability sampling.* A critical decision is whether to use purposive or probability (random) sampling. Although the use of probability (random) sampling has the great advantage that it is possible to estimate the statistical precision of the findings, there are many circumstances in which random sampling is either not possible or not necessary. In the previous section, we discussed the wide range of purposive sampling procedures available, and for many types of evaluation these may be more appropriate than random sampling.

3.2. Selection Procedures in Probability (Random) Sampling

In probability sampling, each unit (person, family, school) has a known, nonzero probability of being selected. Although some texts state that all units have an *equal* probability of selection, this is not correct because there are many types of stratified samples in which the probabilities of selection may be different. For example, small groups such as ethnic minorities or female-headed households may be deliberately oversampled to ensure sufficient appreciation of outcomes for them derived from the sample. The important point is that the probability of selection for each group is known, and weighting procedures can be used in the estimations. Henry (1990:26) points out that it is possible for some units to have a probability of 1 or certainty of being selected. He cites the example of an election study in Illinois where, because of its size and critical importance, Cook County would always be included in the sample. During the estimation process, adjustments would be made to compensate for the different probabilities of selection.[3] The following are the most common types of probability samples:

- *Simple random sample.* Every unit has an equal chance of being selected.
- *Stratified random sample.* The study population is divided into easily identifiable strata such as geographical regions, general health status (on a scale that has already been administered to the whole sample population), or sex and age groups. The strata must be easy to administer, cover the whole survey population, and categorize the population into groups directly related to the purpose of the study. An indicator of a good stratification design is that the within-strata variance of key variables should be significantly smaller than between-strata variation.
- *Systematic sample.* All subjects are listed and assigned sequential numbers from 1 to N (where N is the total number of subjects—for example, 1,000). The required sample size n (for example, 100) is then determined (see later in the chapter), and a sampling fraction (f) is calculated by dividing the total population by n. In this case, $f = 1,000/100 = 10$, so every 10th subject is then selected from the list.
- *Random route.* This is a type of systematic sample that can be used when no listing of the total population is available. A sketch map of the community is drawn, the approximate number of families in the community is estimated, and the number of families to be included in the sample is calculated. A random route is generated by selecting a starting point on the map and then instructing the interviewer to turn left or right or continue straight ahead at each intersection. The interviewer must interview every nth house encountered on this random route.[4]
- *Cluster sampling.* The sample population is divided into naturally occurring clusters such as geographical areas, schools, or places of employment. All the clusters are listed, and a sample of clusters is randomly selected. All subjects in each cluster, or a randomly selected sample of clusters, are then interviewed. See Lohr (1999) for a discussion of cluster sampling procedures.
- *Multistage sampling.* The selection of subjects to be selected for stratified or cluster samples may involve several stages. For example, to select a sample of students attending secondary school in a particular province, a sample of districts may first be selected, then a sample of secondary schools in each district, and then a sample of classes in each school. Finally, a sample of students may be selected within these classes (see Figure 15.1).

---

[3] When strata have different probabilities of selection, weighting is used in the analysis to readjust the numbers from each stratum to their true proportions in the total population. For example, if Stratum X is particularly important for the study, twice as many subjects from Stratum X might be included in the sample. In the analysis, a weighting factor of 0.5 would then be used for Stratum X when making estimates for the total population.

[4] The procedure is slightly more complicated if the sample unit is a certain type of individual in the household (e.g., student attending the local school), but the same general principle applies.

Figure 15.1   A Multistage Sample for Selecting a Sample of Secondary School Students

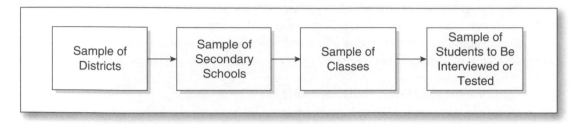

3.3. Sample Design Decisions at Different Stages of the Survey

When designing a sample, a number of decisions must be made before deciding on the best sample design, others must be made during the process of sample design, and yet others must be made after data collection has been completed (Henry 1990). These three types of decisions are summarized next.

Presampling Questions

Before deciding on the best type of sample, it is necessary to consider the following:

- *What is the nature of the study?* Is it exploratory, descriptive, or analytical? Normally, larger samples and more precise estimates are required for analytical studies than for exploratory and descriptive ones.
- *What are the variables and hypotheses of greatest interest?* The characteristics of the key variables (including the size of **standard deviation**) and the nature of the hypotheses to be tested can affect the type of evaluation design and the size and type of sample. For example, the required sample size will be significantly smaller (by as much as 40%) if a **one-tailed** rather than a **two-tailed** significance test can be used (see p. 388, this chapter).
- *What is the target population?* How easily and economically can a good sampling frame (that closely approximates the total target population) be obtained or created?
- *Are there subpopulations or special groups of importance to the study?* When subpopulations must be compared, this will normally increase the sample size.
- *How will the data be collected?* There are significant differences in the cost and time required to administer different data collection instruments.
- *Is sampling appropriate?* There are some situations in which sampling is not possible or appropriate (see earlier discussion, in this chapter).

Questions and Choices during the Sample Design Process

Once the best type of sample design for this evaluation has been decided, there are a number of questions and choices on how to finalize and implement the design:

- *What listing can be used for the sampling frame?* How comprehensive and reliable is this? Could the sampling frame be improved, and would it be worth investing (scarce) resources to improve it?

- *What is the minimum acceptable effect size?* The smaller the expected effect size, the larger the required sample. Is it reasonable to specify a larger effect size so as to reduce the required sample size (see pp. 371–373, this chapter)?
- *What type of sampling technique will be used?* (See earlier discussion, p. 365, this chapter.)
- *Will the probability of selection be equal or unequal if different strata or clusters are used in the sample?*
- *How many participants or units will be selected for the sample?* Is this number affordable, and if not, would it be acceptable to reduce the sample size?
- *For longitudinal studies, what is the expected rate of population change?* Many longitudinal evaluations involve either panel studies where the sample subjects are reinterviewed or where the same sampling frame is used to select a new sample. In many areas, population size and composition can change dramatically as new families move in or others leave. It is not uncommon in informal urban settlements for the number of families or physical structures to increase by 10% to 20% per year. In these cases, it may be necessary to adjust the sample design to ensure that the samples at later points in time are still representative of the total population. The likely sample dropout rate should be estimated, and in some cases the size of the original sample should be increased to compensate for dropouts or turnover. Another practical question concerns the feasibility of locating the same families again for the repeat survey (see Box 15.3).

BOX 15.3
LONGITUDINAL PANEL STUDIES ARE GREAT—BUT WHAT IF YOU CAN'T FIND THE FAMILIES TWO YEARS LATER?

An evaluation of a self-help housing program in informal settlements in El Salvador planned to use a panel study in which the same households would be reinterviewed two years later. Detailed demographic information was collected on each family, and a map was drawn to make sure that all the houses could be correctly identified two years later. Even with all these precautions, it was found that in 10% to 20% of the cases, the researchers were not sure if the same family had been found again. What had previously been two separate buildings had sometimes been combined into one; the front door of some houses had been moved from one street to another; families had decided to change the number of their house. Furthermore, women may have three or four different family names, and they may change from one year to another. Reported ages can also change, depending on how the respondent is feeling. So how does the evaluator know if Maria Rodriguez Martinez, who was 42 years old in 2000 and lived in a single-story house with its entrance on Calle Las Flores, is the same person as 38-year-old Ana Maria Sanchez, who in 2002 lives in a two-story house with its entrance on Calle Los Robles?

Postsampling Questions and Choices

Once the data collection has been completed, there are often a number of questions and choices concerning how the sample should be analyzed. Some of these choices concern how to correct any problems that arose during the administration of the sample, whereas others concern statistical estimations from the sample. For example:

- *How can nonresponse be evaluated?* If the nonresponse rate is relatively high, how might this affect the validity of the conclusions? Are there any adjustments that can be made (such as a rapid follow-up study) to fill in some of the gaps?
- *Is weighting necessary?* Weighting is the process of adjusting the proportion of certain groups included in the sample to their true proportion in the total population. If some small groups were deliberately oversampled (a higher proportion included in the sample than there are in the population) because of their importance to the evaluation, it might be necessary to make an adjustment in the analysis when estimates are being made for the total population. Sometimes weighting is necessary because of a deliberate sampling strategy to over- or underrepresent certain groups. In other cases, weighting is used to adjust for the low response rates of certain groups. For example, it might have proved difficult to interview men who are long-distance truck drivers or deep-sea fishermen because they are away from home for extended periods of time and difficult to contact. If, for example, it is estimated that about 20% of men are deep-sea fishermen but only about 10% of men interviewed were fishermen, then the evaluation team might decide to use a statistical weight to adjust the sample proportion to its true proportion of the population. However, a decision to weight the findings for certain groups is not automatic and always needs careful consideration because weighting can itself introduce a bias. For example, it may be that the fishermen who were interviewed were not typical of all fishermen (perhaps they were older and spent less time at sea), so giving a higher value to those who were interviewed on the assumption that they represented all fisherman could introduce a bias. In this example, the average age of fishermen who were interviewed would be higher than those who were not interviewed.

3.4. Sources of Error in Probabilistic Sample Design

There are two main sources of error affecting the reliability of sample estimates: sampling bias and nonsampling bias (Henry 1990, chap. 3). When samples have to be designed under budget and time constraints, there are often choices to be made about how to address each of these sources of bias. For example, it may not make sense to invest a lot of resources in trying to reduce nonresponse rates if there are some fundamental weaknesses in the sampling frame that cause important sectors of the target population to be excluded from the study.

Assume that an evaluation is being planned to assess the impacts of improved housing on the employment patterns of low-income urban families, many of whom work in small, largely unregistered businesses in the informal sector. The possibility is being considered of using as the sampling frame the list of enterprises compiled by the Ministry of Industry for its periodic employment surveys. The list is very current and easy to use, and it is believed to include almost all registered businesses employing 10 or more workers. However, the evaluation team estimates that the list does not cover at least 25% of the target population working in the informal sector (most of whom work in enterprises with less than 10 employees and are therefore not included in the ministry survey). Two sampling options are being considered: The first is to use the Ministry of Industry sampling frame and to then use statistical techniques to extrapolate from this sample to estimate the characteristics of the smaller businesses not covered by the sample. The second option is to complement the

Ministry of Industry sample with a cluster or quota sample covering some of the areas where many of the small, informal enterprises are located. This second sample would be expensive to select and might have a lower level of statistical precision. Clearly, there are trade-offs of cost and accuracy between these options.

Nonsampling Bias

Samples can never be guaranteed to indicate the true value of the variables covered (e.g., average household income, average absentee rates from third-grade classes, the proportion of families earning over 500 pesos per month). Samples produce estimates that indicate the probability that the true value (e.g., of mean income, absentee rates) will lie within a certain range. This range, which depends on the size of the sample and the standard deviation of the statistic being estimated, is the sampling error. This error can be easily estimated because it is determined by the sample size and the standard deviation of the variable being estimated. However, there are many sources of nonsampling biases that affect estimates from surveys. Some of the important nonsampling biases include the following:

- *The coverage of the sampling frame and the adequacy of listing of subjects.* Some sampling frames approximate the target population quite well, but the quality and comprehensiveness of the listings are questionable. For example, the Ministry of Education may have a complete listing of all schools, but there may be overreporting of children who actually attend.
- *Nonresponse.* Subjects who cannot be located or who refuse to be interviewed usually have different characteristics from willing respondents, so a significant nonresponse rate is likely to introduce important biases in the sample. For example, compared to nonrespondents the respondents may on average be younger, include more women, be better educated, or be from a higher-income group.
- *Measurement error.* Information may be systematically misreported (people understate their income, women do not report domestic violence or that their husband has deserted them), or it may be misrecorded or misinterpreted by the interviewer. For example, the interviewer may assume that the respondent does not know how to read or write, so the questions about literacy are not asked.

Sampling Bias

Certain kinds of biases are also due to the procedures used for sample selection:

- *Selection bias* occurs when not all sectors of the target population have an equal chance of being selected. For example, if one adult is randomly selected from each household, the probability of a particular adult being selected is greater in households with few adults than those with many adults.
- *Estimation bias* occurs when the average calculated from the sample provides a biased estimate of the true population mean. For example, the use of the median will provide a biased estimate of the population mean (Henry 1990:38). It is possible to adjust for most estimation biases during the statistical analysis *as long as the evaluator is aware that a bias exists.*

4. Using Power Analysis and Effect Size for Estimating the Appropriate Sample Size for an Impact Evaluation

4.1. The Importance of Power Analysis for Determining Sample Size for Probability Sampling

Power analysis is a tool for determining the relationship between sample size and the level of statistical precision in a survey or evaluation. It can be used to estimate the sample size required to achieve a specified level of statistical precision, or to estimate the level of statistical precision that can be achieved with a given sample size.

Power analysis is particularly useful for RWE, as reducing the sample size is usually one of the most important options for reducing costs. However, overzealous reductions in sample size can be fatal. Many programs, even if well managed, can only expect to achieve relatively small improvements ("effect size"), and if the sample is too small, the statistical significance tests may commit a "Type II error" (a "false negative") and fail to detect what was in fact a statistically significant project effect. The smaller the effect size, the larger the sample required to detect it. Power analysis is an essential tool for the RWE evaluator providing precise estimates of the sample size required to achieve the objectives of the evaluation. When the effect size is small, power analysis helps avoid selecting a sample that is too small, and conversely when the effect size is relatively large it can avoid wasting time and money through selecting a sample that is larger than necessary.

This is not just an academic concern, as is illustrated in the following example cited by Lipsey. In a review of 556 evaluations of different kinds of juvenile delinquency interventions, it was found that a high proportion of the estimated effect sizes were around 0.3. Many of the programs were designed to reduce recidivism (the likelihood that a juvenile delinquent after leaving the detention center would be reconvicted within a certain period of time, typically six months). It was found that 57% of the studies found an effect size of 0.3 or less, with about one sixth having an effect size close to 0.3, which was equivalent to an average reduction of 24% in recidivism (a 38% recidivism rate for the project groups, compared to 50% for the control group). On the face of it this would seem to be a worthwhile program effect. However, in approximately 75% of the studies reviewed an effect size of 0.3 was not found to be statistically significant. Lipsey's review showed that in many cases the reason was that the sample size was too small (the test was "underpowered") to have been able to detect an effect of this size (Lipsey 1990, chap. 3, and summarized in Rossi et al. 2004, chap. 10). In other words, a high proportion of these evaluation studies were doomed to failure simply because the sample was too small to detect the effect being studied. Table 15.4, pp. 385–386, shows that (with power = 0.8) while an effect size of 0.5 could be detected with a total sample size of 108 (54 in both the project and comparison groups); a sample of 632 would be required to identify an effect size of 0.2. With an effect size as small as 0.1 the total sample size would increase to 2,474!

While a full understanding of the logic of power analysis requires a solid grounding in statistics, the basic principles are easy to understand. For more complicated evaluation designs, or where high levels of statistical precision are required, it is advisable to consult with a statistical specialist. However, it is important for the evaluator to understand the basic principles of power analysis in order to know what questions to ask the statistician and to make sure these questions are addressed.

4.2. Estimating Effect Size

The "effect size" is the size of the change or effect that a program produces or is expected to produce. There are different types of effect sizes, including correlation coefficients and difference between means. In this chapter we will only consider estimates for the difference between means (called "d"). Technically, "d" is *the difference between the outcome measured on program targets receiving the intervention and an estimate of what the outcome for those targets would have been had they not received the intervention.* (Italics added; Rossi et al. 2004:302.) The larger the difference between the means of the two groups being compared (pretest/posttest project group or project and comparison group) the greater the effect size. Where possible, a *standardized effect size* is used so that comparisons can be made across programs or even across different kinds of effects (see next paragraph). However, it is sometimes necessary to use less precise measures, such as the number of points increase on a behavior scale or aptitude test where the meaning of the change can be difficult to interpret. For binary variables, an odds ratio is often used (see Rossi et al. 2004, chap. 10).

To obtain a standardized measure that can be used to compare the findings of different studies, the difference of means is divided by the standard deviation of the population. Thus:

Standardized effect size = $\overline{X}_1 - \overline{X}_2 / \sigma X$

Where:

$\overline{X}_1$ = the mean score for the project group

$\overline{X}_2$ = the mean score for the total population (estimated from the comparison group)

σX = the standard deviation of the total population

For example, assume that after a microcredit program had been operating for two years, the average income of all adult women in the community was 300 pesos, while the average for women who had received loans was 350 pesos, and that the standard deviation for the total population was 100 pesos. The effect size would be calculated as:

Standardized effect size = (350 − 300)/100 = 0.5.

However, if the standard deviation had only been 75 pesos, then the effect size would have been 0.66.

Defining Minimum Acceptable Effect Size (MAES)

The minimum acceptable effect size, also called the critical effect size, is the minimum level of change that the evaluation design must be able to detect. The smaller the effect size that must be detected, the larger the required sample. Table 15.1 describes different criteria that can be used to define the MAES. In some cases the MAES is defined in comparison to an accepted norm or target (for example, average test scores for a particular school grade), in others it is based on a comparison with other similar programs, and in yet other cases policymakers determine what is perceived by politicians and other stakeholders to be the minimum acceptable increase. Also, the MAES may be based on cost-effectiveness calculations. The MAES is normally population-specific, so that the acceptable effect size for a group of young men may be quite different from the acceptable effect size for a group of young women or a group of older people of either sex.

The choice of effect size is a key determinant of the required sample size. Where very small effect sizes must be detected, large samples will be required. Obviously, the MAES cannot be arbitrarily increased just to reduce the sample size. If it is believed that a 10% increase in school enrollment is the most optimistic estimate, it clearly does not make any sense to say, "Let us assume there will be a 25% increase." However, once clients understand the trade-offs between effect size and cost of the evaluation (i.e., sample size), there are sometimes ways to increase effect size. For example, if it is anticipated that enrollment is likely to increase more for girls than for boys, then it would be possible in the first evaluation to study program impact on girls. Obviously, it should be made completely clear to clients and readers that the evaluation does not cover the whole population. Another way to increase effect size is to improve the program design and delivery of services. Assume there is evidence from earlier programs that student math skills increase more when new textbooks are complemented by orientation sessions for teachers. Providing these orientation sessions might improve student performance and hence the effect size. Clearly there are trade-offs, and the client would have to decide whether the additional cost and effort of organizing the orientation sessions was justified.

Another important trade-off is to place less emphasis on statistical significance and greater emphasis on effect size. At least in the developmental stage of a program, it is important to avoid

Table 15.1   Criteria for Determining the Minimum Acceptable Effect Size (MAES)

Criterion	Examples
1. *Difference in the original measurement scale*	When the outcome measure has a clearly understood meaning, the MAES may be stated directly in terms of this unit. For example, the dollar value of health services after the introduction of a new program, or the reduced recidivism rate for juvenile offenders.
2. *Comparison with test norms or performance of a normative population*	For a literacy program the MAES may be defined in terms of reducing the gap below the average grade score in the target scores.
3. *Differences between criterion groups*	Comparison of school with national grade scores.
4. *Proportion over a diagnostic or other success threshold*	A mental health program might use a well-known test of clinical depression such as the Beck Depression Inventory, which defines a score of 17–20 as borderline clinical depression. The MAES could be defined as the proportion with scores below 17.
5. *Proportion over an arbitrary success threshold*	Proportion of families in an employment program with incomes above the federal poverty level.
6. *Comparison with the effects of similar programs*	One of the goals of local irrigation programs is the proportion of farmers paying the water service charges required to maintain the system. MAES could be defined as the average repayment rate found in similar projects.
7. *Conventional guidelines*	Cohen (1988) proposed conventional guidelines, based on meta-evaluations conducted in different sectors of small effects (0.2), medium effects (0.50), and large effects (0.80).
8. *Cost-effectiveness*	The average unit cost of delivering services is compared with alternative programs or what is considered by stakeholders to be a "reasonable" unit cost.

SOURCE: Adapted by the authors from Rossi, Lipsey, and Freeman (2004, pp. 318–19). Criterion 8 was added by the authors.

rejecting a potential program effect due to insistence on a high level of statistical significance. This is referred to as the trade-off between practical significance and clinical or statistical significance. At this stage it is important to identify all potentially credible effects. These can then be assessed more carefully, and more rigorous statistical significance requirements can then be introduced at a later stage. For the present discussion this means that a lower level of statistical power might be used in the program development stage than would be used for full-scale testing of a program at a later stage.

4.3. Type I and Type II Errors

One of the challenges of sample design is to try, within available resources, to reduce two types of error (see Table 15.2):

- **Type I error.** Wrongly concluding that a program has a significant effect on the target variable when, in fact, it does not (error of inclusion or false positive).
- **Type II error.** Wrongly concluding that a program does not have a significant effect on the target variable when, in fact, it does (error of exclusion or false negative).

The relative importance of these two types of error varies according to the research context and the policy objectives. For example, once pilot testing of a new program or treatment (e.g., a conditional cash transfer, secondary school scholarship program, or new drug) has shown positive results, before the program or treatment is launched on a national scale, it will probably be necessary to use a higher statistical significance to avoid a false positive and to demonstrate that the program or treatment really does have a positive effect. In this case you would want a very small Type I error rate to minimize the false positive, and your Type I error rate can be lowered by setting a stricter standard of proof (higher significance level). In this case the financial and human costs of wrong decisions are very high. However, for many types of development programs, the primary concern may be to ensure that small but potentially important effects are not overlooked (Type II error). In this case you would want a very small Type II error rate to reduce the risk of a false negative (concluding the program does not have an effect when, in fact, if does). Type II error rate is lowered by increasing power. Meta-analysis studies in many sectors have found that the "effect size" of even the most successful programs is quite small, and consequently it is important to ensure that these are not overlooked by setting too rigorous criteria for accepting a statistically significant effect or having too little power.

Table 15.2 Type I and Type II Errors in the Interpretation of Evaluation Findings

Results of significance test on sample data	The True Population Circumstance	
	Intervention and control means differ	Intervention and control means do not differ
Significant difference found	Correct conclusion (probability = $1 - \beta$). This is equivalent to the statistical power of the test.	**Type I error (false positive).** Wrongly concluding the project does have a statistically significant impact (probability = α).
No significant difference found	**Type II error (false negative).** Wrongly concluding the project did not have a statistically significant impact (probability = β).	Correct conclusion (probability = $1 - \alpha$).

The probability of making a Type I error (false positive) is set by the researcher. Increasing the sample size (and the cost) will increase the power and thus reduce the risk of making a Type II error. Consequently, it is essential to determine the relative importance of the two types of error and to set the statistical significance levels, and the resultant sample sizes, accordingly.

4.4. The Power of the Test

As indicated earlier, statistical power analysis is one of the key tools for estimating how large a sample is required to be able to find a statistically significant project impact if one really does exist. A number of authors have argued that in cases where a project is not expected to produce a very large impact (effect), many evaluation studies have wrongly assumed that a project did not have a (statistically significant) effect when, in fact, the sample was too small to have been able to detect the effect if it did exist (Lipsey 1990; Rossi et al. 2004). Statistical power is "the probability that an estimate will be statistically significant when, in fact, it represents a real effect of a given magnitude" (Rossi et al. 2004). The normal convention is to set power equal to 0.80, meaning that that there is an 80% chance that a particular sample will reject the null hypothesis (i.e., will find a statistically significant difference) if the program really does have an effect (see Box 15.4).

BOX 15.4
CONVENTIONS FOR DEFINING THE
STATISTICAL POWER OF THE TEST

- The power of the test is conventionally set at 0.80 (an 80% probability that a sample will find a statistically significant result if the null hypothesis is false).
- Power analysis usually assumes that the 0.05 (α) significance level is being used.
- Where greater precision is required power can be set at 0.90 or 0.95 (or even higher), and the significance level can be set at 0.01 (or even higher). However, increasing the precision level will significantly increase the required sample size.
- Estimates of power and the sample size required to achieve a certain power are often approximate because power curves are often steep and precise values difficult to estimate.

Where it is particularly important to avoid Type II errors and to ensure that real program effects are not rejected, it is possible to set power equal to 0.90 or even 0.95 or 0.99. However, the reason why these higher power levels are often not used is that the increase in power requires a significant increase in the sample size. For example, Table 15.4 shows that for a one-tailed test, increasing power from 0.8 to 0.9 may require an increase of between 30 and 38% in the sample size, while raising power from 0.8 to 0.95 may require up to a 75% increase. Box 15.5 points out that when statistical advice is sought on power and effect size calculations, the statistician will probably not be familiar with the particular field, and consequently the evaluator must do his or her homework and come with estimates of the expected effect size.

BOX 15.5

SAMPLING SPECIALISTS ARE OFTEN NOT FAMILIAR WITH THE FIELDS OF APPLICATION ON WHICH THEIR ADVICE IS SOUGHT

"It is not a minor problem that those who are able to do power calculations readily are generally those who least know the fields of application, and those who best know the fields of application are least able to do power calculations."

SOURCE: Kraemer and Thiemann (1987:99).

An Example: The Statistical Power of an Evaluation of Special Instruction Programs on Aptitude Test Scores[5]

This example is a hypothetical study that was conducted to assess the impact of special instruction programs on aptitude scores of fifth-grade students. It was known from previous studies that the mean score for fifth graders on this test was 200 (see Figure 15.2b), and that the population standard deviation (SD) was 48. The standard error (SE) of the distribution of means (some writers use the term *standard deviation of the distribution of means*, e.g., Aron and Aron 2002:157) for a sample size of 64 is calculated as:

$$SE = \sqrt{SD^2/64} = 6$$

This means that for the null hypothesis (that special instruction did not raise aptitude test scores) to be rejected at the 0.05 level, the mean for the treatment group would have to be greater than

$$200 + (6 \times 1.64) = 209.84$$

Where:

1.64 = Z score for the 0.05 significance level.

The shaded area at the right end of the curve in Figure 15.2b represents the area for rejecting the null hypothesis.[6] Note that the numbers on the horizontal axis represent the distribution of means for all possible samples—not individual test scores.

---

[5]This example uses the Z-test procedures to illustrate the stages of the analysis. Many researchers and computer software use the t-test for testing differences between means. The two procedures are similar, although there are some technical differences (see Frankfort-Nachmias and Leon Guerrero 2011:267–68). It is assumed in this example that the conventional power level of 0.8 is used (see Box 15.6). The table also shows that the sample size increases dramatically if higher power levels (0.90 or 0.95) are specified. It is assumed in this example that the conventional power level of 0.8 is used (see Box 15.6). The table also shows that the sample size increases dramatically if a higher power level (0.90 or 0.95) is used.

[6]This is equivalent to a Z score of 1.64 (see Aron and Aron 2002, chap. 2). The Z score is defined as (sample mean − population mean)/standard deviation of the population mean. In this case (209.84 − 200)/6.

It was hypothesized, based on a review of the literature, that the treatment (special instruction) could be expected to raise the mean test score by 8 points, so that the mean of the treatment group would be 208 points.[7] The effect size (ES) is calculated using the equation:

$$ES = X_2 - X_1/SD$$

Where:

X_2 = the sample mean

X_1 = the population mean

SD = the standard deviation

In this case: $ES = (208 - 200)/48 = 0.166$.

As there is only one sample mean, this equation can be used. In cases where two sample means are being compared it is necessary to estimate the adjusted effect size Δ (see Table 15.4).

The shaded area in the upper distribution (Figure 15.2a) shows the probability that a sample of the treatment group would have a mean score sufficiently high (i.e., above 209.84) to reject the null hypothesis, even when the treatment really does have an effect. In this case the probability is only 40% that a sample from the treatment group would find a statistically significant difference (even when the project has produced a real increase in test scores). In other words, the risk of a Type II error is very high (60%).

Why is this so? Many people might assume that a carefully selected sample of the treatment group would always find a statistically significant difference (if, as in this case, the treatment really did have an effect). The reason can be seen by comparing the two distributions in Figure 15.2. It can be seen that the hypothesized increase in test scores (the effect size) is quite small (0.166), and that there is considerable overlap between the two distributions. This means that if the null hypothesis was true and the treatment had no effect, many samples would by chance have means equal to or greater than the hypothesized treatment mean score of 208. Using the 0.05 significance level, the mean score would have to be greater than 209.84 to reject the null hypothesis—even when the treatment does have an effect.

Figure 15.3 shows the effect of an increased effect size on the power of the test. Under this scenario (scenario 2) the average increase in test scores compared to the control group is 16 points (compared to 8 points in the previous example). This represents an effect size of approximately 0.33. It can be seen in the upper half of the figure (Figure 15.3a) that 85% of the distribution is now to the right of the sample mean required to reject the null hypothesis. This means that the power of the test has increased to 0.85, and there is only a 15% risk of rejecting the null hypothesis (false negative).

Calculating Statistical Power

To calculate the statistical power of the test in a particular evaluation it is necessary to know the effect size (see Table 15.3) and the sample size. The statistical power can then be obtained from a power table (see Table 15.4 for a simplified power table). In our example the effect size is 0.166, which is quite small. Our sample size is 67. Consulting a more complete power table than Table 15.4 (Kraemer and Thiemann 1987, p. 105) shows that for an effect size of 0.17 (with a one-sample t-test) and a sample size of 64 the statistical power = 0.40.

---

[7]It was assumed, as is usually done unless other information is available, that the *SD* of the treatment group would be the same as for the total population.

Figure 15.2   Statistical Power Analysis: Testing the Effect of a Program to Raise Mathematical Aptitude Test Scores (Scenario 1)

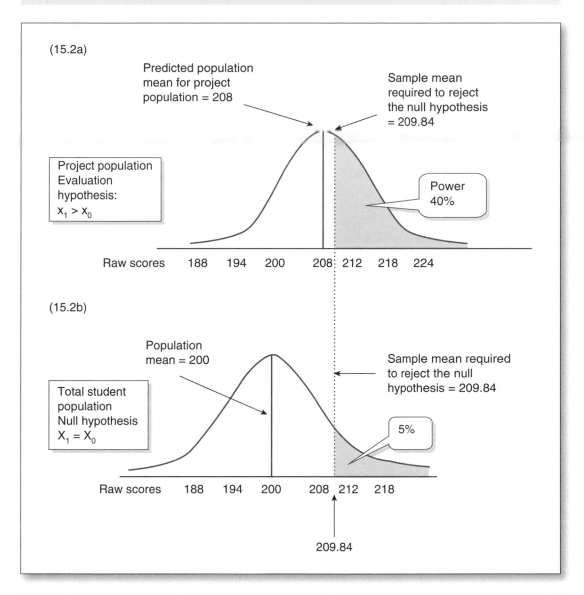

The figure presents the distribution of mean test scores of 64 students on a standardized mathematical aptitude test in a fictional study. The lower curve (Figure 15.2b) is based on the known distribution of means for the total student population and has a mean of 200. The upper distribution (Figure 15.2a) is based on a predicted distribution assuming the evaluation hypothesis (that the treatment raises aptitude score) is correct. It is hypothesized that the mean for the project group is 208, representing an effect size of approximately 0.16. Shaded sections of both curves indicated the areas in which the null hypothesis will be rejected. Power = 0.40, indicating that there is only a 40% probability that any particular sample will reject the null hypothesis, even though the project treatment did produce a statistically significant increase in test scores.

SOURCE: Adapted from Aron and Aron 2002, Figure 7.1. Some of the figures have been slightly adjusted to make the results consistent with the Kraemer and Thiemann power table.

Figure 15.3 Statistical Power Analysis: Testing the Effect of a Program to Raise Mathematical Aptitude Test Scores (Scenario 2)

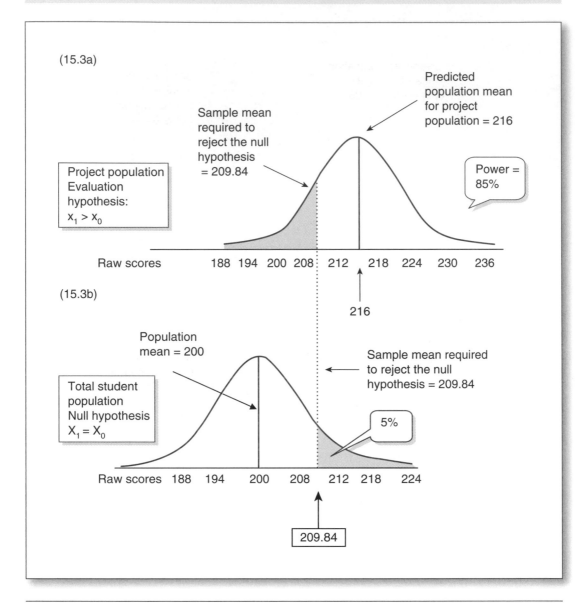

The figure presents the distribution of mean test scores of 64 students on a standardized mathematical aptitude test in a fictional study. The lower curve (Figure 15.3b) is based on the known distribution of means for the total student population and has a mean of 200. The upper distribution (Figure 15.3a) is based on a predicted distribution assuming the evaluation hypothesis (that the treatment raises aptitude score) is correct. It is hypothesized that the mean for the project group is 216, representing an effect size of approximately 0.33. Shaded sections of both curves indicate the areas in which the null hypothesis will be rejected. Power = 0.85, indicating that there is an 85% probability that any particular sample will reject the null hypothesis when the project treatment did produce a statistically significant increase in test scores.

SOURCE: Adapted from Aron and Aron (2002, Figure 7.2). Some of the figures have been slightly adjusted to make the results consistent with the Kraemer and Thiemann power table.

Scenario 1: Project effect size = 8 points test gain (E = 0.166)

Scenario 2: Project effect size = 16 points test gain (E = 0.33)

If the predicted average increase in test scores had been 16 instead of 8 (an effect size of 0.33), then the power of the test would increase to 0.85. In this case the risk of wrongly rejecting a real project effect would drop from 60% in the earlier case to only 15%. Increasing effect size always increases the power of the test, so it is obviously desirable to have as large an effect size as possible. We saw earlier that there are various ways in which the effect size, and consequently the power of the test, can be increased.

So far the discussion of the statistical power of the test has been based upon a sample size of 64. It is important to understand the dramatic effect that the sample size has on the power of the test and consequently on the statistical and operational utility of the findings. If the sample size was significantly larger, the standard error would decrease and the curves in Figure 15.2 would get skinnier. This would mean that there would be less overlap between the top and bottom curves, and the power of the test would increase. This is illustrated in Table 15.3. When the estimated effect size was quite low (0.16) the sample size of 64 only gives a statistical power of 0.40, which is too low to be of any practical utility. If the sample size is increased to 124 the statistical power increases to 0.60, which is higher but still too low to be useful. We can see that a sample size of 211 would be required to achieve a statistical power of 0.80, which is normally considered to be the lowest level to indicate a potentially statistically significant result. Increasing the sample size to 292 and 369 would increase power to 0.90 and 0.95, respectively. On the other hand, when the estimated effect size is 0.32 a sample of 64 already produces an operationally useful power level of 0.85, and the sample would only have to increase to 100 to achieve a 0.95 power level.

Table 15.3 How Sample Size Affects Statistical Power in the Previous Example When Effect Size = 0.16 and 0.32

Effect Size = 0.16		Effect Size = 0.32	
Sample size	Power	Sample size	Power
64	0.40		
93	0.50		
124	0.60		
161	0.70		
211	0.80		
		64	0.85
292	0.90	79	0.90
369	0.95	100	0.95
539	0.99	145	0.99

SOURCE: Statistical power estimated using Kraemer and Thiemann (1987; master table for 5% level and one-tailed test, pp. 105–8).

Deciding How to Set the Power Level

Deciding how to set power involves trade-offs. If a low-power level is used, it will probably be possible to reduce the sample size, but it will be difficult to find results that are statistically significant. So setting a low power level means clients want to pay more attention to effect size than to statistical significance. In the exploratory stage of an evaluation, the goal is often to determine whether there are potentially important effects that should be explored further. From this perspective, it may be worth defining a fairly low power level (increasing the risk of a Type I error) so as not to exclude potentially interesting but small effects.

4.5. One- and Two-Tailed Statistical Significance Tests

Most programs have a clearly defined objective to produce a positive outcome, either by reducing a negative indicator (infant mortality, illiteracy, criminal behavior) or increasing a positive indicator (school attendance rates, household income, agricultural output). When the direction of the desired change is known (to increase school enrollment or reduce malnutrition), a "one-tailed" statistical test can be used. Although this is much less common, the direction of the effect is sometimes not known, and it will be necessary to use a "two-tailed test." For example, introducing school fees might increase enrollment (because the quality of education and the maintenance of the facilities might improve), or it might decrease attendance if many poor families are not able to pay the fees. When a two-tailed test is required the size of the sample will increase between 20–27% when power = 0.8 and 15–23% when power = 0.9.[8] The smaller increases are associated with larger effect sizes.

4.6. Determining the Size of the Sample

The Null Hypothesis, the Evaluation Hypothesis, and Deciding the Power and Statistical Significance Level

To evaluate whether an intervention has had a statistically significant impact, it is necessary to start with a *null hypothesis*. We use a null hypothesis because it is never possible to prove statistically that a hypothesis is true, but only to estimate the probability that an effect size as large as the one observed could have occurred if there really was no difference between the project group and the total population. The null hypothesis states that there is no difference between the total population and the project group with respect to the outcome measure (aptitude test score, household income, proportion of girls attending secondary score, etc.). The null hypothesis (H_0) is specified as follows:

$H_0: x_0 = x_1$

Where:

x_0 = mean or other outcome measure for the total population

x_1 = mean or other outcome measure for the project population

---

[8]Kraemer and Thiemann (1987) include master tables for both one- and two-tailed tests.

The alternative research hypothesis (H_1) is that there is a difference between the project and comparison groups, which is specified as follows:

$$H_1: x_0 \neq x_1$$

A key decision in the evaluation design is the relative importance of (a) ensuring that H_1 is not accepted when it is not true (false positive), and (b) not rejecting H_1 when it is true (false negative). Traditionally researchers have been concerned to avoid the false positive and have required a high standard for rejecting H_0. Conventionally a statistical significance level of 0.05 is used, meaning that H_0 will only be rejected if there is less than a 1 in 20 chance of it being true. The higher the statistical significance requirement for rejecting the null hypothesis, the more difficult it is to accept H_1 and to decide that the project intervention did have an effect. Consequently, evaluators and program managers concerned to identify effective interventions will often use a less stringent significance level so as to increase the likelihood of detecting a project effect. This is particularly important in the development field, where many well-designed programs (e.g., health, education, poverty reduction) are expected to only produce a small improvement (the expected effect size is small). Consequently, the use of stringent significance levels means that many small but important effects may not be detected. So an important challenge for the evaluator is to decide on the relative importance of false positives and false negatives, and to select appropriate statistical significance levels for the testing of H_0 and H_1. In a RealWorld environment the challenge is to satisfy the client's needs for acceptably precise estimates for the purposes of decision making while remaining within the available budget and time.

Evaluability Assessment

Many evaluators become overwhelmed by the statistical calculations required to estimate sample size, and it is often forgotten that there are several important preliminary steps in the evaluation before even thinking about testing and sample sizes. The first step involves a thorough review of the existing evidence from the research literature, reports of similar programs, and if possible, discussions with experts. This will help determine whether the proposed program is likely to have an effect. An exploratory field study should then be conducted to understand the program and how it operates, and to determine whether the program effects can be measured at this point in time, for this particular project, and with the available resources. This *evaluability assessment* may suggest various reasons why an evaluation may not be appropriate. The literature may suggest the program model is unlikely to work, it may be considered too early in the project cycle to measure effects, the target population may be too small to permit the kinds of statistical analysis required, or the proposed effects may be too difficult to quantify and measure. Assuming that none of these problems are considered too serious, it is then possible to begin to plan the evaluation. Henry (1990, chap. 3) and Kraemer and Thiemann (1987, chap. 2) provide useful overviews of these preparatory stages of the evaluation.

Estimating the Required Sample Size for Power Analysis[9]

The choice of sample size cannot be made in a vacuum, as there are trade-offs concerning the most effective way to use the evaluation resources. For example, spending more on sample

---

[9]For a more detailed discussion on the estimation of sample size, see Henry (1990, chap. 7).

size may mean less resources/time for following up on nonresponses to reduce this often important source of nonsampling bias. Each of the steps is illustrated for a hypothetical example in which the required sample size for evaluating the impact of special instructions on student performance on a standardized mathematical aptitude test is estimated. We use the previous example but change several details.

The purpose of the evaluation is to determine whether the special instruction has produced a statistically significant increase in student performance on the standardized mathematical aptitude test. In the present case:

- The mean aptitude test score for the total student population is again 200, and the population standard deviation, based on previous studies, is again estimated to be 48.
- The survey will only cover students who received the special instruction, because the mean and standard deviation of test scores for the total student population are known. Consequently, this is a *single sample comparison* with the population mean.
- The total fifth-grade student population is over 20,000, and the number of fifth-grade students who have received the special instructions is 5,000.
- The null hypothesis to be tested is: $H_0 = H_1$. Where :

    H_0 = the mean aptitude test score for the total fifth-grade student population

    H_1 = the mean aptitude test score for students who have received special instruction.

The following steps must be followed for determining the efficient sample size:

Step 1: Determine the purpose of the evaluation. Smaller sample sizes are usually needed for exploratory studies than for testing hypotheses concerning project effects.

~ **The more precise the required results the greater the required sample size.**

In the example, the Ministry of Education stated that the purpose of the evaluation is to determine whether the special instruction program is a cost-effective way to increase student mathematical skills. The ministry also needs to demonstrate that the program is more effective than other approaches. There are many supporters of alternative mathematics teaching programs who will try to challenge the findings, so the ministry requires "acceptable professional levels of significance testing."

Step 2: Determine if it's a one- or two-tailed test. In most cases a one-tailed test will be used, but the evaluator should always check this.

~ **Using a two-tailed test will increase the sample size by about 40%.**

In the example the purpose is to test whether aptitude scores have increased, so a one-tailed test is appropriate.

Step 3: Estimate the standard deviation (SD) of the population.[10] The size of the SD will affect the estimation of the effect size and consequently the sample size. Sometimes the SD is known from previous studies. In other cases it can be estimated from a small pilot study.[11]

~ **The larger the SD the larger the required sample size.**

In the present example testing has found that the mean test score for fifth-grade students is 200 and the SD is 48. It is assumed that the SD will be similar for the project population.[12]

Step 4: Determine the minimum acceptable effect size (MAES).

~ **The smaller the MAES the larger the required sample size.**

A meta-analysis review of other programs to increase math skills has found that effect sizes range between 0.1 and 0.25. In addition, the ministry indicated that a 5% increase in test scores is the minimum effect that could justify funding to continue the program. This would require an increase of 10 points in the average population test score of 200. With a population SD of 48, this is equivalent to an effect size of:

$$MAES = [210 - 200]/48 = 0.208 \text{ (this is rounded to 0.2 to simplify the calculations)}$$

Step 5: Determine whether the statistical significance of the findings will be tested at the 0.01 level (when a high level of precision is required), at the 0.05 level (the normally accepted level), or at the 0.1 level (for exploratory studies).

~ **The higher the required significance level the larger the sample.**

In the example, it is agreed to use the 0.05 significance level.

Step 6: Decide on the required power of the test.

~ **The higher the required power the larger the sample.**

---

[10]It is important to check that estimates of the *SD* from previous studies are applicable. If different populations were studied or different questions were asked, earlier studies may not provide a good estimate of the *SD* for the present study.

[11]Henry (1990:119) suggests that if no other information is available, a rough estimate can be obtained by dividing the range (the difference between the highest and lowest values of the variable) by 4. However, doing a power analysis for proportions requires a different procedure, which does not require the standard deviation.

[12]It is usually assumed that the project group will have the same standard deviation as the total population. However, in **nonequivalent control group designs** it is possible that the project group could have a different standard deviation. Where sample precision is important, it would be useful to consult with a statistician as to whether an adjustment should be made. For most RWE purposes, this is probably not a major concern.

In the example, the ministry agrees to use the conventional power = 0.8. It initially wished to use the 0.9 power level to achieve a higher level of statistical precision, but when it was advised that this would increase the sample size by more than 200 interviews (increase from 618 to 854) it decided to accept the 0.8 level.

Step 7: Consult a master statistical power table to calculate the required sample size for a given effect size and power level. Table 15.4 is a simplified version of a power table that only covers the 0.05 significance level and only a one-tailed test.[13] The use of the table involves the following steps:

- Determine whether a one- or two-sample comparison is being used. In a one-sample comparison a sample mean is compared with the population mean, as is the case with the present example. When two samples are being compared, as is the case when the project sample is compared with a control group sample, then an adjusted effect size must be used (the second column of Table 15.4).
- When a one-sample model is used the effect size (ES) can be read directly from the master power table. This is the first column in Table 15.4.
- If a two-sample model is used the adjusted effect size is obtained from the second column of Table 15.4.[14]
- Decide the required significance level and then consult the appropriate power table. In our example, Table 15.4 assumes that the significance level is set at 0.05.
- Consult the column for the specified power.
- Consult the row for the effect size or adjusted effect size.
- Locate the intersecting cell to find the required sample size for each group.

In the example:

- The client indicated that normal standards of professional precision should be followed, so the 0.05 significance level will be used.
- The power level is 0.80.
- As this is a one-sample test, the effect size column is consulted and the 0.2 value is used. This is the MAES. The intersection of the power column and 0.2 row shows that 618 interviews would be required.

Step 8: Determine whether to use the finite population correction factor. When the sample represents a high proportion (i.e., more than say 10%) of the total population it is possible to use the finite population correction factor (FPCF) to improve the precision of the estimates (or to produce a slight

---

[13]For more comprehensive master tables covering both one- and two-tailed tests and 0.5 and 0.1 confidence levels, see Kraemer and Thiemann (1987:105–12).

[14]The following equation is used to obtain the adjusted effect size (Δ):

$\Delta = ES/(ES^2 + 1/pq)^{1/2}$

Where: ES = effect size; p and q = the proportion of the sample in group 1 and group 2, respectively.

reduction in the sample size). In the present example the sample size is only about 3% of the total student population of 20,000, so the use of the FPCF is not required.

Estimating Power for Multiple Regression

In this chapter we only discuss the calculation of power for the comparison of sample means. The calculation of power for multiple regression is a little more complicated, as it is necessary to estimate the number of variables in the model, the size of the partial correlation of the variable of interest and the outcome (controlling for all other variables in the model), and the multiple correlation of all the other variables in the model with the outcome. For a discussion of power analysis for linear regression see Kraemer and Thiemann (1987, chap. 6).

4.7. Factors Affecting the Sample Size

In addition to the factors discussed earlier the required sample size is affected by the following:

- The reliability of the instrument used to measure effect. In cases whether effects cannot be reliably measured the variance of the estimates increases and the sample size required to achieve a certain power also increases.
- The evaluation design. More sophisticated evaluation designs that include intervening (mediator) variables can reduce the variance and consequently the required sample size to achieve a certain statistical power.
- The estimated sample drop-out rate (for panel studies).
- Changes in the size and characteristics of the total study population (for longitudinal studies).
- If effect size can be increased this will automatically increase statistical power and/or permit sample size to be reduced. As indicated earlier it may be possible to increase effect size by improving the design and administration of the treatment (special instruction) or by limiting the study to those groups where the effect is expected to be greatest.

Table 15.4 Approximate Sample Sizes for One- and Two-Group Comparisons of Means to Attain Various Criterion Levels of Power for a Range of Effect Sizes with a One-Tail Test and Significance Level = 0.05

Effect Size		Power			
Effect size (ES) for comparing a single sample with the population mean	Adjusted effect size (Δ) for comparison of two sample means	0.95	0.90	0.80	0.60
0.10	0.05	4325	3423	2472	1142
0.20	0.10	1078	854	618	361
0.30	0.15	477	378	274	161
0.40	0.20	267	212	154	91

(Continued)

(Continued)

Effect Size		Power			
Effect size (ES) for comparing a single sample with the population mean	Adjusted effect size (Δ) for comparison of two sample means	0.95	0.90	0.80	0.60
0.50	0.24	184	146	107	64
0.6	0.29	125	100	73	39
0.8	0.37	76	60	45	26
1.0	0.45	50	40	30	19
1.2	0.51	39	26	19	13
1.4	0.57	28	22	16	
1.6	0.62	24	19	14	
1.8	0.67	18	15		
2.0	0.71	16	14		

NOTES:

1. The numbers in the table refer to the required sample size for different combinations of effect size and power. For two-group studies the number refers to the total sample size for the two groups. It is assumed that the sample size will be the same for both groups. If the sample sizes are different this may require a slight adjustment to the estimated total sample size (see note 3).

2. The effect size column is used for one-group analysis (comparing a sample with the total population). This is a slightly simplified estimate, as an adjustment should be made for the single sample t-test (Kraemer and Thiemann 1987, p. 101, and chap. 4, section 4.2), but the effect of the adjustment is very small.

3. The adjusted effect size column is for the comparison of two groups (e.g., comparing project and comparison groups). This uses the adjustment formula for the two sample t-test: $\Delta = ES/(ES^2 + 1/pq)^{1/2}$ where: Δ = adjusted effect size; ES = effect size; p and q = proportion of the sample in group 1 (e.g., project group) and group 2 (e.g., the comparison group) (Kraemer and Thiemann 1987, p. 101, and chap. 4, section 4.3). In the table we have assumed the sample size will be equal for both groups. Sample sizes could be adjusted slightly if the proportions were not equal.

4. The table assumes a one-tailed test at the 0.05 significance level. The required sample size increases between 15%–30% when a two-tailed test is used (depending on the power level). Required sample sizes increase if the 0.01 significance level is used. When the 1% significance level is used there is a significant increase in the required sample size (for example, there is an increase of approximately 45% for the 0.95 power level and approximately 60% for the 0.80 power level).

SOURCE: Calculations by the present authors based on Kraemer and Thiemann (1987, master tables).

5. The Contribution of Meta-Analysis

Meta-analysis is the review and synthesis of all research or evaluation studies that have been conducted in a particular field. Meta-analysis has proved particularly helpful in estimating the range of effect sizes that have been produced by programs in a particular sector. This provides a reference point for defining the effect size that can reasonably be expected for the program being evaluated and, consequently, is a valuable guide for estimating the required sample size. Table 15.5 summarizes some of the average effect sizes found in a meta-analysis of 221 programs addressing aggressive behavior in schools. None of the average effect sizes for any of the five types of intervention exceeds 0.33, and for multimodal approaches the average is only 0.15. If an evaluation of a new social competence program using techniques other than cognitive behavior was being planned, it would seem reasonable to assume that even a very successful intervention would probably not have an effect size greater than 0.3, so the total sample size for the two groups (with power = 0.90) would be around 182. Using power = 0.8, the required sample size for the two groups would be reduced to 132.

Table 15.5 Mean Effect Sizes for Different Interventions Addressing Aggressive Behavior in Schools

Therapy or counseling services	0.33
Social competence training using cognitive-behavioral approaches	0.27
Behavioral and classroom management techniques	0.22
Social competence training using techniques other than cognitive-behavioral approaches	0.20
Multimodal programs	0.15

SOURCE: Rossi, Lipsey, and Freeman (2004:326, Exhibit 10-G).

Another very important finding from this study was that for many programs with an effect size less than 0.3, the sample size was too small to detect a statistically significant effect. The authors conclude that greater attention must be given to estimating the power of the test for small effect sizes to avoid many Type II errors whereby it was incorrectly concluded that programs had no effect.

6. Sampling Issues for Mixed-Method Evaluations

This section provides guidelines for sampling strategies and estimation of sample size for some of the most common mixed-method designs.

6.1. Model 1: Using Mixed Methods to Strengthen a Mainly Quantitative Evaluation Design

With this primarily QUANT evaluation design sample surveys are administered before and after the project treatment (pretest-posttest) or with a control or comparison group design (randomized control trial, regression discontinuity, quasi-experimental design). Qualitative methods are incorporated to strengthen the design. The required sample size for the QUANT surveys are estimated using the effective size and power principles discussed in the previous section. Qualitative methods can be applied at one or more of the following points:

- *Exploratory or diagnostic study to understand the context and issues before the survey instruments are developed.* These can either involve a rapid qualitative study lasting only a few days, or it can involve an anthropologist or sociologist living in, or spending considerable amounts of time in, the communities (sometimes a month or more). In a large project operating in different geographical or ecological regions diagnostic studies might be required in a number of different regions or communities. Sometimes the studies will be conducted by an individual researcher (one researcher per community or region), while in other cases the lead researcher might be assisted by a team of assistants who conduct rapid surveys or conduct participant or nonparticipant observation studies on, for example, community transport systems, women's time use, and production and marketing systems. Although the studies may last for several days or weeks, the primary sampling unit will usually be a community or group, and normally only a few groups or communities will be studied. However, large numbers of individuals may be interviewed using unstructured or semistructured data collection techniques, and in some cases rapid sample surveys may also be conducted.

- *Focus groups conducted with different sectors of the target population.* These can either be conducted during the preparatory stage of the evaluation or after the quantitative surveys have been analyzed and the principal groups of interest have been identified. Ideally, three or four focus groups should be conducted with each economic or demographic group of interest to the evaluation (Teddlie and Tashakkori 2009, Table 8.5), although the numbers of groups will often be smaller when working under budget and time constraints.

- *Specialized semistructured modules can be added to a sample survey and administered to a subsample of respondents.* For example, the main survey may be administered to the household head (who in many cultures may be male), but in a subsample of households the wife may be interviewed. In some cases the same interviewer can administer the special module to the wife (or other household member), but in many cases it may be necessary to arrange a separate interview, often in a location or at a time when the husband or other household members will not be present (and will not bias the responses). Typically these modules are administered to between 10 and 25% of the original sample, although the proportion can vary.

- *Preparation of case studies to complement the survey.* It is often useful to prepare case studies on a small sample of respondents covered in the survey to provide a fuller understanding of the issues of interest to the evaluation. For example, in the evaluation of an agricultural program, case studies might be conducted to illustrate different kinds of farming systems. For an education project, the cases might cover higher- and lower-income families, those who live close to and further from the school, or, where appropriate, families from different religious or ethnic groups. Again, the number of cases will normally be quite small, although the duration may be quite long. When case studies are prepared on organizations (such as schools or agricultural cooperatives) or cover whole communities (for example, to illustrate the effects of improved transport systems), the study will be more complicated, and often significant numbers of individuals will be interviewed for each case.

6.2. Model 2: Using a Mixed-Method Design to Strengthen a Qualitative Evaluation Design

Mixed-method designs can also be used to strengthen a qualitative evaluation design that has mainly used techniques such as focus groups, participant observation, nonparticipant observation, and the preparation of case studies. A challenge for many of these designs is the danger of bias due to the fact that the samples of individuals or groups are not representative. For example, often people who attend focus groups are those who have strong feelings for or against a project, those who have the time and resources to attend (they may have to arrange transport), or in some cases (often without the knowledge of the evaluator), some participants may be sent by the local government or other group with particular interest. Similarly, many researchers feel more comfortable talking to some groups than to others, so there may be a bias in the selection of the case studies. Quantitative techniques, such as a rapid sample survey, can be a useful way to compare the socioeconomic characteristics of the individuals or groups covered in the qualitative studies with the characteristics of the total population. Usually the survey instrument is quite short and the sample is relatively small, but the number of interviews vary depending on the size of the population studied and the required level of precision of the findings.

6.3. Model 3: Using an Integrated Mixed-Method Design

While in most cases the mixed-method designs described in the previous sections are used to complement a quantitative survey or a qualitative evaluation, there are cases in which a more rigorous, integrated mixed-method design might be used. These designs can involve the combination of quantitative and qualitative techniques, as well as specific mixed-method techniques, at each stage of the evaluation. There is no standard way to estimate the sample sizes, as the designs can vary considerably and the sample sizes must be estimated using the approaches discussed in the previous paragraphs.

Table 15.6 Estimated Minimum Sample Sizes Required for Different Types of Qualitative Research Components of Mixed-Method Designs

Type of Qualitative Research Design	Estimated Sample Size Required
Case studies	One can suffice, especially if it is a revelatory case study or has unique characteristics; an upper limit of 15 is suggested by some methodologists. Case studies of institutions often vary from approximately 4 to 12 studies; case studies of individuals may be larger, often ranging from approximately 6 to 24 cases.
Ethnography	Typically, one cultural group is sampled; about 30 to 50 interviews are conducted.
Focus groups	Three to four groups per demographic category are sampled (e.g., white Republican women, African-American Democratic men), with 6 to 8 participants per group.
Grounded theory	Around 20 to 50 interviews are conducted.

SOURCE: Teddlie and Tashakkori, 2009, p. 184, Table 8.5).

7. Sampling Issues for RealWorld Evaluation

Data collection is usually one of the largest budget items for an evaluation, so reducing sample size is usually one of the easiest ways to save costs and time. However, if the sample size or design is inappropriate, the validity of evaluation findings will be jeopardized. In probabilistic sampling, if the sample size becomes too small, there is the danger of committing Type II errors and rejecting real project effects. As discussed earlier, this is a particular problem when the expected effect size is small. The potential benefits and dangers involved in sampling show the importance of the scoping phase (Step 1) of the RWE approach. The evaluator should understand the purposes of the evaluation, how the results will be used, and the types of decisions to which the evaluation will contribute. There are two challenges: (a) to avoid using a larger sample than is required for the purposes of the study, and (b) to ensure that the sample is appropriate and large enough for the types of analysis and findings desired.

One important sampling decision is whether a comparison group is required. In QUANT experimental and quasi-experimental designs, a comparison group is required for both the baseline and the posttest surveying or testing. Complete elimination of the pre- and posttest comparison group would probably reduce the cost of data collection significantly, but the lack of a comparison group would also significantly weaken the validity of the evaluation results. In QUAL and mixed-method designs, comparison groups may also be useful for fully understanding program effects, although, in some cases, they may not be of critical importance for detailing program merits and shortcomings.

When time, personnel, and budget are severe constraints, various options may be worth considering. For example, a QUANT evaluator might choose to use documentary or secondary data rather than to survey or test a comparison group. This may be a way to produce significant cost savings, but again, the trade-offs with respect to validity should be considered. The guidelines in Chapter 5 are designed to help to assess the strengths and weaknesses of a variety of decisions and alternatives concerning the use of documentary data.

7.1. Lot Quality Acceptance Sampling (LQAS): An Example of a Sampling Strategy Designed to Be Economical and Simple to Administer and Interpret

Lot quality acceptance sampling (LQAS) is an example of an approach designed to work with small, economical, and easily administered samples that has recently been gaining in popularity (Valadez and Devkota 2002). Originally developed as an industrial quality-control tool, the first application to social development was to assess the achievement of coverage targets for local health delivery systems. LQAS has now been used to assess immunization coverage, antenatal care, oral rehydration, growth monitoring, family planning, disease incidence, and natural disaster relief.

LQAS is used to assess whether *coverage benchmarks* have been achieved in particular project locations. An example of a benchmark would be ensuring that 80% of families have received oral rehydration kits and orientation, or that 70% of farmers have received information on new seed varieties. A major advantage of this approach is that a sample of 19 (households, farmers, etc.) will normally be sufficient to estimate whether any level of benchmark coverage (above 20%) has been achieved for a particular target area, with no greater than a 10% error. For most operational quality-control purposes a 10% error is considered satisfactory, although for more rigorous evaluation studies a higher confidence level (e.g., 0.05%) might be required, in which case a larger sample would be required. The findings are very simple to analyze, as the number of required positive responses is defined for any given benchmark coverage level. For example, if the target coverage level is 80%, then the sample of 19 families (farms, etc.) must find at least 13 cases where the service had been satisfactorily received. If the target coverage was 60%, then the sample must find at least nine satisfactory cases. So in addition to the advantage of very small samples, an LQAS study is very easy for health workers, agricultural extension workers, and other nonresearch specialists to administer and interpret.

Table 15.7 Lot Quality Acceptance Sampling: Decision Rules for Determining the Minimum Number of Units with Satisfactory Delivery of Information or Services to Accept That a Particular Benchmark Level of Satisfactory Services Has Been Achieved (ß errors > 10%).

Sample size of 19 is considered adequate to test for all benchmark levels greater than 20%									
	Coverage Benchmarks								
Sample size	20%	30%	40%	50%	60%	70%	80%	90%	95%
	Minimum Number of Target Units Where Satisfactory Delivery of Information or Service Has Been Achieved for the Benchmark to Have Been Achieved								
19	1	3	5	7	9	11	13	15	16

SOURCES: Adapted from Valadez and Devkota (2002) and Valadez and Bamberger (1994, chap. 11).

SUMMARY

- Sampling issues are important for both QUAL and QUANT evaluations, but the approaches to sampling tend to be quite different in each case.
- QUAL evaluations tend to use *purposive sampling* to carefully select a small number of cases that represent all the main categories of interest to the study. Although random sampling would not be appropriate with these kinds of small samples, each sample is selected to ensure that the maximum amount of information is obtained.
- In contrast, QUANT evaluations normally use random sampling procedures to ensure that the selected sample is statistically representative of the total population so that generalizations can be made from the sample to this population with a measurable level of statistical precision.
- For QUANT evaluations, questionnaire administration and other forms of data collection usually represent one of the largest cost items in an evaluation; therefore, when RWE constraints require cost reductions, reducing the size of the sample is always a tempting option.
- However, if the sample is too small (as is often the case when there are budget and time constraints), it will not be possible to identify statistically significant relations between the project interventions and the production of the desired outcomes and impacts—even when they do exist.
- Consequently, deciding what is the appropriate sample size to achieve the desired levels of precision of the evaluation findings is one of the critical evaluation design decisions.
- Two key factors in the estimation of sample size are the estimated *effect size* (how large a change the project is expected to produce if it is successful) and statistical *power analysis* (the required level of significance that the project effect will be detected if it really exists). The smaller the expected effect size, the larger the sample

needed to detect the effect. The higher the required level of confidence (power), the larger the required sample size.

• Estimating the effect size and adjusting the power of the test are two of the key factors in estimating sample size.

• When there are cost pressures to reduce sample size, this can be achieved either by accepting a lower power (a higher risk that a real project effect will not be detected) or by finding ways to increase the effect size (e.g., studying only those groups where the project is expected to have a larger effect).

FURTHER READING

Aron, A. and E. Aron. 2002. *Statistics for the Behavioral and Social Sciences: A Brief Course.* 2d ed. Upper Saddle River, NJ: Prentice Hall.

This is a thorough, clear review of all the statistical concepts discussed in the present text. Chapter 7 provides a good overview of statistical power analysis and effect size. There is also a companion study guide and workbook.

Fink, A. 2003b. *How to Sample in Surveys. Vol. 7, The Survey Kit.* 2d ed. Thousand Oaks, CA: Sage.

A useful introduction to sample design.

Henry, G. 1990. *Practical Sampling.* Newbury Park, CA: Sage.

A thorough, clear review of sample design and power analysis.

Khandker, S., G. Koolwal, and H. Samad. 2010. *Handbook on Impact Evaluation: Quantitative Methods and Practices.* Washington, DC: World Bank.

Introduction to the use of econometric methods in impact evaluation. Includes a thorough but readable explanation of techniques such as randomized control trials, propensity score matching, regression discontinuity, and double-difference analysis that are discussed in this book. Also includes large numbers of case studies illustrating how the techniques are used in the field.

Kraemer, H. C. and S. Thiemann. 1987. *How Many Subjects? Statistical Power Analysis in Research.* Newbury Park, CA: Sage.

A comprehensive and quite technical discussion of the estimation of sample sizes with different kinds of statistical tests. Chapters 1 and 10 provide a useful summary of key issues in sample size estimation. This book also contains master tables for estimating sample size with different levels of confidence and for one- and two-tailed tests.

Lohr, S. 1999. *Sampling Design and Analysis.* New York: Duxbury Press.

Covers all the methods and procedures for sample design and analysis, including a chapter on the treatment of nonresponse. Also includes a CD with a comprehensive data set (including survey instruments and complete information on the sampling frame) and a set of exercises that can be used to practice all the different sampling designs. A useful feature for RWE is that the database also includes cost data so that the impact of different sample designs on the evaluation budget can be tested.

Rossi, P., M. Lipsey, and H. Freeman. 2004. *Evaluation: A Systematic Approach.* 7th ed. Thousand Oaks, CA: Sage.

Chapter 10 presents an overview of power analysis and the estimation of sample size.

Sirken, R. 1999. *Statistics for the Social Sciences.* Thousand Oaks, CA: Sage.

Comprehensive and clear coverage of the application of statistics in the social sciences, which pertains to the statistical techniques discussed in this chapter.

Valadez, J. and B. R. Devkota. 2002. "Decentralized Supervision of Community Health Programs: Using LQAS in Two Districts in Southern Nepal." Pp. 169–200 in *Community-Based Health Care: Lessons from Bangladesh to Boston.* Boston, MA: Management Sciences for Health, Inc.

An easy-to-understand explanation of the theory and practical applications in the field of lot quality acceptance sampling.

CHAPTER 16

Evaluating Complicated, Complex, Multicomponent Programs[1]

In this chapter we discuss strategies for evaluating "complicated" and "complex" development interventions that include many different components, cover more than one sector, operate at the national level, or involve cooperation among several different funding agencies. Often they may also provide general budget support to the government without clearly defined objectives and scopes of work. While many donor agencies are investing increasing proportions of their development assistance through these complex interventions, methodologies for evaluating these complex interventions are still at an early stage of development. The chapter begins by discussing the move toward complex, country-level development programming. The terms simple projects, complicated programs, and complex interventions are then defined, and the challenges of evaluating complex interventions are discussed. A range of theory-based, quantitative, qualitative, and mixed-method approaches are then described for the evaluation of these interventions. The final section of the chapter illustrates how the different evaluation techniques can be applied to the evaluation of country assistance strategies—a typical example of a complex program.

1. The Move Toward Complex, Country-Level Development Programming

In 2000 most major international development agencies signed the Millennium Development Goals (MDGs), which recognized the need to define development objectives in terms of eight broad

---

[1]This chapter draws on material developed for the American Evaluation Association (AEA) think tanks in 2009 and 2010 organized by Jim Rugh, Michael Bamberger, and Fred Carden on "Alternative to the Conventional Counterfactual," and also a 2010 International Program for Development Evaluation Training (IPDET) workshop on "Assessing Program Impacts When a Statistical Evaluation Design Is Not Possible," presented by Frans Leeuw and Michael Bamberger. See also Patton (2011) and Rogers (2008). Although they make distinctions between "complicated" and "complex," we use the terms somewhat interchangeably in this book.

development goals and a set of subgoals and specific indicators for each of these (see Box 16.1). These affirmed the growing recognition that in order to focus on the big picture, development should be structured around and evaluated in terms of a set of broad goals that encompassed the main areas of development. The MDGs recognized the need to develop a broad framework for assessing the overall contribution to development of the large number of projects and sector-specific programs being supported by different development agencies, and for assessing the overall impact of the efforts of the government as well as many different development agencies working in a particular country.

BOX 16.1
THE MILLENNIUM DEVELOPMENT GOALS

1. Eradicate extreme poverty and hunger

2. Achieve universal primary education

3. Promote gender equality and empower women

4. Reduce child mortality

5. Improve maternal health

6. Combat HIV/AIDS, malaria, and other diseases

7. Ensure environmental sustainability

8. Develop a global partnership for development

SOURCE : www.un.org/millenniumgoals/

The MDG initiative was also driven by the increasing demands from parliaments, public opinion, civil society, and academia to address the question, "Does aid work?" These concerns were reflected in the 2002 Monterrey Consensus on Financing for Development (Morra-Imas and Rist 2009:76), which sought to distribute more money to the world's poorest people—those living on less than one dollar a day—while at the same time increasing the efficiency and effectiveness with which aid is managed. The Monterrey Consensus also stressed the need for mutual responsibility between donor agencies and recipient countries to improve the quality and management of aid. This had important implications for both the focus of development evaluation (assessing the broader impacts of aid rather than just the impacts of individual, clearly defined projects) and also how evaluations should be managed (greater participation of the recipient country in the management of evaluations and greater cooperation among donor agencies in the conduct of evaluations).

The focus on broader national development objectives was further formalized in the 2005 Paris Declaration on Aid Effectiveness,[2] which was endorsed by more than 100 ministers, heads of agencies, and other senior officials. The indictors and targets were organized around five key principles:

- *Ownership.* Partner countries exercise effective leadership over their development policies and strategies and coordinate development actions.

---

[2]For the Paris Declaration and Accra Accord, see www.oecd.org/document/18/0,3343,en_2649_3236398_35401554_1_1_1_1,00.html

- *Alignment.* Development organizations base their overall support on partner countries' national development strategies.
- *Harmonization.* Development organizations' actions are more harmonized, transparent, and collectively effective.
- *Managing for results.* Governments are moving toward an emphasis on managing resources and improving decision making for results.
- *Mutual accountability.* Development organizations and partners are jointly accountable for development results.

As a result of these and subsequent conventions (such as the 2008 Accra Accords[3]) development has evolved toward a more comprehensive agenda, increasingly addressing country policy reforms, capacity building, and global concerns (Organization for Economic Cooperation and Development/ Development Advisory Committee [OECD-DAC] 2010b). Heath, Grasso, and Johnson (2005, cited by Morra-Imas and Rist 2009) also highlight the implications for development evaluation:

- Reorienting its focus from just project, program, or activity level to the country, sector, thematic, regional, or global level
- Determining how best to aggregate outcomes of interventions at the activity and country level in order to assess global or program-wide results
- Finding ways to assess the influence of program design, partnerships approach, and governance on overall results
- Seeking replicability at a higher level and applicability at the system level

The above kinds of interventions are commonly referred to as *complex* programs or development interventions. The term was coined to reflect the greater difficulties that development agencies experience in trying to assess the effectiveness of these interventions in achieving their often very broad objectives. Conventional evaluation methods that work relatively well for assessing the impacts of individual projects normally cannot be applied to the kinds of broad-based development initiatives described in the previous paragraphs. In particular, it has proved very difficult to define a counterfactual to address several related questions:

- What would have been the situation if the intervention had not taken place?
- How does this hypothetical situation compare with the actual situation after the intervention (or at some point during the implementation of the intervention)?
- To what extent can the difference between the hypothetical no-intervention and the with-intervention situation be attributed to the effect of the intervention?
- Just what is "the intervention" being evaluated, when there are many different policies and programs being implemented by many different agencies?

In the rest of this chapter we will discuss evaluation strategies that can be used to try to develop and apply a credible counterfactual. We will begin by discussing the characteristics of complex interventions, how they differ from other kinds of development interventions, and why they are so difficult to evaluate.

---

[3] www.unctad.org/en/docs//tdxii_accra_accord_en.pdf

2. Simple Projects, Complicated Programs, and Complex Development Interventions

It is helpful to begin by distinguishing between *simple* projects, *complicated* programs, and *complex* development interventions (see Figure 16.1). There is considerable overlap between these three categories but the distinctions are useful as they are associated with important differences in the kinds of evaluation designs that can be used.

"Simple" projects refers to the limited-scope, relatively precise definition of objectives and an organizational structure that does not involve too many actors or levels. "Simple" does not mean that the project is easy to implement or that there is a high probability of success. Many "simple" projects operate in poor and vulnerable communities with high levels of insecurity and conflict. Consequently, success in achieving project objectives will often be quite low, particularly for the kinds of quantitative objectives that funders expect to be achieved in a relatively short time period. "Simple" projects usually have many, but not necessarily all, of the following characteristics:

- They are frequently based on a blueprint approach that is implemented in a very similar way in each project location, and that is intended to produce a uniform set of products or services.
- The number of project components is usually relatively small.
- Although a great deal of time and effort may have gone into their design, the implementation procedures are usually relatively straightforward and require a low level of technical expertise. However, implementation will often require a high level of cultural sensitivity and communication skills.
- They usually have a clearly defined target population that is often, but not always, relatively small.
- The objectives are usually, but not always, clearly defined.
- Projects are often, but not always, time-bound and have clearly defined start and end dates. This is particularly true for externally funded projects, which tend to include a project agreement document indicating duration as well as funding and objectives.
- There is often a defined budget, frequently from one major source.
- Projects are often based on a logic or program theory model that lays out the objectives, stages of implementation, and performance indicators.
- The project implementation process is often described as being relatively linear, with a defined set of inputs expected to produce a defined set of outputs that in turn produce a set of outcomes or impacts.

For a more detailed discussion of simple projects it will usually be necessary to distinguish between (a) projects funded by multilateral or bilateral development agencies, international and national foundations and NGOs, and national governments, on the one hand, and (b) local projects that depend on creative funding campaigns which often generate resources from a number of different sources. For example, a project that is supported by a bilateral development agency will often be based on a signed project document that defines objectives, methods of operation, time horizons, and usually the budget. On the other hand, a local project run by a local NGO, possibly with multiple small sources of funding, will have a very different dynamic and frequently will have less clearly defined goals and objectives, and often no time horizon. These distinctions should be kept in mind when discussing the characteristics of simple projects.

As indicated earlier, it is difficult to draw a clear line between simple, complicated, and complex interventions. In fact, many relatively small activities that satisfy most of the criteria of a simple project actually involve a number of different activities. For example, a project whose main function is to provide information to men and women who are HIV positive and to encourage them to visit a clinic may in some cases find it necessary to provide transport for very poor clients to help them get to the clinic, or may have to provide intervention counseling in cases of domestic violence. So the seemingly "simple" project may include elements of a complicated program. A further complication is that some projects that only provide one or a small number of services may be operating in an area where successful outcomes may require complex processes of behavioral change—which are neither simple to implement nor to evaluate.

One example of a simple project would be a school feeding program designed to increase enrollment, attendance, and possibly educational performance. Another example would be construction of rural feeder roads to enhance access to health clinics and schools, and to increase income for small farmers. A third would be leadership training to strengthen capacity of local communities to manage local development projects.

Simple projects can usually be evaluated using some of the quantitative, qualitative, and mixed-method evaluation designs described in the earlier chapters of this book. Complicated programs usually have the following characteristics:

- They are often a combination of simple projects, each providing a different service. For example, a secondary education improvement program might incorporate projects providing textbooks, school sanitation, teacher training, and school feeding.
- They usually have a broader target population, which is often less precisely defined. Examples include all secondary school–age children, or all villages without basic infrastructure services.
- Often there are different blueprints for different components.
- They have reasonably well-defined objectives, although they are usually broader and less easy to quantify and measure.
- The budget may come from a number of different sources, so it may be less clearly defined.
- There may be a number of different implementing agencies.
- Contextual factors, often described as "noise" in systems analysis, are important.
- Individual projects may approximate linearity, but the whole program has elements of nonlinearity.

One example of a complicated program would be improving the performance of the secondary school system in selected states through teacher training, administrative reform, decentralized financial control, and provision of school textbooks and transport vouchers. Another example would be increasing the income of rural communities through village banks, provision of seeds and fertilizers, improved storage and marketing infrastructure, and technical assistance to commercial banks to cater to small farmers.

It becomes more difficult to evaluate complicated programs using conventional evaluation designs. Sometimes these techniques are applied to individual components of the program (such as school feeding programs or the provision of textbooks) and the overall program performance is assessed by combining findings from the different components with other, broader assessments of management, accessibility to the target population, etc. When there is a systematic design for determining which individuals or organizations (schools, clinics, etc.) receive which services, it may be possible to use a multivariate design that assesses overall outcomes and then assesses the contribution of each main component.

Figure 16.1 Simple Projects, Complicated Programs, and Complex Interventions

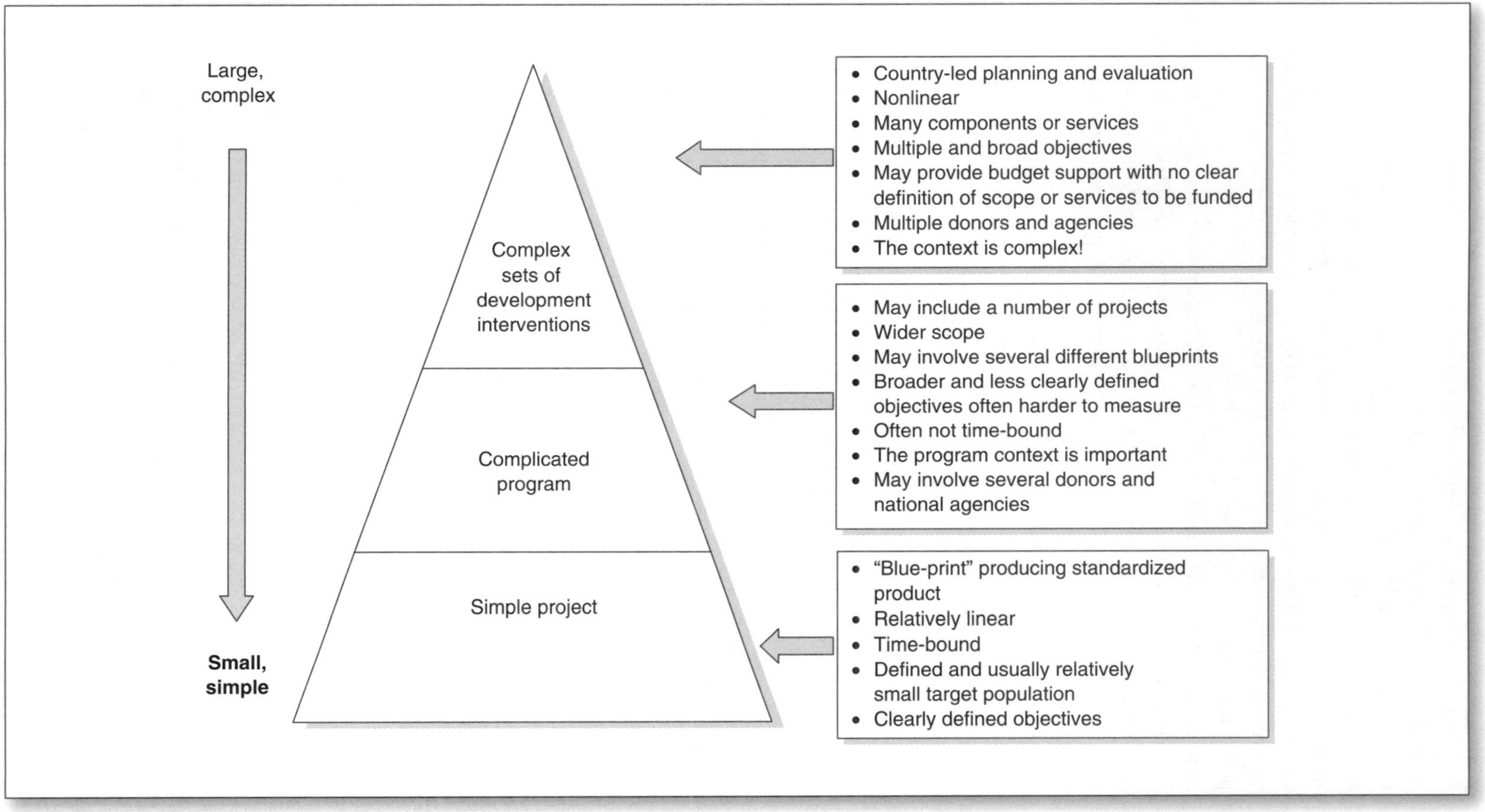

Large,
complex

- Country-led planning and evaluation
- Nonlinear
- Many components or services
- Multiple and broad objectives
- May provide budget support with no clear definition of scope or services to be funded
- Multiple donors and agencies
- The context is complex!

Complex sets of development interventions

- May include a number of projects
- Wider scope
- May involve several different blueprints
- Broader and less clearly defined objectives often harder to measure
- Often not time-bound
- The program context is important
- May involve several donors and national agencies

Complicated program

- "Blue-print" producing standardized product
- Relatively linear
- Time-bound
- Defined and usually relatively small target population
- Clearly defined objectives

Simple project

**Small,
simple**

Complex interventions are more difficult to characterize, as there are many different scenarios (see next section), but they will often have some of the following features:

- They include a number of different components and often a number of distinct programs.
- They are usually large-scale, often covering the whole country.
- Some may even cover a number of different countries, usually but not always in a particular region.
- There are often a number of different donor agencies involved in funding and perhaps implementing different components.
- Increasingly, the interventions are country-led.
- There is often no clear definition of the range of services provided, the target population, or the precise program objectives.
- While some programs cover a particular time period, many others are not time-bound.
- There are usually multiple sources of funding.

One example of a complicated intervention would be the promotion of gender mainstreaming in all of the projects, programs, and development interventions supported by a bilateral donor in a particular country. Another example would be general budget support to a developing country to promote economic development and administrative reform.

The possible approaches to the evaluation of these complex interventions are discussed in the following sections of this chapter.

Patton (2011) suggests that simple, complicated, and complex situations can be distinguished on two dimensions: the degree of certainty and predictability about how to solve a problem and the degree of agreement or conflict about the most appropriate way to solve it. Addressing infectious diseases is an example in which there is both a high degree of agreement that immunization is the best technical way to solve the problem and also that this is the appropriate approach to use. On the other hand, population control would be an example in which there is a high level of agreement about the technical efficacy of different interventions (use of contraceptives) but where there are major disagreements on what is the appropriate approach to use. He also distinguishes between solutions that are technically complicated (sending a rocket to the Moon) and socially complicated (promoting gender equality or population control). The promotion of environmental policies would be an example that is both technically and socially complicated. Figure 16.2 presents a chart that can be used to classify interventions on two dimensions of agreement on the appropriate actions and the degree of certainty concerning the outcomes that will result from different interventions. In this simplified illustration, a simple problem has both close to certainty on the outcome that will result from a particular intervention and close to agreement on the appropriateness of the action. At the other extreme, complex problems have far from agreement on the outcomes resulting from different interventions and far from agreement on the appropriate action to take. In practice the analysis is more complicated, as both dimensions are independent of each other, so that there can be a high degree of certainty on outcomes but far from agreement on the appropriate action to take, and vice-versa.

This framework can also be applied to the definition of the level of simplicity or complexity of an evaluation. When there is a high level of certainty on the outcome of the proposed interventions and on the appropriate approach to use, the evaluation design can be relatively simple, but when the level of certainty is low the evaluation design must be more complex.

The degree of complexity of a situation also depends on a number of other dimensions whose analysis requires what Patton calls "situation recognition." Rogers (2008) identifies five dimensions that must be taken into consideration for situation recognition, program planning, and evaluation design (see Table 16.1). These factors affect the feasibility and difficulty of using logic models, and also the level of difficulty of defining an evaluation design.

Figure 16.2 Two Dimensions for Defining Degree of Complexity

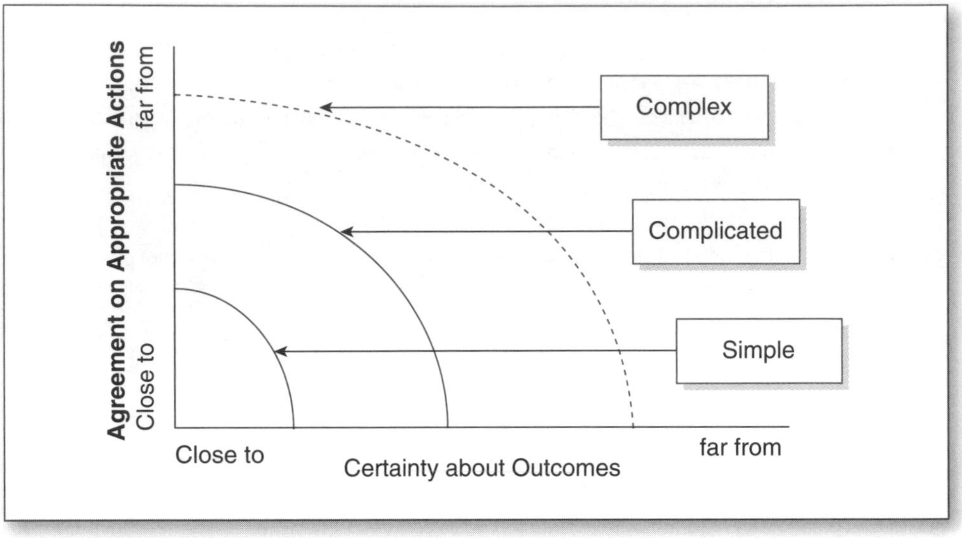

SOURCE: Patton (2011, chap. 4).

Table 16.1 Complicated and Complex Aspects of Interventions

Aspect	Simple Version	Not Simple Version	Challenge for Evaluation	Suggested Label
1. Governance and implementation	Single organization	Multiple agencies	More work required to negotiate agreement about evaluation parameters and to achieve effective data collection and analysis	Complicated
2. Simultaneous causal strands	Single causal strand	Multiple simultaneous causal strands	Effective programs may need to optimize several causal paths; evaluation should both document and support this	Complicated
3. Alternative causal strands	Universal mechanism	Different causal mechanisms operating in different contexts	Replication of effective program may depend on understanding the context that supports it. The counterfactual argument may be inappropriate when there are alternative ways to achieve outcomes	Complicated
4. Nonlinearity (recursive causality) and disproportionate outcomes ("tipping points")	Linear causality, proportional impact	Recursive, with feedback loops	A small initial effect may lead to a large ultimate effect through a reinforcing loop or critical tipping point	Complex
5. Emergent outcomes	Pre-identified outcomes	Emergent outcomes	Specific measures may not be able to be developed in advance, making pre and post comparisons difficult	Complex

SOURCE: Adapted from Rogers (2008).

All of these aspects have significant implications for the types of evaluation design that can be used.

The factors affecting situation recognition relate directly to our discussion in Chapter 2 on "Scoping the Evaluation." In that chapter we identified three dimensions that affect the choice of the appropriate evaluation design:

- *The characteristics of the evaluand (the intervention being evaluated).* These include purpose, level, scale, complexity, and cost.
- *The evaluation context.* At what stage of the intervention was the evaluation commissioned, what is the duration, who is the client, and who is the evaluator commissioned to conduct the evaluation?
- *Methodological dimensions.* These include the level of statistical precision required, and client and evaluator preferences in terms of the quantitative/qualitative continuum and the sources of data.

2.1. The Main Types of Complex Interventions

While the examples in the following section refer mainly to international development programs, principles certainly are appropriate for programs within developed countries as well. Some of the characteristics of complex, country-level programs include the following: that they form part of broad national or sector-level initiatives that often combine a number of different programs or components, that the initiatives will often be supported by a number of different development agencies, that they are intended to support national development policies, and that the goal is to give ownership of the initiative to the recipient country. While some initiatives will support identifiable sector programs or policies, many initiatives provide general budget support, in which case it will often be difficult, or impossible, to identify the specific activities that are being supported. A related goal is to increase the role of the recipient country in the design and implementation of the monitoring and evaluation of these programs.

While there is some overlap, it is useful to classify these initiatives into at least three main types, each with slightly different approaches to its evaluation:

- *Country strategy evaluation.* The purpose is to evaluate the entire country aid program of a particular development agency. The focus is largely normative (rather than statistical), comparing what is being done with what was planned. Performance will often be assessed using the Organization for Economic Cooperation and Development/Development Advisory Committee (OECD/DAC) criteria (see below), although many development agencies add additional criteria.
- *Sector and program evaluation.* These are evaluations of major sectors such as education, health, housing, or transportation, and can focus on a particular country or can assess initiatives operating in a number of different countries (such as health service delivery programs or support for road maintenance supported by a particular development agency in a number of countries). While country program evaluations tend to apply standard methodologies, sector evaluations tend to be conducted in a more ad hoc way, with a variety of different approaches being used.
- *Thematic and cross-cutting evaluation.* These are the evaluation of selected aspects or themes in a number of independent activities. The themes usually emerge from policy statements. The evaluation may cover a range of activities in a given country that affect the outcomes of interest (for example, promoting gender equality or decentralized decision making), or they may cover a number of different countries.

BOX 16.2
EXAMPLES OF THE THREE TYPES OF
COMPLEX EVALUATIONS USED BY AUSAID

Country Strategy Evaluations

- Assessment of the Indonesia country program strategy
- Rapid assessment of the Philippines country program strategy
- Annual program performance reports for Fiji and Papua New Guinea

Sector and Program Evaluations

- Health service delivery in Papua New Guinea, the Solomon Islands, and Vanuatu

Thematic and Cross-Cutting Evaluations

- Education thematic performance report
- Violence against women in Melanesia and East Timor
- Economic governance thematic performance report
- Making a difference in middle-income countries

SOURCE: Various documents available at www.ausaid.gov.au

3. Special Challenges for the Evaluation of Complex, Country-Level Programs

The evaluation of complex, country-level programs involves a number of unique challenges in addition to the general problems faced in the evaluation of the more limited projects and programs that were the main focus or an earlier generation of evaluations. For example:

- *The package of development support is often complex and typically involves a number (often quite large) of different kinds of interventions.* These may include specific and clearly delimited projects, broader-sector programs, country-level interventions, technical assistance and capacity development, and general budgetary support. Conventional impact evaluation designs have only a limited number of outcome or impact indicators, all on similar levels of measurement, so it is difficult to apply those approaches to these more complex interventions.
- *Program objectives are often not clearly defined.* When many different donors and national agencies are involved in negotiating a complex program, the focus is often mainly on the process of funding and setting up the program, with less attention given to the specific objectives. This is even more the case when ownership of the program is being passed to the national government and the policy of the donors is not to impose their own objectives.
- *The scope of many of the interventions is not clearly defined.* Often the program involves a package of interventions that can be applied in different combinations and with different

levels of intensity to different sectors of the target population. Often the target groups are not clearly defined, and different groups may receive different combinations of services in an ad hoc and unpredictable way. To further complicate the analysis, there is often very little documentation on the package of services actually received by different groups.

- *Many programs operate at the national level and intend to cover the total population.* When programs are intended to cover the whole country it is very difficult to identify a comparison group that can be used to define a counterfactual. A similar problem exists for programs covering a total sector (for example: reform of the education sector or promoting decentralization of government financial management). This makes it difficult to isolate the effects of the intervention from the many other changes that are occurring simultaneously.
- *Some interventions cover a number of different countries.* Many thematic programs such as the promotion of gender equality or capacity development cover a number of different countries. Frequently the interventions will be implemented by different agencies in each country, often using different and frequently inadequately documented approaches.

4. Attribution, Contribution, and Substitution

When evaluating clearly defined projects or programs the goal is normally to address two related questions: "To what extent can the observed changes in the project group be attributed to the effects of the project intervention?" and "How confidently can alternative explanations for the changes be eliminated?" For example, assume that free school meals are provided to children in certain schools in a particular geographic region, and that at the end of the school year it is found that school enrollment and attendance rates have increased. How confident can the evaluator be that the increased enrollment and attendance are due to the effects of the school meals and not to other factors such as the following: improvements in the economic conditions of the region; government investments in teaching training; and increased number of textbooks, road improvement programs (that make it easier for children to get to school), or other programs in the same schools that are organized by other donor agencies? These questions are addressed through attribution analysis (see Box 16.3 for a discussion of attribution, contribution, and substitution analysis), in which project schools are matched with a sample of similar schools not participating in the project. The purpose of the comparison is to control for alternative factors that might have contributed to the changes in school enrollment. If the two samples are large enough and well matched, and if there is a statistically significant difference in the change in enrollment and attendance between the two groups of schools, then this provides support for the potential contribution of the project to the observed changes.

BOX 16.3
ATTRIBUTION, CONTRIBUTION, AND SUBSTITUTION ANALYSIS

While project evaluation at times is able to apply experimental or quasi-experimental designs that can control for alternative explanations of the observed changes (outcomes or impacts) in the project group, it is rarely possible to achieve the same level

(Continued)

(Continued)

of rigor in the evaluation of the effects of complex interventions. Consequently, evaluators of complex interventions must decide which of the following levels of analysis can be applied:

- *Attribution analysis.* The project group is matched to a comparison group so that alternative explanations of the observed changes can be controlled for (eliminated). There is then a prima facie case for claiming that statistically significant differences between the project and comparison groups show the project intervention contributed to these changes.
- *Contribution analysis.* The analysis assesses the contribution of a particular development agency to the achievement of the overall changes resulting from the collaborative financial and technical interventions of a number of different development agencies. Sometimes the analysis will also include the programs of national agencies (both government and civil society).
- *Substitution analysis.* An assessment is conducted of the net increase in resources to the target sector or program resulting from the contribution of a particular development agency.

Conventional forms of attribution analysis can only be used when the schools benefiting from the project can be clearly identified, when they all receive the same treatment (in this case school meals), and when a well-matched comparison group can be identified. Unfortunately, for the reasons discussed in the previous section, it is rarely possible to apply these rigorous designs to the evaluation of complex, national-level interventions. Consequently, many development agencies supporting complex programs are resigned to the fact that they will only be able to assess the contribution of their agency to the changes that may be the result of the collaborative activities of many different development agencies and/or national governments, civil society, the economy, etc.

Increasingly, the goal of donor agencies is to support and strengthen national development programs rather than to have separate initiatives managed by and identified with the donor. For example, there will often be a number of donors supporting national development programs such as poverty reduction, HIV/AIDS treatment, or public sector reform. In some cases each donor will have a defined area of responsibility as part of the national program, but in many other cases all resources are pooled so that it would be difficult, if not impossible, to identify how the resources of a particular donor were used. In these cases, which are becoming the major way that many donors operate, it is not possible to conduct attribution analysis to assess the impact of a particular donor. However, national governments, finance ministries, parliaments, and the general public still wish to know what benefits were produced by the often considerable resources their country invested in foreign aid. In these cases contribution analysis is used to identify the value added of a donor's assistance. Even when resources are pooled, foreign aid departments usually present a plan justifying their support to a particular country and sector and indicating some of the objectives they hope to achieve. Agency staff members also receive training and written guidelines indicating how they should operate.

Most agencies also have clear ideas of their goals, what they consider to be the comparative advantage that their agency offers, and what the unique characteristics of their approach are. For example, one agency may believe that it has a better understanding of the local context, greater ability to work with civil society organizations, a stronger commitment to gender equality, more expertise in financial management or in public sector reform, better access to policymakers, or greater financial resources and more flexibility in how these resources can be used.

Based on a review of written documentation, observing training and orientation programs, and interviews with agency staff and counterparts, it is usually possible to define a set of criteria on which the donor agency's performance can be assessed. Contribution analysis will then combine interviews with partners and with agency staff, self-assessment, and review of documents (for example, memoranda of understanding, minutes of meetings, reports of the implementing agencies, and program planning documents) to assess how successfully the donor has performed on each criterion. In some cases it is also possible to track expenditures (budgets have line items even when resources are pooled) to estimate whether the funds have been used as planned.

Another concern of many development agencies is to assess the extent to which the resources they have provided have increased the total resources invested in this programmatic area or sector. The concern is that government may take advantage of the international resources to divert all or part of their own resources budgeted for this sector to a different sector or program so that the net increase in resources to the target sector may be less than the resources provided by the development agency. In extreme cases the net increase in resources to the sector may be close to zero. This is called **substitution analysis.**

Combining attribution and contribution analysis. For the reasons discussed above, many development agencies believe it is not possible to use attribution analysis to assess the impacts of their resources and technical support. When only contribution analysis is used this can lead to the strange situation in which an agency might conclude, "We have been rated as performing well on contribution analysis, but we have no idea whether the programs to which we have contributed have had any significant impact on (for example) poverty, the spread of HIV/AIDS, educational performance, or environmental protection." Obviously, all agencies make educated guesses as to whether the programs they are supporting are producing results, but this frequently is based on output indicators or anecdotal evidence, and it is assumed that no more rigorous evidence can be obtained.

However, even though it may not be possible for an agency to assess the impacts of its particular contribution, it would often be possible to obtain some overall assessment of the effects of the total national program on poverty, HIV/AIDS, etc. In many cases, statistics (of varying quality) or other forms of data are available on overall changes in poverty, HIV infection rates, infant mortality, or school enrollment. The measurement of the MDGs has greatly contributed to the availability of this information. The challenge is then to assess the extent to which the changes can be attributed to international aid or national programs compared to other factors such as changes in export and import prices, migration patterns, or variations in rainfall. We will return to this issue in the following sections, when we discuss strategies for defining the counterfactual.

5. Alternative Approaches for Defining the Counterfactual

Many development agencies have decided that, given the complexity of strategic interventions, and the fact that most of them are intended to cover the total target population (at the country or sector level), it is not possible to define a conventional statistical counterfactual. However, while acknowledging the many difficulties of defining a counterfactual, it is recognized that without some way to estimate what would have been the situation if the intervention had not taken place, it is extremely difficult to make any assessment of the effectiveness of the intervention and to what degree, if at all, it contributed to its intended objectives. Consequently, there is a demand for creative approaches that development agencies can use in real-world contexts to assess what would have been the situation if the program or programs had not taken place: in other words, to define alternatives to the conventional counterfactual.

In recent years a number of options have been proposed for defining an alternative counterfactual, or comparison group. While it is recognized that many of the proposed approaches are methodologically weak, it is argued that in many circumstances these provide sufficient control to permit an approximate assessment of the program impact. Counterfactual designs can be categorized into five main groups (see Figure 16.3):

- *Theory-driven approaches,* which are based on a program theory and usually represented graphically through a logic model (see Chapter 10). The theory describes the nature of the problem that the program is designed to address, the objectives of the program, the steps through which the objectives will be achieved, and the critical assumptions that must be tested. Conventionally the counterfactual is tested by assessing how closely outcomes and processes conform to, or deviate from, the model. Sometimes the counterfactual would be defined more explicitly by formulating an alternative model describing outcomes and processes. Often the alternative model (the counterfactual) will be formulated on the basis of criticisms of the program theory on which the program design is based.
- *Quantitative approaches,* including experimental and quasi-experimental designs, can be considered the conventional approaches to the use of counterfactuals, as well as a number of other quantitative techniques.
- *Qualitative approaches,* in which the counterfactual may be derived from asking individuals or groups what the situation would have been if the project had not taken place, or asking them what things were like before the program began. Participatory group consultation techniques such as participatory rural appraisal (PRA) include exercises whereby groups reconstruct explanations of what changes the program produced and how.
- *Mixed-method designs,* which integrate quantitative and qualitative techniques, building on the strengths of both approaches.
- *Rating scales,* which are widely used to assess the effectiveness and outcomes of complex, country-level programs.

There are also a number of techniques that can be used for strengthening any of these designs, including ways to reconstruct baseline data, creative uses of secondary data, drawing on other completed or ongoing studies, triangulation, and mixed-method approaches.

5.1 Theory-Driven Approaches

Program theory models. A fully articulated program theory model can describe the process through which a program is intended to produce changes; how the changes will be measured; the contextual

Figure 16.3 Statistical and Alternative Counterfactual Designs

Theory-Driven Approaches

- Logic models
- Historical analysis
- General elimination theory

Quantitative Approaches

- Experimental and quasi-experimental designs
- Pipeline design
- Concept mapping
- Statistical analysis of comparator countries
- Citizen report cards and consumer surveys
- Social network analysis

Rating Scales

Qualitative Approaches

- Realist evaluation
- PRA techniques
- Qualitative analysis of comparator countries
- Comparison with other sectors
- Expert judgment
- Key informants
- Public sector comparisons
- Public expenditure tracking

Counterfactual Designs for Assessing the Effects of Development Interventions

- Attribution analysis
- Contribution analysis
- Substitution analysis

Techniques for Strengthening Counterfactual Designs

- Disaggregating complex programs into evaluable components
- Portfolio analysis
- Reconstructing baseline data
- Creative use of secondary data
- Drawing on other studies
- Triangulation
- Mixed-method approaches

Mixed-Method Designs

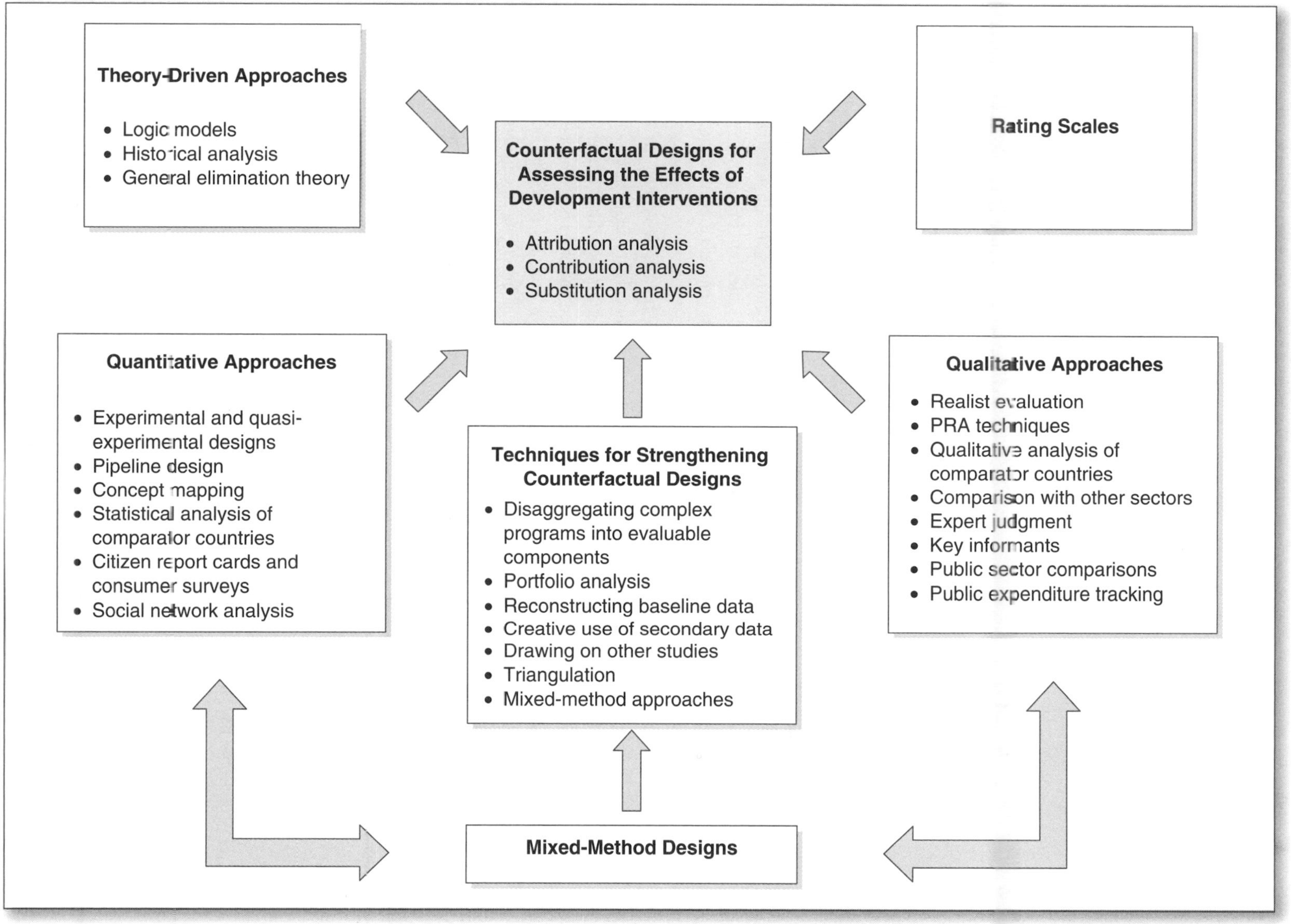

factors that might explain variations in outcomes in different locations; and, through the use of results chain modeling, some of the potential negative outcomes that should be monitored. The characteristics of program theory models are discussed in Chapter 10. The counterfactual can be defined in several ways.

First, the baseline conditions can be assessed through the initial diagnostic study describing the pre-intervention situation. The program theory describes the process of change that will occur if the underlying theory is valid and if the intended outcomes are produced. The validity of the model is tested both by comparing actual outcomes to the theoretically expected outcomes, and also by using process analysis to assess how closely the actual process of change conforms to the model. The analysis of the process strengthens the explanatory power of the model because the situation can occur in which the expected outcomes are achieved but the process of change does not correspond to the model. In this case further analysis is needed to determine the validity of the model—whether it just needs minor refinements or whether the actual process of causality is significantly different from the model, in which case the experimental hypothesis may not have been supported by the evidence.

A second refinement of the model comes with the introduction of contextual analysis. The model can hypothesize how outcomes will be affected by contextual factors such as the local economy, the political context, the characteristics of participating communities, and the level of support from local institutions. Contextual variables can either be analyzed descriptively or, when the project operates in a large number of different locations and quantitative surveys are conducted, it may be possible to incorporate contextual variables into the analysis using dummy variables. In this way it is possible to test the validity of the model's explanations of the role of these contextual factors.

A third refinement is to define one or more alternative models describing what changes will occur if the experimental model is not true. One alternative model is to define a set of outcome indicators assuming the model has not produced any changes that can be defined as the counterfactual. Another model might describe the hypothesized processes and outcomes based on a different set of assumptions. For example, it might be hypothesized that a program providing scholarships to encourage children to enroll in secondary school, instead of benefiting low-income families as intended, would in fact be co-opted by the local elite. In this case the hypothesized outcomes for the alternative model would be increased enrollment by higher-income families but no change, even negative change, for low-income families.

It should be noted that the program theory approach has been criticized on theoretical grounds (including the assumption of linear causality). The models are often too general for it to be possible to falsify them, and they rarely identify and test all of the plausible rival hypotheses (Bamberger, Rugh, and Mabry 2006:187–88; Cook 2000).

Historical analysis. Economic and political historians have often addressed the question of what would have been the consequences if things had worked out differently in the past. In his 1964 book *Railroads and American Economic Growth: Essays in Econometric History,* Fogel used quantitative methods to imagine what the United States would have been like in 1890 if there had never been railroads. He hypothesized that, in the absence of the railroad, America's large canal system would have been expanded and its roads would have been upgraded and paved. As canals and paved roads were already being developed, and as both were economically and technically feasible, it is very likely that they would have been expanded in the absence of railroads. Consequently, the impact of railroads not being there was believed to be very much less than it would have been if the canal and roads options were not available. He estimated that the level of per capita income achieved by January 1, 1890, would have been reached by March 31, 1890, if railroads had never been invented.

Similar approaches could potentially be applied today to evaluate infrastructure projects such as the construction of major roads where no statistical counterfactual is available. The evaluation design would involve defining the available options and defining these as the counterfactual. In some cases investment in railways or water transport might be viable options, whereas in other cases the alternative would be to continue with the previous means of transport, which will usually be an inferior road. However, in this case the counterfactual would have to take into consideration the increased volume of traffic that would have occurred, even on the inferior road, in response to economic growth.

General elimination theory. This approach, developed by Scriven (1976), is similar to the methods often used in crime investigations. It is assumed that observed outcomes have one or more causes. The evaluation begins by preparing a list of possible causes (LOPC). Each LOPC has a modus operandi that is analogous to a trail of evidence or a set of footprints. The trail is short if there is a proximate cause, and longer if there is a remote cause. The facts of the case are documented and the evidence is compared with the steps in the modus operandi for each option in the LOPC. Are all of the steps in the modus operandi for any of the LOPCs present? The credibility of each LOPC is compared and alternative explanations are considered for all potentially credible options. As in crime solving, the credibility of the evidence, the logical consistency of the sequence, and the correct temporal order are all assessed. Again, as for crime solving, there is rarely an incontestable scientific proof, so it is a question of assessing the credibility of the evidence and the argument.

5.2. Quantitative Approaches

Experimental and quasi-experimental designs (discussed in Chapters 11 and 12) all use the conventional counterfactual based on a variation of the project-comparison group design. These are the designs that are typically used to evaluate the impacts of a project when a comparison (control) can be identified and measured.

Pipeline design is a type of quasi-experimental design, but it is discussed separately here because it is widely used as an alternative way to define the counterfactual when an independent control group cannot be identified or measured. Pipeline designs are often used at the project level where a project such as road construction, installation of water supply, or urban renewal is implemented in clearly defined phases over a period of years. The sections of the population that are not scheduled to receive services until the second or later phases can be used as control groups to assess the changes in output/impact indicators for the families/communities receiving benefits under Phase 1. Despite some methodological issues (see Chapter 11 and Appendix F), this design is attractive because it avoids the ethical and other problems and costs of having to select and interview a separate control group that will receive no benefits. It is possible, but usually more difficult, to apply a similar approach at the country or sector level. For example.

- Use regions where the program has not yet been implemented as the comparison group. For example, in Guatemala a new pension benefit was to be provided to all people over the age of 60, but the government did not have the administrative capacity to introduce the program in all regions at the same time.

- (For a program that will cover different agencies), use agencies not yet covered as the comparison group. For example, in Colombia the government was planning to implement an anticorruption program in a number of different ministries and agencies, but a number of administrative procedures had to be completed before the program began in each ministry. The program was therefore launched at different points in time in different agencies.

The methodological challenge in the use of the pipeline approach at the country or sector level is that there are likely to be differences between the regions or agencies that enter the program at different points in time, and these can weaken or invalidate the comparison. For example, the regions that do not enter the pension program in Phase 1 may be poorer regions with less capacity to comply with the administrative requirements, or they may be controlled by an opposition party so that government may deliberately delay their entry. Obviously, it would be necessary to ascertain relevant characteristics of the comparison groups to determine how much those factors affect the kinds of changes being measured.

Concept mapping is a technique that uses interviews with stakeholders or experts to obtain an approximate estimate of program effectiveness, outcomes, or impacts. A comparison of the average ratings for areas receiving different levels of intervention combined with a comparison of ratings before and after the intervention can provide a counterfactual. The approach is described in Appendix G, and an illustration is given of how this could be used to assess the effectiveness and impacts of a gender mainstreaming strategy being implemented in different countries. A similar approach could be applied to evaluate a wide range of programs, including capacity development and technical assistance, as well as programs providing more easily measured services such as health or education. This example shows how the approach could be applied in a multicountry program, but a similar approach can also be used within one country.

Figure 16.4 shows how a baseline reference point can be defined for a multicountry thematic program (such as promoting gender mainstreaming) by asking stakeholders to define the characteristics of a successful program and then to rate each country (or sector) program on each of these criteria. For example, this approach could be used to obtain a baseline measure of gender performance in each of the sampled countries at the start of the program period. The measurement would be repeated at the end of the program, and the changes on the ratings would be used to estimate outcomes or impacts. The design is strengthened if a sample of countries (programs) can also be assessed in which the gender program is not being implemented.

- A variation of this approach can be used in the very common situation in which the evaluation is not commissioned until late in the program. In this case, after defining the key characteristics of a successful gender mainstreaming strategy, the stakeholders/experts are asked to:
  o Rate each country on each scale at the time the program began. Normally this must rely on recall, which introduces a potential source of bias.
  o Rate the present situation of each country on the respective scales. The difference between the two measures provides an estimate of effectiveness or impact.

An alternative approach is to ask respondents to rate the changes that have occurred in each country on each of the scales. Some researchers feel that asking people to rate the amount of change is more reliable than asking them to make two separate preprogram/postprogram ratings.

Figure 16.4 Using Concept Mapping to Evaluate a Thematic Program by Comparing Baseline and End-of-Program Ratings on a Set of Critical Clusters: The Example of Gender Mainstreaming

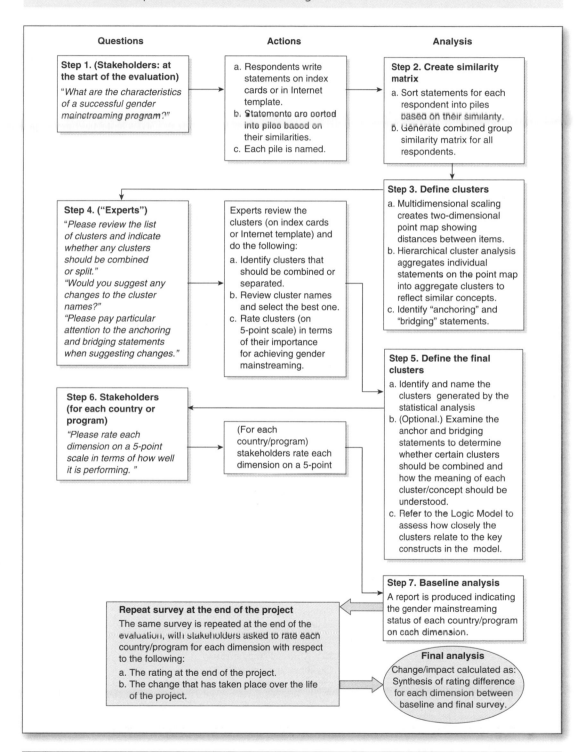

SOURCE: Adapted from Kane and Trochim (2007, chaps. 3, 4, and 6). The example is developed by the present authors.

The reliance on subjective judgment raises issues of validity and reliability, and a key requirement is to include statistical tests for interrater reliability. These are built into the statistical packages used for concept mapping.

Statistical comparison to a set of similar countries. It is sometimes possible to compare the target country to similar countries where the intervention being studied has not taken place. Sometimes the comparison will be made to a small number of countries in the same region (for example, Uganda might be compared to selected countries in East Africa). The selection will be determined partly by the availability of the required comparative data and partly on judgment as to which countries provide the best match. The disadvantage of this approach is that no two countries are identical, so the comparison can only provide a rough approximation. In other cases it may be possible to use one of the increasing numbers of regional or worldwide data sets to obtain comparative data on all countries with similar socioeconomic or other relevant statistics. Table 16.2 gives examples of the kinds of data sets that are now available.

While the data sets in Table 16.2 present carefully constructed statistical indicators that can be compared across countries, there are other data sets that compile all of the available surveys and data sets within a particular country. These are then sometimes combined to construct an index ranking all countries on a particular question. For example, Transparency International compiles all of the available studies and data on corruption and then publishes an annual ranking of most countries on a scale of corruption.

Table 16.2   Examples of International Data Sets Available for Cross-Country Comparisons

Data Set	Examples of Possible Applications for Comparative Purposes
UNDP Human Development Indicators SOURCE: Included in the Annual UNDP Human Development Report. Report for 2010 available at: http://hdr.undp.org/en/reports/global/hdr2010	Annual report covering most countries. Comparative statistics are available in areas such as: • Public expenditure on health • Public expenditure on education • Educational attainment • Under age-five mortality • Life expectancy at birth • Income • Gender equality indicators
Millennium Development Goals SOURCE : www.un.org/millenniumgoals	Detailed statistical data on over 40 indicators covering the areas of: • Poverty and hunger • Primary education • Gender equality and women's empowerment • Child mortality • Maternal health • HIV/AIDS and other diseases • Environmental sustainability
Demographic and Health Surveys SOURCE : www.measuredhs.com	Since 1984 the DHS has developed a database of statistics on demographic, health, and nutritional indicators that covers most developing countries.

Citizen report cards are studies, first used in Bangalore, India, that are based on a survey administered by a respected independent organization to a large random sample of residents in a particular city. They are asked which service agencies they have had to contact (usually during the past 12 months) to resolve a problem. For each agency they have contacted they are asked a number of questions, including how they were treated by the agency, how many visits they had to make, and whether they had to pay bribes. The responses provide a baseline that is used to estimate progress in a follow-up study conducted several years later (Bamberger, MacKay, and Ooi 2004: 8–9, and 2005:13–21). The study can be used as a comparison group either for a similar program in another city or for assessing a different program in the original city. It would also be possible to combine data from a number of citizen report card studies to provide comparison data for assessing a program in a different country. The comparison could either be based on calculating average baseline data from a number of cities or by calculating the range of improvements that occurred between the first and second studies, to provide a yardstick for assessing the amount of change produced in the city or country being evaluated.

Social network analysis techniques ask a sample of respondents to name, for example, the people they know in the community, the people they would go to for help, the people who engage in high-risk behavior, and the people they dislike or are afraid of; they can also be asked to indicate which institutions they know about and have used, or to rate their opinions on these institutions (Carrington, Scott, and Wasserman 2005; Knoke and Yang 2008). The information is combined with socioeconomic data on the respondents to draw community maps and to calculate, for example, density of community networks, friendship patterns and lines of conflict, knowledge of and opinions about community institutions, and identification of opinion leaders.

The techniques have been widely used in the fields of HIV/AIDS, health, and family planning to identify patterns of spread of infection, to identify groups who are particularly active or at risk of unhealthy behavior, or to understand how information is disseminated. There are a number of potential applications for defining counterfactuals, for example:

- Creating indices of social conflict or solidarity that can be used to assess the impacts of community development programs. Project and comparison groups can be scored on the index, or pre- and post comparisons can be made for the project population.
- Providing baseline data on attitudes to or knowledge about community institutions that can be used to assess the effectiveness of information campaigns.

5.3. Qualitative Approaches

Realist evaluations. This approach addresses questions such as: What might work, for whom, and under what circumstances? (Pawson and Tilley 1997; Pawson 2006). It also focuses on the evaluand, understanding exactly what project implementation means in practice. What exactly are the treatments and services that are being delivered, and how are they delivered? The popularity of this approach comes from the recognition that much of the experimental and quasi-experimental design literature has focused on assessing outcomes, implicitly assuming that the program treatment is clearly understood and is implemented as planned. Pawson and Tilley present a methodology, supported with many examples, to illustrate how to understand what really happens during project implementation.

PRA and other participatory group consultation techniques. There are a wide variety of participatory group consultation tools and methods (see Chapter 5) that can be used to identify important changes that have taken place in a community or organization and to explain the factors that contributed to the changes. Kumar (2002, chap. 4) provides examples of how relational techniques such as cause-and-effect diagrams and impact diagrams can be used for this purpose. Similarly, techniques such as process maps and Venn diagrams can assess the contribution of a particular project or external agency to achieving important changes. While these techniques are rarely used to define a counterfactual, the methodology could be applied for this purpose by, for example, asking groups to identify differences in the conditions of communities and households where projects have been implemented and in communities without projects. The value of these techniques is that group participants can both assess the importance of different changes for the welfare of the communities and also describe the processes of change.

Qualitative analysis of comparator countries. In contrast to the quantitative country comparison discussed above, qualitative comparisons normally only involve a small number of countries. Typically a number of countries will be selected from the same geographical region. They are selected judgmentally, either trying to find countries that are similar (for example, in terms of their education level or the quality of their road network) or where there are differences. Often the comparison will be made on broad qualitative indicators such as "the quality of education management," or "the level of corruption." As the evaluation is often to study broad system change or the effectiveness of particular policy measures, the comparison tends to be descriptive and seeking to detect broad patterns of change or quality. (See discussions of expert judgment and key informants below for sources of such information.)

Comparison with other sectors. When the evaluation is assessing broad organizational changes or policy reforms (such as anticorruption policies, decentralization, or citizen participation in decision making) the unit of analysis is often a ministry or government agency. Often the best available comparison group will be another ministry or a sample of ministries not affected or not yet affected by the policy or reform. As each ministry has very different characteristics, it is very difficult to make a comparison between one ministry that has been affected and one that has not. A better option is to make the comparison with a sample of ministries that have not been affected to try to construct an average baseline or performance indicator.

Expert judgment. These techniques use the opinions and judgment of experts to assess both the changes that have been produced by the project and what would have been the situation if the project had not taken place (the counterfactuals). Sometimes methodologies such as concept mapping (discussed earlier) are used to conduct a systematic analysis of the opinions of large numbers of experts, whereas in the majority of cases opinions are obtained more informally through structured, semistructured, or unstructured interviews. When using expert judgment the goal should be to solicit the views of a relatively large number of representative experts, as experts do tend to disagree among themselves.

Key informants. The approach is similar to consultation with experts, but in this case the intention is to obtain opinions from a broad range of individuals who have different experiences and different perspectives on the project. Most of the respondents would not be considered "experts" in the conventional sense, but rather people who know the project and the communities in which it operates. So an evaluation of a program to control illegal substance abuse might include the following among key informants: illegal substance users, their spouses and sexual partners, drug distributors, people in the same demographic groups who do not use illegal substances, neighbors, teachers, community development workers, religious leaders, and the police. All of these respondents can help with the difficult task of assessing what would have been the situation of the community and of the different groups using and affected by substance abuse if the program had not taken place.

Public expenditure tracking (PET) studies. Originating in Uganda, these studies use a very detailed and rigorous methodology to track the flow of approved expenditures for the education, health, or other sectors from the ministry to the intended users (individual schools, health clinics, etc.). The studies monitor both the amount of time taken for the funds to reach the final user and the percentage "leakage" at each stage. The proportion of funds reaching the final user provides a baseline for assessing improvement when the study is repeated a few years later (Bamberger, MacKay, and Ooi 2004:16–17, 2005:45–49). PETS could be used in several ways to construct a counterfactual:

- If time and resources permit, a baseline PET study could be conducted in the country and sector being studied to create a baseline.
- Existing PET studies that had been conducted at two points in other sectors in the country could be used to provide a rough benchmark of the level of improvement that can be achieved. Obviously, the estimates would be more robust if information was available on several sectors.
- Data from other countries could be pooled to provide a benchmark both for initial levels of leakage and to provide parameters for the level of improvement that can be achieved.

Holistic analysis. Holistic assessment of complex programs can be used when one of the objectives of the evaluation is to assess the catalytic role (**plausible contribution**) of one of the agencies participating in a multidonor-funded program in strengthening coordination, improving the delivery of services, and promoting capacity development for the whole program. This design will usually combine one or more of the following approaches:

- Interviews with international and national partners to assess the organizational, technical, and other contributions of the agency being studied
- Focus groups with different partners, key informants, and civil society
- Direct observation of meetings, project locations, and other project activities to observe the style of the agency being studied
- Review of records of agency meetings and other secondary sources that might provide information on agency performance
- Self-assessment by agency staff based on interviews or responses to self-administered questionnaires

A variant involves "reverse construction" of a macro logic model. Whereas typical logic models used in project design begin with the proposed interventions and then predict what outcomes are to be achieved, this approach assesses what change occurred in impact indicators (e.g., improved well-being of the target population) and then uses a variety of means (as discussed above) to assess the relative contributions of various program interventions.

5.4. Mixed-Method Designs

Mixed-method designs (see Chapter 14) are a powerful approach when working with a number of different sources of information, none of which on its own produces a credible counterfactual. Mixed-method designs combine the strengths of both quantitative and qualitative data collection and analysis methods and hence can maximize the efficiency with which available sources of data are used. One of the useful tools of mixed methods is triangulation, which uses two or more independent estimates to assess the validity of each data source, and also provides different perspectives for interpreting data and also the findings of the analysis.

5.5. Tools for Rating Performance of Complex Programs

Given the large number of activities included in many complex programs, and the need to ensure consistency and comparability in the assessment of many different kinds of interventions, most development agencies base their evaluations on a set of rating criteria. The majority of the rating systems are based on the guidelines developed by the OECD/DAC Network for Development Evaluation (OECD/DAC 2010a). This assesses development programs in terms of five criteria:

- *Relevance.* The extent to which the aid activity is suited to the priorities and policies of the target group, recipient, and donor.
- *Effectiveness.* The extent to which an aid activity attains its objectives.
- *Efficiency.* Efficiency measures the outputs—qualitative and quantitative—in relation to the inputs.
- *Impact.* The positive and negative changes produced by a development intervention, directly or indirectly, intended or unintended.
- *Sustainability.* Sustainability is concerned with measuring whether the benefits of an activity are likely to continue after donor funding has been withdrawn. Projects need to be environmentally as well as financially sustainable.

Many agencies add additional criteria. For example, AusAID also uses the criteria of the following:

- Gender equality and equity
- Effectiveness of the M&E system: How effectively does the M&E framework measure progress toward meeting objectives?
- Analysis and learning: How effectively are findings and lessons analyzed and used to improve future activities?

Many agencies use a 4-, 5-, or 6-point scale to rate such criteria. Table 16.3 compares performance rating scales used by the World Bank's Independent Evaluation Group and by AusAID's Office of Development Effectiveness.

Often criteria will be grouped to estimate the proportion of activities that achieve a satisfactory rating or that require improvement. For example, AusAID defines categories 4, 5, and 6 as "Satisfactory," and categories 1, 2, and 3 as "Requires improvement."

Table 16.3 Comparing Performance Rating Scales Used by the World Bank and AusAID

World Bank: Project Performance Results[4]	AusAID: Assessment of Quality at Entry and Quality at Implementation
Highly satisfactory	6. Very high quality
Satisfactory	5. Good quality
Moderately satisfactory	4. Adequate quality: some work to improve needed
Moderately unsatisfactory	3. Less than adequate quality
Unsatisfactory	2. Poor quality
Highly unsatisfactory	1. Very poor quality
SOURCE: IEG Annual Review of Development Effectiveness, 2008.	SOURCE: AusAID Annual Review of Development Effectiveness, 2008.

5.6. Techniques for Strengthening Counterfactual Designs

There are a number of techniques that can be used to strengthen most of the previously described counterfactual designs:

Disaggregating complex programs into simpler components. Many country or sector programs are comprised of a number of different treatments and components, which makes it very difficult to define any kind of counterfactual. Often the program operates at the national level, so it is even more difficult to identify a potential counterfactual. Two alternative strategies can be considered for identifying a counterfactual.

A first option is to disaggregate a multicomponent program into its subcomponents and then conduct separate evaluations of each component. For example, a technical assistance program to support efforts by the Ministry of Transport to increase accessibility of rural communities to agricultural markets and local town centers might include training programs for central office and regional staff, new software for transport planning, commissioning surveys of rural communities, and purchasing vehicles and microcredit to permit farmers and entrepreneurs to acquire intermediate means of transport (motorbikes with trailers, animal traction, etc.). Several of the main components (perhaps those with the largest budget allocations or that had been rated as most important) could each be evaluated separately. The findings would be combined to provide an overall assessment of program effectiveness.

The design of the evaluation could probably be strengthened by developing a program theory model, including a pyramid-style, multilevel, results chain analysis, to define the intended linkages between different levels and the expected outcomes at each level. The program theory model should include a clear identification of the main rival hypotheses that could explain the observed changes together with the collection of evidence to test and eliminate the alternative explanations. For example, an alternative explanation for the increased knowledge and use of planning software could be that all college and university engineering programs now include training on planning software so that all recent recruits to the ministry are familiar with this software. This hypothesis could be tested by comparing knowledge and use of software in departments not affected by the assistance program with departments in the program.

---

[4]For the assessment of sustainability, which is estimating future performance, the ratings are based on the likelihood of achieving sustainability.

Disaggregating National Programs into Regional and Local Levels

A second approach is to recognize that programs that operate at the national level will also produce changes at the regional and often the local level. For example, the previously mentioned assistance program to strengthen rural transport programs and services in the Ministry of Transport should produce changes at the regional level (for example, regional transport plans and budget allocations, communications with local authorities and communities, the content of training programs and outreach activities, and the kinds of staff who are recruited). It should also produce changes at the local level (the kinds of rural roads that are constructed, the number of rural communities with access to roads, and the number of credits authorized for the purchase of intermediate transport services). Another set of measurable indicators might relate to the knowledge that regional and local staff and local communities have about the program and how easy it actually is to obtain the services.

The evaluation will often combine a top-down analysis (tracking how effectively the center has implemented the intended links to the regions, and how effectively the regions have implemented their links to the local level), with a bottom-up analysis (how much the lower levels know about the program and how much access they had to the services that are theoretically being provided). There are often cases where an analysis of plans and documents at the central level, and the knowledge that central level staff have about the program, shows that the program is being implemented as intended. However, when the regional offices are visited it will often be found that many staff have very little information about the program or have been unable to access the services. Similarly, bottom-up analysis might reveal that many communities have prepared and submitted plans or that many farmers have requested loans, but higher-level authorities may claim to have no knowledge of these initiatives. Figure 16.5 illustrates this top-down/bottom-up approach and shows how regions or districts where the program is not (yet) operating can be used to define a counterfactual.

It is often possible to identify regions, districts, or communities that have not yet been affected. These can be used as a comparison group (counterfactual), but care must be taken to assess potential selection bias. However, due to resource constraints many programs are only able to develop pilot programs in a small number of districts or communities, so it is often possible to identify a well-matched comparison group from communities not affected.

Portfolio analysis. Many complex programs, particularly when supported by several different donor agencies, may comprise very large numbers, sometimes into the hundreds of different interventions. Portfolio analysis is an approach that is commonly used in these cases. All interventions are identified (which can in itself be a challenge) and then classified into *performance areas*. A desk review is then conducted to check the kinds of information that are available on these projects, such as the existence of a logic model, monitoring data on inputs and outputs, ratings of quality at entry, quality of implementation and quality at completion, and other kinds of evaluation reports. In many cases there will be no clear delimitation of the projects to be included in the analysis, and boundary analysis may be required to define criteria for determining which projects should and should not be included in the analysis.

If the information is sufficiently complete (which it often is not) the available ratings will be listed and summary indicators will be produced for all of the projects in each performance area. For example, quality at entry or during implementation may be assessed in terms of quality of design, quality of planning, the design and use of the M&E system, and the internal and external efficiency. Where data permit, average ratings will be computed for each of these dimensions and an overall assessment will be produced for quality of entry or implementation. The ratings for the different

Figure 16.5   Disaggregating National Programs into National, Regional, and Local Levels

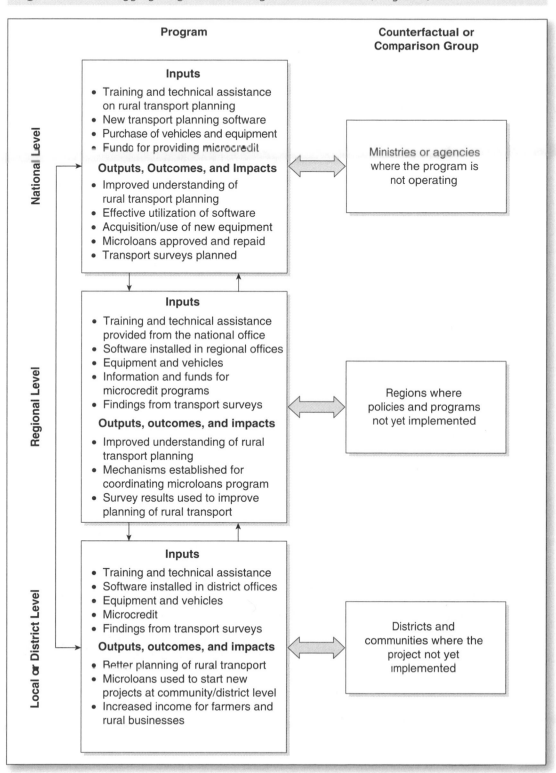

components (quality at entry, etc.) are then combined to obtain an overall assessment for each performance area. Many agencies try to use the OECD/DAC rating criteria, discussed earlier in this chapter, for these overall assessments. Additional criteria such as coherence, integration, and coverage may also be used.

If resources permit, a sample of projects from each performance area will be selected for field studies to compare the data from these secondary sources with experience on the ground. These field studies will normally be conducted with limited time and budget, and will apply the kinds of rapid assessment techniques discussed in earlier chapters.

The findings will then be reviewed by a group of experts and stakeholders, and where there are discrepancies between the draft reports and the feedback from this group, further analysis will be conducted seeking to reconcile or explain the reasons for the discrepancies.

In some cases the kinds of concept mapping techniques described earlier in this chapter may be used as part of the assessment. In cases where field studies are conducted, concept mapping can also be used to help select the countries or projects to be covered.

Reconstructing baseline data. Often the best option for defining the counterfactual will be to estimate the baseline conditions of the project group and a comparison group before the project began. In Chapter 5 we discussed a number of strategies that can be used to reconstruct baseline data.

Creative use of secondary data. There are wide ranges of potentially useful secondary data sources that are often overlooked, many of which are discussed in Chapter 5. However, it is always important to assess these data sources carefully to make sure that the information is of good quality and relevant for the purposes of the evaluation.

Taking advantage of ongoing or planned studies. Sometimes the evaluation can take advantage of other studies that are being conducted or planned by government agencies, other donors, UN agencies, or others. It may be possible to reach agreement with the agency conducting this study to include a few additional questions or to add a special module that will be administered to a subsample of the original sample. If the planned survey covers the universe from which the project population is drawn, it may be possible to use this as the comparison group to construct the counterfactual.

BOX 16.4
APPLYING COMPLICATED AND
COMPLEX EVALUATION DESIGNS TO THE EVALUATION OF
COUNTRY ASSISTANCE STRATEGIES

Appendix H illustrates how the complicated and complex evaluation designs discussed in this chapter can be applied to the evaluation of country assistance strategies. The country assistance evaluation methodology used by the Independent Evaluation Group of the World Bank is used as an example.

SUMMARY

- Development agencies are providing an increasing proportion of their development assistance through complex interventions that may involve multiple components or cover more than one sector, and that frequently operate at the national or international level, often in cooperation with one or more other donor agencies.

- Following the Paris Declaration and a number of follow-up international agreements, the assistance is also being provided more often in the form of general budget support to governments, making it difficult to identify how the funds have been used.

- All of these developments make it more difficult to evaluate the impacts of these interventions. A fundamental methodological challenge is the difficulty of defining a counterfactual that can be used to compare the situation with and without the project.

- Given these methodological challenges, many agencies believe that it is not possible to estimate the impacts that their particular resources and initiative have had; consequently, the focus is often on assessing the *plausible contribution* rather than *direct attribution*.

- Despite these challenges, there are wide ranges of methodologies available that could potentially be used to define alternatives to the conventional statistical counterfactual and that could provide estimates of the impact of the interventions, even though these estimates will often not be as statistically rigorous as is possible when evaluating the direct effects caused by simple project interventions.

- Potential methodologies for assessing impacts of complex programs include quantitative, qualitative, mixed-method, and theory-based approaches. Rating scales, usually adapted from the OECD-DAC evaluation guidelines, are also used by many agencies to rate impacts as well as efficiency, effectiveness, relevance, sustainability, and sometimes other dimensions such as gender equity or systematic procedures for learning and disseminating lessons from the evaluation.

- There are also a number of general strategies that can be used to strengthen all complex evaluation designs: (a) disaggregating programs into simpler and more easily evaluated components; (b) portfolio analysis through which all activities that support a broad development objective are rated on a set of scales assessing the quality of design and implementation and potential outcomes; (c) using the techniques for reconstructing baseline data discussed in Chapter 5 to construct pretest–posttest counterfactuals; (d) creative use of available secondary data; and (e) taking advantage of ongoing or planned studies that could generate program or comparison group data.

FURTHER READING

Funnell, S. and P. Rogers. 2011. *Purposeful Program Theory: Effective Use of Theories of Change and Logic Models.* San Francisco: Jossey-Bass.

Introduction to the concept of complexity and the challenges of applying logic models to complex programs. Also includes a review of recent developments in logic modeling that help address the challenges of modeling complex programs.

Kane, M. and W. Trochim. 2007. *Concept Mapping for Planning and Evaluation.* Thousand Oaks, CA: Sage.

A thorough but not too technical explanation of how concept mapping can be used for the design, implementation, and interpretation of an evaluation. The approach, which largely relies on consultations with stakeholders and experts, is well suited to the evaluation of complex programs.

Morra-Imas, L. and R. Rist. 2009. *The Road to Results: Designing and Conducting Effective Development Evaluations.* Washington, DC: World Bank.

A comprehensive review of recent trends in international development evaluation with a strong emphasis on the move toward complex, multidonor programs.

OECD-DAC. 2010. *Evaluation in Development Agencies.* Paris: OECD-DAC. Available electronically at www.oecdbook shop.org/oecd/display.asp?sf1=identifiers&st1=978 9264094857

Publication also reviews recent trends in the focus of the kinds of evaluations that these agencies support.

Patton, M. Q. 2011. *Developmental Evaluation: Applying Complexity Concepts to Enhance Innovation and Use.* New York: Guilford.

Detailed but very readable discussion of the concepts of complexity and why it is so difficult to apply conventional experimental evaluation designs to real-world development programs. Large numbers of detailed and very informative case studies are included throughout.

World Bank. 2008. *CAE Methodology Guide to IEG's Country Evaluation Rating Methodology.* Washington, DC: World Bank. Available at: http://web.worldbank.org/ WBSITE/EXTERNAL/EXTOED/EXTCOUASSEVAL/0,, contentMDK:2110704 6~menuPK:4620176~pagePK:6 4829573~piPK:64829550~theSitePK:4425762,00.html

Complete description of the World Bank Independent Evaluation Group's (IEG) methodology for the evaluation of complex country programs and country assistance strategies. Many other bilateral and multilateral development agencies have drawn on the IEG approach.

PART III

Organizing and Managing Evaluations and Strengthening Evaluation Capacity

For readers involved with the funding and management of evaluations

CHAPTER 17

Organizing and Managing the Evaluation Function

T his is the first of two chapters discussing the organization and management of evaluations. It begins by discussing a number of organizational and political issues affecting the design, implementation, and use of evaluations. It then discusses the main steps in the planning and management of evaluations: preparing the evaluation, recruiting the evaluators, designing the evaluation, managing the implementation of the evaluation, reporting and disseminating the findings, and coordinating the management response to the findings and recommendations and ensuring follow-up on the agreed actions to be taken to implement the recommendations that are accepted. In Chapter 18, we will discuss approaches for strengthening the capacities of managers and evaluators to plan and conduct evaluations.

1. Organizational and Political Issues Affecting the Design, Implementation, and Use of Evaluations

All evaluations are developed, managed, and used within particular administrative systems and within particular political contexts. Administrative systems are designed to operate in a particular way, and they also have their own traditions and beliefs concerning how things should be done. So an evaluation approach that works well within one administrative system, as well as within a particular context, might be much less successful in a different administrative context and with a different political dynamic. For example, a particular approach to evaluation might work well in a highly centralized administrative system with a very powerful Ministry of Finance, whereas a different approach might be more successful in a decentralized political system where the Ministry of Planning was the driving force. Similarly, a newly elected government that wishes to introduce ambitious new social programs might have a very different attitude to a broad-based evaluation program than an administration that is facing a difficult election and may not wish to have its flagship programs assessed too critically. In this section, we discuss some of the political and administrative issues that define the framework within which an evaluation system must be developed and managed and some of the challenges and constraints that affect the system.

Political and organizational factors can influence decisions and actions at all stages of the evaluation, from decisions as to whether to commission an evaluation and what should be evaluated to how the findings are presented and disseminated. Table 6.1 (Chapter 6) illustrates how political and organizational factors can have influence during

- *The evaluation design phase:* the criteria for selecting the evaluators, the choice of the evaluation design, data collection methods, the choice of indicators, which stakeholders to involve or consult, the professional orientation of the evaluation, and the allocation of budget and time
- *The evaluation implementation phase:* the changing role of the evaluator at different stages of the evaluation, the selection of audiences to receive progress reports and to provide feedback and comments, and the evolving dynamics of the evaluation
- *The analysis, dissemination, and use phase:* defining who prepares and can veto the executive summary and the cover note that accompanies the report, deciding who should review the evaluation reports, choice of the language(s) in which the report will be presented, choice of the style and technical level of the report, and how and to whom the final report is presented

2. Planning and Managing the Evaluation

This section discusses the planning and management of an individual evaluation. In Step 3, the section on designing the evaluation, we will discuss the different strategies that an agency can adopt for organizing the overall evaluation function. The planning and management of an evaluation can be broken down into six steps (see Figure 17.1). These steps apply to all development evaluations, whether this is an assessment of a small (simple) project providing health services for a small number of villages; a (complicated) sector program such as strengthening secondary education throughout the country, which involves a number of different components, often supported by different donors and with different methodologies and objectives; or a (complex) national-level intervention providing broad-based support in a number of different areas and often with no clearly defined objectives (see Chapter 16). The steps apply to government programs as well as to activities managed by nongovernmental organizations (NGOs) or private-sector agencies. This section draws on evaluation management approaches recommended by AusAID, Swedish International Development Cooperation Agency (Sida), Department for International Development (DFID), and United Nations Development Programme (UNDP):

- Step 1: Preparing the evaluation
- Step 2: Recruiting the evaluators
- Step 3: Designing the evaluation
- Step 4: Managing the implementation of the evaluation
- Step 5: Reporting and disseminating the findings
- Step 6: Management response and follow-up

Figure 17.1 Managing the Evaluation Process

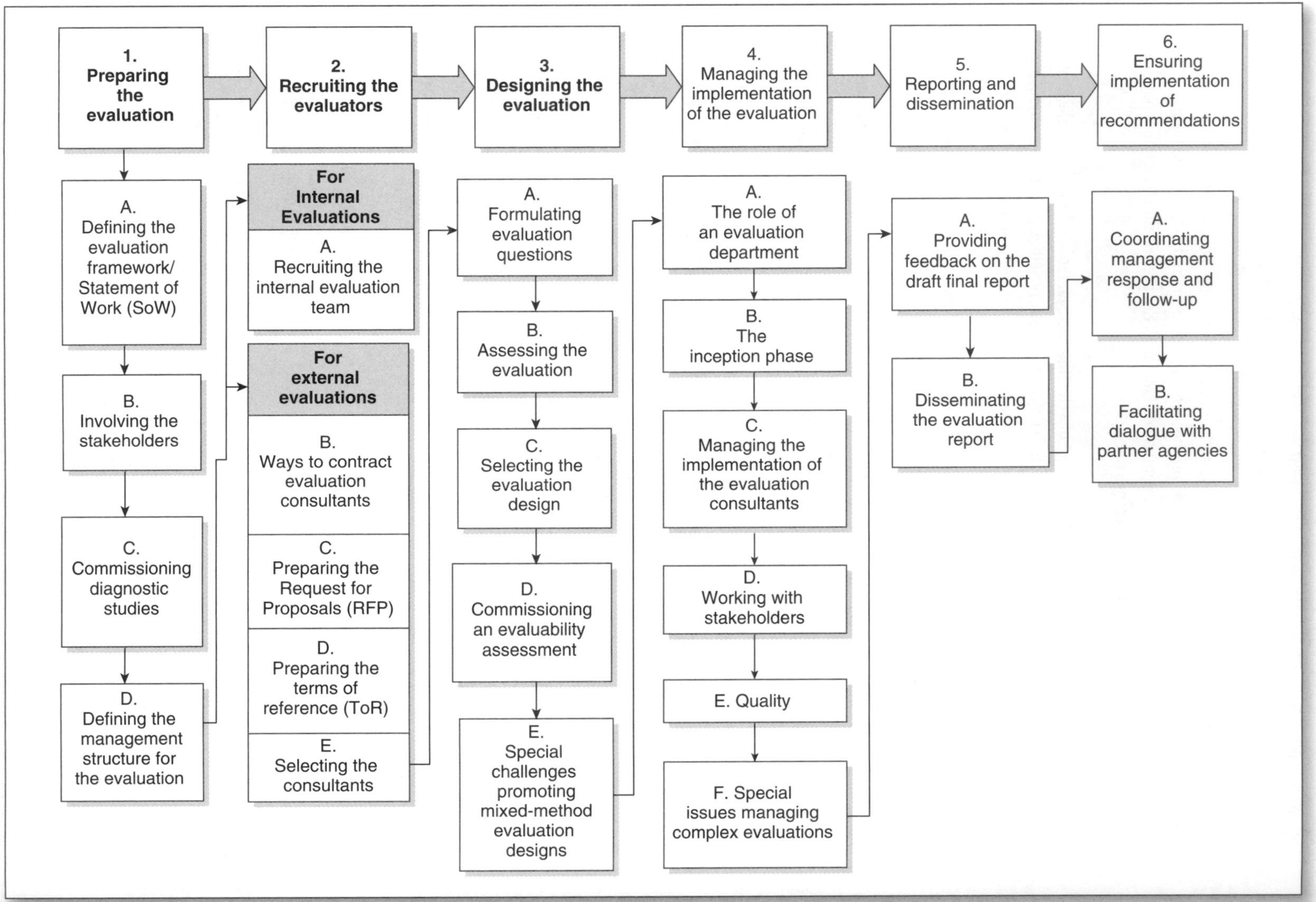

2.1. Step 1: Preparing the Evaluation

Before planning or commissioning an evaluation, it is important to understand the context within which the evaluation will be conducted, involving the main stakeholders, and agreeing on how the evaluation will be conducted and managed. This will normally involve the following activities.

Step 1-A: Defining the Evaluation Framework or the Scope of Work (SoW)

A key stage in the organization of an evaluation is to define a clear framework, agreed to among all parties. Some organizations refer to this as the Evaluation Framework (UNDP 2009), while others refer to this as the Scope (or Statement) of Work (SoW; Morra-Imas and Rist 2009; United States Agency for International Development [USAID] 2010). The situation is confused by the fact that other agencies use the term *Statement of Work* to define the Terms of Reference for consultants. Evaluation Frameworks and Statements of Work are discussed separately, although there is considerable overlap. Box 17.1 explains the potential confusion arising from the fact that different agencies use the term *Scope of Work* (SoW) in different ways and proposes a way in which the meaning of the terms can be clarified.

The Evaluation Framework. Evaluation Frameworks are used extensively by the UNDP (2009) and are considered particularly important for collaborative evaluations that involve more than one development partner (UNDP 2009, chap. 3). The framework should clarify the following:

- What is to be evaluated
- The activities needed to evaluate
- Who is responsible for different evaluation activities
- Timing of the evaluation activities
- The proposed methods
- What resources are required and where do they come from

BOX 17.1
EVALUATION FRAMEWORKS, SCOPE OF WORK, AND EVALUATION TERMS OF REFERENCE

There are some potential confusions concerning the terms *Evaluation Framework, Scope of Work* (*SoW*), and *Terms of Reference* (*ToR*) as they are used differently by different agencies.

Evaluation Framework. This is an internal planning document used by the UNDP to define the purpose and scope of the evaluation, timing, responsibilities, resource requirements, and proposed methodologies. If this is a collaborative evaluation, the framework will be shared with partners. Once agreement has been reached on the framework, this will be used to define the Terms of Reference that will be included in the Request for Proposals that is communicated to interested consultants.

(Continued)

(Continued)

Scope of Work (SoW). Agencies such as USAID use the SoW in a similar way to the UNDP's evaluation framework as defining the scope, timing, responsibilities, resource requirements, and proposed methodology. One of the purposes of the SoW is to prepare the budget, time, and other resource requirements. These must be approved before the evaluation begins. Often the SoW covers a broad program of activities that may include a number of different specific evaluations, so often this will lay out the whole evaluation strategy for a multiyear program.

The confusion arises because other agencies use the term *Scope of Work* to refer to the Terms of Reference that are given to consultants defining the scope of the evaluation, the questions that must be addressed, and so on.

Terms of Reference (ToR). This a general term referring to a document that defines the responsibilities of any consultant contracted for a particular purpose, including but not limited to the design and implementation of an evaluation. In the case of an evaluation ToR, this will describe the purposes of the evaluation, the deliverables to be produced, the timing, and the available resources.

The confusion arises because what some agencies call the Terms of Reference to be given to consultants, other agencies call the Scope of Work.

How we use the terms: To avoid confusion, we will use the term *Agency* Scope of Work to refer to the internal planning document used by an agency to plan and budget an individual evaluation or an evaluation program and the term *Evaluator* Scope of Work to refer to the document that is given to prospective evaluation consultants. Based on these definitions:

- Agency Scope of Work and Evaluation Framework have similar meanings.
- Consultant Scope of Work and Evaluation Terms of Reference have similar meanings.

The UNDP recommends that the evaluation framework normally has three components: a narrative component describing how (international and national) partners will undertake evaluation activities and the accountabilities assigned to each group, a results framework, and a planning matrix (see UNDP 2009:87 for an example of an evaluation plan/matrix). Some of the considerations for planning the evaluation system include the following:

- Uses, purposes, and timing
- Resources available and required
- The likelihood of future initiatives in the same area
- Anticipated problems
- Need for lessons learned
- (When several development agencies are involved) alignment and harmonization

It can also be useful to check "evaluability readiness" (UNDP 2009:148). This involves questions such as the following:

- Does the subject of the evaluation have a clearly defined results map?
- Is there a clearly defined results framework?
- Is there sufficient capacity to provide required data for the evaluation?
- Is the planned evaluation still relevant?
- Will political, social, and economic factors allow for an effective conducting and use of the evaluation?
- Are there sufficient resources?

Additional issues arise when planning a joint evaluation involving a number of different partners. The partners must be selected, and there must be agreement on the scope of work, the funding modality, the process for selecting the evaluators, the reporting and dissemination strategies, and the modality for management response.

The Agency Scope of Work (SoW). While agencies use the term *Statement of Work* or *Scope of Work* (SoW), to avoid confusion (see Box 17.1), we will refer to this planning document as the *Agency* Scope of Work. The Agency SoW, as used by organizations such as USAID (2010), can be broader than the evaluation framework as it may lay out a monitoring and evaluation strategy for a complete program lasting several years, which may involve a number of distinct evaluation activities, some conducted internally and some subcontracted. It may also define roles and responsibilities for the management and implementation of the evaluation within the contracting agency, as well as the overall budget and staffing requirements for all of the evaluation activities, including the resources for internal activities as well as for external contracts. For many organizations, the Agency SoW is a standard planning and budgeting mechanism used for all program activities, not just evaluations. This means that evaluation plans must be defined using the same procedures as other program activities, which can introduce some additional constraints and issues in large and complex organizations where administrative departments are processing very large numbers of diverse contracts.

The Agency SoW for an evaluation spells out the mutual obligations between client and the evaluation team—whether internal, external, or mixed. It explains the evaluation parameters and the resources available for conducting it.

- Start with the constraints within which the evaluation must operate:
  o The budget
  o Timing
  o What are other RealWorld constraints on the evaluation? (lack of baseline or counterfactual data, political pressures, etc.)
- The SoW should be considered as a first step in developing the evaluation utilization plan
- Key elements of the SoW
  o Program implementation: what, where, when (start and end dates)
  o Evaluation fundamentals: purpose, main questions
  o Technical requirements: design, methods, staffing
  o Management information: schedule, budget
  o Present the theory of change (logic model/development hypothesis/results format)

- ○ Target groups and areas
- ○ Critical assumptions
- ○ Information available on the project and its context

- Evaluation fundamentals

  - ○ Primary users of the evaluation
  - ○ How it will be used
  - ○ Technical requirements of the evaluation design

    - Key questions
    - Sources of data
    - Data collection methods
    - Data quality expected
    - Data analysis
    - How the data will be disaggregated and presented

- Management requirements

  - ○ Team qualifications and size

    - Local personnel

  - ○ Deliverables
  - ○ Schedule
  - ○ Logistics
  - ○ LOE (level of effort)/budget
  - ○ Estimated costs for each step
  - ○ Reporting

Box 17.2 lists the elements of a good evaluation SoW identified by USAID.

BOX 17.2
THE ELEMENTS OF A GOOD EVALUATION
STATEMENT OF WORK (SOW)

1. Describe the activity, program, or process to be evaluated

2. Provide a brief background

3. State the purpose and use of the evaluation

4. Clarify the evaluation questions

5. Identify the evaluation methods

6. Identify existing performance information

7. Specify deliverables and timelines

8. Discuss the composition of the evaluation team

9. Address scheduling, logistics, and other support

10. Clarify requirements for reporting and dissemination

11. Include a budget

SOURCE: USAID (2010).

Step 1-B: Involving Stakeholders

Stakeholders are the people and organizations (in addition to the client who asks for and will pay for the evaluation) with stakes in the intervention or in the evaluation (Morra-Imas and Rist 2009:144). They include policy and planning agencies, organizations involved in the implementation of the program or who may be affected by it, beneficiaries, and groups benefiting from, affected by, or potentially suffering as a result of the program. It also involves groups excluded from the program. Stakeholders can be involved in the evaluation in different ways: They may use the results to make policy or operational decisions, may provide inputs to the evaluation or comments, or may be academics or others generally interested in the evaluation. All evaluation handbooks and textbooks emphasize the importance of involving stakeholders from an early stage of the evaluation. This is important for a number of reasons, including the following: to ensure buy-in to increase the likelihood that the results will be used; to avoid opposition to the evaluation, for reasons of equity; or to receive guidance on the design and implementation of the evaluation. Where possible, it is recommended that a stakeholder analysis be conducted at the start of the evaluation to systematically capture the areas of interest and concern of each stakeholder group (Patton 2008; Morra-Imas and Rist 2009:147–48; UNDP 2009:93–94).

Table 17.1 is an example of a chart that can be used to identify all potential stakeholders. While it is important to involve all stakeholders, it is equally important to define their respective roles. In particular, it is important to clarify which individuals or groups are only to receive information on the evaluation, which ones will be invited to give opinions, and which individuals have any kind of veto power. A common danger is to give too many people the right to approve the evaluation plan or the right to comment before the plan is approved. This can result in long delays while waiting for people to respond or unnecessary and time-consuming negotiations with people who feel obliged to propose changes in the plan.

Table 17.1 Roles of Stakeholders in an Evaluation

Stakeholders	To Make Policy	To Make Operational Decisions	To Provide Input to Evaluation	To React	For Interest Only
Developers of the program					
Funders of the program					
Authorizing official, board, or agency					
Providers of other resources (facilities, supplies, in-kind contributions)					
Heads of implementing agencies and senior managers					
Program managers responsible for implementation					
Program staff					

(Continued)

(Continued)

Stakeholders	To Make Policy	To Make Operational Decisions	To Provide Input to Evaluation	To React	For Interest Only
Monitoring or evaluation staff					
Direct beneficiaries of the program					
Indirect beneficiaries of the program					
Potential adopters of the program					
People excluded from the program (e.g., by entry criteria)					
People perceiving negative effects of the program or the evaluation					
People losing power as a result of the program					
People losing opportunities as a result of the program					
Members of the community or the general public					
Others					

SOURCE: International Bank for Reconstruction and Development/The World Bank: *The Road to Results* (Morra-Imas and Rist 2009).

Step 1-C: Commissioning Diagnostic Studies

It will often be helpful to commission an exploratory diagnostic study to better understand the context within which the intervention operates (see Chapters 2 and 11). An important function of this study will often be to determine whether the intervention to be evaluated is simple, complicated, or complex (see Chapters 11 and 16) as this will determine the possible evaluation approach and design.

Step 1-D: Defining the Management Structure for the Evaluation

There is no single best way to organize an evaluation as the decision will be determined by a number of factors, including the following:

- Whether the evaluation is to be conducted internally or externally
- The evaluation capacity of sector and central government agencies. In some cases, a sector agency may have the capacity to manage an evaluation, but their managers may not have the time. This is often the case when a new program is being launched.

- The purpose of the evaluation: For a formative evaluation, it is important to involve the implementing agency to the greatest possible extent, whereas when the purpose is accountability or to ensure an objective summative assessment of the project outcomes and impacts, it may be more important to have the evaluation conducted by an external agency.
- Is this a single evaluation that is not likely to be repeated or is it one of a series? If this is part of an ongoing series of evaluations, it may be more important to ensure an active participation of the implementing agency, but if this is a single evaluation, it may make more sense to commission an outside agency that has the necessary expertise and resources.
- The importance that is attached to evaluation capacity development of agency staff, partners, and/or independent evaluators in the host country

If one of the goals of an evaluation program is to strengthen the evaluation capacity of line ministries and regional/local agencies, it is possible to make these agencies responsible for managing the evaluation but to provide technical and logistical assistance from local consultants or international agencies. Many development loans and grants include funds to contract a resident evaluator adviser who will spend several months or, in some cases, several years helping an agency to strengthen its capacity to commission, manage, and perhaps implement evaluations (more on this subject in Chapter 18).

A goal of most development agencies, particularly since the Paris Declaration,[1] has been to strengthen the responsibility of national agencies for management and evaluation of development programs. Similarly, many governments and international development agencies seek to decentralize the evaluation function by strengthening the capacity and responsibility of line ministries and regional and local agencies in all stages of the evaluation.

Boxes 17.3 and 17.4 present two examples of how different actors can be involved in different stages of the evaluation. In the first case, an evaluation of how effectively gender issues are addressed in the design and implementation of an international food security program, two international evaluators were commissioned to conduct the evaluation, and they brought in several national evaluators to conduct data collection in several of the six sample countries selected for the in-depth evaluations. The evaluation department of the client was actively involved in discussions on the evaluation design and in coordinating contacts with different departments at headquarters. Country offices of the client were involved in coordinating interviews in each project and in arranging meetings with community groups. This evaluation illustrates a typical compromise between the needs to ensure independence of the evaluation and the practical needs, given budget and time constraints, to rely on client staff at the country or local level to coordinate interviews and to facilitate meetings with community groups, many of whom do not speak the national language. The second example (Box 17.4) illustrates a situation where different stakeholders have different priorities and where the international consultant was required to develop a compromise solution to satisfy the information needs and methodological priorities of different stakeholders.

Each stage of the evaluation process can be implemented by a range of different actors,[2] including *a sector or local agency* (e.g., the project executing agency or a local or regional agency), a

---

[1]For a description of the Paris Declaration, see Organization for Economic Cooperation and Development (OECD) 2008).

[2]For examples of how different agencies identify the main actors and stakeholders and their roles in the evaluation, see Department of International Development (DFID) (2005), AusAID (2008), and Morra-Imas and Rist (2009:246–51).

national-level agency (e.g., national planning or financial agencies, an NGO or consortium of NGOs, a consulting firm, a university or research institute, or a national foundation), or an *international development or consulting agency* (e.g., a bilateral agency, a multilateral agency, and international NGO or NGO consortium, a foundation, an individual consultant, or a consulting firm). The choice of agency to implement each stage of the evaluation has important implications for the focus and technical quality of the evaluation as well as the "ownership" and utilization of the evaluation. Agencies or stakeholders that do not feel involved will often be less likely to use the findings and recommendations of the evaluation.

Sometimes all or most stages will be the responsibility of a single agency, but frequently different stages will be the responsibility of different agencies. It is also quite common to have a number of different agencies involved in a particular stage, with some playing a more major role than others. A potential source of conflict or confusion is when the respective responsibilities of different agencies are not clearly defined.

BOX 17.3
THE ACTORS INVOLVED IN AN EVALUATION OF HOW GENDER EQUALITY ISSUES WERE ADDRESSED IN AN INTERNATIONAL FOOD SECURITY PROGRAM

Two individual consultants were commissioned to conduct an evaluation of the gender policies of an international agency promoting food security in low-income countries around the world. It was agreed that fieldwork would be conducted in a sample of six representative countries in Africa, Asia, and Latin America and that this would be combined with existing documentation from other countries and interviews with agency headquarters staff. The principal actors involved in the evaluation were (a) the two international consultants; (b) local consultants contracted by the international consultants to conduct data collection in several countries; (c) the evaluation department of the development agency, which was actively involved in developing detailed guidelines for the evaluation, working actively with the consultants, and organizing videoconferences to obtain feedback from staff in a wider range of countries than the sample countries selected for fieldwork; (d) country offices in the sample countries, which coordinated the interview schedule, coordinated field trips, and accompanied consultants on some of the field visits; (e) the gender focal points in country offices in sample countries, which coordinated the distribution and collection of a survey administered to agency staff; (f) partner government agencies in sample countries, which provided additional statistical data requested by consultants following field visits; (g) NGO implementing agencies in sample countries, which helped facilitate community meetings in beneficiary communities (including providing interpretation into local languages); (h) key informants from agencies such as the district health department and the police, familiar with the communities but not involved in the project so as to avoid bias from obtaining information only from beneficiaries and agencies directly involved in the project; and (i) the gender unit of the client agency, which provided comments on the evaluation design and the survey instruments and provided background documentation but were not directly involved in the implementation of the evaluation.

The evaluation design sought to ensure impartiality and objectivity by using external evaluators while accepting the practical necessity (due to time and budget constraints) to involve the country offices of the client in coordinating interview schedules, distributing surveys, and, in some cases, facilitating and providing interpretation for community meetings. Consultants were aware of the potential biases that involvement of the client implied and sought to control for this through triangulation (interviews with other stakeholders, review of secondary data, requests for additional data from government and NGO implementing agencies and through consultation with agencies not involved in the project).

SOURCE: Unpublished personal experience of one of the present authors.

BOX 17.4
AN EXAMPLE OF ACTORS INVOLVED IN THE EVALUATION OF A NATIONAL HOUSING PROGRAM THAT WAS PART OF A COMPARATIVE INTERNATIONAL EVALUATION

In the early 1970s, the World Bank began funding low-cost housing programs in different developing regions. To assess the social and economic impacts of these housing programs, the World Bank and the International Development Research Centre in Canada (IDRC) agreed to co-finance a 5-year longitudinal impact evaluation of three of these projects. The main actors in the evaluation in a typical country (e.g., El Salvador) were the following:

(a) The IDRC, which funded and managed the national evaluation teams and participated in the annual review meetings

(b) The World Bank, which funded and supervised the international consultant who spent 3 years in (in this case) El Salvador and whose economic research staff were actively involved in the evaluation design, implementation, and analysis of findings

(c) The resident international consultant who helped create the national evaluation unit, supervised all stages of the evaluation during the first 2 years, and gradually passed responsibility over to the national evaluation team so that they were able to completely manage the evaluation during the final 2 years after the departure of the international consultant. He was also responsible for preparing (different) progress reports for the World Bank and the national project implementing agency (the Salvadorian Foundation for Low-cost Housing [FSDVM]) and for ensuring that the interests of all parties were adequately reflected in the evaluation.

(Continued)

(Continued)

(d) The FSDVM, which insisted on having direct responsibility for the evaluation and had strong views on the overall focus of the evaluation (see below)

(e) The national monitoring and evaluation unit under the FSDVM that implemented the evaluation

(f) A local university that was contracted to conduct some of the surveys so as to ensure greater independence and objectivity of the findings

(g) The national steering committee that included representatives from the planning and housing ministries as well as other national stakeholders

The proposed arrangements were designed to achieve a compromise between the interests of the different stakeholders. The World Bank was concerned to ensure a strong economic focus so as to assess the cost-effectiveness of the housing model as an efficient delivery system for providing housing for low-income families. This required strong technical input from the World Bank, while the IDRC, although interested in the technical (but less the econometric) quality of the findings, was more concerned to ensure building national evaluation capacity and a strong voice for the FSDVM at all stages of the evaluation. FSDVM had a strong social activist orientation, considering that families working together on housing construction was a form of political empowerment, and wanted the evaluation to assess the social and political outcomes of the housing programs. It became clear at an early stage that while there was agreement among the main stakeholders with respect to many aspects of the evaluation, there were significant disagreements concerning other questions. While the FSDVM felt that the World Bank was too narrowly focused on the economic outcomes, many people in the World Bank felt that the FSDVM wished to address political and social issues that were either not of interest or in some cases considered inappropriate. The resulting compromise was to request the international consultant to prepare separate progress reports for the World Bank and for the FSDVM. Core survey instruments were developed that covered the basic information needs of all parties, and then a number of additional studies were conducted at the request of particular parties.

SOURCE: Unpublished personal experience of one of the present authors.

2.2. Step 2: Recruiting the Evaluators

For Evaluations to Be Conducted Internally

Step 2-A: Recruiting the Internal Evaluation Team

When an evaluation is to be conducted internally, it will normally be the responsibility of the monitoring and evaluation (M&E) unit if they are combined or the evaluation unit if it is separate. In some cases, particularly for a new program, there may not be a unit with responsibility for evaluation, in which case a special arrangement will have to be made (e.g., a special unit may be created in the office of the general manager or the director of operations of the agency responsible for implementing the program).

While some agencies have the staff to conduct data collection and analysis, very often the evaluation will be managed by the respective internal unit, but interviewers or data analysts will be subcontracted to an outside individual or agency (market research firm, university, national statistics bureau). Often a donor agency may provide technical support through visits from an international consultant or by providing a resident evaluation adviser.

The decision on how much of the evaluation will be subcontracted will depend in part on the professional capacity of the agency but also on whether this is seen as a one-off evaluation or as the start of an evaluation capacity development program. In the former case, the policy may be to contract parts of the evaluation to the best-qualified local evaluators, whereas in the latter case, the preference may be to use in-house staff as much as possible—possibly paired with more experienced outsiders.

For Evaluations to Be Conducted Externally

Step 2-B: Different Ways to Contract External Evaluation Consultants

When and How to Use Consultants. Consultants are individuals, firms, or research institutions such as universities or social, economic, or scientific research institutes that provide technical support in the design or analysis of an evaluation and who are often responsible for conducting the evaluation. Evaluation consultants can be divided into two broad categories: *evaluation implementers,* who carry out the evaluation, and *evaluation technical support consultants,* who provide support to the agencies that are commissioning evaluations or developing their own evaluation capacity.

Some of the ways that *evaluation technical support consultants* can be used include the following:

- Organizing training programs to strengthen the evaluation capacity of stakeholders and possibly local consultants
- Technical assistance in scoping and/or designing the evaluation, including help in developing the Terms of Reference or Scope of Work for an evaluation
- Assessing evaluation proposals from potential consultants responding to the request for proposals
- Evaluation of quality assurance: providing feedback to evaluation clients on the quality of the evaluation work of *evaluation implementers* at the design, implementation, and analysis phases
- Resident evaluation adviser who provides long-term support to an agency in developing its capacity to formulate, design, commission, manage, implement, and use evaluations

Contracting the Evaluation Consultants. Evaluators can be contracted directly or through a competitive process. Governments have procedures specifying the required recruiting and contracting processes based on the size and nature of the contract and sometimes the source of funding. Donor agencies also have similar requirements. Working within the required contracting procedures, there are often a number of factors to be considered when recruiting consultants:

- *Fixed cost or level of effort.* A fixed-cost contract specifies the deliverables (evaluation reports, training activities, etc.) to be provided and the time scale for their delivery. This has the advantage that the contracting agency and the consultant know the budget commitment in advance. This procedure works well when the nature of the product is clearly understood and when it can be quantified (e.g., conducting a certain number of interviews). However, a fixed-cost procedure works less well in a new field where the appropriate evaluation design must be developed, tested, and possibly revised and where it is difficult to know in advance how long this will take. The consultant has an incentive to complete the design as quickly and cheaply as possible so as not to lose money on the contract, and consequently there is a danger of producing a poor quality design.

  On the other hand, the level-of-effort contract is more flexible as the number of consultant days can be adjusted as the design requirements become clear. This also provides the flexibility to conduct follow-up interviews if the need arises. However, the potential disadvantage is that the consultant may have the incentive to spend more time than is really required.

- *Contracting a firm versus an individual consultant.* Hiring an individual consultant will usually be much cheaper and may work well if the client is familiar with the field and knows which consultant to hire. The danger is that if the consultant is not able to deliver (she or he is overcommitted or becomes sick, for example), there may not be a backup team member available, and the completion of the contract may be delayed or the quality may suffer. Contracting through an experienced and well-established firm has the advantage that they can draw on a wider range of professional expertise and have more logistical resources for conducting evaluations. However, when working with a firm, it is important to clarify who will actually work on the contract as some firms list a number of well-known professionals in the proposal, but these people may have relatively little direct involvement in the design or implementation of the evaluation.

- *Broadening the range of research expertise.* Many consultants and firms have developed their expertise in particular research fields such as econometrics and quantitative survey research or qualitative and participatory evaluations. With the growing interest in mixed-method evaluations that combine a broad range of quantitative and qualitative techniques, consultants will often be requested to broaden the range of data collection and analysis techniques they use. This will often result in an evaluation design that is not well integrated. For example, a number of not very well-selected focus groups or in-depth case studies may be added to a sample survey, or a rapid and not well-designed survey may be added to a set of case studies to permit generalization to a broader population. In these cases, the client may wish to contract a *technical support consultant* to define the requirements for these mixed-method designs and to assess the quality of the proposals.

Different Procedures for Selecting and Contracting Consultants. Different agencies use different procedures for selecting and contracting consultants, and the procedures can also vary depending on the size, duration, and complexity of the contract. Often simpler procedures will be used for smaller contracts, and in some cases for small contracts, a single consultant or firm can be selected without going through a competitive bidding process. Some of the steps and options, described in more detail in the following sections, include the following:

a. For many large organizations, the first stage is the use of a broad planning framework such as an Evaluation Framework or Statement of Work (SoW) that defines the overall purpose, approach, and resource requirements of the evaluation (discussed earlier in Step 1-A). Often the SoW will cover the total monitoring and evaluation for a multiyear program that might involve a number of different evaluation contracts.

b. *Invitation to submit an Expression of Interest (EOI).* Often for large contracts, but sometimes also for smaller ones, interested firms and individual consultants can be invited to submit an EOI indicating their interest in submitting a proposal. Sometimes an announcement will be posted, and all interested consultants can respond, while in other cases, the invitation is only sent to a selected short list. The EOI will include background on the firm/consultant and usually initial ideas on the proposed approach.

c. *Request for Proposals (RFP).* This document provides detailed information on the purpose and scope of the proposed evaluation and procedures for submitting a proposal. In some cases, all interested firms/consultants can submit proposals, while in other cases, there will be a preliminary screening process, often based on responses to the EOI.

d. *Terms of Reference (ToR).* Sometimes the ToR will be completely defined in the RFP, but in other cases, the RFP will invite firms to comment on the draft ToR, and this may be revised and finalized during negotiations with the selected or short-listed firms.

e. *Inception Report.* Once consultants have been selected, many agencies require, at least for large contracts, that an inception report be prepared. This provides consultants an opportunity to revise their methodology after having spent some time in the field assessing the feasibility of the proposed methodology, and this may result in revisions to the ToR or SoW.

Step 2-C: Preparing the Request for Proposals (RFP)

The process of recruiting consultants normally begins with the preparation of an RFP. Depending on the organization and contract rules and procedures, the contract may be awarded on a sole-source basis, from invitations to a few contractors to bid, or from open competition. The winning proposal may be selected by the evaluation manager or by an appointed panel that makes its recommendation based on prespecified criteria. Most agencies have very precisely defined selection and contracting procedures, and many have a policy of transparency.

A source of frustration to agencies wishing to fund and launch evaluations or to consultants interested in winning an evaluation contract is the long and complex selection process used by many agencies. It is not unusual for the selection process to last several months, particularly when RFPs have to be advertised for a certain period of time. As discussed earlier, many evaluations involve a large number of actors and stakeholders (see Table 17.1), and the process of reaching agreement on the purpose and proposed design can also be time-consuming. So it is important for the agency funding or promoting the evaluation to understand the selection process that will be used and to factor in a realistic amount of time to complete this process.

An RFP should include the following (Hawkins 2005, cited in Morra-Imas and Rist 2009:443):

- Purpose of the evaluation
- Background and context of the study
- Key information requirements
- Evaluation objectives
- Deliverables required
- Timeframe
- Criteria for tender selection
- Contract details for the project manager
- Deadline for proposals
- Budget and other resources

Step 2-D: Preparing the Terms of Reference (ToR)

As discussed earlier, the ToR will be included in the RFP, but it may be revised and finalized later to address comments that consultants include in their proposals or on the basis of feedback from the inception report (see Step 4-B). According to the Organization for Economic Cooperation and Development (OECD 2001), a ToR for an evaluation is a written documentation that should present the following:

- The purpose and scope of the evaluation
- The methods to be used
- The standard against which performance is to be assessed or analyses are to be conducted
- The resources and time allocated
- Reporting requirements

Some agencies include a Consultant Statement of Work (SoW) as an element of a solicitation for an evaluation. The SoW for an evaluation spells out the mutual obligations between client and the evaluation team—whether internal, external, or mixed. It explains the evaluation parameters and the resources available for conducting it.

Expanding on the OECD/Development Advisory Committee (DAC) list cited above, the ToR typically includes the following (Morra-Imas and Rist 2009:445):

- A short descriptive title
- A description of the project or program
- The reasons for and expectations of the evaluation
- A statement of the scope and focus of the evaluation
- Identification of stakeholder involvement
- A description of the evaluation process
- A list of deliverables
- Identification of necessary qualifications of the evaluators
- Cost projection based on activities, time, number of people, professional fees, travel, and other costs

The process of preparing the ToR provides an opportunity to ensure all key stakeholders are involved in the process and that the purposes of the evaluation are clarified. Different stakeholders will frequently have different expectations and requirements, and it will often be necessary to have a process of negotiation. It is important to avoid placing too many demands on the evaluation, and sometimes it will be necessary to prioritize the requirements of different stakeholders.

Common Problems Concerning ToR for RealWorld Evaluations. While many of the following issues may affect the preparation of ToR for many different types of evaluation, they tend to be particularly challenging for evaluations conducted under RealWorld budget and time constraints:

- The budget estimates are unrealistically low, and it would not be possible to respond to all of the conditions of the ToR within this budget.
- The time constraints, particularly the time for data collection in the field and data analysis, are unrealistically short, and it would not be possible to implement a sufficiently rigorous design within this time limit. Very commonly, the time required to plan field trips (coordinating with government and other local agencies, arranging air or ground transport, obtaining security clearance to travel, etc.) is underestimated.
- Often the time allowed for in-country travel and number of consultant days is determined according to a set administrative formula, which may not reflect the realistic requirements in a particular country. For example, the number of days allocated for travel often does not take into account the time (often several days) waiting for travel clearance or the time waiting to get a seat on World Food Program flights (often the only means of transport) into high-security regions.
- The ToR often requires types of information or analysis that are not possible or realistic to provide. There are several common reasons for this. First, if the evaluation is commissioned at a relatively early stage in the project cycle, it is too soon to be able to measure impacts and sometimes even outcomes. Despite this, ToRs frequently state that the evaluation will estimate project impacts. A second reason is that the approved budget is not sufficient to permit the kind of large and carefully selected sample that would be required to conduct the kinds of statistical analysis that are proposed. A third reason is that the evaluation is commissioned late in the project cycle and no baseline data have been collected, so it is not possible to use a rigorous pretest–posttest comparison group evaluation design. Fourth, the target population is too small to permit the sample sizes required for rigorous statistical analysis. Finally, there may be logistical, methodological, or ethical reasons why a control group cannot be identified or included.
- When the programs to be evaluated involve various different funding agencies or different national agencies, the challenges of coordinating the evaluation may limit the kind of evaluation that can be conducted.

The Consequences of Unrealistic or Poorly Defined ToR. The above problems can have serious consequences for the validity (and utility) of the evaluation. A common problem is that the time and resource constraints mean that the evaluators are able to spend only a short time visiting the project sites and interview the groups who are most easily accessible. These will often be the individuals or groups that have benefited from the project interventions, most of whom are likely to have a relatively positive impression of the project. Often the evaluator does not have time or the resources to meet with sectors of the intended target population who did not benefit (e.g., ethnic minorities, landless, or illegal immigrants), and under these circumstances, there is even less opportunity to meet with sectors of the population who may be worse off as a result of the project (Bamberger 2009e). For example, some families may have been forced to move or have had their houses demolished for road construction without receiving compensation. In other cases, some women may be subjected to domestic violence because they participated in a microcredit or food for work program without their husband's permission. For all of these reasons, the evaluation may have a positive bias, overstating the positive benefits of the project, underestimating the sectors of the intended target population who did not have access to the project services, and ignoring the negative outcomes. This may lead funders, implementing agencies, and policymakers to continue funding programs that have fewer benefits than expected or to fail to recognize that the project is not reaching certain sectors, often the most vulnerable.

The positive bias of the evaluation or other threats to validity resulting from the budget and time constraints may be worsened in cases where the ToRs do not clearly define the required methodology, so that the consultant is not required to ensure a minimum level of representativity of the sample, even when working under resource and time constraints.

The fact that many evaluation reports present the project in a favorable light, suggesting that it has achieved its objectives, means that funding agencies and implementing agencies may feel less concerned about the weak methodology than they would have been if this resulted in the findings being more negative and critical.

Tips for Strengthening the ToR. Table 17.2 provides general guidelines for strengthening evaluation ToRs and identifies some of the key areas and issues for developing evaluation ToRs when operating under RealWorld budget, time, and data constraints. Often the ToRs for RealWorld Evaluation (RWE) are methodologically quite weak as many agencies have come to accept that the quality will be low when resources are limited. However, there are a number of practical ways in which evaluation designs can be strengthened, even when operating under severe budget constraints, and strengthening the ToR is an important element in ensuring better quality evaluations.

The table identifies a number of preparatory steps that must be taken before the ToR is issued, ways to strengthen the ToR, and follow-up steps once interested consultants have responded to the RFP.

A number of important preparatory activities must be carried out before the ToR is prepared. These include consultations with stakeholders to clarify their information needs and how they plan to use the evaluation findings, as well as conducting a preliminary feasibility (evaluability) analysis to determine whether it will be possible to achieve the stated evaluation objectives with the current resource envelope and timelines. This preliminary analysis, which is often not conducted, will often show that the stated objectives of the evaluation are not feasible, in which case further discussion with stakeholders is required before the ToR is issued.

Some important points to stress in the ToR, particularly for RWE, are as follows:

- Provide a clear and explicit statement of the objectives of the evaluation, how the findings will be used, the required level of precision, and the kinds of management and/or policy decisions to which the findings will contribute.
- Define clearly the required minimum acceptable methodological standards for the evaluation. Some of the minimum requirements for evaluations operating on a limited budget and

tight timeline might include (a) the definition of a counterfactual together with an explanation of the sources of data that will be used to test it; (b) a specified minimum number of meetings with nonbeneficiaries; (c) identifying and obtaining information on groups who may be negatively affected by the project; (d) selection of a sample of key informants who are both familiar with the project and with the broader political, economic, and sociocultural context within which it operates; and (e) methodological procedures for selecting participants for focus groups (if these are to be used) and for conducting the discussions and reporting the findings.

- The possibility should be considered of including additional resources to allow the evaluation team to contract a local resource person to assist in the planning and organization of the evaluation. This can include identification and assessment of potential secondary data sources, preparing field trips, identifying key informants, organizing focus groups, and ensuring that the sample of informants will not be limited to project beneficiaries.
- Do not simply state the objectives of the evaluation in technical or process terms. State clearly how the evaluation is expected to help the organization, particularly managers and policy-makers.
- State clearly the quality assurance procedures (see Chapter 7 and Chapter 18 section 1) that will be used and the criteria that will be used to monitor and assess the quality of the evaluation design, implementation, and analysis. If a Threats-to-Validity Checklist is used (see Chapter 18), this should be included as an attachment to the ToR so that consultants fully understand the criteria to be used in the quality assurance.
- Avoid choosing too many questions.
- Require the sources to be given for each finding and recommendation in the evaluation report and check on the accuracy and adequacy of the sources. The executive summaries of many evaluation reports include statements like "many respondents stated that . . ." or "most women had encountered problems with respect to. . . .". Quite often "many" or "most" in fact only refer to one or two people attending focus groups or who were included in case studies. In other cases, some findings are not consistent with the evidence presented in the main report, or sometimes there is no evidence to support the statements. It is not unusual for the Executive Summary to present a more positive assessment of project effects than the evaluation findings actually justify. Many readers only read the Executive Summary, and if this presents their program in a favorable light, they may not check the validity of the findings[3] or the evidence on which they are based.

    At the time of contract negotiation, the evaluators should be advised that all of their findings will be checked for accuracy and all must be documented. It is of course essential

---

[3]An evaluation was commissioned in a South American country to assess the impact of rural roads on access to health, education, and other services. The executive summary reported that the construction of rural roads significantly increased women's utilization of rural health centers. This finding was widely quoted by the Ministry of Transport. In fact, the main report indicated that the impact of rural roads on women's use of health centers was quite limited, partly because the husband controlled the household budget and would often not give his wife the money for the bus fare if she "didn't look sick" or if he would have to mind the children while she was traveling, and partly because many rural communities did not believe in the utility of modern medicine. Unfortunately, not many people actually read the main report, so the positive impacts of rural roads continued to be cited.

that the agency commissioning the evaluation does in fact systematically follow up and actually check the sources. Where the findings are not supported by the evidence, the consultants must be asked to revise the report or even in some cases to return to the field.

Step 2-E: Selecting the Consultants

Criteria for selecting consultant (Hawkins, cited in Morra-Imas and Rist 2009:443–44) include:

- Has the RFP been adequately addressed?
- Is there a detailed explanation of how the evaluation will be implemented?
- What communication and reporting strategy is being proposed?
- Is there evidence of competence? What is the consultant's record of past accomplishments?
- What is the estimated cost? Is it specified in detail?

Some of the follow-up activities should include further discussions with consultants on the feasibility of complying with the ToR and agreement on how the scope and outputs can be adjusted to the available resources and timelines. This is important because consultants usually have an incentive to agree to comply with all of the scope of the ToR in order not to be disqualified.

Table 17.2   Guidelines for Strengthening Evaluation ToR and Key Issues When Working under RealWorld Constraints

General Guidelines	Key Issues for RealWorld Evaluations
Note: Depending on the scope of the responsibilities given to consultants, it is possible that some of the activities classified as "Preparatory" might be assigned to consultants and included in the ToR.	
A. Preparatory activities	

1. Define the purposes of the evaluation and ensure the participation of key stakeholders.
  a. Clarify the information needs and expectations of different stakeholders.
  b. Prioritize information needs and if necessary determine how these could be reduced.
	Consider the possibility of reducing the information needs (see Chapter 5) to accommodate budget and time constraints.

2. Define the resources and timelines.
  a. Define the budget (which may come from several sources). Clarify whether there is flexibility and circumstances in which the budget could be increased (or decreased).
  b. Define staff, other resources, information, and support to be provided by different stakeholders to the evaluation.
  c. Define the start and end dates of the evaluation and deadlines for deliverables. Clarify what determines the deadlines and how much (if any) flexibility there is.
	Review strategies for addressing budget and time constraints (see Chapters 3 and 4) and assess whether any of these could be applied.

General Guidelines	Key Issues for RealWorld Evaluations
3. Assess the viability of producing the required analysis and deliverables within the available budget and timelines. a. If possible, conduct an assessment of the main sources of secondary data in terms of their availability, quality, and appropriateness for the present evaluation.	This is particularly critical in RWE contexts as budget and time constraints often mean that great reliance must be placed on secondary data. • Consider commissioning an assessment (prior to issuing the ToR) of the availability and adequacy of secondary data. • Use the program theory model (or create a theory model if it does not already exist) to define the time trajectory over which outcomes and impacts are expected to be achieved. Compare this with the evaluation timeline to determine whether it is feasible to generate the estimates of outcomes and impacts specified in the ToR. • If the proposed analysis is not feasible, consider the possibility of either extending the duration of the evaluation or reducing the kinds of analysis that are required.
B. Writing the ToR	

1. State clearly the objectives of the evaluation and define the following:
 	
   a. The evaluation questions to be addressed
   b. Key stakeholders and their expected uses of the evaluation
   c. The overall evaluation approach to be adopted
   d. The products expected from the evaluation, when each needs to be submitted, and how each will be used
   e. The expertise required from evaluation team members
   f. Logistical arrangements
	Given the resource constraints, it is important to define clearly the minimum methodological requirements for the evaluation design. For example, the ToR may state that a methodology must be proposed for identifying and collecting data on sectors of the target population that have not had access to the project.

2. Do not simply state the objectives in technical or process terms but make sure they will be understood by all stakeholders. Be clear on how the evaluation is expected to help the organization.	
3. Avoid choosing too many questions. It is better to have an evaluation that examines a few issues in depth than to look into a broad range of issues superficially.	Use the strategies discussed in Chapter 3 to identify any areas where the number or complexity of the questions could be reduced.
C. Follow-up (quality assurance) activities	
1. Encourage consultants to indicate the feasibility of complying with the deliverables and analysis defined in the ToR.	For many RWEs, the stated outputs of the evaluation cannot be achieved within the time limits of the evaluation. It is essential to give consultants an incentive and opportunity to negotiate the ToR; to question the proposed scope of the evaluation without fear of being disqualified.
2. Conduct an evaluability assessment to assess whether the proposed evaluation is feasible and whether it would be able to deliver the proposed outputs and analysis.	The ToRs for many RWEs make unrealistic demands, but many consultants accept the contract knowing that it will not be possible to comply with all of the conditions.
3. Be prepared to renegotiate either the scope of the evaluation and the resources or the timeline.	Renegotiation is required for many RWE ToRs.

SOURCE: International Bank for Reconstruction and Development/The World Bank: *The Road to Results* (Morra-Imas and Rist 2009: 443–444).

2.3. Step 3: Designing the Evaluation

Step 3-A: Formulating Evaluation Questions

A key element for ensuring the quality and usefulness of the evaluation is the selection of the appropriate evaluation questions. Evaluation questions come from a number of different sources (Fitzpatrick, Sanders, and Worthen 2004, cited in Morra-Imas and Rist 2009:222–34):

- Questions, values, and concerns of stakeholders
- Evaluation models
- Frameworks and approaches
- Research and evaluation findings raised in the literature
- Professional standards, checklists, and guidelines
- Views and knowledge of experts
- The evaluator's own professional judgment

Different kinds of questions should be asked at different points in the causal chain, so the types of questions will vary depending on the stage of the program at which the evaluation is conducted. This is clearly demonstrated in a logic model that describes inputs, activities, outputs, and short- and long-term results.

The types of questions can be classified as follows:

- *Descriptive:* These refer to "what is" and can cover the project as well as the context within which it is being implemented. These questions also provide information on the problems to be addressed and the opinions of different stakeholders with respect to the problems.
- *Normative:* These compare what is with what should be. This can include opinions of different stakeholders on the problems to be addressed and the priorities in terms of services and target groups.
- *Cause and effect:* Determine what difference the intervention made. This involves questions in the baseline study to provide a reference on the changes to be measured as well as information on intervening variables that might affect outcomes. At the end of the project, information is collected on the changes in the dependent variables and the intervening variables. Qualitative evaluations may also include questions on the perception of different stakeholder groups on both what has changed and the causes. Participatory group techniques such as participatory rural appraisal (PRA) include a number of techniques for obtaining group perceptions on the change process and outcomes.

How the questions will be formulated will determine whether the evaluation approach should be mostly quantitative, qualitative, or mixed. The purpose of the evaluation will also determine the scope and focus of the questions.

Morra-Imas and Rist (2009:230–32) suggest that the process of identifying and selecting questions will often include a *divergent phase* in which a long list of possible questions is identified and a *convergent phase* in which the list of questions is narrowed down, either by the evaluator or through a consultative process and perhaps group discussion. A number of computer-based techniques such as concept mapping (Kane and Trochim 2007) can be used for synthesizing a large number of questions into a set of indicators or scales. Several factors must be taken into consideration when determining the number of questions. On one hand, it is desirable to limit the number of key questions to be asked, both to ensure the evaluation is clearly focused and to reduce the costs and time of data collection. This is also important because the greater the number of questions, the lower the quality of the information. On the other hand, many evaluations involve a large number of stakeholders, many of whom are interested in different kinds of information. So arbitrarily limiting the number of key questions, as some textbooks recommend, will often mean ignoring the interests of some stakeholders. Also, large agencies have several different organizational levels within a particular country (e.g., project managers, sector or thematic managers, and country management teams). Each of these levels may request different kinds of information from the evaluation, so again, limiting the number of questions may mean that the information needs of important groups within the agency may be ignored.

Morra-Imas and Rist (2009:232–34) provide some useful guidelines for developing good questions (see also Presser et al. 2004a, 2004b).

Step 3-B: Assessing the Evaluation Scenario

In order to select the appropriate evaluation design and to adapt the design to the RealWorld constraints, it is essential for both evaluation managers and evaluation specialists to understand the context within which the evaluation will be implemented. Chapter 11 (Table 11.1) presents a checklist for identifying key factors that should be assessed.

Step 3-C: Selecting the Appropriate Evaluation Design

Chapter 11 describes an eight-step process for selecting the most appropriate evaluation design (summarized in Figure 11.1). The evaluation manager is responsible for working with the evaluation specialists and the different groups who will use the evaluation to ensure that these steps are followed.

Step 3-D: Commissioning an Evaluability Assessment

Before the evaluation design is finally approved and the evaluation is commissioned, a final check should be to ensure that the proposed design is feasible and realistic within the RealWorld constraints and that it will be able to address all of the questions included in the ToR. This is achieved through an *evaluability assessment* (Sida 2007:72–74; Morra-Imas and Rist 2009:183–85). This examines the following:

- Assessment of whether it will be possible to achieve the evaluation objectives within the proposed budget and time. This is particularly critical for the many evaluations that are commissioned with a very tight budget and timeline as it is often the case that when questioned, the evaluation manager recognizes that the resources are inadequate but states that it would be difficult or impossible to get them increased. For example, the timeline in a recent evaluation of Central Asian projects was based on the assumption that it would be possible to arrange flights to different regions of each country without major delays. However, everyone involved in approving the ToR was fully aware that there would be major travel delays, but no allowance was made for this.
- The coherence and specificity of the logic model

- The availability of the relevant data
- Access to key informants
- Assessment of political and stakeholder pressures and how they might affect the ability to select and implement an appropriate evaluation design (see Chapter 6 for a discussion of political and organizational constraints and Chapter 11 for evaluation designs)
- The timing of the evaluation and the ability to address key questions at this point in the project. A key issue is whether it will be possible to assess outcome, impacts, and (where required) sustainability or whether it is too early to collect the required information.

The evaluability assessment *should* provide a critical input to the evaluation manager prior to the final approval of the evaluation design and work program and should indicate, where appropriate, that the proposed evaluation ToR and work program are not realistic. However, the evaluability assessment is often somewhat of a formality, and it is quite common that it is not sufficiently used as a decision-making tool.

Step 3-E: Special Challenges in Promoting the Use of Mixed-Method Evaluations

There is a growing recognition in the evaluation community of the benefits of using mixed methods, combining a range of quantitative and qualitative techniques for the design, data collection, and analysis of an evaluation. However, there are a number of special challenges for an evaluation office (EO) in promoting the use of mixed methods. First, these methods tend to be more expensive and time-consuming, so that must be factored into the evaluation planning and budgeting. Second, mixed methods require the active participation of researchers from a wider range of professions, which presents additional challenges for team building. Finally, there are challenges to market mixed methods to clients familiar with or who think they prefer quantitative or qualitative evaluations.

2.4. Step 4: Implementing the Evaluation

Step 4-A: The Role of the Evaluation Department of a Funding Agency, Central Government Ministry, or Sector Agency

There are a number of options with respect to how the roles of an EO are defined with respect to the management of evaluations. How these functions are defined and implemented can have important consequences for the technical quality and the utilization of the evaluations. Experience suggests that many EOs tend to give too much independence to the evaluation consultants with respect to the evaluation methodology, how it is implemented, and how the findings are presented. In particular, there is often insufficient oversight concerning the methodological rigor of the evaluation. This has proved to be a particular challenge for EOs when commissioning evaluation under budget and time constraints. Consequently, it is recommended that development agencies consider carefully which of the following options is the most appropriate way for their EO to manage evaluations:

Option 1: All department staff members are, or are being trained to become, evaluation specialists. Under this option, EO staff would take an active role in defining the evaluation methodology and would actively supervise and contribute to the technical parts of the consultant's methodology.

- In addition to a minimum level of general competence in evaluation methodology, each team member would probably specialize in a particular methodology and would be a resource to other team members.
- The EO would probably develop its own evaluation "brand" and might seek to promote EO as a cutting-edge evaluation agency.
- The EO might conduct or commission research to develop and test new evaluation tools and techniques (e.g., using recall, participatory group techniques, and other methods for reconstructing baseline data).
- This option would require the EO to have an active evaluation capacity development program for its own staff.

Option 2: Most staff will be evaluation managers, but the EO would have a team of in-house (or external) evaluation specialists who would assist staff in the formulation of the evaluation and in working with consultants.

- This would be a scaled-down version of Option 1 with the EO still taking an active role in defining the evaluation methodologies and providing guidance to consultants.
- The goal might be to move from Option 2 to Option 1 over time as the internal evaluation capacity of the EO develops.

Option 3: EO staff would mainly manage evaluations and would rely more heavily on consultants to design the evaluations and to develop the methodologies.

It is possible to combine these options. For example, most evaluations might be managed using Option 2 or 3, but the EO might be more actively involved in a few high-profile evaluations itself. Also, the EO strategies might evolve over time. For example, the strategy might be to gradually strengthen the role of EO staff in the management of the evaluations. When the EO is created, it might not be clear how many evaluations they would manage, their complexity, or the capacity of local consultants to help design and implement the evaluations. Once the situation becomes clearer, an assessment might be commissioned and the longer term strategy defined.

Step 4-B: The Inception Report

When responding to the RFP, evaluators usually do not have all of the information that they require to prepare a detailed evaluation design and to assess the feasibility of implementing this design. Consequently, many clients require that once the evaluation contract has been approved, the consultants prepare an inception report. This addresses questions such as the following (Sida 2007:81–82):

- An assessment of any evaluability issues affecting the feasibility of complying with the SoW and the ToR. These can include issues relating to the availability of data, the time and cost and any logistical questions, and other issues such as the willingness or availability of key stakeholders or informants to be interviewed or provide required information.
- Any remaining questions concerning how the ToR should be interpreted
- The proposed methodology for data collection and analysis
- The evaluation work plan

Normally the client has to respond to these questions, discuss and propose modifications, and approve the work plan before the evaluation can begin.

Sometimes the inception report is produced within a short period of time and without major consultant inputs, but in other cases, this might require significant resources and time. There are also many evaluations where no inception report is required. Probably in most cases, the inception report does not involve travel, but for a large and complex evaluation, the consultants may be required to meet with stakeholders and make preliminary visits to project areas.

The inception report has the advantage of ensuring that there is agreement among all parties on the purpose of the evaluation, how the ToR should be interpreted, and the proposed evaluation design, as well as resolving any logistical and administrative issues. This avoids the unfortunate situation where it is only when clients receive the draft of the final evaluation report that they realize this is not focusing on their priority issues and information needs. Despite these benefits, the risk with an inception report is that it can produce significant delays in the launch of the evaluation and can absorb a significant proportion of the evaluation resources. In some cases, the inception report becomes a major document with a great deal of time spent producing graphs and annexes and a great deal of unnecessary detail just to make the document look impressive. However, a more serious problem, particularly for evaluations working with a tight deadline, is that the design of the evaluation cannot start until feedback and clearance have been received from a number of busy stakeholders. These delays can significantly reduce the time available for conducting the evaluation itself, including data collection and analysis.

Step 4-C: Managing the Evaluation

The responsibilities of the evaluation manager include the following (Morra-Imas and Rist 2009:449–50):

During the preparation phase:

- Select, recruit, and brief evaluators on the purpose of the evaluation, the work plan, and the evaluation design matrix.
- Oversee the development and testing of data collection instruments and the collection of existing data.
- Ensure that background documentation and materials are submitted well in advance of the evaluation so that the evaluation team has time to digest the material.
- Oversee the field visit plan.
- Ensure the availability of funds to carry out the evaluation.
- Avoid and mitigate conflicts of interest.

During implementation of the evaluation:

- Ensure the evaluators have full access to files, reports, publications, and other relevant information.
- Follow the progress of the evaluation, and provide feedback and guidance to evaluators during all phases of implementation.
- Assess the quality of the evaluation reports, and discuss strengths and limitations with evaluators to ensure the draft report satisfies the ToR, evaluation findings are defensible, and recommendations are realistic. (See Chapter 7 and Appendixes A–E for detailed guidance on assessing the validity and quality of evaluation reports.)

- Arrange for a meeting with evaluators and key stakeholders to discuss and comment on the draft report.
- Approve the end product, and ensure presentation of evaluation results to stakeholders.

During follow-up:

- Evaluate the performance of evaluators and put it on record.
- Disseminate the evaluation results to key stakeholders and other audiences.
- Promote the implementation of recommendations and the use of evaluation results in present and future programming, and monitor regularly to ensure that recommendations are acted on.
- Lead the team in a learning review to assess what went well and should be repeated and what, in hindsight, might have been done differently.

During all three stages, the evaluation manager may act as a facilitator during team meetings, enabling all participants to share their views and ideas. As a facilitator, the manager is responsible for

- Setting an agenda
- Helping the group stick to the agenda
- Ensuring that all views are heard
- Overseeing a process for decision making (consensus or a voting process)

Step 4-D: Working with Stakeholders

It is important for evaluation offices to work closely with agency management and other stakeholders to limit the scope and expectations for impact and other kinds of evaluation so as to produce a more realistic Scope of Work. Stakeholders can also be involved in the application of techniques such as rating scales (using concept mapping and related techniques) to help with sample selection, definition of performance indicators, and rating the relative importance of each indicator. (See Chapter 16 for a discussion of concept mapping.) The active participation of stakeholders in evaluation design is also important to help ensure that evaluations are designed to be useful and that the findings and recommendations are actually used.

In participatory evaluations, stakeholders can play a number of different roles during design, implementation, and dissemination. Selected stakeholders may form part of the evaluation team, involving them in question development, data collection, and analysis. The World Bank's (1996) *Participation Sourcebook* provides guidelines for involving stakeholders in participatory evaluations, but many of the strategies can be applied more widely to the involvement of stakeholders in all kinds of evaluation.

It is also important to engage critics of the program at an early stage so that their concerns can be addressed in the selection of questions to be answered, the design of the evaluation, and the interpretation of the findings. Frequently, critics are not involved until comments are solicited on the draft final report, by which time it is too late to address many of the criticisms, which can result in the evaluation being discredited among certain groups. In Chapter 10, we discussed the possibility of formulating two or more logic models, one based on the program's theory of change and one on an alternative theory of change proposed by the critics.

The following are some of the roles of stakeholders defined by the UNDP (2009). Stakeholders can play a particularly important role in joint evaluations as they represent the interests of the different funding agencies:

- Define or confirm the profile, competencies, and roles and responsibilities of the evaluation manager and the evaluation team (this is an important role for a joint evaluation).
- Clear candidates proposed for the role of evaluation manager and principal evaluator.
- Participate in the drafting and review of the ToR.
- Assist in collecting some of the required data.
- Oversee the progress and conduct of the evaluation.
- Review the draft evaluation report and ensure the final draft meets the defined quality standards.

Step 4-E: Quality Assurance (QA)

Whichever option or options are used to manage evaluations, it is important for the EO to put in place quality assurance procedures to ensure that evaluations fully respond to the terms of reference and that they follow accepted evaluation standards. The quality assurance (QA) standards can be applied to assess evaluations conducted by EO staff or by outside consultants.

An important element in QA is the incorporation of evaluability assessments. This point is stressed because if the ToR are not realistic, no amount of subsequent quality assurance can ensure a methodologically sound and useful evaluation. It would be impossible for many evaluations to achieve the objectives stated in the ToR within the stipulated time and resources for one or more of the following reasons:

- It is too early in the project or program cycle to estimate outcomes and impacts (or even outputs). This is probably the main reason why evaluations are likely to fail.
- The time available for data collection and analysis is too short. Agencies always underestimate the time required to coordinate evaluations in the field and to set up focus groups and other kinds of data collection. Consultants either collect poor-quality data (e.g., focus groups are not properly prepared, survey instruments are not pilot tested) or much of the agreed-to data are not collected.
- The proposed methodologies are not appropriate or adequate to conduct the proposed analysis (e.g., it is proposed to estimate attributable impact without any kind of counterfactual).

Evaluability analysis (or something similar) might be required at the following points:

- When the board or senior management requests an evaluation or provides guidance on the types of evaluations that are required. Sometimes senior management will state that certain kinds of technically difficult evaluations (e.g., rigorous impact evaluations) must be conducted, and staff then feel obliged to follow these instructions—even if they believe they are not feasible.
- When deciding what kinds of evaluation should be commissioned, when they should be commissioned and completed, and the appropriate scope and level of rigor
- When a proposal or inception report is received from consultants (or from an internal research team)

Step 4-F: Special Issues Managing Multiagency and Complex, Multicomponent Evaluations

An important development (over the past decade) has been the partial shift in the architecture of development cooperation from a fragmented system of project support to a more integrated system of program support where donors align their contributions with partner country policies and seek to harmonize procedures between themselves. This change affects monitoring and evaluation along with everything else. In sector-based programs, where the inputs of several donors cannot be separately evaluated, various forms of joint evaluation are becoming the norm. For the time-being, joint evaluations tend to be dominated by donors, but as the evaluation capacity of partner countries grows the balance will change (Sida 2007:22).

Joint evaluations can be conducted by

- Two or more donors
- A donor + a partner country
- Multidonor + multipartner
- Partner + partner

When a joint evaluation involves only a few agencies, the management structure can be relatively simple (though not as simple as an evaluation commissioned by one agency acting alone). One of the main decisions is whether all agencies will be equally involved in the management or whether one or more agencies should be given a leadership role with other agencies only evaluating key outputs.

When more agencies are involved or for very large joint evaluations, the evaluation will commonly have a two-tier system consisting of a broad membership steering committee and a smaller management group. The OECD's (2001) *Effective Practices in Conducting a Multi-Donor Evaluation* identifies the following key steps for planning and conducting a joint multidonor evaluation:

- Deciding on the need for a joint multidonor evaluation
- Deciding on evaluation partners
- Planning the evaluation's management structure
- Preparing the scope of work
- Selecting the evaluation team
- Preparing the evaluation team
- Collecting, analyzing, and reporting results
- Reviewing, communicating, and following up on evaluation results

2.5. Step 5: Reporting and Dissemination

Step 5-A: Providing Feedback on the Draft Report

Most evaluation ToRs require that consultants submit a draft version of the final report for review and revision before the final version is prepared. This is a critical step in ensuring a high-quality final report, and it is essential to ensure that sufficient time is allowed to provide feedback from key stakeholders and to allow time for the evaluator to make required revisions. The evaluation manager plays a critical role in this process as there is a tendency for the review period to get shortened because the draft report is submitted late, because stakeholders delay submitting their comments, or because there are impending deadlines for management to make decisions that were supposed to be informed by the evaluation.

Often a briefing meeting will be organized with internal and external stakeholders to present the key findings of the draft report and to obtain feedback. These briefing meetings can be very valuable but should be planned ahead and ideally specified in the ToR so that the evaluator does not suddenly find that a large amount of time, which was budgeted to work on the final report, now has to be spent on preparing this presentation. An important but often politically sensitive role for the evaluation manager is to agree with stakeholders on a deadline for submitting their comments. Evaluators will often receive feedback from important stakeholders at the very last moment, often with an apologetic note from the evaluation manager saying, "I know this is very late but I really would like you to address these suggestions because the support of this Regional Director is critical for the implementation of the evaluation recommendations."

Another related problem is when senior management requests a summary or briefing on the final report before it is submitted, and given the fact that it is politically difficult to change key findings after this briefing, the effective time for preparing the final report is significantly reduced. A key challenge for the evaluation manager is to do everything possible, within the political realities of the agency, to protect the time allocated for the review of the draft report. However, many evaluation managers are more concerned about creating a good impression on their own senior management than in ensuring the technical quality of the final report, and many evaluators have had the frustrating experience of finding that they have lost significant amounts of time that had been allocated to preparing the final report.

An important management decision that should be addressed in the ToR is how much time and resources should be committed in the evaluation budget for revisions to the draft report. Frequently, the data analysis either identifies some inconsistencies or unexplained findings or identifies some interesting issues (such as higher than expected participation in the project by certain sectors of the target population). It is frequently the case that time (and staff resources) has not been budgeted to follow up on these questions. Many potentially interesting issues are simply mentioned in the final reports as questions that should be addressed in a future study. Where possible, time and budget should be included to follow up on some of these questions and, where practical, resources could also be allocated to allow rapid follow-up visits to some of the project areas (where the evaluation team has local affiliates). Chapter 14 (Mixed-Method Evaluations) gives examples of the benefits of follow-up field visits.

Step 5-B: Disseminating the Evaluation Report

The findings and recommendations of many evaluations are underused because the report is either not disseminated to key stakeholders or not written or disseminated in the preferred communication style or even language of different stakeholders. (See Chapter 8 for a discussion of communication strategies.) It is the responsibility of the evaluation manager to design and implement an effective communication strategy.

2.6. Step 6: Ensuring Implementation of the Recommendations

Step 6-A: Coordinating the Management Response and Follow-Up

The effective implementation of evaluation recommendations requires a process for coordinating the response of management, defining responsibility for follow-up actions, and monitoring the implementation of agreed actions. Agencies that regularly commission evaluations usually have a standard procedure for management review and follow-up (see, e.g., Sida 2007:93–94), but for agencies that do not regularly commission evaluation, the evaluation manager may be required to work with the evaluator to set up a follow-up action plan.

The International Finance Corporation, in cooperation with the World Bank Independent Evaluation Group, developed the Management Action Tracking Record (MATR), which comprises two matrices: an indicator cycle and a monitoring cycle (Morra-Imas and Rist 2009:474–76).

On a broader level, to strengthen the overall quality of agency evaluations, some agencies commission independent evaluators to conduct a metaevaluation (review of the methodological rigor and quality of findings) of a sample of evaluations. When this is done, a challenge for the evaluation manager is to ensure that there is an institutional learning process so that findings of these evaluations are built into the policies for defining and managing future evaluations. These evaluation reviews can be built into a more systematic metaevaluation system that reviews the overall evaluation strategies of the agency.[4]

6-B: Facilitating Dialogue with Partners

For multidonor evaluations, it may be necessary to develop follow-up consultations on lessons learned for each agency and possible follow-up collaborative activities.

SUMMARY

All evaluations are developed, managed, and used within a particular administrative system and within a particular political context, both of which affect how the evaluation is designed, implemented, disseminated, and used. An approach to evaluation that works well in one administrative system might work less well in a different system. There is also a wide range of ways in which the political system can influence how evaluations are designed, implemented, disseminated, and used.

The planning and management of an evaluation typically involves six main steps (see Figure 17.1):

Step 1: Preparing the evaluation. This requires (1) the preparation of the evaluation framework or a Statement of Work (SoW) and the definition of what is to be evaluated, the activities needed to do the evaluation, responsibilities for each stage, timing, proposed methods, and resources, as well as where they will come from; (2) involving the stakeholders; and (3) defining the management structure. Often an additional preparation

---

[4]See Chapter 12 for an example of a meta-evaluation conducted by CARE International in which some 70 evaluations reports were reviewed. See also Sida (2007) for another example of an agency review of its evaluation strategies.

activity will be to commission a diagnostic study to help understand the context and nature of the program being studied.

Step 2: Recruiting the evaluators. A first decision is to decide whether the evaluation should be conducted internally or whether external evaluators should be commissioned. External evaluators can provide two main services: evaluation implementation and evaluation technical support. The latter can include a training program to strengthen evaluation capacity, assistance in scoping the evaluation, assessing evaluation proposals, evaluation quality assurance, and providing a resident evaluation adviser to provide long-term support.

Each organization has its own contracting procedures. There are a number of factors to be considered during the recruitment process: deciding whether to use a fixed-cost contract or level of effort (number of consultant days), whether to contract a firm or an individual consultant, and broadening the range of research expertise. With respect to the latter, many agencies traditionally draw on a limited range of evaluation expertise (e.g., mainly quantitative or mainly qualitative research), and the decision may be made to design the selection process to encourage a broader range of evaluators to participate.

Typical stages in consultant selection and recruitment include inviting EOI, issuing the RFP, and preparing the ToR (which will be included in the RFP but may be revised based on consultants' comments on the RFP or feedback from the inception report). Many agencies require an Inception Report, which can be used to revise and finalize the ToR.

Step 3: Designing the evaluation. (Evaluation design is discussed in more detail in Chapter 11.) This will typically involve the following: (1) formulating the main evaluation questions, (2) assessing the evaluation scenario, (3) selecting the appropriate evaluation design, and (4) commissioning an evaluability assessment.

Step 4: Implementing the evaluation. This typically involves the following steps: (1) defining the role of the evaluation department, (2) preparing and reviewing an inception report, (3) managing the implementation of the evaluation, (4) working with stakeholders, and (5) building in quality assurance procedures. There are additional issues to address when managing multiagency and complex evaluations.

Step 5: Reporting and dissemination. This involves providing feedback on the draft report and dissemination of the final report (see Chapter 8).

Step 6: Ensuring implementation of the recommendations. It is important to have clearly defined procedures to ensure that agreed actions on the recommendations are implemented. This involves coordinating the management response and follow-up and facilitating dialogue with partners.

FURTHER READING

Engela, R. and T. Ajam. 2010. *Implementing a Government-wide Monitoring and Evaluation System in South Africa.* Independent Evaluation Group. The World Bank. http://siteresources.worldbank.org/EXTEVACAPDEV/Resources/ecd_wp_21_south_africa.pdf

This paper is interesting because it draws on the experience of an African country, whereas most of the earlier literature focuses on Latin America. The paper analyzes the process of designing and implementing a government-wide monitoring and evaluation (GWM&E) system in South

Africa. South Africa has followed a "big bang" approach in its efforts to build a national M&E system, starting as recently as 2005. The country has pursued capacity building and system building with an initial focus on monitoring; a conscious decision was made to pursue evaluation later. M&E development is being allowed to evolve, rather than follow a completed and detailed blueprint. A number of major M&E initiatives have been pursued over the past few years, and considerable success has already been achieved. The paper assesses the remaining challenges, including the barriers to achieving more of a performance culture in the government and civil service.

Mackay, K. 2007. *How to Build M&E Systems to Support Better Government.* Independent Evaluation Group. Washington, DC: World Bank. http://web.worldbank.org/WBSITE/ EXTERNAL/EXTOED/EXTEVACAPDEV/0,,contentMDK: 22294993~menuPK:4585748~pagePK:64829573~piPK: 64829550~theSitePK:4585673,00.html

Comprehensive review of the features of a successful national M&E system and the steps required to implement and sustain the system. This mainly draws on the experience of Latin America, where more progress has been made in the institutionalization of national M&E systems.

Morra, L. and R. Rist. 2009. *The Road to Results: Designing and Conducting Effective Development Evaluations.* Washington, DC: World Bank. Also available in electronic format at www.worldbank.org/r2r

This very useful reference publication is written by the two co-directors of the International Program for Development Evaluation Training (IPDET) and draws on the experience of 10 years of evaluation training by some of the leading specialists in this field. The main sections cover the following: Foundations (of international development evaluation), Preparing and Conducting Effective Development Evaluations, Designing and Conducting (development evaluations), Meeting Challenges, and Leading (which covers managing evaluations, presenting results, guiding the evaluator, and looking to the future).

Swedish International Development Agency (Sida). 2007. *Looking Back, Looking Forward. Sida Evaluation Manual.* Second revised edition.

Part Two provides step-by-step guidelines for Sida staff on the management of development evaluations.

U.K. Department for International Development (DFID). 2005. *Guidance on Evaluation and Review for DFID Staff.*

Another example of guidelines on how to manage development evaluations.

Wholey, J., H. Hatry, and K. Newcomer, eds. 2010. *Handbook of Practical Program Evaluation.* San Francisco: Jossey-Bass.

A useful reference source covering evaluation planning and design, data collection, data analysis, and use of evaluation. Although referring to U.S. experience, many of the principles are relevant for international development evaluation. The final section on "Use of Evaluation" is particularly relevant for the present chapter.

CHAPTER 18

Strengthening Evaluation Capacity at the Agency and National Levels

T his chapter discusses four issues that are critical for strengthening the capacity of managers and policy-makers in donor agencies and developing countries to design, implement, and use evaluations. First, we discuss ways to put in place quality assurance systems to identify aspects of the evaluation design that affect the quality (validity) of the findings and recommendations of the evaluation. Once "threats to validity" have been identified, there should be standard procedures for addressing and, as far as possible, correcting the threats. Appendixes A to E present worksheets that can be used to assess and address threats to validity for quantitative, qualitative, and mixed-method evaluations, respectively. Appendix D illustrates how the worksheet can be used with a typical project evaluation to provide managers with the information needed to assess the degree of confidence that they can place in the evaluation findings and recommendations. We then discuss the importance of collaboration between evaluators and program management at the program planning stage to create conditions to facilitate the use of strong evaluations designs ("evaluation-ready program designs"). The third topic concerns evaluation capacity development strategies to strengthen the ability of the different stakeholders to commission, design, implement, and use evaluations. Finally, we discuss alternative strategies for strengthening (institutionalizing) evaluation systems at the sector and national levels.

1. Building in Quality Assurance Procedures

Quality assurance refers to standardized management procedures for assessing the quality of the evaluation design, implementation, analysis, and dissemination. A key concern is to assess the extent to which the findings and recommendations of the evaluation are supported by the evaluation methodology and how it was implemented. Quality assurance procedures can include the following:

- *Preliminary feasibility analysis* to ensure that there is a reasonable possibility that the purposes of the evaluation stated in the Terms of Reference (ToR) could be achieved with the available resources, within the proposed time frame, and at this point in the project cycle. The feasibility analysis should be conducted before the ToR is issued to avoid embarking on an evaluation that could not achieve its stated objectives. A number of factors must be considered. Two common reasons why the stated objectives could not be achieved are that the budget is insufficient to implement the proposed design and collect the required data and that insufficient time is allowed for the different stages of the design, implementation, and analysis of the evaluation. Timing must also take into account factors such as the onset of the rainy season or events such as public holidays, the start of an election campaign, and periods when national agencies will not be able to be actively involved in the evaluation due to pressures to prepare the annual budget or other priority activities. Another common issue is that the evaluation is commissioned when it is still too early in the project cycle to be able to measure the required outcomes or impacts. Finally, funding agencies often underestimate the time required for administrative arrangements such as approval and implementation of the project budget by the host government, the need to complete the hiring of key program staff before work can begin on the evaluation, procurement of local consultants or other local services, or the time required for review and approval of inception reports.
- *Evaluability analysis.* Once evaluation proposals are received (from agency staff if it is to be conducted internally or from consultants), an evaluability assessment may be conducted to determine whether (a) the proposal fully responds to the terms of reference, (b) the proposed methodology is technically sound, (c) it will be possible to implement the methodology within the budget and time constraints, and (d) there is a reasonable likelihood that the required data can be collected (either from secondary sources or through the proposed primary data collection procedures).
- *Application of a threats-to-validity worksheet.* A threats-to-validity worksheet can be used to identify potential threats to the validity of the evaluation findings and recommendations. The worksheet can be used at various points in the evaluation cycle: at the start of the evaluation as part of the evaluability analysis, midway through the evaluation, to assess the draft final report, or when the final report has been submitted. The worksheet can be used by funding agencies, the evaluation team, the project implementation agency, or national planning and policymaking agencies. Threats-to-validity checklists are discussed later in this section.

The application of a threats-to-validity worksheet is discussed in Chapter 7, where it is pointed out that different approaches are required for assessing the validity of QUANT, QUAL, and mixed-method designs.

Why does the assessment of evaluation validity matter? If the conclusions of the evaluations are not methodologically sound, there is a risk that

- Programs that do not work or that are not efficient and cost-effective may continue or be expanded.
- Good programs may be discontinued.

- Priority target groups may not have access to project benefits.
- Important lessons concerning which aspects of a program do and do not work and under what circumstances may be missed.

Even where methodologically rigorous QUANT, QUAL, or mixed-method evaluation designs are used, there are always factors that pose threats to the validity of the evaluation findings and recommendations (see Bamberger and White 2007). Unfortunately, in the RealWorld of development evaluation, it is frequently not possible to use the strongest evaluation designs, so the risks of arriving at wrong conclusions and providing wrong or misleading policy advice are much greater.

1.1. Using the Threats-to-Validity Worksheet

The worksheets for assessing validity for QUANT, QUAL, and mixed-method designs all have three parts, each of which is targeted to a different audience (see Figure 18.1):

- *Part 1.* The cover sheet provides a one-page summary for senior management and for partner agencies. This explains the purpose of the evaluation and the reason for conducting the threats-to-validity assessment. It also summarizes the main conclusions of the validity assessment and the recommended follow-up actions. If the assessment concludes that the evaluation methodology was sound, the recommendation will normally be to accept the findings and recommendations of the evaluation report. However, if methodological weaknesses are identified, the assessment might recommend that

  o The evaluation report be accepted but that a covering memorandum might flag some of the areas where the findings and recommendations should be treated with caution
  o The consultants be requested to clarify some points
  o The consultants be required to conduct further analysis or in some cases return to the field to verify some of the information or to fill in gaps in the data (e.g., to interview some groups not represented in the focus groups)
  o The report be rejected as methodologically unsound

- *Part 2.* The summary assessment for each component is intended for mid-level management. It presents a half-page text summary of the validity assessment of each of the 4-5 components and a summary numerical rating (1 = very strong to 5 = serious problems). This provides sufficient detail for mid-level management to understand the main strengths and weaknesses of the evaluation and how these affect the validity of the findings and recommendations. In cases where only a general assessment of the evaluation quality is required, only Parts 1 and 2 of the worksheet may be used. However, when a more rigorous and comprehensive validity assessment is required, Part 3 can also be used.
- *Part 3.* This includes a set of checklists that assesses dimensions such as objectivity, internal design validity, statistical conclusion validity, construct validity, external validity, and utilization validity. The checklists vary depending on whether the evaluation used a quantitative, qualitative, or mixed-method design. Rating scales are used to assess the seriousness and importance of each threat to validity. A set of summary scores is included in Part 2 to provide evaluation managers, many of whom are not evaluation specialists, with the key findings from the assessment and the recommended actions that should be taken.

Most quality assurance assessments will only use Parts 1 and 2 described above, as this provides a short, easy to understand, and relatively economical assessment of the strengths and weaknesses of an evaluation. The assessment can be prepared internally by an experienced researcher from the evaluation office or by an external consultant.

For a small number of the largest or most important evaluations, or where it is essential to ensure credibility when sensitive or controversial programs are being evaluated, a more comprehensive validity assessment may be required. In these cases, Part 3 can also be used. This provides a more in-depth and technical assessment, and in most cases, an external evaluation specialist will be contracted to conduct the assessment. This is both because of the technical nature of the assessment but also to ensure independence when credibility of the assessment is important.

When and How to Use the Validity Worksheet

The worksheet can be used at various points in an evaluation:

- During the evaluation design phase to identify potential threats to validity or adequacy. When important problems or threats are identified, it may be possible to modify the design to address them. In other cases, if some of the potential threats could seriously compromise the purpose of the evaluation, further consultations may be required with the client or funding agency to consider either increasing the budget or the duration of the evaluation (where this would mitigate some of the problems) or agreeing to modify the objectives of the evaluation to reflect these limitations. In some extreme cases, the evaluability assessment may conclude that the proposed evaluation is not feasible, and all parties may agree to cancel or postpone the evaluation.
- During the implementation of the evaluation (for example a midterm review). If the worksheet had also been administered at the start of the evaluation, it is possible to assess if progress has been made in addressing the problems. Where serious problems are identified, it may be possible to adjust the evaluation design (e.g., to broaden the sample coverage or to refine or expand some of the questions or survey instruments).
- Toward the end of the evaluation—perhaps when the draft final report is being prepared. This may still allow time to correct some (but obviously not all) of the problems identified.
- When the evaluation has been completed. While it is now too late to make any corrections, a summary of the worksheet findings can be attached to the final report to provide a perspective for readers on how to interpret the evaluation findings and recommendations and to understand what caveats are required.
- For organizations that regularly commission or conduct evaluations, a very useful exercise is to conduct a meta-analysis to compare the ratings for different evaluations to determine whether there is a consistent pattern of methodological weaknesses in all evaluations (or all evaluations in a particular country, region, or sector). We discussed earlier how the worksheet can be used at different points in the evaluation—for example, at the evaluation design stage, during implementation, and when the draft final report is being prepared. When the scale is applied at these different points, it is possible to detect whether any of the threats are corrected or mitigated over time or whether, on the other hand, some of them get worse. Differential sample attrition (between the project and control groups) is a familiar example where a problem may get worse over time as differences between the characteristics of subjects remaining in the project and the control samples may increase.

Figure 18.1 Structure, Audience, and Responsibility for the Different Parts of the Threats-to-Validity Worksheet

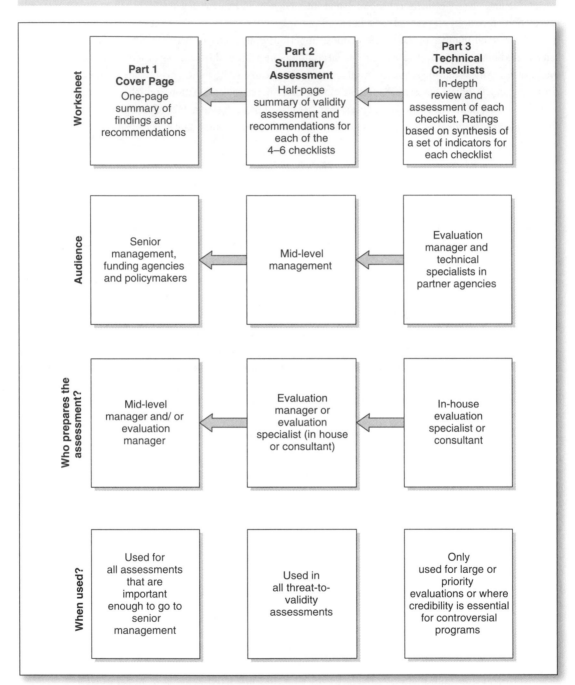

1.2. Other Checklists

In addition to the checklists developed by Shadish, Cook, and Campbell (2002), Guba and Lincoln (1989), and Miles and Huberman (1994) referred to earlier in this chapter, a number of other checklists have been developed for assessing the quality of evaluations or the validity of their conclusions (see also Chapter 9 for a discussion of evaluation guidelines and standards). The following are some widely used examples:

The Western Michigan University Evaluation Checklist Project[1] provides refereed checklists for designing, budgeting, contracting, staffing, managing, and assessing evaluations of programs, personnel, students, and other evaluands; collecting, analyzing, and reporting evaluation information; and determining merit, worth, and significance. Each checklist is a distillation of valuable lessons learned from practice. The site's stated purpose is to improve the quality and consistency of evaluations and enhance evaluation capacity through the promotion and use of high-quality checklists targeted to specific evaluation tasks and approaches. The checklists are classified into the following groups: Evaluation Management, Evaluation Models, Evaluation Values and Criteria, Meta-Evaluation, and Evaluation Capacity Development and Institutionalization. Many, but not all, of the checklists focus on the education sector.

The site includes a number or widely cited checklists, among which are the following: Michael Scriven's *Key Evaluation Checklist* (2007), Daniel Stufflebeam's *Program Evaluations MetaEvaluation Checklist* (1999) and *CIPP Model* (2007), and Michael Patton's *Qualitative Evaluation Checklist* (2003) and *Utilization Focused Evaluation Checklist* (2002c).

The American Evaluation Association's *Guiding Principles for Evaluators* (2004), which provides guidance to evaluators in five areas: Systematic Enquiry, Competence, Integrity/Honesty, Respect for People, and Responsibilities for General and Public Welfare.

The Organization for Economic Cooperation and Development/Development Advisory Committee (OECD/DAC) *Quality Standards for Development Evaluation* (2010b). This provides standards for (1) the rationale, purpose, and objectives of an evaluation; (2) evaluation topic; (3) context; (4) evaluation methodology; (5) information sources; (6) independence; (7) evaluation ethics; (8) quality assurance; (9) relevance of the evaluation results; and (10) completeness.

While these three sources are extremely valuable resources, they focus mainly on ensuring quality in the design and implementation of the evaluation and ensuring that evaluators follow appropriate professional standards. There is little direct discussion of threats to validity and how they can be addressed.

2. Designing "Evaluation-Ready" Programs

An evaluation design can often be strengthened if the evaluator can coordinate with the implementing agency to build the evaluation into the design of the project. For example, it often would have been possible to have used a strong evaluation design such as a randomized controlled trial (RCT; if participants had been selected randomly) or a regression discontinuity (RD) design (if beneficiaries had been selected using a clearly designed cutoff point). However, the evaluator is often not contracted or

---

[1]For information on the Western Michigan University Evaluation Center Checklist Project, see http://www.wmich.edu/evalctr/checklists/checklist_topics.

consulted until the project selection procedures have already been defined, by which time it is too late to use either the RCT or RD design. The challenge in these and many other cases is to arrange for the evaluators to be involved during the project design stage.

In many other cases, the criteria used to select the communities that will receive services (e.g., basic infrastructure in urban slums, conditional cash transfers or scholarships) are not clearly defined, so it is difficult for the evaluator to select a well-matched comparison group or to assess the effects of selection procedures on accessibility of the project to different sectors of the target population. Sometimes the original participant selection criteria are changed in some municipalities or communities without documenting the changes. This again makes it difficult to ensure a rigorous evaluation design. In all of these cases, the quality of the evaluation design could have been improved if the implementing agencies had been requested and had agreed to document their selection procedures and any changes that were introduced in these procedures. Again, this would require close coordination between the evaluator and project management from the start of the project.

Many projects collect extensive monitoring and other kinds of administrative information that could be used to provide data on the baseline conditions of the project group or to document how the actual project implementation schedule and procedures compared with the original plan. Data are also often collected on the benefits received by project participants and sometimes on the outcomes and impacts (e.g., income generated by small-business loan programs; changes in diseases rates or school grade scores and attendance). However, evaluators often assume that these data were collected and filed in a form that they could use for the evaluation design only to discover when they were preparing to use these data that this was not the case. Sometimes, much of the information was not actually collected, the quality was poor, or it was not saved. In other cases, it was filed in a way that made it difficult to use, or the required identification numbers were not recorded or were changed arbitrarily.

In all of the above cases, the quality of the evaluation design and the availability of secondary data on the project, as well as sometimes the control population, could have been greatly improved if the evaluator had been consulted on how the project was designed and how administrative data were collected and filed. However, it is often not easy to involve the evaluator at the start of the project, and organizational and administrative changes might be required to make this possible. For example, the country programs department often does not consult with the evaluation department until it has already been decided which projects will be evaluated, and this decision is often not made until the project is already under way. When consultants are to be contracted, the procurement process often cannot start until the project has been launched.

Table 18.1 illustrates different ways in which lack of coordination between the project agency and the evaluator during the project design can impede the quality of the evaluation design. In each case, closer coordination between the evaluator and project management during the program design phase could have strengthened the evaluation design and/or the analysis of findings.

Table 18.1   Ways in Which Lack of Coordination between Project Management and the Evaluator Can Weaken the Evaluation Design

How the project was designed	How this affected the quality of the evaluation
1. Baseline data were not collected in a timely manner or they were incomplete or of poor quality.	It was not possible to use the project data as the baseline for the evaluation design.

How the project was designed	How this affected the quality of the evaluation
2. Participant selection criteria were not clearly defined or implemented.	Variations in selection criteria and lack of documentation on these procedures make it difficult to correct for variations in the criteria.
3. Project beneficiaries are not clearly identified (e.g., in urban development projects).	It is hard to identify the beneficiary and control groups, which weakens the evaluation design.
4. Changes in the package of project services (treatments) are not documented.	Not knowing who received which treatments seriously weakens the evaluation design.
5. Due to administrative problems (such as distribution of materials, medicines, etc.) to project locations, not all beneficiaries receive all of the intended services. However, lack of documentation means it is not possible to determine who received which services.	Without these data, the evaluator must normally assume that all participants receive the complete package of services. However, if this is not the case, this seriously weakens the analysis and interpretation of the evaluation findings.

3. Evaluation Capacity Development

3.1. Target Groups for Evaluation Capacity Building

At least five groups of actors are actively involved in the evaluation process, and the success of most evaluations is dependent on the support and understanding of all of these stakeholder groups, each of which has different roles in the evaluation process and requires different sets of skills or knowledge. An evaluation capacity-building strategy should define ways to strengthen the evaluation skills of each of these groups:

- *Agencies that commission and fund evaluations.* These include donor agencies, foundations, government budget and funding agencies, and national and international nongovernmental organizations (NGOs).
- *Evaluation practitioners who design, implement, analyze, and disseminate evaluations.* These include evaluation units of line ministries, planning and finance ministries, national and international NGOs, foundations and donor agencies, evaluation consultants, and university research groups.
- *Evaluation users.* These include government, donor, and civil society organizations that use the results of evaluations to help formulate policies, allocate resources, and design and implement programs and projects.
- *Groups affected by the programs being evaluated.* These include community organizations, farmers organizations, trade associations and business groups, trade unions and workers organizations, and many other groups affected directly or indirectly by the programs and policies being evaluated.
- *Public opinion.* This includes broad categories such as the general public, the academic community, and civil society.

3.2. Required Evaluation Skills

Each of the different target groups is concerned with different aspects of the evaluation process and requires different skills or knowledge. Some of the broad categories of skills and knowledge include the following:

- Knowing when evaluations are required
- Understanding what evaluations can and cannot achieve and knowing what questions to ask
- Defining what evaluation clients "really want to know"
- Assessing the cost, time, and technical requirements for an evaluation
- How to promote, commission, or finance evaluations
- How to design, conduct, analyze, and disseminate evaluations
- How to use evaluation findings
- Designing evaluations that will be used
- How to assess the quality and utility of evaluations
- Adapting "ideal" evaluation methodology to RealWorld constraints

Table 18.2 summarizes the types of evaluation skills typically required by each of the five target groups. While there is obviously some overlap, the focus of the evaluation capacity needs is significantly different for each group. For example, the *agencies that fund evaluations* (Target Group 1) require skills in how to identify evaluation needs and when evaluations are needed, evaluating and selecting consultants, assessing evaluation proposals, estimating evaluation resource requirements, and understanding what questions an evaluation can and cannot answer.

On the other hand, *the groups affected by programs and policies* (Target Group 4) must be able to define when evaluations are required; negotiate with evaluators and funding agencies on the content, purpose, use, and dissemination of evaluations; ensure that the right questions are asked, that information is collected from the right people, and that the questions are formulated so as to avoid bias; understand, use, and disseminate the evaluation findings; and conduct an independent evaluation if it is necessary to challenge the findings of the "official" evaluation.

3.3. Designing and Delivering Evaluation Capacity Building

Evaluation capacity building can be delivered in many different ways, formally and informally, in long university or training institution programs or very rapidly. In many cases, the target groups may not consider that they are involved in an evaluation process and may not even recognize that they are in a capacity-building exercise.

Some of the common evaluation capacity-building approaches include the following:

- Formal university or training institute programs. These can range from one or more academic semesters to seminars lasting from several days to several weeks.
- Workshops lasting from less than a day to 2–3 days
- Distance learning and other online programs
- Mentoring
- On-the-job training where evaluation skills are learned as part of a package of work skills
- As part of a community development program
- As part of a community or group empowerment program

Table 18.3 illustrates different methods for evaluation capacity development and how they can be applied to different audiences. For example, **evaluation users** can strengthen their capacity to

Table 18.2 Evaluation Skills Required by Different Groups

Group	Examples	Evaluation Skills Needed
1. Funding agencies	➤ Donor agencies ➤ Ministry of finance and ministry finance departments ➤ Foundations ➤ International NGOs	• Defining when evaluations are required • Evaluating evaluation consultants • Assessing proposals • Estimating evaluation resource requirements (budget, time, human resources)
2. Evaluation practitioners	➤ Evaluation units of line ministries ➤ Evaluation departments of ministries of planning and finance ➤ Evaluation units of NGOs ➤ Evaluation consultants ➤ Universities	• Defining client needs • Adapting theoretically sound designs to RealWorld budget, time, data, and political constraints • Understanding and selecting among different evaluation designs • Data collection and analysis • Sampling • Supervision • Institutional development • Adapting evaluation methodologies to the Real World
3. Evaluation users	➤ Central government agencies (finance, planning, etc.) ➤ Line ministries ➤ NGOs ➤ Foundations ➤ Donor agencies	• Assessing the validity of quantitative evaluation designs and findings • Assessing the adequacy and validity of qualitative and mixed-method evaluation designs
4. Beneficiary populations (target groups)	➤ Community organizations ➤ Farmers organizations ➤ Trade associations and business groups ➤ Trade unions and workers organizations	• Defining when evaluations are required • Negotiating with evaluators and funding agencies on the content, purpose, use, and dissemination of evaluations • Asking the right questions • Understanding and using evaluation findings • Participatory evaluations
5. Public opinion	➤ The general public ➤ The academic community ➤ Civil society	• How to get evaluations done • Participatory evaluations • Making sure the right questions get asked • Understanding and using evaluation findings

understand and use evaluation findings through briefings and short workshops, often with additional documentation available on websites.

An example of distance learning is the Brazilian Interlegis program organized by the Brazilian Senate to train municipal government functionaries on how to use social development indicators and evaluation studies to help identify priority areas for action. A particularly important function is helping mayors and other elected officials to use social indicators to compare their municipality with neighboring municipalities on key indicators such as school attendance, infant mortality, unemployment, and crime. This is useful not only to identify priority areas but also to evaluate performance. For functionaries at this level, it is much more meaningful to compare progress with neighboring municipalities than to try to understand and use the overwhelming amounts of information available from national Millennium Development Goal or Human Development Reports.

Table 18.3   Examples of Different Capacity-Building Approaches Customized for Different Audiences

Audience	Type of Training	Duration	Example
Funding agencies	Workshops and seminars	½–3 days	➢ Chile: briefings to Ministry of Finance and Parliamentary Budget Committee on findings and recommendations of evaluations of government programs[2]
Evaluation practitioners	Short courses on theory and practice using evaluation tools and techniques	1–2 weeks	➢ IPDET: 2-week basic course on evaluation principles and review of evaluation methods and approaches ➢ AEA: 1-day workshop on RealWorld Evaluation. How to assess the validity and adequacy of evaluation designs and how to estimate budget, time, and human resources to conduct the evaluation[3]
Evaluation users	• Debriefing workshop presenting the findings of an evaluation • Distance learning • Case studies and other short publications on how evaluations are used	0.5–1 day Short sessions once a week over a period of months UNICEF "webinars"	➢ Briefing workshops on the evaluation of World Bank Gender Policies ➢ Beneficiary assessment studies ➢ National Millennium Development Goals (MDG) workshops. Supported by mass media campaigns, publications, and websites. ➢ Brazil: Interlegis distance learning program for municipal governments on how to use social development indicators and research findings to identify priority areas of action[4] ➢ *Influential Evaluations:* Eight development evaluation case studies where there is convincing evidence the report influenced policy formulation or program design[5]
Affected populations	Participatory assessment and community consultations	0.5 day to 1 week	➢ Ethiopia: Assessing the impacts of participatory agricultural extension programs[6]
Public opinion	Mass media campaigns to disseminate Citizen Scorecards	Intensive campaign over several weeks consisting of short workshops, briefings, and extensive mass media coverage	➢ "Holding the State to Account" Citizen Report Card study in Bangalore, India. Mass media reporting on citizen attitudes to the quality of public services supported by workshops organized by NGOs[7]

[2] For more information on the Chile program of impact evaluations and evaluations of government programs (in Spanish), see http://www.dipres.cl/fr_control.html.

[3] International Program for Development Evaluation Training (IPDET). This program, organized by the World Bank in cooperation with Carleton University and supported by other donor agencies, is probably the most comprehensive training program available for development evaluation practitioners (see IPDET.org).

[4] For more information about the Interlegis program (in Portuguese), see http://www.interlegis.gov.br.

[5] "Influential Evaluations: Evaluations That Improved Performance and Impacts of Development Programs." 2004. Evaluation Capacity Development, Operations Evaluation Department. World Bank. Available at www.worldbank.org/oed/ecd

[6] A presentation on this study was made at the American Evaluation Association Conference in 2004.

[7] A summary of this study is included in "Influential Evaluations" (see Note 5). For a more detailed assessment, see Adikeshavalu Ravindra, "An Assessment of the Impact of the Bangalore Citizen Report Cards on the Performance of Public Agencies" (also available at www.worldbank.org/oed/ecd).

4. Institutionalizing Impact Evaluation Systems at the Country and Sector Levels

4.1. The Importance of Impact Evaluation for Development Assistance Programs

In order to assess the effectiveness of development assistance programs in contributing to poverty reduction, economic growth, and sustainable development, it is important to conduct systematic analysis of development effectiveness. Many assessments of development effectiveness are based either on data that are only collected from project beneficiaries *after the project has been implemented* or on the use of monitoring and evaluation (M&E) or results-based management to measure changes that have taken place in the target population over the life of the project. In all these cases, data are generated only on the target population, and no information is collected on sectors that do not benefit from the project or that in some cases may even be worse off as a result of the project. With all of these approaches, there is a tendency for the evaluation to overestimate the true benefits or effects produced by the project (Bamberger 2010). Typically, only project beneficiaries are interviewed, none of the families or communities that do not benefit are interviewed, and the evaluation does not present any information on the experiences or opinions of these nonbeneficiary groups. Many of these evaluations are methodologically weak and often biased, and consequently, there is a serious risk that development agencies will continue to fund programs that are producing smaller impacts than are reported and that may even be producing negative consequences for some sectors of the target population.

Although no hard statistics are available, it is quite likely that rigorous impact evaluation (IE) designs are only used in perhaps 10% of development impact evaluations. Given the widespread recognition by development agencies of the importance of rigorous IEs, why are so few conducted? There are many reasons, including the limited evaluation budgets of many agencies, most evaluations are not commissioned until late in the project cycle, and consultants are given only a very short time to conduct data collection. Also, many government agencies see evaluation as a threat or something that will demand a lot of management time without producing useful findings. Also, as many evaluations produce a *positive bias,* showing programs in a positive light, many agencies do not feel the need for more rigorous (as well as more expensive and time-consuming) evaluation methodologies. One of the challenges for the institutionalization of IE is to convince both development agencies and host country governments that rigorous and objective impact evaluations can become valuable budgetary, policy, and management tools.

4.2. Institutionalizing Impact Evaluation

Institutionalization of IE at the sector or national level occurs when (a) the evaluation process is country led and managed by a central government ministry or sector agency; (b) there is strong "buy-in" from key stakeholders; (c) there are well-defined procedures for selecting, implementing, and using IEs; (d) IE is integrated into national M&E systems that generate much of the evaluation data; (e) IE is integrated into national budget formulation and development planning; and (f) there is a focus on evaluation capacity development (ECD). Institutionalization is a process, and at any given point, it will have advanced further in some sectors than others. How IE is institutionalized will also vary from country to country, reflecting different political and administrative systems and historical factors such as donor support for particular sectors.

Many IEs have not been able to achieve their potential contributions to program management, budget planning, and policymaking because evaluations were selected and funded in an ad hoc and opportunistic way determined by the interests of donor agencies or individual ministries rather than by national planning priorities. The value of IEs as a policymaking tool can be greatly enhanced once selection, dissemination, and use of the evaluations becomes part of a national IE system. This requires an annual plan for selection of the government's priority programs on which decisions have to be made concerning continuation, modification, or termination and where the evaluation framework permits the comparison of alternative interventions in terms of cost-effectiveness and contribution to national development goals.

No single strategy is always successful in the institutionalization of IE. Countries that have made progress have built on existing evaluation experience, political and administrative traditions, and the interest and capacity of individual ministries, national evaluation champions, or donor agencies. Figure 18.2 identifies three alternative pathways to the institutionalization of IE. *The ad hoc or opportunistic approach* evolves from individual evaluations that took advantage of available funds and the interest of a senior government official or a particular donor. The approaches were gradually systematized as experience was gained in selection criteria, effective methodologies, and how to achieve both quality and utilization. A central government agency, usually finance or planning, is involved from the beginning or becomes involved as the focus moves toward a national system. Colombia's national M&E system illustrates this pathway with the Ministry of Planning responsible for managing the National System for Evaluation of Public Sector Performance (SINERGIA). Although initially, selection of evaluations was somewhat ad hoc and strongly influenced by donor interests, as the program of IE evolved, the range of methodologies was broadened, and technical criteria in the selection of programs to be evaluated were formalized through policy documents (with more demand-side involvement from the agencies managing the programs being evaluated) and in how the findings are used. Most of the IEs use rigorous econometric evaluation techniques (Mackay 2007:31–36; Bamberger 2009a).

The second pathway is where IE expertise is developed in a priority sector supported by a dynamic government agency and where there are important policy questions to be addressed and strong donor support. Once the operational and policy value of these evaluations has been demonstrated, this becomes a catalyst for developing a national system. The evaluations of the PROGRESA conditional cash transfer programs in Mexico are an example of this approach (Mackay 2007:56; Bamberger 2008). A series of rigorous evaluations of the PROGRESA programs conducted over a number of years convincingly demonstrated the effectiveness of conditional cash transfers as a way to improve the welfare (particularly education and health) of large numbers of low-income families. The evaluations are considered to have been a major contributing factor in convincing the new government that came to power in 2002 to continue these programs started by the previous administration. The evaluations also convinced policymakers of the technical feasibility and policy value of rigorous IEs and contributed to the passing of a law by Congress in 2007 mandating the evaluation of all social programs. This law also created the National Commission for the Evaluation of Social Programs, which was assigned the responsibility for regulating the development of monitoring and evaluation functions in the social sectors.

The World Bank Africa Impact Evaluation Initiative (AIM) is a regional initiative helping governments strengthen their overall M&E capability and systems that is currently supporting some 90 experimental and quasi-experimental IEs in 20 African countries.[8] At least 40 countries in Asia, Latin America, and the Middle East are now implementing sectoral approaches to IE with World Bank support. A number of international evaluation initiatives are being promoted through collaborative organizations such as the Network of Networks for Impact Evaluation (NONIE)[9] and the International Initiative for Impact Evaluation (3IE).[10]

---

[8]For more information on the Africa Impact Evaluation Initiative, see http://worldbank.org/afr/impact.

[9]http://www.worldbank.org/ieg/nonie/index.html

[10]http://www.3ieimpact.org

Figure 18.2   Three Pathways for the Evolution of Institutionalized IE Systems

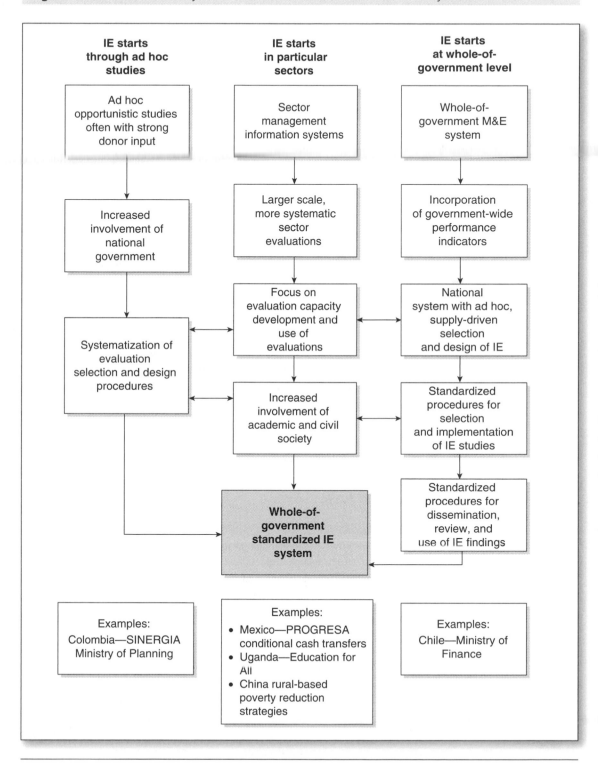

SOURCE: International Bank for Reconstruction and Development/The World Bank: *Institutionalizing Impact Evaluation within the Framework of a Monitoring and Evaluation System* (Bamberger 2009d).

The third pathway is where a program of IEs was developed as one component of a whole-of-government system, managed and championed by a strong central government agency, usually the Ministry of Finance or Planning. Chile is a good example of a national M&E system with clearly defined criteria and guidelines for the selection of programs to be evaluated, their conduct and methodology, and how the findings will be used (Mackay 2007:25–30; Bamberger 2008). Starting in 1994, a system of performance indicators was developed; rapid evaluations of government programs were incorporated in 1996; and in 2001, a program of rigorous impact evaluations was introduced. There are two clearly defined IE products. The first are rapid ex-post evaluations that follow a clearly defined and rapid commissioning process, where the evaluations are used by the Ministry of Finance as part of the annual budget process. The second are more comprehensive evaluations that can take up to 18 months and cost $88,000 on average. The strength of the system is that it has defined and cost-effective procedures for commissioning, conducting, and reporting of IEs; a defined audience (the Ministry of Finance); and a clearly understood use (the preparation of the annual budget). The disadvantages are that the studies only cover issues of interest to the Ministry of Finance, and the buy-in from the agencies being implemented is typically low.

Integrating IE into sector and/or national M&E and other data collection systems. The successful institutionalization of IE requires that selection, design, and use are integrated into national M&E systems and data collection programs. This is critical for several reasons. First, much of the data required for an IE can be obtained efficiently and economically from program M&E systems. Second, IE findings that are widely disseminated provide an incentive for agencies to improve the quality of M&E data they collect and report. For example, the Ministry of Education in Uganda reported that the wide dissemination of the Education for All evaluations contributed to improvements in the quality of monitoring reporting. Third, national household survey programs provide valuable sources of secondary data for strengthening the methodological rigor of IE design and analysis (e.g., the use of propensity score matching to reduce sample selection bias). Some IEs have cooperated with national statistical offices to piggy-back information required for the IE onto an ongoing household survey or to add a special module.

Creating Demand for IE

Efforts to strengthen IE and other kinds of M&E systems are often viewed as technical fixes—mainly involving better data systems and the conduct of good-quality evaluations. Although the creation of evaluation capacity to provide high-quality evaluation services is important, these *supply-side interventions* will have little effect unless there is sufficient *demand* for quality IE. This requires that quality IEs are seen as important policy and management tools in at least one of the following areas: (a) budget resource allocation, (b) policy formulation and analytical work, (c) management and delivery of government services, and (d) accountability.

Creating demand requires powerful incentives within government to commission IE, create a good level of quality, and use IE information intensively. A key factor is a public-sector environment supportive of the use of evaluation findings as a policy and management tool. MacKay (2007, Table 11.1) suggests some *positive incentives* ("carrots") such as building ownership and financing to build better IE systems; *sanctions and threats* ("sticks") such as laws and decrees mandating the planning, conduct, and reporting of IEs; and *positive messages from key figures* ("sermons") such as high-level statements of endorsement and conferences on good IE practice to help generate demand for IE among potential users.

Strategies to promote utilization are discussed in Chapter 8, and Box 8.3 summarizes lessons learned.

SUMMARY

1. Most evaluations are intended to provide information on program performance and recommendations on actions that management or policymakers should take to improve performance of ongoing programs or the selection and design of future programs. It is important to build in quality assurance procedures to ensure the findings are accurate and unbiased and that recommendations are based on all available evidence.

2. Some of the most common quality assurance procedures are (1) preliminary feasibility studies to ensure that the evaluation objectives could be achieved, (2) evaluability analysis to assess whether the proposed evaluation design could answer all of the questions in the Terms of Reference, and (3) a threats-to-validity analysis. The chapter presented three complementary threats-to-validity analyses designed to evaluate quantitative, qualitative, and mixed-method evaluations.

3. Threats-to-validity have traditionally focused on internal threats to validity (reasons why conclusions about the contribution of project and program interventions to explaining observed changes in the beneficiary population may not be valid) and external threats to validity (reasons why recommendations about the replicability of the program in other settings may not be valid). The approaches proposed in this chapter also assess utilization validity (arguing that if stakeholders do not use the evaluation findings, there must be questions about the validity of the design).

4. The threats-to-validity assessment for mixed-method evaluations is more complicated as this must assess both how effectively quantitative and qualitative methods are used as well as how well these approaches are integrated into a mixed-method approach at each stage of the evaluation.

5. Appendixes A, B, and C present worksheets that can be used to assess validity for quantitative, qualitative, and mixed-method approaches, respectively. Each worksheet includes three parts, each targeted for a different audience: a one-page summary for senior management summarizing the findings of the assessment and recommended actions that might be required before the evaluation report is accepted; a half-page summary of each component of the assessment for mid-level management, providing more detail on the reasons for the ratings given to each component; and checklists providing a detailed set of technical indicators for assessing the methodological quality of each component. This latter will be used when a detailed technical assessment is required and an evaluation specialist, either from within the client agency or contracted externally, will normally be required to conduct this technical assessment.

6. The second topic concerns ways in which closer coordination between evaluators and program management can improve the quality of evaluation design. Frequently, the evaluator has no involvement in the design of the program, and as a result, opportunities to use participant selection procedures such as randomized selection or regression discontinuity may be missed. Similarly, project data sources such as baseline studies, information about beneficiaries and those not selected, or monitoring data on project implementation, which could be very valuable for the evaluation, are collected or archived in ways that cannot easily be used for the evaluation. Another major frustration for many evaluations is that changes are made in how beneficiaries are selected or in the packages of services provided by the program, but these changes are not systematically documented. Consequently, it is very difficult for the evaluator to know the criteria on which different participants were selected or what services different groups of participants actually received. Finally, it is frequently the case that, due to administrative problems or resource constraints, not all beneficiaries receive all of the planned services. Frequently, the failure to deliver services as planned is not documented, so the evaluation may be designed on the assumption

that everyone receives the complete package of services, while this may not be the case. Where closer cooperation between evaluators and program management can be achieved, which is admittedly often difficult to ensure, it is possible to design programs that are "evaluation ready," and the quality of the evaluation findings and recommendations can be improved.

7. The third topic concerns strategies for evaluation capacity development. While much evaluation training is targeted for the evaluation practitioners who conduct the evaluations, an effective evaluation program requires that five main groups between them have the capacity to understand how to define the need for evaluation and the kind of evaluation that is required at a given point in time, how to select the appropriate evaluation design, how to implement or manage the evaluation, and how to disseminate and use the evaluation findings and recommendations. Evaluation capacity can be developed in a number of ways, including courses and workshops, on-the-job training, guidance manuals and publications, and study tours.

8. The final topic covered is the institutionalization of evaluation systems. International and national donors have supported the conduct of high-quality evaluations in many countries, but there are still very few countries in which these individual evaluations have resulted in the development of a nationally managed evaluation system. One of the reasons for this is that many donors support evaluations that respond to their information needs and do not necessarily address the priority questions of concern to national governments. Similarly, the choice of evaluation methods is often strongly influenced by the methodological preferences of the donor.

9. Progress toward institutionalization involves most of the following: country ownership of the evaluation system, including the selection of the policies or programs to be evaluated; an increasing proportion of evaluation funding comes from national sources; there is a system for the selection, commissioning, design, implementation, dissemination, and use of evaluation with clearly defined audiences and purposes; and systems are put in place to strengthen the capacity of national evaluators. It has also been argued that the system must include "carrots," "sticks," and "sermons" to provide incentives, sanctions, and moral support to agencies to build evaluation into the programs they manage.

10. In countries that have made progress toward the institutionalization of evaluations, one of three paths tends to have been followed. The first starts with ad hoc selection of evaluations, taking advantage of funding opportunities or the interest of a strong figure in government. As these evaluations are found to be useful, central agencies gradually become more involved in the selection, management, and dissemination of the evaluations. Colombia is cited as an example of this approach. The second path is where a concerted effort is made to implement high-quality evaluations in a particular sector such as education, health, or cash payments to the poor. Where these evaluations are found to be useful and where they gain international recognition, the decision may be made to expand the rigorous approaches to other sectors. Mexico is an example of this approach. The third path, and the least common, is where a national government makes a commitment to develop a national evaluation system that is introduced step by step over a period of years. Chile is an example of this approach.

11. At the time of writing, most progress has been made toward the institutionalization of evaluation in Latin America. However, progress is being made in other regions, and it is likely that over the next five years, it will be possible to cite a number of countries in Africa, South and East Asia, and perhaps the Middle East and Eastern Europe that have made significance progress toward the institutionalization of their evaluation systems.

FURTHER READING

Bamberger, M. 2008. *Institutionalizing Impact Evaluation within the Framework of a Monitoring and Evaluation System.* Independent Evaluation Group. Washington, DC: World Bank. http://siteresources.worldbank.org/EXTEVACAPDEV/Resources/4585672-12514618 75432/inst_ie_framework_me.pdf

This publication complements the previous publication by Mackay (2007) by focusing in more detail on the institutionalization of impact evaluations, while Mackay discusses basic M&E systems. Discussion of alternative ways to institutionalize national impact evaluation systems and steps required to implement, strengthen, and sustain the systems. Case studies are presented describing the national systems in Chile, Colombia, Mexico, and Uganda.

Bamberger, M. and A. Kirk (eds.). 2009. *Making Smart Policy: Using Impact Evaluation for Policy Making.* Case Studies on Evaluations that Influenced Policy. Doing Impact Evaluation Series No. 14. Thematic Group on Poverty Analysis, Monitoring and Impact Evaluation. Poverty Reduction and Economic Management. Washington, DC: The World Bank.

Presentation of 12 case studies on impact evaluations in the education, health, antipoverty, and sustainable development sectors that appear to have influenced policymakers. Identification of factors that contribute to the utilization of evaluations.

Bamberger, M., K. Mackay, and E. Ooi. 2004 and 2005. *Influential Evaluations: Evaluations That Improved Performance and Impacts of Development Programs.* Operations Evaluation Department. Washington, DC: World Bank. http://sitere sources.worldbank.org/EXTEVACAPDEV/Resources/4585672-1251727474013/influential_evaluation_case_studies.pdf

Presentation of eight case studies on evaluations that were influential at the program, planning, and policy levels. The 2004 publication summarizes the cases, while the 2005 publication presents the cases in more detail and also describes the attribution analysis methodologies. While the 2009 publication referenced above (Bamberger and Kirk 2009) focuses only on impact evaluations, the present publications cover a number of different types of process, output, and outcome evaluations.

Engela, R., and T. Ajam. 2010. *Implementing a Government-wide Monitoring and Evaluation System in South Africa.* Independent Evaluation Group. Washington, DC: World Bank. http://siteresources.worldbank.org/EXTEVACAPDEV/Resources/ecd_wp_21_south_africa.pdf

This paper is interesting because it draws on the experience of an African country, whereas most of the earlier literature focuses on Latin America. The paper analyzes the process of designing and implementing a government-wide monitoring and evaluation (GWM&E) system in South Africa. South Africa has followed a "big bang" approach in its efforts to build a national M&E system, starting as recently as 2005. The country has pursued capacity building and system building with an initial focus on monitoring; a conscious decision was made to pursue evaluation later. M&E development is being allowed to evolve rather than follow a completed and detailed blueprint. A number of major M&E initiatives have been pursued over the past three years, and considerable success already has been achieved. The paper assesses the remaining challenges, including the barriers to achieving more of a performance culture in the government and civil service.

Mackay, K. 2007. *How to Build M&E Systems to Support Better Government.* Independent Evaluation Group. Washington, DC: World Bank. http://web.worldbank.org/WBSITE/EXTERNAL/EXTOED/EXTEVACAPDEV/0,,contentMDK:22294993~menuPK:4585748~pagePK:64829573~piPK:64829550~theSitePK:4585673,00.html

Comprehensive review of the features of a successful national M&E system and the steps required to implement and sustain the system. This mainly draws on the experience of Latin America, where more progress has been made in the institutionalization of national M&E systems.

Morra, L., and R. Rist. 2009. *The Road to Results: Designing and Conducting Effective Development Evaluations.* Washington, DC: World Bank. Also available in electronic format at www.worldbank.org/r2r

This very useful reference publication is written by the two co-directors of the International Program for Development Evaluation Training (IPDET) and draws on the experience of 10 years of evaluation training by some of the leading specialists in this field. The main sections cover the following: Foundations (of international development evaluation), Preparing and Conducting Effective Development Evaluations, Designing and Conducting (development evaluations), Meeting Challenges, and Leading (which covers managing evaluations, presenting results, guiding the evaluator, and looking to the future).

CHAPTER 19

Conclusions and Challenges for the Road Ahead

1. Conclusions

1.1. The RWE Perspective on the Methods Debate

There are a wide variety of purposes, evaluands, contexts, designs, and methods for conducting evaluations. Some of them were introduced in Chapters 2 and 11. Nevertheless, our main focus in this book has been on evaluations whose main purpose is to ascertain the impact of programs. There are also a variety of ways to design and conduct impact evaluations. But since this is still such a hotly debated subject among evaluators and those who call for "rigorous impact evaluation," we feel the need to clarify our perspectives on this important issue.

Experimental and quasi-experimental (QED) impact evaluation designs[1] are an essential part of the evaluation toolkit. In situations where randomized controlled trials (RCTs) can be used, they are able to statistically control for selection bias, a major cause of misinterpretation of evaluation findings. When only QEDs can be applied, they are able to partially control for selection bias and also, when properly applied, can identify the issues that have not been controlled for and the implications for the interpretation of findings and recommendations. Even in the many situations where experimental designs cannot be used, the logic of the experimental design can still provide a reference framework against which to judge the validity of findings from nonexperimental or weaker QED evaluation designs.

While the continuing debate on impact evaluation designs has had many positive effects, one of the unfortunate consequences has been that the often heated debates have caused many evaluators to react against what they consider the exaggerated claims of some advocates of RCTs. Consequently, the important reference point that experimental designs can provide for understanding potential threats to validity of nonexperimental designs has been ignored by many evaluators from other camps. On the other side of the debate, many of the websites promoting RCTs and other strong statistical designs

---

[1]We use "experimental" designs as a generic term covering randomized designs and strong quasi-experimental designs.

could be accused of a selective presentation of the evidence as most of these sites only present examples where experimental designs have been used successfully, and it is extremely difficult to find any information on these sites about the frequency with which efforts to use these designs were not successful. So unsuspecting visitors to these websites could get the impression that experimental designs almost always work well and that they should be used wherever possible. However, experienced evaluators know there are many situations in which attempts to use experimental designs have run into problems (e.g., because of changes in the project design and treatments, changes in the participant selection criteria, problems in maintaining the comparison group, difficulties in implementing the project as planned, and external events that dramatically changed the project context). So there is still a need for a franker assessment of what the experience has been in the use of these designs and more objective discussions of when they are and are not likely to work.

It is also important to make a clearer distinction between *statistically strong* designs (designs that incorporate a robust counterfactual and control for selection bias) and *methodologically strong* designs. While experimental and strong QEDs provide statistically strong designs, they do not automatically ensure that the overall design is methodologically sound, and the logic on which these designs are based exposes them to a number of potential methodological vulnerabilities:

- *Inflexibility.* Most experimental designs require the replication of the same or a similar data collection instrument in the pre- and posttest applications to measure change.
- *Hard to adapt sample to changing circumstances.* They also require that the same, or a similar, sample be used in the pre- and posttest comparisons.
- *Hard to adapt to changing circumstances.* These requirements make it difficult to adapt the design to situations where the project design (services provided) or participant selection criteria may change. They also make it difficult for changes in the control group when, for example, parts of the control group are incorporated into the project or may vanish due to migration, urban renewal, or other factors.
- *Problems with collecting sensitive information.* Experimental designs usually require the use of a structured questionnaire that is often administered in a formal setting.
- *Monomethod bias.* Many experimental designs rely on one principal method of data collection and do not systematically incorporate triangulation. This is always a potential weakness, particularly for studying complex, multidimensional constructs such as poverty, empowerment, and vulnerability.
- *Difficult to identify and interview difficult to reach groups.* Many evaluations require interviewing difficult to reach groups such as the homeless, sex workers, people who are HIV positive, the landless, and illegal squatters/immigrants. Reaching these groups often requires a more qualitative approach that can be difficult to incorporate into the experimental design and sample frame.
- *Lack of attention to the project implementation process.* Many experimental designs rely on a pretest–posttest methodology that does not adequately assess the process of project implementation (the so-called black box problem). As most projects experience some deviations from the implementation plan, and there are often serious implementation problems, it is difficult to judge whether failure to achieve expected outcomes is due to *design failure* or to *implementation failure.*
- *Lack of attention to context.* Many experimental designs do not systematically analyze contextual factors such as the local and national economic, political, organizational,

sociocultural, and natural environmental factors that can affect outcomes in different project locations.

- *Focus on one intervention.* Typically, experimental designs test one intervention at a time. The unstated ideal is that of a "silver bullet" or "panacea"—one relatively simple intervention that will, by itself, lead to desired impact. In most RealWorld situations, combinations of multiple interventions (by more than one agency) or preconditions are required to achieve higher-level impact. In other words, they call for multilayered, more complex logic models, where plausible contributions from multiple sources are acknowledged and taken into account when determining what led to any observed changes in impact-level indicators.

- *Limitation of direct cause-effect attribution.* Again, the typical RCT tests directly attributable results of an intervention, redefining *impact* to be what others may consider short-term or intermediate outcomes rather than *impact* defined as higher-level, long-term, sustainable improvements in human well-being (like the indicators of the Millennium Development Goals (MDGs).[2]

Here's another way to express the caveat regarding RCTs: For an individual evaluator to attempt to conduct an impact evaluation of a program using only one predetermined tool is to suffer from myopia, which is unfortunate. On the other hand, to prescribe to donors and senior managers of major agencies that there is a single preferred design and method for conducting all impact evaluations can and has had unfortunate consequences for all of those who are involved in the design, implementation, and evaluation of national and international development programs. There is much more to impact, to rigor, and to "the scientific method" than RCTs. Serious impact evaluations require a more holistic approach.

In any case, experimental designs, whatever their merits, can only be applied in a very small proportion of impact evaluations in the real world.

A crucial issue that often gets overlooked in the methods debate is the fact that experimental designs can only be applied in a very small proportion of program impact evaluations where it is feasible (and ethical) to randomly select "intervention" and "control" subjects. While no hard statistics are available, it is often estimated that RCTs can probably only be applied in less than 5% of impact evaluations, and many would estimate the figure is much lower. Even strong quasi-experimental designs have been applied in perhaps only 10% to 25% of impact evaluations. So for many evaluators, the debate on the merits of experimental designs is largely academic as they may never have a chance to apply these in their whole professional career as evaluators.

Furthermore, most development agencies are moving from support of individual projects to support of broad development programs, often with multiple components, many different funding and implementing agencies, and often a lack of defined objectives or even target population. For most of these complicated and complex programs, conventional (relatively simplistic) experimental and quasi-experimental designs are generally not applicable.

So for all of these reasons, we are left with the question, "What kinds of impact evaluation designs are appropriate for the vast majority of development interventions where conventional experimental designs do not apply?" In contrast to the very large literature on rigorous, quantitative

---

[2]As a reminder, the oft-quoted definition of impact by the Organization for Economic Cooperation/Development Advisory Committee (2002:24) is "the positive and negative, primary and secondary long-term effects produced by a development intervention, directly or indirectly, intended or unintended. These effects can be economic, sociocultural, institutional, environmental, technological or of other types."

experimental research designs, the evaluation literature has had very little to offer to the majority of funding and implementing agencies and evaluators. *This is a "missing piece" where we hope the RealWorld Evaluation (RWE) approach will make a contribution.*

1.2. How Does RealWorld Evaluation Fit into the Picture?

The RWE approach was designed to address situations where evaluations have to be conducted under budget, time, and data constraints (see Chapters 3–5) and where it is necessary to reconcile different political interests (see Chapter 6) and to accommodate organizational structures and administrative procedures that may add further complications to the design, implementation, dissemination, and use of the evaluation (see Chapter 17). Strategies are proposed for addressing all of these challenges while at the same time seeking the most rigorous methodology that is possible within each context. An important component of the strategy is the use of a "threats to validity" worksheet to assess the methodological validity of each component of the evaluation, to identify potential threats to validity that affect the achievement of the evaluation's objectives, and to propose actions to address the challenges (see Chapter 7 and Appendixes A–E). The worksheet is designed in three parts so that the findings of the technical assessment of validity can be communicated in a brief and nontechnical language to various stakeholders, including program participants, evaluation managers, donor agency senior management, partner agencies, and (where appropriate) policymakers.

1.3. Selecting the Appropriate Evaluation Design

RWE also identifies a wide range of evaluation design options that could be considered in different situations. In Chapters 2 and 11, we proposed an eight-step strategy for selecting the appropriate evaluation design. In addition to a technical analysis of feasible design options, the process involves consultation and sometimes negotiation with the clients (see Figure 11.1, page 210). It is essential that they understand and are in agreement with the proposed design. Where trade-offs must be made to accommodate to budget, time, data, administrative, and political constraints, it is essential that clients fully understand the methodological and political consequences of decisions to cut budgets, reduce time, or respond to priorities or concerns of key stakeholders.

We start with the premise that there is no single "best" evaluation design that will work well for all kinds of evaluation. It is essential to begin with a scoping study (Step 1 of the RWE approach—see Chapter 2) to fully understand the following:

- What is the purpose of the evaluation, how do clients intend to use the evaluation, and what key kinds of information do they require?
- In addition to the clients paying for the evaluation, who are the other key stakeholders, what are their perspectives on the program and the purpose of the evaluation, how do they relate to each other, what roles should they play in the evaluation, and what kinds of information would be useful to them?
- What are the contextual factors likely to influence the choice of evaluation questions, how the evaluation will be implemented, the kinds of constraints that will be faced, and how the findings will be used (or not used)?
- What are the key characteristics of the "evaluand" (the program or activity being evaluated)? This will include dimensions such as purpose, size, budget, implementation strategy,

previous experience, qualifications of the staff, and relations with the target population (including whether and how they were involved in the choice and design of the project).

It is then necessary to understand the circumstances and context within which the evaluation will be conducted, including the following:

- Why is the evaluation being conducted?
- What is it supposed to achieve?
- Who promoted it, who supports it, and who does not? What are the opinions of the clients? Are they in favor or opposed? Do they understand the proposed methodology and do they agree with it?
- What are the preferred methodologies of the funding agency, the national government agencies, and the implementers? Do they have strong preferences for or against quantitative and qualitative methods? Do they support or oppose participatory approaches?

To assist with this process, RWE identifies 7 basic evaluation design framework scenarios (see Table 11.2, page 217) and a total of 19 more nuanced evaluation design options (see Table 11.3, page 220) that take into consideration the following:

- When the evaluation primary data collection is conducted (at the start of the project, during implementation, at the time the project closes, or sometime afterwards)
- What is used as a counterfactual—that is, whether a comparison group is used (at some or all points of the evaluation) and how it is matched with the project group (random assignment, statistically matched quasi-experimental comparison group, or judgmental matching), or whether secondary data or key informants or recall or other methods are used to determine an adequate counterfactual.
- Whether relevant baseline data were collected and used and how they were obtained (primary data collection, use of secondary data or through "reconstruction" of the baseline when the evaluation does not begin until late in the project cycle)

The choice of the appropriate design is critical and must involve both the findings of the scoping study (see Chapter 2) and methodological considerations and an evaluability assessment to determine if the preferred design is feasible. It is important to recognize that there is almost always more than one possible design option, and the final choice must combine technical considerations as well as the purpose of the evaluation, client preferences, and a full understanding of the evaluation context. Although many clients will expect the evaluation "expert" to tell them which is the "best" design or the appropriate sample size, it is important to understand that there are political dimensions to the choice and that the client and other key stakeholders must be fully involved in the decision.

1.4. Mixed Methods: The Approach of Choice for Most RealWorld Evaluations

Almost all program evaluations require a combination of depth, to understand the lived experiences of individuals and groups affected by the program, and breadth, to generalize from in-depth qualitative methods to the broader population (see Chapter 14). This requires a judicious combination of quantitative (QUANT) and qualitative (QUAL) methods. While many and perhaps most evaluators claim to have used mixed methods, in many cases, they are only including one additional method of data collection to complement an approach that is mainly QUANT or QUAL. In fact, mixed methods is an integrated approach to evaluation that has a unique approach to all stages of the evaluation from hypothesis development through sample design, data collection, data analysis and triangulation, interpretation, and dissemination of findings. Among the many contributions that mixed methods make to RWE are the following:

- Hypothesis development strategies that combine deductive (QUANT) hypotheses that can be tested statistically on one hand, and inductive, emergent (QUAL) hypotheses, on the other hand, that have the flexibility to adapt as more information is obtained on the program and its context
- Sample designs that permit the use of QUAL purposive sampling to select a small sample of subjects that provides the highest value for the purposes of the evaluation, with QUANT random sampling procedures that permit generalizations from the QUAL sample to the broader program population
- Triangulation that helps strengthen the reliability and validity of data by using two or more independent methods to check for consistency or to provide a broader context for understanding the complexity and multidimensionality of what initially appeared to be "simple" concepts.

1.5. Greater Attention Must Be Given to the Management of Evaluations

When we first began organizing workshops on "shoestring" evaluation and, later, "RealWorld" evaluations, we had assumed that budget, time, and data would be the main constraints. But it quickly became clear that for many evaluators, the main challenges involve accommodating different organizational priorities and perspectives, as well as having to work within administrative systems that are often inflexible and not designed to accommodate the real world within which evaluations are designed, implemented, and used. So while all evaluators would always like more time and money, as well as easy access to all of the required information, often their major headaches concern things such as:

- Pressures from their own organization or partner agencies (e.g., other donors or host country government agencies) to not "rock to boat" by being "too negative" and to avoid raising sensitive questions
- Pressures to not interview certain groups, including control groups and critics of the program, and not to address certain issues
- Inflexible procurement arrangements for hiring consultants
- Unrealistically short amounts of time that consultants can spend in the field. Allowable days in each country often ignore the significant amounts of time that everyone knows are required to obtain travel clearance from government (once in the country) or the logistical problems and delays in arranging in-country travel.
- Long delays in obtaining feedback on evaluation designs, inception, and progress reports

- Difficulties in obtaining information from partner agencies or arranging interviews with key people in these agencies
- Internal coordination problems (not to mention rivalries) within partner agencies

For reasons such as these, two additional chapters were added to this second edition of the RWE book: "Organizing and Managing the Evaluation Function" (Chapter 17) and "Strengthening Evaluation Capacity at the Agency and National Level" (Chapter 18). Some of the key conclusions from these chapters and from the many references to these issues in earlier chapters include the following:

- The importance of developing an evaluation framework (some agencies call this the "Terms of Reference"; others call it a "Scope of Work" or "Statement of Work") that spells out the basic purpose, objectives, major questions to be answered, proposed methodology, division of responsibilities, resource requirements and sources, timelines, and deliverables. This should be developed and negotiated in consultation with all partners. This step is crucial to avoid confusions or misunderstanding at a later point. It is also important to ensure that all budget requirements have been realistically estimated and that budgetary approval has been obtained.
- Ensure that the evaluation proposal reviews alternative designs and explains why a particular design has been proposed. This is important because many clients (and evaluators) have preferred designs that they propose for all evaluations without studying the specific requirements of each evaluation.
- Commission an evaluability analysis to ensure that the proposed evaluation design is feasible within the RealWorld constraints and that it can respond to all of the information requirements. Sometimes evaluations are commissioned too early in the life of the project before it is possible to have achieved and measured outcomes and impacts, so this should receive particular attention.
- An important aspect of the evaluability analysis is the trajectory analysis in which the way impacts are expected to evolve (both in terms of time and the shape of the impact trajectory) is assessed (see also Chapter 10). Evaluations that are conducted too early or too late (in cases where impacts are not expected to have a very long duration) can fail to capture impacts that may really have occurred.
- A follow-up plan to ensure agreed-to recommendations are acted on is critical. Due to the pressure of other activities, often the agreements are forgotten, so a management log that tracks implementation of agreements can be helpful.
- The following section emphasizes that an important management function is to build in a quality assurance system so that the quality of evaluation findings and recommendations are routinely assessed.

1.6. Quality Assurance

Many evaluation departments and agencies that commission evaluations do not have systematic procedures for assessing the quality of the evaluation and for taking actions to address any weaknesses that are identified. Sometimes evaluations are assessed through a peer review process where reviewers are not given clear guidance on the assessment criteria and where consequently each reviewer uses his or her own assessment criteria. Often, as a result, important aspects of the evaluation design may not get assessed. Even more frequently, there is no plan, budget, or time to follow up on any recommendations concerning issues with the design or findings. Consequently, it is recommended that the Terms of Reference (ToR) for the evaluation should include budget and time to allow for any follow-up actions that might be required, and consultants must agree to ensure the appropriate members of their team would be available to respond to these requests.

Experience shows that the success of quality assurance depends to a significant degree on the specificity of the ToR concerning the methodology and responsibilities of the consultants. Frequently, the consultants will respond to critiques or requests for further analysis by stating, often with justification, that these requirements were not clearly stated in the ToR.

Chapter 7 proposes a set of threats to validity worksheets and checklists that can be used to assess the validity of findings and recommendation of QUANT, QUAL, and mixed-method evaluations. Appendixes A to C present the worksheets, and Appendix D gives an example of a completed worksheet. Part 3 of each worksheet permits a detailed technical assessment of validity on each major dimension, Part 2 provides a short summary for evaluation managers, and Part 1 presents a one-page summary of the assessment and proposed follow-up actions for senior management and for other partners.

1.7. The Challenge of Institutionalization

In many countries, donors have been supporting impact evaluations for many years, and many of these evaluations have been of a high technical quality. However, much less attention has been given to helping governments build a *national monitoring and evaluation system* to ensure that central planning and finance agencies have a strategy for identifying each year the evaluation questions that have the greatest policy relevance, commissioning evaluations that will address these questions, and ensuring that the findings contribute to key budget planning and policy decisions. This requires a clearly defined strategy by donors and governments for promoting the institutionalization of impact evaluation at the national and sector levels. This remains a weakness in most donor approaches to evaluation.

1.8. The Importance of Competent Professional and Ethical Practice

In recent years, a number of important standards and best practice guidelines have been developed for evaluators and the agencies that commission and use evaluations (see Chapter 9). While these are widely, but not universally, used in many Western countries such as the United States, Canada, and Europe, they have been less frequently used in development evaluation. There is an even bigger gap with respect to ethical standards, and while the U.S. federal government and many other agencies have strict standards for research on human subjects (most research has to go through an institutional review board, also known as an independent ethics committee or ethical review board), this is not always the case in international evaluation. For example, many international development agencies do not have formal guidelines covering human subject research, and guidelines on how to implement a "do no harm" policy are often not clearly defined.

However, ethical issues affecting evaluation practice are often complex[3] and are even more challenging when working in a different culture.[4] They are made more difficult when having to

---

[3]The wide range of topics covered in the *American Journal of Evaluation*'s Ethical Challenges section, as well as the complex and subtle nature of many of these issues, illustrates the difficulties of addressing these issues, even when the evaluator is working in her or his own country.

[4]See the American Evaluation Association (2011).

accommodate different cultures and different national government policies. Some agencies try to follow government policies, but this can lead to further complications when working in countries that have different approaches to privacy, gender equality, rights of minorities, and dissemination of information. These are important issues that require greater attention and discussion.

1.9. Basing the Evaluation Design on a Program Theory Model

The RWE approach stresses the importance of basing the evaluation design on a program theory model (theory of change or logic model). While a conventional experimental design can assess whether a particular outcome has been achieved and whether it is reasonable to attribute this to the program intervention, this result tells us little about why and how the program contributed to the outcome, what were the key elements of the approach, and under what circumstances would similar outcomes be achieved if the program were replicated in a different setting. Even more important, if outcomes were not achieved or were different than expected, an experimental design, when used in isolation, offers little to help us answer these questions.

A well-designed program theory will spell out all of the steps through which outcomes are to be achieved, the key assumptions and hypotheses to be tested, and how outcomes are likely to be affected by contextual factors, including assumptions concerning expected conditions and contributions by external sources. It is useful to spell out this process in more detail in a results chain, which can also identify potential negative outcomes at each stage if the model does not operate as planned. The theory model also helps define the key inputs, process, output, outcome, and impact indicators that should be measured and helps identify the hypothesis that should be tested. Although this is more controversial, many authors argue that a well-articulated program theory model can also help test causality.[5]

So a well-articulated program theory model can greatly strengthen the evaluation design and the interpretation of findings. However, despite this great potential, many program theory/logic models have proved to be of very limited practical utility. One of the most common reasons is that once they have been developed, often at the instigation of the funding agency prior to approval of funds for a proposed project, they are often subsequently put in a drawer and forgotten. In other cases, the level of detail (pages and pages of indicators) is so overwhelming that no one in the agency understands how to use them. Another common problem is that the process of designing the program theory is guided by the donor, and therefore implementation agency staff do not feel they have ownership of the process or may feel embarrassed to suggest the basic indicators that they would like to use when the planning workshop is directed by a highly paid international consultant who has flown halfway around the world to direct the workshop.[6]

---

[5]If implementation proceeds according to the program theory and if the expected outcomes are achieved, this gives some credibility to the claim that that the program contributed to the outcomes. However, the claims are more credible if alternative models are developed to test rival hypotheses.

[6]Michael Patton (personal communication) talks about program theory workshops being seen as a "guessing game" where participants believe that the instructor knows the correct answer and that they are being asked to guess this answer—which makes participants feel they are being treated as schoolchildren.

1.10. The Importance of Context

How programs are formulated, designed, and implemented, as well as what benefits they produce and for whom, are all affected by the particular constellation of economic, political, organizational, socio-cultural, and environmental (to name but a few) factors that operate in that particular context. So to explain why the program was not implemented exactly (or even approximately) as planned, why certain outcomes were or were not achieved, and why certain groups did or did not benefit, it is essential to understand how the program interacted with its setting and how it was influenced by the particular constellation of contextual factors.

Many programs consist of multiple subprojects that operate in quite a few different settings, and in most cases the characteristics of many of these contextual factors will vary from location to location. Consequently, their individual and combined influence on program implementation and outcomes is likely to vary from location to location. Thus, the identification and analysis of these contextual factors are critical for explaining variations in project performance and outcomes in different locations, and the evaluation design should include a framework for the analysis of contextual factors and for assessing their influence.

Unfortunately, most QUANT impact evaluations do not include a systematic analysis of contextual factors. Often discussion will be limited to the presentation of anecdotal evidence to explain one particular variation in outcome. While QUAL evaluations will usually include a discussion of context, it is not always done systematically.

1.11. The Importance of Process

As we discussed earlier, projects are rarely implemented exactly as planned, and sometimes how a project is actually implemented can be significantly different from the original design (sometimes for good reasons). Also, as we've already mentioned, when projects operate in different locations, implementation will often vary from location to location. Sometimes the differences are due to unantici-pated problems, poor management, or because more effective ways were found to implement the intended program. There are other cases where the original objectives may have changed due to changed circumstances or new government policies or because the intended beneficiaries were able to adapt the program to their needs. Ray Pawson's (2006) *realist evaluation* approach also argues that every beneficiary influences how a program evolves. People tell their neighbors and friends what they did and did not like about the program or perhaps how they can manipulate the rules to obtain more or different benefits.

Box 19.1 gives an example showing how a school feeding program was dramatically changed during implementation. The program was originally designed to provide breakfast to children enrolled in the school to provide an incentive to attend more regularly. However, siblings not enrolled in the school gradually began to arrive at breakfast time, and soon many schools were providing breakfast for two or three times the number of children enrolled. This had a major impact on how the schools were organized and also resulted in other activities related to nutrition being organized by the communities themselves.

Even when the stated purpose of the evaluation is to assess outcomes, it is clearly important to understand these processes as they can dramatically affect the achievement of outcomes. Many impact evaluations either ignore implementation processes or only study them through project reports or interviews with project staff, both of which can be very misleading.

BOX 19.1
PROGRAMS DRAMATICALLY
CHANGED DURING IMPLEMENTATION:
THE EXAMPLE OF A SCHOOL FEEDING PROGRAM

In an evaluation of a school feeding program with which one of the authors was involved, families began to bring other children not enrolled in school to obtain free meals. Some schools agreed to feed all children who came, and others did not, and the effects on the original program were quite dramatic. One school, which had around 50 students, was providing meals for more than 150 children, and the community became actively involved in building and running a food kitchen, which led to other related activities. Men, who previously had little involvement with their children's education, became actively involved with building the school kitchen and then rewiring the school electrical system. Whether or not these outcomes were considered positive in terms of the original program objectives, it is obviously important to understand and follow through on these processes. It may well have been the case that the community, and perhaps the health ministry, found this a positive development, but the education ministry may have had concerns about the additional food expenses and the disruptive effect on teaching.

1.12. The Evaluation of Complicated and Complex Programs

As discussed earlier, during recent years, international donor agencies have moved toward broad program support for packages that involve many different activities and often involve a number of different donors and government agencies. These interventions are defined as complicated or complex because they have multiple and often not clearly defined objectives, no clearly defined target populations, no clear start and end dates, and often multiple sources of funding.

Given these complexities, it is usually impossible to apply conventional experimental and quasi-experimental impact evaluation designs. Many donor agencies believe that it is not possible to conduct a rigorous assessment of such complex interventions, and often they have come to rely on commissioning consultants to apply a set of rating scales, sometimes adapted from the Organization for Economic Cooperation/Development Advisory Committee (OECD/DAC), where it is often difficult to judge the basis on which the assessments were made.[7]

One of the messages of the RWE approach (see Chapter 16) is that a wide range of promising approaches can provide a credible level of evidence in many contexts. However, there are currently very few widely accepted and tested approaches, so creativity is required, with strong emphasis on the use of multiple methods and triangulation to assess consistency of the estimates from different sources.

---

[7]While it is certainly possible to apply the OECD/DAC rating scales in a rigorous way with precisely defined criteria on which the ratings are based, these rigorous procedures are often not followed.

2. The Road Ahead

In this section, we identify some of the key challenges that RWE, and program impact evaluation in general, must address over the next few years.

2.1. Developing Standardized Methodologies for the Evaluation of Complex Programs

As we have discussed, there are few standardized approaches for the evaluation of complex development interventions, such as country assistance strategies, generalized budget support, thematic evaluations (such as gender mainstreaming or strengthening local capacity for the planning and management of evaluations), or postconflict reconstruction. In Chapter 16, we presented a number of promising approaches, and a goal over the next few years will be to test these approaches in different contexts and to develop some guidelines on how they can be incorporated into the evaluation toolkit of development agencies and national partners.

2.2. Creative Approaches for the Definition and Use of Counterfactuals

There remains a widely held perception that a statistically matched (randomly chosen) comparison group is the only acceptable form of counterfactual and that where such a counterfactual cannot be used, it is not possible to conduct methodologically sound impact evaluation. We totally agree that the experimental counterfactual is a powerful tool whose use should be considered where feasible and appropriate, usually as one of several complementary evaluation techniques. However, as Rieper, Leeuw, and Ling (2010) and Scriven (2009) point out, many if not most social and natural sciences (including qualitative evaluation; criminal justice; forensics; many branches of economics, including economic history; geology and astronomy) rarely if ever have access to experimental designs requiring randomly assigning subjects to treatment and control groups. Instead, they use other logical and reasoning approaches to present credible evidence that supports conclusions "beyond a reasonable doubt." A challenge for RealWorld evaluations is to draw on these approaches, as well as the many similar approaches already being used within the evaluation field to broaden the range of what can be considered "credible evidence" to support a broader range of logically defensible counterfactuals.

Government and donor agency decision makers are almost never presented with statistically significant tests proving that a particular intervention was responsible for an observed outcome. When making a decision on whether to continue or modify a program, they normally have to weigh evidence and recommendations from many different sources, and what they seek is analysis that compares alternative possible explanations of what policies, programs, or external events contributed to particular outcomes. What they seek is credible evidence that the program being studied has made a significant contribution to the desired outcomes beyond a reasonable doubt. Strengthening the generation and assessment of credible evidence is one of the important challenges for RWE over the next few years.

2.3. Strengthening Quality Assurance and Threats to Validity Analysis

We have discussed the RWE approach being used to strengthen quality assurance through the use of threats to validity analysis that can be operationalized by using the threats to validity worksheets described in Chapter 7 and in Appendixes A to E. This is still very much a work in progress, and it is hoped that we and others will work with agencies that are interested in testing out the approach on the evaluations they support, to test and refine the approach.

2.4. Defining Minimum Acceptable Quality Standards for Conducting Evaluations under Constraints

The RWE approach has now developed sets of guidelines for addressing budget, time, data, political, organizational, and administrative constraints and challenges. A number of observers have pointed out that these approaches do not provide clear guidance for defining minimum acceptable standards. There is a danger that evaluators following this approach could produce evaluations that result in findings and recommendations that are based on "we did the best we could under the circumstances" but are methodologically questionable. While the threats to validity checklists provide general pointers, the RWE approach would benefit from more specific guidelines and examples on how to determine what minimum acceptable standards might be. For example, how do we judge what is the minimum time required in the field to conduct methodologically sound data collection, how do we assess whether data collected through reconstructing baselines are of an acceptable validity, and what is the minimum time and level of financial and professional resources required for the analysis of different kinds of data?

Separate but complementary guidelines will be required for evaluations that use predominantly QUANT, QUAL, and mixed-method approaches.

2.5. Further Refinements to Program Theory

Program theory is a key building block of the RWE approach, and a goal will be to introduce further refinements to strengthen applications to RWE. This will include but not be limited to the following:

- Strengthening contextual analysis, including methods for transforming descriptive assessments into dummy variables or ordinal scales that can be integrated into regression analysis
- Strengthening methodologies for process analysis and for assessing the influence of contextual factors on the efficiency of project implementation
- Using results chain analysis to help generate hypotheses, identify unexpected outcomes, and identify key data to be collected
- Further work on the use and limitations of program theory for causal analysis
- Further work on trajectory analysis to help identify the appropriate time horizon for estimating outcomes and impacts

2.6. Further Refinements to Mixed-Method Designs

The use of mixed methods is another key component of the RWE approach, and the goal will be to develop and test further refinements with respect to, among others, the following:

- Guidelines for mixed-method sampling to strengthen the representativity of findings from small samples of case studies or in-depth interviews. A key question will be to develop guidelines for estimating the required sample size for the qualitative samples.

- Ways to combine multiple data collection and analysis methods to strengthen the validity of data obtained under budget and time constraints
- Guidelines for strengthening the conceptual framework by integrating QUANT deductive hypotheses with QUAL inductive hypotheses

2.7. Further Work on Sampling to Broaden the Use of Small Samples

We introduced into this edition Lot Quality Acceptance Sampling (LQAS) as one strategy that permits the assessment of many types of program performance with small samples, but we plan to explore other options for obtaining statistically robust estimates of outcomes and impacts through small samples.

2.8. Feedback Is Welcome

In this concluding chapter, we have hinted at some of the ongoing exploratory work that is needed to make the RWE approach even more practical and useful to a broad number of institutions and practitioners. We invite you, as a colleague who has taken the time to read this book, to share your experiences as you experiment with these and similar approaches. We invite you to contribute to the continued expansion of our networks of colleagues who collectively share in this journey. One way to do so is to join the RealWorld Evaluation listserv by sending an e-message to RealWorldEval-subscribe@yahoogroups.com. Also, note that we periodically add more materials to the www.RealWorldEvaluation.org website. We look forward to your company on the road ahead!

Appendix A

Worksheet for Assessing Threats to the Validity
of the Findings and Recommendations of
Quantitative (Experimental and Quasi-Experimental)
Impact Evaluation Designs[1]

Part 1: Summary of the Findings of
the Assessment of the Evaluation

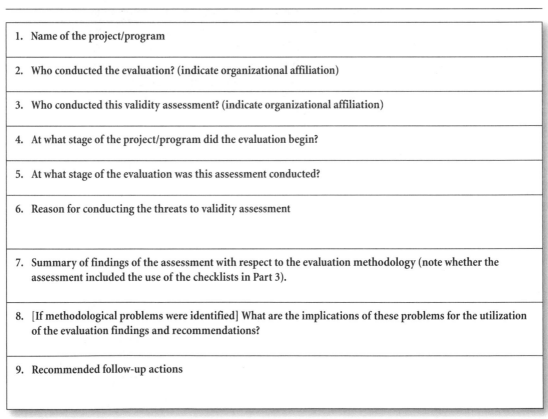

1. Name of the project/program
2. Who conducted the evaluation? (indicate organizational affiliation)
3. Who conducted this validity assessment? (indicate organizational affiliation)
4. At what stage of the project/program did the evaluation begin?
5. At what stage of the evaluation was this assessment conducted?
6. Reason for conducting the threats to validity assessment
7. Summary of findings of the assessment with respect to the evaluation methodology (note whether the assessment included the use of the checklists in Part 3).
8. [If methodological problems were identified] What are the implications of these problems for the utilization of the evaluation findings and recommendations?
9. Recommended follow-up actions

[1]SOURCE: The checklists in Part 3 are adapted from Shadish, Cook, and Campbell (2002, Tables 2.2, 2.4, 3.1, and 3.2). Additional material, including the proposed rating systems, has been included in the checklists, and the present authors are solely responsible for the adaptation and interpretation of the data.

Part 2: Summary Assessment for Each Component

A. Threats to Internal Design Validity: *Reasons why inferences about a causal relationship between two variables may be incorrect*
Summary assessment and recommendations (identify most serious operational problems)
• The quality of the methodology of this component: Rating[2]: • The number of methodological problems that could affect the utilization of the evaluation:
B. Threats to Statistical Conclusion Validity: *Reasons why inferences about a statistical association between two variables (e.g., project treatment and outcome) may be incorrect*
Summary assessment and recommendations (identify most serious operational problems)
• The quality of the methodology of this component: Rating: • The number of methodological problems that could affect the utilization of the evaluation:

(Continued)

---

[2]Note on ratings: 1 = the design and implementation of the methodology for this component are sound and there are no problems or issues; 5 = the design and/or implementation of the methodology for this component are weak, and many issues could affect the validity of the findings and recommendations.

(Continued)

C. Threats to Construct Validity: *Reasons why inferences about the constructs used to define implementation processes, outputs, outcomes, and impacts may be incorrect*
Summary assessment and recommendations (identify most serious operational problems)
• **The quality of the methodology of this component: Rating:** • **The number of methodological problems that could affect the utilization of the evaluation:**
D. Threats to External Validity: *Reasons why inferences about how study results would hold over variations in persons, settings, treatments, and outcomes may not be correct*
Summary assessment and recommendations (identify most serious operational problems)
• **The quality of the methodology of this component: Rating:** • **The number of methodological problems that could affect the utilization of the evaluation:**

Part 3: Checklists Used to Assess the Four Components Describing Potential Threats to the Adequacy and Validity of a Quantitative Impact Evaluation

NOTE: Part 3, which involves a more in-depth, technical, and expensive assessment, is normally used only for large, high-priority evaluations or where the controversial nature of the topic requires a high level of credibility of the assessment. For these reasons, Part 3 would normally be conducted by an external consultant.

Dimension 1: Internal Validity
  Checklist 1: Threats to internal design validity
  Checklist 2: Threats to statistical conclusion validity
  Checklist 3: Threats to construct validity

Dimension 2: External Validity
  Checklist 4: Threats to external validity

Checklist 1. Threats to Internal Design Validity: *Reasons why inferences about a causal relationship between two variables may be incorrect*

	Rating (see footnote on use of ratings)	
	A	B
1. **Temporal precedence of interventions and effects.** Was it clearly established that the intervention actually occurred before the effect that it was predicted to influence? A cause must precede its effect. However, it is often difficult to know the order of events in a project. Many projects (e.g., urban development programs) do not have a precise starting date but get going over periods of months or even years.		
2. **Project selection bias.** Were potential project selection biases identified and were measures taken to address them in the analysis? Project participants are often different from comparison groups either because they are self-selected or because the project administrator selects people with certain characteristics (the poorest farmers or the best-organized communities).		
3. **History.** Were the effects of history identified and addressed in the analysis? Participation in a project may produce other experiences unrelated to the project treatment that might distinguish the project and control groups. For example, entrepreneurs who are known to have received loans may be more likely to be robbed or pressured by politicians to make donations, or girls enrolled in high school may be more likely to get pregnant.		
4. **Maturation.** Maturation produces many natural changes in physical development, behavior, knowledge, and exposure to new experiences. It is often difficult to separate changes due to maturation from those due to the project.		
5. **Regression toward the mean.** If subjects are selected because of their extreme scores (e.g., weight, physical development), there is a natural tendency to move closer to the mean over time—thus diminishing or distorting the effects of the program.		
6. **Attrition.** Was there significant attrition over the life of the project, and did this have different effects on the composition of the project and comparison groups? Even when project participants originally had characteristics similar to the total population, selective dropout over time may change the characteristics of the project population (e.g., the poorest or least educated might drop out).		
7. **Testing.** Being interviewed or tested may affect behavior or responses. For example, being asked about expenditures may encourage people to cut down on socially disapproved expenditures (cigarettes and alcohol) and spend more on acceptable items.		
8. **Instrumentation.** As researchers gain more experience, they may change how they interpret rating scales, observation checklists, and so on.		
9. **Potential biases or distortion during the process of recall.**** Respondents may deliberately or unintentionally distort their recall of past events. Opposition politicians may exaggerate community problems while community elders may romanticize the past.		
10. **Information is not collected from the right people, or some categories of informants are not interviewed.**** Sometimes information is collected from and about only certain sectors of the target population (men but not women, teachers but not students), in which case estimates for the total population may be biased.		

(Continued)

(Continued)

Checklist 1. Threats to Internal Design Validity: *Reasons why inferences about a causal relationship between two variables may be incorrect*		
	Rating (see footnote on use of ratings)	
	A	**B**
11. **Use of less rigorous designs due to budget and time constraints.**** Many evaluations are conducted under budget, time, and data constraints, which require reductions in sample size, time for pilot studies, amount of information that can be collected, and so on. These constraints increase vulnerability to threats to internal validity.		
Summary score		███
No. of methodological issues affecting the use of the evaluation	███	
General comments on this component		

Notes on the four checklists:

1. ** = additional categories included by the present authors.

2. How to use the checklist: Column A = the existence or seriousness of each threat to validity. It is possible to simply check issues that exist or a rating scale can be used. A typical rating scale: 1 = the methodology is sound, and there are no issues or problems; 5 = there are major methodological problems and issues. **Column B** = the importance of this threat for the purposes of this particular evaluation. The same two options exist. The first is to simply check each item rated as 4 or 5 in Column A that has important implications for the purposes of this evaluation. The second option is to rate the importance of this threat for the purposes of the present evaluation. For example: 1 = the threat does not have important implications for this evaluation and 5 = the threat has serious implications for the purposes of this evaluation.

Summary scores for each column: The summary score for Column A can be calculated either as the number of items that have been checked as having methodological problems, or when a rating scale is used, the mean rating can be calculated (the sum of all scores divided by the number of indicators rated). For Column B, this will normally be the number of items in Column A that were rated as having problems that were considered to have important policy or operational implications for the use of the evaluation. If mean scores are calculated, it is important to be aware of the dangers of treating ordinal variables as if they were interval (calculating means, etc.).

SOURCE: Adapted from Shadish, Cook, and Campbell (2002). Checklists A, B, C, and D are adapted from Tables 2.2, 2.4, 3.1, and 3.2, respectively. The proposed rating systems and the categories indicated by ** were included by the present authors.

Checklist 2. Threats to Statistical Conclusion Validity: *Reasons why inferences about statistical association (covariation) between two variables may be incorrect*	A	B
1. **The sample is too small to detect program effects (low statistical power).** The sample is not large enough to detect statistically significant differences between project and control groups even if they do exist. Particularly important when effect sizes are small.		
2. **Some assumptions of the statistical tests have been violated.** Many statistical tests require that observations are independent of each other. If this assumption is violated (e.g., studying children in the same classroom, or patients in the same clinic who may be more similar to each other than the population in general), this can increase the risk of Type I error (false positive), wrongly concluding the project had an effect.		
3. **"Fishing" for statistically significant results.** A certain percentage of statistical tests will show "significant" results by chance (1 in 20 at the .05 significance level). Generating large numbers of statistical tables will always find some of these spurious results.		
4. **Unreliability of measures of change of outcome indicators.** Unreliable measures of, for example, rates of change in income, literacy, and infant mortality always reduce the likelihood of finding a significant effect.		
5. **Restriction of range or extrapolation from a truncated or incomplete data base.**** If only similar groups are compared, the power of the test is reduced and the likelihood of finding a significant effect is also reduced. If the sample only covers part of the population (e.g., only the poorest families, or only people working in the formal sector), this can affect the conclusions of the analysis and can bias generalizations to the total population.		
6. **Unreliability of treatment implementation.** If the treatment is not administered in an identical way to all subjects, the probability of finding a significant effect is reduced.		
7. **External events influence outcomes (extraneous variance in the experimental setting).** External events or pressures (power failure, community violence, election campaigns) may distract subjects and affect behavior and program outcomes.		
8. **Diversity of the population (heterogeneity of units).** If subjects have widely different characteristics, this may increase the variance of results and make it more difficult to detect significant effects.		
9. **Inaccurate effect size estimation due to outliers.** A few outliers (extreme values) can significantly reduce effect size and make it less likely that significant differences will be found.		
10. **Project and comparison group samples do not cover the same populations.**** It is often the case that the comparison group sample is not drawn from the same population as the project sample. In these cases, differences in outcomes may be due to the differences in the characteristics of the two samples and not to the effects of the project.		
11. **Information is not collected from the right people, or some categories of informants not interviewed.**** Sometimes information is collected from and about only certain sectors of the target population (men but not women, teachers but not students), in which case estimates for the total population may be biased.		
Summary score		
No. of methodological issues affecting the use of the evaluation		
General comments on this component		

Checklist 3. Threats to Construct Validity: *Reasons why inferences about the constructs used to define implementation processes, outputs, outcomes, and impacts may be incorrect*

	A	B
1. **Inadequate explanation of constructs.** Constructs (the effects/outcomes) being studied are defined in terms that are too general or are confusing or ambiguous, thus making it impossible to have precise measurement (examples of ambiguous constructs include quality of life, unemployed, aggressive behavior, hostile work environment, sex discrimination).		
2. **Indicators do not adequately measure constructs (construct confounding).** The operational definition may not adequately capture the desired construct. For example, defining the unemployed as those who have registered with an employment center ignores people not working but who do not use these centers. Similarly, defining domestic violence as cases reported to the police significantly underrepresents the real number of incidents.		
3. **Use of single indicator to measure a complex construct (mono-operation bias).** Using a single indicator to define and measure a complex construct (such as poverty, well-being, domestic violence) will usually produce bias.		
4. **Use of a single method to measure a construct (monomethod bias).** If only one method is used to measure a construct, this will produce a narrow and often biased measure (e.g., observing communities in formal meetings will produce different results than observing social events or communal work projects).		
5. **Only one level of the treatment is studied (confounding constructs with levels of constructs).** Often a treatment is administered at only one, usually low, level of intensity (only small business loans are given), and the results are used to make general conclusions about the effectiveness (or lack of effectiveness) of the construct. This is misleading as a higher level of treatment might have produced a more significant effect.		
6. **Program participants and comparison group respond differently to some questions (treatment-sensitive factorial structure).** Program participants may respond in a more nuanced way to questions. For example, they may distinguish between different types and intensities of domestic violence or racial prejudice, whereas the comparison group may have broader, less discriminated responses.		
7. **Participants assess themselves and their situation differently than comparison group (reactive self-report changes).** People selected for programs may self-report differently from those not selected even before the program begins. They may wish to make themselves seem more in need of the program (poorer, sicker) or they may wish to appear more meritorious if that is a criterion for selection.		
8. **Reactivity to the experimental situation.** Project participants' interpretation of the project situation may affect their behavior. If they believe the program is run by a religious organization, they may respond differently than if they believe it is run by a political group.		
9. **Experimenter expectancies.** Experimenters also have expectations (about how men and women or different socioeconomic groups will react to the program), and this may affect how they react to different groups.		
10. **Novelty and disruption effects.** Novel programs can generate excitement and produce a big effect. If a similar program is replicated, the effect may be less as novelty has worn off.		

(Continued)

(Continued)

Checklist 3. Threats to Construct Validity: *Reasons why inferences about the constructs used to define implementation processes, outputs, outcomes, and impacts may be incorrect*	A	B
11. **Compensatory effects and rivalry.** Programs create a dynamic that can affect outcomes in different ways. There may be pressure to provide benefits to nonparticipants, comparison groups may become motivated to show what they can achieve on their own, or those receiving no treatment or a less attractive treatment may become demoralized.		
12. **Using constructs developed in other countries without pretesting in the local context.**** Many evaluations import theories and constructs from other countries and may not adequately capture the local project situation. For example, many evaluations of the impacts of microcredit on women's empowerment in countries such as Bangladesh use international definitions of empowerment that may not be appropriate for Bangladeshi women.		
Summary score		■
No. of methodological issues affecting the use of the evaluation	■	

General comments on this component

	A	B
Checklist 4. Threats to External Validity: *Reasons why inferences about how study results would hold over variations in persons, settings, treatments, and outcomes may be incorrect*		
1. **Sample does not cover the whole population of interest.** Subjects interviewed may come from one sex or from certain ethnic or economic groups, or they may have certain personality characteristics (e.g., depressed, self-confident). Consequently, it may be different to generalize from the study findings to the whole population.		
2. **Different settings affect program outcomes (interaction of the causal relationship over treatment variations).** Treatments may be implemented in different settings, which may affect outcomes. If pressure to reduce class size forces schools to construct extra temporary and inadequate classrooms, the outcomes may be very different than having smaller classes in suitable classroom settings.		
3. **Different outcome measures give different assessments of project effectiveness (interaction of the causal relationship with outcomes).** Different outcome measures can produce different conclusions on project effectiveness. Microcredit programs for women may increase household income and expenditure on children's education but may not increase women's political empowerment.		
4. **Program outcomes vary in different settings (interactions of the causal relationships with settings).** Program success may be different in rural and urban settings or in different kinds of communities. So it may not be appropriate to generalize findings from one particular setting to different settings,		
5. **Programs operate differently in different settings (context-dependent mediation).** Programs may operate in different ways and have different intermediate and final outcomes in different settings. The implementation of community-managed schools may operate very differently and have different outcomes when managed by religious organizations, government agencies, and nongovernmental organizations.		
6. **The attitude of policymakers and politicians to the program.**** Identical programs will operate differently and have different outcomes in situations where they have the active support of policymakers or politicians than in situations where they face opposition or indifference. When the party in power or the agency head changes, it is common to find that support for programs can vanish or be increased.		
7. **Seasonal and other cycles.**** Many projects will operate differently in different seasons, at different stages of the business cycle, or according to the internal terms of trade for key exports and imports. Attempts to generalize or project findings from pilot programs must take these cycles into consideration.		
Summary score		
No. of methodological issues affecting the use of the evaluation		
General comments on this component		

Appendix B

Worksheet for Assessing Threats to the Validity of the Findings and Recommendations of Qualitative Impact Evaluation Designs

Part 1: Summary of the Findings of the Assessment of the Evaluation

1. Name of the project/program
2. Who conducted this validity assessment? (indicate organizational affiliation)
3. At what stage of the project/program did the evaluation begin?
4. At what stage of the evaluation was this assessment conducted?
5. Reason for conducting the threats to validity assessment
6. Summary of findings of the assessment with respect to the evaluation methodology (note whether the assessment included the use of the checklists in Part 3)
7. [If methodological problems were identified] What are the implications of these problems for the utilization of the evaluation findings and recommendations?
8. Recommended follow-up actions

Part 2: Summary Assessment for Each Component

A. Confirmability: *Are the conclusions drawn from the available evidence, and is the research relatively free of researcher bias?*
Summary assessment and recommendations (identify most serious operational problems)
• The quality of the methodology of this component: Rating[1]: _____ • The number of methodology problems that affect the utilization of the evaluation:
B. Dependability: *Is the process of the study consistent, coherent, and reasonably stable over time and across researchers and methods? If emergent designs are used, are the processes through which the design evolves clearly documented?*
Summary assessment and recommendations (identify most serious operational problems)
• The quality of the methodology of this component: Rating: • The number of methodology problems that affect the utilization of the evaluation:

(Continued)

---

[1]Note on ratings: 1 = the design and implementation of the methodology for this component is sound and there are no problems or issues; 5 = the design and/or implementation of the methodology for this component are weak, and many issues could affect the validity of the findings and recommendations.

(Continued)

C. **Credibility:** *Are the findings credible to the people studied and to readers, and do we have an authentic portrait of what we are studying?*
Summary assessment and recommendations (identify most serious operational problems)
• The quality of the methodology of this component: Rating: • The number of methodology problems that affect the utilization of the evaluation:
D. **Transferability:** *Do the conclusions fit other contexts, and how widely can they be generalized?*
Summary assessment and recommendations (identify most serious operational problems)
• The quality of the methodology of this component: Rating: • The number of methodology problems that affect the utilization of the evaluation:

Part 3: Checklists Used to Assess the Five Components Describing Potential Threats to the Adequacy and Validity of a Qualitative Impact Evaluation

NOTE: Part 3, which involves a more in-depth, technical, and expensive assessment, is normally only used for large, high-priority evaluations or where the controversial nature of the topic requires a high level of credibility of the assessment. For these reasons, Part 3 would normally be conducted by an external consultant.

Dimension 1: Internal Validity
  Checklist 1: Confirmability
  Checklist 2: Dependability
  Checklist 3: Credibility

Dimension 2: External Validity
  Checklist 4: Transferability

Dimension 3: Utilization
  Checklist 5: Utilization

Checklist 1. Confirmability:[2] *Are the conclusions drawn from the available evidence, and is the research relatively free of researcher bias?*

	Rating (see footnote on use of ratings)	
	A	B
1. Are the study's methods and procedures adequately described? Are study data retained and available for reanalysis?		
2. Are data presented to support the conclusions?		
3. Has the researcher been as explicit and self-aware as possible about personal assumptions, values, and biases?		
4. Were the methods used to control for bias adequate?		
5. Were competing hypotheses or rival conclusions considered?		
Summary score		
No. of methodological issues affecting the use of the evaluation		

General comments on this component

Notes on the five checklists:

1. ** = additional categories included by the present authors.

2. How to use the checklist: Column A = the existence or seriousness of each threat to validity. There are two options: (1) Simply check all indicators where methodological problems exist, or (2) use a rating scale to indicate the severity of the issue. A typical rating scale: 1 = the methodology is sound and there are no issues or problems; 5 = there are major methodological problems and issues. Column B = the importance of each methodological threat identified in Column A for the purposes of the present evaluation. In this case, all items that have important implications for the present evaluation are checked.

Summary scores for each column: The summary score for Column A can be calculated either as the number of items that have been checked as having methodological problems, or when a rating scale is used, the mean rating is calculated (the sum of all scores divided by the number of indicators rated). If mean scores are calculated, it is important to be aware of the dangers of treating ordinal variables as if they were interval (calculating means, etc.). For Column B, this will normally be the number of items in Column A that were rated as having problems that were considered to have important policy or operational implications for the use of the evaluation.

[2]SOURCE: Adapted from Miles and Huberman (1994, chap. 10, Section C). See also Guba and Lincoln (1989). The rating scales were developed by the present authors. Items indicated by ** were added by the present authors.

Checklist 2. Dependability: *Is the process of the study consistent, coherent, and reasonably stable over time and across researchers and methods? If emergent designs are used, are the processes through which the design evolves clearly documented?*

	A	B
1. Are findings trustworthy, consistent, and replicable across data sources and over time?		
2. Were data collected across the full range of appropriate settings, times, respondents, and so on?		
3. Did all fieldworkers have comparable data collection protocols?		
4. Were coding and quality checks made, and did they show adequate agreement?		
5. Do the accounts of different observers converge? If they do not (which is often the case in QUAL studies), is this recognized and addressed?		
6. Were peer or colleague reviews used?		
7. Were the rules used for confirmation of propositions, hypotheses, and so on made explicit?		
Summary score		
No. of methodological issues affecting the use of the evaluation		

General comments on this component

Checklist 3. Credibility: *Are the findings credible to the people studied and to readers, and do we have an authentic portrait of what we are studying*

	A	B
1. How context-rich and meaningful ("thick") are the descriptions? Is there sufficient information to provide a credible/valid description of the subjects or the situation being studied?**		
2. Does the account ring true, make sense, or seem convincing? Does it reflect the local context?		
3. Did triangulation among complementary methods and data sources produce generally converging conclusions? If expansionist qualitative methods are used where interpretations do not necessarily converge, are the differences in interpretations and conclusions noted and discussed?**		
4. Are the presented data well linked to the categories of prior or emerging theory? Are the findings internally coherent, and are the concepts systematically related?		
5. Are areas of uncertainty identified? Was negative evidence sought, found? How was it used? Have rival explanations been actively considered?		
6. Were conclusions considered accurate by the researchers responsible for data collection?		
Summary score		■
No. of methodological issues affecting the use of the evaluation	■	

Gender comments on this component

Checklist 4. Transferability: *Do the conclusions fit other contexts, and how widely can they be generalized?*	A	B
1. Are the characteristics of the sample of persons, settings, processes, and so on described in enough detail to permit comparisons with other samples?		
2. Does the sample design theoretically permit generalization to other populations?		
3. Does the researcher define the scope and boundaries of reasonable generalization from the study?		
4. Do the findings include enough "thick description" for readers to assess the potential transferability?		
5. Does a range of readers report the findings to be consistent with their own experience?		
6. Do the findings confirm or are they congruent with existing theory? Is the transferable theory made explicit?		
7. Are the processes and findings generic enough to be applicable in other settings?		
8. Have narrative sequences been preserved? Has a general cross-case theory using the sequences been developed?		
9. Does the report suggest settings where the findings could fruitfully be tested further?		
10. Have the findings been replicated in other studies to assess their robustness. If not, could replication efforts be mounted easily?		
Summary score		
No. of methodological issues affecting the use of the evaluation		

General comments on this component

Checklist 5. Utilization: *How useful were the findings to clients, researchers, and the communities studied?*		
	A	B
1. Are the findings intellectually and physically accessible to potential users?		
2. Were any predictions made in the study and, if so, how accurate were they?		
3. Do the findings provide guidance for future action?		
4. Do the findings have a catalyzing effect leading to specific actions?		
5. Do the actions taken actually help solve local problems?		
6. Have users of the findings experienced any sense of empowerment or increased control over their lives? Have they developed new capacities?		
7. Are value-based or ethical concerns raised explicitly in the report? If not, do some exist that the researcher is not attending to?		
Summary score		
No. of methodological issues affecting the use of the evaluation		

General comments on this component

Appendix C

Integrated Worksheet for Assessing Threats to the Validity of the Findings and Recommendations of Mixed-Method Evaluation Design (Standard Version)

Part 1: Summary of the Findings of the Assessment of the Evaluation

1. Name of the project/program
2. Who conducted this validity assessment? (indicate organizational affiliation)
3. At what stage of the project/program did the evaluation begin?
4. At what stage of the evaluation was this assessment conducted?
5. Reason for conducting the threats to validity assessment
6. Summary of findings of the assessment with respect to the evaluation methodology (note whether the assessment included the use of the checklists in Part 3)
7. [If methodological problems were identified] What are the implications of these problems for the utilization of the evaluation findings and recommendations?
8. Recommended follow-up actions

Part 2: Summary Assessment for Each Component

A. **Objectivity (Confirmability):** *Are the conclusions drawn from the available evidence, and is the research relatively free of researcher bias?*

Summary assessment and recommendations (identify most serious operational problems)

- The quality of the methodology of this component: Rating:
- The number of methodological problems that could affect the utilization of the evaluation:

B. **Internal Design Validity (Reliability/Dependability/Credibility/Authenticity):** *Are the findings credible to the people studied and to readers, and do we have an authentic portrait of what we are studying? Is the process of the study consistent, coherent, and reasonably stable over time and across researchers and methods? If emergent designs are used, are the processes through which the design evolves clearly documented?*

Summary assessment and recommendations (identify most serious operational problems)

- The quality of the methodology of this component: Rating:
- The number of methodological problems that could affect the utilization of the evaluation:

C. Statistical Conclusion Validity: *Reasons why inferences about statistical association (covariation) between two variables may be incorrect*

Summary assessment and recommendations (identify most serious operational problems)

- The quality of the methodology of this component: Rating:
- The number of methodological problems that could affect the utilization of the evaluation:

D. Construct Validity: *Do the constructs used to define processes, outcomes and impacts, and contextual variables adequately capture the essential elements of what is being measured? Are the constructs sufficiently comprehensive to capture the multidimensionality of many of the constructs?*

Summary assessment and recommendations (identify most serious operational problems)

- The quality of the methodology of this component: Rating:
- The number of methodological problems that could affect the utilization of the evaluation:

(Continued)

(Continued)

E. External Validity (Transferability and Fittingness): *Do the conclusions fit other contexts, and how widely can they be generalized? Do they provide credible evidence on how the program would perform in other settings?*
Summary assessment and recommendations (identify most serious operational problems)
<ul><li>The quality of the methodology of this component: Rating:</li><li>The number of methodological problems that could affect the utilization of the evaluation:</li></ul>
F. Utilization: *How useful were the findings to clients, researchers, and the communities studied?*
Summary assessment and recommendations (identify most serious operational problems)
<ul><li>The quality of the methodology of this component: Rating:</li><li>The number of methodological problems that could affect the utilization of the evaluation:</li></ul>

Part 3: Checklists Used to Assess the Six Components Describing Potential Threats to the Adequacy and Validity of a Quantitative Impact Evaluation

NOTE: Part 3, which involves a more in-depth, technical, and expensive assessment, is normally only used for large, high-priority evaluations or where the controversial nature of the topic requires a high level of credibility of the assessment. For these reasons, Part 3 would normally be conducted by an external consultant.

Checklist 1: Objectivity (Confirmability)

Checklist 2: Internal Design Validity (Reliability/Dependability/Credibility/Authenticity)

Checklist 3: Statistical Conclusion Validity

Checklist 4: Construct Validity

Checklist 5: External Validity

Checklist 6: Utilization

Checklist 1. Objectivity (Confirmability): *Are the conclusions drawn from the available evidence, and is the research relatively free of researcher bias?*

| | Ratings (see footnote on use of ratings) | |
	A	B
1. Are the study's methods and procedures adequately described? Are study data retained and available for reanalysis?		
2. Are data presented to support the conclusions?		
3. Has the researcher been as explicit and self-aware as possible about personal assumptions, values, and biases?		
4. Were the methods used to control for bias adequate?		
5. Were competing hypotheses or rival conclusions considered?		
Summary score		
No. of methodological issues potentially affecting the use of the evaluation		

General comments on the component

Notes and Sources:

How to use the checklist: Column A = the existence or seriousness of each threat to validity. It is possible to simply check issues that exist or a rating scale can be used. A typical rating scale: 1 = the methodology is sound and there are no issues or problems; 5 = there are major methodological problems and issues. **Column B** = the importance of this threat for the purposes of this particular evaluation. The same two options exist. The first is to simply check each of the items rated as 4 or 5 in Column A that have important implications for the purposes of this evaluation. The second option is to rate the importance of this threat for the purposes of the present evaluation. For example: 1 = the threat does not have important implications for this evaluation and 5 = the threat has serious implications for the purposes of this evaluation.

Summary scores for each column: The summary score for Column A can be calculated either as the number of items that have been checked as having methodological problems, or when a rating scale is used, the mean rating can be calculated (the sum of all scores divided by the number of indicators rated). For Column B, this will normally be the number of items in Column A that were rated as having problems that were considered to have important policy or operational implications for the use of the evaluation. If mean scores are calculated, it is important to be aware of the dangers of treating ordinal variables as if they were interval (calculating means, etc.).

Sources for the six checklists: Items in normal text (i.e., those used most commonly in qualitative evaluations) are adapted from Miles and Huberman (1994, chap. 10, Section C) and from Teddlie and Tashakkori (2009), especially Chapter 12. See also Guba and Lincoln (1989). Items in italics (i.e., those most commonly used in quantitative evaluations) are adapted from Shadish, Cook, and Campbell (2002, Tables 2.2, 2.4, 3.1, and 3.2). The rating scales were developed by the present authors.

**Indicates items added by the present authors.

Checklist 2. Internal Design Validity (Reliability/Dependability/Credibility/Authenticity): *Are the findings credible to the people studied and to readers, and do we have an authentic portrait of what we are studying?*	A	B
1. How context-rich and meaningful ("thick") are the descriptions? Is there sufficient information to provide a credible/valid description of the subjects or the situation being studied?		
2. Does the account ring true, make sense, or seem convincing? Does it reflect the local context?		
3. Did triangulation among complementary methods and data sources produce generally converging conclusions? If expansionist qualitative methods are used where interpretations do not necessarily converge, are the differences in interpretations and conclusions noted and discussed?**		
4. Are the presented data well linked to the categories of prior or emerging theory? Are the findings internally coherent, and are the concepts systematically related?		
5. Are areas of uncertainty identified? Was negative evidence sought, found? How was it used? Have rival explanations been actively considered?		
6. Were conclusions considered accurate by the researchers responsible for data collection?		
7. Are findings trustworthy, consistent, and replicable across data sources and over time?		
8. Were data collected across the full range of appropriate settings, times, respondents, and so on?		
9. Did all fieldworkers have comparable data collection protocols?		
10. Were coding and quality checks made, and did they show adequate agreement?		
11. Do the accounts of different observers converge? If they do not (which is often the case in QUAL studies), is this recognized and addressed?		
12. Were peer or colleague reviews used?		
13. Were the rules used for confirmation of propositions, hypotheses, and so on made explicit?		
14. *Temporal precedence of interventions and effects. Was it clearly established that the intervention actually occurred before the effect that it was predicted to influence? A cause must precede its effect. However, it is often difficult to know the order of events in a project. Many projects (e.g., urban development programs) do not have a precise starting date but get going over periods of months or even years.*		
15. *Project selection bias. Were potential project selection biases identified and were measures taken to address them in the analysis? Project participants are often different from comparison groups either because they are self-selected or because the project administrator selects people with certain characteristics (the poorest farmers or best-organized communities).*		
16. *History. Were the effects of history identified and addressed in the analysis? Participation in a project may produce other experiences unrelated to the project treatment that might distinguish the project and control groups. For example, entrepreneurs who are known to have received loans may be more likely to be robbed or pressured by politicians to make donations, or girls enrolled in high school may be more likely to get pregnant.*		

(Continued)

(Continued)

Checklist 2. Internal Design Validity (Reliability/Dependability/Credibility/Authenticity): *Are the findings credible to the people studied and to readers, and do we have an authentic portrait of what we are studying?*	A	B
17. **Maturation.** *Maturation produces many natural changes in physical development, behavior, knowledge, and exposure to new experiences. It is often difficult to separate changes due to maturation from those due to the project.*		
18. **Regression toward the mean.** *If subjects are selected because of their extreme scores (e.g., weight, physical development), there is a natural tendency to move closer to the mean over time—thus diminishing or distorting the effects of the program.*		
19. **Attrition.** *Was there significant attrition over the life of the project, and did this have different effects on the composition of the project and comparison groups? Even when project participants originally had characteristics similar to the total population, selective dropout over time may change the characteristics of the project population (e.g., the poorest or least educated might drop out).*		
20. **Testing.** *Being interviewed or tested may affect behavior or responses. For example, being asked about expenditures may encourage people to cut down on socially disapproved expenditures (cigarettes and alcohol) and spend more on acceptable items.*		
21. **Instrumentation.** *As researchers gain more experience, they may change how they interpret rating scales, observation checklists, and so on.*		
22. **Potential biases or distortion during the process of recall.**** Respondents may deliberately or unintentionally distort their recall of past events. Opposition politicians may exaggerate community problems while community elders may romanticize the past.		
22. **Information is not collected from the right people, or some categories of informants not interviewed.**** Sometimes information is collected from and about only certain sectors of the target population (men but not women, teachers but not students), in which case estimates for the total population may be biased.		
23. **Use of less rigorous designs due to budget and time constraints.**** Many evaluations are conducted under budget, time, and data constraints, which require reductions in sample size, time for pilot studies, amount of information that can be collected, and so on. These constraints increase vulnerability to threats to internal validity.		
Summary score		■
No. of methodological issues potentially affecting the use of the evaluation	■	
General comments on the component		

NOTE: Items in italics are those normally used in the assessment of quantitative evaluations, while items in normal text are commonly used in the assessment of qualitative evaluations.

Checklist 3. Threats to Statistical Conclusion Validity: *Reasons why inferences about statistical association (covariation) between two variables may be incorrect*	A	B
1. ***The sample is too small to detect program effects (low statistical power).*** *The sample is not large enough to detect statistically significant differences between project and control groups even if they do exist. Particularly important when effect sizes are small.*		
2. ***Some assumptions of the statistical tests have been violated.*** *Many statistical tests require that observations are independent of each other. If this assumption is violated (e.g., studying children in the same classroom, or patients in the same clinic who may be more similar to each other than the population in general), this can increase the risk of Type I error (false positive), wrongly concluding the project had an effect.*		
3. ***"Fishing" for statistically significant results.*** *A certain percentage of statistical tests will show "significant" results by chance (1 in 20 at the .05 significance level). Generating large numbers of statistical tables will always find some of these spurious results.*		
4. ***Unreliability of measures of change of outcome indicators.*** *Unreliable measures of, for example, rates of change in income, literacy, and infant mortality, always reduce the likelihood of finding a significant effect.*		
5. ***Restriction of range or extrapolation from a truncated or incomplete database.*** *** If only similar groups are compared, the power of the test is reduced, and the likelihood of finding a significant effect is also reduced. If the sample only covers part of the population (e.g., only the poorest families, or only people working in the formal sector), this can affect the conclusions of the analysis and can bias generalizations to the total population.*		
6. ***Unreliability of treatment implementation.*** *If the treatment is not administered in an identical way to all subjects, the probability of finding a significant effect is reduced.*		
7. ***External events influence outcomes (extraneous variance in the experimental setting).*** *External events or pressures (power failure, community violence, election campaigns) may distract subjects and affect behavior and program outcomes.*		
8. ***Diversity of the population (heterogeneity of units).*** *If subjects have widely different characteristics, this may increase the variance of results and make it more difficult to detect significant effects.*		
9. ***Inaccurate effect size estimation due to outliers.*** *A few outliers (extreme values) can significantly reduce effect size and make it less likely that significant differences will be found.*		
10. ***Project and comparison group samples do not cover the same populations.*** *** It is often the case that the comparison group sample is not drawn from the same population as the project sample. In these cases, differences in outcomes may be due to the differences in the characteristics of the two samples and not to the effects of the project.*		
11. ***Information is not collected from the right people, or some categories of informants not interviewed.*** *** Sometimes information is collected from and about only certain sectors of the target population (men but not women, teachers but not students), in which case estimates for the total population may be biased.*		
Summary score		
No. of methodological issues affecting the use of the evaluation		

General comments on this component

	A	B
Checklist 4. Construct Validity: *Reasons why inferences about the constructs used to define implementation processes, outputs, outcomes, and impacts may be incorrect*		
1. **Inadequate explanation of constructs.** Constructs (the effects/outcomes) being studied are defined in terms that are too general or are confusing or ambiguous, thus making it impossible to have precise measurement (examples of ambiguous constructs include quality of life, unemployed, aggressive behavior, hostile work environment, and sex discrimination).		
2. **Indicators do not adequately measure constructs (construct confounding).** The operational definition may not adequately capture the desired construct. For example, defining the unemployed as those who have registered with an employment center ignores people not working but who do not use these centers. Similarly, defining domestic violence as cases reported to the police significantly underrepresents the real number of incidents.		
3. **Use of single indicator to measure a complex construct (mono-operation bias).** Using a single indicator to define and measure a complex construct (such as poverty, well-being, domestic violence) will usually produce bias.		
4. **Use of a single method to measure a construct (monomethod bias).** If only one method is used to measure a construct, this will produce a narrow and often biased measure (e.g., observing communities in formal meetings will produce different results than observing social events or communal work projects).		
5. *Only one level of the treatment is studied (confounding constructs with levels of constructs). Often a treatment is administered at only one, usually low, level of intensity (only small business loans are given), and the results are used to make general conclusions about the effectiveness (or lack of effectiveness) of the construct. This is misleading as a higher level of treatment might have produced a more significant effect.*		
6. *Program participants and comparison group respond differently to some questions (treatment-sensitive factorial structure). Program participants may respond in a more nuanced way to questions. For example, they may distinguish between different types and intensities of domestic violence or racial prejudice, whereas the comparison group may have broader, less discriminated responses.*		
7. *Participants assess themselves and their situation differently than comparison group (reactive self-report changes). People selected for programs may self-report differently from those not selected even before the program begins. They may wish to make themselves seem more in need of the program (poorer, sicker) or they may wish to appear more meritorious if that is a criterion for selection.*		
8. *Reactivity to the experimental situation. Project participants' interpretation of the project situation may affect their behavior. If they believe the program is run by a religious organization, they may respond differently than if they believe it is run by a political group.*		
9. *Experimenter expectancies. Experimenters also have expectations (about how men and women or different socioeconomic groups will react to the program), and this may affect how they react to different groups.*		
10. *Novelty and disruption effects. Novel programs can generate excitement and produce a big effect. If a similar program is replicated, the effect may be less as novelty has worn off.*		

(Continued)

(Continued)

Checklist 4. **Construct Validity:** *Reasons why inferences about the constructs used to define implementation processes, outputs, outcomes, and impacts may be incorrect*		
	A	B
11. ***Compensatory effects and rivalry.*** *Programs create a dynamic that can affect outcomes in different ways. There may be pressure to provide benefits to nonparticipants; comparison groups may become motivated to show what they can achieve on their own, or those receiving no treatment or a less attractive treatment may become demoralized.*		
12. **Using constructs developed in other countries without pretesting in the local context.**[**] *Many evaluations import theories and constructs from other countries and may not adequately capture the local project situation. For example, many evaluations of the impacts of micro-credit on women's empowerment in countries such as Bangladesh use international definitions of empowerment that may not be appropriate for Bangladeshi women.*		
Summary score		
No. of methodological issues affecting the use of the evaluation		
General comments on this component		

Checklist 5. External Validity: *Do the conclusions fit other contexts and how widely can they be generalized?*		
	A	**B**
1. *Sample does not cover the whole population of interest.*		
2. *Different settings affect program outcomes.*		
3. *Different outcome measures give different assessments of project effectiveness.*		
4. *Program outcomes vary in different settings.*		
5. *Programs operate differently in different settings.*		
6. *Does the attitude (positive or negative) of policymakers and politicians to the program affect implementation or outcomes?*		
7. *Do seasonal and other cycles affect implementation or outcomes?*		
8. *Is there an adequate description of sample characteristics?*		
9. *Does the sample design permit generalization to other populations?*		
10. Does the researcher define the scope and boundaries of reasonable generalization from the study?		
11. Do the findings include enough "thick description" for readers to assess the potential transferability?		
12. Does a range of readers report the findings to be consistent with their own experience?		
13. Do the findings confirm or are they congruent with existing theory? Is the transferable theory made explicit?		
14. Are the processes and findings generic enough to be applicable in other settings?		
15. *Have narrative sequences been preserved? Has a general cross-case theory using the sequences been developed?*		
16. *Have the findings been replicated in other studies to assess their robustness? If not, could replication efforts be mounted easily?*		
Summary score		
No. of methodological issues potentially affecting the use of the evaluation		
General comments on the component		

Checklist 6. Utilization: *How useful were the findings to clients, researchers, and the communities studied?*		
	A	**B**
1. Are the findings intellectually and physically accessible to potential users?		
2. Were any predictions made in the study and, if so, how accurate were they?		
3. Do the findings provide guidance for future action?		
4. Do the findings have a catalyzing effect leading to specific actions?		
5. Do the actions taken actually help solve local problems?		
6. Have users of the findings experienced any sense of empowerment or increased control over their lives? Have they developed new capacities?		
7. Are value-based or ethical concerns raised explicitly in the report? If not, do some exist that the researcher is not attending to?		
8. Did the evaluation report reach the key stakeholder groups in a form that they could understand and use [Note: This question can be asked separately for each of the main stakeholders]?		
9. Is there evidence that the evaluation had a significant influence on future project design?		
10. Is there evidence that the evaluation influenced policy decisions?		
Summary score		
No. of methodological issues potentially affecting the use of the evaluation		
General comments on the component		

Appendix D

Example of a Completed Threats-to-Validity Worksheet

Using the Worksheet to Assess an Already Completed Evaluation of a Low-Cost Housing Project

This example illustrates the use of the integrated worksheet to assess the validity of a fictitious but fairly typical housing project in Central America. The 3-year low-cost housing project began in June 2007 and ended in December 2010. A baseline study was conducted with project beneficiaries at the start of the project, and the survey was repeated about 6 months before the project closing date. The baseline survey covered a sample of 500 households selected randomly from the five project locations. A panel study design was used in which as many as possible of the original project households were reinterviewed for the posttest survey 3 years later. Approximately 85% were reinterviewed, and a random sample of 75 project households was selected to replace those who could not be reinterviewed. It was originally intended to include a comparison group, but this was cut out both because of budget constraints and because the Ministry of Housing did not wish to raise expectations that families interviewed as part of the comparison group would become eligible to obtain houses in a second phase of the project. When the posttest survey was being commissioned, the Ministry of Housing recognized the need to obtain comparison data to support their claim that the project had produced significant social and economic impacts, and consultants were requested to identify and interview a group of households with similar characteristics to the project participants. A matched comparison group was selected and interviewed. Project impacts were estimated by combining a posttest comparison of the project and comparison groups and a pretest–posttest estimate of the changes in the project group. The analysis found (a) the project group scored significantly higher than the comparison group on a number of economic and social indicators, and (b) the project group scores on the same indicators had improved over the life of the project. It was concluded that the project had produced a significant impact on both the economic and social conditions of participants, and it was recommended that the project should be replicated on a larger scale as part of the national poverty reduction strategy.

Integrated Worksheet for Assessing Threats to the Validity of the Findings and Recommendations of Mixed Method Evaluation Design (Standard Version)

Part 1: Summary of the Findings of the Assessment of the Evaluation

---

1. **Name of the project/program:** *Central America Low-Cost Housing Project*

2. **Who conducted the evaluation?** *A national consulting firm contracted by the Ministry of Housing*

3. **Who conducted this validity assessment? (indicate organizational affiliation)** *An international consultant hired by the funding agency*

4. **At what stage of the project/program did the evaluation begin?** *At the start of the project*

5. **At what stage of the evaluation was this assessment conducted?** *Several months after the project closed and the final evaluation report had been submitted*

6. **Reason for conducting the threats-to-validity assessment:** *Requested by the international funding agency as a standard procedure for all projects lasting more than 24 months.*

7. **Summary of findings of the assessment with respect to the evaluation methodology (note whether the assessment included the use of the checklists in Part 3).**

    [NOTE: *The assessment did include the use of the checklists.*] *The decision of the Ministry not to include a baseline survey of a comparison group seriously affected the validity of the evaluation findings. While there were statistically significant differences between the project group and the comparison group interviewed at the end of the project, the lack of baseline data on the comparison group makes it very difficult to assess the conditions of the comparison group at the start of the project and how they compared with the project group. If the comparison group scored lower than the project group on the economic and social indicators, then the post-project differences may have been at least partly due to the existing differences between the groups at the start of the project. The lack of a baseline comparison group also affected the interpretation of the observed improvements in the project group over the life of the project. It may be that the improvements were at least partly due to general improvements in the economy (for example, general wage increases and increased employment opportunities). However, it is not possible to control for these external factors without having data on the corresponding changes in the comparison group.*

    Due to these evaluation design issues, it is necessary to qualify the conclusion that housing is an effective way to improve the economic and social conditions of low-income households, and caution is needed with respect to the recommendation that the project should be expanded as part of the national poverty reduction strategy.

    While the evaluation consultants were not responsible for the decision not to include a baseline comparison group survey, they could be criticized for not having pointed out to the Ministry (which did not have any previous experience with impact evaluations) the problems that this decision would cause with respect to the interpretation of the evaluation findings. The consultants could also have proposed strategies in the posttest survey for estimating the conditions of the comparison group at the start of the project and for identifying and estimating the impacts of external factors during the 3 year period of project implementation. For example, consultants did not consult any of the household income and employment surveys that the government conducts every year and which could have provided information on changing earnings and employment opportunities.

(Continued)

(Continued)

8. **[If methodological problems were identified] What are the implications of these problems for the utilization of the evaluation findings and recommendations?**

The weaknesses in the evaluation design seriously affect the findings and recommendations. The finding that housing increased income and improved social indicators of the project families is not fully supported by the evaluation design. As indicated in the previous section, it is not possible to determine to what extent the improved indicators are due to external factors such as improved economic conditions or increased availability of schools and health clinics. It is also not possible to judge whether the differences in the economic and social conditions of the project and comparison groups is due to the project or whether this might be due to differences between the two groups at the time the project began.

Consequently, the recommendations that housing has been shown to be an effective way to increase income and improve social indicators and that the project should be replicated on a larger scale as part of a national poverty reduction strategy should be carefully assessed.

9. **Recommended follow-up actions:**

If resources and time permit, it would be useful to commission a rapid follow-up study to review secondary data from the household income and employment surveys and other sources, to estimate how much of the increased income and access to services of the project population was due to a general trend affecting all low-income households in the cities where the project operates.

If similar evaluations are to be commissioned in future, it is strongly recommended that baseline and posttest data should be collected on both the project population and a comparison group.

Part 2: Summary Assessment for Each Component

1. **Objectivity (Confirmability):** *Are the conclusions drawn from the available evidence, and is the research relatively free of researcher bias?*

Summary assessment and recommendations (identify most serious operational problems):

The conclusions are based on the available evidence, but the analysis does not take into consideration the methodological problems resulting from the absence of baseline data on a comparison group. There are some indications (based on interviews with the consultant and the clients) that given the positive reaction of the Ministry of Housing and the international funding agency to the favorable findings, the consultant may have been less rigorous in pointing out the limitations of the findings than he or she should have been.

- The quality of the methodology of this component: Average rating: 2.8
- The number of methodological problems that could affect the utilization of the evaluation: 2

2. **Internal design validity (reliability/dependability/credibility/authenticity):** *Are the findings credible to the people studied and to readers, and do we have an authentic portrait of what we are studying? Is the process of the study consistent, coherent, and reasonably stable over time and across researchers and methods? If emergent designs are used, are the processes through which the design evolves clearly documented?*

Summary assessment and recommendations (identify most serious operational problems):

The findings were favorably received and considered credible by the client because they presented the project in a favorable light and concluded that it had achieved its objectives. The findings would have seemed less credible to professional evaluators and researchers, but they were not consulted.

- The quality of the methodology of this component: Average rating: 2.7
- The number of methodological problems that could affect the utilization of the evaluation: 5

(Continued)

(Continued)

3. **Statistical conclusion validity:** *Reasons why inferences about statistical association (covariation) between two variables may be incorrect*
Summary assessment and recommendations (identify most serious operational problems):
The absence of baseline comparison group data weakens the statistical estimation of project impacts. A number of econometric procedures could have been used to strengthen the analysis, but these were not used.
• The quality of the methodology of this component: Average rating: 1.5 • The number of methodological problems that could affect the utilization of the evaluation: 1
4. **Construct validity:** *Does the adequacy of the constructs used to define processes, outcomes and impacts, and contextual variables capture the essential elements of what is being measured? Are the constructs sufficiently comprehensive to capture the multidimensionality of many of the constructs?*
Summary assessment and recommendations (identify most serious operational problems):
The constructs used to estimate changes in income are weakened by an inadequate definition of income from the informal sector and from other sources such as rent and remittances, so household income may have been underestimated.
• The quality of the methodology of this component: Average rating: 1.9 • The number of methodological problems that could affect the utilization of the evaluation: 2

5.   **External validity (transferability and fittingness):** *Do the conclusions fit other contexts and how widely can they be generalized? Do they provide credible evidence on how the program would perform in other settings?*

Summary assessment and recommendations (identify most serious operational problems):

The evaluation recommends that the project should be replicated on a larger scale and estimates that it would produce significant impacts on income and other social indicators. However, no analysis is made of any of the special characteristics of the household populations, the project locations, or the support from government agencies and politicians that might have affected project outcomes and that might not exist in other locations where a larger project might operate. Consequently, caution is required when stating that the project would have similar outcomes in other locations.

- **The quality of the methodology of this component: Average rating: 3.2**
- **The number of methodological problems that could affect the utilization of the evaluation: 3**

6.   **Utilization:** *How useful were the findings to clients, researchers, and the communities studied?*

Summary assessment and recommendations (identify most serious operational problems):

The findings were considered very useful by the Ministry of Housing and the donor and were used to support the proposal to fund a larger second phase. The project community was not involved in the planning or review of the evaluation, and they were not informed about the findings or recommendations.

- **The quality of the methodology of this component: Average rating: 3.2**
- **The number of methodological problems that could affect the utilization of the evaluation: 3**

Part 3: Checklists Used to Assess the Six Components Describing Potential Threats to the Adequacy and Validity of a Quantitative Impact Evaluation

Checklist 1: Objectivity (Confirmability)

Checklist 2: Internal Design Validity (Reliability/Dependability/Credibility/Authenticity)

Checklist 3: Statistical Conclusion Validity

Checklist 4: Construct Validity

Checklist 5: External Validity

Checklist 6: Utilization

Checklist 1: Objectivity (Confirmability)		
Are the conclusions drawn from the available evidence, and is the research relatively free of researcher bias?	**Ratings** (see footnote on use of ratings)	
	A	**B**
1. Are the study's methods and procedures adequately described? Are study data retained and available for reanalysis?	1	
2. Are data presented to support the conclusions?	2	
3. Has the researcher been as explicit and self-aware as possible about personal assumptions, values, and biases?	2	
4. Were the methods used to control for bias adequate?	4	√
5. Were competing hypotheses or rival conclusions considered?	5	√
Summary score (average rating)	2.8	
No. of methodological issues potentially affecting the use of the evaluation		2

General comments on the component:

The conclusions are based on the available evidence, but the analysis does not take into consideration the methodological problems resulting from the absence of baseline data on a comparison group. There are some indications (based on interviews with the consultant and the clients) that given the positive reaction of the Ministry of Housing and the international funding agency to the favorable findings, the consultant may have been less rigorous in pointing out the limitations of the findings than he or she should have been.

Notes and Sources

How to use the checklist: Column A = the existence or seriousness of each threat to validity. It is possible to simply check issues that exist or a rating scale can be used. A typical rating scale: 1 = the methodology is sound and there are no issues or problems; 5 = there are major methodological problems and issues. **Column B** = the importance of this threat for the purposes of this particular evaluation. The same two options exist. The first is to simply check each of the items rated as 4 or 5 in Column A that have important implications for the purposes of this evaluation. The second option is to rate the importance of this threat for the purposes of the present evaluation. For example: 1 = the threat does not have important implications for this evaluation and 5 = the threat has serious implications for the purposes of this evaluation.

Summary scores for each column: The summary score for Column A can be calculated either as the number of items that have been checked as having methodological problems, or when a rating scale is used, the mean rating can be calculated (the sum of all scores divided by the number of indicators rated). For Column B, this will normally be the number of items in Column A that were rated as having problems that were considered to have important policy or operational implications for the use of the evaluation. If mean scores are calculated, it is important to be aware of the dangers of treating ordinal variables as if they were interval (calculating means, etc.).

Sources for the six checklists: Items in normal text (i.e., those used most commonly in qualitative evaluations) are adapted from Miles and Huberman (1994, chap. 10, Section C) and from Teddlie and Tashakkori (2009), especially Chapter 12. See also Guba and Lincoln (1989). Items in italics (i.e., those most commonly used in quantitative evaluations) are adapted from Shadish, Cook, and Campbell (2002), Tables 2.2, 2.4, 3.1, and 3.2. The rating scales were developed by the present authors.

**Indicates items added by the present authors.

Checklist 2: Internal Validity (Credibility, Authenticity)		
Are the findings credible to the people studied and to readers, and do we have an authentic portrait of what we are studying?	**A**	**B**
1. How context-rich and meaningful ("thick") are the descriptions? Is there sufficient information to provide a credible/valid description of the subjects or the situation being studied?	4	
2. Does the account ring true, make sense, or seem convincing? Does it reflect the local context?	3	
3. Did triangulation among complementary methods and data sources produce generally converging conclusions? If expansionist qualitative methods are used where interpretations do not necessarily converge, are the differences in interpretations and conclusions noted and discussed?**	4	
4. Are the presented data well linked to the categories of prior or emerging theory? Are the findings internally coherent, and are the concepts systematically related?	3	
5. Are areas of uncertainty identified? Was negative evidence sought, found? How was it used? Have rival explanations been actively considered?	4	√
6. Were conclusions considered accurate by the researchers responsible for data collection?	2	
7. Are findings trustworthy, consistent, and replicable across data sources and over time?	4	√
8. Were data collected across the full range of appropriate settings, times, respondents, and so on?	5	√
9. Did all fieldworkers have comparable data collection protocols?	1	
10. Were coding and quality checks made, and did they show adequate agreement?	2	
11. Do the accounts of different observers converge? If they do not (which is often the case in QUAL studies), is this recognized and addressed?	2	
12. Were peer or colleague reviews used?	4	√
13. Were the rules used for confirmation of propositions, hypotheses, and so on made explicit?	3	
14. ***Temporal precedence of interventions and effects.*** *Was it clearly established that the intervention actually occurred before the effect that it was predicted to influence? A cause must precede its effect. However, it is often difficult to know the order of events in a project. Many projects (for example, urban development programs) do not have a precise starting date but get going over periods of months or even years.*	2	
15. ***Project selection bias.*** *Were potential project selection biases identified, and were measures taken to address them in the analysis? Project participants are often different from comparison groups either because they are self-selected or because the project administrator selects people with certain characteristics (the poorest farmers or best-organized communities).*	3	
16. ***History.*** *Were the effects of history identified and addressed in the analysis? Participation in a project may produce other experiences unrelated to the project treatment that might distinguish the project and control groups. For example, entrepreneurs who are known to have received loans may be more likely to be robbed or pressured by politicians to make donations, or girls enrolled in high school may be more likely to get pregnant.*	5	√

(Continued)

(Continued)

Checklist 2: Internal Validity (Credibility, Authenticity)		
Are the findings credible to the people studied and to readers, and do we have an authentic portrait of what we are studying?	**A**	**B**
17. **Maturation.** *Maturation produces many natural changes in physical development, behavior, knowledge, and exposure to new experiences. It is often difficult to separate changes due to maturation from those due to the project.*	3	
18. **Regression toward the mean.** *If subjects are selected because of their extreme scores (e.g., weight, physical development), there is a natural tendency to move closer to the mean over time—thus diminishing or distorting the effects of the program.*	n/a	
19. **Attrition.** *Was there significant attrition over the life of the project, and did this have different effects on the composition of the project and comparison groups? Even when project participants originally had characteristics similar to the total population, selective dropout over time may change the characteristics of the project population (e.g., the poorest or least educated might drop out).*	3	
20. **Testing.** *Being interviewed or tested may affect behavior or responses. For example, being asked about expenditures may encourage people to cut down on socially disapproved expenditures (cigarettes and alcohol) and spend more on acceptable items.*	1	
21. **Instrumentation.** *As researchers gain more experience, they may change how they interpret rating scales, observation checklists, and so on.*	1	
22. **Potential biases or distortion during the process of recall.** ** *Respondents may deliberately or unintentionally distort their recall of past events. Opposition politicians may exaggerate community problems while community elders may romanticize the past.*	n/a	
23. **Information is not collected from the right people or some categories of informants not interviewed.** ** *Sometimes information is collected from and about only certain sectors of the target population (men but not women, teachers but not students), in which case estimates for the total population may be biased.*	1	
24. **Use of less rigorous designs due to budget and time constraints.** ** *Many evaluations are conducted under budget, time, and data constraints, which require reductions in sample size, time for pilot studies, amount of information that can be collected, and so on. These constraints increase vulnerability to threats to internal validity.*	n/a	
Summary score (average rating)	2.7	
No. of methodological issues potentially affecting the use of the evaluation		5

General comments on the component:

The researchers followed appropriate procedures for sample selection and for quality control of data. The weaknesses concerned not having collected baseline data on the comparison group and not having collected data to control for economic and other events during the 3 years that might have affected outcomes.

NOTE: Items in italics are those normally used in the assessment of quantitative evaluations, while items in normal text are commonly used in the assessment of qualitative evaluations.

Checklist 3: Threats to Statistical Conclusion Validity		
Reasons why inferences about statistical association (covariation) between two variables may be incorrect	**A**	**B**
1. **The sample is too small to detect program effects (low statistical power):** *The sample is not large enough to detect statistically significant differences between project and control groups even if they do exist. Particularly important when effect sizes are small.*	1	
2. **Some assumptions of the statistical tests have been violated:** *Many statistical tests require that observations are independent of each other. If this assumption is violated (e.g., studying children in the same classroom, or patients in the same clinic who may be more similar to each other than the population in general), this can increase the risk of Type I error (false positive) wrongly concluding the project had an effect.*	3	
3. **"Fishing" for statistically significant results:** *A certain percentage of statistical tests will show "significant" results by chance (1 in 20 at the .05 significance level). Generating large numbers of statistical tables will always find some of these spurious results.*	1	
4. **Unreliability of measures of change of outcome indicators:** *Unreliable measures of, for example, rates of change in income, literacy, and infant mortality, always reduce the likelihood of finding a significant effect.*	1	
5. **Restriction of range or extrapolation from a truncated or incomplete database.**** *If only similar groups are compared, the power of the test is reduced and the likelihood of finding a significant effect is also reduced. If the sample covers only part of the population (e.g., only the poorest families, or only people working in the formal sector), this can affect the conclusions of the analysis and can bias generalizations to the total population.*	1	
6. **Unreliability of treatment implementation:** *If the treatment is not administered in an identical way to all subjects, the probability of finding a significant effect is reduced.*	1	
7. **External events influence outcomes (extraneous variance in the experimental setting):** *External events or pressures (power failure, community violence, election campaigns) may distract subjects and affect behavior and program outcomes.*	5	√
8. **Diversity of the population (heterogeneity of units):** *If subjects have widely different characteristics, this may increase the variance of results and make it more difficult to detect significant effects.*	1	
9. **Inaccurate effect size estimation due to outliers:** *A few outliers (extreme values) can significantly reduce effect size and make it less likely that significant differences will be found.*	1	
10. **Project and comparison group samples do not cover the same populations.**** *It is often the case that the comparison group sample is not drawn from the same population as the project sample. In these cases, differences in outcomes may be due to the differences in the characteristics of the two samples and not to the effects of the project.*	3	
11. **Information is not collected from the right people, or some categories of informants not interviewed.**** *Sometimes information is collected from and about only certain sectors of the target population (men but not women, teachers but not students), in which case estimates for the total population may be biased.*	1	
Summary score (average rating)	**1.5**	
No. of methodological issues affecting the use of the evaluation		**1**

General comments on this component:

The sample design and the statistical tests were correctly administered. The problem was that only very biased statistical tests (comparison of single means) were used, and some of the more powerful econometric tests that could have partially controlled for the absence of baseline data were not used.

Checklist 4: Construct Validity		
Reasons why inferences about the constructs used to define implementation processes, outputs, outcomes, and impacts may be incorrect	**A**	**B**
1. **Inadequate explanation of constructs:** Constructs (the effects/outcomes) being studied are defined in terms that are too general or are confusing or ambiguous, thus making it impossible to have precise measurement (examples of ambiguous constructs include quality of life, unemployed, aggressive behavior, hostile work environment, and sex discrimination).	1	
2. **Indicators do not adequately measure constructs (construct confounding):** The operational definition may not adequately capture the desired construct. For example, defining the unemployed as those who have registered with an employment center ignores people not working but who do not use these centers. Similarly, defining domestic violence as cases reported to the police significantly underrepresents the real number of incidents.	4	√
3. **Use of a single indicator to measure a complex construct (mono-operation bias):** Using a single indicator to define and measure a complex construct (such as poverty, well-being, and domestic violence) will usually produce bias.	3	
4. **Use of a single method to measure a construct (monomethod bias):** If only one method is used to measure a construct, this will produce a narrow and often biased measure (e.g., observing communities in formal meetings will produce different results than observing social events or communal work projects).	3	
5. *Only one level of the treatment is studied (confounding constructs with levels of constructs): Often a treatment is only administered at one, usually low, level of intensity (only small business loans are given), and the results are used to make general conclusions about the effectiveness (or lack of effectiveness) of the construct. This is misleading as a higher level of treatment might have produced a more significant effect.*	1	
6. *Program participants and comparison group respond differently to some questions (treatment-sensitive factorial structure): Program participants may respond in a more nuanced way to questions. For example, they may distinguish between different types and intensities of domestic violence or racial prejudice, whereas the comparison group may have broader, less discriminated responses.*	2	
7. *Participants assess themselves and their situation differently than comparison group (reactive self-report changes): People selected for programs may self-report differently from those not selected even before the program begins. They may wish to make themselves seem more in need of the program (poorer, sicker) or they may wish to appear more meritorious if that is a criterion for selection.*	1	
8. *Reactivity to the experimental situation: Project participants' interpretation of the project situation may affect their behavior. If they believe the program is run by a religious organization, they may respond differently than if they believe it is run by a political group.*	1	
9. *Experimenter expectancies: Experimenters also have expectations (about how men and women or different socioeconomic groups will react to the program), and this may affect how they react to different groups.*	4	√
10. *Novelty and disruption effects: Novel programs can generate excitement and produce a big effect. If a similar program is replicated, the effect may be less as novelty has worn off.*	1	
11. *Compensatory effects and rivalry: Programs create a dynamic that can affect outcomes in different ways. There may be pressure to provide benefits to nonparticipants, comparison groups may become motivated to show what they can achieve on their own, or those receiving no treatment or a less attractive treatment may become demoralized.*	1	

(Continued)

(Continued)

Checklist 4: Construct Validity		
Reasons why inferences about the constructs used to define implementation processes, outputs, outcomes, and impacts may be incorrect	A	B
12. **Using constructs developed in other countries without pretesting in the local context**:** *Many evaluations import theories and constructs from other countries and may not adequately capture the local project situation. For example, many evaluations of the impacts of microcredit on women's empowerment in countries such as Bangladesh use international definitions of empowerment that may not be appropriate for Bangladeshi women.*	1	
Summary score (average rating)	1.9	
No. of methodological issues affecting the use of the evaluation		2

General comments on this component:

The definition and measurement of income did not adequately capture informal sector earnings or nonearned income such as rent and remittances. Consequently, income may have been underestimated.

Experimenter expectancies concerning a positive project outcome may have made researchers less critical of the weak evaluation design and the potential bias of the findings.

Checklist 5: External Validity		
Do the conclusions fit other contexts, and how widely can they be generalized?	**A**	**B**
1. *Sample does not cover the whole population of interest.*	*3*	
2. *Different settings affect program outcomes.*	*3*	
3. *Different outcome measures give different assessments of project effectiveness.*	*1*	
4. *Program outcomes vary in different settings.*	*3*	
5. *Programs operate differently in different settings.*	*3*	
6. *Does the attitude (positive or negative) of policymakers and politicians to the program affect implementation or outcomes?*	*3*	
7. *Do seasonal and other cycles affect implementation or outcomes?*	*3*	
8. *Is there an adequate description of sample characteristics?*	*3*	
9. *Does the sample design permit generalization to other populations?*	*5*	√
10. Does the researcher define the scope and boundaries of reasonable generalization from the study?	*4*	√
11. Do the findings include enough "thick description" for readers to assess the potential transferability?	*4*	√
12. Does a range of readers report the findings to be consistent with their own experience?	n/a	
13. Do the findings confirm or are they congruent with existing theory? Is the transferable theory made explicit?	n/a	
14. Are the processes and findings generic enough to be applicable in other settings?	*3*	
15. *Have narrative sequences been preserved? Has a general cross-case theory using the sequences been developed?*	n/a	
16. *Have the findings been replicated in other studies to assess their robustness? If not, could replication efforts be mounted easily?*	*4*	
Summary score (average rating)	**3.2**	
No. of methodological issues potentially affecting the use of the evaluation		**3**

General comments on the component:

Many of the issues mentioned in the checklist have not been addressed. The main weakness is that the factors affecting potential replicability have not been assessed.

Checklist 6: Utilization		
How useful were the findings to clients, researchers, and the communities studied?	A	B
1. Are the findings intellectually and physically accessible to potential users?	3	
2. Were any predictions made in the study and, if so, how accurate were they?	n/a	
3. Do the findings provide guidance for future action?	4	√
4. Do the findings have a catalyzing effect leading to specific actions?	4	√
5. Do the actions taken actually help solve local problems?	3	
6. Have users of the findings experienced any sense of empowerment or increased control over their lives? Have they developed new capacities?	4	
7. Are value-based or ethical concerns raised explicitly in the report? If not, do some exist that the researcher is not attending to?	1	
8. Did the evaluation report reach the key stakeholder groups in a form that they could understand and use? (Note: This question can be asked separately for each of the main stakeholders.)	3	
9. Is there evidence that the evaluation had a significant influence on future project design?	2	
10. Is there evidence that the evaluation influenced policy decisions?	4	√
Summary score	3.2	
No. of methodological issues potentially affecting the use of the evaluation		3

General comments on the component:

The main problem is that the evaluation recommended that the project should be replicated based on questionable analysis. Policy makers have been influenced by these recommendations and used them to support a proposal to finance a second and larger project.

Appendix E

Integrated Worksheet for Assessing Threats to the Validity of Findings and Recommendations of a Mixed-Method Impact Evaluation[1] (Advanced Version)

Part 1: Summary of the Findings of the Assessment of the Evaluation

1. Name of project/program
2. Who conducted the evaluation? (indicate organizational affiliation)
3. Who conducted this validity assessment? (indicate organizational affiliation)
4. At what stage of the project/program did the evaluation begin?
5. At what stage of the evaluation was this assessment conducted?
6. Reason for conducting the threats to validity assessment
7. Summary of findings of the assessment (note whether the assessment included the use of the checklists in Part 3)
8. [If methodological problems were identified] What are the implications of these problems for the utilization of the evaluation findings and recommendations?
9. Recommended follow-up actions (if any)

[1] SOURCE: Adapted from Teddlie and Tashakkori (2009, chap. 12, Tables 12.5 and 12.6). Additional material included from Appendixes A and B of the present publication (additional sources cited in the two appendixes).

Part 2: Summary Assessment for Each Dimension and Category (see Part 3 for more detailed assessments)

Dimension 1: Internal Threats to Validity
Level 1: Overall design quality: *How suitable was the mixed-method design for the purposes of the evaluation? How well were the QUANT and QUAL procedures and design components implemented and analyzed, and how well were both integrated into a mixed-method approach? (see Checklist 1)*
Summary assessment and recommendations
• The quality of the methodology of this component: Summary Rating[2]: • The number of methodology problems that affect the utilization of the evaluation:
Level 2: Quality assessment for each stage of the evaluation (see Checklist 2)
Summary assessment and recommendations

	1	2	3	4	5	N/A
Data quality						
Data analysis						
Inference						
Integration						
Overall rating						

---

[2]Note on ratings: If the Part 3 checklists are not used, then judgmental ratings will be used on a 5-point scale where 1 = this aspect of the evaluation methodology is sound and there are no issues affecting the findings and recommendations and 5 = this aspect of the evaluation methodology has serious problems that affect the findings and recommendations. The rating system is described in more detail in the note to Checklist 1. If the Part 3 checklists are used, the summary rating and number of methodological problems are included from the respective checklists.

Dimension 2: External Threats to Validity (Checklist 3)
How well will the findings and recommendations apply to different groups and in different settings? Have these differences been adequately addressed in the reports?
Summary assessment and recommendations
• The quality of the methodology of this component: Rating: • The number of methodology problems that affect the utilization of the evaluation:

Dimension 3: Utilization Validity (Checklist 4)
How useful were the findings to clients, researchers, and the communities studied? Is there evidence that the findings and recommendations influenced policymakers or the design of future projects?
Summary assessment and recommendations
• The quality of the methodology of this component: Rating: • The number of methodology problems that affect the utilization of the evaluation:

Dimension 4: Interpretative Rigor (see Checklist 5)
Are the findings credible on the basis of the results obtained in the evaluation?
Summary assessment and recommendations
• The quality of the methodology of this component: Rating: • The number of methodology problems that affect the utilization of the evaluation:

Part 3: Checklists Used to Assess Each Dimension and Component

Checklist		Dimension		Level
1	1	Internal threat to validity	1	Overall design quality
2	1	Internal threat to validity	2	Quality assessment for each stage of the evaluation
3	2	External validity		
4	3	Utilization validity		
5	4	Interpretative rigor		

Checklist 1: Dimension 1: Internal Threats to Validity Level 1: Overall Design Quality		
How suitable was the mixed-method design for the purposes of the evaluation? How well were the QUANT and QUAL procedures and design components implemented, analyzed, and integrated into a mixed-method approach?		
	Ratings[3]	
	Threat	**Importance**
	A	**B**
1. Design suitability: *Was the design appropriate for the purpose of the study?*		
a. Are the methods of the study appropriate for answering the research questions? Does the design match the research questions?		
b. Does the mixed-methods design match the stated purpose for conducting an integrated study?		
c. Do all the strands of the mixed-methods study address the same research questions?		
Summary score for design suitability		
2. Internal design validity: *Does the design adequately address threats to internal design validity?* (see Part 4: Guidelines for Checklist 1)		
a. Temporal precedence of interventions and effects		
b. Project selection bias		
c. History		
d. Attrition		
e. Maturation		
f. Regression toward the mean		
g. Testing		
h. Instrumentation		
i. Potential biases or distortion during the process of recall		
j. Information not collected from the right people		
Summary score for internal design validity		
3. Construct validity: *The adequacy and comprehensiveness of constructs used to define processes, outcomes, impacts, and contextual variables (see Part 4 guidance for explanation)*		
a. Inadequate explanation of constructs		
b. Indicators do not adequately measure constructs		
c. Use of a single indicator or method to measure a complex construct		
d. Use of a single method to measure a construct (monomethod bias)		
e. Only one level of the treatment is studied		
f. The implicit program theory model is not well documented		
g. Program participants and comparison groups respond differently to some questions		
h. Participants assess themselves and their situation differently from comparison group		

(Continued)

[3]See note at the end of the checklist.

(Continued)

Checklist 1: Dimension 1: Internal Threats to Validity Level 1: Overall Design Quality		
How suitable was the mixed-method design for the purposes of the evaluation? How well were the QUANT and QUAL procedures and design components implemented, analyzed, and integrated into a mixed-method approach?		
(3. Construct validity continued)	**Ratings**	
	Threat	**Importance**
	A	**B**
i.	Reactivity to the experimental situation		
j.	Experimenter expectancies		
k.	Novelty and disruption effects		
l.	Compensatory effects and rivalry		
m.	Using indicators and constructs developed in other countries without pretesting in the local context		
n.	The process of "quantizing" or "qualitizing" changes the nature or meaning of a variable in a way that can be misleading		
o.	Does multilevel, mixed-method analysis accurately reflect how the project operates and interacts with its environment?		
	Summary score for construct validity		
4. Design fidelity: Are the QUANT, QUAL, and mixed-method procedures (sampling, data collection, etc.) implemented with the necessary quality and rigor? (refer to Checklist 2)			
a.	QUANT data collection		
b.	QUAL data collection		
c.	QUANT data analysis		
d.	QUAL data analysis		
	Summary score for design fidelity		
5. Within-design consistency: consistency among all elements of the design			
a.	Do the components of the design fit together in a seamless manner?		
b.	Do the strands of the MM study follow each other (or are they linked) in a logical and seamless manner?		
	Summary score for within-design consistency		
6. Analytic adequacy: *Was the analytic strategy appropriate and adequate?*			
a.	Are the data analysis procedures/strategies appropriate and adequate to provide possible answers to research questions?		
b.	Are the mixed-method analytic strategies implemented effectively?		
	Summary score for analytic adequacy		

(Continued)

(Continued)

Checklist 1: Dimension 1: Internal Threats to Validity Level 1: Overall Design Quality		Ratings	
How suitable was the mixed-method design for the purposes of the evaluation? How well were the QUANT and QUAL procedures and design components implemented, analyzed, and integrated into a mixed-method approach?			
		Threat	Importance
		A	B
7.	**Objectivity:** *Are the conclusions drawn from the available evidence and is the research relatively free of researcher bias?*		
a.	Are the conclusions and recommendations presented in the executive summary consistent with, and supported by, the information and findings in the main report?		
b.	Are the study's methods and procedures adequately described? Are study data retained and available for reanalysis?		
c.	Are data presented to support the conclusions? Is evidence presented to support all findings?		
d.	Has the researcher been as explicit and self-aware as possible about personal assumptions, values, and biases?		
e.	Were the methods used to control for bias adequate?		
f.	Were competing hypotheses or rival conclusions considered?		
	Summary score for objectivity		
	Summary score for Checklist 1		
	No. of methodological issues affecting the use of the evaluation		
General comments and conclusions for this component			

Notes on the five checklists:

1. ** = additional categories included by the present authors.

2. How to use the checklist: Column A = the existence or seriousness of each threat to validity. There are two options: (1) Simply check all indicators where methodological problems exist, or (2) use a rating scale to indicate the severity of the issue. A typical rating scale:

1 = the methodology is very strong and there are no issues or problems; 2 = the methodology is sound and there are no major weaknesses; 3 = the methodology is generally sound but there are some areas of weakness; 4 = the methodology has a number of important weaknesses; 5 = there are major methodological problems and issues. Column B = the importance of each methodological threat identified in Column A for the purposes of the present evaluation. In this case, all items that have important implications for the present evaluation are checked.

Summary scores for each column: The summary score for Column A can be calculated either as the number of items that have been checked as having methodological problems, or when a rating scale is used, the mean rating is calculated (the sum of all scores divided by the number of indicators rated). If mean scores are calculated, it is important to be aware of the dangers of treating ordinal variables as if they were interval (calculating means, etc). For Column B, this will normally be the number of items in Column A that were rated as having problems that were considered to have important policy or operational implications for the use of the evaluation.

		Rating[4]	
		Threat	Importance
		A	B
1.	Data collection: The adequacy of the data collection methods and the quality of the data		
1A.	**Quantitative data collection (see Part 4 guidelines for explanations)**		
a.	The sample is too small to detect program effects (low statistical power)		
b.	Unreliability of measures of change in outcome indicators		
c.	Restriction of range		
d.	Diversity of the population (heterogeneity of units)		
e.	Project and comparison group samples do not cover the same population		
f.	Information is not collected from the right people, or some categories of informants are not interviewed		
g.	Did budget, time, or data constraints affect the quality of the data? If so, were adequate measures taken to address these limitations?		
h.	Data collection methods not appropriate for collecting information on sensitive topics or for interviewing difficult to reach groups		
1B.	**Qualitative data collection**		
a.	How context rich and meaningful ("thick") are the descriptions? Is there sufficient information to provide a credible/valid description of the subjects or the situation being studied?		
b.	Are findings trustworthy, consistent, and replicable across data sources and over time?		
c.	Were data collected across the full range of appropriate settings, times, respondents, and so on?		
d.	Did all fieldworkers have comparable data collection protocols?		
e.	Were coding and quality checks made, and did they show adequate agreement?		
f.	Do the accounts of different observers converge? If they do not (which is often the case in qualitative studies), is this recognized and addressed?		
g.	Were peer or colleague reviews used?		
h.	Did budget, time, or data constraints affect the quality of the data? If so, were adequate measures taken to address these limitations?		
i.	Does the account ring true, make sense, or seem convincing? Does it reflect the local context?		
j.	Did triangulation among complementary methods and data sources produce generally converging conclusions? If expansionist qualitative methods are used where interpretations do not necessarily converge, are the differences in interpretations and conclusions noted and discussed?		
k.	Are the presented data well linked to the categories of prior or emerging theory? Are the findings internally coherent, and are the concepts systematically related?		
l.	Are areas of uncertainty identified? Was negative evidence sought, found? How was it used? Have rival explanations been actively considered?		
m.	Were conclusions considered accurate by the researchers responsible for data collection?		
	Summary score for data collection		

Checklist 2: Dimension 1: Internal Threats to Validity
Level 2: quality assessment for each stage of the evaluation

How well were the QUANT and QUAL procedures and design components implemented, analyzed, and integrated into a mixed-methods approach?

(Continued)

[4]See note at end of Checklist 1.

(Continued)

Checklist 2: Dimension 1: Internal Threats to Validity Level 2: Quality Assessment for Each Stage of the Evaluation			
How well were the QUANT and QUAL procedures and design components implemented, analyzed, and integrated into a mixed-methods approach?			
		Rating	
		Threat	Importance
		A	B
2.	**Data analysis and the validity of how data are interpreted (inference)**		
2A.	Quantitative data analysis and inference (see Part 4 guidelines for more details)		
a.	The sample is too small to detect program effects (low statistical power)		
b.	Some assumptions of the statistical tests have been violated		
c.	"Fishing" for statistically significant results		
d.	Restriction of range		
e.	Unreliability of treatment implementation not captured in the analysis		
f.	Diversity of the population reduces the statistical power of the analysis		
g.	Extrapolation from a truncated or incomplete database		
h.	Project and comparison group samples do not cover the same population		
i.	The sample is too small to detect statistically significant effects		
j.	Sample size for group- and community-level variables is too small to permit statistical significance testing		
2B.	**Qualitative data analysis and inference**		
a.	Were the rules used for the confirmation of propositions and hypotheses made explicit?		
b.	Were coding and quality checks made, and did they show adequate agreement?		
	Summary score for data analysis		
3.	**Integration of quantitative and qualitative approaches at all stages of the evaluation**		
a.	Hypotheses development		
b.	Developing the conceptual framework and the program theory model		
c.	Same design		
d.	Data collection		
e.	Data analysis		
	Summary score for Integration of Quantitative and Qualitative Approaches		
	Summary score for Checklist 2		
	No. of methodological issues affecting the use of the evaluation		
General comments on this component			

Checklist 3: Dimension 2: External Validity

Reasons why inferences about how study results would hold over variations in persons, settings, treatments, and outcomes may be incorrect (see Part 4 guidelines for explanations)

	Rating[5]	
	Threat	**Importance**
	A	**B**
1. Sample does not cover the whole population of interest		
2. Different settings affect program outcomes		
3. Different outcome measures give different assessments of project effectiveness		
4. Program outcomes vary in different settings		
5. Programs operate differently in different settings		
6. The attitude of policymakers and politicians to the program		
7. Seasonal and other cycles		
8. Adequate description of sample characteristics		
9. Does the sample design permit generalization to other populations?		
10. Does the researcher define the scope and boundaries of reasonable generalization from the study?		
11. Do the findings include enough "thick description" for readers to assess the potential transferability?		
12. Does a range of readers report the findings to be consistent with their own experience?		
13. Do the findings confirm or are they congruent with existing theory? Is the transferable theory made explicit?		
14. Are the processes and findings generic enough to be applicable in other settings?		
15. Have narrative sequences been preserved? Has a general cross-case theory using the sequences been developed?		
16. Does the report suggest settings where the findings could fruitfully be tested further?		
17. Have the findings been replicated in other studies to assess their robustness? If not, could replication efforts be mounted easily?		
Summary score		■■■
No. of methodological issues affecting the use of the evaluation	■■■	

General comments on this component

---

[5]See note at the end of Checklist 1.

Checklist 4: Dimension 3: Utilization

How useful were the findings to clients, researchers, and the communities studied?

	Rating[6]	
	Threat	**Importance**
	A	**B**
1. Are the findings intellectually and physically accessible to potential users?		
2. Were any predictions made in the study and, if so, how accurate were they?		
3. Do the findings provide guidance for future action?		
4. Do the findings have a catalyzing effect leading to specific actions?		
5. Do the actions taken actually help solve local problems?		
6. Have users of the findings experienced any sense of empowerment or increased control over their lives? Have they developed new capacities?		
7. Are value-based or ethical concerns raised explicitly in the report? If not, do some exist that the researcher is not attending to?		
8. Did the evaluation report reach the key stakeholder groups in a form that they could understand and use? (Note: This question can be asked separately for each of the main stakeholders.)		
9. Is there evidence that the evaluation had a significant influence on future project design?		
10. Is there evidence that the evaluation influenced policy decisions?		
Summary score		
No. of methodological issues affecting the use of the evaluation		

General comments on this component

---

[6]See note at the end of Checklist 1.

Checklist 5: Dimension 4: Interpretative Rigor			
Are the interpretations credible on the basis of the results obtained in the evaluation?			
		Rating[7]	
		Threat	Importance
		A	B
1.	**Interpretative consistency**		
a.	Do the inferences closely follow the relevant findings in terms of type, scope, and intensity?		
b.	Are multiple inferences made on the basis of the same findings consistent with each other?		
2.	**Theoretical consistency**		
a.	Are the inferences consistent with theory and state of knowledge in the field?		
3.	**Interpretive agreement**		
a.	Are other scholars likely to reach the same conclusions on the basis of the same results?		
b.	Do the inferences match participants' constructions?		
4.	**Interpretive directness**		
a.	Is each inference distinctively more credible/plausible than other possible conclusions that might be made on the basis of the same results?		
5.	**Integrative efficacy (mixed and multiple methods)**		
a.	Do the meta-inferences adequately incorporate the inferences that are made in each strand of the study?		
b.	If there are credible inconsistencies between the inferences made within/across strands, are the theoretical explanations for these inconsistencies explored and possible explanations offered?		
6.	**Interpretive correspondence**		
a.	Do the inferences correspond to the stated purposes/questions of the study? Do the inferences made in each strand address the purposes of the study in that strand?		
b.	Do the meta-inferences meet the stated need for using a mixed-method design?		
	Summary score		
	No. of methodological issues affecting the use of the evaluation		
General comments, conclusions and recommendations from this component			

---

[7]See note at the end of Checklist 1.

Part 4: Guidelines for Using the Checklists

NOTE: *Explanations are only provided for technical questions that may be more difficult to interpret.*

Guidelines for Checklist 1: Overall Design Quality: *How suitable was the mixed-methods design for the purposes of the evaluation? How well were the QUANT and QUAL procedures and design components implemented, analyzed, and integrated into the mixed-methods approach?*

Question No.	Question	Explanation
1	Design suitability	*No explanation required*
2.	**Internal design validity**	
a.	Temporal precedence of interventions and effects	*Was it clearly established that the intervention actually occurred before the effect that it was predicted to influence? A cause must precede its effect. However, it is often difficult to know the order of events in a project. Many projects (e.g., urban development programs) do not have a precise starting date but get going over periods of months or even years.*
b.	Project selection bias	*Were potential project selection biases identified and were measures taken to address them in the analysis? Project participants are often different from comparison groups either because they are self-selected or because the project administrator selects people with certain characteristics (the poorest farmers or the best-organized communities).*
c.	History	*Were the effects of history identified and addressed in the analysis? Participation in a project may produce other experiences unrelated to the project treatment that might distinguish the project and control groups. For example, entrepreneurs who are known to have received loans may be more likely to be robbed or pressured by politicians to make donations, or girls enrolled in high school may be more likely to get pregnant.*
d.	Attrition	*Was there significant attrition over the life of the project, and did this have different effects on the composition of the project and comparison groups? Even when project participants originally had characteristics similar to the total population, selective dropout over time may change the characteristics of the project population (e.g., the poorest or least educated might drop out).*
e.	Maturation	*Maturing produces many natural changes in physical development, behavior, knowledge, and exposure to new experiences. It is often difficult to separate changes due to maturation from those due to the project.*
f.	Regression toward the mean	*If subjects are selected because of their extreme scores (e.g., weight, physical development), there is a natural tendency to move closer to the mean over time, thus diminishing or distorting the apparent effects of the program.*
g.	Testing	*Being interviewed or tested may affect behavior or responses. For example, being asked about expenditures may encourage people to cut down on socially disapproved expenditures (cigarettes and alcohol) and spend more on acceptable items.*

(Continued)

(Continued)

Guidelines for Checklist 1: Overall Design Quality: *How suitable was the mixed-methods design for the purposes of the evaluation? How well were the QUANT and QUAL procedures and design components implemented, analyzed, and integrated into the mixed-methods approach?*		
Question No.	**Question**	**Explanation**
h.	Instrumentation	*As researchers gain more experience, they may change how they interpret rating scales, observation checklists, and so on.*
i.	Potential bias or distortion during the process of recall	*Respondents may deliberately or unintentionally distort their recall of past events. Opposition politicians may exaggerate community problems while community elders may romanticize the past.*
j.	Information not collected from the right people	*Sometimes information is collected from and about only certain sectors of the target population (men but not women, teachers but not students), in which case estimates for the total population may be biased. Some categories of informants are not interviewed.*
3. Construct validity		
a.	Inadequate explanation of constructs	*Constructs (e.g., implementation processes, effects/outcomes) being studied are defined in terms that are too general or are confusing or ambiguous, thus making it impossible to have precise measurement. Examples of ambiguous constructs include quality of life, unemployed, aggressive behavior, hostile work environment, and sex discrimination.*
b.	Indicators do not adequately measure constructs *(construct confounding)*	*The operational definition may not adequately capture the desired construct. For example, defining the unemployed as those who have registered with an employment center ignores people not working but who do not use these centers. Similarly, defining domestic violence as cases reported to the police significantly under-represents the real number of incidents.*
c.	Use of single indicator to measure a complex *construct (mono-operation bias)*	*Using a single indicator to define and measure a complex construct (such as poverty, well-being, and domestic violence) will usually produce bias.*
d.	Use of a single method to measure a construct *(mono-method bias)*	*If only one method is used to measure a construct, this will produce a narrow and often biased measure (e.g., observing communities in formal meetings will produce different results than observing social events or communal work projects).*
e.	Only one level of the treatment is studied	*Often a treatment is only administered at one, usually low, level of intensity (e.g., only small business loans are given), and the results are used to make general conclusions about the effectiveness (or lack of effectiveness) of the construct. This is misleading as a higher level of treatment might have produced a more significant effect.*
f.	The implicit program theory model on which the project is based is not well documented	*This makes it difficult to identify how the key constructs were understood by program planners.*
g.	Program participants and comparison group respond differently to some questions	*Program participants may respond in a more nuanced way to questions. For example, they may distinguish between different types and intensities of domestic violence or racial prejudice, whereas the comparison group may have broader, less discriminated responses.*

(Continued)

(Continued)

Guidelines for Checklist 1: Overall Design Quality: *How suitable was the mixed-methods design for the purposes of the evaluation? How well were the QUANT and QUAL procedures and design components implemented, analyzed, and integrated into the mixed-methods approach?*

Question No.	Question	Explanation
h.	Participants assess themselves and their situation differently than comparison group	*People selected for programs may self-report differently from those not selected even before the program begins. They may wish to make themselves seem more in need of the program (poorer, sicker) or they may wish to appear more meritorious if that is a criterion for selection.*
i.	Reactivity to the experimental situation	*Project participants try to interpret the project situation, and this may affect their behavior. If they believe the program is being run by a religious organization, they may respond differently than if they believe it is run by a political group.*
j.	Experimenter expectancies	*Experimenters have expectations (e.g., about how men and women or different socioeconomic groups will react to the program), and this may affect how they react to different groups.*
k.	Novelty and disruption effects	*Novel programs can generate excitement and produce a big effect. If a similar program is replicated, the effect may be less as novelty has worn off.*
l.	Using indicators and constructs developed in other countries without pretesting in the local context	*Many evaluations import theories and constructs from other countries, and these may not adequately capture the local project situation. For example, many evaluations of the impacts of micro-credit on women's empowerment in countries such as Bangladesh have used international definitions of empowerment that may not be appropriate for Bangladeshi women.*
m.	The process of "quantizing" (transforming qualitative variables into interval or ordinal variables) or "qualitizing" (transforming quantitative variables into qualitative) changes the nature or meaning of a variable in a way that can be misleading	*One example of "quantizing" is to convert contextual variables (the local economic, political, or organization context affecting each project location) into dummy variables to be incorporated into regression analysis.*
n.	Does multilevel, mixed-method analysis accurately reflect how the project operates and interacts with its environment?	*The reviewer may consult with key informants, beneficiaries, and stakeholders, requesting them to review and comment on the descriptions included in the evaluation reports.*

Guidelines for Checklist 2: Dimension 1: Internal Threats to Validity:
Level 2: Quality Assessment for Each Stage of the Evaluation

Question No.	Question	Explanation
1B. Qualitative data collection		
a.	How context rich and meaningful ("thick") are the descriptions?	*Is there sufficient information to provide a credible/ valid description of the subjects or the situation being studied?*
j.	Did triangulation among complementary methods and data sources produce generally converging conclusions?	*Where interpretations do not converge, are the differences in interpretation and conclusion noted and discussed?*
k.	Are the data well linked to the categories of prior or emerging theory?	*Are the findings internally coherent, and are the concepts systematically related?*
2A. Quantitative data analysis		
a.	The sample is too small to detect program effects (low statistical power).	*The sample is not large enough to detect statistically significant differences between project and control groups even if they do exist. Particularly important when effect sizes are small.*
b.	Some assumptions of the statistical tests have been violated.	*Computer software analysis packages make it simple to run statistical tests without understanding the assumptions on which they are based. Sometimes this can invalidate or weaken the findings and how they are interpreted.*
c.	"Fishing" for statistically significant results	*If large numbers of regressions or other statistical tests are run, a certain number will come out "positive" due to the laws of probability. To avoid these spurious findings, it is important to base the analysis design on a set of hypotheses derived from the program theory.*
d.	Restriction of range	*Many evaluations only cover part of a population (e.g., only the poorest sectors are studied), and this can weaken the strength of some kinds of analysis.*
e.	Unreliability of treatment implementation not captured in the analysis	*If the treatment is not administered in an identical way to all subjects, the probability of finding a significant effect is reduced.*
f.	Diversity (heterogeneity) of the population	*If subjects have widely different characteristics, this may increase the variance of results and make it more difficult to detect significant effects.*
g.	Extrapolation from a truncated or incomplete database	*If the sample only covers part of the population (e.g., only the poorest families or only people working in the formal sector), this can affect the conclusions of the analysis and can bias generalizations to the total population.*

(Continued)

(Continued)

Guidelines for Checklist 2: Dimension 1: Internal Threats to Validity: Level 2: Quality Assessment for Each Stage of the Evaluation		
Question No.	**Question**	**Explanation**
h.	Project and comparison group samples do not cover the same populations.	*It is often the case that the comparison group sample is not drawn from the same population as the project sample. In these cases, differences in outcomes may be due to the differences in the characteristics of the two samples and not to the effects of the project.*
i.	The sample is too small to detect program effects (low statistical power).	*The sample is not large enough to detect statistically significant differences between project and control groups even if they do exist. Particularly important when effect sizes are small.*
j.	Sample size for group- and community-level variables is too small to permit statistical significance testing.	*When the unit of analysis is the group, organization, or community, the sample size tends to be significantly reduced (compared to data collected from household sample surveys), and the power of the test is lowered so that it may not be possible to conduct statistical significance testing. This is frequently the case when data are collected at the group level to save time or money.*

Guidelines for Checklist 3: External Validity

	Question	Explanation
1.	Sample does not cover the whole population of interest.	*Subjects may only come from one sex or from certain ethnic or economic groups, or they may have certain personality characteristics (e.g., depressed, self-confident). Consequently, it may be different to generalize from the study findings to the whole population.*
2.	Different settings affect program outcomes.	*Treatments may be implemented in different settings, which may affect outcomes. If pressure to reduce class size forces schools to construct extra temporary and inadequate classrooms, the outcomes may be very different than having smaller classes in suitable classroom settings.*
3.	Different outcome measures give different assessments of project effectiveness.	*Different outcome measures can produce different conclusions on project effectiveness. Micro-credit programs for women may increase household income and expenditure on children's education but may not increase women's political empowerment.*
4.	Program outcomes vary in different settings.	*Program success may be different in rural and urban settings or in different kinds of communities. So it may not be appropriate to generalize findings from one setting to different settings.*
5.	Programs operate differently in different settings.	*Programs may operate in different ways and have different intermediate and final outcomes in different settings. The implementation of community-managed schools may operate very differently and have different outcomes when managed by religious organizations, government agencies, and nongovernmental organizations.*
6.	The attitude of policymakers and politicians to the program	*Identical programs will operate differently and have different outcomes in situations where they have the active support of policymakers or politicians than in situations where they face opposition or indifference. When the party in power or the agency head changes, it is common to find that support for programs can vanish or, alternatively, be increased.*
7.	Seasonal and other cycles	*Many projects will operate differently in different seasons, at different stages of the business cycle, or according to the terms of trade for key exports and imports. Attempts to generalize findings from pilot programs must take these cycles into account.*
8.	Are the characteristics of the sample of persons, settings, processes, and so on described in enough detail to permit comparisons with other samples?	*This may require presenting information on the social and economic characteristics of the study population and of comparison groups.*
9.	Does the sample design theoretically permit generalization to other populations?	*Does the program theory explain the factors determining success or failure of the project, and are these presented in a way that makes it possible to assess the potential for replication in other settings?*

	Question	Explanation
10.	Does the researcher define the scope and boundaries of reasonable generalization from the study?	*Does the analysis assess the extent to which these characteristics are likely to be present in the areas where the program might be replicated?*
13.	Do the findings confirm or are they congruent with existing theory? Is the transferable theory made explicit?	*Is there a review of existing theory, and does this discuss how the program theory relates to current theory? Is the program theory consistent with current theory, and if not, is there a credible case made for the differences?*
14.	Are the processes and findings generic enough to be applicable in other settings?	*Does the study present sufficient evidence to show whether processes are unique to this setting or can be generalized? Is the evidence convincing?*
15.	Have narrative sequences been preserved? Has a general cross-case theory using the sequences been developed?	*Is a significant amount of the original narrative preserved or are only the researchers' notes and interpretations available? Is sufficient narrative available to test whether the findings and interpretations are consistent across cases?*

Guidelines for Checklists 4 and 5: External Validity: *Explanations were not considered necessary for these two checklists.*

Appendix F

A More Detailed Look at the RealWorld Evaluation Design Frameworks

This appendix describes in more detail all the designs described in Chapter 11. The designs are presented in the same order as in Table F.1 (which reproduces Table 11.3 from Chapter 11).[1] Examples are given illustrating how each of these designs has been applied in the field. All the following designs can be strengthened if used in combination with the methods described in Chapter 11. Table F.3 (reproduced from Table 11.5) summarizes some of the strategies that can be used to strengthen all of the designs discussed in this appendix. First the longitudinal (Design 1) and then the randomized control trial (RCT; Design 2.1) designs are discussed in more detail to explain some of the basic procedures used in all the subsequent designs.

To make it easier for the reader to navigate all the evaluation designs addressed in this rather long appendix, we provide below a Table of Contents just for Appendix F.

---

[1]The numbering of the designs discussed in this appendix follow the numbering used in Table 11.3, in that the lead number reflects the number of the seven basic designs of Table 11.2, and the second number represents a variant of that basic design.

(Continued)

(Continued)

3.	**Weaker Statistical Designs**	
3.1	Pipeline Design (Design 2.4)	
	When to Use	
	The Evaluation Design	
	Table F.8	Design 2.4: Pipeline Design
	Box F.8	Example of Design 2.4 Pipeline Design: A Quasi-Experimental Pipeline Design to Evaluate a Social Protection Program in Argentina
3.2	Pretest–Posttest Project and Comparison Group Design with Judgmental Matching of the Two Samples (Design 2.5)	
	When to Use	
	The Evaluation Design	
	Table F.9	Design 2.5: Quasi-Experimental Design with Judgmental Matching of the Two Samples
	Box F.9	Case Study for Design 2.5A: Using Judgmental Matching to Evaluate the Impacts of Improved Housing on Household Income in El Salvador
3.3	Truncated Pretest–Posttest Project and Comparison Group Design (Design 3.1)	
	When to Use	
	Description of the Design	
	Table F.10	Design 3: Truncated Pretest–Posttest Project and Comparison Group Design Starting at the Time of the Midterm Review
3.3.3	Incorporating mixed methods into the design	
	Box F.10	Case Study for Design 3 (Truncated Design) Combined with Design 2.5B (Judgmental Matching Pretest–Posttest): Assessing the Social and Economic Impacts of a Feeder Roads Project in Eritrea
3.4	Elimination of the Baseline Comparison Group (Pretest–Posttest Project Group Combined with Posttest-Only Analysis of Project and Comparison Group) (Design 4.1)	
	When to Use	
	Description of the Design	
	Table F.11	Design 4: Elimination of the Baseline Comparison Group (Pretest–Posttest Project Group Combined with Posttest Analysis of Project and Comparison Groups)
	Incorporating Mixed-Method Approaches into the Design	
	Box F.11	Case Study for Design 4.1 (with Elements of Design 1): Comparing the Effects of Resettlement on Project Beneficiaries and Nonbeneficiaries in the Second Maharashtra Irrigation Project, India

3.5	Posttest-Only Comparison Group Design (Design 5)	
	When to Use	
	Description of the Design	
	Table F.12	Design 5: No Baseline Data (Posttest-Only Project and Comparison Groups)
	Box F.12	Case Study for Design 5: Assessing the Impacts of Microcredit on the Social and Economic Conditions of Women and Families in Bangladesh
	Incorporating Mixed-Method Approaches into the Design	
	Box F.13	Example of Design 5B: Posttest Comparison Combining Statistical Matching with a Mixed-Method Design—Evaluating Nicaragua's School-Based Reform: A Retrospective, Mixed-Method Design with Statistical Matching
4.	**Nonexperimental designs (NEDs) (Designs 6 and 7)**	
4.1	Pretest–Posttest No-Comparison Group Designs (Designs 6)	
	When to Use	
	Description of the Design	
	Table F.13	Design 6: Basic Pretest–Posttest Project Group Design with No Comparison Group
	Box F.14	Case Study for Design 6.1: Using a Before-and-After Survey of Resettled Households to Evaluate the Impact of the Khao Laem Hydroelectric Project in Thailand
	The Single-Case Design (SCD)	
	Box F.15	Design 6.1: Single-Case Design: Treating a Schoolgirl with Asperger's Disorder
	Longitudinal NED Design (Design 6.2)	
	Box F.16	Design 6.2: Longitudinal Design without Comparison Group: The 12–18 Project—Making Lives Modern in Australia
	Interrupted Time Series (Design 6.3)	
	Box F.17	Design 6.3: Interrupted Time Series: Estimating the Effects of Raising the Drinking Age
	Case Study Designs	
	Box F.18	Example of a More Rigorous Nonexperimental Design: Evaluating the Effectiveness of the Natural Resources Leadership Program
4.2	Data Collected Only on the Posttest Project Group (Design 7)	
	When to Use	
	Description of the Design	
	Strengthening the Design	
	Table F.14	Design 7: Posttest Analysis of Project Group without a Baseline or Comparison Group
	Incorporating Mixed-Method Approaches into the Design	
	Box F.19	Case Study for Design 7: Assessing the Impacts of the Construction of Village Schools in Eritrea

Table F.1 List of Experimental, Quasi-Experimental, and Nonexperimental Evaluation Design Options, with a Focus on How the Counterfactual Is Determined (Duplication of Table 11.3)

Design	Start of Project T_1	Intervention	Midterm T_2	End of Project T_3	Post-Project T_4	Stage of Project When Evaluation Commissioned
Experimental (Randomized) Designs						
1.1[a] Longitudinal design starting with randomized selection of intervention and control group	P_1 C_1	X	P_2 C_2	P_3 C_3	P_4 C_4	Start
2.1 Randomized control trial with only pretest and posttest	P_1 C_1	X		P_3 C_3		Start
Quasi-Experimental Designs						
1.2 Longitudinal design (without randomized selection)	P_1 C_1	X	P_2 C_2	P_3 C_3	P_4 C_4	Start
2.2 Option A. Pretest–posttest comparison group design with statistical matching of samples. Evaluation commissioned at start of project.	P_1 C_1	X		P_2 C_2		Start
2.2. Option B. Pretest–posttest comparison group design with statistical matching of samples. Evaluation commissioned at end of project.[b]	(P_1) (C_1)	X		P_2 C_2		End
2.3 Regression discontinuity	P_1 C_1	X		P_2 C_2		Start

		Start of Project	Intervention	Midterm	End of Project	Post-Project	Stage of Project When Evaluation Commissioned
2.4. Pipeline comparison group design. Can be used when projects are implemented in phases. Individuals, households or communities entering in Phase 2 (P2), and later phases, can be used as the comparison group for those entering in Phase 1 (P1). Note that $C1_2$ becomes $P2_1$, $C2_2$ becomes $P3_1$, etc.	Phase 1	$P1_1$ $C1_1$	X_1	$P1_2$ $C1_2$			Start
	Phase 2			$P2_1$ $C2_1$	X_2	$P2_2$ $C2_2$	
	Phase 3					$P3_1$	
2.5 Option A. Pretest–posttest comparison group design with judgmental matching. Evaluation commissioned at start of project.		P_1 C_1	X		P_2 C_2		End
2.5 Option B. Pretest–posttest comparison group design with judgmental matching. Evaluation commissioned at end of project. Recall or secondary data used to reconstruct initial status of both project and comparison groups.		(P_1) (C_1)	X		P_2 C_2		End
3.1 Pretest–posttest comparison group design in which initial data collection (delayed baseline) is not conducted until project has been underway for some time.			X	P_1 C_1	P_2 C_2		During implementation.
4.1 Option A. Posttest comparison group design combined with collection of baseline data on project. Evaluation commissioned at start of project.		P_1	X		P_2 C_1		Start
4.1 Option B. Posttest comparison group design combined with collection of baseline data on project. Evaluation commissioned at end of project. Recall or secondary data used to reconstruct initial status of project group.		(P_1)	X		P_2 C_1		End
5.1 Posttest-only comparison group design.			X		P_1 C_1		End

(Continued)

	Start of Project	Intervention	Midterm	End of Project	Post-Project	Stage of Project When Evaluation Commissioned
Nonexperimental Designs						
6.1 Pretest–posttest single case project group design with no external comparison group. *Note:* Though it looks similar to the pipeline design, it is based on single cases, not group observations. This design is complicated to represent because the methodology requires that the treatment is applied sequentially in three separate cases, so more cells are required to represent all three phases.	C1 [(P1$_1$)]	X$_1$	C1 [P1$_2$] C2 [P2$_1$] X$_2$	C2 [P2$_2$] C3 [P3$_1$] X$_3$	C3 [P3$_2$]	Start
6.2 Longitudinal design with no comparison group	P$_1$	X	P$_2$	P$_3$	P$_4$	Start
6.3 Interrupted time series: This is a special case of Design 6.2, where more frequent observation points are available.	P$_1$ P$_2$ P$_3$ P$_4$ P$_5$	X	P$_6$ P$_7$ P$_8$	P$_9$ P$_{10}$ P$_{11}$	P$_{12}$ P$_{13}$ P$_{14}$	Before start
6.4 Option A. Pretest–posttest project group design without comparison group. Evaluation commissioned at start of project.	P$_1$	X		P$_2$		Start
6.4 Option B. Pretest–posttest project group design without comparison group. Evaluation commissioned at end of project.	(P$_1$)	X		P$_2$		End
7.1 Posttest analysis of project group without a baseline or comparison group.		X		P$_1$		End

a. Initial number refers to design frameworks in Table 11.2; second digit refers to a variant of the basic design.

b. The parentheses, e.g., (P$_1$) and (C$_1$), indicate designs in which the evaluation was not commissioned until late in the project cycle and baseline conditions of participants and comparison groups need to be estimated either through the use of secondary data from surveys conducted by other agencies or through the baseline reconstruction techniques discussed in Chapter 5.

1. Longitudinal Design with Pre-, Midterm, Post- and Ex-Post Observations on the Project and Comparison Groups (Design 1)

1.1. When to Use

This is the strongest RealWorld Evaluation (RWE) design framework. Although not all variants of this design involve randomly assigning units into experimental and control groups, random assignment is possible. Box F.1 illustrates a longitudinal design that did use random assignment, and Box F.2 gives an example where the project and comparison groups were statistically compared. Longitudinal designs require more observations than the typical pretest–posttest comparison group designs classified as Design 2. A longitudinal design framework requires collecting data on both the project and comparison groups during at least four different points in time. It also requires the evaluation to continue throughout and even after the life of a project. The first round of data is collected at the start of the project (baseline), and the final round of data is not collected until some time after the project has ended (ex-post). The advantages of this design are that it provides the most comprehensive and methodologically robust assessment of project impacts and **sustainability** as well as getting "inside the **black box**" to describe the process of project implementation, as well as trends over time.

Although more expensive than other RWE designs, this design is recommended for projects that have an important research function, to thoroughly test an experimental strategy or approach and where the evaluation will be used to guide future decisions on the continuation, modification, or expansion of a major project. The design can be used only when the evaluation begins at the start of the project so that relevant baseline data can be collected. It also requires the evaluation to continue over a relatively stable environment in which the project is expected to continue to operate more or less as planned and where it will be possible to revisit the comparison groups over a number of years. It may be difficult, for example, to apply the design to a large-scale, low-income urban development project because it is likely that the housing of many of the comparison groups will be demolished or dramatically restructured over the life of the project (even though the comparison groups are expected to remain largely intact during the period of project implementation).

1.2. Description of the Longitudinal Design

As for all designs, the design should be based on a program theory model (see Chapter 10). Design 1 compares the project and a comparison group at the start of the project (T_1), at midterm or even more frequently during the life of the project (T_2), at project completion (T_3), and some time (preferably several years) after the project has ended (T_4) to assess sustainability (see Table F.2). Among the advantages of having multiple observations made during the life of project implementation are being able to describe and assess the implementation process and to identify trends in outcome indicators over time.

A comparison or nonequivalent control group (C) is selected at the start of the project to approximate as closely as possible the project beneficiary group (P). The observations from the comparison group represent the **counterfactual,** or what the conditions of the project group would have been like if the project's interventions had not taken place. In other words, if the average household income of the comparison group increases between T_1 and T_3, it needs to be known whether there would have been a similar increase in the project group if the project intervention had not taken place.

Our use of the term *comparison* group, rather than *control* group, reminds us that it is rarely possible to assign subjects randomly to the project and control groups, so differences may exist between the characteristics of the two groups that could distort the interpretation of the findings. It also acknowledges that in the real world, communities not participating in our project cannot be "controlled" in terms of external factors or alternative developmental activities undertaken in those communities by other agencies.

Both groups are interviewed at Time 1 (T_1) before the project begins, and information is obtained on a set of indicators ($I_1, I_2 \ldots I_n$) measuring the variables that the project is intended to affect (e.g., household income, daily travel time, number of children attending school).

Information is also collected on the social and economic characteristics of the individuals or families, called **intervening variables,** that might affect project outcomes. Data collection is repeated at Time 3 (T_3) at the completion of project implementation (e.g., occupation of new houses, turning on the water supply, completion of the rural roads) and again a relevant amount of time after the project has been completed, to assess the sustainability of any impacts (T_4). Ideally, the analysis should also include the contextual factors and how they may have changed over the life of the project.

Table F.2   Design 1: Longitudinal Design

	Time	T_1 (baseline)	Project Intervention (over time)	T_2 (midterm)	T_3 (end of project)	T_4 (after project)
	Sample selection procedure					
Project group	While randomized selection is occasionally used, in most cases, participants will either be self-selected or selected by the project agency. Quasi-experimental matching procedures will be used for the comparison group: either using statistical matching (the strongest option) or judgmental matching.	P_1	X	$P_{2(n)}$	P_3	P_4
Comparison group		C_1		$C_{2(n)}$	C_3	C_4

T_1 = pre-project observation.

T_2 = observation(s) during project implementation period.

T_3 = project completion (when project funding ends).

T_4 = ex-post follow-up evaluation some time after project completion to determine sustainability.

P_1 and C_1 = baseline observations on the project and comparison groups before start of the project.

$P_{2(n)}$ and $C_{2(n)}$ = periodic (longitudinal) observations on both groups during project implementation to observe the processes of change; (n) indicates the number of observation points during implementation. Some evaluation designs use panel informants (a small subsample of the participants and perhaps comparison groups) to track trends over time. If only one observation is made at the midterm review, this would be simplified to P_2 and C_2.

X = implementation of the project (construction of schools, water system, etc.). It is important to remember that project implementation is a process that continues over time and is not a finite event occurring at a specific point in time.

If the observations P_1, P_3, C_1, C_3 and so on refer to the mean scores for each group (e.g., average income, average educational test scores, or average anthropometric scores) before and after, as well as with and without, project implementation, then a statistical test such as the *t*-test for the difference of means is used to determine whether the observed difference is statistically significant. If, on the other hand, the values refer to proportions (e.g., the proportion of children attending school or the proportion correctly answering a test question), then the appropriate statistical test would be a measure such as the *Z*-score for difference of proportions (Moore and McCabe 1999, chap. 8; see also Chapter 12 of the present book).

The advantages of this design are that it examines the processes and outcomes of project implementation over time, and it addresses the important issues of sustainability, which are ignored in many evaluations. This is the evaluation design that ideally would be most compatible with the program theory model presented in Chapter 2 and discussed in more detail in Chapter 10. It can serve both formative and summative evaluation purposes. Design 1 is a very robust design that can address many of the "threats to validity" discussed in Chapter 7. However, it also requires sizable resources in terms of budget and personnel because the survey questionnaire, or similar data collection instrument, is administered at four or more points in time during (and after) the life of a project, both within the beneficiary population and a comparison community.

As we will discuss in the RCT section below, it is rarely feasible to randomly allocate subjects to the project or control groups in most RealWorld social development programs. In these cases, multivariate analysis can be used to statistically control for differences between the project and comparison groups. Many refinements can be introduced into the basic design to assess multiple treatments or to capture impacts that evolve gradually over time (Shadish, Cook, and Campbell 2002; Valadez and Bamberger 1994).

The GAIN welfare-to-work program in California (see Box F.1) is an example of a longitudinal design that used random assignment to determine who would receive assistance with job search, basic education, vocational training, and unpaid work experience.

BOX F.1
AN EXAMPLE OF DESIGN 1.1 (LONGITUDINAL DESIGN WITH RANDOMIZED ASSIGNMENT): THE EVALUATION OF GAIN: A WELFARE-TO-WORK PROGRAM IN CALIFORNIA

GAIN was created in 1985 by the California legislature as California's main welfare-to-work program for recipients of Aid to Families with Dependent Children (AFDC). The program was designed to provide welfare recipients with job search assistance, basic education, vocational training, postsecondary education, and unpaid work experience to help them prepare for and find employment. Welfare recipients assigned to the program were required to participate in these activities. Those refusing to cooperate without "good cause" could have their welfare payments reduced as a penalty. The evaluation addressed four main goals: (1) to learn about the counties' experiences in turning this ambitious legislation into an operating program and welfare recipients' participation and experiences in it; (2) to determine GAIN's effects or impacts on recipients' employment, earnings, welfare, and other outcomes and whether positive

(Continued)

(Continued)

effects could be achieved in a variety of settings; (3) to assess how different program strategies influence those results; and (4) to determine the program's economic costs and benefits. Implementation issues were studied in 13 counties, and the full evaluation was concentrated in a subset of 6 of these counties, representing diverse areas of the state.

The evaluation made use of an array of QUANT and QUAL data, including employment and welfare administration records, program case data, staff and recipient surveys, field research, and fiscal data from a wide range of agencies. For the impact evaluation, more than 33,000 welfare recipients were randomly assigned to GAIN or a control group. The control group did not have access to GAIN services and was not subject to a participation mandate as a condition of receiving their full welfare grants. However, they remained free to enroll themselves in any services normally available in the community. Program impacts were analyzed using data from existing administrative records on employment, earning, welfare receipt, and food stamp payments (for all sample members) and the recipient survey (for a subsample). A cost-benefit analysis was used to estimate the overall financial gain or loss caused by the program for welfare recipients, government budgets and taxpayers, and society as a whole. The GAIN participant and control samples were interviewed regularly over a 5-year period.

SOURCE: Fitzpatrick, Christie, and Mark (2009).

The Bolivian Social Investment Fund evaluation (Box F.2) is an example of a longitudinal design that used statistical matching to evaluate two of the three components (health and water/sanitation) and randomized assignment for the third component (education).

BOX F.2
EXAMPLE OF DESIGN 1.2: LONGITUDINAL
DESIGN WITH STATISTICAL MATCHING: EVALUATING
THE BOLIVIAN SOCIAL INVESTMENT FUND

The Bolivian Social Investment Fund (SIF) was established in 1991 as a financial institution promoting sustainable investments in the social sectors, notably health, education, and sanitation. The program directs investments to poor communities that have been largely neglected by public service networks. The SIF was the first institution of its kind and has served as a prototype for programs in Latin America, Africa, Asia, and the Middle East.

The evaluation began in 1991 at the start of the project and continued over a period of 10 years. A baseline study was conducted in 1991, a second study was conducted in 1993 at the start of the second phase, and a follow-up study was conducted in 1997. A number of other studies were conducted up to 2000. It also included separate studies of the education, health, and water projects. The evaluation uses a wide range of techniques to assess the effectiveness of the targeting systems in reaching the poor: the impact of the social service investments on desired social outcomes such as improved school enrollment rates, health conditions and water availability, and the overall cost-effectiveness of the SIF as a mechanism for delivering social services to low-income communities.

For the health and water supply components, interested communities applied to participate in the project. These communities were then statistically matched with comparison communities using socio data from project records and other sources.

The evaluation design used random assignment for the education component with eligible communities being randomly assigned to the treatment and control groups, while for the health and water components, communities that elected to participate were statistically matched with comparison communities. Three subsamples were used: (a) a random sample of all households in rural Bolivia (plus the Chaco region), (b) a sample of households that live near the schools in the project and comparison areas (for the evaluation of the education component), and (c) a sample of households that would benefit from the water and sanitation component. The evaluation combined various data collection techniques at the level of the community and the household, and data were collected over a 10-year period.

The comparison of findings from randomized allocation designs and statistically matched designs (in education) found that randomization produced better-matched samples and detected some positive outcomes, such as improvements in school infrastructure in the project areas, that were not detected by the judgmentally matched samples.

SOURCE: Baker (2000).

1.3. Tools and Techniques for Strengthening All of the Basic Impact Evaluation Designs Described in This Appendix

All of the designs presented in Table F.1 and described in this appendix depict only the frameworks or scenarios under which these evaluation designs operate. The methodological validity and practical utility of all of these designs can be enhanced by incorporating one or more of the refinements described in Table F.3. These refinements are as follows:

- Basing the design on a program theory model that incorporates a theory of change and a theory of action (see Chapter 10)
- Incorporating process analysis to understand how the project is actually implemented and to assess how any deviations from the intended implementation plan affect efficiency, accessibility, and outcomes (see Chapter 10)
- Incorporating contextual analysis to understand the interaction between the project and the economic, political, institutional, and sociocultural context within which it operates

- Using mixed-method approaches that combine quantitative and qualitative design, data collection, and analysis methods so as to combine breadth (the ability to generalize from the sample to the total population) with depth of understanding of the lived experience of individual families, groups, or communities (see Chapter 14)
- Maximizing the use of all available types of secondary data
- Using triangulation to combine data and interpretation of findings from two or more independent sources so as to increase reliability and validity of the findings

Many of these techniques can also be combined to help reconstruct baseline data when the evaluation is not commissioned until late in the project cycle (see Chapter 5 for a full discussion of strategies for reconstructing baseline data).

Many of the examples of RealWorld evaluation designs presented in this appendix illustrate how evaluators incorporate these different techniques to strengthen the basic designs. For example, the evaluation of the GAIN welfare-to-work program (Box F.1) strengthened the longitudinal design with randomized assignment by incorporating a range of quantitative and qualitative methods to understand how different groups responded to the different components of the program and to understand how the program actually operated in different contexts.

Table F.3   Tools and Techniques to Strengthen Any of the Basic Impact Evaluation Designs (Reproduction of Table 11.5)

The tools and techniques described in this table can enhance the methodological rigor of all of these designs, including the designs that are considered to be statistically rigorous.

Essential Tools and Techniques	Why Required	How to Implement
1. Basing the evaluation on a theory of change and a program logic model	The purpose of an evaluation is not just to estimate "how much" change has occurred but also to explain "why" and "how" the changes were produced. Clients also wish to know to what extent the changes were due to the intervention and whether similar changes would be likely to occur if the program is replicated in other contexts. To achieve the above objectives, it is necessary to explain the underlying theory and the key assumptions on which the program is based and to identify how these can be tested in the evaluation.	The design and use of program theory is discussed in Chapter 10. That chapter also illustrates how the theory can be articulated graphically through a logic model.
2. Process analysis	Project outcomes are affected by how well a project is implemented and by what happens during implementation. Without process analysis, it is not possible to assess whether failure to achieve outcomes is due to design failure or to implementation failure.	See Chapters 10, 11 and 17
3. Contextual analysis	Projects implemented in an identical way in different locations will often have different outcomes due to different local economic, political, or organizational contexts or different socioeconomic characteristics of target communities. This can result in wrong estimations of project impact, often leading to underestimation of impacts (due to increased variance of the estimations).	See Chapters 10 and 11

Essential Tools and Techniques	Why Required	How to Implement
4. Using mixed-method approaches to strengthen evaluation design, data collection, and analysis	Most evaluation designs can be strengthened by combining QUANT techniques that ensure the statistical representativity of the data with QUAL methods that permit in-depth analysis and assessment of the quality of implementation, outputs, and outcomes.	See Chapters 12, 13, and 14
5. Identification and use of available secondary data	Many evaluations do not identify and use all of the available secondary data. Secondary data can often reduce the costs of primary data collection and provide independent estimates of key variables.	See Chapter 5
6. Triangulation	The validity of the data and the quality and depth of the interpretation of the findings are enhanced when two or more independent estimates can be compared.	See Chapters 13 and 14
7. Reconstructing baseline data	When evaluations are not commissioned until late in the project, it will frequently be the case that no baseline data had been collected. Several of the techniques described above (mixed methods, secondary data, and program theory models) can be combined to "reconstruct" and estimate the baseline conditions of the project and comparison groups.	See Chapter 5

All of these techniques can be used singly or in combination to strengthen all of the designs described in this appendix, but for reasons of space and to avoid repetition, the importance of incorporating these techniques will not be repeated.

1.4. Threats to Validity and Adequacy of the Conclusions

Design Framework 1 is the methodologically strongest RWE scenario (data collected at multiple times during and after the life of a project, with relevant counterfactual). Thus, if it is applied appropriately, most threats to validity and adequacy (see Chapter 7) should be less serious than for most of the subsequent design frameworks, especially if the design is complemented with appropriate QUAL methods. However, under RealWorld conditions, it is never possible to design a perfect evaluation, so it is always important to review the Integrated Checklist (Appendix C) to identify potential problems. Table F.4 identifies from this checklist some of the potentially important threats to conclusion validity affecting this design to which particular attention should be paid. Most of these threats to validity also affect the subsequent designs, but again, for reasons of space and to avoid repetition, we will not address threats to validity for each individual design.

These potential threats should be examined during the design phase and at later points during the evaluation. Where possible, corrective measures (see Chapter 7) should be taken. If this is not possible, the evaluation report must clearly identify the existence of these threats and how they affect the findings and conclusions.

Table F.4 Some Threats to Validity That Must Be Checked for Designs 1 and 2

Threats to statistical conclusion validity	
1. *Low statistical power*	The sample is too small to be able to detect statistically significant effects (see Chapter 12).
2. *Unreliability of measures*	The indicators do not adequately measure key variables.
3. *Restriction of range*	The sample does not cover the whole population. For example, the lowest or highest income groups are excluded, or the sample covers only enterprises employing more than 10 people.
4. *Unreliability of treatment implementation*	The treatments were not applied uniformly to all subjects, and often there is no documentation of the differences in application. For example, some mothers received malaria tablets and guidance from the nurse, but others received only the tablets.
Threats to internal validity	
1. *Selection bias*	Differences between project and comparison groups with respect to factors affecting outcomes
2. *Attrition*	While the project group is initially representative of the total population, certain subgroups (e.g., the less educated, women with small children, the self-employed) have higher dropout rates, so the people who are actually exposed to the project are no longer representative of the whole population.
3. *Reactivity to the data collection instruments*	Responses may be affected by how subjects react to the interview or other data collection methods. For example, respondents may report that they are poorer than they really are or that the project has not produced benefits because they are hoping the agency will provide new services or reduce the cost of current services.
Threats to construct validity	
1. *Inadequate explanation of constructs and program theory model*	The basic concepts of the model are not clearly explained or defined.
Threats to external validity	
6. *Influence of policymakers on program outcomes*	Support or opposition of policymakers in particular locations may affect program outcomes in ways that might be difficult to assess.
7. *Seasonal cycles*	Many surveys are conducted at only one time in the year and may not adequately capture important seasonal variations.

a. See Checklists 1 to 4 in Appendix A for the full list of threats. The numbers in the left column correspond to those given in the checklists.

2. Strong Statistical Designs

2.1. Randomized Control Trial (Design 2.1)

When to Use

RCTs are a powerful statistical design because, when the sample is sufficiently large to estimate the significance of changes given a particular effect size, they can eliminate selection bias (initial differences between the project and control groups that might explain part of the change that was assumed due to the project intervention). Thus, this design can be useful when it is important to obtain credible estimates of impact of a major social or economic development project or program. The designs work best when there is a single intervention that can be administered in a standard way and where the effects can be quantified (e.g., increase in income, increase in school enrollment rates, reduction in infant mortality). The designs also work better for large projects reaching large numbers of people and being implemented in many different locations. In this way, the effects of particular local contextual factors can be cancelled out and the average effect size estimated.

A number of factors, however, limit scenarios in which this design can be used. As indicated earlier (see Chapters 11 and 12), RCTs can only be used when subjects can be randomly assigned to treatment and nontreatment groups. In many cases, projects use participant self-selection, or participants are selected by the agency responsible for implementing the project. In other cases, there are political or ethical objections to the use of this model. The RCT design also only works well in a stable project environment where participant selection and service delivery can be implemented according to the project guidelines and in a stable way. The project environment must also remain relatively stable. A final limitation is that the basic RCT only estimates average project effect (it averages out contextual factors or participant attributes that can affect implementation and outcomes). So while this is useful for estimating the average effect of a large project, it makes it more difficult to use the findings to assess potential replicability in other locations with different population groups and different contextual factors.

The promotion of RCTs for the evaluation of international development programs, as well as within the United States, has sparked many heated debates among evaluators, donors, and other stakeholders (see Chapter 19 for a summary of the limitations of RCTs).

Description of the Design

Table F.5 illustrates a typical RCT design. The design can be represented as follows:

Table F.5 Experimental Design 2.1: Randomized Control Trial (RCT)

	Time	T_1		T_2
	Sample selection procedure		Project intervention[a]	
Project group	Subjects randomly assigned to project and control groups[b]	P_1	X	P_2
Control group		C_1		C_2

a. With RCT, the treatment is often administered at a specific point in time (e.g., a drug), but it can also continue to be administered over time (e.g., school meals, the use of a flip chart throughout the school year).

b. Random assignment will often be done in two or more stages, with one reason being to increase both external and internal validity (Khandker, Koolwal, and Samad 2010, chap. 9).

Box F.3 illustrates how a randomized control trial was used to assess the efficacy of a vaginal microbicide gel in reducing the likelihood that a woman would become infected with HIV after sex.

> ## BOX F.3
> ## EXAMPLE OF DESIGN 2.1: RANDOMIZED
> ## CONTROL TRIAL TESTING A VAGINAL MICROBICIDE GEL TO
> ## REDUCE THE LIKELIHOOD OF HIV INFECTION
>
> The Centre for the AIDS Program of Research in South Africa (CAPRISA) announced breakthrough research in 2010 on testing a vaginal microbicide gel containing an antiretroviral drug known as Tenofovir. Randomized control trials found that women who used the drug before and after sex were 39% less likely to become infected with HIV compared to the placebo gel users. The risk fell by 54% for women who used the drug consistently, and the risk of acquiring herpes simplex virus fell by more than half. The research, which is largely funded by USAID under the President's Emergency Plan for AIDS Relief (PEPFAR), is considered to be the first "proof of concept" of the efficacy of a vaginal gel that women can apply themselves without having to face the problems of negotiating the use of condoms with their sex partner. Susan Brems, the senior deputy assistant administrator in the Bureau for Global Health, stated, "This is the first ever 'proof of concept' (meaning that it works) that a vaginal microbicide can reduce the risk of sexually transmitted HIV. We all know that science consists of trial and error, and previous studies of microbicide candidates had not proved promising. While further testing is necessary, we now have renewed hope for a microbicide as we move forward."
>
> ---
>
> SOURCE: http://blog.usaid.gov/2010/12microbicide-gel-offers-protection-against-hiv-transmission

2.2. Pretest–Posttest Project and Comparison Group Designs with Statistical Matching (Designs 2.2–2.5)

When to Use

These designs are used under similar conditions to Design 1, but they are used more frequently because they cover a shorter time period (ending around the same time as the project) and are also relatively less expensive than the longitudinal design (Design 1) (although still more expensive than the less robust quasi-experimental designs [QED]) because data are collected at only two points in time rather than four or more. There are at least three variants of this design. If there is random selection of participants and a control group, it is a randomized control trial (Design 2.1 described above). In one variant (Design 2.2), the size of the sample and the quality of data make it possible to statistically match the two samples (see below), thus reducing selection bias. In another variant (Design 2.3), the two samples are matched using judgment (because the available statistical base is weaker) so that the potential selection bias is larger. In both cases, the design can only be used when it is possible to select a reasonably well-matched comparison group and to collect baseline data on both groups. This design is still fairly robust and is often the design of choice when the evaluation starts at the same time as the project and when a fairly rigorous project impact evaluation is justified (and, of course, when the resources are available). Design 2.3 (the judgmental matching of treatment and comparison groups) is a widely used and useful design, but greater care is needed to address the potential selection bias and to strengthen the design using the RWE techniques discussed earlier.

Description of the Design

Design 2.2 represents a simplified version of Design 1. It involves comparison of the project and nonequivalent comparison groups at the start of the project (T_1) and again at project completion (T_4). As always, it is recommended that the design should be based on a program theory model and should be combined with a process evaluation to analyze the project implementation and a contextual analysis to assess the influence of the economic, political, organizational, and natural environment within which the different project sites operate and to study the influence of cultural characteristics of the affected populations on program outcomes.

Table F.6   Design 2.2: Pretest–Posttest (Quasi-Experimental) Design with Statistical Matching of the Two Samples

Time		T_1 (baseline)	Project Intervention	T_3 (end of project)
	Sample selection procedure			
Project group	The project group is selected either through self-selection or administrative selection by the project agency.	P_1	X	P_2
Comparison group	Where secondary data are available from previously conducted surveys, it is possible to use techniques such as propensity score matching (PSM) (see Box F.5), or instrumental variables can be used to improve the matching. Where a large sample survey is possible, techniques such as PSM can also be used. Also, large samples permit the use of multiple regression to statistically control for the effect of subject attributes such as income, education, farm size, and so on.	C_1		C_2

Box F.4 presents an example of how this design was used to evaluate a conditional cash transfer program in Colombia (*Familias en Accion*).

BOX F.4
EXAMPLE OF DESIGN 2.2A: PRETEST–POSTTEST COMPARISON WITH STATISTICAL MATCHING—OPTION A: EVALUATION COMMISSIONED AT THE START OF THE PROJECT

Familias en Accion (FeA) is a conditional cash transfer (CCT) program launched in Colombia in 2001 and funded by the World Bank and the Inter-American Development Bank (IDB). It promoted increased access to health and education by providing monthly grants to poor families on the condition that children were brought to the local clinic for regular health check-ups and vaccinations and that children attended school regularly. All payments were made to the mother on the assumption that the money was more likely to benefit children. The program operated in municipalities with populations of less than 100,000 and required a bank branch to which funds could be transferred. Beneficiaries were selected from the lowest stratum of the social security register (Sisben).

A pretest–posttest comparison group design was used with the comparator groups selected from municipalities ineligible to participate in the program, in most cases because there was no bank branch to handle the funds transfer. The availability of good secondary data permitted the use of propensity score matching to reduce sample selection bias. The baseline studies were conducted in 2002 with follow-ups in 2003 and 2006. A total of 57 project and 65 control municipalities were sampled with approximately 100 interviews per municipality. Political pressures due to the upcoming elections forced FeA to advance the program launch, and families in a number of municipalities had already received payments before the baseline study was conducted. The World Bank and IDB were able to convince the government to delay program launch in some areas until the baseline studies could be conducted. Consequently, the baseline was divided into two groups: those who had not received any payments prior to the baseline and those who had.

Positive results could already be seen at the time of the first follow-up study one year after project launch (2003), particularly in rural areas. The results of the second 2006 follow-up were similar to the 2003 study: There was increased primary school enrollment in rural but not urban areas, increased secondary school enrollment in rural and urban areas, some improvements in nutritional status in rural areas but not in urban areas, and an impact on diarrhea occurrence for younger rural children but not for children older than 36 months. A major concern was the lack of effects on anemia, which affects half of all poor children. Reservations were expressed in the report and in conversations with policymakers concerning the extent to which findings from the small municipalities could be extrapolated to urban areas.

SOURCE: Bamberger and Kirk (2009).

Refinements to the Design

The design presented in this section is in fact the most basic design framework for pretest–posttest comparison group evaluations. Although cost and time constraints mean that this design is more likely to be used than the longitudinal Design 1 in RWE applications, a number of refinements can significantly strengthen the design (Shadish et al. 2002, chap. 5). Several of the refinements increase the number of pretest or posttest observation points, whereas others reverse the treatment between the project and comparison groups at different points. It is also possible to use **cohort analysis** in which successive groups passing through the same cycle (e.g., third-grade students, medical trainees, women receiving microcredit loans, families who will receive houses or public services in different phases of a project) are compared. One variant of this is to use subjects who will receive services or benefits in the next phase of a project as a comparison group for subjects who received the services in the first phase (see description of pipeline Design 2.4).

BOX F.5
PROPENSITY SCORE MATCHING (PSM)

PSM uses logistical regression to strengthen the match of the project and comparison group samples. The technique is most commonly used when a large sample survey is available that covers the geographical areas of interest to the evaluation and the appropriate information has been collected on the appropriate population groups. The technique is used both to reconstruct baseline data or for ex-post surveys. PSM can also be used when a sufficiently large primary sample survey is being conducted, but this application is less common. The technique involves the following steps:

a. Logistical regression (Logit) analysis is conducted with a combined sample of project participants and nonparticipants from areas that are considered appropriate as a comparison group. The first stage of the analysis, covering the project group, determines subject characteristics that are good predictors of participation.

b. For each subject in the project sample, around five "nearest neighbors" are selected from the comparison population who match the subject closely on all of these characteristics.

c. Baseline scores on the indicators to be used to measure changes in outcome variables are recorded for each participant, and the average score for the "nearest neighbors" of each subject are also computed.

d. The posttest scores are then calculated for each participant and the nearest neighbors, and a "change score" is calculated as the difference in the change for each participant compared to the average change for the nearest neighbors.

e. All of the individual change scores are summed to estimate the total change score.

The *Familias en Accion* evaluation discussed under Design 2.2A (Box F.4) is an example of the use of PSM.

SOURCE: Baker (2000:48–52) and Khandker et al. (2010, chap. 4).

Box F.6 illustrates how Design 2.2B was used to evaluate the effectiveness of a scholarship program in increasing girls' secondary school enrollment in Cambodia.

BOX F.6

EXAMPLE OF DESIGN 2.2B: PRETEST–POSTTEST DESIGN COMMISSIONED POSTTEST AND USING STATISTICAL MATCHING: EVALUATING THE EFFECTS OF A SCHOLARSHIP PROGRAM IN CAMBODIA IN INCREASING GIRLS' SECONDARY SCHOOL ENROLLMENT

The Japanese Fund for Poverty Reduction (JFPR) in Cambodia awarded scholarships to poor girls who were completing sixth grade and who wished to enter secondary school. The goal of the program was to encourage girls from poor families to enroll in secondary school and to complete the full three years of lower secondary school. The program covered 15% of all secondary schools, and in each, a maximum of 45 girls were awarded scholarships.

As the evaluation was not commissioned until late in the project, a retrospective evaluation design was used. Two sources of data were used: application forms for the scholarship program (information on parental education, household composition, ownership of assets, housing materials, and distance to the nearest secondary school) and data on school enrollment and attendance collected during unannounced school visits. Regression analysis was used to statistically control for socioeconomic characteristics of the households after the data had been collected on the project and comparison groups (i.e., it was not possible to use propensity score matching to match samples before data collection).

The evaluation found that scholarship recipients had significantly lower socioeconomic status than nonrecipients, confirming that the program had been successful in targeting poorer girls, After controlling for household characteristics, it was found that girls receiving scholarships had an almost 30% higher enrollment and attendance rate than nonrecipients and that the effects were greatest for the most disadvantaged girls.

In the evaluation of a follow-up World Bank project, the Ministry of Education had become aware of the benefit of a well-designed evaluation, and the evaluation was built into the project design. It was originally proposed to use a randomized control trial, but the Ministry was concerned that this would not permit targeting of the poorest families, so it was agreed to use a regression discontinuity design.

SOURCE: Adapted from Bamberger and Kirk (2009).

2.3. Regression Discontinuity (RD) (Design 2.3)

When to Use

RD is an evaluation technique that was used widely in the 1960s and 1970s in fields such as criminal justice (e.g., to assess the impacts of different treatments on recidivism rates). Its use then appeared to decline, but there has been renewed interest in recent years. RD can be used when the population of interest can be ranked on an ordinal or interval scale (assignment variable) that is used as the eligibility criteria for selection to participate in the project. A numerical eligibility cutoff point is defined on the scale; people above this cutoff are always accepted, and people below the cutoff are always rejected. Examples of assignment variable scales are number of hours of vocational training that prisoners received while in jail, a rating on a scale of psychological disorder or stress, or a rating on a scale of likelihood of success in a women's entrepreneurial management training program.

There are three very attractive features with RD: one methodological, one political and ethical, and one logistical. The methodological advantage is that when properly designed and administered, an RD design can produce unbiased estimates of project impact. The political and ethical advantage is that experts or program management can define the eligibility criteria for project participation. For example, an agricultural development project could be targeted for the smallest and poorest farmers (defined, for example, in terms of hectares of land owned), a school feeding program could be targeted for children from the poorest households (using an appropriate indicator of wealth, expenditure, or consumption), and a women's entrepreneurial development program could be targeted either to women considered most likely to succeed (based on an assignment variable scale rated by experts or managers) or to the poorest and most needy women. In all cases, eligibility criteria are determined by clients and stakeholders, thus avoiding political concerns that managers and influential stakeholders have no control over who receives benefits and the ethical concerns that benefits are withheld from the neediest groups while other less needy people might participate based on the luck of the lottery or other randomization process.

The logistical advantage is that the comparison group is generated automatically through the selection process (all falling below the cutoff eligibility criterion). In many cases, it is a major challenge to identify a comparison group, so having the group already selected can be a significant advantage.[2]

Description of the Design

The design requires the definition of a target population (e.g., prisoners being released from jail, high school students in low-income areas, small farmers). An assignment variable must then be identified. Normally this will be related either to need (poverty, low school test scores, low agricultural productivity) or to likelihood of success (hours of vocational training received, rating on a likelihood of entrepreneurial success scale). The scale must be ordinal or interval with precise and measurable scale positions, and it must be possible to rate everyone on the scale. A precise and measurable eligibility cutoff must also be defined, and it must be clear who falls above and below the cutoff.

A strict selection procedure must be applied so that everyone above the cutoff point is accepted and everyone below the cutoff is rejected. In practice, the strict application of the selection rule has proved to be a challenge. Sometimes the data are not available to apply the rating (hectares of land are not known, it is difficult to determine household wealth or income), sometimes there are pressures to relax the criteria to accept friends or people with political contacts, and in other cases, the administrative procedures are not well monitored.

---

[2]Some programs also provide a small benefit to the comparison group so as to give them an incentive to cooperate with the study. For example, an entrepreneurial training program invited members of the comparison group to attend a workshop on how to obtain information resources on the Internet. This benefit was considered a sufficient incentive to encourage people to cooperate with the study but not sufficient to affect their entrepreneurial activities.

Once selection has been completed and the program is implemented, the evaluation involves comparing subjects just above the eligibility cutoff point with those just below it. A regression is calculated between the score on the assignment variable and the posttest outcome score. If the project had an effect, there will be a discontinuity ("jump") in the regression line at the cutoff point. This is illustrated in Figure F.1 to assess the effect of constructing new schools and complementary interventions on school enrollment rates where the assignment variable is average household income in each school district and the cutoff point is average household income of $100 per month. In this case, the unit of analysis is the school district (not the family with school-age children). It can be seen that there appears to be a significant discontinuity around the $100 cutoff point. Of course, the significance of this break has to be calculated statistically.

One practical issue with the RD design is that it requires a relatively large target population because the sample for the evaluation only compares subjects falling just above or just below the cutoff point. As a rule of thumb, the 25% above the cutoff point are compared with the 25% just below it. So if a sample of 100 was required to obtain statistically significant results, it would be necessary to start with a target population of 200.

Box F.7 illustrates the use of a regression discontinuity design to evaluate the effects of a social safety net program in Jamaica.

BOX F.7

EXAMPLE OF DESIGN 2.3: REGRESSION DISCONTINUITY COMBINED WITH A MIXED-METHOD DESIGN: EVALUATING THE EFFECTS OF A SOCIAL SAFETY NET BASED ON A POVERTY INDEX IN JAMAICA

In 2001, the government of Jamaica initiated the Program of Advancement through Health and Education (PATH) to increase investments in human capital and improve the targeting of welfare benefits to the poor. The program provided health and education grants to children in eligible poor households, conditional on school attendance and regular health care visits. Eligibility for the program was determined by a scoring formula with a clearly defined cutoff. A regression discontinuity (RD) analysis was conducted comparing families 2 to 15 points below and above the cutoff. Researchers justified the use of the RD design because a baseline study showed that the treatment and comparison groups had similar levels of poverty and also had similar levels of motivation as both groups had applied to participate in the program. The RD was strengthened by using a mixed-method design that gathered data using information systems, interviews, focus groups, and household surveys.

The analysis found that the PATH program increased school attendance for children ages 6 to 17 by an average of 0.5 days per month, which is significant given an already high attendance rate of 85%. Also, health care visits by children ages 0 to 6 increased by approximately 38%.

SOURCE: Adapted from Gertler et al. (2011).

Table F.7   Design 2.3: Regression Discontinuity (RD)

	Sample selection procedure	T_1 Start of project	T_2 Implementation	T_3 End of project
Project group	The 25% of subjects above and closest to the eligibility criteria cutoff point	P_1	X	P_2
Comparison group	The 25% of subjects below and closest to the eligibility cutoff point	C_1	Sometimes the group is given a small service as an incentive to cooperate with the study	C_2

Figure F.1   Example of Regression Discontinuity (Design 2.3): Assessing Impact of School Construction and Complementary Interventions on School Enrollment Rates Where Assignment Variable Is Average Household Income in School District

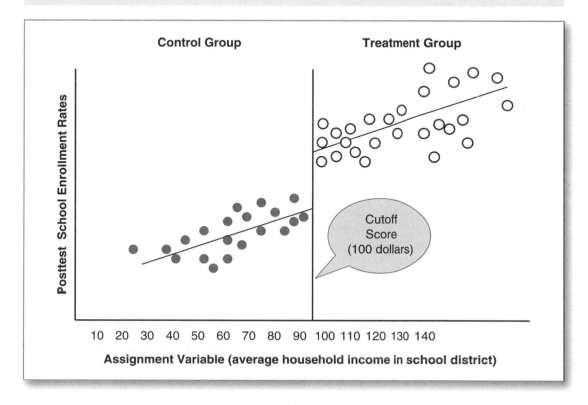

3. Weaker Statistical Designs

3.1. Pipeline Design (Design 2.4)

When to Use

This design is used when a project is implemented in phases and where communities or people who will not benefit until the second or a subsequent phase can be used as the comparison group for Phase 1. The design works best where the communities or individuals in each phase are similar, where the implementation schedule for each phase is known in advance, where all phases will eventually receive similar benefits, and where communities or individuals in Phase 2 and subsequent phases do not have access to benefits during Phase 1. In the real world, many projects do not satisfy all these conditions. For example, in a slum upgrading project, families in Phase 2 may walk several kilometers to collect water from the drinking water standpipes being installed for Phase 1. Also, it is quite common that the characteristics of communities in each phase are not identical.

The Evaluation Design

As mentioned above, it is first necessary to determine that the project will be implemented in clearly defined phases with an implementation schedule that is known in advance. It is also necessary to check that the characteristics of individuals or communities in each phase are similar and that people or communities in Phase 2 and subsequent phases will not have access to services during Phase 1. Once the project begins, monitoring studies should be conducted periodically to ensure that these conditions are satisfied in practice.

Assuming these conditions are met, a sample of households or communities that will participate in Phase 1 is randomly selected. A decision will then be made as to how the comparison group sample will be selected. If a project is implemented in several phases, it would be possible to only select the comparison group from Phase 2 (geographically closest to Phase 1 and probably more similar than communities further away) or to include households or communities from all subsequent phases or even to only select from the final phase. While Phase 2 families may be more similar to Phase 1, there are two potential disadvantages of using them as the comparison group. First, they can serve only as a comparison group until the time they begin to receive project benefits in Phase 2. Consequently, they can only be used to assess initial changes in Phase 1 up to the point when Phase 2 begins. Because in many cases, each phase is completed in one year or less, Phase 2 cannot be used to assess changes that take place more slowly. The second issue is that given its greater proximity, Phase 2 subjects are more likely to start having access to some project benefits before Phase 2 officially begins. The advantage of selecting the comparison group from Phase 3 or later is that they can continue to be used as a comparison over several years. Also, given their greater distance, they are less likely to gain access to the benefits of Phase 1. However, their greater distance might increase the likelihood that the group will have different characteristics from the participants in Phase 1. There is also the disadvantage of interviewing people from later phases because they may lose patience while waiting for the project's interventions to reach them.

For projects that are not geographically based but that provide cash or other services to people who may be distributed over a wider area, the considerations in selecting the comparison group may be slightly different. For example, the "leakage" of benefits such as access to water might not be a consideration when families are receiving cash payments.

Table F.8   Design 2.4: Pipeline Design

		T_1	T_2	T_3	T_4	T_5
	Sample selection procedure	Start of Phase 1	Implementation Phase 1	Start of Phase 2	Implementation Phase 2	Start of Phase 3
Project group for Phase 1	Random sample of Phase 1 households or communities	$P1_1$	X_1	$P1_2$		
Comparison group for Phase 1 [$C1_1$ and $C1_2$] which is also the project group for Phase 2 [$P2_1$ and $P2_2$]	Random sample of households or communities from Phase 2, from a later phase or from all phases after Phase 1	$C1_1$		$C1_2 = P2_1$	X_2	$P2_2$
Comparison group for Phase 2	Random sample of households or communities from Phase 3, from a later phase or from all phases after Phase 2			$C2_1$		$C2_2 = P3_1$

BOX F.8
EXAMPLE OF DESIGN 2.4 PIPELINE DESIGN: A QUASI-EXPERIMENTAL PIPELINE DESIGN TO EVALUATE A SOCIAL PROTECTION PROGRAM IN ARGENTINA

A large-scale social protection program, Jefes y Jefas (translation: male and female household heads), was launched in Argentina in 2001 in response to the financial crisis. The program was a public safety net that provided income to families with dependents for whom their main source of earnings was lost in the crisis. There were questions about how strictly the eligibility rules had been enforced, so it was decided to use a quasi-experimental design to assess the impacts of the program.

The evaluation design (Galasso and Ravallion 2004) took advantage of the fact that the program was scaling up rapidly, so it was possible to construct a comparison group of families who had not yet received benefits from the program. Propensity score matching (see Boxes F.4 and F.5) was used to match the project and comparison groups on a number of socioeconomic household characteristics. Panel data were also collected by the central government before and after the crises, and these were used to help remove fixed unobserved heterogeneity through double difference analysis.

(Continued)

(Continued)

The analysis found that the program's eligibility criteria were not enforced, with about one third of those receiving program benefits not satisfying the eligibility criteria. Also, about 80% of the adults who were eligible did not receive the program. Using double-difference analysis to control for selection bias, the study did find some positive benefits from the program—most important, a reduction in the drop of income that would have occurred without participation.

SOURCE: Adapted from Khandker et al. (2010).

3.2 Pretest–Posttest Project and Comparison Group Design with Judgmental Matching of the Two Samples (Design 2.5)

When to Use

This design (Table F.9) is similar to Designs 2.1 and 2.2 except that the two samples have to be matched judgmentally because secondary survey data are not available to permit statistical matching and the sample is not large enough to permit close matching through regression analysis. So typically, Design 2.5 is used in cases where a project is being implemented in a number of specific locations (e.g., low-cost housing, slum upgrading, micro-catchment irrigation projects) and where the evaluator must use judgment to select comparison communities or areas that match as closely as possible the project locations. Typically, the selection will be based on consultations with local experts and community leaders, review of secondary data (studies, maps, etc.), and where possible rapid visits to possible comparison sites. The evaluator then uses his or her judgment to select the best match.

The Evaluation Design

Table F.9 Design 2.5: Quasi-Experimental Design with Judgmental Matching of the Two Samples

Time		T_1 (baseline)	Project Intervention	T_3 (end of project)
	Sample selection procedure			
Project group	The project group is selected either through self-selection or administrative selection by the project agency.	P_1	X	P_2
Comparison group	The comparison group is selected through judgmental matching where consultations with experts, community leaders, and other relevant groups are combined with information from secondary sources (agency records, maps, any studies that have been conducted) and, where possible, rapid visits to possible comparison sites. The evaluator then uses judgment to select the best locations or groups.	C_1		C_2

Box F.9 illustrates how a pretest–posttest comparison group design with judgmental matching was used to evaluate the social and economic impacts of a low-cost housing program in El Salvador.

BOX F.9
CASE STUDY FOR DESIGN 2.5A: USING JUDGMENTAL MATCHING TO EVALUATE THE IMPACTS OF IMPROVED HOUSING ON HOUSEHOLD INCOME IN EL SALVADOR

A four-year evaluation was conducted in El Salvador between 1976 and 1980 to assess the impacts of improved housing on poor households in San Salvador, the capital. In 1976, a randomly selected sample of households was interviewed shortly before they entered a self-help housing construction project. A comparison group was selected by combining samples of randomly selected families from the three main types of inner-city housing from which project participants were selected. The samples were repeated in 1980. The survey was combined with various QUAL methods such as participant observation during project workdays and in comparison group communities, case studies of individual families, and interviews with key informants. These assessed the quality of implementation, examined factors affecting the participation of particular groups such as female-headed households and the self-employed, and also documented the influence of certain contextual variables such as the local economy and the involvement of government housing agencies.

It was found that between T_1 and T_3, the average household income for project participants had increased by 70.0% compared with an increase of 74.6% for the comparison group. Therefore, there was no evidence that improved housing had a positive impact on income, and in fact, the income of the comparison group rose slightly faster. This illustrates the importance of a carefully selected comparison group. If only project participants had been studied, one might have concluded that "improved housing has a significant impact on household income because the income of participants in the low-cost housing project increased by 70% in four years."

SOURCE: Valadez and Bamberger (1994).

3.3. Truncated Pretest–Posttest Project and Comparison Group Design (Design 3.1)

When to Use

This design is used when an adequate budget is available but the major constraint is that the evaluation did not begin until the project was already under way for some time. Often the initial evaluation event will be part of the midterm project review, which is often commissioned between two and three years after the start of a five-year project. The size of the sample and the complexity of the design can be adapted according to whether this is a pilot project or a well-tested program, and according to the types of decisions to which the evaluation will contribute. As with any evaluation design, the pretest–posttest impact assessment should be complemented with a process evaluation.

Description of the Design

The truncated QED design is used when the evaluation cannot begin until around midterm, when the project has already been operating for some time but at least another 18 months remain in its operational cycle. The first observation is considered a proxy (delayed) baseline, while recognizing that there is reduced time to produce and measure outcomes. If there is time (e.g., several more years), observations could be repeated at several points between the midterm and end of the project to observe the process of project implementation. The final observation is then made at T_3, around the time of project completion.

Table F.10 Design 3: Truncated Pretest–Posttest Project and Comparison Group Design Starting at the Time of the Midterm Review

Time	Sample selection procedure	T_1 (baseline)	Project Intervention (continues past midterm)	T_2 (midterm)	T_3 (end of project)
Project group	Selection of the comparison group will be based on statistical or judgmental matching. The approach is similar to Designs 2, except selection is made when the project has already been operating for some time (there was no initial baseline).		X	P_1	P_2
Comparison group				C_1	C_3

As always, it is recommended that the design be based on a program theory model and include a contextual analysis to assess the influence of the economic, political, organizational, and natural environment within which the different project sites operate and to study the influence of cultural characteristics of the affected populations on program outcomes. Box F.10 illustrates how QUAL and mixed methods were incorporated into the design of an evaluation of a feeder roads project (rural roads connecting villages to the main road network) in Eritrea. These were used for purposes of triangulation (comparing secondary sources with observational estimates of the volume and types of road transport), conducting a process analysis of project implementation, and evaluating the quality of road construction and maintenance. Observational techniques were also used to reduce the costs of obtaining data on vehicular and pedestrian traffic.

BOX F.10
CASE STUDY FOR DESIGN 3 (TRUNCATED DESIGN) COMBINED WITH DESIGN 2.5B (JUDGMENTAL MATCHING PRETEST–POSTTEST): ASSESSING THE SOCIAL AND ECONOMIC IMPACTS OF A FEEDER ROADS PROJECT IN ERITREA

This evaluation did not begin until the project had reached midterm. It combined an end-of-project survey of the project areas combined with a simple longitudinal study to observe the process of change. The purpose of the evaluation was to assess impacts of the road on access to schools (increased enrollment), use of local health facilities, and volume and prices of agricultural produce sold. The evaluation was not able to identify a comparison group that would serve to assess the three different outcomes, so judgmental matching was used to identify separate comparison groups for assessing each outcome:

- A sample of schools in the same regions as the roads that did not have access to the newly constructed roads. School attendance records were used to measure changes in enrollment in the year prior to the construction of the road and in the year the road was constructed.
- A sample of local health centers in the same region as the roads but that did not have access to the newly constructed roads. Records on the average number of patients attended to each week in the year before the road was constructed and the year the road was constructed were analyzed.
- Almost all agricultural produce was bought and sold in the local cooperative markets. A sample of agricultural markets was selected that served both the villages with access to the new roads and those that did not have access. Volumes and prices of sales and purchases were compared in the year prior to road construction and the year of construction.

Observations were made at three points during the approximate nine-month period of road construction to document changes such as the number of small businesses operating along the route of the future road, the number of pedestrians, the number of trucks and buses, and the number of people visiting the health clinic. Observation was also used during road construction workdays to assess the efficiency of organization and the quality of construction and maintenance. Data reliability was strengthened through triangulation of findings from focus groups, key informant interviews, and direct observation. Baseline conditions were reconstructed through recall, and secondary data compensated for the lack of a comparison group.

SOURCE: Unpublished national consultant report. The study was supervised by one of the present authors.

3.4. Elimination of the Baseline Comparison Group (Pretest–Posttest Project Group Combined with Posttest-Only Analysis of Project and Comparison Group) (Design 4.1)

When to Use

This design is used either when the evaluation begins at the start of the project (Option A) or when the evaluation starts later but previously secondary or recall data representing baseline conditions for the project group can be obtained (Option B). Baseline data are not collected on comparison groups for a number of reasons: to save money, because of technical or ethical difficulties in collecting the data, or because management does not consider this necessary. It is quite common that when the project begins, management does not feel it is necessary to include a comparison group because they feel the purpose of the evaluation is simply to compare the project group before and after the project intervention. However, as the project evolves and there is a need to justify an extension or the launch of a new project, the need for a comparison group is understood. Consequently, it is not uncommon for the evaluator to be asked to create a comparison group for the end-of-project evaluation.

Description of the Design

In this design (Option A), a baseline survey is conducted with the intended project beneficiaries before the project begins, but no comparison group is used at this stage. Only at the time of the final project evaluation (in T_3) is a survey conducted that includes both project and comparison groups. This design works reasonably well for assessing how a project is being implemented and whether it is able to produce the intended outputs. It is also able to compare the characteristics of the project group and the comparison group at the time the project completes its work. If, retrospectively, it can be adequately documented that the comparison group was essentially the same as the project group at the time the project started (T_1), this design may be sufficient to demonstrate project effects.

For example, with a rural road construction project, surveys and participatory consultations with the community may have identified a number of factors affecting the willingness of the community to participate in the project and the benefits they obtain from the road. These factors might include whether local culture permits women to participate in road construction and to travel to the market, the distance from the local market, and the agricultural surplus available to sell. A comparison group, if it is well selected, could rate other local communities on these variables and hence determine the likelihood that the project would be well received and would have an impact in other areas. The project and comparison groups could also be compared on indicators such as amount of produce sold in the local markets, average number of trips and distance traveled, and kinds of consumer goods available in community shops.

As always, the design should be based on a program theory model and should be combined with a process evaluation and a contextual analysis.

Table F.11   Design 4: Elimination of the Baseline Comparison Group (Pretest–Posttest Project Group Combined with Posttest Analysis of Project and Comparison Groups)

Time		T_1 (baseline)	Project Intervention	T_3 (end of project)
	Sample selection procedure			
Project group	Purposeful selection of project participants	P_1	X	P_2
Comparison group	No baseline comparison group. Posttest comparison group selected statistically or judgmentally depending on the availability of secondary data and the sample size.			C_1

Incorporating Mixed-Method Approaches into the Design

In addition to the incorporation of a process and contextual analysis, a mixed-method approach can be very helpful for reconstructing the baseline conditions of the comparison group. For the interpretation of the findings, it is important to have the best information possible on how similar the characteristics of the project and comparison groups were at the time the project started. In the case of the Maharashtra (India) irrigation project (see Box F.11), QUAL methods (informal conversations with neighbors and key informants) were used to identify former residents who had not been eligible for compensation of new land and who had moved out of the area. A **tracer study** was then conducted with these families to compare their situation with the project families who had received compensation.

BOX F.11
CASE STUDY FOR DESIGN 4.1 (WITH ELEMENTS OF DESIGN 1): COMPARING THE EFFECTS OF RESETTLEMENT ON PROJECT BENEFICIARIES AND NONBENEFICIARIES IN THE SECOND MAHARASHTRA IRRIGATION PROJECT, INDIA

Sample surveys were conducted periodically between 1978 and 1985 in areas from which families were to be resettled as a consequence of a large-scale irrigation project. The study covered only families who were eligible to receive land or housing plots in the relocation areas. The surveys were repeated in 1990 after project families had been

(Continued)

(Continued)

relocated. An ex-post comparison group survey was conducted in 1990 with a sample of families who had remained in the command area of the irrigation project. This was not an ideal comparison as many of the sample households forced to move as a result of the dam had remained in the project, so their situation did not really represent families not affected by the dam. Recognizing that no information was available on the approximately 45% of families who were forced to relocate but who were not eligible for compensation, a tracer study was conducted in 1990 to try to identify these families. The study found that the economic conditions of most families receiving compensation had improved. The situation concerning the families who had not received compensation was more mixed, but in general, forced resettlement appeared to have had less negative consequences than had been expected.

SOURCE: Valadez and Bamberger (1994:264–66, summarizing World Bank 1993).

3.5. Posttest-Only Comparison Group Design (Design 5)

When to Use

This design is used when the evaluation does not begin until near the end of project implementation or the project has recently been completed. Despite the late start, evaluations using this design are often quite well funded, and it is often possible to administer surveys to quite large samples of subjects in both the project and comparison groups. In other cases, the evaluation is based on secondary data from household, agricultural, labor force, and other surveys that had been collected for some other purposes.

Description of the Design

This design relies entirely on an end-of-project comparison between the project group and a non-equivalent control group (comparison group), and no baseline data were collected on either the project or comparison areas. It can be used to obtain an approximate estimate of project impacts. The design works better in isolated communities where the project is the only major outside intervention so that it is less important to isolate the effects of other interventions taking place at the same time. It can also be used to compare the characteristics of project participants with people from other similar communities. If project households have similar characteristics to other communities (other than those characteristics affected by the project's interventions), then it is more likely that the results of the pilot project can be generalized. If, on the other hand, there are significant differences between the two groups, it will be more difficult to generalize.

The fact that large, carefully selected samples are often used means that the analytical **power** of the design can be strengthened through the use of multivariate analysis to statistically control for differences between the two groups.

Table F.12   Design 5: No Baseline Data (Posttest-Only Project and Comparison Groups)

Time	Sample selection procedure	T_1 (baseline)	Project Intervention	T_3 (end of project)
Project group	Purposeful selection of project participants	P_0 secondary data sometimes permit the reconstruction of baseline data (see Chapter 5)	X	P_1
Comparison group	Many evaluations use secondary data to select the sample and to use statistical matching. In some cases, secondary data are also available at the time of project launch as this is used to reconstruct baseline data. When secondary survey data are not available, judgmental matching must be used.	C_0 secondary data are sometimes available to reconstruct a baseline comparison group. See Chapter 5 for a discussion of ways to address the issue of missing variables (also called "unobservables")		C_1

BOX F.12

CASE STUDY FOR DESIGN 5: ASSESSING THE IMPACTS OF MICROCREDIT ON THE SOCIAL AND ECONOMIC CONDITIONS OF WOMEN AND FAMILIES IN BANGLADESH

In 1991–1992, a random sample of households was interviewed in a sample of villages where some of the leading village bank programs were operating in rural Bangladesh. A comparison group was interviewed in villages where none of these village bank programs were operating. The surveys were conducted ex-post when the village banks had already been operating for several years. No baseline information had been collected on the condition of families before the banks began to operate. It was found that borrowing from a village bank had a much greater impact on women than on men (although the latter also benefited). Per capita household expenditures increased almost twice as fast when women received loans rather than men, housing conditions improved, and personal savings increased. Interestingly, it was found that contraceptive usage declined for women borrowers, and their fertility increased. The lack of baseline data made it difficult to determine to what extent the observed differences between the project and comparison groups were due to the effects of the project or whether they were due, at least in part, to differences that already existed before the project began.

SOURCES: Khandker (1998), Baker (2000, Annex 1.2), and World Bank (2001).

Incorporating Mixed-Method Approaches into the Design

Often this design relies exclusively on QUANT data collection and analysis, particularly when the evaluation is based on survey data collected for some other purpose. A fundamental weakness of the design is that it does not control for historical events or for preexisting differences between the project and comparison groups. Mixed methods can significantly strengthen the design by obtaining information on the characteristics of the two groups at the time the project began. This can be obtained through focus groups, participatory appraisal (PRA) techniques (see Chapter 5), or interviews with key informants. For example, in the evaluation of the impacts of microcredit programs in Bangladesh (Box F.12), the analysis found that when women obtained loans, this had a greater impact on household expenditures, investment in housing, and children's school enrollment than when men obtained loans. It was assumed that the difference was due to the strong emphasis of the credit groups on group development and strengthening women's self-confidence. However, an alternative hypothesis, which could not be tested on the basis of the survey data, would be that the women who decided to apply for loans already had more self-confidence and perhaps entrepreneurial experience. This hypothesis could have been tested through some of the mixed-method approaches described above. This assumes, of course, that it would be possible for the researchers to go to the field to apply these techniques.

BOX F.13

EXAMPLE OF DESIGN 5B: POSTTEST COMPARISON COMBINING STATISTICAL MATCHING WITH A MIXED-METHOD DESIGN—EVALUATING NICARAGUA'S SCHOOL-BASED REFORM: A RETROSPECTIVE, MIXED-METHOD DESIGN WITH STATISTICAL MATCHING

The decentralization reform in Nicaragua was a principal element of the coalition government that replaced the Sandinista regime in 1990. The reform aimed to give schools power over key managerial and pedagogical decisions and transfer financial administration directly to the schools. By the end of 1995, more than 100 secondary schools had signed a contract with the Ministry of Education to establish a directive council and become autonomous. The three questions addressed in the first phase of the evaluation were as follows:

- Whether autonomous public schools exercise greater control over their management than do traditional public schools
- Whether (and which) local stakeholders (directors, teachers, council members) affect school decisions
- How local stakeholders perceive the changes that have occurred in schools since autonomy

The evaluation was not commissioned until 1995, at the start of Phase 3 of the reform program but when the program had already been under way for five years. Consequently, a retrospective mixed-method evaluation design was used. The mixed-method design permitted the use of triangulation to first *corroborate* the quantitative findings and to ensure *convergent* validity and, second, to use qualitative techniques for *elaboration* to expand our understanding of the reform as presented by the initial results of the quantitative studies.

A matched comparison group design was used in which autonomous (reformed) schools were compared with nonautonomous (traditional, nonreformed) schools. Matching was based on the timing of the reform and the school's size and location. The lack of pre-reform baseline data meant that the matching was not as precise as when secondary data permitted the use of propensity score matching. Three quantitative data collection instruments were used:

- A school survey using a random sample of 242 schools, including both autonomous and nonautonomous schools at both the primary and secondary levels. The survey covered, among other indicators, enrollment, level of absenteeism, grade repetition and dropout, physical resources, training and experience of staff, and changes since reform. A special questionnaire was developed to determine whether the school made important decisions and to determine whether respondents felt influential in the decision-making process.
- A household survey covering 3,000 randomly selected students from the surveyed schools and followed to their household. This determined the socioeconomic status of the households and parents' participation in school affairs.
- Achievement tests in math and language were applied to a sample of third-grade primary and second-year secondary students to compare schools' academic performance.

Qualitative methods were applied in a subsample of 18 schools to develop typologies, assess beneficiary perspectives, examine the context in which the reform was introduced, and examine the decision-making dynamics in each school. The aim was to detect patterns and to highlight variations across schools and actors. Methods included focus groups with parents, teachers and school council members, and key informant surveys with the school director and local officials from the Ministry of Education.

The initial findings showed that the reforms were successful in expanding the role of the schools in governance. In the quantitative surveys, about half of the respondents reported that school performance had improved in the reform schools, while the other half said there was no change.

SOURCE: Rawlings (2000).

4. Nonexperimental Designs (NEDs) (Designs 6 and 7)

We classify nonexperimental designs (NEDs) into two categories: those that include baseline data on the project group (so that a pretest–posttest project group–only design can be used) and designs that only collect data on the project group at one point in time, normally toward the end of the project cycle. There is another important distinction that we emphasize and that concerns the reasons for selecting an NED. Many evaluation textbooks assume that NEDs are used only as a last resort when budget and time constraints do not permit the use of a "stronger" evaluation design. However, there are many situations in which experienced evaluators select an NED, considering it the strongest design for assessing causality in a given context. So we make a distinction between situations in which a "basic" NED is used as a default option due to budget and time constraints and situations in which NEDs are considered the strongest available design.

4.1. Pretest–Posttest No-Comparison Group Designs (Designs 6)

When to Use

With this design, the evaluation begins at the start of the project, but for budget, technical, or political reasons, baseline data are collected only on the project group, and there is no comparison group, either at the beginning or at the end of the project. In some cases, this design is selected in consultation with the client due to budget constraints. However, there are other situations in which it was originally intended to collect baseline data on a comparison group, but this proved to not be possible due to political or technical reasons. The design works reasonably well for projects using "best practice" interventions that have been previously proven to work under very similar conditions—for example, the construction of a village school or clinic where there was previously no such facility within easy access. It can also work well when the purpose of the evaluation is to understand the project implementation process and where QUANT assessment of impacts is less important.

Description of the Design

This design is based on a comparison of baseline data collected on the project population at the start of the project (pretest), with similar posttest data collected toward the end of the project. No comparison group is included, and consequently, it is not possible to use a conventional counterfactual to control for alternative explanations of the observed changes. In its basic form, this design is very weak because it implicitly assumes that all of the observed changes in outcome indicators are due to the project intervention.

As always, the design should be based on a program theory model and should be combined with a process evaluation and a contextual analysis. However, in many cases, none of these options are included due to budget and time constraints.

An Option B will sometimes be used when the evaluation is commissioned at the end of the project and baseline data are "reconstructed" using some of the strategies discussed earlier.

Table F.13 presents the basic design.

Table F.13   Design 6: Basic Pretest–Posttest Project Group Design with No Comparison Group

Time		T_1 (baseline)	Project Intervention	T_3 (end of project)
	Sample selection procedure			
Project group	Random sample of project participants at start of the project. If a panel sample is used, the same subjects will be reinterviewed in T_3 (with appropriate procedures to adjust for subjects who cannot be reinterviewed or new subjects who have entered) (see Chapters 11 and 12). A second option is to select a new random sample in T_3.	P_1	X	P_2
Comparison group	No comparison group was included in the design.			

Box F.14 illustrates how this basic design was used to evaluate the impact of a hydroelectric project in Thailand on households that were resettled.

BOX F.14
CASE STUDY FOR DESIGN 6.4: USING A BEFORE-AND-AFTER SURVEY OF RESETTLED HOUSEHOLDS TO EVALUATE THE IMPACT OF THE KHAO LAEM HYDROELECTRIC PROJECT IN THAILAND

The project called for the involuntary resettlement of 41 affected villages with a total of 1,800 families. A survey of 50% of the intended beneficiaries was conducted in 1978–1979 prior to the start of the project, and a follow-up survey was conducted in 1989–1990 with 200 resettled families. No formal comparison group was used either before or after resettlement, although the research team consulted available secondary sources. While the comparison of quantitative surveys conducted before and after resettlement showed that families were better off on the basis of a set of economic indicators, a qualitative survey found that the majority of families considered themselves to be worse off. No information was available on the families who did not move to resettlement areas or on the 30% who did not remain in the project.

SOURCE: Valadez and Bamberger (1994:259–61).

The Single-Case Design (SCD)

This design has traditionally been used in the behavioral and health sciences to assess the effects of a treatment on an individual or small group, for example, in a school classroom or a managed health care facility. However, there has recently been renewed interest in this design due to the recommendation of a panel of experts convened by the Department of Education that the SCD, when properly administered, could be considered a methodologically rigorous design for assessing a range of educational interventions (Kratochwill et al. 2010). According to Kratochwill et al. (2010), SCDs have the following features:

- An individual "case" is the unit of intervention and the unit of data analysis. A case may be a single participant or a cluster of participants (e.g., a classroom or community).
- Within the design, the case provides its own control for purposes of comparison. For example, the case's series of outcome variables are measured prior to the intervention and compared with the measurements taken during and (after) the intervention.
- The outcome variable is measured repeatedly within and across different conditions or levels of the independent variable. These different conditions are referred to as phases (e.g., baseline, intervention phase).

Very rigorous evidence standards must be applied before the results can be considered convincing evidence of a causal relationship. The present authors are not aware of the SCD approach having been applied outside school, clinical, and managed health care settings, so it is not yet clear whether and how the approach could be used in development evaluation. However, the SCD approach is potentially attractive for the evaluation of development interventions at the level of a village or small group because an analysis of the specific group context and behavioral dynamics might produce change. It would then be possible to test whether similar results were found in similar settings to assess how far it would be possible to generalize the results. This approach is at the other end of the spectrum from RCT and other statistical designs that estimate average effect for a large population but can say nothing about the likely effect of the treatment on a particular individual or group.

Box F.15 illustrates how SCD was used to evaluate the effectiveness of a behavioral therapy for a schoolgirl with Asperger's disorder. This study used the "withdrawal design" (defined as ABA) in which the baseline condition is observed and measured for some time to obtain a stable measurement, and the treatment is administered for a certain time (which can be as short as a few minutes or may last several weeks) and is then withdrawn. This treatment cycle is repeated several times (at least three times under similar conditions and ideally four or five times), and if the same pattern of change is observed (and if this is rated as large enough to be significant) in each cycle, this is considered evidence that the treatment has been successful. For research purposes, the cycle would be repeated in other similar situations to build a body of evidence on the conditions under which the treatment appears to be successful.

BOX F.15
DESIGN 6.1: SINGLE-CASE DESIGN: TREATING A SCHOOLGIRL WITH ASPERGER'S DISORDER

Lakeesha was a 12-year-old African-American girl beginning seventh grade and diagnosed with Asperger's disorder. Some of the symptoms included difficulty in interacting with peers, reduced eye contact, "odd" facial expressions and gestures, a lack of social or emotional reciprocity, and failure to develop appropriate peer relationships. The treatment involved the most common single-case "withdrawal design" in which baseline measurements are made, usually based on observation, followed by the administration and then withdrawal of the treatment. The behavioral indicators are recorded during treatment and again after withdrawal. This is referred to as the ABA single-case design. The ABA cycle is repeated three or, ideally, four times: ABA ABA ABA ABA. A group of experts reviews the observational data, and if significant behavioral change has occurred in each cycle, this is considered credible evidence that the treatment had an effect.

In the case of Lakeesha, the "buddy" system was used in which another child with similar interests (in this case, interest in solving geometry proofs and interest in animal tracks) was trained to help Lakeesha master and use five sets of skills in which she had been coached: (a) sharing ideas, (b) complimenting others, (c) offering help or encouragement, (d) recommending changes nicely, and (e) exercising self-control. The peer buddy was asked to reinforce Lakeesha simply by smiling at her or telling her she was going a great job when she engaged in one of these skills.

Prior to initiating the program, Lakeesha's behavior was tracked over a four-week baseline period. On one of the indicators, initiating conversations with others, she did not initiate any conversations over the four-week observation period. During the first five-week treatment period, the number of conversations Lakeesha initiated increased steadily to nine per week. During the first withdrawal period, the number dropped steadily to zero after three weeks. During the second treatment period, the number of conversations initiated rose steadily to eight. By chance, the initial peer buddy moved to another school and was no longer able to participate, and a new buddy was trained. The results were similar with the second buddy, thus reinforcing the conclusion that the treatment was effective.

This summary greatly oversimplifies the design and the care that is needed during administration and analysis to control for internal and external threats to validity.

SOURCE: Adapted from Morgan and Morgan (2009).

Longitudinal NED Design (Design 6.2)

A longitudinal NED involves the continued observation of a sample of individuals or groups over a long period of time (but no comparison group). Observations are made on the same sample on a regular basis to observe the process of change. Often the design will include a pretest–posttest comparison to measure changes that have occurred over the life of the project, but the periodic observations also make it possible to study the process of change, focusing on both how the program is implemented and how implementation and the response of the subjects are affected by local contextual factors. As the NED does not include a comparison group, the effects of the intervention are estimated by detailed description of the processes of change.

Longitudinal NED designs can also be used to provide a broad analysis of the contextual factors that influence the operation of a particular institution such as a school. These studies can help define the broader contextual factors that need to be taken into consideration when evaluating the effectiveness of programs designed to improve the performance of institutions such as schools or to increase their accessibility to low-income and vulnerable groups.

Box F.16 describes a seven-year longitudinal study that examined the interactions between school and education for teenage girls and boys from different backgrounds in Australia.

BOX F.16

DESIGN 6.2: LONGITUDINAL DESIGN WITHOUT COMPARISON GROUP: THE 12–18 PROJECT—MAKING LIVES MODERN IN AUSTRALIA

The 12–18 Project was a study of subjectivity, schooling, and social change funded by the Australian Research Council. Over a seven-year period (1993–2000), the researchers interviewed and videotaped 26 young Australians (14 girls and 12 boys) as they aged from 12 to 18 years The young people came from diverse backgrounds and attended four different types of schools. Interviews were undertaken twice annually over the high school years and twice in the year afterwards. In the researchers' words, "We listened to these students talk about their sense of self, their values, attitudes to the future, and their experiences of school. Their individual narratives illuminate the uneven and differentiated impact of contemporary social and gender change, and the profound influence of school, community and culture on the shaping of subjectivity" (McLeod and Yates 2006:2).

Central to the research design of the study was a focus on *school culture,* and the sample of 26 was carefully constructed to include young people from similar class backgrounds going to different schools, as well as those from a different class background in the same school—avoiding the conflation of the "habitus" of school and family that characterizes so much educational research. So although the study followed individuals over time, it was also a comparative study of institutional culture and the way that institutions shape subjectivities.

SOURCE: McLeod and Thomson (2009).

Interrupted Time Series (Design 6.3)

An interrupted time-series design can be used when there is a continuous series of data that begins well before the intervention being studied and continues during the implementation and for some time afterwards (Shadish et al. 2002, chap. 6). Typical examples include information on traffic accidents or arrests of drivers, records of malnutrition or low birth weight children, school enrollment and attendance records or school test scores, and recidivism rates (the proportion of criminals released from jail who are rearrested within a certain time, often six months). The design is used to determine whether there is a significant break in the time series or a change in the slope at the point where an intervention, such as a change in the traffic laws or the legal drinking age or an incentive program to increase school enrollment, is introduced. For example, traffic accidents or driving arrests might fall after a new law is introduced, or school enrollment might increase.

Box F.17 presents an example of an interrupted time-series analysis used to assess the effect of raising the legal drinking age on the number of drinking-related traffic accidents.

BOX F.17
DESIGN 6.3: INTERRUPTED TIME SERIES: ESTIMATING THE EFFECTS OF RAISING THE DRINKING AGE

During the early 1980s, many U.S. states raised the minimum drinking age from 18 to 21, especially after passage of the Uniform Drinking Age Act of 1984, which reduced highway construction funds to states that maintained a drinking age younger than 21. Wisconsin raised its drinking age to 19 in 1984 and then to 21 in 1986. To assess the impact of these changes, David Figlio (1995) examined an 18-year time series of monthly observations of alcohol-related traffic accidents, stratified by age, that was available from the Wisconsin Department of Transportation from 1976 to 1993. Statistical time-series models were fit to the data for 18-year-olds (who could legally drink prior to 1984), for 19- and 20-year-olds (who could legally drink prior to 1986), and for those older than 21 (who could legally drink over the whole time period). The outcome variable in these analyses was the rate of alcohol-related crashes per thousand licensed drivers in the respective age group.

The results showed that for 18-year-olds, raising the minimum drinking age to 19 reduced the alcohol-related crashes by an estimated 26% from the prior average of 2.2 per month per 1,000 drivers. For 19- and 20-year-olds, raising the minimum age to 21 reduced the monthly crash rate by an estimated 19% from an average of 1.8 per month per 1,000 drivers. By comparison, the estimated effect of the legal changes for the 21 and older group was only 2.5% and statistically nonsignificant. The evaluator's conclusion was that the imposition of increased minimum drinking ages in Wisconsin had immediate and conclusive effects on the number of teenagers involved in drinking-related crashes, resulting in substantially fewer crashes than prelegislation trends would have generated.

SOURCE: Rossi, Lipsey, and Freeman (2004, Exhibit 9-H, p. 293). Adapted from Figlio (1995).

Case Study Designs

"Case studies explore real-life events in a natural setting" (Yin 2004:xii). Chapter 13 described a number of different ways that case study designs can be used in program evaluation and the different sample selection procedures that can be used depending on the purpose of the study. Case studies collect detailed information on a relatively small number of cases (individuals, groups, schools, communities, etc). It is also possible to conduct a single case: for example, the effects of a mass vaccination program of the American public in the 1970s or a methadone maintenance program in Syracuse (Yin 2004). The cases may be conducted at one point in time, or they can collect information over time. Normally, the purpose of a case study is to help understand what meaning people give to a program, how they perceive its purpose, their attitudes and expectations, how they respond to it, how their response is affected by contextual factors, and what effects it has on them. Cases can be selected to be representative of the broader population, or they can be selected to include subjects with particular characteristics (those who benefited most or least from the program, outliers with unusual responses, etc.). Due to the costs and time involved in conducting case studies, the number of cases will normally be quite small, so their selection is very important if the purpose is to generalize from these cases to the broader population.

Box F.18 describes a rigorous case study evaluation of a Natural Resources Protection Program that was selected as an example of an exemplary evaluation design for inclusion in "Evaluation in Action: Interviews with Expert Evaluators" (Fitzpatrick, Christie, and Mark 2009). The evaluation is based on a detailed analysis of six training courses and combined document review, observation of the training programs, interviews with participants and their managers, monitoring of a one-year practicum that followed the training and follow-up interviews to assess the effects of the program.

BOX F.18
EXAMPLE OF A MORE RIGOROUS NONEXPERIMENTAL DESIGN: EVALUATING THE EFFECTIVENESS OF THE NATURAL RESOURCES LEADERSHIP PROGRAM

The Natural Resources Leadership Program (NRLP) was designed to introduce new approaches to the resolution of environmental conflicts for natural resources leaders in three southeastern states. These new ideas focused on reframing conflicts as opportunities for progress, rather than as fights to be won or lost, and on re-envisioning leadership as facilitating a consensual agreement rather than as persuasion to a claimed position. The leadership program was offered to approximately 150 leaders from public and private sectors and from environmental activist groups and industry. The program was implemented through a series of five 2½-day sessions of residential instruction, spaced out over a period of six months in communication and conflict-resolution skills, leadership development, and government and public policy resources, complemented by a trip to Washington and a year-long practicum.

The evaluation design was organized around case studies of each of the six leadership programs. The evaluation began with an intensive case study of the first pilot training program that included a review of all program materials, observation of all instructional sessions, interviews during the sessions with most participants, repeated interviews in person and over the phone with program staff, attendance at Advisory Board meetings, and in later years follow-up phone interviews and surveys of participants. This intensive study provided the evaluation team with a deep understanding of the program as designed, implemented, and experienced and permitted grounded development of later instruments.

The case studies of the other five leadership programs were less intensive as the evaluation resources had to be distributed across states and time. In each case, two training sessions were observed, and follow-up data were collected through phone

(Continued)

(Continued)

interviews and surveys. It was also necessary to track the practicum experiences and the longer term program outcomes for the participants.

An important aspect of the evaluation was to assess how the program affected the ability of the graduates to engage differently in "real-life" environmental disputes. This was done by surveying Advisory Board members, conducting mini-case studies of selected participant practicum projects, and surveying supervisors and other key individuals in participants' work sites. The "best" of the practicums were sampled to understand how the program had contributed to their success.

The evaluation determined that the NRLP was generally successful in realizing its learning aims. Most participants reported that the program changed their conceptual understanding of environmental conflict and changed their ideas of successful leadership in conflict situations, and they learned new skills and techniques for organizing people and information toward the resolution of conflicts. In terms of effects on practice, only a few participants were able to enact the new lessons learned in the field.

SOURCE: Fitzpatrick et al. (2009).

4.2. Data Collected Only on the Posttest Project Group (Design 7)

When to Use

Design Framework 7 is statistically weak because the design does not include either a baseline or a matched comparison group. The absence of a pretest makes it difficult to know if a change has occurred, and the absence of a nontreatment comparison group makes it difficult to know what would have happened without the project treatment (Shadish et al. 2002:106). It is also difficult to obtain precise QUANT estimates of project outcomes or impacts. Despite these limitations, by default, Design 7 is probably the most widely used RWE evaluation scenario, mainly because, all too typically, evaluation was not planned from the beginning of the project, nor was it considered necessary or practical to include a counterfactual. In addition, all too often when asked to conduct an evaluation at the end of a project, the evaluator is given very little time (sometimes as little as one or two weeks) and a very limited budget (sometimes as little as a few thousand dollars).

Nevertheless, it is important to appreciate that a wide range of different evaluation approaches can help to strengthen Design 7, and many qualitative and mixed-method evaluations are considered methodologically sound within their respective paradigms and use nonstatistical approaches to assess outcomes and impacts.

There are three main situations in which this design is used. The first is where the project being evaluated is very small, perhaps operating in only one location, or where this is an exploratory study where the main purpose is to obtain an initial assessment of whether the project "works" and whether it seems potentially able to achieve its stated objectives. In this context, *works* might mean any of the following:

- Are women able and willing to apply for loans and invest the proceeds in a small business?
- Do most residents use the community toilets, and are they maintained in good working order?
- Are teachers able to apply the new teaching tools and methods, and are there preliminary indications that they affect students' behavior and performance?

The second situation is where the project is quite large and clients are interested in obtaining estimates of outcomes and impacts, but there was no life-of-project evaluation plan or even a baseline. In this context, the evaluators are aware that they have to do the best they can with a methodologically weak evaluation design.

The third situation is where the evaluation was planned using a mixed-method or QUAL design and where the focus was on understanding the implementation process, the influence on the project context, and the perspectives and experiences of different groups affected by the project (including groups who did not benefit or might even have been affected negatively). Some of these designs are discussed in Chapters 13 and 14.

When using Design 7, the scoping of the evaluation (Step 1, see Chapter 2) is particularly important to fully understand the client's information needs and how the evaluation results will be used.

Description of the Design

In this design, only the project population is studied, and they are surveyed only after the project has been implemented. Data may be collected from a small, rapid sample survey; from QUAL methods (PRA, focus groups, secondary sources, key informants, etc.); or from a mixed-method design combining QUANT and QUAL methods.

Strengthening the Design

Given its methodological weaknesses when used under severe budget and time constraints, it is important to strengthen the design by using some of the approaches described earlier in this appendix. Maximum use should be made of mixed-method approaches (see Chapter 14). Even when operating under time pressures, efforts should be made to construct at least a simple program theory model using the techniques described in Chapter 10 to obtain an approximate estimate of causality. This permits the use of logical deduction through techniques such as pattern matching (Campbell 1966) or coherence (Rosenbaum 1995) and through the nine strategies proposed by Davidson (2000:21–2), described in Chapter 10. Some of these approaches have been described as being analogous to detective work in which a causal sequence is deducted from observing all the clues, and alternative explanations are eliminated through evidence. Readers should also be aware of the criticisms of the use of program theory to estimate causality (Cook 2000:29–32).

Table F.14   Design 7: Posttest Analysis of Project Group without a Baseline or Comparison Group

Time		T_1 (baseline)	Project Intervention	T_3 (end of project)
	Sample selection procedure			
Project group	$[P_0]$ Baseline data may be reconstructed from project records or from the other techniques discussed in Chapter 5.		X	P_1

Time		T_1 (baseline)	Project Intervention	T_3 (end of project)
Comparison group	$[C_0]$ Small purposively selected samples might be used.	QUAL techniques such as PRA, in-depth interviews, and secondary data may be used to reconstruct baseline data.		Secondary data or QUAL techniques may be used to ask key informants and even project participants how they think they compare to persons who did not participate in the project.

Incorporating Mixed-Method Approaches into the Design

The evaluation of village schools in Eritrea (Box F.19) illustrates the use of a mixed-method approach. To try to make up for the lack of pretest and comparison data, recall was used to assess school attendance prior to the construction of the school, and these estimates were triangulated with key informant interviews and a review of school attendance records.

BOX F.19

CASE STUDY FOR DESIGN 7: ASSESSING THE IMPACTS OF THE CONSTRUCTION OF VILLAGE SCHOOLS IN ERITREA

In the evaluation of the Eritrea Social Fund, an end-of-project survey was conducted in 48 communities representing the catchment area for 10 newly constructed primary schools. No comparison group was used. Baseline data on school attendance prior to the construction of the schools were estimated by asking families to recall the situation before the schools were built. Recall data seem to have been reliable because it was easy for families to recall whether their children attended school before the village school was built and also because they did not have any incentive to give wrong information. Triangulation was used to compare estimates from recall with key informant

(Continued)

(Continued)

interviews and a review of school attendance records. The analysis focused on the following topics:

- Process evaluation: More than 90% confirmed that the school was a high priority, but only 37% had attended meetings to participate in planning the project.
- Accessibility, impact, and gender: The schools were successful in reaching the poorest sectors of the community; it was more difficult to involve recently returned refugees because they were still unsettled and not motivated to send their children to school; families are equally motivated to send boys and girls to school, but if they have to choose for economic reasons, they normally give priority to a boy.
- Social impact: Local school construction reduced travel time (to other schools) for students by one half to two thirds.
- Sustainability: Despite extreme poverty, almost all households contributed the required 10% of the cost of the school in cash, labor, or materials.

SOURCE: Unpublished national consultant report.

Appendix G

*Using Concept Mapping as
a Tool for Program Evaluation*[1]

Many thematic programs have multiple interventions and objectives, and consequently, it is often not possible to use the conventional project evaluation designs where one or two outcome and impact indicators can be precisely defined and measured. As discussed earlier, this makes it difficult to apply logic models. It is proposed that one approach that could be considered for the evaluation of complex, multicomponent, multi-outcome programs is *concept mapping*. This approach is designed to capture the views of multiple stakeholders on the issues and concepts that must be taken into consideration in the planning or evaluation of complex programs.

This annex presents three examples of the potential applications of concept mapping in thematic evaluations. The first example illustrates the use of concept mapping to improve the representativity of countries or programs selected for in-depth case studies, the second illustrates the use in a pretest–posttest evaluation, and the third shows how concept mapping could help define the scope and characteristics of the portfolio to be covered by the evaluation. A hypothetical assessment of gender mainstreaming strategies is used in all three examples. The approach is based on Kane and Trochim's (2007) *Concept Mapping for Planning and Evaluation,* and readers are referred to this publication for more details on the different stages of the concept mapping approach.

Example 1: Using Concept Mapping to Improve the Sample Selection of Case Studies

Table G.1 summarizes the main steps in using concept mapping to select a representative sample of countries or programs on which case studies would be prepared to assess the effectiveness of a donor

---

[1]This Appendix is adapted from a report prepared by Michael Bamberger for an Experts Workshop on Thematic Evaluation organized by the UNDP Evaluation Office, New York, February 2009.

supported gender mainstreaming strategy. A similar strategy could be used in sampling for many other thematic programs. This is a simplified example to illustrate the general principles of the approach.

Step 1: A group of stakeholders are contacted either through a face-to-face meeting or through a website.[2] After an initial briefing on the purpose of the evaluation, they are asked a question (or a series of questions) such as the following:

> "In your opinion what are the characteristics of a successful donor supported gender mainstreaming program?"

Stakeholders are asked to write as many statements as they wish, either on index cards or in an Internet template. Each response should include only one idea, and complex ideas should be divided into separate statements. Stakeholders sort their statements into piles based on the similarity of the items. Sometimes stakeholders are left to decide whether they wish to have many small piles or a few larger ones, but sometimes they are encouraged to avoid having too many small piles with only one or two statements in each. They are then asked to suggest a name for each pile.

Step 2: All of the statements/items mentioned by the respondents are numbered, and a *similarity matrix* is produced manually or using concept mapping software. This is done in two stages. In Stage 1, a *binary matrix* is produced for each respondent indicating which items were grouped together (Kane and Trochim 2007:90–93). In Stage 2, matched items are summed across all respondents to produce a *combined group similarity matrix.*

Step 3: Clusters are defined. Stage 1 may use *multidimensional scaling* to create a *two-dimensional point map* showing distances between items (Kane and Trochim 2007:97, Figure 5.5). *Stress analysis* can be used to measure the degree to which the distances on the map are discrepant from the distances in the input similarity matrix. In Stage 2, *hierarchical cluster analysis* can be used to combine individual statements on the point map into clusters of statements that reflect similar concepts (Kane and Trochim 2007:100, 104, Figures 5.6 and 5.7). As an optional third stage, the names respondents gave to their sorted piles can be listed and their frequencies indicated.

Step 4: A group of "experts" is assembled to assess the groupings. They could include some of the original stakeholders or they could be Evaluation Office staff plus other evaluation specialists. In Stage 1, the group is asked to review the clusters and to indicate whether any of them should be combined to represent a broader dimension or whether any clusters should be divided into two or more groups describing different concepts. The revised list can be called "dimensions." In Stage 2, a new list of dimensions is generated that incorporates these suggestions. In Stage 3, the experts are asked to give a name to each dimension and to rank the dimensions in terms of their importance for sample selection.

Step 5: The dimensions proposed by the experts can be compared with the key indicators and constructs defined in the logic model. Any major inconsistencies should be reviewed and adjustments made either to the proposed dimensions or to the logic model.

---

[2]Kane and Trochim (2007) mention Concept Systems Incorporated 2004 as an example of an Internet program for conducting concept mapping.

Step 6: The evaluators, possibly in consultation with the experts, decide how many dimensions will be used in the sample selection. Normally all of the highest rated dimensions will be included, and the main decision concerns the cut-off point of how many dimensions to use. The number of dimensions should be sufficient to reflect all important indicators identified by stakeholders while keeping to a reasonable number (probably no more than 10 dimensions). The sample may be divided into two groups representing countries that scored high and low on the overall ratings, or a middle group might also be included. The choice between two and three groups will depend on the total number of countries to be selected.

Step 7: Stakeholders are asked to rate each country on a (usually) 5-point scale for each selected dimension.

Step 8: Stakeholder ratings are combined and average ratings computed. If there are large discrepancies on a particular dimension, this will either be eliminated or, if the dimension is considered important, could be subdivided into two or more categories. However, in this case, stakeholders would have to be asked to repeat the rating process—which will often not be practical. The agreed number of high and low (and possibly intermediate) rated countries or programs will then be selected. Sometimes the sample will be subdivided by region, by size of the program, or by other relevant characteristics. The sample can then be chosen by randomly selecting the required number of cases from each category.

Example 2: Using Concept Mapping for Evaluating Program Effectiveness, Outcomes, and Impacts

Concept mapping can also be used to evaluate complex, multicomponent, multicountry thematic programs. Table G.2 illustrates the process of designing an evaluation for the same gender mainstreaming program. In this example, concept mapping is used to select indicators to be measured in a baseline survey, which is then repeated at the end of the program. It can also be used in cases when only an ex-post evaluation design is used.

The process is similar but not identical to sample selection. A group of stakeholders are again asked to identify the characteristics of a successful gender mainstreaming program (or a similar question on the factors determining the success of gender mainstreaming). When concept mapping is used for sample selection, normally only a small number of dimensions will be used, but when it is applied to program evaluation, the number of dimensions will often be larger. In a more sophisticated option and where a high level of respondent cooperation is anticipated, it is possible to complement the assessment of the dimensions with rating some of the individual statements included in particular clusters/dimensions. Conventional attitude scale development techniques could be used to select statements with high interrater correlations.

A further refinement is to identify what are called "anchor" and "bridging" statements. Anchor statements are those considered central to the meaning of a cluster, while bridging statements are those that seem to link two different clusters. This analysis can provide a deeper semantic and conceptual understanding of the composition of the clusters and could guide decisions on whether any clusters should be combined or where some should be subdivided.

A wider group of stakeholders is then asked to rate each country or program on each dimension.[3] The analysis is used to generate the baseline or benchmark data. Ideally, stakeholders would be asked to complement their ratings with their explanation of why particular countries have performed well or badly on the different dimensions.

The survey would then be repeated at the end of the evaluation (e.g., at the end of the four-year program cycle). Stakeholders would be asked to rate the current status of each country on every dimension and also to assess how much change had occurred over the period of the study. The two measures can sometimes reveal different perspectives, particularly when a respondent's understanding of what can realistically be achieved over four years may have changed. Depending on the focus of the evaluation, the questions could ask about outcomes and impacts or about efficiency or effectiveness. Depending on the time that respondents are willing to spend on the survey, the ratings can also be complemented with questions about the particular challenges faced in different countries or the factors that contributed to success (or lack of success) in particular countries.

An important benefit from using concept mapping to enhance the representativity of the sample is that during the analysis, it is possible to assess the extent to which findings can be generalized to the total population of countries or programs where gender mainstreaming is, or was intended to have been, implemented.

Example 3: Using Concept Mapping to Help Define the Portfolio to Be Assessed

As we discussed earlier, the scope of many thematic programs is often not clearly defined and may vary among countries. The range of services or treatments, the implementation methodology, and the range of participating agencies and/or final beneficiaries may also vary. Consequently, it may be difficult to define and delimit the portfolio to be assessed. If the evaluation team makes the decision on how to delimit the program, there is the danger that stakeholders may later complain either that the study is too broad or that important elements, participating agencies, or beneficiary groups have been left out.

Concept mapping can help to reach consensus on these questions. A similar methodology to the earlier examples would be used to consult stakeholders on the key elements, participating agencies, and beneficiary groups that should be covered in the assessment. If a very broad and diverse set of elements, agencies, and beneficiary groups were mentioned, stakeholders might be asked to rank the different elements and groups in terms of their importance or centrality to the program (and consequently to the evaluation).

---

[3]Depending on their level of knowledge, stakeholders may only be asked to rate countries or programs in their region, or they may be asked to rate all programs worldwide.

Table G.1   Using Concept Mapping to Select a Sample of Countries or Programs for Thematic Evaluation Case Studies: The Example of Gender Mainstreaming

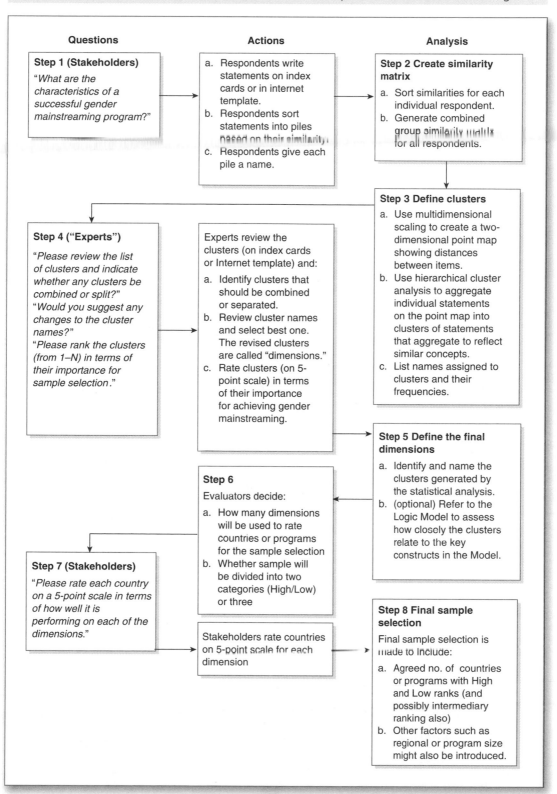

Questions

Step 1 (Stakeholders)

"What are the characteristics of a successful gender mainstreaming program?"

Actions

a. Respondents write statements on index cards or in internet template.
b. Respondents sort statements into piles based on their similarity.
c. Respondents give each pile a name.

Analysis

Step 2 Create similarity matrix

a. Sort similarities for each individual respondent.
b. Generate combined group similarity matrix for all respondents.

Step 3 Define clusters

a. Use multidimensional scaling to create a two-dimensional point map showing distances between items.
b. Use hierarchical cluster analysis to aggregate individual statements on the point map into clusters of statements that aggregate to reflect similar concepts.
c. List names assigned to clusters and their frequencies.

Step 4 ("Experts")

"Please review the list of clusters and indicate whether any clusters be combined or split?"
"Would you suggest any changes to the cluster names?"
"Please rank the clusters (from 1–N) in terms of their importance for sample selection."

Experts review the clusters (on index cards or Internet template) and:

a. Identify clusters that should be combined or separated.
b. Review cluster names and select best one. The revised clusters are called "dimensions."
c. Rate clusters (on 5-point scale) in terms of their importance for achieving gender mainstreaming.

Step 5 Define the final dimensions

a. Identify and name the clusters generated by the statistical analysis.
b. (optional) Refer to the Logic Model to assess how closely the clusters relate to the key constructs in the Model.

Step 6

Evaluators decide:

a. How many dimensions will be used to rate countries or programs for the sample selection
b. Whether sample will be divided into two categories (High/Low) or three

Step 7 (Stakeholders)

"Please rate each country on a 5-point scale in terms of how well it is performing on each of the dimensions."

Stakeholders rate countries on 5-point scale for each dimension

Step 8 Final sample selection

Final sample selection is made to include:

a. Agreed no. of countries or programs with High and Low ranks (and possibly intermediary ranking also)
b. Other factors such as regional or program size might also be introduced.

Table G.2 Using Concept Mapping to Evaluate a Thematic Program by Comparing Baseline and End-of-Program Ratings on a Set of Critical Clusters: The Example of Gender Mainstreaming

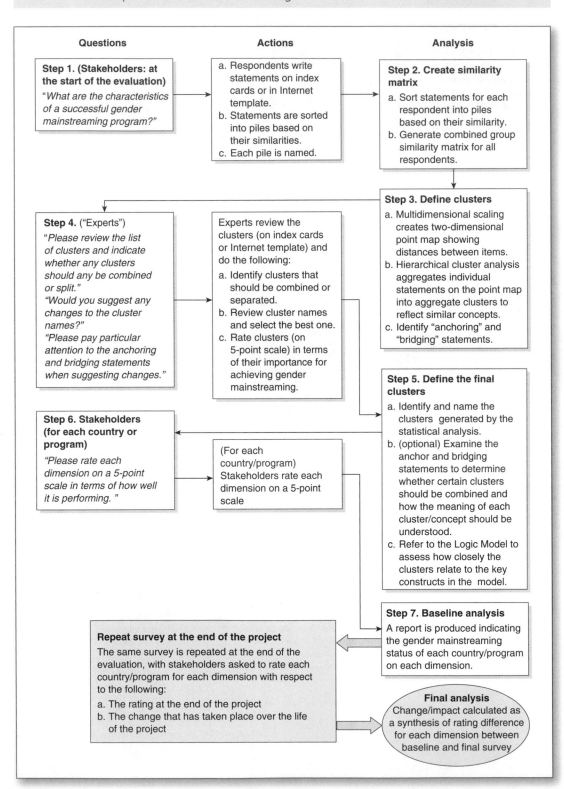

Appendix H

Applying the Complicated and Complex Program Evaluation Methodologies Discussed in Chapter 16 to the Evaluation of Country (Assistance) Strategies

This section illustrates how the evaluation tools and techniques discussed in Chapter 16 (see particularly Section 5) can be applied to the evaluation of country strategies. Donor country programs will often combine a number of different kinds of interventions, including specific projects, broader programs, a package of support for a particular sector, country-level policy interventions, financial support (either targeted for a specific purpose or general budget support), and a range of capacity development and technical assistance programs. While some of the interventions will be specific to the aid agency being studied, increasingly the support is part of a multidonor cooperation.

The country strategy evaluation may have one or more of the following objectives:

- Assess the strategic relevance of the country strategy relative to country needs.
- Test the implementation of agency-wide outcomes to determine whether the intended outcomes were achieved.
- Identify the successes and failures in different sectors or of different approaches used in the country and identify the factors contributing to the performance.
- Identify the effectiveness of a donor's aid to a particular country.

The evaluation of these complex, multicomponent country programs presents many challenges, including the following:

- The overall program may lack coherent goals and clearly defined outcomes or even distinct interventions.
- Similar interventions may be funded from different sources, making attribution difficult. Often the similarities and differences between the approaches used by different agencies are not clearly defined, and even the areas of operation and package of services provided may be difficult to determine.
- There is usually no overall mapping of the assistance different agencies are providing to the country.

- Political sensitivities may make it difficult to evaluate or criticize the work of other international partners, and agencies (both international and national) may be reluctant to recognize weaknesses in their programs.
- Many interventions are intended to have complete coverage of the country or of a particular sector, making it very difficult to identify a comparison group (counterfactual).

The evaluation of country strategies will normally be based on a combination of several of the evaluation techniques discussed in Chapter 16 Section 5 and summarized in Figure 16.3. *Attribution analysis* is not normally used due to the complexity of the country programs, but it may be applied occasionally when a major component of the donor program being evaluated is part of a multidonor initiative with defined and measurable objectives (such as reducing infant mortality). In this case, attribution analysis may be conducted to estimate the overall impacts of the multidonor program before using *contribution analysis* to assess the value added of the activities of a particular donor. The contribution analysis is sometimes combined with *substitution analysis* to estimate the net increase of resources to these programs after taking into consideration the possibility that the host country may divert some of the funding it had previously budgeted for this sector to other programs.

Box H.1 summarizes the methodology used by the World Bank's Independent Evaluation Group (IEG) in the evaluation of World Bank country assistance strategies (CAS). The CAS is a good example of a complex program as the strategies will often include support to individual projects, broad sector programs, technical assistance at the national and sector levels, capacity development, and policy reform. The lending portfolio for a large country program may include dozens of large loans as well as even larger numbers of smaller activities, plus extensive policy dialogue. Box H.1 shows that the evaluation strategy combines a top-down assessment of the extent to which the Bank achieved its policy objectives and how relevant these objectives were to the national development priorities; with a bottom-up review of the Bank's products and services used to achieve these objectives.

BOX H.1
AN EXAMPLE OF A COMPLEX EVALUATION STRATEGY: THE WORLD BANK COUNTRY ASSISTANCE EVALUATION METHODOLOGY

The World Bank has developed a standard methodology (country assistance evaluation—CAE) for the assessment of its country assistance strategies (CAS; World Bank 2008). The following description of a typical World Bank CAE methodology is adapted from Box 11.1 of Morra-Imas and Rist (2009:422):

The main objectives of the country strategy are clarified on the basis of a document review and consultations with key stakeholders. For each of the main objectives, the CAE evaluates the following:

- The relevance of the objective
- The relevance of the Bank's strategy toward meeting the objective, including the balance between lending and nonlending instruments
- The efficacy with which the strategy was implemented
- The results achieved

The evaluation is conducted in two steps:

- A top-down review of whether the Bank's program achieved a particular Bank objective or planned outcome and had a substantive influence on the country's development
- A bottom-up review of the Bank's products and services used to achieve the objectives

The CAE assesses the extent to which the major strategic objectives were relevant and achieved. Country programs often express their goals in terms of higher order objectives such as MDGs and poverty reduction. The CAS often establishes intermediate goals such as improved targeting of social services, and the CAE will seek to validate whether these achieved satisfactory net benefits and whether the results chain specified in the CAS was valid. The CAE also assesses the degree to which clients demonstrate ownership of international development priorities (World Bank 2008).

Glossary of Terms and Acronyms

Authenticity: The fidelity of the work to the real world. In education and educational testing, authentic tasks refer to those that simulate professional or nonacademic work outside classrooms. In evaluation, accurate presentation of stakeholder perspectives and experiences may be considered to give an evaluation an air of authenticity. See Chapters 6 and 13 and Appendix B.

Bibliometrics: Methods for documenting the number of citations and publications of program products and descriptions. See Chapter 13.

Black box evaluation: A term used to describe evaluation designs that do not articulate a program theory about how the project is expected to operate or to achieve the intended outcomes and impacts. It also refers to evaluations that measure indicators of outcomes without examining the process (quality of project interventions) that supposedly led to changes in those outcome indicators. The term is frequently used to describe and critique many randomized and quasi-experimental designs where pretest–posttest comparisons are made of the project population but where the project itself is a "black box" about which no information is obtained. See Chapters 10 and 12.

Case study: Study of a particular case because of its intrinsic interest or because it is an instance of a phenomenon of interest. See Chapters 13 and 14.

Clientism: Providing overly positive evaluation findings to avoid conflict with clients and ensure future work. See Chapter 6.

Clients/evaluation clients (see also stakeholders): Those for whom an evaluation is conducted—for example, those who commission the evaluation and sign the contract, as well as sponsoring or funding agencies of the project to be evaluated. These are the groups to whom the evaluators are directly accountable. See Chapters 2, 6, and 17.

Cohort analysis: The analysis of data about a particular group. Cohort analysis may involve comparing successive groups passing through a cycle of activity (e.g., third-grade students, medical trainees, families who receive public services). One variant is using subjects scheduled to receive services or benefits in later phases of a project as a control or comparison group for subjects who received services in an earlier phase (sometimes referred to as "pipeline comparison"). See Chapter 11.

Comparison group/nonequivalent control group or matched control group (see also comparison group): A group selected to match as closely as possible the project (experimental) group with respect to relevant internal and external characteristics, except that the comparison group did not receive the interventions of the project being evaluated. A comparison group is used when it is not possible to randomly assign subjects (individuals, communities, groups) to the project and control situations as would be done in a randomized experimental design. See Chapters 11, 12, and 14.

Confirmability: The extent to which the conclusions drawn can be confirmed by the available evidence. See Chapter 7 and Appendix B.

Connoisseurship evaluation: Evaluation relying on the enlightened eye of the expert to recognize program quality, including subtleties not easily discerned by nonexperts (Eisner 1991). See Chapter 13.

Construct validity: Incorrect inferences about the constructs identifying what a project is intended to achieve. Because constructs tend to be intangible (e.g., student knowledge acquisition, improved quality of life), there may be some ambiguity regarding operational definitions or exactly what is being scrutinized or measured. See Chapter 7 and Appendix A.

Constructivist: Another term for QUAL paradigm.

Contextual variables (or factors): Factors in the community or region that can affect how a project is implemented, how—and how successfully—it achieves its outcomes and impacts and which sectors of the target population do and do not benefit. Contextual variables may include economic, political, institutional, environmental, security, and sociopsychological factors and the sociocultural environment. See Chapters 2, 10, and 14.

Contextuality: The extent to which aspects of a program's setting are considered in the evaluation. Qualitative inquiry is *contextual,* recognizing that a unique array of contexts influences the program and its outcomes, such as policy and political contexts, ideological and value contexts, and organizational and sociological contexts. See Chapter 13.

Control group (see also comparison group): When experimental evaluation designs are used with random assignment of subjects to treatment and nontreatment groups, the control group consists of subjects who will not receive the experimental treatment (project services) and with whom the experimental group that does receive services will be compared. Where large groups are available, random assignment of persons to experimental and control groups is considered to result in comparable or equivalent groups, differing only in their participation (or not) in the project. When it is not possible to randomly assign subjects to the experimental and control groups, as is the case with most quasi-experimental designs, a matched *comparison group* is used. When sufficiently detailed secondary data are available, it may be possible to use statistical matching techniques such as propensity scores, but in most real-world contexts, judgmental matching must be used. When the number of persons available is too small for random assignment or

quasi-experimental designs, to ensure that the two groups will be equivalent, matched groups may be formed and designated as experimental and comparison groups. See Chapters 11, 12, 14, and 16.

Counterfactual: What would have happened to a population if it had not participated in the program or received its services or benefits? For quantitative evaluations, a control or comparison group may serve as a counterfactual. However, in many cases, a counterfactual may be constructed based on documentary data or interviews asking respondents to reconstruct what they think would have happened without the project. See Chapters 11, 12, and 16.

Credibility: The extent to which the data and findings from an evaluation are accepted as true by audiences. All types of evaluations, evaluation data, and evaluation findings are vulnerable to being considered to lack credibility, even when evaluators have attempted to collect appropriate and sufficient data and to base findings on the data (cf. *validity*) and to include stakeholder perspectives and consideration of contexts. See Chapters 7 and 13 and Appendixes B and C.

Criteriality: Judging programs against explicit criteria. The criteria may be prespecified and external (e.g., an accreditation review), or they may be prespecified but created specifically for this program. See Chapter 13.

Critical ethnography: Ethnographic study focused on power structures and the cultural assumptions, institutions, and relationships that contribute to the disenfranchisement or oppression of dominated groups. See Chapter 13.

Deontological: An approach to ethics that judges the morality of an action based on the action's adherence to a rule or rules. See Chapter 9.

Dependability: The degree to which data are stable. This term, from Lincoln and Guba (1985), is often preferred by interpretivists to the term *reliability,* which refers to replicability, a related concept. See Chapter 13 and Appendix B.

Design/evaluation design: We use design in two ways. The first is the plan for conducting an evaluation, including methods and sources of data collection, deliverables, methods of analysis, and a timeline. The evaluation design is distinct from the project design or theory. Design also refers to the first stage in the model of the project cycle. See Chapters 2, 10, 11, and 12. We also use the term **evaluation scenario** to refer to the situation under which an evaluation must be conducted (e.g., whether the evaluation was planned at the beginning of a project and whether there was a comparable baseline) and **evaluation design framework** that basically identifies the times during the life of a project when primary data will be collected and whether there will be data collected from a comparison group (counterfactual). These are illustrated in Table 11.2. See Appendix F for examples of all the evaluation designs.

Developmental evaluation: As defined by Patton (2011:36), developmental evaluation guides action and adaptation in innovative initiatives facing high uncertainty. Where predictability and control are relatively low, goals, strategies, and what gets done can be emergent and changing rather than predetermined and fixed. Developmental evaluation supports innovation by bringing data to bear to inform and guide ongoing decision making as part of innovative processes. See Chapter 2.

Disaggregated analysis: Breaking down the analysis of overall findings on project outcomes or impacts into more detailed comparative analysis for subcategories such as sex, age, social class, different project sites or regions of the country, or types of services received. Determining whether and what types of disaggregated analysis of outcomes and impacts are required is critical when operating under budget constraints because disaggregated analysis usually requires increasing sample size and hence the cost of the evaluation. See Chapters 3, 12, and 15.

Dummy variables: A technique used in multivariate analysis to transform information such as whether a household is participating in the project, or whether a family owns its own house, into a variable with values of 1 (e.g., participates in the project) and 0 (e.g., does not participate in the project). The purpose of these transformations is to permit statistical analysis of this information. A common use of dummy variables in impact evaluation is to determine the effect of project participation on an outcome variable such as household income or education test scores. The coefficient of the dummy variable indicates the proportion of the variance (in household income, for example) explained by project participation. In RealWorld Evaluation (RWE), dummy variables can also be used to transform contextual information (local government does/does not support the project; the local economy is growing/is not growing) into variables that can be subjected to statistical analysis. See Chapter 12.

Effect size: The size of the change or effect that a project produces or is expected to produce. In quantitative approaches to evaluation, the effect size is calculated as the measurable difference between the outcome measured on the project group receiving the intervention or treatment and outcomes for control or comparison groups. The *standardized effect size* is the difference between the sample and population means divided by the population standard deviation, permitting comparison of effect sizes for different projects. The *minimum acceptable effect size* (MAES), or critical effect size, is the minimum level of change that the evaluation design must be able to detect. In quantitative studies, the smaller the effect size that must be detected, the larger the required sample. See Chapters 5 and 15.

Emergent design (see also developmental evaluation): Evaluation designs that emerge as researchers and evaluators gradually learn about the phenomena and programs they examine. An evaluation client's information needs and available data sources may serve for initial planning of the focus and methods of an evaluation. From this somewhat tentative beginning, as critical features and issues come more clearly into view, early questions and methods are to be refined, a process called *progressive focusing*, which is useful for both QUAL and mixed-methods designs. See Chapter 13.

Emic: The perspective of interest in qualitative approaches that seeks to obtain the insider's understanding and meanings rather than an *etic* or outsider's perspective. See Chapter 13.

Empowerment evaluation (see also participatory evaluation and PRA): Evaluation intended to improve not only program understanding but also the effectiveness of participant involvement in program development and decision making (Fetterman 1996). See Chapters 2 and 5.

Enumerators: Research staff who administer structured questionnaires or survey instruments. This is contrasted with interviewers who administer less structured data collection instruments or who conduct interviews without a questionnaire. Interviewers normally require a higher level of training and more field experience. See Chapters 13 and 15.

Ethnography: Sustained field studies to understand the ethos or culture of a group or society. See Chapter 13.

Ethnomethodology: The study of human perceptions, meanings, interactions, and how they maintain social structure. See Chapter 13.

Etic: Evaluation approaches based on an outsider's perspectives rather than an *emic* or insider's perspective. See Chapter 3.

Evaluability assessment: A determination as to whether a program can be evaluated using the type of evaluation planned with the available resources and within the proposed time frame. See Chapters 2, 7, and 17.

Evaluand: The project or program being evaluated.

Evaluation capacity building/evaluation capacity development: Strengthening the capacity of stakeholders to commission, design, implement, interpret, and use evaluations. This may be achieved through formal training or through interactive evaluation capacity development. See Chapter 18.

Evaluation designs: Different approaches to evaluation that prioritize different elements such as purposes, stakeholders, and procedures. Stufflebeam (2001a) identifies 22 evaluation designs (see also Mathison 2005:256–8; Patton 2008:300–5; Patton 2011:23–6; and Shadish, Cook, and Campbell 2002, among others). See Chapter 11 and Appendix F.

Evaluation design framework: See design/evaluation design.

Evaluation practitioners: People who conduct evaluations, including staff of government and funding agencies, nongovernmental organizations (NGOs),

consulting firms, academics, independent consultants, and external evaluators. See Chapter 18.

Evaluation scenario: See design/evaluation design.

Evaluation users: All those who may potentially use the evaluation findings. These include funding agencies, government planning and finance ministries, agencies implementing the project being evaluated, intended project beneficiaries and groups that may be affected by the project, academics, evaluation consultants, and civil society. See Chapters 2 and 18.

Evidence: The information used to support conclusions. This can include data from surveys, observation, documents, and interviews.

Evidence-based evaluation (evidence-based practice): A treatment practice or service delivery system based on consistent scientific evidence showing that it improves client/participant outcomes in both clinically (scientifically) controlled and everyday settings. Although widely used, the approach has proved difficult to apply in fields such as education due to disagreement concerning what are the acceptable evaluation methods and standards of evidence. See Chapters 11 and 12.

Experimental designs: A research design in which subjects are randomly assigned (allocated) to the experimental (treatment) group and the control (nontreatment) group. Both groups are tested or measured through a survey or other instrument before the experiment begins. The experimental treatment is then applied to the experimental group but not to the control group. The conditions of the two groups are then carefully regulated during the period of the experiment to eliminate any external factors that might influence outcomes. The test or survey is then administered again to the two groups. Any significant difference in the change in the mean value of the outcome variable between the experimental and control groups is interpreted as an initial indication of a potential treatment effect. The experiment should be repeated several times to test for consistency of the findings. For the purposes of RealWorld Evaluation, it is important to distinguish between *true experimental designs*, which combine randomization with careful regulation of the conditions of the two groups through the period required for the treatment to take effect, and *randomized (randomization) designs,* where in most RWE evaluations, the conditions of the two groups cannot be regulated or held constant during project implementation. See Chapters 11 and 12 and Appendix F.

External validity: The generalizability of study results to other groups, settings, treatments, and outcomes. See Chapters 7 and 11 and Appendixes A to E.

Findings: Stated judgments and interpretations regarding program quality and impacts. Warranted findings are adequately and appropriately based on relevant and comprehensive data. See Chapter 7.

Focus group: A group of people, usually between six and eight, interviewed regarding the research focus. A set of questions is often used that is deliberately sequenced or focused to move the discussion toward concepts of interest to the researcher. A number of sessions with different groups sharing characteristics (e.g., age, sex, socioeconomic status, type of project participation) may be of interest to the purposes of the evaluation. See Chapters 5, 13, and 14.

Formative evaluation: An evaluation intended to help improve the implementation and outcomes of the ongoing project or program being evaluated. By contrast, a *summative evaluation* is intended to assess the impacts or effects of a completed program but not usually to improve its implementation. See Chapter 8.

Fourth-generation evaluation: Evaluation involving sensitive, systematic attention to context and to stakeholders' perceptions and meanings, verifiable by audit trails and by member checking with groups of stakeholders to ensure the validity of data and findings (Guba and Lincoln 1989). See Chapters 7 and 13.

Geographical Information Systems (GIS): GIS systems create electronic maps that define the precise location of physical features (e.g., roads, rivers); services (e.g., hospitals, stores, public service facilities); populations classified by socio-economic or other characteristics (income, ethnicity, number of children) or events (crime, high incidence of disease, infant mortality, etc.). It is also possible to overlay different GIS maps to compare, for example, high infant mortal-ity rates with socio-economic data such as household income, education, ethnicity, or availability of public transport. See Chapter 5.

Hermeneutics: Interpretive study of human expression and intention often attentive to the relationship between the subject and the enquirer; study of human meaning making, including how experiences, conscious and unconscious purposes, and multiple contexts affect meanings as they are locally perceived and expressed. See Chapter 13.

Ideological evaluation: Evaluation intended to promote identified ideologies or values, such as social justice or deliberative democracy (House 1993; Mertens 1999, 2001). See Chapters 9 and 13.

Impact: The long-term effects on identifiable populations or groups produced by a project or program. Impacts may be direct or indirect, intended or unintended, economic, sociocultural, institutional, environmental, technological, or other. See Chapters 2, 11, and 12.

Implementation process: The running or putting into effect of a program. Also the third stage of the project cycle: the operational procedures used to transform project inputs into project outputs. See Chapters 2 and 10.

Incommensurability: The belief that two perspectives are so fundamentally different that there can be no mutual understanding, agreement, or collaboration. See Chapters 7 and 13.

Inputs: The money, materials, equipment, staff, consultants, and other resources available to a project. The project implementation process is intended to transform *inputs* into *outputs.* See Chapters 2 and 10.

Instrumental variable (IV): A statistical technique used in quasi-experimental designs to control for project participant *selection bias* due to variables not measured in the survey instrument (*unobservables*). These variables influence program participation (e.g., geographical differences in program availability) but do not affect outcomes once someone is selected. IVs model the participant selection process to separate the effect of the selection process on outcomes from the effects of the project intervention. IV analysis is often combined with **propensity scores** (see separate entry). See Chapters 11 and 12.

Integrated checklist: RWE's nine categories for assessing the threats to the adequacy and validity of quantitative, qualitative, and mixed-method evaluation designs. The five categories for assessing qualitative and mixed-method designs are adapted from the work of Guba and Lincoln (1989) and Miles and Huberman (1994), and the four categories for evaluating quantitative designs are adapted from Shadish, Cook, and Campbell (2002). See Chapter 7 and Appendix C.

Interpretative rigor: A criteria for assessing the credibility of the findings and interpretations of mixed-method evaluations. "Are the interpretations credible on the basis of the results obtained from the evaluation?" This assesses the integration of quantitative and qualitative dimensions of the evaluation in terms of: interpretative and theoretical consistency, interpretive agreement and directness, integrative efficacy, and interpretative correspondence. See Chapter 7 and Appendix E.

Internal validity: The accuracy of the data in reflecting the reality of the program. See Chapters 7 and 11.

Intervening variables (see also moderators and mediators): Factors that may explain differences in the level or direction of project outcomes from the anticipated outcomes or for different groups. See Chapters 10, 11, and 12.

Interviewer: Research staff members who collect information from subjects either in an informal context without any survey instrument or using an unstructured data collection instrument. This is contrasted with *enumerators*, who administer structured questionnaires or survey instruments. Being an interviewer normally requires a higher professional level and more experience than being an enumerator. See Chapter 13.

Logical framework analysis/LFA, logframe, logic modeling: A matrix, flowchart, or graphic that translates program theory into a series of indicators facilitating the monitoring and assessing of factors related to achievement or nonachievement of program goals. Logframes or other forms of logic models, including results-based

monitoring, are widely used as program monitoring and evaluation tools by international development agencies and also agencies such as the Department of Education and the Centers for Disease Control and Prevention in the United States. See Chapter 10.

Logic model: See **program theory model/logic model.**

MAES (minimum acceptable effect size): See **effect size.**

Mediators: Intervening variables that influence program outcomes and that program interventions can modify. See Chapters 10 and 11.

Meta-evaluation: Evaluation of an evaluation. Meta-evaluation is particularly needed where evaluation results may influence critical or resource-consuming decisions. See Chapters 7, 15, and 16.

Microcredit/microcredit program: Programs providing small-scale loans and technical assistance to low-income individuals to help promote the creation or expansion of small businesses. Many microcredit programs require the creation of small groups of families who form a "solidarity group," which in addition to reviewing and approving all loan proposals also creates community organizations and promotes other social and economic development activities. Microcredit is considered one of the most successful mechanisms for strengthening the economic conditions of the poorest sectors of society, particularly women and female-headed households, and microcredit programs, organized by government, international agencies, or NGOs, are now operating in most developing countries.

Mixed-method designs: Designs involving the planned use of both quantitative and qualitative methods. See Chapter 14.

Moderators: Intervening variables that influence program outcomes and that a program cannot modify. See Chapter 10.

Naturalistic inquiry: Study focusing on ordinary events in natural settings described in ordinary language. *Naturalistic inquiry*, a term introduced by

Lincoln and Guba (1985), involves time at the program's site or sites and data collection unobtrusive enough to minimize altering or interfering with ordinary activities. See Chapter 13.

Non-Experimental Designs (NED): Evaluation designs that do not include a matched comparison group. While these designs are often considered to be methodologically weak for causal analysis, there are a number of potential sound NEDs. See Appendix F.

NGO/nongovernmental organization (also known as PVOs/private voluntary organization): A group or institution entirely or largely independent of government with humanitarian rather than commercial objectives. International NGOs (INGOs) are private, not-for-profit agencies based mainly but not exclusively in industrial countries that support international relief and development. Local or national NGOs are indigenous groups organized regionally or nationally. In some cases, these may be membership-run groups in villages, although these are more commonly referred to as community-based organizations (CBOs). NGOs include charitable and religious associations that mobilize private funds for development, respond to emergencies, distribute food and family-planning services, promote community organization, and provide other forms of direct service or policy advocacy. These and other civil society organizations (CSOs) also include independent cooperatives, community associations, water user societies, women's groups, and pastoral associations.

Nonequivalent control group: See **comparison group/nonequivalent control group or matched control group.**

Nonprobability sampling/purposive sampling: Sampling procedures involving relatively small samples. Each subject or case is selected individually to ensure that the maximum information is obtained. Sometimes all subjects or cases will be selected at the same time, but additional cases may be added as need and opportunity emerge. Purposive sampling strategies include typical case samples, range samples, maximum variation samples, quota samples, unique case samples, snowball samples, critical case samples, reputational samples, and comparable case samples. See Chapters 13 and 15.

Null hypothesis: A hypothesis in quantitative evaluations stating that there is no statistically significant difference between the experimental and control/comparison groups. According to statistical theory, it is never possible to prove that a hypothesis is true (i.e., that a project or intervention does have an effect), so proving a null hypothesis (or series of null hypotheses) false, at a given level of statistical significance, is taken as corroborative evidence of an intervention or project's effect. See Chapters 12 and 15.

Omitted variable problem/"unobservables": A variable not included in a study's design or analysis that may have influenced program results, for example, when important characteristics of experimental and comparison groups do not match. See Chapters 11 and 12.

One-tailed test: When testing for statistical significance, a one-tailed test is used when the direction of the expected change or difference is known (e.g., to test whether there has been a significant increase in a mathematical aptitude test score or whether the proportion of the project population with household income below the poverty line has decreased). The one-tailed test indicates the probability of finding a result as large as the test score if there really is no difference between the two groups being compared (e.g., the project and comparison groups). If the direction of the expected change is not known, then a *two-tailed test* must be used. See Chapter 15.

Outcomes: Medium and long–term program effects (e.g., changes in what others do), as influenced by a project's outputs. Project staff have little direct control over outcomes. See Chapters 2 and 10.

Outputs: Products and services resulting directly from project activities; program results over which project personnel have direct control. See Chapters 3, 10, and 11.

Paradigm: A perspective or point of view affecting what is recognized, known, valued, and done. For example, those who adhere to the positivist paradigm consider to be "true" only that which they can observe to be in one-to-one correspondence with an objective reality, while those who adhere to the interpretivist paradigm consider reality to be subjectively constructed and apprehended. See Chapters 13 and 14.

Participant observation: Study in which data are collected while the researcher is a full or partial member of the group studied. See Chapters 5, 13, and 14.

Participatory evaluation: Evaluation intended not only to improve program understanding but also to transform program-related working relationships through broad local participation in evaluation processes. See Chapter 8.

Phenomenology: Study of things as they are perceived, without regard for whether they are objectively real, to understand people's perceptions and experiences and the meanings they give to events and concepts. See Chapter 13.

Plausible contribution: An assessment of the contribution one intervention or project made that, combined with those of other actors, contributed to the achievement of a higher level impact. The "plausibility" of such a contribution can be strengthened by demonstrating an attributable cause-effect relationship at least up to the intermediary outcome level of a multi-layered, multiproject program logic model. It can also be determined by "working down" from the top of such a logic model to ascertain the proportional contributions of two or more interventions to the achievement of any discernable changes. See Chapter 16.

Power of the test/statistical power of the test: The probability that a statistical test of project impact will correctly identify that there is a statistically significant impact when the impact really does exist. The normal convention is to set power equal to 0.80, meaning that there is an 80% chance that a particular sample will correctly identify a project effect if the program really does have an effect. The power level can be set higher (reducing the risk of rejecting a statistically significant project effect but requiring a larger sample) or lower (reducing the sample size but increasing the risk of incorrectly rejecting a significant project effect). See Chapter 15.

PRA: Originally an abbreviation for participatory rural appraisal, PRA is now used as a generic term covering a range of participatory research methods, including RRA (rapid rural appraisal) and participatory learning and action (PLA). All these approaches are based on the principle of empowering the community to conduct its own analysis of its needs and priorities and translate these into a plan of action. All the approaches work through community groups rather than individuals, relying heavily on mapping and other graphical techniques that can be used with populations having low literacy rates. See Chapter 5.

Precision: The level of statistical significance used to accept that an observed project effect does not occur by chance. The convention is to accept a 95% confidence level (a 1 in 20 possibility that the apparent project effect is due to chance). If a higher level of precision is required, the confidence level can be increased to 99% (only a 1 in 100 possibility that the result is due to chance) or even higher. See Chapter 15.

Probability sample: See **random sampling/ probability sampling.**

Process evaluation: An evaluation that studies and assesses the way in which a project is implemented and how it is affected by the context within which it operates. This may be a stand-alone evaluation or combined with an outcome-oriented evaluation that identifies project effects. See Chapters 2, 10, 11, and 14.

Program: See **project (development project).**

Program theory model/logic model: A program theory is a theory or model of how a program is expected to cause the intended or observed outcomes. Program theories identify program resources, activities, and intended outcomes and specify a chain of causal hypotheses linking program resources, activities, intermediate outcomes, and ultimate program goals. Many program theories also identify the contextual variables (economic, political, organizational, psychological, environmental, and cultural) that influence program implementation and outcomes in each site or location. See Chapter 10.

Project (development project): A time-bound intervention involving multiple activities intended to provide a defined set of services or to produce a defined set of outcomes or impacts usually for a specified population group. While the terms *project* and *program* are sometimes used interchangeably, a program is usually understood to include a number of different projects and is intended to produce broader and possibly longer term outcomes and impacts. See Chapters 2, 10, and 16.

Project cycle: The different stages through which a project intends to achieve its objectives. The project cycle usually comprises seven stages: design, inputs, implementation process, outputs, outcomes, impacts, and sustainability. See Chapters 2 and 10.

Propensity score matching (PSM): A technique used in quasi-experimental designs whereby each subject in the project sample is statistically matched (using logistical regression or a similar technique) to a group of nonparticipants ("nearest neighbors") on a set of relevant characteristics. The mean value of the outcome variable is calculated for the nearest neighbors, and this is compared with the outcome score for the project participant to estimate the *gain score*. Propensity scores are often combined with **instrumental variable** analysis (see separate entry). See Chapter 12.

Pseudoevaluation: An evaluation undertaken to serve a public relations function. See Chapter 13.

Purposive sampling: See **nonprobability sampling/purposive sampling.**

QED/quasi-experimental design: A set of quantitative evaluation designs used where randomized assignment of subjects to the experimental and control conditions is not possible. In this book, seven quasi-experimental designs are described that are widely used in RealWorld evaluation contexts. The strongest design uses a pretest–posttest project and comparison group design but without randomization. The other designs address budget, time, and data constraints by eliminating one or more of the four data collection points. See Chapter 11.

QUAL: Abbreviation for *qualitative*. The abbreviations QUAL and QUANT were introduced by Rossi (1994).

QUANT: Abbreviation for *quantitative*.

Random sampling/probability sampling: In simple random sampling, all units (e.g., individuals, schools, households) in the population have the same probability of being selected to participate in the study. Selection procedures may use random number tables, select every *n*th unit, or use other techniques, such as a lottery, ensuring equal probability of selection. Random selection helps to ensure the comparability of experimental and control groups, requiring that these groups be large enough to neutralize the unique

characteristics of individuals in consideration of group trends. See Chapters 12 and 15.

Randomization/randomized control trials (RCTs). See **experimental designs.**

Recall: Techniques used to elicit information on, among other things, behavior (e.g., contraceptive use, time use), access to public services (e.g., water, education, health), economic status (e.g., income, employment, agricultural production), attitudes, knowledge, or beliefs (e.g., attitudes to child care, contraception, opinions about community or government agencies) at an earlier point in time—usually around the time the project began. Recall techniques include questionnaire items, in-depth interviews, life course research, and PRA techniques (see **PRA**). See Chapter 5.

Responsive evaluation: Evaluation more attentive to emerging issues than to an initial design (Stake 1975). See Chapter 13.

Results chain: A diagram showing the sequence of steps linking the project design to the intended outcome. At each step, the results chain shows the desired outcome and the possible alternative negative or nondesired outcomes. The preparation of a results chain can be used in conjunction with logical framework analysis to identify the critical assumptions and the key indicators to be incorporated into the logframe. See Chapters 2 and 10.

RWE (RealWorld Evaluation): An approach developed for evaluations operating under budget, time, data, or political constraints intended to maximize the rigor of methods and the validity of findings. See Chapter 1.

Sampling frame/pool: A list of all of the units in the population to be sampled that is used to identify the units to be included in the sample. See Chapter 15.

Scenarios: Common situations that an evaluation may face. See Chapters 1 and 2.

Semiotics: Study of signs, what they denote, and what effects they have within cultural settings. See Chapter 13.

Social funds/social investment funds: Funds used to support social infrastructure projects identified by local communities (e.g., water supply, schools, roads, health centers, etc.) and usually constructed by local government agencies with a high level of community involvement.

Stakeholders: Individuals, groups, or organizations having an interest in a program. Stakeholders may include funding agencies, policymakers, planners, advocacy groups, the communities, or groups that the program is intended to benefit and other groups that might be affected negatively or positively. See Chapters 2, 6, 8, 16, and 17.

Standard deviation: A widely used statistical measure to describe how widely dispersed sample scores are around the sample mean. The more widely dispersed the scores, the greater the value of the standard deviation. An important characteristic of the standard deviation for most distributions is that approximately 65% of all observations will lie within one standard deviation of the mean, and approximately 95% will lie within two standard deviations of the mean. For example, if the average household income is $200 per month with a standard deviation of $25, that means that approximately 65% of households would have a monthly income between $175 and $225 (within $25 of the mean), and 95% would have monthly incomes between $150 and $250. See Chapters 15 and 18.

Standardized effect size: See **effect size.**

Statistical conclusion validity: The analysis of evaluation findings may arrive at incorrect conclusions as to whether the project had an effect due to weaknesses in the sample design or to the incorrect application or interpretation of statistical tests. See Chapter 7 and Appendix A.

Substitution analysis: A process for determining whether, or how much, budget support funds provided by a donor were used by the recipient government or other organization to reallocate other funds to different purposes, thus reducing the total available for the purpose the donor wished to support. See Chapter 16.

Summative evaluation: An evaluation conducted to determine the quality, merit, worth, or shortcomings of a program. By contrast, *formative evaluation* is intended to provide information to help improve the program during its implementation. See Chapter 11.

Sustainability: Whether a project or its effect will continue over time. Sustainability can either be predicted prospectively to estimate future effects or determined retrospectively some time after the project has ended (ex-post evaluation). See Chapters 2 and 10.

Target population: The population eligible to receive program services or benefits.

Terms of reference (ToR): A document prepared by the evaluation client specifying the objectives, contents, organization, and timeline for the evaluation and defining the scope of work and responsibilities for the evaluation consultant(s). Often used interchangeably with Statement of Work (SoW). See Chapter 17.

Thick description: The term was first used by the anthropologist Clifford Gertz in The Interpretation of Cultures (1973) to describe human behavior and the context within which it takes place. The purpose was to provide a sufficiently detailed and contextualized description to make the behavior meaningful to an outsider.

Tracer study: The location and reinterviewing of subjects in an earlier study where records do not list their present location, often through knowledgeable people from the same community.

Transferability: In qualitative evaluations, a concept analogous to the quantitative concept of generalizability or external validity. See Chapters 7 and Appendix B.

Triangulation: Improving the validity of evaluation findings by drawing information from different sources, through different methods of inquiry, by different investigators, or through analysis from different theoretical or conceptual frameworks. See Chapters 11, 13, and 14.

Trustworthiness: A term used in qualitative evaluation with approximately the same meaning as validity in quantitative evaluation. See Chapter 13.

Two-tailed test: See **one-tailed test.**

Type I error/false positive: Wrongly concluding that a program had a statistically significant impact on the outcome variable when in fact it does not. See Chapter 15.

Type II error/false negative: Wrongly concluding that a program does *not* have a statistically significant impact on the outcome variable when in fact it does. See Chapter 15.

Utilization: Whether and how evaluation findings are used. See Chapters 8 and 18.

Unobservables: See **omitted variable problem.**

Utilization-focused evaluation: Evaluation responsive to the information needs of "primary intended users," facilitating their use of evaluation results or catalytic validity (Patton 2002a, 2002b). See Chapters 2 and 8.

Useful Websites Pertinent to RealWorld Evaluation

Websites

International Organization for Cooperation in Evaluation (IOCE): www.IOCE.net

Umbrella organization linking professional evaluators and evaluation associations. Includes database of national, regional, and international associations, societies, and informal networks. Promotes many forms of evaluation capacity building.

Center for Global Development (CGD): www.cgdev.org

Published the critical "When Will We Ever Learn? Improving Lives through Impact Evaluation" article in 2006 that has promoted much reexamination by international development agencies on what should be involved in rigorous impact evaluations. Includes links to a large number of impact evaluations that use randomized controlled trials (RCTs) and other statistical designs.

Abdul Latif Jameel Poverty Action Lab (J-PAL) at MIT: www.povertyactionlab.org

According to their website, J-PAL is dedicated to the "use of Randomized Evaluations to answer questions critical to poverty alleviation."

Network of Networks for Impact Evaluation (NONIE): www.worldbank.org/ieg/nonie and www.nonie2011.org

Formed by the major international donor agencies, NONIE initially brought together three networks: Organization for Economic Cooperation and Development/Development Advisory Committee (OECD/DAC) bilateral donors, multilateral development banks (like the World Bank), and UN agencies (like United Nations Development Programme [UNDP] and United Nations Children's Fund [UNICEF]). In 2008, a fourth network led by IOCE was invited to join NONIE, representing professional evaluators, especially those working in developing countries.

International Initiative for Impact Evaluation 3ie: www.3ieimpact.org

Formed with the encouragement of CGD, NONIE, and others, with strong financial support by the Gates Foundation, 3ie promotes rigorous impact evaluations of many issues of interest to the international development community. The site also includes links to the series of systematic reviews of the evaluation research literature on topics such as water, sanitation, and hygiene to combat childhood diarrhea in developing countries; community-based intervention packages for preventing maternal morbidity and mortality and improving neonatal outcomes; agriculture; education; and social development.

American Evaluation Association (AEA): www.eval.org

Comprehensive and sophisticated website of the 6,500-member AEA. Highly recommended hub for searching for many useful resources related to evaluation.

Better Evaluation: http://betterevaluation.org

"We advocate for systematic and informed choices of methods, based on an understanding of what is available. We advocate for building and sharing information on methods based on evidence of their utility and feasibility. We advocate for learning across sectors, across countries, and across evaluators, evaluation managers, and evaluation users."

My M&E portal: www.mymande.org

Set up by Marco Segone of UNICEF, **My M&E** is an interactive WEB 2.0 platform to share knowledge on country-led monitoring and evaluation (M&E) systems worldwide. In addition to being a learning resource, **My M&E** facilitates the strengthening of a global community, while identifying good practices and lessons learned about program monitoring and evaluation in general and on country-led M&E systems in particular.

Millennium Development Goals: www.un.org/ millenniumgoals

The UN system's website for information on the millennium development goals (MDGs) that provide specific goals and indicators to measure progress toward the reduction of global poverty. Also includes information on the large number of national MDG reports that are now being produced regularly by many developing countries.

The Campbell Collaboration: http://www .campbellcollaboration.org

The goal of this website is to help people make well-informed decisions by preparing, maintaining, and disseminating systematic reviews in education, crime and justice, and social welfare. Most of the reviews are based on RCTs.

The Cochrane Collaboration: http://www.thecochrane library.com/view/0/index.html

This is an international, independent, not-for-profit organization of over 28,000 contributors from more than 100 countries, dedicated to making up-to-date, accurate information about the effects of health care readily available worldwide. Contributors work together to produce systematic reviews of health care interventions, known as Cochrane Reviews, which are published online in *The Cochrane Library.* Cochrane Reviews are intended to help providers, practitioners, and patients make informed decisions about health care and are the most comprehensive, reliable, and relevant source of evidence on which to base these decisions. The reviews seek to achieve the highest possible level of evidence-based findings, in most cases using RCTs.

The World Bank Poverty Website: http://www1 .worldbank.org/prem/poverty/ie/evaluationdb.htm

The Bank's website includes various catalogues of impact evaluations. Most but not all of the evaluations use RCTs. Also includes a section on impact evaluation methodologies and a wide range of publications, most of which are available free of charge.

What Works (in Education) Clearinghouse: http:// ies.ed.gov/ncee/wwc/publications_reviews

This site includes synthetic reviews of the evaluations that have been conducted of a wide range of education interventions, mostly based on RCTs. It also includes guidelines on different impact evaluation methodologies that the clearinghouse considered "rigorous." This includes detailed guidelines on RCTs, regression discontinuity, and single-case evaluations.

DAC Network on Development Evaluation: http:// www.oecd.org/document/5/0,3746,en_21571361_34 047972_34079941_1_1_1_1,00.html

The DAC evaluation site is maintained by the Development Advisory Committee of the Organization for Economic Cooperation and Development (OECD). It contains links to dozens of other evaluation websites as well as a wide range of OECD/DAC publications and guidelines on development evaluation.

USAID: www.usaid.gov and www.usaid.gov/policy/ evalweb

Includes a link to the 2011 United States Agency for International Development (USAID) Evaluation Policy and other evaluation resources.

RealWorld Evaluation: www.RealWorldEvaluation .org

Authors of the present book share PowerPoint presentations in many languages, handouts, and other resources they have used in many training workshops in many countries, typically as part of conferences organized by evaluation associations. There is a page addressed to alternative counterfactuals and also a page dedicated to supplemental materials directly related to this second edition of the *RealWorld Evaluation* book.

Other Resources

Morra-Imas, L., and R. Rist. 2009. *The Road to Results.* Washington, DC: World Bank.

This is a hard-copy book that contains one of the most extensive sets of website references. An electronic version of the book, containing all of the electronic links, is available for purchase at www.worldbank.org/ r/2r.

References and Additional Resources

Abma, T. 1997. "Sharing Power, Facing Ambiguity." Pp. 105–19 in *Evaluation and the Postmodern Dilemma*, edited by L. Mabry. Greenwich, CT: JAI Press.

Alderman, H. 2000. "Anthropometry." Pp. 251–72 in *Designing Household Survey Questionnaires for Developing Countries: Lessons from 15 Years of the Living Standards Measurement Study*, vol. 1, edited by M. Grosh and P. Glewwe. Washington, DC: World Bank.

Altschuld, J. and D. Kumar. 2010. *Needs Assessment: An Overview.* Thousand Oaks, CA: Sage.

Alwin, D. 2009. "Assessing the Validity and Reliability of Timeline and Event History Data." Pp. 277–301 in *Calendar and Time Diary Methods in Life Course Research*, edited by R. Belli, F. Stafford, and D. Alwin. Thousand Oaks, CA: Sage.

American Anthropological Association. 1998. *Code of Ethics of the American Anthropological Association.* Arlington, VA: American Anthropological Association. Retrieved from www.aaanet.org/committees/ethics/ethcode.htm

American Association of University Professors. 2001. "Protecting Human Beings: Institutional Review Boards and Social Science Research." *Academe* 87(3):55–67.

American Evaluation Association. 1995. "Guiding Principles for Evaluators." Pp. 19–26 in *Guiding Principles for Evaluators*, edited by W. R. Shadish, D. L. Newman, M. A. Scheirer, and C. Wye. New Directions for Program Evaluation, No. 66. San Francisco: Jossey-Bass.

American Evaluation Association. 2003. "Response to U.S. Department of Education Notice of Proposed Priority, 'Scientifically Based Evaluation Methods.'" *Federal Register*, November 4, RIN 1890-ZA00. Retrieved October 3, 2005 (www.eval.org/doestatement.htm).

American Evaluation Association. 2004. *Guiding Principles for Evaluators.* Retrieved November 15, 2005 (www.eval.org/Guiding%20Principles.htm).

American Evaluation Association. 2011. *American Evaluation Association Public Statement on Cultural Competence in Evaluation.* Fairhaven, MA: American Evaluation Association. Retrieved April 22, 2011 (www.eval.org/ccstatement.asp).

American Psychological Association. 2007. *Ethical Principles of Psychologists and Code of Conduct.* Washington, DC: American Psychological Association. Retrieved from www.apa.org/ethics/code2002.html

American Sociological Association. 1997. *Code of Ethics.* Washington, DC: American Sociological Association. Retrieved from www.asanet.org/members/ecoderev.html

Anderson, G. A. 1989. "Critical Ethnography in Education: Origins, Current Status, and New Directions." *Review of Educational Research* 59(3):249–70.

Aron, A. and E. Aron. 2000. *Statistics for the Behavioral and Social Sciences: A Brief Course.* 2d ed. Upper Saddle River, NJ: Prentice Hall.

Aron, A., E. Coups, and E. Aron. 2010. *Statistics for the Behavioral and Social Sciences: A Brief Course.* 5th ed. Upper Saddle River, NJ: Prentice Hall.

Atkinson, P. and A. Coffey. 2004. "Analyzing Documentary Realities." Pp. 45–62 in *Qualitative Research: Theory, Method and Practice*, 2d ed., edited by D. Silverman. Thousand Oaks, CA: Sage.

Atkinson, P. and M. Hammersley. 1994. "Ethnography and Participant Observation." Pp. 2248–261 in *Handbook of Qualitative Research*, edited by N. K. Denzin and Y. S. Lincoln. Thousand Oaks, CA: Sage.

AusAID. 2008. *Manage the Independent Evaluation of an Aid Activity.* Guidelines Series. Canberra, Australia: AusAID.

Australasian Evaluation Society. 2006. *Guidelines for Ethical Conduct of Evaluations.* Retrieved from www.aes.asn.au

Australian Institute of Aboriginal and Torres Strait Islander Studies. 2000. *Guidelines for Ethical Research in Indigenous Studies.* Canberra: Australian Institute of Aboriginal and Torres Strait Islander Studies.

Baker, J. 2000. *Evaluating the Impacts of Development Projects on Poverty: A Handbook for Practitioners.* Directions in Development. Washington, DC: World Bank.

Bamberger, M. 2000a. "The Evaluation of International Development Programs: A View from the Front." *American Journal of Evaluation* 21(1):95–102.

Bamberger, M. 2000b. "Opportunities and Challenges for Integrating Quantitative and Qualitative Research." Pp. 3–36 in *Integrating Quantitative and Qualitative Research in Development Projects,* edited by M. Bamberger. Directions in Development. Washington, DC: World Bank.

Bamberger, M. 2001. "Evaluation in Developing Countries: Experience with Agricultural Research and Development and the Annotated Bibliography of International Program Evaluation." *American Journal of Evaluation* 21(1):117–22.

Bamberger, M. 2008. *Institutionalizing Impact Evaluation Within the Framework of a Monitoring and Evaluation System.* Independent Evaluation Group. Washington, DC: World Bank.

Bamberger, M. 2009a. *Institutionalizing Impact Evaluation Opportunities for ODA Agencies.* Trends in Development Assistance Series 5. Tokyo: Foundation for Advanced Studies on International Development.

Bamberger, M. 2009b. "Strengthening Impact Evaluation Designs through the Reconstruction of Baseline Data." *Journal of Development Effectiveness* 1(1):37–59.

Bamberger, M. 2009c. "Checklist for Assessing Threats to the Validity of Findings and Recommendations of Impact Evaluations." Workshop on Conducting Impact Evaluations under Constraints, International Program for Development Evaluation Training, Ottawa. www.realworldevaluation.org

Bamberger, M. 2009d. *Institutionalizing Impact Evaluation Within the Framework of a Monitoring and Evaluation System.* Independent Evaluation Group. Washington, DC: World Bank.

Bamberger, M. 2009e. "Why Do Many Evaluations Have a Positive Bias? Should We Worry?" *Evaluation Journal of Australasia* 9(2):39–49.

Bamberger, M. and A. Kirk, editors. 2009. *Making Smart Policy: Using Impact Evaluation for Policy Making.* Case Studies on Evaluations That Influenced Policy. Doing Impact Evaluation Series No. 14. Thematic Group on Poverty Analysis, Monitoring and Impact Evaluation. Poverty Reduction and Economic Management. The World Bank. http://siteresources.worldbank.org/INTISPMA/Resources/383704-1146752240884/Doing_ie_series_14.pdf

Bamberger, M., K. Mackay, and E. Ooi. 2004. *Influential Evaluations: Evaluations That Improved Performance and Impacts of Development Programs.* Knowledge Programs and Evaluation Capacity Development. Operations Evaluation Department. Washington, DC: World Bank. www.worldbank.org/ieg/ecd

Bamberger, M., K. Mackay, and E. Ooi. 2005. *Influential Evaluations.* Detailed Case Studies. Operations Evaluation Department. Washington, DC: World Bank.

Bamberger, M., V. Rao, and M. Woolcock. 2010. "Using Mixed Methods in Monitoring and Evaluation: Experiences from International Development," in *SAGE Handbook of Mixed Methods Research,* 2d ed., edited by Charles Teddlie and Abbas Tashakkori. Thousand Oaks, CA: Sage.

Bamberger, M., J. Rugh, M. Church, and L. Fort. 2004. "Shoestring Evaluation: Designing Impact Evaluations under Budget, Time and Data Constraints." *American Journal of Evaluation* 25(1):5–37.

Bamberger, M., J. Rugh, and L. Mabry. 2006. *RealWorld Evaluation: Working under Budget, Time, Data and Political Constraints.* Thousand Oaks, CA: Sage.

Bamberger, M. and H. White. 2007. "Using Strong Evaluation Designs in Developing Countries: Experience and Challenges." *Journal of Multidisciplinary Evaluation* 4(8):58–73.

Ban, R. and V. Rao. 2009. *Is Deliberation Equitable? Evidence from Transcripts of Village Meetings in South Asia.* Policy Research Working Paper No. 4928. Washington, DC: World Bank.

Banerjee, A. 2007. *Making Aid Work.* Cambridge: MIT Press.

Barritt, L., T. Beekman, H. Bleeker, and K. Mulderij. 1985. *Researching Educational Practice.* Grand Forks: University of North Dakota, Center for Teaching and Learning.

Beebe, J. 2001. *Rapid Assessment Process: An Introduction.* Walnut Creek, CA: Altamira Press.

Begley, S. 2002, November 1. "Review Boards Pose Threat to Tough Work by Social Scientists." *Wall Street Journal,* p. B1.

Belli, F., F. Stafford, and D. Alwin. 2009. *Calendar and Time Diary Methods in Life Course Research.* Thousand Oaks, CA: Sage.

Berliner, D. C. 2002. "Educational Research: The Hardest Science of All." *Educational Researcher* 31(8):18–20.

Bernard, H. R. and G. W. Ryan. 2010. *Analyzing Qualitative Data: Systematic Approaches.* Thousand Oaks, CA: Sage.

Best, J. 2001. *Damned Lies and Statistics: Untangling Numbers from the Media, Politicians and Activists.* Los Angeles: University of California Press.

Best, J. 2004. *More Damned Lies and Statistics: How Numbers Confuse Public Issues.* Los Angeles: University of California Press.

Best, S. and C. H. Harrison. 2009. "Internet Survey Methods" in *The SAGE Handbook of Applied Social Research Methods,* 2d ed., edited by L. Bickman and D. Rog. Thousand Oaks, CA: Sage.

Bickman, L., editor. 1987. *Using Program Theory in Evaluation.* New Directions for Program Evaluation No. 33. San Francisco: Jossey-Bass.

Bickman, L., C. A. Heflinger, D. Northrup, S. Sonnichsen, and S. Schilling. 1998. "Long-Term Outcomes to Family Caregiver Empowerment." *Journal of Child and Family Studies* 7(3):269–82.

Bickman, L. and D. Rog, eds. 2009. *The SAGE Handbook of Applied Social Research Methods,* 2d ed. Thousand Oaks, CA: Sage.

Blake, W. c.1798–1809. *Annotations to Sir Joshua Reynolds's Discourses.* London.

Boruch, R., D. Weisburd, H. M. Turner III, A. Karpyn, and J. Littell. 2009. "Randomized Control Trials for Evaluation and Planning." Pp. 147–81 in *The SAGE Handbook of Applied Social Research Methods,* 2d ed., edited by L. Bickman and D. Rog. Thousand Oaks, CA: Sage.

Bourgois, P. 2002. "Respect at Work: Going Legit." Pp. 15–35 in *Ethnographic Research: A Reader,* edited by S. Taylor. Thousand Oaks, CA: Sage.

Brandt, R. S., ed. 1981. *Applied Strategies for Curriculum Evaluation.* Alexandria, VA: Association for Supervision and Curriculum Development.

British Educational Research Association. 2004. *Revised Ethical Guidelines for Educational Research.* Notts, UK: Author.

Bronfenbrenner, U. 1979. *The Ecology of Human Development.* Cambridge, MA: Harvard University Press.

Brown, A. L. and A. S. Palincsar. 1989. "Guided Cooperative Learning and Individual Knowledge Acquisition." In *Knowing, Learning, and Instruction: Essays in Honor of Robert Glaser,* edited by L. B. Resnick. Hillsdale, NJ: Lawrence Erlbaum.

Brown, G. 2000. "Evaluating the Impact of Water Supply Projects in Indonesia." Pp. 107–13 in *Integrating Quantitative and Qualitative Research in Development Projects,* edited by M. Bamberger. Directions in Development. Washington, DC: World Bank.

Caldwell, J. 1985. "Strengths and Limitations of the Survey Method Approach for Measuring and Understanding Fertility Change: Alternative Possibilities." Pp. 45–63 in *Reproductive Change in Developing Countries: Insights from the World Fertility Survey,* edited by J. Cleland and J. Hobcraft. Oxford, UK: Oxford University Press.

Campbell, D. T. 1966. "Pattern Matching as an Essential in Distal Knowing." Pp. 81–106 in *The Psychology of Egon Brunswick,* edited by K. R. Hammond. New York: Holt, Rinehart.

Campbell, D. T. 1978. "Qualitative Knowing in Action Research." Pp. 184–209 in *The Social Context of Methods,* edited by M. Brenner, P. Marsh, and P. Brenner. London: Croom Helm.

Campbell, D. T. and J. C. Stanley. 1963. *Experimental and Quasi-Experimental Designs for Research.* Boston: Houghton Mifflin.

CARE International. 2003. *Program Standards Framework.* www.globaldev.org/m&e

Carlsson, J., M. Eriksson-Baaz, A. M. Fallenius, and E. Lövgren. 1999. *Are Evaluations Useful? Cases from Swedish Development Cooperation.* Sida Studies in Evaluation, 99/1. Stockholm: Swedish International Development Agency. Retrieved September 1, 2005 (www.sida.se/Sida/articles/5400-5499/5452/STUD99-1.PDF).

Carrington, P., J. Scott, and S. Wasserman. 2005. *Models and Methods in Social Network Analysis.* Structural Analysis in the Social Sciences No. 27. New York: Cambridge University Press.

Carter, K. 1993. "The Place of Story in the Study of Teaching and Teacher Education." *Educational Researcher* 22(1):5–12, 18.

Carvalho, S. and H. White. 2004. "Theory Based Evaluation: The Case of Social Funds." *American Journal of Evaluation* 25(2):141–60.

Center for Global Development. 2006. "When Will We Ever Learn? Improving Lives through Impact Evaluation." http://www.dochas.ie/pages/resources/documents/WillWeEverLearn.pdf

Centers for Disease Control and Prevention. 1999. "Summary of the Framework for Program Evaluation in Public Health." *Morbidity and Mortality Weekly Report* 48 (No. RR-11):1–43. Retrieved August 10, 2005 (www.cdc.gov/eval/framework.htm).

Centre for Social Research and Evaluation. 2004. *Guidelines for Research and Evaluation with Maori.* Wellington, New Zealand: Ministry of Social Development, Centre for Social Research and Evaluation.

Chambers, R. 1983. *Rural Development: Putting the Last First.* Essex, UK: Longman.

Chambers, R. 1997. *Whose Reality Counts? Putting the First Last.* London, UK: ITDG.

Chambers, R. 2002. *Participatory Workshops: A Sourcebook of 21 Sets of Ideas and Activities.* Sterling, VA: Earthscan.

Chelimsky, E. 1994. "Evaluation: Where We Are." *Evaluation Practice* 15(3):339–45.

Chelimsky, E. 1997. "The Political Environment of Evaluation and What It Means for the Development of the Field." Pp. 53–68 in *Evaluation for the 21st Century,* edited by E. Chelimsky and W. R. Shadish. Thousand Oaks, CA: Sage.

Chelimsky, E. 1999. "The Political Environment of Evaluation and What It Means for the Development of the Field." *Evaluation Practice* 16(3):215–25.

Chelimsky, E. 2007. "Factors Influencing the Choice of Methods in Federal Evaluation Practice." Pp. 13–33 in *Informing Federal Policies on Evaluation Methodology: Building the Evidence Base for Method Choice in Government Sponsored Evaluation,* edited by G. Julnes and D. Rog. New Directions for Evaluation No. 113. San Francisco: Jossey-Bass.

Chelimsky, E. and W. R. Shadish, eds. 1997. *Evaluation for the 21st Century: A Handbook.* Thousand Oaks, CA: Sage.

Chen, H. T. 2005. *Practical Program Evaluation: Assessing and Improving Planning, Implementation, and Effectiveness.* Thousand Oaks, CA: Sage.

Clemmer, G. 2010. *The GIS: 20 Essential Skills.* Redlands, CA. ESRI Press.

Cohen, J. 1988. *Statistical Power Analysis for the Behavioral Sciences.* 2d ed. Hillsdale, NJ: Lawrence Erlbaum.

Community Tool Box. 2005. *Developing a Framework or Model of Change: Part J. Evaluating Community Programs and Initiatives.* http://ctb.ku.edu/tools/en/chapter_1036.htm

Cook, T. D. 2000. "The False Choice between Theory-Based Evaluation and Experimentation." Pp. 27–34 in *Program Theory in Evaluation: Challenges and Opportunities,* edited by P. Rogers, T. Hacsi, A. Petrosino, and T. Huebner. New Directions for Evaluation No. 87. San Francisco: Jossey-Bass.

Cook, T. D. and D. T. Campbell. 1979. *Quasi-Experimentation: Design & Analysis Issues for Field Settings.* Chicago: Rand McNally.

Coryn, C. L. S. 2009. "The Fundamental Characteristics of International Models and Mechanisms for Evaluating Government-Funded Research." *Access: Critical Perspectives on Communication, Cultural & Policy Studies* 27(1/2):9–25.

Coryn, C. L. S. and M. Scriven. 2007. "Are National-Level Research Evaluation Models Valid, Credible, Useful, Cost-Effective, and Ethical?" *Journal of Multidisciplinary Evaluation* 4(8):92–96.

Creswell, J. 2003. *Research Design: Qualitative, Quantitative and Mixed-Methods Approaches.* Thousand Oaks, CA: Sage.

Creswell, J. C., V. L. Clark, M. L. Gutmann, and W. Hanson. 2003. "Advanced Mixed Method Research Designs." Pp. 209–40 in *Handbook of Mixed Methods in Social & Behavioral Science,* edited by A. Tashakkori and C. Teddlie. Thousand Oaks, CA: Sage.

Dane, F. 2011. *Evaluating Research: Methodology for People Who Need to Read Research.* Thousand Oaks, CA: Sage.

Dart, J. 2010. *Collaborative Outcomes Reporting Techniques (CORT).* http://evaluationrevisited.files.wordpress.com/2010/05/overview-of-cort.pdf

Datta, L. 2007. "Looking at the Evidence: What Variations in Practice Might Indicate." Pp. 35–54 in *Informing Federal Policies on Evaluation Methodology: Building the Evidence Base for Method Choice in Government Sponsored Evaluation,* edited by G. Julnes and D. Rog. New Directions for Evaluation No. 113. San Francisco: Jossey-Bass.

Davidson, J. 2000. "Ascertaining Causality in Theory-Based Evaluation." Pp. 17–26 in *Program Theory in Evaluation: Challenges and Opportunities,* edited by P. Rogers, T. Hacsi, A. Petrosino, and T. Huebner. New Directions for Evaluation No. 87. San Francisco: Jossey-Bass.

Dayal, R., C. van Wijk, and N. Mukherjee. 2000. *Methodology for Participatory Assessments with Communities, Institutions and Policy Makers: Linking Sustainability with Demand, Gender and Poverty.* Washington, DC: World Bank, Water and Sanitation Program.

de Cervantes Saavedra, M. 1615/1964. *Don Quixote.* New York: Signet.

Deaton, A. 2005. "Measuring Poverty in a Growing World (or Measuring Growth in a Poor World)." *Review of Economics and Statistics* 87(1):1–19.

Deaton, A. 2009. "Instruments of Development: Randomization in the Tropics, and the Search for the Elusive Keys to Economic Development." The Keynes Lecture, British Academy.

Deaton, A. and M. Grosh. 2000. "Consumption." Pp. 91–134 in *Designing Household Survey Questionnaires for Developing Countries: Lessons from 15 Years of the Living Standards Measurement Study,* vol. 1, edited by M. Grosh and P. Glewwe. Washington, DC: World Bank.

DeMers, M. 2009. *GIS for Dummies.* Hoboken, NJ: John Wiley.

Denzin, N. K. 1989. *The Research Act: A Theoretical Introduction to Sociological Methods.* 3d ed. Englewood Cliffs, NJ: Prentice Hall.

Denzin, N. K. 1997. *Interpretive Ethnography: Ethnographic Practices for the 21st Century.* Thousand Oaks, CA: Sage.

Denzin, N. K. 2003. "IRBs and the Turn to Indigenous Research Ethics." Paper presented at the Human Subject Protection Regulations and Research Outside the Biomedical Sphere Conference, College of Law, University of Illinois Champaign-Urbana, April.

Denzin, N. K. and Y. S. Lincoln. 2000. *Handbook of Qualitative Research.* 2d ed. Thousand Oaks, CA: Sage.

Department of International Development (DFID). 2005. *Guidance on Evaluation and Review for DFID Staff.* Glasgow: Evaluation Department.

DeStefano, L. 1992. "Evaluating Effectiveness: A Comparison of Federal Expectations and Local Capabilities for Evaluation among Federally Funded Model Demonstration Programs." *Educational Evaluation and Policy Analysis* 14(2):157–68.

Dewey, J. 1916. *Democracy and Education: An Introduction to the Philosophy of Education.* New York: Macmillan.

Dewey, J. D., B. E. Montrosse, D. C. Schröter, C. D. Sullins, and J. R. Mattox. 2008. "Evaluator Competencies: What's Taught versus What's Sought." *American Journal of Evaluation* 29(3):268–87.

Dilthey, W. 1883/1976. *Einleitung in die Geisteswissenschaften (Introduction to the Human Sciences).* Pp. 157–263 in *W. Dilthey: Selected Writings,* edited by H. P. Richman. Cambridge, UK: Cambridge University Press.

Dimitrov, T. 2005. "Enhancing the Performance of a Major Environmental Project through a Focused Mid-Term Evaluation: The Kombinat za Cvetni Metali Environmental Improvement Project in Bulgaria." Pp. 50–57 in *Influential*

Evaluations: Evaluations That Improved Performance and Impacts of Development Programs. Operations Evaluation Department. Washington, DC: World Bank. http://worldbank.org/oed/ecd

Donaldson, S. 2003. "Theory Driven Program Evaluation in the New Millennium." Pp. 109–41 in *Evaluating Social Programs and Problems,* edited by S. Donaldson and M. Scriven. Mahwah, NJ: Lawrence Erlbaum.

Donaldson, S. 2007. *Program Theory-Driven Evaluation Science: Strategies and Applications.* Thousand Oaks, CA: Sage.

Donaldson, S., C. Christie, and M. Mark. 2009. *What Counts as Credible Evidence in Applied Research and Evaluation Practice?* Thousand Oaks, CA: Sage.

Duflo, E. and M. Kremer. 2005. "Use of Randomization in the Evaluation of Development Effectiveness." In *Evaluating Development Effectiveness,* edited by G. Pitman, O. Feinstein, and G. Ingram. New Brunswick, NJ: Transaction Publishers.

Duignan, P. 2011. *Impact/Outcome Evaluation Design Types: An Outcomes Theory Knowledge Basic Topic.* Version 65. http://knol.google.com/k/paul-duignan-phd/impact-outcome-evaluation-design-types/2m7zd68aaz774/10

Eisenhart, M. and L. Towne. 2003. "Contestation and Change in National Policy on 'Scientifically Based' Education Research." *Educational Researcher* 32(7):31–38.

Eisner, E. W. 1985. *The Art of Educational Evaluation: A Personal View.* London: Falmer.

Eisner, E. W. 1991. *The Enlightened Eye: Qualitative Inquiry and the Enhancement of Educational Practice.* New York: Macmillan.

Engela, R. and T. Ajam. 2010. *Implementing a Government-wide Monitoring and Evaluation System in South Africa.* Independent Evaluation Group. Washington, DC: World Bank. http://siteresources.worldbank.org/EXTEVACAPDEV/Resources/ecd_wp_21_south_africa.pdf

Erickson, F. 1986. "Qualitative Methods in Research on Teaching." Pp. 119–61 in *Handbook of Research on Teaching,* 3d ed., edited by M. C. Wittrock. New York: Macmillan.

Erickson, F. and K. Gutierrez. 2002. "Culture, Rigor, and Science in Educational Research." *Educational Researcher* 31(8):21–24.

Evaluation Center. n.d. *Evaluation Checklists.* Kalamazoo, MI: The Evaluation Center. www.wmich.edu/evalctr/checklists

Evergreen, S. D. H. and A. Cullen. 2010. "Moving to Genuine: Credible Cultural Competence." *Journal of Multidisciplinary Evaluation* 6(13):130–39.

Fetterman, D. M. 1996. *Empowerment Evaluation: Knowledge and Tools for Self-Assessment and Accountability.* Thousand Oaks, CA: Sage.

Feuer, M. J., L. Towne, and R. J. Shavelson. 2002. "Scientific Culture and Educational Research." *Educational Researcher* 31(8):4–14.

Figlio, D. 1995. "The Effect of Drinking Age Laws and Alcohol-Related Crashes: Time Series Evidence from Wisconsin." *Journal of Policy Analysis and Management* 14(4):555–66.

Fink, A. 2003a. *How to Design Survey Studies: Vol. 6. The Survey Kit.* 2d ed. Thousand Oaks, CA: Sage.

Fink, A. 2003b. *How to Sample in Surveys: Vol. 7. The Survey Kit.* 2d ed. Thousand Oaks, CA: Sage.

Fink, A. 2003c. *How to Manage, Analyze, and Interpret Survey Data: Vol. 9. The Survey Kit.* 2d ed. Thousand Oaks, CA: Sage.

Fink, A. 2003d. *How to Report on Surveys: Vol. 10. The Survey Kit.* 2d ed. Thousand Oaks, CA: Sage.

Fink, A. 2008. *Practicing Research: Discovering Evidence That Matters.* Thousand Oaks, CA: Sage.

Fink, A. 2009. *How to Conduct Surveys: A Step-by-Step Guide.* 4th ed. Thousand Oaks, CA: Sage.

Firestone, W. A. 1993. "Alternative Arguments for Generalizing from Data as Applied to Qualitative Research." *Educational Researcher* 22(4):16–23.

Fisher, C. B. 2003. *Decoding the Ethics Code: A Practical Guide for Psychologists.* Thousand Oaks, CA: Sage.

Fitzpatrick, J., C. Christie, and M. Mark. 2009. *Evaluation in Action: Interviews with Expert Evaluators.* Thousand Oaks, CA: Sage.

Fitzpatrick, J. L. and M. Morris, eds. 1999. *Current and Emerging Ethical Challenges in Evaluation.* New Directions for Evaluation No. 82. San Francisco: Jossey-Bass.

Flinders, D. J. 1992. "In Search of Ethical Guidance: Constructing a Basis for Dialogue." *Qualitative Studies in Education* 5(2):101–15.

Fogel, R. W. 1964. *Railroads and American Economic Growth: Essays in Econometric History.* Baltimore: Johns Hopkins University Press.

Fontana, A. and J. H. Frey. 1994. "Interviewing: The Art of Science." Pp. 361–76 in *Handbook of Qualitative Research,* edited by N. K. Denzin & Y. S. Lincoln. Thousand Oaks, CA: Sage.

Foucault, M. 1980. *Power/Knowledge.* Cambridge, MA: Harvard University Press.

Fowler, F. J. and C. Cosenza. 2009. "Design and Evaluation of Survey Questions." Pp. 375–412 in *The SAGE Handbook of Applied Social Research Methods,* 2d ed., edited by L. Bickman and D. Rog. Thousand Oaks, CA: Sage.

Frankfort-Nachmias, C. and A. Leon-Guerrero. 2011. *Social Statistics for a Diverse Society.* 6th ed. Thousand Oaks, CA: Sage.

Freeman, M., ed. 2010. *Critical Social Theory and Evaluation Practice.* New Directions for Evaluation No. 127. San Francisco: Jossey-Bass.

Frick, U. 2007. *Managing Quality in Qualitative Research.* Thousand Oaks, CA: Sage.

Funnell, S. 1997. "Program Logic: An Adaptable Tool." *Evaluation News and Comment* 6(1):5–17.

Funnell, S. 2000. "Developing and Using a Program Theory Matrix for Program Evaluation and Performance Monitoring." Pp. 91–102 in *Program Theory in Evaluation: Challenges and Opportunities,* edited by P. Rogers, T. Hacsi, A. Petrosino, and T. Huebner. New Directions for Evaluation, No. 87. San Francisco: Jossey-Bass.

Funnell, S. and P. Rogers. 2011. *Purposeful Program Theory: Effective Use of Theories of Change and Logic Models.* San Francisco: Jossey-Bass.

Gadamer, H.-G. 1960. *Truth and Method,* 2nd rev. ed. Translated by J. Weinsheimer and D. G. Marshall. New York, NY: Crossroad.

Galasso, E. and M. Ravallion. 2004. "Social Protection in a Crisis: Argentina's Plan Jefes y Jefas." *World Bank Economic Review* 18(3):367–400.

Geertz, C. 1973. *The Interpretation of Cultures: Selected Essays.* New York: Basic Books.

General Accounting Office. 1995. *Program Evaluation: Improving the Flow of Information to the Congress.* GAO/PEMD-95–1. Washington, DC: GAO.

Gertler, P., S. Martinez, P. Premand, L. Rawlings, and C. Vermeersch. 2011. *Impact Evaluation in Practice.* Washington, DC: World Bank.

Gibson, C. and M. Woolcock. 2008. "Empowerment, Deliberative Development and Local Level Politics in Indonesia: Participatory Projects as a Source of Countervailing Power." *Studies in Comparative International Development* 43(2):151–80.

Gibson, J. 2006. "Statistical Tools and Estimation Methods for Poverty Measures Based on Cross-Sectional Household Surveys." In *United Nations Handbook on Poverty Statistics: Concepts, Methods and Policy Use.* http://unstats.un.org/unsd/methods/poverty/chapter5l.htm

Glaser, B. G. and A. I. Strauss. 1967. *The Discovery of Grounded Theory.* Chicago: Aldine.

Glewwe, P. 2000. "Education." Pp. 143–76 in *Designing Household Survey Questionnaires for Developing Countries: Lessons from 15 years of the Living Standards Measurement Study,* vol. 1, edited by M. Grosh and P. Glewwe. Washington, DC: World Bank.

Glewwe, P., M. Kremer, S. Moulin, and E. Zitzewitz. 2004. "Retrospective vs. Prospective Analyses of School Inputs: The Case of Flip Charts in Kenya." *Journal of Development Economics* 74:251–68. Retrieved October 3, 2005 (www.povertyactionlab.com/projects/project.php?pid=26).

Gomez, L. 2000. *Gender Analysis of Two Components of the World Bank Transport Projects in Lima, Peru: Bikepaths and Busways.* http://web.worldbank.org/WBSITE/ EXTERNAL/TOPICS/ EXTGENDER/EXTGENDERTRANSPORT/0,,contentMDK:20202435~menuPK:522654 ~pagePK:148956~piPK:216618~theSitePK:338726,00 .html#Peru_Bike

Gray, D. 2004. *Doing Research in the Real World.* Thousand Oaks, CA: Sage.

Greene, J. C. 1997. "Participatory Evaluation." Pp. 171–89 in *Evaluation and the Postmodern Dilemma,* edited by L. Mabry. Greenwich, CT: JAI Press.

Greene, J. C. 2005. "Mixed Methods." Pp. 255–56 in *Encyclopedia of Evaluation,* edited by S. Mathison. Thousand Oaks, CA: Sage.

Greene, J. C. 2007. *Mixed Methods in Social Enquiry.* San Francisco: John Wiley.

Greene, J. C. and V. J. Caracelli. 2003. "Making Paradigmatic Sense of Mixed Methods Practice." Pp. 91–110 in *Handbook of Mixed Methods in Social & Behavioral Research,* edited by A. Tashakkori and C. Teddlie. Thousand Oaks, CA: Sage.

Greene, J. C., V. Caracelli, and W. F. Graham. 1989. "Toward a Conceptual Framework for Multimethod Evaluation Designs." *Educational Evaluation and Policy Analysis* 11:255–74.

Grosh, M. and P. Glewwe, editors. 2000. *Designing Household Survey Questionnaires for Developing Countries: Lessons from 15 Years of the Living Standards Measurement Study.* 3 vols. Washington, DC: World Bank.

Guba, E. G. 1978. *Toward a Methodology of Naturalistic Inquiry in Educational Evaluation.* Monograph 8. Los Angeles: UCLA Center for the Study of Evaluation.

Guba, E. G. 1990. *The Paradigm Dialog.* Thousand Oaks, CA: Sage.

Guba, E. G. and Y. S. Lincoln. 1989. *Fourth Generation Evaluation.* Newbury Park, CA: Sage.

Guba, E. G. and Y. S. Lincoln. 1994. "Competing Paradigms in Qualitative Research." Pp. 105–17 in *Handbook of Qualitative Research,* edited by N. K. Denzin and Y. S. Lincoln. Thousand Oaks, CA: Sage.

Guba, E. G. and Y. S. Lincoln. 2005. "Paradigmatic Controversies, Contradictions, and Emerging Confluences." Pp. 191–216 in *Handbook of Qualitative Research,* 3d ed., edited by N. K. Denzin and Y. S. Lincoln. Thousand Oaks, CA: Sage.

Gubbels, P. and C. Koss. 2000. *From the Roots Up: Strengthening Organizational Capacity through Guided Self-Assessment.* Oklahoma City, OK: World Neighbors.

Guggenheim, S. E. 2006. "Crises and Contradictions: Explaining a Community Development Project in Indonesia." Pp. 111–44 in *The Search for Empowerment: Social Capital as Idea and Practice at the World Bank,* edited by A. Bebbington, S. E. Guggenheim, W. Olsen, and M. Woolcock. Bloomfield, CT: Kumarian Press.

Habermas, J. 1975. *Legitimation Crisis.* Translated by T. McCarthy. Boston: Beacon Press.

Habermas, J. 1981/1987. *Lifeworld and System: A Critique of Functionalist Reason.* In *The Theory of Communicative Action,* vol. 2. Translated by T. McCarthy. Boston: Beacon Press.

Habermas, J. 1987. *The Philosophical Discourse of Modernity.* Translated by F. Lawrence. Cambridge: MIT Press.

Handwerker, W. P. 2001. *Quick Ethnography.* Walnut Creek, CA: Altamira Press.

Harvey, A. S. and M. E. Taylor. 2000. "Time Use." Pp. 249–74 in *Designing Household Survey Questionnaires for Developing Countries: Lessons from 15 Years of the Living Standards Measurement Study,* vol. 2, edited by M. Grosh and P. Glewwe. Washington, DC: World Bank.

Hashemi, S., S. R. Schuler, and A. P. Riley. 1996. "Rural Credit Programs and Women's Empowerment in Bangladesh." *World Development* 24(4):635–53.

Heath, C. 2004. "Analyzing Face to Face Interaction: Video and the Visual and Material." Pp. 283–304 in *Qualitative Research: Theory, Method and Practice,* edited by D. Silverman. Thousand Oaks, CA: Sage.

Heath, J., P. Grasso, and J. Johnson. 2005. *World Bank Country, Sector and Project Evaluation Approaches.* Ottawa: International Program for Development Evaluation Training (IPDET).

Heidegger, M. 1927/1996. *Being and Time.* Translated by J. Stambaugh. Albany, NY: State University of New York Press.

Henry, G. 1990. *Practical Sampling.* Applied Social Science Methods Series, Vol. 21. Newbury Park, CA: Sage.

Hentschel, J. 1999. "Contextuality and Data Collection Methods: A Framework and Application to Health Service Utilization." *Journal of Development Studies* 35(4):64–94.

Hochschild, A. 1998. *King Leopold's Ghost.* Boston: Houghton Mifflin.

Hodder, I. 1994. "The Interpretation of Documents and Material Culture." Pp. 403–12 in *Handbook of Qualitative Research,* edited by N. K. Denzin and Y. S. Lincoln. Thousand Oaks, CA: Sage.

Holley, K. A. and J. Colyar. 2009. "Rethinking Texts: Narrative and the Construction of Qualitative Research." *Educational Researcher* 38(9):680–86.

Holstein, J. A. and J. F. Gubrium. 1994. "Phenomenology, Ethnomethodology, and Interpretive Practice." Pp. 262–72 in *Handbook of Qualitative Research,* edited by N. K. Denzin and Y. S. Lincoln. Thousand Oaks, CA: Sage.

Hood, S., R. K. Hopson, and H. Frierson, editors. 2005. *The Role of Culture and Cultural Context in Evaluation: A Mandate for Inclusion, the Discovery of Truth, and Understanding in Evaluative Theory and Practice.* Greenwich, CT: Information Age.

Horton, D. and R. Mackay, eds. 1999. "Evaluation in Developing Countries: Experience with Agricultural Research and Development." *Knowledge, Technology and Policy* 11(4, Special Issue).

House, E. 1972. "The Conscience of Educational Evaluation." *Teachers College Record* 73(3):405–14.

House, E. 1990. "Trends in Evaluation." *Educational Researcher* 19(3):24–28.

House, E. R. 1991. "Evaluation and Social Justice: Where Are We?" In *Evaluation and Education: At Quarter Century,* edited by M. W. McLaughlin and D. C. Phillips. Ninetieth Yearbook of the National Study for the Study of Education. Chicago: University of Chicago Press.

House, E. R. 1993. *Professional Evaluation: Social Impact and Political Consequences.* Newbury Park, CA: Sage.

House, E. R. 1994. "Integrating the Quantitative and Qualitative." Pp. 13–22 in *The Qualitative-Quantitative Debate: New Perspectives,* edited by C. S. Reichardt and S. F. Rallis. New Directions for Program Evaluation No. 61. San Francisco: Jossey-Bass.

House, E. R. 1995. "Principled Evaluation: A Critique of the AEA Guiding Principles." Pp. 27–34 in *Guiding Principles for Evaluators,* edited by W. R. Shadish, D. L. Newman, M. A. Scheirer, and C. Wye. New Directions for Program Evaluation No. 66. San Francisco: Jossey-Bass.

House, E. R., G. V. Glass, L. D. McLean, and D. F. Walker. 1978. "No Simple Answer: Critique of the Follow Through Evaluation." *Harvard Educational Review* 48:128–60.

House, E. R. and K. R. Howe. 1998. "The Issue of Advocacy in Evaluation." *American Journal of Evaluation* 19(2):233–36.

House, E. R. and K. R. Howe. 1999. *Values in Evaluation and Social Research.* Thousand Oaks, CA: Sage.

House, E. R. and K. R. Howe. 2000. "Deliberative Democratic Evaluation." Pp. 3–12 in *New Directions for Evaluation 85,* edited by K. Ryan and L. DeStefano. San Francisco: Jossey-Bass.

Humphreys, L. 1970. *Tearoom Trade: Impersonal Sex in Public Places.* Chicago: Aldine De Gruyter.

Hunter-Gault, C. 1997, May 16. "An Apology 65 Years Too Late." *Online NewsHour.* www.pbs.org/newshour/bb/health/may97/tuskegee_5-16

International Military Tribunals. 1949. *Trials of War Criminals before the Nuremberg Military Tribunals under Control Council Law No. 10, October 1946–April 1949.* Vol. 2. Washington, DC: Government Printing Office. Retrieved July 10, 2006 (www.csu.edu.au/learning/ncgr/gpi/odyssey/privacy/NurCode.html).

International Organization for Migration. 2006. *IOM Evaluation Guidelines.* Geneva, Switzerland: Office of the Inspector General.

International Program for Development Evaluation Training. 2004. *Evaluation Models.* Ottawa, Canada: International Program for Development Evaluation Training.

Jalan, J. and M. Ravallion. 1998. "Are There Dynamic Gains from a Poor-Area Development Program?" *Journal of Public Economics* 67 (1):65–85.

Jha, S., Rao, V., and Woolcok, M. 2007. "Governance in the Gullies: Democratic Responsiveness and Community Leadership in Delhi's Slums." *World Development* 35(2), 230–246.

Johnson, R. B. and A. J. Onwuegbuzie. 2004. "Mixed Methods Research: A Research Paradigm Whose Time Has Come." *Educational Researcher* 33(7):14–26.

Joint Committee on Standards for Educational Evaluation. 1988. *The Personnel Evaluation Standards: How to Assess Systems for Evaluating Educators.* Newbury Park, CA: Corwin.

Joint Committee on Standards for Educational Evaluation. 1994. *The Program Evaluation Standards: How to Assess Evaluations of Educational Programs.* 2d ed. Thousand Oaks, CA: Sage.

Joint United Nations Programme on HIV/AIDS(UNAIDS). 2000, May. *Ethical Considerations in HIV Preventive Vaccine Research (04.07E).* Geneva, Switzerland: UNAIDS. http://pre.ethics.gc.ca/english/links/links.cfm

Jolliffe, D. 2001. "Measuring Absolute and Relative Poverty: The Sensitivity of Estimated Household Consumption to Survey Design." *Journal of Economic and Social Measurement* 27(1):1–23.

Jones, J. H. 1993. *Bad Blood: The Tuskegee Syphilis Experiment.* New York: Free Press.

Jones, P. W. 1992. *World Bank Financing of Education: Lending, Learning and Development.* London: Routledge.

Julnes, G. and D. Rog, editors. 2007. *Informing Federal Policies on Evaluation Methodology: Building the Evidence Base for Method Choice in Government Sponsored Evaluations.* New Directions for Evaluation No. 113. San Francisco. Jossey-Bass.

Justice, J. 1986. *Policies, Plans and People: Culture and Health Development in Nepal.* Berkeley: University of California Press.

Kane, M. 1994. "Validating the Performance Standards Associated with Passing Scores." *Review of Educational Research* 64(3):425–561.

Kane, M. and W. Trochim. 2007. *Concept Mapping for Planning and Evaluation.* Thousand Oaks, CA: Sage.

Kane, M. and W. Trochim. 2009. "Concept Mapping for Applied Social Research." *In The SAGE Handbook of Applied Social Research Methods,* edited by L. Bickman and D. Rog. Thousand Oaks, CA: Sage.

Khandker, R. S., G. B. Koolwal, and H. A. Samad. 2010. *Handbook on Impact Evaluation: Quantitative Methods and Practices.* Washington, DC: World Bank.

Khandker, S. 1998. *Fighting Poverty with MicroCredit: Experience in Bangladesh.* Oxford, UK: Oxford University Press.

Kim, J., H. Alderman, and P. Orazem, 1999. "Can Private School Subsidies Increase Schooling for the Poor? The Quetta Urban Fellowship Program." *World Bank Economic Review* 13(3):443–66.

King, J., L. Stevahn, G. Ghere, and J. Minnema. 2001. "Toward a Taxonomy of Essential Evaluator Competencies." *American Journal of Evaluation* 22(2):229–47.

Klugman, J. 2002. *A Sourcebook for Poverty Reduction Strategies.* 2 vols. Washington, DC: World Bank.

Knoke, D. and S. Yang. 2008. *Social network analysis.* 2d ed. Quantitative Applications in the Social Sciences No. 154. Thousand Oaks, CA: Sage.

Kovach, H. and Y. Lansman. 2006, June. *World Bank and IMF Conditionality: A Development Injustice.* Brussels, Belgium: European Network on Debt and Development (Eurodad) report. www.globalpolicy.org/socecon/bwi-wto/wbank/index.htm

Kraemer, H. C. and S. Thiemann. 1987. *How Many Subjects? Statistical Power Analysis in Research.* Newbury Park, CA: Sage.

Kratochwill, T. R., J. Hitchcock, R. H. Homer, J. R. Levin, S. L. Odom, D. M. Rindskopf, and W. R. Shadish. 2010. *Single-Case Design Technical Documentation. What Works Clearinghouse.* Retrieved August 9, 2011 (http://ies.ed.gov/ncee/wwc/pdf/wwc_scd.pdf).

Krueger, R. A. 2005. "Focus Groups." Pp. 158–60 in *Encyclopedia of Evaluation,* edited by S. Mathison. Thousand Oaks, CA: Sage.

Krueger, R. A. and M. A. Casey. 2000. *Focus Groups: A Practical Guide for Applied Research.* 3d ed. Thousand Oaks, CA: Sage.

Kuhn, T. 1962. *The Structure of Scientific Revolutions.* Princeton, NJ: Princeton University Press.

Kumar, K. ed. 1993. *Rapid Appraisal Methods: Regional and Sectoral Studies.* Washington, DC: World Bank.

Kumar, S. 2002. *Methods for Community Participation: A Complete Guide for Practitioners.* London: ITDG.

Kusek, J. and R. Rist. 2004. *Ten Steps to a Results-Based Monitoring and Evaluation System.* Washington, DC: World Bank.

Lather, P. 1993. "Fertile Obsession: Validity after Poststructuralism." *The Sociological Quarterly,* 34(4):673–93.

Lee, H. 1960. *To Kill a Mockingbird.* Philadelphia: Lippincott.

Leeuw, F. 2003. "Reconstructing Program Theories: Methods Available and Problems to Be Solved." *American Journal of Evaluation* 24(1):5–20.

Leeuw, F. and J. Jos Vaessen. 2009. *Impact Evaluations and Development. NONIE Guidance on Impact Evaluation.*

Draft prepared for the Cairo International Evaluation Conference, April 2009, Network of Networks on Impact Evaluation (NONIE).

Lenne, B. and H. Cleland. 1987. *Describing Program Logic*. Program Evaluation Bulletin No. 2. Sydney, Australia: Public Service Board of New South Wales.

Lewis, O. 1961. *The Children of Sanchez*. New York: Random House.

Lewis, O. 1965. *La Vida: A Puerto Rican Family in the Culture of Poverty in San Juan and New York*. New York: Random House.

Lincoln, Y. S. and E. G. Guba. 1985. *Naturalistic Inquiry*. Beverly Hills, CA: Sage.

Linn, R. L. 2000. "Assessments and Accountability." *Educational Researcher* 29(2):4–16.

Lipsey, M. W. 1990. *Design Sensitivity: Statistical Power for Experimental Research*. Newbury Park, CA: Sage.

Lipsey, M. W. 1993. "Theory as Method: Small Theories of Treatment." Pp. 5–38 in *Understanding Causes and Generalizing about Them*, edited by L. Sechrest and A. Scott. New Directions for Program Evaluation No. 57. San Francisco: Jossey-Bass.

Litwin, M. 2003. *How to Assess and Interpret Survey Psychometrics*. 2d ed. The Survey Kit, Vol. 2. Thousand Oaks, CA: Sage.

Lohr, S. 1999. *Sampling Design and Analysis*. New York: Duxbury Press.

Mabry, L., ed. 1997. *Evaluation and the Postmodern Dilemma*. Greenwich, CT: JAI Press.

Mabry, L. 1998. "Case Study Methods." Pp. 155–70 in *Evaluation Research for Educational Productivity*, edited by H. J. Walberg and A. J. Reynolds. Greenwich, CT: JAI Press.

Mabry, L. 1999. "Circumstantial Ethics." *American Journal of Evaluation* 20(2):199–212.

Mabry, L. 2001. "Representing the Truth about Program Quality or the Truth about Representing Program Quality." Pp. 19–27 in *Visions of Quality: How Evaluators Define, Understand, and Represent Program Quality*, edited by A. Benson, D. M. Hinn, and C. Lloyd. Amsterdam: JAI Press.

Mabry, L. 2003. "In Living Color: Qualitative Methods in Educational Evaluation." Pp. 167–85 in *International Handbook of Educational Evaluation*, edited by T. Kellaghan and D. L. Stufflebeam. Boston: Kluwer-Nijhoff.

Mabry, L. 2008a. "Case Study in Social Research." Pp. 214–27 in *Handbook of Social Research Methods*, edited by P. Alasuutari, L. Bickman, and J. Brannen. London: Sage.

Mabry, L. 2008b. "Consequences of NCLB on Evaluation Purpose, Design, and Practice." Pp. 21–36 in *Consequences on NCLB on Educational Evaluation*, edited by T. Berry and R. Eddy. New Directions for Evaluation No. 119. San Francisco: Jossey-Bass.

Mabry, L. 2009, October. "The Responsibility of Evaluation." Keynote address to the German Educational Science Association (DeGEval) and to the International Organisation for Cooperation in Evaluation (IOCE), Muenster, Germany.

Mabry, L. and J. Z. Snow. 2004. "Three Innovative Evaluation Methods: Online Surveys, Video-Stimulated Focus Groups, and Think-Aloud Interviews." Presentation to the Oregon Program Evaluators Network annual meeting, October, Portland, OR.

Mabry, L. and J. Z. Snow. 2005. "Individual Laptop Computers to Support Learning of High-Risk Elementary Students and Classroom Culture Change." Paper presented at the annual meeting of the American Educational Research Association, April 12, Montreal.

Mabry, L. and J. Z. Snow. 2006. "Laptops for High-Risk Students: Empowerment and Personalization in a Standards-Based Learning Environment." *Studies in Educational Evaluation* 32(4):289–316.

Mabry, L., D. Stufflebeam, R. Hambleton, C. Ovando, R. O'Sullivan, B. Page, M. Wakely, and C. Swartz. 2000. "Both Sides Now: Perspectives of Evaluators and Stakeholders in Educational Evaluations." Paper presented at the annual meeting of the American Educational Research Association, April, New Orleans, LA.

Mackay, K. 2007. *How to Build M&E Systems to Support Better Government*. Independent Evaluation Group. Washington, DC: World Bank. http://web.worldbank.org/WBSITE/EXTERNAL/EXTOED/EXTEVACAPDEV/0,,contentMDK:22294993~menuPK:4585748~pagePK:64829573~piPK:64829550~theSitePK:4585673,00.html

Macklin, R. 2004. *Double Standards in Medical Research in Developing Countries*. Cambridge, UK: Cambridge University Press.

Madaus, G. F., M. S. Scriven, and D. L. Stufflebeam, eds. 1987. *Evaluation Models: Viewpoints on Educational and Human Services Evaluation*. Boston: Kluwer-Nijhoff.

Mahoncy, K. K. 1999. "Peer Mediation: An Ethnographic Investigation of an Elementary School's Program." Ph.D. dissertation, Indiana University, Bloomington, IN.

Malone, D. L. 1997. "Namel manmeri: Language and Culture Maintenance and Mother Tongue Education in the Highlands of Papua New Guinea." Ph.D. dissertation, Indiana University, Bloomington, IN.

Mathison, S., ed. 2005. *Encyclopedia of Evaluation*. Thousand Oaks, CA: Sage.

Maxwell, J. A. 1992. "Understanding and Validity in Qualitative Research." *Harvard Educational Review* 62(3):279–300.

Maxwell, J. A. 2004. "Causal Explanation, Qualitative Research, and Scientific Inquiry in Education." *Educational Researcher* 33(2):3–11.

Mayer, S. 1996. "Building Community Capacity with Evaluation Activities That Empower." Pp. 332–75 in *Empowerment Evaluation: Knowledge and Tools for Self-Assessment and Accountability,* edited by D. Fetterman, S. Kaftarian, and A. Wandersman. Thousand Oaks, CA: Sage.

McLeod, J. and R. Thomson. 2009. *Researching Social Change.* Thousand Oaks, CA: Sage.

McLeod, J. and L. Yates. 2006. *Making Modern Lives: Subjectivity, Schooling and Social Change.* Albany, NY: State University of New York Press.

McNamara, C. 2002. *Basic Guide to Program Evaluation.* Free Management Library. Retrieved August 9, 2011 (www .managementhelp.org/evaluatn/fnl_eval.htm).

MercyCorps. 2005. *Design, Monitoring and Evaluation Guidebook.* Portland, OR: MercyCorps.

Mertens, D. M. 1999. "Inclusive Evaluation: Implications of Transformative Theory for Evaluation." *American Journal of Evaluation* 20(1):1–14.

Mertens, D. M. 2001. "Inclusivity and Transformations: Evaluation in 2010." *American Journal of Evaluation* 22(3):367–74.

Mertens, D. M. 2003. "Mixed Methods and the Politics of Human Research: The Transformatory-Emancipatory Perspective." Pp. 135–66 in *Handbook of Mixed Methods in Social & Behavioral Research,* edited by A. Tashakkori and C. Teddlie. Thousand Oaks, CA: Sage.

Mertens, D. M. 2010. *Research and Evaluation in Education and Psychology: Integrating Diversity with Quantitative, Qualitative, and Mixed Methods* (3rd ed.) Thousand Oaks, CA: Sage.

Messick, S. 1989. "Validity." Pp. 13–103 in *Educational Measurement,* 3d ed., edited by Robert L. Linn. New York: Macmillan.

Miles, M. and M. Huberman. 1994. *Qualitative Data Analysis.* 2d ed. Thousand Oaks, CA: Sage.

Milgram, S. 1963. "Behavioral Study of Obedience." *Journal of Abnormal and Social Psychology* 67:371–78.

Milgram, S. 1974. *Obedience to Authority: An Experimental View.* New York: HarperCollins.

Mill, J. S. 1863/1891. *Utilitarianism.* 11th ed. London: Longmans, Green, & Co.

Moore, D. and G. McCabe. 1999. *Introduction to the Practice of Statistics.* 3d ed. New York: Freeman.

Morgan, D. and R. Morgan. 2009. *Single-Case Research Methods for the Behavioral and Health Sciences.* Thousand Oaks, CA: Sage.

Morra-Imas, L. and R. Rist. 2009. *The Road to Results: Designing and Conducting Effective Development Evaluations.* Washington, DC: World Bank.

Morris, M., ed. 2008. *Evaluation Ethics for Best Practice: Cases and Commentaries.* New York: Guilford.

Morris, M. and R. Cohn. 1993. "Program Evaluators and Ethical Challenges: A National Survey." *Evaluation Review* 17(6):621–42.

Morse, J. M. 2003. "Principles of Mixed Methods and Multimethod Research Design." Pp. 189–208 in *Handbook of Mixed Methods in Social & Behavioral Research,* edited by A. Tashakkori and C. Teddlie. Thousand Oaks, CA: Sage.

Narayan, D. 2002. *Empowerment and Poverty Reduction: A Sourcebook.* Washington, DC: World Bank.

National Association of Social Workers. 1996/1999. *Code of Ethics.* Washington, DC: National Association of Social Workers. www.socialworkers.org/pubs/code/default.asp

National Commission for the Protection of Human Subjects in Biomedical and Behavioral Research. 1979. *The Belmont Report: Ethical Principles and Guidelines for the Protection of Human Subjects of Research.* Washington, DC: U.S. Department of Health, Education, and Welfare.

National Council on Measurement in Education, American Educational Research Association. 1995. *Code of Professional Responsibility in Educational Assessment.* Washington, DC: National Council on Measurement in Education, American Educational Research Association.

Newman, C. 2001. *Gender, Time Use, and Change: Impacts of Agricultural Export Employment in Ecuador.* Policy Research Report on Gender and Development, Working Paper Series No. 18. Washington, DC: World Bank, Poverty Reduction and Economic Management Network/Development Research Group. http://scholar .google.com/scholar?hl=en&lr=&q=cache:UOHVbCs-SRgJ:www.worldbank.org/gender/prr/wp18.pdf+new man,+c.+2001+Gender,+time+use+and+change

Newman, D. L. and R. D. Brown. 1996. *Applied Ethics for Program Evaluation.* Thousand Oaks, CA: Sage.

No Child Left Behind Act. 2002. Public Law No. 107-110. 107th Congress, 110 Congressional Record 1425, 115 Stat.

Oakes, J. M. 2002. "Risks and Wrongs in Social Science Research: An Evaluator's Guide to the IRB." *Evaluation Review* 24:443–78.

O'Cathain, A. 2010. "Assessing the Quality of Mixed Methods Research: Towards a Comprehensive Framework." Pp. 531–55 in *SAGE Handbook of Mixed Methods in Social and Behavioral Research,* edited by A. Tashakkori and C. Teddlie. Thousand Oaks, CA: Sage.

Operations Evaluation Department. 2004. *Influential Evaluations: Evaluations That Improved Performance and Impacts of Development Programs.* Washington, DC: World Bank. http://worldbank.org/oed/ecd

Operations Evaluation Department. 2005. *Influential Evaluations: Evaluations That Improved Performance and Impacts of Development Programs.* Washington, DC: World Bank.

Organization for Economic Cooperation and Development (OECD). 1986. *Methods and Procedures in Aid Evaluation.* Paris: OECD.

Organization for Economic Cooperation and Development (OECD). 2001. *Effective Practices in Conducting a Multi-Donor Evaluation.* Paris: OECD.

Organization for Economic Cooperation and Development (OECD). 2008. *The Paris Declaration on Aid Effectiveness (2005) and the Accra Agenda for Action (2008).* Paris: OECD. http://www.oecd.org/dataoecd/11/41/34428351.pdf

Organization for Economic Cooperation and Development (OECD). 2010a. *Evaluating Development Cooperation: Summary of Key Norms and Standards.* 2d ed. Paris: OECD. http://www.oecd.org/dataoecd/12/56/41612905.pdf

Organization for Economic Cooperation and Development (OECD)/Development Advisory Committee. 2010b. *Quality Standards for Development Evaluation.* DAC Guidelines and Reference Series. Paris: OECD. Retrieved August 4, 2011 (http://www.oecd.org/dataoecd/55/0/44798177.pdf)

Organization for Economic Cooperation and Development/Development Advisory Committee. 2002. *Glossary of Key Terms in Evaluation.* Retrieved August 14, 2005 (www.oecd.org/findDocument/ 0,2350,en_2649_3443 5_1_119678_1_1_1,00.html).

Patton, M. Q. 1997. *Utilization-Focused Evaluation.* 3d ed. Thousand Oaks, CA: Sage.

Patton, M. Q. 2002a. "A Vision of Evaluation That Strengthens Democracy." *Evaluation* 8(1):125–39.

Patton, M. Q. 2002b. *Qualitative Research and Evaluation Methods.* Thousand Oaks, CA: Sage.

Patton, M.Q. 2002c. *Utilization Focused Evaluation: Checklist.* Kalamazoo, MI: Western Michigan University, The Evaluation Center. http://www.wmich.edu/evalctr/archive_checklists/ufe.pdf

Patton, M. Q. 2003. *Qualitative Evaluation Checklist.* Kalamazoo, MI: Western Michigan University, The Evaluation Center. http://www.wmich.edu/evalctr/archive_checklists/qec.pdf

Patton, M. Q. 2008. *Utilization-Focused Evaluation.* 4th ed. Thousand Oaks, CA: Sage.

Patton, M. Q. 2011. *Developmental Evaluation: Applying Complexity Concepts to Enhance Innovation and Use.* New York: Guilford.

Paul, S. 2002. *Holding the State to Account: Citizen Monitoring in Action.* Bangalore: Books for Change ActionAid.

Pawson, R. 2006. *Evidence-Based Policy: A Realist Perspective.* London: Sage.

Pawson, R. and N. Tilley. 1997. *Realist Evaluation.* London: Sage.

Pebley, A., N. Noreen, and M. K. Choe. 1986. "Evaluation of Contraceptive History Data in the Republic of Korea." *Studies in Family Planning* 17(1):22–35.

Peirce, C. S. 1931–1958. *The Collected Papers of Charles Sanders Peirce.* Edited by C. Hartshorne and P. Weiss (vols. 1–6) and A. W. Burks (vols. 7–8). Cambridge, MA: Harvard University Press.

Pellegrino, J. W. and S. R. Goldman. 2002. "Be Careful What You Wish for—You May Get It: Educational Research in the Spotlight." *Educational Researcher* 31(8):15–17.

Perlman, J. 1976. *The Myth of Marginality: Urban Poverty and Politics in Rio de Janeiro.* Berkeley: University of California Press.

Perlman, J. 2002. "The Metamorphosis of Marginality: Rio's Favelas 1969–2002." Paper presented at the World Bank Conference, May 7. Retrieved August 8, 2005 (www.kas.de/upload/dokumente/megacities/janiceperlman.pdf).

Phillips, D. C. 1987. "Validity in Qualitative Research: Why the Worry about Warrant Will Not Wane." *Education and Urban Society* 20:9–24.

Piaget, J. 1955. *The Language and Thought of the Child.* New York: World.

Picciotto, R. 2002. *Development Cooperation and Performance Evaluation: The Monterrey Challenge.* Washington, DC: World Bank, Operations Evaluation Department.

Picciotto, R. 2005. "The Value of Evaluation Standards: A Comparative Assessment." *Journal of Multidisciplinary Evaluation* 3:30–59.

Polanyi, M. 1958. *Personal Knowledge: Towards a Post-Critical Philosophy.* Chicago: University of Chicago Press.

Posavac, E. J. and R. J. Carey. 2003. *Program Evaluation: Methods and Case Studies.* 6th ed. Upper Saddle River, NJ: Prentice Hall.

Poverty Action Lab. 2005. *Fighting Poverty: What Works? No. 1 Primary Education for All.* http://www.povertyactionlab.org/sites/default/files/publications/Fighting%20Poverty%2C%20What%20works%20Issue%201.pdf

Pratt, C., W. McGuigan, and A. Katzev. 2002. "Measuring Program Outcomes: Using Retrospective Pretest Methodology." *American Journal of Evaluation* 21(5):341–50.

Presser, P., M. Couper, J. Lessler, M. Martin, J. Martin, J. Rothgeb, and E. Singer. 2004a. *Methods for Testing and Evaluating Survey Questionnaires.* New York: John Wiley.

Presser, P., M. Couper, J. Lessler, M. Martin, J. Martin, J. Rothgeb, and E. Singer. 2004b. "Methods for Testing and Evaluating Survey Questions." *Public Opinion Quarterly* 68(1):109–30.

Pretty, J., I. Guijt, J. Thompson, and I. Scoones. 1995. *Participatory Learning and Action.* London: International Institute for Environment and Development.

Psacharopoulos, G. and M. Woodhall. 1991. *Education for Development: An Analysis of Investment Choices.* New York: Oxford University Press.

Rao, V. 2000. "Price Heterogeneity and Real Inequality: A Case Study of Poverty and Prices in Rural South India." *Review of Income and Wealth*, 46(2), 201–212.

Rao, V. 2001. "Celebrations and Social Investments: Festival Expenditures, Unit Price Variation and Social Status in Rural India." *Journal of Development Studies*, 37(1), 71–97.

Rao, V., Gupta, I., Lokshin, M., and Jana, S. 2003. "Sex Workers and the Cost of Safe Sex: The Compensating Differential for Condom Use in Calcutta." *Journal of Development Economics*, 71(2), 585–603.

Rao, V. and M. Woolcock. 2003. "Integrating Qualitative and Quantitative Approaches in Program Evaluation." Pp. 165–90 in *The Impact of Economic Policies on Poverty and Income Distribution: Evaluation Techniques and Tools,* edited by F. J. Bourguignon and L. Pereira da Silva. New York: Oxford University Press.

Ravallion, M. 2008. "Evaluating Anti-Poverty Programs." In *Handbook of Development Economics,* vol. 4, edited by edited by Paul Schultz and John Strauss. Amsterdam: North-Holland.

Ravindra, A. 2004. *Assessment of the Impact of the Bangalore Citizen Report Cards on the Performance of Public Agencies.* Washington, DC: World Bank. Available at www.worldbank.org/oed/ecd

Rawls, J. 1971/1999. *A Theory of Justice.* Rev. ed. Cambridge, MA: Belknap Press.

Rawlings, L. 2000. "Evaluating Nicaragua's School-Based Management Reform." In *Integrating Quantitative and Qualitative Research in Development Projects,* edited by M. Bamberger. Washington, DC: World Bank.

Reforma, M. and R. Obusan. 1981. *Household Networks and Survival Strategies among the Urban Poor: Monetary and Non-Monetary Transfers among Selected Families in Tondo.* Urban and Regional Report 81-22. Washington, DC: World Bank.

Reichardt, C. 2005. "Quasi-Experimental Designs." Pp. 351–55 in *Encyclopedia of Evaluation,* edited by S. Mathison. Thousand Oaks, CA: Sage.

Reichardt, C. S. and S. F. Rallis, eds. 1994. *The Qualitative-Quantitative Debate: New Perspectives.* New Directions for Program Evaluation No. 61. San Francisco: Jossey-Bass.

Rieper, O., F. Leuw, and T. Ling, editors. 2010. *The Evidence Book: Concepts, Generation and Use of Evidence.* Comparative Policy Evaluation, vol. 15. London: Transaction Publishers.

Rietberger-McCracken, J. and D. Narayan 1997. *Participatory Rural Appraisal. Module III of Participatory Tools and Techniques: A Resource Kit for Participation and Social Assessment.* Washington, DC: World Bank. Environment Department.

Roche, C. 1999. *Impact Assessment for Development Agencies: Learning to Value Change.* Oxford, UK: OXFAM.

Rogers, P. 2008. "Using Programme Theory to Evaluate Complicated and Complex Aspects of Interventions." *Evaluation* 14(1):29–48.

Rogers, P., T. Hacsi, A. Petrosino, and T. Huebner, eds. 2000. *Program Theory in Evaluation: Challenges and Opportunities.* New Directions for Evaluation No. 87. San Francisco: Jossey-Bass.

Rogers, P., A. Petrosino, T. Huebner, and T. Hacsi. 2000. "Program Theory Evaluation: Practice, Promise and Problems." Pp. 5–13 in *Program Theory in Evaluation: Challenges and Opportunities,* edited by P. Rogers, T. Hacsi, A. Petrosino, and T. Huebner. New Directions for Evaluation No. 87. San Francisco: Jossey-Bass.

Roodman, D. and J. Morduch. 2009. *The Impact of Microcredit on the Poor in Bangladesh: Revisiting the Evidence.* Working Paper 174. Washington, DC: Center for Global Development.

Rosenbaum, P. R. 1995. "Design Sensitivity in Observational Studies." *Biometrika* 91(1):153–64.

Rossi, P. H. 1994. "The War between the Quals and the Quants: Is a Lasting Peace Possible?" Pp. 23–36 in *The Qualitative-Quantitative Debate: New Perspectives,* edited by C. S. Reichardt and S. F. Rallis. New Directions for Program Evaluation No. 61. San Francisco: Jossey-Bass.

Rossi, P., M. Lipsey, and H. Freeman. 2004. *Evaluation: A Systematic Approach.* 7th ed. Thousand Oaks, CA: Sage.

Rossman, G. B. and S. F. Rallis. 1998. *Learning in the Field: An Introduction to Qualitative Research.* Thousand Oaks, CA: Sage.

Rugh, J. 1986. *Self-Evaluation: Ideas for Participatory Evaluation of Rural Community Development Projects.* Oklahoma City, OK: World Neighbors.

Russell, B. and G. W. Ryan. 2010. *Analyzing Qualitative Data.* Thousand Oaks, CA: Sage.

Russon, C. 2005. *The Mega 2004 Evaluation (Meta-Evaluation of Goal Achievement of CARE Projects).* Atlanta, GA: CARE International. www.globaldev.org/m&e

Russon, C. and G. Russon, editors. 2005. *International Perspectives on Evaluation Standards.* New Directions for Evaluation No. 104. San Francisco: Jossey-Bass.

Salkind, N. 2008. *Statistics for People Who (Think They) Hate Statistics.* Thousand Oaks, CA: Sage.

Salkind, N. 2011. *EXCEL Statistics: A Quick Guide.* Thousand Oaks, CA: Sage.

Salmen, L. F. 1987. *Listen to the People: Participant Observer Evaluation of Development Projects.* New York: Oxford University Press.

Salmen, L. F. 1992. *Beneficiary Assessment: An Approach Described.* Washington, DC: World Bank.

Schutz, A. 1970. *On Phenomenology and Social Relations.* Chicago: University of Chicago Press.

Schwarz, N. and D. Oyserman. 2001. "Asking Questions about Behavior: Cognition, Communication, and Questionnaire Construction." *American Journal of Evaluation* 22(2):127–60.

Scott, C. and B. Amenuvegbe. 1991. "Recall Loss and Recall Duration: An Experimental Study in Ghana." *Inter-Stat* 4(1):31–55.

Scott, K. and W. Okrasa. 1998. *Analysis of Latvia Diary Experiment.* Washington, DC: World Bank, Development Research Group.

Scrimshaw, S. and E. Hurtado. 1987. *RAP: Rapid Assessment Procedures for Nutrition and Primary Health Care.* Tokyo: United Nations University.

Scriven, M. 1972. "Pros and Cons about Goal-Free Evaluation." *Evaluation Comment* 3:1–7.

Scriven, M. 1976. "Maximizing the Power of Causal Investigation: The Modus Operandi Method." Pp. 120–39 in *Evaluation Studies Annual Review 1,* edited by G. V. Glass. Beverley Hills, CA: Sage.

Scriven, M. 1991. *Evaluation Thesaurus.* 4th ed. Newbury Park, CA: Sage.

Scriven, M. 1997. "Truth and Objectivity in Evaluation." Pp. 477–500 in *Evaluation for the 21st Century: A Handbook,* edited by E. Chelimsky and W. R. Shadish. Thousand Oaks, CA: Sage.

Scriven, M. 1998. "An Evaluation Dilemma: Change Agent vs. Analyst." Paper presented at the annual meeting of the American Evaluation Association, November 6, Chicago.

Scriven, M. 2005. *The Logic and Methodology of Checklists.* www.mich.edu/evalctr/checklists

Scriven, M. 2007. "Key Evaluation Checklist." www.wmich.edu/evalctr/checklists

Scriven, M. 2009. "Demytholizing Causation and Evidence." Pp. 134–52 in *What Counts as Credible Evidence in Applied Research and Evaluation Practice?* edited by S. Donalson, C. Christie, and M. Mark. Thousand Oaks, CA: Sage.

Shadish, W., T. Cook, and D. Campbell. 2002. *Experimental and Quasi-Experimental Designs for Generalized Causal Inference.* Boston: Houghton Mifflin.

Shadish, W. R., D. Newman, M. Scheirer, and C. Wye. 1995. *Guiding Principles for Evaluators.* New Directions for Program Evaluation No. 66. San Francisco: Jossey-Bass.

Shavelson, R. and L. Towne, editors. 2002. *Scientific Research in Education.* Committee on Scientific Principles for Educational Research. Washington, DC: National Academy Press.

Shaw, I. F. 2003. Ethics in Qualitative Research and Evaluation. *Journal of Social Work* 3(1):9–29.

Sheinfeld, S. N. and G. L. Lord. 1981. "Ethics of Evaluation." *Evaluation Review* 5:377–91.

Sida. 2007. *Looking Back, Moving Forward.* 2d ed. Stockholm: Swedish International Development Agency.

Silverman, D. 2004. *Qualitative Research: Theory, Method and Practice.* 2d ed. Thousand Oaks, CA: Sage.

Sirkin, R. 1999. *Statistics for the Social Sciences.* Thousand Oaks, CA: Sage.

Smith, L. 1978. "An Evolving Logic of Participant Observation, Educational Ethnography and Other Case Studies." Pp. 316–77 in *Review of Research in Education,* vol. 6, edited by L. Schulman. Itasca, IL: Peacock.

Spector, P. 1991. *Summated Rating Scale Construction: An Introduction.* Quantitative Applications in the Social Sciences, vol. 82. Newbury Park, CA: Sage.

Stack, C. 1996. *Call to Home: African Americans Reclaim the Rural South.* New York: Basic Books.

Stake, R. E. 1975. *Evaluating the Arts in Education: A Responsive Approach.* Columbus, OH: Merrill.

Stake, R. E. 1986. *Quieting Reform: Social Science and Social Action in an Urban Youth Program.* Urbana: University of Illinois Press.

Stair, T. O., C. R. Reed, M. S. Radeos, G. Koski, and C. A. Camargo. 2001. "Variation in Institutional Review Board Responses to a Standard Protocol for a Multicenter Clinical Trial." *Academic Emergency Medicine* 8(6):636–41.

Stern, E. 2009. "Evaluation Policy in the European Union and Its Institutions." *New Directions for Evaluation, 123,* 67–85.

Stevahn, L., J. King, G. Ghere, and J. Minnema. 2005. "Establishing Essential Competencies for Program Evaluators." *American Journal of Evaluation* 26(1):43–59.

Stevens, C. J. and M. Dial, editors. 1994. *Preventing the Misuse of Evaluation.* New Directions for Evaluation No. 64. San Francisco: Jossey-Bass.

Strauss, A. and J. Corbin. 1990. *Basics of Qualitative Research: Grounded Theory Procedures and Techniques.* Newbury Park, CA: Sage.

Strauss, A. and J. Corbin 1994. "Grounded Theory Methodology: An Overview." Pp. 273–85 in *Handbook of Qualitative Research,* edited by N. K. Denzin and Y. S. Lincoln. Thousand Oaks, CA: Sage.

Stronach, I., J. Allan, and B. Morris, 1996. "Can the Mothers of Invention Make Virtue Out of Necessity? An Optimistic Deconstruction of Research Compromises in Contract Research and Evaluation." *British Educational Research Journal* 22(4):493–509.

Stufflebeam, D. L. 1987. "The CIPP Model for Program Evaluation." Pp. 117–41 in *Evaluation Models: Viewpoints on Educational and Human Services Evaluation,* edited by G. F. Madaus, M. S. Scriven, and D. L. Stufflebeam. Boston: Kluwer-Nijhoff.

Stufflebeam, D. L. 1994. "Empowerment Evaluation, Objectivist Evaluation, and Evaluation Standards: Where the Future of Evaluation Should Not Go and Where It Needs to Go." *Evaluation Practice* 15(3):321–38.

Stufflebeam, D. L. 1997. "A Standards-Based Perspective on Evaluation." Pp. 61–88 in *Evaluation and the Postmodern Dilemma*, edited by L. Mabry. Greenwich, CT: JAI Press.

Stufflebeam, D. L. 1999. *Program Evaluations Metaevaluation Checklist (Based on the Program Evaluation Standards)*. Kalamazoo, MI: Western Michigan University. The Evaluation Center. http://www.wmich.edu/evalctr/archive_checklists/program_metaeval.pdf

Stufflebeam, D. 2001a. *Evaluation Models*. New Directions for Evaluation No. 89. San Francisco: Jossey-Bass.

Stufflebeam, D. L. 2001b. "The Metaevaluation Imperative." *American Journal of Evaluation* 22(2): 183–209.

Stufflebeam, D. L. 2007. *The CIPP Evaluation Model Checklist*. 2d ed. Kalamazoo, MI: Western Michigan University. The Evaluation Center. http://www.wmich.edu/evalctr/archive_checklists/cippchecklist_mar07.pdf

Stufflebeam, D. L., M. Q. Patton, D. Fetterman, J. G. Greene, M. S. Scriven, and L. Mabry. 2001. "Theories of Action in Program Evaluation." Panel presentation at the annual meeting of the American Evaluation Association, November 9, St. Louis, MO.

Stufflebeam, D. and A. Shinkfield. 2007. *Evaluation Theory, Models and Applications*. San Francisco: Jossey-Bass.

Sudman, S. and N. Bradburn. 1982. *Asking Questions*. San Francisco: Jossey-Bass.

Tashakkori, A. and C. Teddlie, eds. 2003. *Handbook of Mixed Methods in Social & Behavioral Research*. Thousand Oaks, CA: Sage.

Teddlie, C. and A. Tashakkori. 2009. *Foundations of Mixed Methods Research: Integrating Quantitative and Qualitative Approaches in the Social and Behavioral Sciences*. Thousand Oaks, CA: Sage.

Tashakkori, A. and C. Teddlie, editors. 2010. *SAGE Handbook of Mixed Methods in Social and Behavioral Research*. Thousand Oaks, CA: Sage.

Theis, J. and H. Grady. 1991. *Participatory Rapid Appraisal for Community Development: A Training Manual Based on Experiences in the Middle-East and North Africa Region*. London: Save the Children/International Institute for Environment and Development.

Thomas, A. and G. Mohan. 2007, eds. *Research Skills for Policy and Development: How to Find Out Fast*. London: Sage/The Open University.

Thurston, P. W., J. C. Ory, P. W. Mayberry, and L. A. Braskamp. 1984. "Legal and Professional Standards in Program Evaluation." *Educational Evaluation and Policy Analysis* 6(1):15–26.

Tobin, J. J., D. Y. H. Wu, and D. H. Davidson. 1989. *Preschool in Three Cultures: Japan, China, and the United States*. New Haven, CT: Yale University Press.

Tolstoy, L. 1889. *Anna Karenina*. New York: Crowell.

United Nations Development Programme (UNDP). 2009. *Handbook on Planning, Monitoring and Evaluating for Development Results*. New York: UNDP.

United Nations General Assembly. 1948. *The Universal Declaration of Human Rights*. www.un.org/Overview/rights

United Nations General Assembly. 1966, December 16. *International Covenant on Civil and Political Rights*. New York: United Nations General Assembly.

United Nations General Assembly. 1990, December 14. *Guidelines for the Regulation of Computerized Personal Data (Resolution 45/95)*. New York: United Nations General Assembly.

United Nations General Assembly. 2005, March 8. *United Nations Declaration on Human Cloning (Resolution 59/280)*. New York: United Nations General Assembly.

United Way. 1999. *Achieving and Measuring Community Outcomes*. Retrieved September 2, 2005 (http://national.unitedway.org/files/pdf/outcomes/cmtyout1.pdf).

United Way. 2005. *Connecting Program Outcome Measurement to Community Impact*. Retrieved September 2, 2005 (http://national.unitedway.org/files/pdf/outcomes/ConnectingPOM_toCI% 20Final.pdf).

U.S. Agency for International Development. 2010. "Preparing an Evaluation Statement of Work." Performance Monitoring and Evaluation TIPS. No. 3. http://www.usaid.gov/policy/evalweb/documents/TIPS-PreparinganEvaluationStatementofWork.pdf

U.S. Agency for International Development. 2011. *Evaluation Policy*. Washington, DC: USAID.

U.S. Department of Education. 2003, November 4. "Notice of Proposed Priority: Scientifically Based Evaluation Methods (RIN 1890-ZA00)." *Federal Register* 68(213):62445–47.

U.S. Department of Education. 2005, January 25. "Scientifically Based Evaluation Methods (RIN 1890-ZA00)." *Federal Register* 70(15):3586–89.

U.S. Department of Health and Human Services. 2010. *Head Start Impact Study: Final Report*. Washington, DC: Office of Planning, Research and Evaluation Administration for Children and Families.

Valadez, J. and M. Bamberger. 1994. *Monitoring and Evaluating Social Programs in Developing Countries: A Handbook for Policymakers, Managers and Researchers*. Washington, DC: World Bank.

Valadez, J. and B. R. Devkota. 2002. "Decentralized Supervision of Community Health Programs: Using LQAS in Two Districts of Southern Nepal." Pp. 169–200 in

Community-Based Health Care: Lessons from Bangladesh to Boston, edited by RaJ Wyon. Boston: Management Sciences for Health.

Van de Walle, D. 1999. *Assessing the Poverty Impact of Rural Road Projects.* Washington, DC: World Bank.

Vaughan, R. J. and T. F. Buss. 1998. *Communicating Social Science Research to Policy Makers.* Applied Social Research Methods Series No. 48. Thousand Oaks, CA: Sage.

Viadero, D. 2004. "What Works Research Site Unveiled." *Education Week,* July 14, p. 33.

Viadero, D. 2007. "AERA Stresses Value of Alternatives to 'Gold Standard.'" *Education Week* 29(33):12–13.

van Wright, G. H. 1971. *Explanation and Understanding.* London: Routledge and Kegan Paul.

Vygotsky, L. S. 1978. *Mind in Society: The Development of Higher Mental Process.* Cambridge, MA: Harvard University Press.

W. K. Kellogg Foundation. 1998. *Evaluation Handbook.* Retrieved September 5, 2005 (www.wkkf.org/Pubs/ Tools/Evaluation/Pub770.pdf).

Waddington, H., B. Snilsveit, H. White, and L. Fewtrell. 2009. *Water, Sanitation and Hygiene Interventions to Combat Childhood Diarrhea in Developing Countries.* Synthetic Review No. 1. New Delhi, India: International Initiative for Impact Evaluation.www.3ieimpact.org

Walker, D. 1997. "Why Won't They Listen? Reflections of a Formative Evaluator." Pp. 121–37 in *Evaluation and the Postmodern Dilemma,* edited by L. Mabry. Greenwich, CT: JAI Press.

Wansbrough, G., D. Jones, and C. Kappaz. 2000. "Studying Interhousehold Transfers and Survival Strategies of the Poor in Cartagena, Colombia." Pp. 69–84 in *Integrating Quantitative and Qualitative Research in Development Projects,* edited by M. Bamberger. Directions in Development. Washington, DC: World Bank.

Weber, M. 1904/1949. *The Methodology of the Social Sciences.* Edited and translated by E. A. Shils and H. A. Finch. New York: Free Press.

Weinberg, S. L. and S. K. Abramowitz. 2002. *Data Analysis for the Behavioral Sciences Using SPSS.* Cambridge, UK: Cambridge University Press.

Weiss, C. H. 1993. "Where Politics and Evaluation Research Meet." *Evaluation Practice* 14(1):93–106.

Weiss, C. H. 1995. "Nothing as Practical as Good Theory: Exploring Theory-Based Evaluation for Comprehensive Community Initiatives for Children and Families." Pp. 65–92 in *New Approaches to Evaluating Community Initiatives: Concepts, Methods and Contexts,* edited by J. P. Connell, A. C. Kubisch, L. B. Schorr, and C. H. Weiss. Washington, DC: Aspen Institute.

Weiss, C. H. 1997. "How Can Theory-Based Evaluation Make Greater Headway?" *Evaluation Review* 21: 501–24.

Weiss, C. H. 2000. "Which Links in Which Theories Shall We Evaluate?" Pp. 35–45 in *Program Theory in Evaluation: Challenges and Opportunities,* edited by P. J. Rogers, T. A. Hacsi, A. Petrosino, and T. A. Huebner. New Directions for Evaluation No. 87. San Francisco: Jossey-Bass.

Weiss, C. H. 2001. "Theory-Based Evaluation: Theories of Change for Poverty Based Programs." Pp. 103–14 in *Evaluation and Poverty Reduction,* edited by O. Feinstein and R. Picciotto. New Brunswick, NJ: Transaction.

Weitzman, B., D. Silver, and K. N. Dillman. 2002. "Integrating a Comparison Group Design into a Theory of Change Evaluation: The Case of the Urban Health Initiative." *American Journal of Evaluation* 23(4):371–86.

White, H. and M. Bamberger. 2008. *Impact Evaluation in Official Development Agencies.* Sussex, UK: IDS Bulletin.

Wholey, J. S. 1987. "Evaluability Assessment: Developing Program Theory." Pp. 35–46 in *Using Program Theory in Evaluation,* edited by L. Bickman. New Directions for Program Evaluation No. 33. San Francisco: Jossey-Bass.

Wholey, J., H. Hatry, and K. Newcomer, eds. 2010. *Handbook of Practical Program Evaluation.* San Francisco: Jossey-Bass.

Wholey, J., J. Scanlon, H. Duffy, J. Fukumoto, and L. Vogt. 1970. *Federal Evaluation Policy: Analyzing the Effects of Public Programs.* Washington, DC: Urban Institute.

Wolcott, H. F. 1994. *Transforming Qualitative Data: Description, Analysis, and Interpretation.* Thousand Oaks, CA: Sage.

Woolcock, M. 2009. "Toward a Plurality of Methods in Project Evaluation: A Contextualized Approach to Understanding Impact Trajectories and Efficacy." *Journal of Development Effectiveness* 1(1):1–14.

World Bank. 1993. *Early Experience with Involuntary Resettlement: Impact Evaluation on India: Maharashtra Irrigation Project.* Operations Evaluation Department. Washington, DC: World Bank.

World Bank. 1996. *Participation Sourcebook.* Washington, DC: World Bank. www.world bank.org/wbi/sourcebook/ sbpdf.htm

World Bank. 2001. *Engendering Development: Through Gender Equality in Rights, Resources and Voice.* Oxford, UK: Oxford University Press.

World Bank. 2004. *Influential Evaluations: Evaluations that Improved Performance and Impacts of Development Programs.* Evaluation Capacity Development, Operations Evaluation Department. Washington, DC: World Bank.

World Bank. 2008. *CAE Methodology Guide to IEG's Country Evaluation Rating Methodology.* Washington, DC: World Bank. http://web.worldbank.org/WBSITE/ EXTERNAL/EXTOED/EXTCOUASSEVAL/0,,contentM DK:21107046~menuPK:4620176~pagePK:648295 73~piPK:64829550~theSitePK:4425762,00 .html

World Bank Independent Evaluation Group. 2006. *From Schooling Access to Learning Outcomes: An Unfinished Agenda; Evaluation of World Bank Support to Primary Education.* Washington, DC: World Bank Independent Evaluation Group.

World Medical Association General Assembly. 1964/1996. *Declaration of Helsinki: Ethical Principles for Medical Research Involving Human Subjects (Document 17.C).* Helsinki, Finland. Retrieved July 6, 2007 (www.wma .net/e/policy/b3.htm).

Yarbrough, D. B., L. M. Shulha, R. K. Hopson, and F. A. Caruthers. 2011. *The Program Evaluation Standards: A Guide for Evaluators and Evaluation Users.* 3d ed. Thousand Oaks, CA: Sage.

Yin, R. K. 1994. *Case Study Research: Design and Methods.* 2d ed. Applied Social Research Methods Series, vol. 5. Thousand Oaks, CA: Sage.

Yin, R. 2003. *Case Study Research: Design and Methods.* 3d ed. Thousand Oaks, CA: Sage.

Yin, R., editor. 2004. *The Case Study Anthology.* Thousand Oaks, CA: Sage.

Yin, R. K. and D. Davis. 2007. "Adding New Dimensions to Case Study Evaluations: The Case of Evaluating Comprehensive Reforms." Pp. 75–93 in *Informing Federal Policies on Evaluation Methodology: Building the Evidence Base for Method Choice in Government Sponsored Evaluation,* edited by G. Julnes and D. Rog. New Directions for Evaluation No. 113. San Francisco: Jossey-Bass.

Author Index

Subject Index